Disk Operating
System with
DOS 6.0

ISBN 0-03-000638-4

1

DOS 6.0

*Commonly Used
DOS Commands*

DOS

OBJECTIVES

After completing this chapter you will be able to:

1 Explain the difference between internal and external DOS commands.

2 Describe the procedures to boot up and exit DOS.

3 Explain the concept of a default drive and describe the technique
to change it.

4 Describe the need for disk formatting and differentiate among the various
FORMAT commands.

5 Explain and illustrate basic DOS commands, including FORMAT, DIR,
COPY, XCOPY, SYS, RENAME, ERASE, DISKCOPY, COMP, and DISK-
COMP.

6 Name the two wildcard characters and explain their use.

DOS3

O V E R V I E W   This chapter introduces you to the basics of PC-DOS and MS-DOS—standard disk operating systems in the microcomputer world. You will learn how to start the microcomputer and how to use the system software to perform basic "housekeeping" chores associated with proper file management. The concept of internal and external commands is presented, and tutorials allow you to explore commands such as FORMAT, DIR, SYS, COPY, XCOPY, RE-NAME, ERASE, and so on. The tutorials are based on DOS version 6.0, but most will also work with earlier DOS versions.

Although you can sit at a microcomputer and try each of the commands presented in the tutorials, it is best to read the text first and examine the screens in preparation for the hands-on session and as a review. All commands are shown in uppercase letters for clarity, but DOS does not require them in this form; you may type commands in lowercase letters with the same effect. Also, your version of DOS may differ from the one presented here, and thus the procedures and screens may vary slightly.

Each set of tutorials is followed by a "Checkpoint"—a set of questions or tasks that quickly tests your mastery of the skills presented in that section. Do not proceed to the next section if you cannot get past the Checkpoint questions. Review the material and try again.

Getting Started

Embarking on any new learning experience is both exhilarating and frightening. This is especially true when you are using new technology. Some experiences may frustrate you, especially when your commands are ignored or misunderstood. Remember, however, that the computer is just a tool that merely responds to *your* instructions. A mistyped command, no matter how slight the error, can have unwanted effects. Take time to type words, spaces, colons, and periods exactly as they are shown—do not add any, nor take any away. A semicolon will not work in place of a colon; the lowercase letter *l* cannot be used for the number one, nor the uppercase letter *O* for zero.

All this having been said, relax. You cannot hurt the computer, nor can it hurt you. Do not be afraid to experiment with commands and techniques as you gain confidence in their use. As the old adage says, practice makes perfect.

Handling Disks and Hardware

Like automobiles, microcomputers can provide reliable service for years if they are used and maintained wisely. Careful handling of your hardware and disks can significantly extend their life and reduce maintenance costs and downtime.

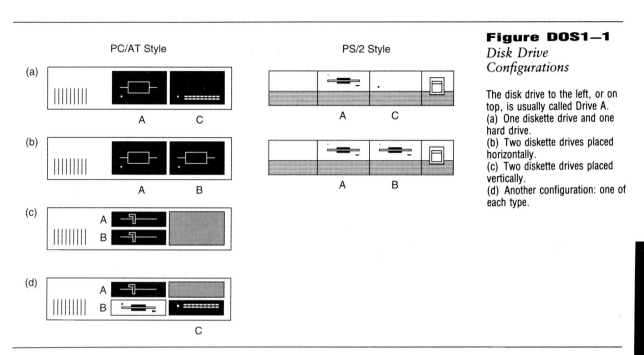

Figure DOS1—1

*Disk Drive
Configurations*

The disk drive to the left, or on top, is usually called Drive A.
(a) One diskette drive and one hard drive.
(b) Two diskette drives placed horizontally.
(c) Two diskette drives placed vertically.
(d) Another configuration: one of each type.

Not only should you avoid such obvious risks as hitting the hardware or banging on the keyboard, but you should also keep your work environment clean.

To complete this tutorial, you will need a blank disk and either a hard-disk system or network that contains the DOS files or a DOS system disk (a disk that contains the DOS start-up and command files). It is assumed that your computer hardware is configured with at least one disk drive (called Drive A) and a hard-disk drive (called Drive C) as shown in Figure DOS1—1a. If you are using a system with a single disk drive, it is called Drive A. If you are using two disk drives placed horizontally, side by side (as in Figure DOS1—1b), Drive A is on the left and Drive B is on the right. If the drives are placed vertically, one above the other (as in Figure DOS1—1c), then Drive A is on top. Of course, you may also have some combination of disk drives, such as the one shown in DOS1—1d, which includes drives for 5¼-inch disks (Drive A) and 3½-inch disks (Drive B), as well as a hard-disk drive (Drive C). These drives may be either contained within the system unit itself or attached to it as external components.

As you read through the rest of this chapter, pay particular attention to the numbered steps in each section, and follow them while sitting at your computer. Instructions that differ between hard-disk and dual-diskette systems are shown in two columns. Network instructions are shown as needed. Follow the one appropriate for your disk configuration.

The procedure for booting DOS on a microcomputer system is similar whether you are using a system that contains a hard-disk drive or one that uses only diskettes. The only difference is whether you need to place a diskette in Drive A before you turn on the system unit.

Booting DOS

Hard-Disk Start-up

1. Do *not* place any disk in Drive A

2. Turn on the system unit

3. Turn on the monitor's separate power switch if it has one

Dual-Diskette or Network Start-up

1. Place a DOS system disk in Drive A

2. Close the drive door if you are using 5¼-inch disks

3. Turn on the system unit

4. Turn on the monitor's separate power switch if it has one

The Boot Procedure.   You should now hear some whirring sounds (from the internal fan and disk drive) and perhaps see some numbers or symbols on the monitor as your computer system is booting up. Your screen may display the message "Starting MS-DOS...." During **booting**, the computer may run some self-check programs, and certain DOS commands are brought into the computer's main memory (RAM) from disk so that they can be accessed quickly. Booting can take a few seconds or well over a minute depending on the hardware you are using, so be patient.

There are really two types of booting procedures. Starting a computer by turning on its power is called a *cold boot*. You can also restart a computer that is already on by performing a **warm boot**. This is accomplished with three keys: you press and hold the Ctrl and Alt keys, tap the Del key, and then release all three. The computer will start without the need to turn it off and back on again. It will also skip its normal self-check routine.

Date and Time Prompts.   When DOS has booted, you will usually see a screen message asking you to enter the current date, as in Figure DOS1–2a. It is a good practice to enter the correct date and time when booting. This way, your files will correctly show when they were last saved or modified. Some computers have an internal clock maintained by a long-life battery. In these computers, you

---

Figure DOS1—2
Date and Time Prompts

(a) During the boot process, the computer displays the current date and prompts you for a new one, which should be entered in month-day-year order.
(b) Time is entered in hours and minutes separated by a colon.

```
Current date is Fri 03-26-1993
Enter new date (mm-dd-yy):_
```

```
Current time is 9:05:41.11a
Enter new time:_
```

(a)

(b)

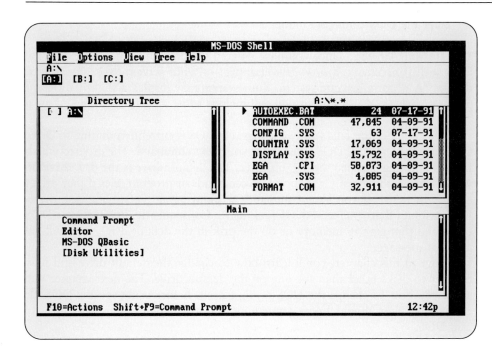

Figure DOS1—3
The DOS Shell Program Menu Is a Graphic Extension of DOS

It can be exited by pressing the F3 key.

need not enter the date or time. Of course, you may choose to skip date or time by simply pressing the Enter key in response to the date and time prompts. If you choose to enter a date, it must be entered in month-day-year order. For example, if today was October 7, 1994, you would type *10-7-94* and then press the Enter key. Notice that the month comes first, followed by the day and year, each separated by a dash (or minus sign). Do *not* type the day of the week. If your screen requests it, enter today's date into your computer now, as follows:

1.   Type the **<month>-<day>-<year>** (as in *10-07-94*)

2.   Press ↵

If your screen responds with "Invalid Date," you have typed something wrong. Review the sample and type the date again. Then press the Enter key.

Once you have entered the date, DOS will normally prompt you for the time, as in Figure DOS1–2b. Time is generally input in hours and minutes separated by a colon. For example, *10:08* means 10:08 A.M., and *19:45* means 7:45 P.M. (in 24-hour military time). If your screen requests it, type in the time now as follows:

3.   Type the hours:minutes (as in *10:08*)

4.   Press ↵

If an "Invalid Time" message appears on the screen, reenter the time correctly.

The DOS Shell.   Depending on how your system starts, you may now see a menu resembling Figure DOS1–3. This is a graphic extension of DOS called a *shell* program. The shell program presents you with items that can be selected with a few keystrokes or a mouse. In the future, you may want to examine this menu on your own, but since this module concentrates on the command-driven version of DOS, you must exit the shell before you can continue. For this exercise,

1.   If there is no shell menu on your screen, continue to the next section

2. If the shell menu is on your screen, press **F3** to exit the DOS shell and enter the DOS command mode

The Default Drive.   Once you have entered the date and time and exited the DOS shell if necessary, a *prompt* will appear on your screen: "C>" for a hard disk or "A>" for a diskette system. Your system may display a slightly different prompt (such as "C:\>") but it will still include some indication of an "A" or a "C."

The DOS prompt tells you two things: (1) DOS is currently pointing to Drive C (or Drive A), and (2) DOS is ready for your next command. The drive to which DOS is pointing is called the **default drive**. The default drive is the disk drive on which DOS automatically will look for commands or program files if they aren't already in RAM. If you issue commands without naming a specific disk drive, DOS assumes that you mean the default drive. Consequently, if you issue a DOS command that isn't in memory or on the disk in the default drive, you will get an error message.

Later in this chapter, you'll learn how to change the default drive and how to refer to disks other than the one on the default drive. The next chapter will show you how to change the DOS prompt itself. Before using specific DOS file commands, you should know something about DOS filenames and how to quit DOS.

☞ Tip: DOS version 6.0 offers a help feature invoked by typing *HELP* and pressing the Enter key or typing the command followed by /? (as in FORMAT /?) and pressing the Enter key.

Naming Files in DOS

Like other operating systems, DOS has a convention for naming and handling files. A file can contain program instructions or data. It might be a word-processed document, a spreadsheet, a program, or even a collection of DOS commands.

DOS Filenames.   A DOS file is typically specified by three components, separated respectively by a colon and a period. Consider the DOS *filename* A:DATA1994.JAN, shown in Figure DOS1–4a.

The first (optional and temporary) component of the filename is the drive specification, which indicates the drive on which the file can be found. It is necessary to type this component only when the file is located on a drive other than the default drive. So, for instance, you would have to type the *A:* in front of DATA1994.JAN if Drive C was the default drive. If Drive A was the default, you would not need to include the *A:*. The drive specification is not part of the filename but merely a locating device placed in front of the actual filename. As you will see in the next chapter, the drive specification may also include additional information concerning the location of a file.

The second (mandatory) component is the main part of the filename, which consists of one to eight characters. In many software packages, this component must begin with a letter and cannot contain special characters. In general, you should not use a space as part of a filename, nor characters reserved for DOS commands, such as * and ?. In addition, DOS will truncate (eliminate) all characters after the first eight you type. For example, BUDGET1992 and BUDGET1993 would have the same filename (based on the first eight characters), namely, BUDGET19.

The third (optional) component is the *extension* part of the filename. The extension consists of one to three characters. Extensions are useful for qualifying related files; for example, BUDG1994.JAN and BUDG1994.FEB are different filenames.

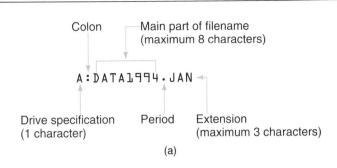

Figure DOS1—4
*The Anatomy
of a Filename*

(a) A filename consists of an
optional drive specification, a
required main part, and an
optional extension.
(b) Filenames may include path
identifiers to indicate
subdirectories and disk drives.

Filename	Refers to
TEST	The file TEST on the current (default) disk drive.
TEST.ONE	The file TEST (with extension ONE) on the default disk.
\CLASS\TEST	The file TEST in the subdirectory CLASS on the default disk.
C:\CLASS\TEST	The file TEST in the subdirectory CLASS on the C: drive.

(b)

At times, the file you seek may be located in another portion of your disk (called a subdirectory). When this occurs, you can add a *path identifier* between the drive specification and the main filename, as in C:\ACCT\BUDG1994.JAN. Figure DOS1–4b displays a few samples of filenames. The next chapter will present subdirectories in detail.

You must be careful when choosing filenames, because a particular filename (the main part and extension) cannot be used more than once with the same disk specification. In DOS, saving a file with a filename that already exists on the disk will cause the new file to replace the old one—erasing the old file! For this reason, many software packages ask for verification before they replace existing files with new files with the same filename; DOS, however, does not.

Special Extensions.   DOS and many software packages use special extensions to differentiate among certain types of files. For example, Lotus 1-2-3 uses the extension .WK1 on its worksheets (Quattro uses .WQ1), .PRN for print files, and .PIC for graphs. Similarly, dBASE uses the extension .DBF for database files, .NDX for individual indexes, and .TXT for text files. Paradox identifies its table files with .DB.

Because many programs (such as Lotus 1-2-3 and Quattro) can tell by context the type of file in which you are working, you need not refer to such extensions when using these programs. When you're working in DOS, however, you must explicitly refer to these extensions; DOS does not make any assumptions about extensions since it works with so many different software packages.

Wildcard Characters.   Wildcard characters save you work when referring to filenames, so a single command can be used to copy or erase several files with similar characters in their names. A **wildcard** character is a special character that can stand for one or more regular characters in a filename. DOS offers two wildcard characters: the question mark (?) and the asterisk (*).

The *?* (question mark) wildcard stands for a *single* character in a filename. For instance, if you wanted to erase four files named DATA1, DATA2, DATA3, and DATA4, you could tell DOS to erase DATA?. When the ? wildcard is used, each question mark acts as a substitute for any one character that occupies that position in the filename. It will also refer to any filename that matches all the characters up to the question mark. For example, the previous command, *ERASE DATA?*, would also erase a file named *DATA*. Similarly, the command *ERASE M??.TXT* would erase MOM.TXT but would remove MO.TXT and M.TXT as well.

The * (asterisk) wildcard stands for *several* character positions in a filename; for instance, *DATA** would refer to any file that started with the characters "DATA"; any remaining characters of the filename are ignored.

Both wildcard characters can be used as references in the same filename; for instance, *D*.A?B* would refer to any file that started with *D* and whose extension started with *A* and ended with *B*.

Wildcard characters are extremely useful but can prove disastrous if you make mistakes. For instance, if you told DOS to erase *D*.**, it would erase all files that start with *D*—some that you might have wanted to keep on the disk. Use wildcards carefully.

Choosing Filenames.   You should also be careful and systematic when choosing names for your files. Filenames that follow a pattern and have some meaning are easier to locate and manipulate than those that have obscure, randomly assigned names. For instance, if all your letters home are named HOME0101.LTR, HOME0122.LTR, HOME0425.LTR, and so on, you can refer to all of them with HOME*.LTR. Similarly, if all your letters have the extension .LTR, you could refer to these with *.LTR.

Quitting DOS

Quitting from the DOS system is quite simple. Anytime you are at the DOS prompt (C> or A>, for example) and want to quit, follow these steps:

1. Remove any diskettes from the disk drives

If they are 5¼-inch, place them in their protective envelopes.

2. Turn off the system unit's power switch
3. If the monitor has a separate power switch, turn it off as well

Checkpoint

☐ Start your computer and get to the DOS prompt.

☐ Name five files that are referenced by the filename DA??.W*.

☐ Exit from DOS and correctly turn off the computer.

Manipulating Files: DOS Commands

DOS contains a rich set of commands for manipulating program and data files. Here, you'll investigate the most important of the basic commands. The next chapter will present a more advanced set.

If computer memory was infinite, every command could be placed into RAM for immediate availability. Unfortunately, it is not. To conserve space in memory, DOS provides two types of commands: internal and external.

Internal and External Commands

Internal Commands.   **Internal commands** are those loaded into RAM during booting. They remain in RAM until you turn off your computer. Because these commands are kept in the computer's memory, you may invoke them at any time, whether or not DOS is in the default drive. Internal commands include those that are used most often in normal operation, such as COPY, ERASE, DIR, and RENAME. Some software packages also offer programs called *resident* or *TSR (Terminate and Stay Resident)* programs; like internal DOS commands, they remain conveniently in RAM until you turn off the computer.

External Commands.   **External commands**, on the other hand, are not loaded into RAM when the system is booted but remain on the DOS disk. Normally, to issue an external command, you must have DOS in the default drive (or on the hard-disk drive). When an external command is invoked, the appropriate program is copied from the DOS disk into RAM and executed; upon completion, it is removed from RAM to save space. Typically, external commands—such as FORMAT and SYS—are not used often. Like external DOS commands, most software packages' programs are placed in RAM when invoked and removed from RAM when you quit the program. Such programs are called *transient*— they remain in RAM only while in use.

In a dual-diskette system, there is a clear difference between invoking an internal and an external command. Internal commands are acted upon immediately (since they are already in RAM); external commands must first be located on the default diskette and then loaded into RAM. In a hard-disk system or network, this distinction between internal and external DOS commands is less evident to the user. External commands are still kept on disk, but the disk itself is contained within the system unit (or is available on the network), and the hard-disk drive has such a fast access speed that it requires only a fraction of a second to locate and load a command.

Figure DOS1–5 provides a capsule summary of the DOS commands you'll be learning in this chapter. Each of the commands must be issued after DOS has displayed its command prompt; for example, A> or B> (for dual-diskette drives), C> or C:\> (for a hard-disk drive). Here, for simplicity, assume a hard-disk system that contains the DOS files in a portion of the disk—called a subdirectory—that has the name "DOS" (more about subdirectories later). If you have a dual-diskette system, the commands can be issued directly from Drive A, which contains the DOS disk. (If you are using a network, check with your instructor or lab technician.) After you type in a command, you must press the Enter key to send the command into the system unit.

The **FORMAT** command lets you prepare a disk for use on your computer. Every new disk must be formatted (organized) for your computer before you can store anything on it. The FORMAT command sets up the disk's directory and File Allocation Table and divides the disk into addressable storage locations. It will also check for defective tracks on the disk and seal them off from further use. You can use the FORMAT command on a disk that has previously been formatted; it will erase the disk's files and set up a new blank directory.

Formatting a Disk

DOS

Figure DOS1—5

A Summary of DOS Commands Presented in this Chapter

Command	Type	Description
A: (or C:)	I	Changes default drive to the named disk drive
CHKDSK	E	Checks a disk for errors and provides a report
CLS	I	Clears the screen
COMP	E	Compares the contents of two files
COPY	I	Duplicates a specified file
DATE	I	Displays and sets the system date
DIR	I	Lists a disk's files in a directory
DISKCOMP	E	Compares two disks
DISKCOPY	E	Copies an entire diskette to another diskette
ERASE (also DEL)	I	Deletes a specified file(s)
FORMAT	E	Prepares a disk for use with MS-DOS or PC-DOS
LABEL	E	Labels a disk
REN	I	Renames a file
SYS	E	Copies MS-DOS or PC-DOS system files to a named disk
TIME	I	Displays and sets the time
UNDELETE	E	Returns files that have been erased
VER	I	Displays the DOS version number
VOL	I	Displays a disk's volume label
XCOPY	E	Alternate method for duplicating files or directories

I = Internal   E = External   Note: Not all external commands will work on a network.

FORMAT is an external command, so your DOS files must be available on the network or Drive C (or a DOS disk must be present in Drive A) when you issue the command. To prepare for this exercise, boot up your computer. Remember how?

1. Place a DOS disk in Drive A if your computer has no hard-disk drive, otherwise leave Drive A empty
2. Turn on the system unit
3. If requested, answer the date and time prompts to arrive at the DOS prompt

Formatting Double-Density Diskettes on High-Density Drives and Other Options.   If your computer system has a high-density disk drive, it can recognize both high-density and double-density formatted disks. However, when

Modifier	Description
/1	Formats a single side of a diskette
/4	Formats a 5¼-inch, 360K diskette in a high-density drive. *Warning:* Some 360K disk drives may not be able to read these disks.
/S	Copies the operating system files from the default disk to a newly formatted disk
/T:#	Specifies the number of tracks to be formatted on a 3½-inch diskette—as in /T:80
/N:#	Specifies the number of sectors per track to be formatted on a 3½-inch diskette—as in /N:9
/V:label	Specifies the volume label to use
/F:#	Specifies the size of the diskette to format. Values include the following (each size can be expressed as a number, or a number followed by *K*, *KB*, *M*, or *MB*—as in 360KB):

Disk type:	Size:	Example:
5¼″ 360K double-sided	360	FORMAT A:/F:360
5¼″ 1.2M high-density	1200, 1.2M	FORMAT A:/F:1200
3½″ 720K double-sided	720	FORMAT A:/F:720
3½″ 1.44M high-density	1440, 1.44M	FORMAT A:/F:1440

you *format* disks on this drive, the system will always attempt to format them as high density. Unless you indicate otherwise, DOS will attempt to format each disk for the maximum capacity of the drive. To format double-density disks, you must add a /4 or /F:360 option to the FORMAT command. This tells the system to use double-density (360K) formatting. You can also use this option to format a high-density disk so that it can be read by a double-density drive (a waste of disk space to be sure, but necessary sometimes when you are moving files from one computer to another). A similar FORMAT option is available for high-density 3½-inch disks as well. Figure DOS1–6 lists the common formatting options.

☞ **Tip: DOS includes an UNFORMAT command that can restore much of a diskette (or hard disk) that was reformatted by mistake (provided you have not saved any files on it yet). Use the HELP feature or see the DOS Appendix for details.**

The FORMAT Command. If you are using a hard-disk system or network, format your blank disk in Drive A, following the directions that appear in the left column of the page. However, if you are using a dual-diskette system, use Drive B for formatting, leaving the DOS disk in Drive A. In this case, follow the directions shown in the right column, using B: as the disk identifier. If you are using a network, there may be another procedure you must use. Check with your instructor or lab technician.

Hard-Disk System

1. Type **CD DOS** (or **CD** followed by the name of the subdirectory that contains your DOS files) and

   press ↵

2. At the C> (or C:\>) prompt, type

   FORMAT A: and press ↵

Note: If you are formatting a disk of less capacity than the disk drive, add the appropriate option (/f:and a number).

Make sure to leave a blank space between the command and the disk specification.

A screen message now asks you to place a new disk in Drive A and then to strike the Enter key.

3. Put a blank disk in Drive A (and close the door if needed)

4. Press ↵ to begin formatting

Dual-Diskette System

1. At the A> prompt, type
   FORMAT B:

Make sure to leave a blank space between the command and the disk specification.

2. Press ↵

A screen message now asks you to place a new disk in Drive B and then to strike the Enter key.

3. Put a blank disk in Drive B (and close the door if needed)

4. Press ↵ to begin formatting

If an error message appears, check the position of your disk and try again.

☞ **Tip: Issuing the FORMAT command *without* a disk specifier (permitted in earlier DOS versions before 4.0) will destroy all the data on whatever disk is in the default drive, so it is safer *always* to include a drive identifier after the FORMAT command.**

The system will check to see if the disk is already formatted. If it is, it will save the information in case you decide to "unformat" this disk later. The computer system will now begin to format the disk. This may take a minute or more depending on disk capacity and computer speed. Your screen may display its progress as it works. When the formatting is finished, DOS will ask for a "Volume label" to help identify your disk in the future.

5. When the volume label message appears, type your last name and press

   DOS will then inform you of its success. If the format was totally successful, you should see a message similar to the one in Figure DOS1–7. Or the message may identify bad disk areas, as in Figure DOS1–8. Your numbers may differ depending on the disk you formatted. The disk is still usable, however; DOS has formatted the good parts and will work around the bad ones.

   You can now format another disk or, if your disk had some bad sectors, you can format the same disk again by pressing Y and the Enter key at this time. Often, a second format will fix some of the bad sectors identified in the first format attempt.

6. Press **N** ↵ to answer "No" to "Format another disk?"

The DOS prompt will reappear.

☞ **Tip: DOS also offers a FORMAT/Q command to quickly reformat a previously formatted disk that has no bad sectors.**

```
C:\DOS>format a:
Insert new diskette for drive A:
and press ENTER when ready...

Checking existing disk format.
Formatting 1.2M
Format complete.

Volume label (11 characters, ENTER for none)?

    1213952 bytes total disk space  ◄────────── Your numbers
    1213952 bytes available on disk             may differ
                                                from these
       512 bytes in each allocation unit.
      2371 allocation units available on disk.

Volume Serial Number is 1433-1700

Format another (Y/N)?n


C:\DOS>
```

Figure DOS1—7
A Successful DOS Format Displays the Total Storage Area Available on Your Disk (Double-density disk would show 362496)

```
C:\>FORMAT A:
Insert new diskette for drive A:
and press ENTER when ready...

Checking existing disk format.
Saving UNFORMAT information.
Verifying 1.2M
Format complete.

Volume label (11 characters, ENTER for none)? LASTNAME

    1213952 bytes total disk space
     453120 bytes in bad sectors
     760832 bytes available on disk

       512 bytes in each allocation unit.
      1486 allocation units available on disk.

Volume Serial Number is 2D5E-12D7

Format another (Y/N)?
```

Figure DOS1—8
The Format Process also Identifies Any Bad Disk Areas, Which Will Result in Less Storage Space Even though the Disk Is Still Usable

Formatting with System. The FORMAT command creates a disk with the maximum available space for data. However, you can add additional symbols to invoke various formatting options. (Remember to add an /f: option if needed.) Try this command sequence:

Hard-Disk System	**Dual-Diskette System**
1. Type **FORMAT A:/S**	1. Type **FORMAT B:/S**
2. Press ↵	2. Press ↵
3. Check to make sure your disk is in Drive A	3. Check to make sure your disk is in Drive B
4. Press any key to continue	4. Press any key to continue

Figure DOS1—9

FORMAT /S Copies System Files to the Disk, Which Can Then Be Used to Boot Up the Computer

```
C:\>format a:/s
Insert new diskette for drive A:
and press ENTER when ready...

Checking existing disk format.
Saving UNFORMAT information.
Verifying 1.2M
Format complete.
System transferred

Volume label (11 characters, ENTER for none)?

   1213952 bytes total disk space
    119808 bytes used by system
   1094144 bytes available on disk

       512 bytes in each allocation unit.
      2137 allocation units available on disk.

Volume Serial Number is 0B47-1703

Format another (Y/N)?
```

By specifying /S in the FORMAT command, some operating system files will be copied from the default drive to the disk being formatted. These include a few hidden files (IBMBIO.COM and IBMDOS.COM in PC-DOS, or IO.SYS and MSDOS.SYS in MS-DOS) and a COMMAND.COM file. The screen will notify you when the disk has been formatted and the system transferred (copied) to the new disk. While this type of formatting is unnecessary on a hard-disk system, it is useful when preparing disks to be used on a dual-diskette system or a network. A disk formatted with the /S option is now a *system disk* and can be used to boot the computer without the need for a separate DOS disk.

When the format is finished, note that the available space on the formatted disk has been reduced by the system files that have been copied onto it, as shown in Figure DOS1—9.

5. Press **N** to answer "No" to "Format another disk?"

Installing the System

At times, you may want to transfer the operating system from the default drive to a disk that has already been formatted. Remember that the FORMAT /S command will destroy any existing files on the disk (which you may not want to do). For example, you may have purchased a software disk that has space for the DOS system files but does not yet contain them. You may want to copy the necessary start-up files to this disk so that it can boot your computer. In this instance, DOS provides a command called **SYS** that transfers the hidden DOS files to the specified disk. If you are using a network, check with your instructor or lab technician. In a hard-disk or dual-diskette system, do the following:

Hard-Disk System

1. Be sure that your disk is in Drive A

2. Type **CD DOS** (or use the subdirectory name that contains your DOS files)

3. Press ↵

4. Type **SYS A:** and press ↵

Dual-Diskette System

1. Be sure that a DOS disk is in Drive A and that your disk is in Drive B

2. At the A> prompt, type **SYS B:**

3. Press ↵

If the proper space is available, the hidden DOS files will be transferred to the disk. SYS is an external command and thus requires that DOS files be available on the default drive. Note that in earlier DOS versions, SYS does not copy the COMMAND.COM file to the disk. If you wanted to use this disk to boot the computer system, you would also have to copy COMMAND.COM separately to the disk (more on copying in a moment). In addition, SYS does not work in a network environment and may not work with some disks (if not, an error message will appear on the screen).

At times, you will want to change the default drive. Try one of these two procedures (depending on your system).

Changing the Default Drive

Hard-Disk System

1. Keep your disk in Drive A

2. At the C>, type **A:**

3. Press ↵ to change the default drive to A

The computer now prompts with *A>* (or *A:\>*). To switch to Drive C:

4. At the A>, type **C:**

5. Press ↵

Dual-Diskette System

1. Keep your disk in Drive B

2. At the A>, type **B:**

3. Press ↵ to change the default drive to B

The computer now prompts with *B>*. To switch to Drive A:

4. At the B>, type **A:**

5. Press ↵

In many networks, a Drive "F" specification is used to hold network files. You can use this same technique to switch to Drive A and back to F as needed. The command to change the default drive is an internal command.

Listing a Disk Directory

The **DIR** command displays the names of the files that are stored on a disk. For example, to list a disk directory for the default drive:

1. Type **DIR**

2. Press ↵

This produces a list of filenames similar to that shown in Figure DOS1–10. Although your list may contain different information, its arrangement should match fairly closely. The list generated by the DIR command shows the filename of each file, its extension (if any), its size expressed in bytes, and the date and time it was last saved. The topmost line identifies any disk volume label that was specified; the bottom line displays a file count, the total space used by the files, and the space remaining on the disk (measured in bytes).

If the directory of files exceeds one screen, you can add a "pause" option to the DIR command as follows:

3. Type **DIR /P**

4. Press ↵

The listing will pause after each screen is filled. Striking any key will produce the next screen, and so on.

An alternative method is to use a "wide" option with the DIR command as follows:

5. Type **DIR /W**

6. Press ↵

Figure DOS1—10

The DIR Command Displays the Names of the Files That Are Stored on a Disk

(Your list will differ.)

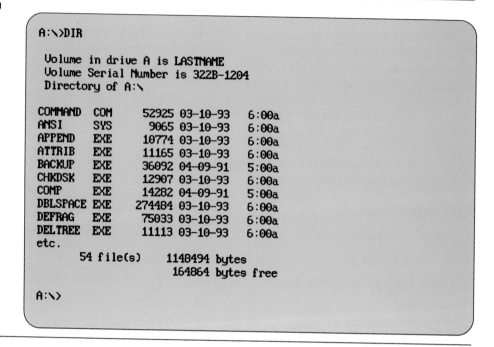

```
A:\>DIR

Volume in drive A is LASTNAME
Volume Serial Number is 322B-1204
Directory of A:\

COMMAND  COM     52925 03-10-93   6:00a
ANSI     SYS      9065 03-10-93   6:00a
APPEND   EXE     10774 03-10-93   6:00a
ATTRIB   EXE     11165 03-10-93   6:00a
BACKUP   EXE     36092 04-09-91   5:00a
CHKDSK   EXE     12907 03-10-93   6:00a
COMP     EXE     14282 04-09-91   5:00a
DBLSPACE EXE    274484 03-10-93   6:00a
DEFRAG   EXE     75033 03-10-93   6:00a
DELTREE  EXE     11113 03-10-93   6:00a
etc.
        54 file(s)     1148494 bytes
                        164864 bytes free

A:\>
```

This produces a display of filenames only, five columns wide, allowing you to view over 100 filenames at a time.

By specifying a drive other than the default, as in *DIR B:*, you can list the files on other drives as well. Try the following:

Hard-Disk System or Network

7. Be sure that your disk is in Drive A

8. Type **DIR A:**

9. Press ⏎

Dual-Diskette System

7. Be sure that your disk is in Drive B

8. Type **DIR B:**

9. Press ⏎

If you have followed the commands presented so far, the list you now see on your screen should resemble Figure DOS1–11a. One file—COMMAND.COM—appears in the disk's directory. On the other hand, a disk that has been formatted but contains no files on it as yet (other than hidden files) will display the directory shown in Figure DOS1–11b.

☞ Tip: Using the DIR command is a quick way to determine if a disk has been formatted. If a directory appears (even the message "File not found"), then the disk is formatted. If the message "General failure error" appears, then the disk is not formatted or the disk and drive are not compatible.

The DIR command can also be used with DOS wildcard characters to produce a selective list of filenames. For example, *DIR *.COM* would display all files whose extension was COM. The command *DIR DATA?.** would list all files with four or five characters in their filename starting with the word *DATA*. The command *DIR *.** lists *all* files (any filename, any extension). You may want to try the three DIR commands shown in Figure DOS1–12 and compare the results on your screen with the lists in the figure. Of course, your list may differ in the number and names of the files it displays but should accurately reflect the contents of the disk in the default drive.

DOS

```
C:\>DIR A:

 Volume in drive A is LASTNAME
 Volume Serial Number is 322B-1204
 Directory of A:\

COMMAND  COM      52925 03-10-93   6:00a
         1 file(s)      52925 bytes
                      1041219 bytes free

C:\>
```
(a)

```
C:\>DIR A:

 Volume in drive A is OTHER
 Volume Serial Number is 3B76-12CC
 Directory of A:\

File not found

C:\>
```
(b)

Figure DOS1—11
DIR Displays the Contents of Any Disk

(a) The DIR of your data disk displays that one file—COMMAND.COM—is in the directory. The hidden DOS system files do not appear as part of the directory.
(b) A formatted disk that contains no files (other than hidden files) will display "File not found."

```
DIR C*.EXE

CHKDSK   EXE     12907 03-10-93   6:00a
COMP     EXE     14282 04-09-91   5:00a


DIR *.COM /W

COMMAND.COM    ASSIGN.COM    CHOICE.COM    CV.COM       DISKCOPY.COM
DOSKEY.COM     EDIT.COM      FAKEMOUS.COM  FORMAT.COM   GRAFTABL.COM
GRAPHICS.COM   HELP.COM      KEYB.COM      LOADFIX.COM  MIRROR.COM
MODE.COM       MORE.COM      MOUSE.COM     MSHERC.COM   PRINTFIX.COM
SYS.COM        TREE.COM      UNFORMAT.COM  USAFE.COM


DIR F*.*

FAKEMOUS COM       307 03-10-93   6:00a
FASTOPEN EXE     12050 04-09-91   5:00a
FORMAT   COM     22717 03-10-93   6:00a
FDISK    EXE     57224 04-09-91   5:00a
FIND     EXE      6770 04-09-91   5:00a
```

Figure DOS1—12
DIR Commands Using Wildcards and the /W Modifier

DIR is an internal command and can be issued in combination with /P, /W, and the wildcard characters ? and * as needed.

Copying Files

The **COPY** command allows you to duplicate a file. COPY is an internal command and thus does not require the DOS disk to be in the default drive. You can copy a file to the same disk or from one disk to another; you may use the same filename (with one exception as you will shortly see) or create a new one. COPY can also be used with DOS wildcard characters to copy related files. Prepare to try some COPY exercises:

Hard-Disk System	Dual-Diskette System or Network
1. If your computer is off, boot it up and get to the C> prompt	1. If your computer is not yet on, place a DOS disk in Drive A and boot up the system to get to the A> prompt
2. Place your formatted disk in Drive A	
3. Type **CD DOS** (or whatever subdirectory name contains your DOS files)	2. Place a formatted disk in Drive B (if you have no Drive B, skip this step)
4. Press ⏎	

Copying from One Disk to Another. In a hard-disk system or network, the general form for copying a file from the default drive to Drive A is

```
COPY FILE1.EXT A:FILE2.EXT
```

This command will locate a file named FILE1.EXT on the default drive and make a duplicate of it on Drive A, in a file named FILE2.EXT.

In a dual-diskette system, this same command could be typed as

```
COPY FILE1.EXT B:FILE2.EXT
```

This would copy the file from the default drive (Drive A) to Drive B with the name FILE2.EXT. Try this on your computer:

Hard-Disk System	Single- or Dual-Diskette System
1. Type **COPY COMMAND.COM A:TEST1.COM**	1. Type **COPY COMMAND.COM B:TEST1.COM**
2. Press ⏎	2. Press ⏎

Notice that the light on each drive glows momentarily, indicating that the disk is in use, as the file is located and copied. You should not open disk-drive doors, or try to remove disks, while the light remains lit.

There should now be a file named TEST1.COM on your data disk. To verify this:

Hard-Disk System	Dual-Diskette System
1. Type **DIR A:**	1. Type **DIR B:**
2. Press ⏎	2. Press ⏎

The directory now shows this new file as in those of Figure DOS1–13a. Note that TEST1.COM's file size and date are identical to those of COMMAND.COM.

To copy a file (such as TREE.COM) from the default drive to your data disk *with the same name*, simply omit the new name from the COPY command, as seen here in general form:

```
COPY FILE1.EXT A:
```

To see this in action, follow these steps:

Hard-Disk System	Dual-Diskette System
1. Type **COPY TREE.COM A:**	1. Type **COPY TREE.COM B:**
2. Press ⏎	2. Press ⏎

Figure DOS1—13

The DIR Command Can Be Used to Confirm Successful Copies

```
C:\>DIR A:

Volume in drive A is LASTNAME
Volume Serial Number is 322B-1204
Directory of A:\

COMMAND  COM     52925 03-10-93   6:00a
TEST1    COM     52925 03-10-93   6:00a
        2 file(s)       105850 bytes
                        988294 bytes free

C:\>
```

(a)

(a) The COMMAND.COM file has been copied into a new file called TEST1.COM—note the size, date, and time are identical.
(b) TREE.COM has been copied from the DOS disk and added to your data disk.

```
C:\>DIR A:

Volume in drive A is LASTNAME
Volume Serial Number is 322B-1204
Directory of A:\

COMMAND  COM     52925 03-10-93   6:00a
TEST1    COM     52925 03-10-93   6:00a
TREE     COM      6898 03-10-93   6:00a
        3 file(s)       112748 bytes
                        981396 bytes free

C:\>
```

(b)

Note: If you have only one disk drive, you will now be prompted to switch disks. Remove the source disk, replace it with the disk that will hold the copy, and press the Enter key to continue.

If the message "File not found" appears on your screen, then either you typed the command incorrectly or the TREE.COM file does not exist on the default drive. Retype the command correctly if necessary, or simply continue if TREE.COM is not available.

When the copying is finished, type *DIR A:* (or *DIR B:*) to verify that TREE.COM has indeed been copied to your disk, as in Figure DOS1–13b.

For each of the remaining COPY exercises, watch the disk drive lights and, after the copy routine has finished, generate a directory to verify that a new file has been created.

☞ **Tip: This is a good habit to establish when copying files—watch the drive lights while copying and check the directory when copying has ended.**

Before continuing, change the default drive as follows:

Hard-Disk System or Network	**Dual-Diskette System**
1. Leave your disk in Drive A	1. Leave your disk in Drive B
2. Type **A:**	2. Type **B:**
3. Press ↵	3. Press ↵

The new prompt appears on the screen.

Copying on the Same Disk.   The general form for copying a file from the default drive onto the same disk is

```
COPY FILE1.EXT FILE2.EXT
```

This command will duplicate a file named FILE1.EXT on the default drive in a file named FILE2.EXT. Try this on your computer:

1.   Type **COPY TEST1.COM TEST2.COM**

2.   Press   ↵

To see that TEST1.COM and TEST2.COM are now on the default disk:

3.   Type **DIR** and press   ↵

The DOS COPY command puts one restriction on copying—it will not copy a file to the same disk directory unless it is given a new name. Thus, the commands *COPY TEST1.COM, COPY A:TEST1.COM A:,* or *COPY B:TEST1.COM B:,* will not work. Try one if you like. The screen will respond with a message such as "File cannot be copied onto itself."

Copying with DOS Wildcards.   As with DIR, the COPY command can use DOS wildcard characters. For instance, if you want to copy to your data disk all the files in DOS that start with *D* and have the extension .COM, try this:

Hard-Disk System

1.   Type **COPY   C:\DOS\D∗.COM   A:**

The extra *\DOS* after the *C:* is necessary to locate the DOS subdirectory. (You will learn more about subdirectories in the next chapter.) Replace *DOS* with the name of the appropriate DOS subdirectory on your hard disk.

2.   Press   ↵

Dual-Diskette System

1.   Type **COPY   A:D∗.COM   B:**

2.   Press   ↵

☞ Tip: You can still issue this command with only *one* disk drive. The program will prompt you when to switch disks.

A number of files (perhaps four) may be found among the DOS files and copied to your disk as shown in Figure DOS1–14a. You may have different files than the ones shown in the figure, or none at all.

☞ Tip: Since the default drive is set to the one that contains your disk, you could omit the *A:* (or *B:*) from the COPY command in this example.

Here's a slightly more complicated variation using one drive that shows the versatility of the COPY command:

1.   Type **COPY   D∗.∗   G∗.BAK**

2.   Press   ↵

All files that start with *D* are copied to new files on the same disk whose names start with *G* and end with the extension *.BAK,* as you can see in Figure DOS1–14b.

3.   Type **DIR**

4.   Press   ↵

Examine the directory to verify that the copying has occurred. Many variations are possible. For example, *COPY C:∗.∗ A:* copies all files on Drive C to Drive

Chapter 1   *Commonly Used DOS Commands*   **DOS23**

```
A:\> COPY C:\DOS\D*.COM A:
C:\DOS\DOSKEY.COM
C:\DOS\DOSSHELL.COM
C:\DOS\DISKCOMP.COM
C:\DOS\DISKCOPY.COM
        4 file(s) copied

A:\>
```
(a)

```
A:\>DIR

Volume in drive A is LASTNAME
Volume Serial Number is 322B-1204
Directory of A:\

COMMAND  COM    52925 03-10-93   6:00a
TEST1    COM    52925 03-10-93   6:00a
TREE     COM     6898 03-10-93   6:00a
TEST2    COM    52925 03-10-93   6:00a
DOSKEY   COM     5883 03-10-93   6:00a
DOSSHELL COM     4623 04-09-91   5:00a
DISKCOMP COM    10652 04-09-91   5:00a
DISKCOPY COM    11879 03-10-93   6:00a
GOSKEY   BAK     5883 03-10-93   6:00a
GOSSHELL BAK     4623 04-09-91   5:00a
GISKCOMP BAK    10652 04-09-91   5:00a
GISKCOPY BAK    11879 03-10-93   6:00a
       12 file(s)    231747 bytes
                     862397 bytes free

A:\>
```
(b)

Figure DOS1—14
Using Wildcards in the COPY Command

(a) The COPY C:\DOS\D*.COM command copies any file on the DOS subdirectory that starts with a D and has a .COM extension (you may have different files than the ones shown in the figure, or none at all).
(b) The DIR command displays that the COPY D*.* G*.BAK command has duplicated the files starting with D but has renamed them to start with "G" and have a .BAK extension.

A using the same names (assuming there is ample space for all the files). Similarly, on a dual-diskette system, *COPY A:*.* B:* copies all files from Drive A to Drive B.

Copying with Verification.   Although copying errors are rare, you may want DOS to verify that a file has been correctly copied. This can be done by adding /V at the end of the COPY command, as in *COPY TEST1.COM TEST2.COM /V*. This option causes the COPY command to run more slowly but may increase your peace of mind when copying critical data.

Using XCOPY.   The DOS command **XCOPY** can be used to copy files, directories, and subdirectories. It has the form

```
XCOPY file1 file2
```

By adding options to the end of the command, you can further control which files are copied. For example, adding a /d:date option tells DOS to copy only those files modified on or after the specified date. Thus, XCOPY A: B: /D:04/25/93 will copy all files from Drive A to Drive B that were modified on or after April 25, 1993.

The option /s will copy all directories and subdirectories unless they do not contain files. An /e option will copy *all* directories and subdirectories, even if they are empty. Thus, XCOPY A: B: /s will copy all nonempty directories (and their files) from Drive A to Drive B.

Refer to the Appendix and your software manual for additional information about XCOPY.

Copying the Contents of an Entire Diskette

DISKCOPY is an external command that allows you to copy the entire contents of one diskette onto a similar diskette. (Of course, this command should be used only where it does not violate a copyright.) In addition, if the target diskette is not yet formatted, the DISKCOPY command also formats as it copies. Like FORMAT, DISKCOPY erases any files already on the target diskette and should be used with caution. Because the contents of a hard disk cannot fit onto one diskette, DISKCOPY *cannot* be used to copy from hard disk onto a diskette. In general, the disks used in DISKCOPY must be of similar data capacity. It is obvious that you cannot diskcopy a 720K diskette to a 360K one, but you also cannot use DISKCOPY to duplicate a 360K diskette on to one that holds 1.2 Meg.

Do *not* issue this command now, but review the procedure for future use in copying your own diskettes. Assuming DOS is in Drive A (the default), the command would be *DISKCOPY A: B:*.

The system would now prepare to copy the contents of the disk in Drive A (called the *source diskette*) onto the disk in Drive B (called the *target diskette*). The system would prompt you as shown in Figure DOS1–15. At this point, you would place your source disk (the disk you want to copy from) in Drive A, and a target disk (the disk you want to copy to) in Drive B. Then, you would strike any key to begin the actual copy procedure.

☞ Tip: If you have only one disk drive, you can still issue the command as *DISKCOPY A: B:* and place the source disk in Drive A. The screen would then prompt you to change back and forth between the target and source disks as each is needed.

Renaming Files

At times, you will want to change the name of a file. The **RENAME** command (abbreviated as **REN**) enables you to do this easily. It has the form *REN FILE1.EXT FILE2.EXT*, which changes the name of FILE1.EXT to FILE2.EXT. Try this example:

1. Set the default drive to the disk drive where your formatted disk is located (A: for hard-disk systems, B: for two-disk systems)

Figure DOS1–15
The DISKCOPY Command Screen Prompt

```
C:\>DISKCOPY A: B:

Insert SOURCE diskette in drive A:

Insert TARGET diskette in drive B:

Press any key to continue . . .
```

2. Type **REN TEST1.COM PRACTICE**

3. Press ⏎

You can type *DIR* to verify that TEST1.COM has been renamed PRACTICE. The RENAME command can be used with DOS wildcard characters as well, as in *REN FILE∗.TXT DATA∗.BAK* and so on. RENAME is an internal command.

DOS offers two erase commands: **ERASE** and **DEL** (Delete). Since the commands are identical in effect, only one is presented here. ERASE, which is an internal command, is particularly useful for removing unwanted files from a disk that is reaching capacity.

Erasing Files

Erasing One File. Any file can be erased by typing the command ERASE followed by the full filename. First, verify that the DOS prompt still shows the default disk is set as it was in the RENAME exercise. If not, change it. Now try this:

1. Type **ERASE TEST2.COM**

2. Press ⏎

3. Type **DIR**

4. Press ⏎

A directory will verify that the filename has been removed.

Erasing with DOS Wildcards. As with other DOS commands, ERASE can be used with the DOS wildcards to remove more than one file at a time. Be careful, since a carelessly stated ERASE command can remove the wrong files. Follow these steps:

1. Type **ERASE ∗.COM**

2. Press ⏎

All files on the default disk with the extension .COM have been erased. To erase all the files in a disk's directory, do the following:

Hard-Disk System or Network	**Dual-Diskette System**
1. Type **ERASE A:∗.∗**	1. Type **ERASE B:∗.∗**
2. Press ⏎	2. Press ⏎

Note the use of a named disk drive in this ERASE command. It is a good idea to state the disk drive explicitly in an ERASE command of this magnitude to reduce the chance of error.

Since removal of all the files on a disk is a drastic action, the system will now ask "Are you sure (Y/N)?" You must verify the erase command by pressing Y (*yes*) or N (*no*).

3. Press **Y** ⏎ to continue

A directory will show that all files on your disk have been erased. Try it now. The directory should resemble the earlier Figure DOS1–11b.

Erased, but Gone Forever? A final note about erasing. When you erase a file, DOS does not really remove it from the disk, but simply replaces the first character in its filename with a special initial character. This character tells the system to ignore the file and use its space allocation, even though the file is still physically left on the disk. Although its name does not appear in the directory, the file's contents are not written over until another file is saved on the disk.

This opens up the possibility of *un*erasing a file. As long as you haven't copied or saved another file on the disk, you can identify the erased files and put them back on the directory, in effect "unerasing" them.

DOS includes an **UNDELETE** command, which can unerase a file if invoked as the next command after an erase or delete. The form is *UNDELETE XX* (where *XX* is the deleted filename).

Try this exercise to "undelete" the COMMAND.COM file that you just erased.

Hard-Disk System or Network	**Dual-Diskette System**
1. Type **C:** ↵	1. Type **A:** ↵
2. Type **CD DOS** ↵	2. Place the DOS disk in Drive A
3. Place your disk in Drive A	3. Place your disk in Drive B
4. Type **UNDELETE A:COMMAND.COM**	4. Type **UNDELETE B:COMMAND.COM**
5. Press ↵	5. Press ↵

The program locates the file and asks "Undelete (Y/N)?"

6. Press **Y** for "Yes"

You are now asked to replace the first character of the file. Although you can type any letter, it makes sense to use the original letter (if you remember it). In response to "first character,"

7. Type **C**

The file is successfully undeleted. It is now available for use and will appear in a directory.

☞ **Tip: Typing *UNDELETE* followed by a disk identifier (such as *A:* or *B:*) will find *all* files that can be unerased and prompt you to undelete each one in sequence.**

Checkpoint

☐ List the command that will prepare a blank diskette on Drive A so that it can be used to start your computer.

☐ At the DOS prompt, change the default drive to the one that contains your data disk, and list the contents of the disk on the screen.

☐ Copy the COMMAND.COM file on your data disk to a file named REVIEW.TXT on the same disk; then erase the REVIEW.TXT file.

Additional DOS Commands

The DOS commands presented so far are the basic ones that you will use most often. However, there are a few more that can help you manage disk space and maintain files.

The **CHKDSK** (Check Disk) command analyzes a disk's directory and File Allocation Table, checks for errors, and produces a report that indicates available space on the disk and in RAM. If you add the characters /V to the end of the CHKDSK command, CHKDSK will display messages as it progresses and provide detailed information about any errors it may find. Try the following:

Checking Free Disk Space

Hard-Disk System or Network	**Dual-Diskette System**
1. Set the default drive to C: (or the network)	1. Set the default drive to A:
2. Type **CD DOS** to change to the DOS subdirectory if it isn't already there (or **CD** followed by the subdirectory name that contains your DOS files)	2. Place the DOS disk in Drive A
	3. Place your disk in Drive B
	4. Type **CHKDSK B:**
	5. Press ↵
3. Place your disk in Drive A	
4. Type **CHKDSK A:**	
5. Press ↵	

Your screen should present useful information, such as that shown in Figure DOS1–16. Notice the hidden files; these are the DOS system files that still remain on the disk. The last number on the screen displays the amount of RAM memory still available for your use. CHKDSK is an external DOS command.

At times, you may want to know if two files contain the same data. Even if you don't use COPY /V, you can still determine if files are the same by issuing the **COMP** (Compare files) command. This external command takes the form *COMP A:FILE1.EXT B:FILE2.EXT* and can be used to compare the contents of files on one or two disks. It can also be used in combination with wildcards to compare a set of files. For instance, *COMP A:*.TXT B:*.BAK* would cause each file with an extension of .TXT on Drive A to be compared with a file of the same name but with an extension of .BAK, on Drive B.

Comparing Files

```
C>CHKDSK A:

Volume LASTNAME    created 03-27-1993 10:59a
Volume Serial Number is 322B-1204

  1213952 bytes total disk space
    71680 bytes in 2 hidden files
    48128 bytes in 1 user files
   115200 bytes in bad sectors
   978944 bytes available on disk

      512 bytes in each allocation unit
     2371 total allocation units on disk
     1912 available allocation units on disk

   655360 total bytes memory
   593680 bytes free

C>
```

Figure DOS1–16
The CHKDSK Command Displays Information about the Named Disk, Including Volume Label, Total Space Used by All Files, and the Remaining Space on Disk and in RAM

If the files are identical, the screen displays "Files compare OK." Otherwise, a set of mismatches will be generated, indicating that the file contents differ.

Comparing Disks

A similar external command exists to compare entire disks with each other. The command, called **DISKCOMP** (Compare Diskettes) takes the form *DISKCOMP A: B:*. It is most useful if issued after a DISKCOPY operation to ensure that two disks are, indeed, identical.

Changing Date and Time

Whenever you are at the DOS prompt, you may view the date or time, or change either one, by simply typing the internal command **DATE** or **TIME** and pressing the Enter key. Try this:

1. Type **DATE**

2. Press ⏎

The current date appears on your screen. You may change it by typing a new date, or simply press the Enter key to return to the DOS prompt.

3. Press ⏎

The TIME command allows you to view or change the time in a similar fashion. If you want to supply a new date or time without seeing the current setting, you can type a new date or time immediately after the appropriate command—as in *DATE 11-01-94*—and then press the Enter key.

Other House-keeping Commands

There are other DOS commands that you may want to use for general "housekeeping"—keeping your files and disks in order. Four basic commands include CLS (Clear Screen), **VER** (Version), **VOL** (Volume), and **LABEL**. The first three are internal commands; LABEL is external.

Clearing the Screen.   To clear your screen,

1. Type **CLS**

2. Press ⏎

The screen will be erased and the DOS prompt will reappear at the upper left. Although you do not need to clear your screen to issue commands, you may want to clear old messages from the screen.

Identifying the DOS Version.   There may be times when you need to verify which version of DOS you are using. For example, you may want to check compatibility with an applications software package. To identify the DOS version, do this:

1. Type **VER**

2. Press ⏎

A statement such as "MS-DOS Version 6.00" will appear to indicate the DOS version in use.

Displaying or Setting the Volume Label.   Although volume labels are optional, they are useful for identifying each disk. Volume labels are normally displayed as part of the DIR command but can be shown separately as follows:

1. Type **VOL A:** (or **VOL B:** in a dual-diskette system)

2. Press ⏎

Note that the command *VOL* alone will display the volume label for the default disk. Once the command is issued, the screen will display a message similar to "Volume in Drive A is LASTNAME" or, if there is no label, "Volume in Drive A has no label." DOS will also display a volume serial number on the line beneath the label. The serial number is a unique code given to each disk when it is formatted. Although it provides additional identification, it has no use for our purposes.

To create, change, or delete a volume label, you could type the command *LABEL A:* (or *LABEL B:* in a dual-diskette system) and press the Enter key. The volume will be displayed once again, and you will be prompted to enter a label and then press the Enter key. Any characters you enter will become the new volume label for that disk. *Note:* If you press the Enter key without typing any characters (and then verify by pressing *Y*), the current volume label will be deleted.

Invoking Applications Software

While systems software coordinates the overall operation of the computer system, *applications software* (also called *productivity software*) instructs the computer to perform specific tasks that serve you directly. Such tasks include the creation of word processing documents or spreadsheets. Each software package has its own start-up command. This command can usually be invoked directly from the A> prompt in a dual-diskette system. If you use a hard disk, you may first have to change to the subdirectory that contains the program (more on this in the next chapter). Networks and hard drives often provide their own menu to facilitate the selection of application software.

To use productivity software in a dual-diskette drive computer system, you typically boot up your computer and get to the A> prompt. Then you replace the DOS disk in Drive A with the disk that contains the desired productivity software. The software is started by issuing a specific command, such as *WP* for WordPerfect, *123* for Lotus 1-2-3, or *DBASE* for dBASE. The software then takes over.

In a hard-disk system, you boot up your computer and get to the C> (or C:\>) prompt. At this point, you can issue a CD (*change directory*) command to activate the portion of the disk that contains the desired program. The software can then be started by issuing its specific command.

In a network, you typically boot the computer as you would a dual-diskette system. Then, at the A>, invoke the network with a specific command (often LAN). Once in the network, you would follow the menu to access the desired software.

You might also use the DOS shell itself to invoke applications software from the appropriate menu. The use of the shell screen is not included in this module, but you might want to investigate it on your own.

Checkpoint

☐ Determine the free space available on your data disk.

☐ Determine if DOS's COMMAND.COM file is exactly the same as the COMMAND.COM file saved on your disk.

☐ Change the volume label on your disk so that it includes your last name (up to nine characters) followed by an underline symbol and your first initial, as in LASTNAME_F.

Summary

- DOS (Disk Operating System) contains commands for manipulating program and data files. **Internal commands** are those loaded into RAM during the start-up process. **External commands** are kept on disk, loaded into RAM when invoked, and then removed from RAM when completed.
- The process of starting a computer system is known as **booting.** During booting, DOS commands are brought into RAM from DOS files. The steps include placing a DOS disk in Drive A in a dual-diskette system, turning on the power, and typing the date and time, to arrive at a DOS prompt. The DOS prompt, such as C>, indicates the default drive that is currently set.
- DOS filenames are typically specified by three components: a one-letter drive specification (optional), the main filename (consisting of a maximum of eight characters), and an optional file extension (consisting of up to three characters).
- **Wildcard** characters are special characters that can be used in DOS commands when referring to filenames to stand for one or more regular characters. The asterisk (*) can represent several characters, while the question mark (?) represents one character.
- **FORMAT** is an external command that enables you to prepare a disk for use on your computer. Every new disk must be formatted once before use. FORMAT can be used with modifiers such as /S (system) and /V (volume label). DOS also offers a quick format /Q modifier and an UNFORMAT command.
- **SYS** is an external command that transfers the operating system to another disk. COMMAND.COM is also transferred in DOS Version 6.0.
- Changing the **default drive** is accomplished by typing the letter of the desired drive followed by a colon (as in C:).
- **DIR** is an internal command that displays the names of files stored on a disk. It may also display file size and the date and time the file was last saved. DIR can be used with wildcards or with modifiers such as /W (wide display) and /P (pause after page).
- **COPY** is an internal command that is used to duplicate files on the same disk or on another disk. COPY can be used with wildcards or with the modifier /V (copy with verification). **XCOPY** is an alternate copy command that provides added controls over what is copied.
- **DISKCOPY** is an external command that copies the entire contents of a diskette onto another diskette.
- **RENAME** is an internal command that allows you to change the name of a file.
- **ERASE** and **DEL** (*delete*) are internal commands that can remove a filename from the disk's directory. Both can be used with wildcards. DOS also offers an **UNDELETE** command to unerase files.
- Other DOS commands include **CHKDSK** (check disk), **COMP** (compare files), **DATE** (see or set date), **TIME** (see or set time), **CLS** (clear the screen), **VER** (see DOS version number), and **VOL** and **LABEL** (see or set volume label).

Key Terms

Shown in parentheses are the page numbers on which key terms are boldfaced.

Booting (DOS6)
CHKDSK (Check Disk) (DOS27)
CLS (Clear Screen) (DOS28)
COMP (Compare) (DOS27)
COPY (DOS19)
DATE (DOS28)
Default drive (DOS8)
DIR (Directory) (DOS17)
DISKCOMP (Disk Compare) (DOS28)

DISKCOPY (DOS24)   SYS (System) (DOS16)
ERASE or DEL   TIME (DOS28)
  (DOS25)   UNDELETE (DOS26)
External   VER (Version)
  command (DOS11)   (DOS28)
FORMAT (DOS11)   VOL (Volume)
Internal command   (DOS28)
  (DOS11)   Warm boot (DOS6)
LABEL (DOS28)   Wildcard (DOS9)
REN (Rename)   XCOPY (DOS23)
  (DOS24)

Quiz

True/False

1. In a two-drive system, the DOS disk is normally placed in Drive A.
2. The date is entered in the computer in year-month-day format.
3. A DOS filename must contain a drive specification, main filename, and extension.
4. The wildcard character *?* stands for a single character in a filename.
5. Internal DOS commands are loaded into RAM during booting.
6. The FORMAT /S command creates a disk with the maximum space available for data storage.
7. DOS files can be transferred to a formatted disk with the SYS command.
8. DIR is an external DOS command.
9. In DOS, you may not copy a file to the same disk directory unless you give it a new name.
10. The ERASE command physically removes a file from the designated disk.

Multiple Choice

11. Certain DOS commands are brought into RAM during
    a. date entry.
    b. booting.
    c. prompting.
    d. hard-disk use.
12. The disk drive to which DOS is pointing is called the
    a. prompt drive.
    b. main drive.
    c. RAM.
    d. default drive.
13. Which of these filename components are mandatory?
    a. Main filename
    b. Drive specification
    c. File extension
    d. All of the above
14. Which one of these files is *not* referenced by the filename B:DATA?.* (with wildcards as shown)?
    a. B:DATA1.TXT
    b. B:DATA5.WK1
    c. B:DATA21.TXT
    d. B:DATAX.DBF

15. External command files arc typically kept
    a.   in RAM.
    b.   on the disk in Drive B.
    c.   on a formatted data disk.
    d.   on the disk in the default drive.

16. Which FORMAT command prepares a disk that can boot up a computer system?
    a.   FORMAT B:/S
    b.   FORMAT B:/V
    c.   FORMAT B:
    d.   FORMAT B:/4

17. Which of these commands will change the default disk to Drive B?
    a.   DIR B:
    b.   B:
    c.   SYS B:
    d.   FORMAT B:

18. What will DOS do if you attempt to copy a file from Drive A to Drive B if Drive B already contains a file with the same name?
    a.   Warn you of the problem and ask for verification
    b.   Replace the old file with the new one
    c.   Produce an error message and cancel the command
    d.   Copy the file to the default disk instead

19. Which two DOS commands have exactly the same meaning?
    a.   FORMAT B:/S and SYS B:
    b.   REN and DIR
    c.   ERASE and DEL
    d.   COPY and DISKCOPY

20. Which DOS command should be issued to retrieve a file that was erased by mistake?
    a.   UNDELETE
    b.   UNERASE
    c.   FIND
    d.   XCOPY

Matching

Select the term that best matches each phrase below:

a.	Booting	g.	CHKDSK
b.	Default drive	h.	COPY
c.	Wildcard	i.	ERASE
d.	Internal command	j.	COMP
e.	External command	k.	DIR
f.	FORMAT	l.	DISKCOPY

21. The type of DOS command that is not loaded into RAM when the computer is started up

22. A DOS command that enables you to remove a file from a disk's directory

23. The disk drive to which the operating system (or active applications program) is currently pointing

24. The type of DOS command that is loaded into RAM when the computer is started up

25. A DOS command that displays the names of files on a disk

26. A DOS command that compares the contents of two files

27. A DOS command that prepares a disk for use

28. A character that acts as a stand-in for other characters in a filename

29. A DOS command that enables you to duplicate a file

30. The process of getting a computer system ready to use by reading certain commands into RAM

Answers

True/False: 1. T; 2. F; 3. F; 4. T; 5. T; 6. F; 7. T; 8. F; 9. T; 10. F
Multiple Choice: 11. b; 12. d; 13. a; 14. c; 15. d; 16. a; 17. b; 18. b; 19. c; 20. a
Matching: 21. e; 22. i; 23. b; 24. d; 25. k; 26. j; 27. f; 28. c; 29. h; 30. a

Exercises

I. Operations

Provide the DOS command required to do each of the operations shown below. For each operation, assume a system with two disk drives, A and B, and assume the default drive indicated in parentheses after the operation.

1. Format the disk in Drive B (A>).

2. Copy files named ZUBIE, ZIPCODE, ZODIAC, ZOO, and ZEBRA, all located on the A-drive disk, to the B-drive disk. Assume that these are the only files starting with the letter Z on the A-drive disk (A>).

3. Change the default drive to B (A>).

4. Erase everything with the extension .MAT from the B-drive disk (B>).

5. List the names of all files stored on the B-drive disk (A>).

6. Copy the contents of the disk in the A drive to the disk in the B drive, thereby making the two disks identical (A>).

7. Erase a file named INVTY.DAT from the B-drive disk (A>).

8. Change the name of a file named SKATE.DAT, located on the A-drive disk, to SKATER.TXT (A>).

9. Copy a file named DITTO.WK1 from the disk on Drive A to the disk on Drive B (A>).

10. Get a summary status report on the default disk showing the byte capacity of the disk, the total number of bytes of disk space available, and the total amount of disk space used (A>).

II. Commands

Describe fully, using a dozen or fewer words in each case, what is accomplished by each of the DOS commands given below. Assume that each exercise part is independent of any previous parts. Be aware that some commands may result in error messages; where this is the case, respond "Error message" and state the reason for the message. Assume that the computer system contains two diskette drives, A and B; also assume that the disk in Drive A is the default disk and contains DOS's external commands and that the following user-created files are on the disks in the A and B drives: (A) MARTY.F1 MARTY.F2 LYNN.DAT (B) MICRO.ABC MICRO.A MICRO.B MARY.J1 MARTY.F3 MARTY.F4 WILLIAM ED.B

1. ERASE *.*

2. COPY MA*.* B:

3. XCOPY MARTY B:

4. RENAME MARTHA LYNN

5. COPY LYNN.DAT JOAN.DAT

6. ERASE WILLIAM

7. ERASE B:*.B

8. UNDELETE B:MICRO

9. RENAME LYNN.DAT JOAN

III. Applications

Perform the following operations using your computer system. You will need a DOS disk (or a hard-disk drive or network) and one additional blank disk to complete this exercise. In a few words (or by copying the screen to your printer with the PrtSc key) describe the resulting screen or message that appears after each operation.

1. Boot your computer system and answer DATE and TIME.

2. Format a diskette in Drive A (or B in a dual-diskette system) with the system modifier. (Use your last name as the volume label.)

3. Using the appropriate directory command, find out how many files are on the disk in the default drive and how much space is still available on the disk.

4. Copy all the files from DOS whose filename begins with the letter A to the formatted data diskette. How many files were copied? How much space is still available on the data disk?

5. Change the default drive to the one containing your data disk.

6. Erase any files on the data disk whose extension is .COM. How many files are left in the directory? Now undelete one file.

7. Rename the ANSI.SYS file on the data disk to SAMPLE.TXT.

8. Erase all files from the data disk. How much space is available on this disk now?

9. Format the disk in Drive A *without* a system. How much space is now available? Why is the space different from that shown in Exercise 8 above?

10. Format the disk with the system once again.

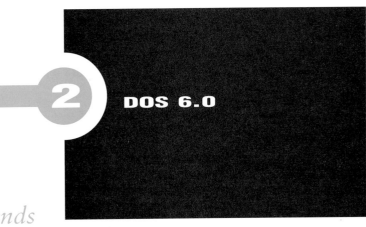

2 DOS 6.0

Advanced DOS Commands

DOS

O B J E C T I V E S

After completing this chapter you will be able to:

1 Explain the need for hierarchical directories.

2 Describe the procedure to create, use, and delete subdirectories.

3 Demonstrate how to create, modify, or remove prompts and paths.

4 Explain the use of a batch file and AUTOEXEC.BAT.

5 Demonstrate the use of the COPY CON and TYPE commands.

6 Name several useful pipes and filters in DOS.

7 Identify several DOS 6.0 utilities and explain their use.

O V E R V I E W   In the previous chapter, you were introduced to DOS and its basic commands. This chapter extends your understanding of DOS by examining additional commands that allow you to manage large numbers of files, automate commands, and manipulate files and screens.

The chapter begins with a look at hierarchical directories and the commands necessary to create and manage them—such as MKDIR, CHDIR, RMDIR, TREE, PROMPT, and PATH. Next, batch files and automated commands are presented with the related commands necessary to create, view, and modify these files.

The chapter concludes with special DOS commands that control the movement of data among files and peripheral equipment and a discussion of a few DOS utilities. You may want to review the concepts in this chapter after you have developed a number of your own files and worked with a few application software packages.

Hierarchical Disk Storage

If you use diskettes for program and data storage, then the standard directory is sufficient for most needs. However, disks with larger storage capacities (such as high-density disks and hard disks) typically contain many more files, sometimes numbering in the hundreds or even thousands. Such disks are better managed if their files are organized in a hierarchical manner with related files grouped together for easy access. Hard disks, whose capacities typically exceed 100 Mb, are prime candidates for this DOS feature.

Subdirectories

A larger-capacity disk can be treated, in effect, as a collection of smaller disk portions that contain groups of related files. These self-contained file "packages" are called subdirectories. As shown in Figure DOS2–1, the main directory, known as the **root directory**, is at the top of the hierarchy, with separate **subdirectories** subordinate to it. Each subdirectory, in turn, may be further subdivided into its own collection of subordinate subdirectories.

The root directory of a hard disk will often contain key operating system and boot files. Of course, any files can be placed into it, but good housekeeping rules suggest that most files be stored in appropriate subdirectories, rather than in the root directory. As in Figure DOS2–1, the first subdirectory level is often used for DOS files, for applications software files, and for language translators. For example, Figure DOS2–1 shows that the first subdirectory level contains DOS (DOS files), WP (for a word processing program), DT (for a desktop publishing system), DB (for a database management system), and SS (for a spreadsheet program).

The WP subdirectory is further subdivided into second-level subdirectories of LETTERS and RESEARCH; DB is divided into ROSTER and CONSULT. Notice that subdirectory names, like filenames, are limited to eight characters.

Subdirectories are most useful on large-capacity disks, but they may be used on any diskette to group related files. For illustration purposes, you will now create the hierarchical scheme in Figure DOS2-1 on your data diskette. *Do not attempt* this on your hard disk drive—it may ruin existing subdirectories or confuse the arrangement. To reduce the chance of conflicts, you will use names that do not exist on your hard-disk drive or diskette by starting each with an X. This is not a requirement of DOS, but simply a precaution for these exercises.

To prepare for these exercises,

1. If you haven't already done so, boot DOS and get to the DOS prompt

Figure DOS2—1

*The Main Directory—
the Root Directory—Is
at the Top of the
Hierarchy with Separate
Subdirectories
Subordinate to It*

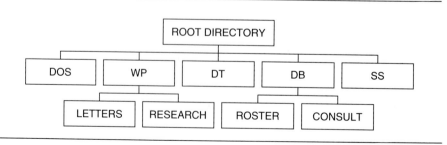

You will need a disk that has been formatted with the FORMAT /S command to complete the exercises in this chapter.

2. Use the disk that you created in the last chapter or reformat a disk now with FORMAT /S

Review the FORMAT section in the first DOS chapter if you need assistance with this procedure.

Change the default drive to this formatted disk as follows:

Hard-Disk System or Network	**Dual-Diskette System**
1. Type **A:**	1. Type **B:**
2. Press ↵	2. Press ↵
The DOS prompt should now appear as A> (or A:\>).	The DOS prompt should now appear as B>.

The first step in establishing a hierarchical directory is to create a subdirectory with the **MD** or **MKDIR (Make Directory)** command. This is done by specifying a path through the hierarchy using a backward slash key to separate subdirectory names. Try this:

1. Type **MD \XDOS**

2. Press ↵

This creates a subdirectory called XDOS. (Remember the peculiar name "XDOS" is simply a safeguard against using existing directory names as you practice.) The operating system allows you to leave out the path to the directory if you are already located in the directory, or subdirectory, that is directly above it. Since you are currently in the root directory, you could have typed *MD XDOS* with the same effect.

☞ Tip: You can also type the complete (or absolute) path to a subdirectory, such as *MD A:\XDOS* (or *MD B:\XDOS* for dual-diskette), including the drive specification as well. This command can be issued from any default disk or subdirectory, since it leaves no question about where the new directory will be created.

Create the other subdirectories as follows:

1. Type **MD \XWP** and press ↵
2. Type **MD \XDT** ↵
3. Type **MD \XDB** ↵
4. Type **MD \XSS** ↵

Now create the second-level subdirectories:

5. Type **MD \XWP\LETTERS** and press ↵
6. Type **MD \XWP\RESEARCH** ↵
7. Type **MD \XDB\ROSTER** ↵
8. Type **MD \XDB\CONSULT** ↵

MD is an internal DOS command and can be used to create new subdirectories at any time.

Making a Directory

DOS

Using Subdirectories

Once you have created subdirectories, you may refer to them in DOS commands simply by including the path of the subdirectory in the command. Try the following COPY command as an example:

1. Type **COPY COMMAND.COM \XDOS**

2. Press ↵

By including the path \XDOS as the destination in the command, you instruct the operating system to copy the file COMMAND.COM from the root directory to the subdirectory called XDOS on the default disk as shown in Figure DOS2–2a. Try one more:

3. Type **COPY \XDOS\COMMAND.COM \XWP**

4. Press ↵

This copies the COMMAND.COM file from the XDOS subdirectory (on the default drive) to the XWP subdirectory, as shown in Figure DOS2–2b. Note that the file COMMAND.COM is now stored three times on the same disk—in the root directory and the XDOS and XWP subdirectories. This is fine as long as the same filename is not used in the same subdirectory.

TREE.   One problem with subdirectories is that you may, over time, create so many of them that it is easy to forget their names or how they are related to one another. Fortunately, the **TREE** command enables DOS to supply this information. This command is aptly named, for you can picture the hierarchy as an upside-down tree—the root directory forms the trunk and the subdirectories form the branches. TREE is an external command and requires access to the DOS disk. Try the following:

Hard-Disk System or Network

1. Type **C:** (or network identifier)

2. Press ↵

3. Type **CD DOS** (or name of subdirectory with DOS)

4. Press ↵

5. Type **TREE A:**

6. Press ↵

Dual-Diskette System

With a DOS disk in Drive A and your data disk in Drive B,

1. Type **A:**

2. Press ↵

3. Type **TREE B:**

4. Press ↵

Figure DOS2–2

Copying Files Using Subdirectory Paths

(a) COPY COMMAND.COM \XDOS has copied the COMMAND.COM file from the root directory to the subdirectory called XDOS.
(b) The COPY \XDOS\COMMAND.COM \XWP copies the COMMAND.COM file from the XDOS subdirectory to the XWP subdirectory.

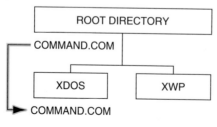

(a) COPY COMMAND.COM \XDOS

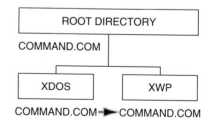

(b) COPY \XDOS\COMMAND.COM \XWP

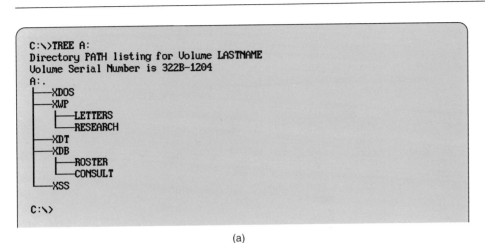

Figure DOS2–3
The TREE Command

(a) The TREE command lists each subdirectory and its relation to the root directory or its subordinates.
(b) The TREE A:/F command also includes the names of the files contained in each subdirectory.

This command creates a list similar to that shown in Figure DOS2–3a. You can easily see each level of subdirectory and its relation to the root directory or its subordinates.

On the other hand, the command *TREE A:/F* lists not only the information in Figure DOS2–3a, but also all of the names of the files contained in each subdirectory as shown in Figure DOS2–3b. This can be a lengthy report if there are many files on the disk.

Using DIR with Subdirectories.   Issuing the DIR command with a disk specifier alone or a single backslash normally displays only the root directory's contents. For example,

Hard-Disk System or Network	**Dual-Diskette System**
1. Type **DIR A:** (or **DIR A:**)	1. Type **DIR B:** (or **DIR B:**)
2. Press ↵	2. Press ↵

Figure DOS2—4

Using DIR with Subdirectories

(a) The DIR command normally displays only the root directory's contents. Subdirectories are shown by the identifier "<DIR>".

(b) Adding a subdirectory path to DIR displays the directory listing for the named subdirectory only.

```
C:\>DIR A:

Volume in drive A is LASTNAME
Volume Serial Number is 322B-1204
Directory of A:\

COMMAND  COM     52925 03-10-93    6:00a
XDOS          <DIR>       03-27-93   11:55a
XWP           <DIR>       03-27-93   11:55a
XDT           <DIR>       03-27-93   11:55a
XDB           <DIR>       03-27-93   11:55a
XSS           <DIR>       03-27-93   11:55a
        6 file(s)       52925 bytes
                       908099 bytes free

C:\>
```

(a)

```
A:\>DIR \XWP

Volume in drive A is LASTNAME
Volume Serial Number is 322B-1204
Directory of A:\XWP

.             <DIR>
..            <DIR>       03-27-93   11:55a
LETTERS       <DIR>       03-27-93   11:55a
RESEARCH      <DIR>       03-27-93   11:55a
COMMAND  COM     52925 03-10-93    6:00a
        5 file(s)       52925 bytes
                       908099 bytes free

C:\>
```

(b)

This command creates the directory listing shown in Figure DOS2—4a. Note that the root directory (A:\ or B:\) appears at the top of the screen. The single backslash (\) denotes the root directory. The root directory shows the COMMAND.COM file and the subordinate subdirectories XDOS, XWP, XDT, XDB, and XSS. There may also be files left over from the exercises in the first DOS chapter as well. Note that each of the subdirectories is identified by "<DIR>" where the number of bytes normally appears. Now, add a path in the command as follows:

Hard-Disk System or Network

1. Change the default disk to **A:**

2. Type **DIR \XWP**

3. Press ⏎

Dual-Diskette System

1. Change the default disk to **B:**

2. Type **DIR \XWP**

3. Press ⏎

This command creates the directory listing shown in Figure DOS2—4b. Notice that COMMAND.COM appears, as well as the two second-level subdirectories. The dots at the beginning of the list indicate that this is not the root directory, but a subdirectory.

Changing the Active Directory. Although you can access a file in a subdirectory by including its path as part of any command you issue, there will be

(a) CD \XDB activates the XDB subdirectory.

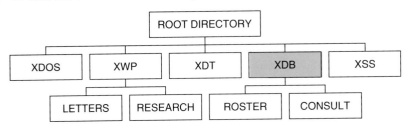

Figure DOS2–5
The CD (Change Directory) Command

(a) The command *CD \XDB* changes to, or activates, the XDB subdirectory.
(b) The command *CD * returns control to the root directory.

(b) CD \ makes the root directory active.

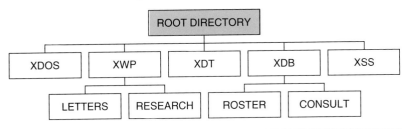

DOS

times when you want to move into the subdirectory itself so that subsequent commands need not include the path. This is called changing the active (or working) directory. It is the file hierarchy equivalent to changing the default disk drive. That is, the default drive and the active directory will be the ones used by the operating system if no other is specified in a DOS command. The **CD** or **CHDIR (Change Directory)** command is available for this purpose. For example,

1. Type **CD \XDB**

2. Press ↵

The command changes to, or activates, this subdirectory as shown in Figure DOS2–5a. Any commands you now issue (without specifying a path) will affect this subdirectory only. For example, if you now type *DIR* and press the Enter key, you would see the directory of this subdirectory.

To move back to the root directory, type the command with the root identifier—a single backwards slash (\), but no path, as follows:

3. Type **CD ** (to return to the root directory)

4. Press ↵

The active directory has been returned to the root directory as shown in Figure DOS2–5b. CD is an internal DOS command.

Relative Path versus Absolute Path. As you have seen, paths can be written as *complete* (absolute) paths or *partial* (relative) paths. An absolute path (such as *C:\XWP\LETTERS\NOTE*) specifies the *entire* path, from start to finish, that leads to a desired file (or files). Thus, an absolute path must include a disk identifier and all subdirectories and can be issued regardless of the active disk or directory. On the other hand, a relative path (such as *\LETTERS\NOTE*) simply indicates the *rest* of the path that must be followed from the active disk and directory to lead to a desired file. Either one can be used as needed.

Removing a Directory

If you no longer need a particular subdirectory, you can use the **RD** or **RMDIR** (Remove Directory) command to get rid of it.

The internal RD command requires that the subdirectory meet two conditions. First, it must be empty—it can contain no files or subordinate subdirectories. Second, it cannot be the active directory. To use the tree analogy, you cannot cut off a branch on which you are currently sitting.

To see how the RD command works, try the following:

1.   Type **RD \XDB** and press ↵

This command attempts to remove the XDB subdirectory. A screen error message appears, "Invalid path, not directory, or directory not empty." The XDB subdirectory is not empty—it has subordinate subdirectories. You must first remove these subdirectories as follows:

2.   Type **RD \XDB\ROSTER** and press ↵

☞ **Tip: If the active subdirectory is XDB, you could also type the relative path as** *RD ROSTER.*

3.   Type **RD \XDB\CONSULT** and press ↵

Now, issue the RD command again, as follows:

4.   Type **RD \XDB** and press ↵

A TREE or DIR command will reveal that the XDB subdirectory has been removed.

DOS also offers a powerful combination of the REMOVE DIRECTORY and ERASE commands, called DELTREE. When invoked, it removes the named subdirectory and *all subordinate* subdirectories and files. Try this:

5.   Type **DELTREE \XSS** and press ↵

A DIR command will show that the XSS subdirectory is gone.

Managing Directories

As you begin to use subdirectories, you will appreciate two other DOS commands that allow you to keep track of the active subdirectory, as well as tell DOS where to find needed files. These commands are called PROMPT and PATH, respectively. Both are internal DOS commands.

PROMPT.   The **PROMPT** command lets you modify the standard DOS prompt to display more information than just the default disk drive. As shown in Figure DOS2–6, there are many characters that you can use to define how your screen prompt will appear. For example, you could do the following:

1.   Type **PROMPT DBTBNG**

2.   Press ↵

This command produces a prompt that shows the date, time, and default drive, as shown in Figure DOS2–7a. Although it displays a lot of information, it is also confusing. When using subdirectories, the most useful prompt is one that displays the working (active) directory. This PROMPT command is issued as follows:

3.   Type **PROMPT PG**

4.   Press ↵

The active directory will now be displayed followed by the ">" symbol. Your screen shows "A:\>" (or "B:\>"). To see its effect, change the active directory to XWP\LETTERS as follows:

Prompt Character	Description
$T	The current time
$D	The current date
$P	The active directory of the default drive
$V	The DOS version number
$N	The default drive
$G	The > symbol
$B	The ¦ symbol
$_	Enter (line feed)

(a) PROMPT DBTBNG

    Fri 11-01-94¦10:08:41.01¦A>

You can get carried away with designing prompts. This one displays the date, time, and default drive, separated with vertical bars.

(b) PROMPT PG after CD \XWP\LETTERS

    A:\XWP\LETTERS>

This configuration is most helpful, showing the default drive and active subdirectory followed by the normal prompt ">."

(c) PROMPT PG at the root directory after CD\

    A:\>

The extra "\" after the colon indicates that the root directory is active.

(d) PROMPT at the root directory

    A>

The prompt set back to the standard setting only shows the default drive.

"A" is used for illustration only. The active default disk drive will be shown in the prompt.

5. Type **CD \XWP\LETTERS**

6. Press ↵

Notice how the prompt now displays the complete subdirectory path, including the default disk and active directory, as in Figure DOS2–7b. To change the directory back to the root directory,

7. Type **CD **

8. Press ↵

The prompt now returns to "A:\>" (or "B:\>") as shown in Figure DOS2–7c. The backward slash after the colon indicates that the root directory is active.

Figure DOS2—8

The Command PATH \XDOS Establishes a Search Path through the XDOS Subdirectory

Any time you issue a .BAT, .EXE, or .COM command, DOS will also look in the XDOS subdirectory if the file cannot be found.

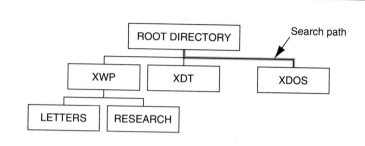

If you wanted to return the prompt to its standard form (as in Figure DOS2–7d), you would type *PROMPT* and press the Enter key. However, most users find the *PG* prompt to be most helpful in keeping track of their current subdirectory location.

PATH. When using subdirectories, you may, at times, issue a command that refers to a file not contained in the active subdirectory. Such commands typically involve files with extensions of .COM, .EXE, or .BAT. Since subdirectories are separate file packages, DOS will not be able to locate the required file. For example, if you use a separate subdirectory for your DOS files, you would not be able to issue an external DOS command unless the DOS subdirectory was the active one.

Fortunately, DOS's **PATH** command enables you to get around this problem by setting up a command search path. The PATH command tells DOS which subdirectories it should search (after it searches the active one) to find the command file. For example,

1. Type **PATH \XDOS**

2. Press ↵

This command establishes a search path through the XDOS subdirectory as shown in Figure DOS2–8. Any time you issue a .BAT, .EXE, or .COM command now, the computer will first search the active directory and then look in the XDOS subdirectory if the file could not be found. You can include as many subdirectories in the PATH as you want. For example, you might type *PATH \XDOS;\XWP;\XWP\LETTERS* to have DOS search the XDOS, XWP, and XWP\LETTERS subdirectories—in that order (note that each subsequent path is separated with a semicolon). If a listed subdirectory does not exist, DOS will simply ignore it. To set the path back to the active directory only (called the NUL path), do this:

3. Type **PATH;**

4. Press ↵

You can also establish paths through specific disk drives by specifying them as absolute paths within the path statement, such as *PATH A:\XDOS;C:\XWP* and so on. On a hard-disk system, listing the C: within the PATH statement will ensure that the hard disk is searched for needed command files if they are not available on the diskette in use. *Note:* Typing *PATH* by itself will show the current path setting.

Make sure you do these Checkpoint activities before continuing. You will need them in the upcoming sections.

Checkpoint

☐ Change the DOS prompt to display the default disk and active subdirectory.

☐ Delete the COMMAND.COM file in \XWP, and then remove the subdirectories named \XDT and \XWP\LETTERS.

Automating Commands

DOS commands are typically issued one at a time, as they are needed. However, you may use a particular series of commands often and not want to bother typing the sequence each time. For example, you may want to change the prompt, create a path, and set an active directory each time you boot your computer. You might also want to switch to another subdirectory and invoke an applications software program without having to issue all the commands involved. DOS provides a way to automate a series of commands by combining them into a group (or "batch") known as a batch file.

Batch Files

A **batch file** is a text file that contains a series of DOS commands, each command on a separate line. To allow the operating system to recognize them as such, all batch file filenames must end with the extension *.BAT*. For example, the following batch file, named START.BAT, includes three separate commands. When executed, this batch file will set the path to the XDOS subdirectory, change to a more useful prompt, and then set the active subdirectory to XWP:

```
PATH \XDOS
PROMPT $P$G
CD \XWP
```

Creating Batch Files with COPY CON

Batch files can be created a number of ways, but perhaps the most direct is to use the **COPY CON** command, which literally means "*copy* keystrokes from the *con*sole (or keyboard) into a file." Create the START.BAT batch file as follows:

1. Set the default drive to A: (or B: in a dual-diskette system)

2. Type **COPY CON START.BAT** and press ↵

3. Type **PATH \XDOS** and press ↵

4. Type **PROMPT PG** and press ↵

5. Type **CD \XWP** and press ↵

To mark the end of the batch file,

6. Press **F6**

Your screen should now resemble Figure DOS2–9. The symbols "∧Z" placed at the end of your batch file when you pressed the F6 function key indicate the file's end. You could also have generated these symbols by holding the Ctrl key and pressing Z once. To save the file to your disk,

7. Press ↵

Once a batch file has been created, you can invoke its functions at any time by simply typing its name (as you would any DOS command) and pressing the Enter

DOS

Figure DOS2–9

The Completed START Batch File

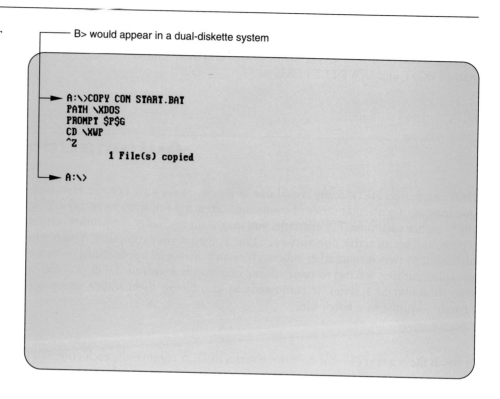

B> would appear in a dual-diskette system

```
A:\>COPY CON START.BAT
PATH \XDOS
PROMPT $P$G
CD \XWP
^Z
        1 File(s) copied

A:\>
```

Figure DOS2–10

Typing the Main Filename of a Batch File Will Invoke Its Commands Immediately and in Sequence

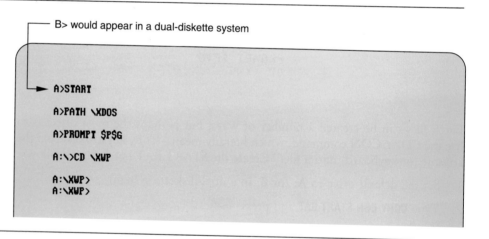

B> would appear in a dual-diskette system

```
A>START

A>PATH \XDOS

A>PROMPT $P$G

A:\>CD \XWP

A:\XWP>
A:\XWP>
```

key. You need not type its file extension. Since batch files remain on disk, they are similar to external DOS commands in that the subdirectory in which they reside must be active or included in the PATH command. Issue the START command now as follows:

8. Type **START**

9. Press ↵

Notice how the commands within the START.BAT batch file are issued in sequence, as in Figure DOS2–10.

☞ Tip: If you do not want the list of commands in the batch file to show on the screen, include the command ECHO OFF at the beginning of the batch file.

```
┌──── B> would appear in a dual-diskette system
│
│
│
└──► A:\>TYPE START.BAT
     PATH \XDOS
     PROMPT $P$G
     CD \XWP

     A:\>
```

Batch files can be created whenever you want to automate a set of DOS procedures. They can also be used to begin an applications software program with one
or two keystrokes. For example, if the WordPerfect program was contained in
your XWP subdirectory, you might create a batch file named W.BAT that would
change the active subdirectory to C:\XWP and then invoke the WP command to
start WordPerfect. Another batch file, named S.BAT perhaps, might switch to
another subdirectory and start a spreadsheet program. Using these batch files,
you could invoke your word processor by pressing *W* and the Enter key, or start
your spreadsheet by pressing *S* and the Enter key. There are many creative ways
that you can use batch files.

At times, you may want to review a batch file's contents. Perhaps you have
forgotten what it contains, or want to change it. Any text file (which includes all
batch files) can be displayed easily with the **TYPE** command. Try this:

**Reading
Batch
Files with
TYPE**

1.   Type **CD ** to select the root directory

2.   Type **TYPE   START.BAT**

3.   Press ↵

☞ **Tip: If the message "File not found" appears, make sure you are in the root directory
and have typed the filename correctly.**

A list of START.BAT will appear on the screen, as in Figure DOS2–11. Notice
that you must include the full filename (main name and extension) in the TYPE
command. TYPE is an internal DOS command.

There may be times when you want to modify the contents of a batch file. Of
course, you can simply retype the batch file using the COPY CON command,
but you can also modify parts of the file with other methods: (1) Use a word
processing program that can read and save ASCII files, (2) use **EDLIN**—a limited
line editor offered by DOS, or (3) Use DOS's full-screen editor. To use the editor,
use the command *EDIT* followed by the text filename to invoke it; when finished,
choose *EXIT* from the file menu. (See the Appendix.)

**Editing
Batch
Files**

Until now, you have been starting DOS in the standard manner—answering date
and time to arrive at the DOS prompt. It is possible (and often necessary) to
modify the start-up procedure to take greater advantage of the operating system.
For example, you could reconfigure the system to increase the number of memory
blocks or files available for use. You could also create a batch file to change the

**Automat-
ing the
Boot
Process**

prompt, path, and other useful parameters each time you boot your computer. DOS reserves two special files for these purposes—CONFIG.SYS and AUTO-EXEC.BAT.

CONFIG.SYS.   When you start DOS, it automatically searches for a file named CONFIG.SYS on the root directory. **CONFIG.SYS** is a text file of commands that changes the standard DOS configuration of available memory blocks, files, or devices. If CONFIG.SYS isn't found, DOS uses its default settings. When you create a CONFIG.SYS file, you use various commands to specify the changes you want to make. There are a number of good reasons for creating a CONFIG.SYS file:

- Many applications programs require more memory blocks (called *disk buffers*) to hold data during reading or writing operations than those normally opened. For instance, word processors work better when 10 to 20 disk buffers are available—you may want to use 30 if you use many subdirectories. The BUFFERS command addresses this problem.
- Applications may also require that more files be open at one time than the eight normally allowed by DOS. A better setting is 20. The FILES command is used to change this setting.
- As you add new devices to your system, appropriate instructions for their use (called device drivers) must be made known to DOS through the CONFIG.SYS file. **Device drivers** are programs that let DOS recognize devices not part of the computer itself. Such devices include a mouse, scanner, modem, printer, or external disk drive. Some device drivers (for keyboards, disk drives, and printers) are already installed in DOS. Others are supplied on an installation disk that comes with each device you purchase. The DEVICE command is used to initiate the installation.

You can create a CONFIG.SYS file (which should be placed on the root directory of the boot disk) by using COPY CON, a word processor that saves in ASCII format, or DOS's EDIT command. Although a CONFIG.SYS file can grow rather complicated for sophisticated applications, a basic CONFIG.SYS is quite simple.

If you already have a CONFIG.SYS file on your disk, *do not create this new one.* Generate a directory of your data disk to see if one is listed. If it is not listed, use COPY CON to create this file *on your data diskette:*

1. Type **A:** (or **B:** on a dual-diskette system)

2. Press ↵

3. Type **CD** \ and press ↵

These commands set the default drive to your disk and ensure that the root directory is active.

4. Type **COPY CON CONFIG.SYS** and press ↵

5. Type **BUFFERS = 20** and press ↵

6. Type **FILES = 20** and press ↵

7. Press **F6** ↵ to end

If you were to boot up your system with your disk, the CONFIG.SYS file would instruct the operating system to set aside space for 20 file buffers and 20 active files. These particular commands are recommended by most modern software manufacturers and will improve the performance of most software.

There may be another CONFIG.SYS file on your hard-disk drive or DOS start-up diskette. Use the TYPE command to list it as follows:

Hard-Disk System	**Dual-Diskette System or Network**
1. Type **TYPE C:\CONFIG.SYS**	1. Type **TYPE A:\CONFIG.SYS**
2. Press ↵	2. Press ↵

Note that the backslash between the colon and the filename tells the operating system to search for the file on the root directory. This is important in case you made some other subdirectory active earlier.

Examine the file that appears. If a "File not found" message appears (and you typed the command correctly), there is no CONFIG.SYS on the root directory.

AUTOEXEC.BAT. An AUTOEXEC.BAT file is invoked automatically when you start DOS. After DOS has looked for the CONFIG.SYS file, it searches for a file on the root directory named AUTOEXEC.BAT. If it finds one, it bypasses the normal date and time prompts and follows the batch file instead. If it does not find the file, it continues normally. Any batch file can be selected as the automatic start-up by naming it AUTOEXEC.BAT. You can create a new batch file, or you can RENAME or COPY an existing batch file with the new name.

Before you attempt this exercise, check if an AUTOEXEC.BAT file already exists on your data disk. Type *DIR AUTOEXEC.BAT* or *TYPE AUTO-EXEC.BAT* and press the Enter key. If the message "File not found" appears, there is no AUTOEXEC.BAT on the disk and you may continue. However, if a text listing or filename appears, *do not* create a new AUTOEXEC.BAT file—it will erase the one on your disk. Instead, read the exercise, but continue to the next section *without* creating a file.

If there is no AUTOEXEC.BAT file on your disk, try the following to see how this works.

1. Type **A:** (or **B:** on a dual-diskette system)

2. Press ↵

3. Type **COPY CON AUTOEXEC.BAT** and press ↵

4. Type **DATE** and press ↵

5. Type **PROMPT PG** and press ↵

6. Type **PATH \XWP** and press ↵

7. Press **F6** ↵ to end

Booting with an AUTOEXEC.BAT File. Since you formatted your disk with the FORMAT /S command, it can boot DOS. Try this exercise to see the effect of your AUTOEXEC.BAT file.

1. Remove all diskettes from the disk drives

2. Place your diskette (*not* the DOS diskette) in Drive A

Invoke a "warm boot" as follows:

3. Depress and hold **Ctrl** and **Alt**

4. Press **Del** and then release all three keys

As you've learned, holding the Ctrl and Alt keys while pressing the Del key and then releasing all three (a "warm boot") will restart your computer quickly.

5. Enter the date when prompted

Note that you were asked for the date only (not time) and that the path and prompt were then set as listed in the batch file, without your having to type in any additional commands. You may create any AUTOEXEC.BAT file that you want.

☞ **Tip: It is good practice to first create the file with a name other than AUTOEXEC.BAT (such as AUTOTRY.BAT), test it by typing its name, and then copy it or rename it as AUTOEXEC.BAT only after you are sure it works.**

Checkpoint

☐ Create a batch file named REVIEW.BAT on your data disk that will set a path to \XDOS.

☐ Retype the REVIEW.BAT file to insert a date command before the path command.

☐ View the contents of the REVIEW.BAT file, print it (with Shift + PrtSc) and then erase the REVIEW.BAT file from your disk.

Redirecting Input and Output

Usually, DOS receives input from the keyboard and sends output to the screen. However, DOS has a few useful command modifiers that let you redirect file input and output. These modifiers include redirection symbols, pipes, and filter commands.

You will need to access some DOS external commands for this section, so restart your computer now as follows:

Hard-Disk System

1. If your computer is on, remove your diskette from Drive A and "warm boot" the computer

2. If your computer is off, boot it up normally

3. Place your diskette in Drive A

4. Set the PATH to **C:\DOS** (or the correct subdirectory)

5. Change the default drive to A:

Dual-Diskette System

1. If your computer is on, place the DOS disk in Drive A and "warm boot" the computer

2. If your computer is off, boot it up normally

3. Place your diskette in Drive B

4. Change the default drive to B:

If you're using a network, boot your computer and change the default to A:. Set the path to the disk and subdirectory where DOS is located.

Symbols and Pipes

DOS reserves three symbols for redirecting input or output. They are:

>	(greater than symbol)	redirects output
<	(less than symbol)	redirects the source of input
¦	(vertical line symbol)	called a "pipe," for using the output of one command as the input for another

When used alone or in combination, these symbols alter the normal path of input or output to suit your needs.

Output Redirect.   By default, DOS sends the output of most commands to the screen. However, there are times when you might want to "capture" output in a text file. This can be done by adding the output redirect symbol (>) and a filename after the command. For example, to redirect a DIR list to a text file named LISTING, do this:

1.   Type **DIR>LISTING**

2.   Press   ↵

The directory of the default disk will be sent to a file on your data disk called LISTING.

☞ Tip: Using drive identifiers (such as *DIR B:>B:LISTING)* can control which directory is produced and which drive is used to save the results.

If LISTING does not exist, DOS creates it; if it already exists, its contents will be replaced with the new data. Such a text file could now be modified or even incorporated into another word-processed document. To see the result for now,

3.   Type **TYPE LISTING**

4.   Press   ↵

The TYPE command lets you see LISTING on the screen. The list should resemble the results of the DIR command shown in Figure DOS2–12a.

☞ Tip: To add new data to a file that already exists *without* replacing its contents, use two output redirect symbols (>>) instead of one, to tell DOS to *append* the new data to the end of an existing file rather than replace it.

Input Redirect.   At times, it may be useful to have input for a command come from a file instead of the keyboard. This can be accomplished with the input redirect symbol (<) as in the expression *SORT<LISTING*, which would use the commands in the SORT file to alphabetically sort the LISTING file (and send the output to the screen). Figure DOS2–12b displays an input redirect to a file called LISTING. You will learn more about SORT in a moment.

The Pipe Symbol.   A pipe is used to connect two DOS commands together. That is, the output from one command can be used as input for another command. This is done by separating the commands with the pipe symbol (┊)—a vertical bar. This symbol can be generated on newer keyboards by holding the Shift key and depressing the key immediately above the Enter key. For example, to send the output from the DIR command as input to the SORT command,

1.   Type **DIR ┊ SORT** and press   ↵

Your screen should resemble Figure DOS2–13. The number and names of files may differ from those in the figure, but the directory should present the list of filenames on the default disk's root directory in alphabetical order.

You can also combine pipes with redirection symbols as in this exercise:

2.   Type **DIR ┊ SORT>LISTING2** and press   ↵

This command sorts the output of the DIR command and then saves it in a disk text file called LISTING2.

Figure DOS2—12

Input and Output Redirect Symbols

(a) The output redirect symbol (>) in DIR>LISTING has redirected directory output to a file called LISTING.
(b) The input redirect symbol (<) in SORT<LISTING> LISTING2 has sent input from the LISTING file through a sort routine with the result redirected to a file called LISTING2.

```
A:\>TYPE LISTING

Volume in drive A is LASTNAME
Volume Serial Number is 322B-1204
Directory of A:\

COMMAND  COM     52925 03-10-93   6:00a
XDOS        <DIR>       03-27-93  11:55a
XWP         <DIR>       03-27-93  11:55a
START    BAT        34 03-27-93  12:14p
CONFIG   SYS        26 03-27-93  12:16p
AUTOEXEC BAT        30 03-27-93  12:17p
LISTING             0 03-27-93  12:19p
        7 file(s)       53015 bytes
                       908009 bytes free

A:\>
```

(a)

```
A:\>SORT<LISTING>LISTING2

A:\>TYPE LISTING2

                      908009 bytes free
        7 file(s)       53015 bytes
   Directory of A:\
Volume in drive A is LASTNAME
Volume Serial Number is 322B-1204
AUTOEXEC BAT        30 03-27-93  12:17p
COMMAND  COM     52925 03-10-93   6:00a
CONFIG   SYS        26 03-27-93  12:16p
LISTING             0 03-27-93  12:19p
START    BAT        34 03-27-93  12:14p
XDOS        <DIR>       03-27-93  11:55a
XWP         <DIR>       03-27-93  11:55a

A:\>
```

(b)

Figure DOS2—13

The Pipe Symbol (¦) in DIR¦SORT Sends the Directory Listing through the SORT Filter, before Displaying It on the Screen

The files on your screen may be different, but all will be in alphabetical order.

```
A:\>DIR¦SORT

                      907093 bytes free
       10 file(s)       53931 bytes
   Directory of A:\
Volume in drive A is LASTNAME
Volume Serial Number is 322B-1204
AMBFCABH            0 03-27-93  12:21p
AMBFCBBF            0 03-27-93  12:21p
AUTOEXEC BAT        30 03-27-93  12:17p
COMMAND  COM     52925 03-10-93   6:00a
CONFIG   SYS        26 03-27-93  12:16p
LISTING           458 03-27-93  12:19p
LISTING2          458 03-27-93  12:20p
START    BAT        34 03-27-93  12:14p
XDOS        <DIR>       03-27-93  11:55a
XWP         <DIR>       03-27-93  11:55a

A:\>
```

Figure DOS2—14
*The Pipe Symbol in
DIR ¦ MORE Sends the
Directory Listing
through the MORE
Filter, Which Pauses at
the End of Each Screen*

```
Volume in drive C is EGM
Volume Serial Number is 322B-1204
Directory of C:\DOS

.              <DIR>       02-17-93    2:21p
..             <DIR>       02-17-93    2:21p
4201     CPI       6404 04-09-91    5:00a
4208     CPI        728 04-09-91    5:00a
5202     CPI        378 04-09-91    5:00a
ANSI     SYS       9065 03-10-93    6:00a
APPEND   EXE      10774 03-10-93    6:00a
ASSIGN   COM       6399 04-09-91    5:00a
ATTRIB   EXE      11165 03-10-93    6:00a
BACKUP   EXE      36092 04-09-91    5:00a
CHKDSK   EXE      12907 03-10-93    6:00a
CHKSTATE SYS      41600 03-10-93    6:00a
CHOICE   COM       1754 03-10-93    6:00a
COMMAND  COM      52925 03-10-93    6:00a
COMP     EXE      14282 04-09-91    5:00a
COUNTRY  SYS      17066 03-10-93    6:00a
--More--
```

Filters

A **filter** is a command that reads input, modifies it in some way, and then outputs it, typically to a screen. In a sense, data are filtered into another form. DOS offers three filters: MORE, SORT, and FIND. All are external DOS commands.

MORE.   The **MORE** filter displays the contents of a file one screenful at a time. This is useful on large files that are displayed too quickly to be read. Try this:

Hard-Disk System

1. Change the default drive to C:
2. Set the active directory to \DOS (or the correct DOS subdirectory)
3. Type **DIR ¦ MORE**

Dual-Diskette System

1. Change the default drive to A:
2. Set the active directory to the root directory

(Be sure to place the pipe symbol between the two commands.)

4. Press ↵

Your display should resemble Figure DOS2–14. Notice that the screen display halts when it has been filled, and that "—More—" appears at the bottom to indicate there is more output to follow.

5. Press any key to move to the next screen
6. Continue to press any key to change screens until the directory listing is finished

(The listing is finished when there is no "—More—" message and the DOS prompt has returned.)

The MORE command can be used with other DOS commands whenever you want to view long documents on your screen. For example, the command *TYPE A:LISTING2¦MORE* (or *B:* on a dual-diskette system) would list the text file LISTING2 on screen, pausing if needed to display each filled screen.

SORT. The SORT filter allows you to alphabetize a file according to a character in a specified column. SORT will normally alphabetize in ascending order (*A–Z*) according to the first column of a file. You can change the order (or character position) with additional command modifiers. First, restart your computer if needed.

Hard-Disk System or Network	**Dual-Diskette System**
1. Set the path to C:\DOS (or to the disk and path in your network that contains DOS)	1. Place your disk in Drive B
2. Set the default drive to A:	2. Set the default drive to B:

Now, try these sort commands:

3. Type **DIR ¦ SORT** ⏎

The directory will be listed in alphabetical order according to the first character of each line, as shown in Figure DOS2–15a. SORT does not distinguish between uppercase and lowercase letters.

☞ **Tip: You could add ¦ *MORE* if needed at the end of the command to pause after each screen is full.**

4. Type **DIR ¦ SORT / R** ⏎

The addition of the /R modifier reverses the order of the sort as shown in Figure DOS2–15b. That is, the list will be sorted from *Z* to *A*, and then from *9* to *0*.

5. Type **DIR ¦ SORT / +9** ⏎

The /+9 modifier sorts the directory based on the *9th* column on each line. Note that the 9th column is where DIR starts the file extension name, as shown in Figure DOS2–15c, so that this command presents the directory in file extension order. You can choose any column by specifying its number in the /+ modifier. Choosing an appropriate column can produce many useful sorts.

FIND. The FIND filter allows you to search for a specific series of characters (known as a text "string") within an ASCII file. For example, the command *FIND "Frog Prince" STORY.TXT* (also written as *STORY.TXT ¦ FIND "Frog Prince"*) would display all the lines from the file STORY.TXT that contained the text string "Frog Prince." You can also add the modifier /C to count the number of lines, or /N to display each line's relative line number within the file. This exercise lists DIR file names that contain the extension .BAT:

1. Type **DIR ¦ FIND "BAT"** ⏎

This produces a listing similar to that shown in Figure DOS2–16a.
   Placing the modifier /N in a FIND command, as in *DIR ¦ FIND /N "LIST,"* adds bracketed numbers in front of each entry identifying its location in the file. For example, to produce a listing similar to that shown in Figure DOS2–16b,

2. Type **DIR ¦ FIND /N "LIST"** ⏎

A /C modifier will simply count the entries that match the search:

3. Type **DIR ¦ FIND /C "LIST"** ⏎

The result is shown in Figure DOS2–16c.

```
A:\>DIR:SORT

                       907093 bytes free
          10 file(s)       53931 bytes
 Directory of A:\
 Volume in drive A is LASTNAME
 Volume Serial Number is 322B-1204
 AMBFCABH                0 03-27-93  12:21p
 AMBFCBBF                0 03-27-93  12:21p
 AUTOEXEC BAT           30 03-27-93  12:17p
 COMMAND  COM        52925 03-10-93   6:00a
 CONFIG   SYS           26 03-27-93  12:16p
 LISTING              458 03-27-93  12:19p
 LISTING2             458 03-27-93  12:20p
 START    BAT          34 03-27-93  12:14p
 XDOS        <DIR>        03-27-93  11:55a
 XWP         <DIR>        03-27-93  11:55a

 A:\>
```

(a)

```
A:\>DIR:SORT/R

 XWP         <DIR>        03-27-93  11:55a
 XDOS        <DIR>        03-27-93  11:55a
 START    BAT          34 03-27-93  12:14p
 LISTING2             458 03-27-93  12:20p
 LISTING              458 03-27-93  12:19p
 CONFIG   SYS           26 03-27-93  12:16p
 COMMAND  COM        52925 03-10-93   6:00a
 AUTOEXEC BAT           30 03-27-93  12:17p
 AMBJBMDN                0 03-27-93  12:25p
 AMBJBMEP                0 03-27-93  12:25p
 Volume Serial Number is 322B-1204
 Volume in drive A is LASTNAME
 Directory of A:\
          10 file(s)       53931 bytes
                       907093 bytes free

 A:\>
```

(b)

```
A:\>DIR:SORT/+9

                       907093 bytes free
 AMBKAKCK                0 03-27-93  12:21p
 AMBKALEF                0 03-27-93  12:21p
 LISTING              458 03-27-93  12:19p
 LISTING2             458 03-27-93  12:20p
 XDOS        <DIR>        03-27-93  11:55a
 XWP         <DIR>        03-27-93  11:55a
 AUTOEXEC BAT           30 03-27-93  12:17p
 START    BAT          34 03-27-93  12:14p
 COMMAND  COM        52925 03-10-93   6:00a
 CONFIG   SYS           26 03-27-93  12:16p
          10 file(s)       53931 bytes
 Volume in drive A is LASTNAME
 Directory of A:\
 Volume Serial Number is 322B-1204

 A:\>
```

(c)

Figure DOS2—15
The SORT Filter

(a) The SORT command presents a file in alphabetical order according to the first character of each line.
(b) The use of an /R modifier reverses the order of the sort.
(c) The / + number modifier (as in DIR : SORT/ + 9) sorts the lines in a file based on the named column (in this case, the 9th).

Note: You may have different files on your screen

DOS

Figure DOS2–16

The FIND Filter

(a) The FIND ''string'' filter lists lines that contain the named string, in this case, DIR ¦ FIND ''BAT'' lists all files with a .BAT extension.
(b) The /N modifier (as in DIR ¦ FIND /N ''LIST'') adds bracketed numbers in front of each item, identifying its line in the original file.
(c) The /C modifier displays a simple count of the items that match the search criteria.

```
A:\>DIR¦FIND "BAT"
START    BAT        34 03-27-93   12:14p
AUTOEXEC BAT        30 03-27-93   12:17p


A:\>DIR¦FIND /N "LIST"
[12]LISTING             458 03-27-93   12:19p
[13]LISTING2            458 03-27-93   12:20p


A:\>DIR:FIND /C "LIST"
2
```

Checkpoint

☐ Redirect the output of a DIR command (sorted by file size) of your data disk to a file named DOS2.TXT on your data disk.

☐ Append to the DOS2.TXT file the results of TYPE commands showing the contents of the START.BAT, CONFIG.SYS, and AUTOEXEC.BAT files. (Hint: TYPE START.BAT>>DOS2.TXT)

☐ Find all filenames on your data disk's directory that contain the text string "TXT."

House-keeping

As you have seen, "housekeeping" refers to proper management of disk files—selecting meaningful filenames, using subdirectories when appropriate, making backup files for safekeeping, and erasing files or subdirectories that are no longer needed. Before you continue in the text, perform the following housekeeping chores on *your data disk*:

1. Remove the XDOS directory and its contents
2. Remove the \XWP\RESEARCH directory
3. Erase all files that start with LISTING and START

If you are using a network or a dual-diskette system, you may need to boot your computer with your data disk. You must therefore retain in the root directory the COMMAND.COM file and any special AUTOEXEC.BAT or CONFIG.SYS file.

4. If AUTOEXEC.BAT or CONFIG.SYS is not needed, delete it

Your disk directory should now show only the XWP subdirectory, COMMAND.COM, and DOS2.TXT (and AUTOEXEC.BAT and CONFIG.SYS if you left them on the disk).

Note: If you do not need your disk to boot your system, it is better to reformat it without the /S option to maximize its storage space.

For your convenience and further study, the DOS appendix provides a comprehensive reference for most DOS commands, including those that were not presented in detail in this module.

DOS Utilities

Utility programs can enhance a computer's power and the ease with which you can access files. However, because most of DOS's utilities operate automatically or serve specialized purposes, they are presented for your information only (without tutorials). Refer to the Appendix and the *DOS 6.0 Reference Manual* for further details about their use.

DOS 6.0 offers three utilities that increase disk storage, namely, DoubleSpace, DblBoot and Defrag. In addition, Backup (a backup utility) provides a quick way to create safe copies of hard-disk files on floppy disks.

Hard–Disk Utilities

DoubleSpace. DoubleSpace is a data-compression program that reduces the space occupied by most files on your hard disk to as little as half their original size. In effect, this almost doubles the storage capacity of your disk without the need for new hardware. (*Note:* An increase of disk capacity of about 50 percent is more likely, since not all files can be compressed to the same extent and some not at all.)

Once installed, DoubleSpace works automatically and "transparently" (without any noticeable difference in normal operation), uncompressing disk files for use and then recompressing them when saved. DOS also includes an EXPAND command that lets you uncompress files when needed.

DblBoot. DblBoot is the data-compression equivalent of the *FORMAT /S* command. With DoubleSpace installed, the DblBoot command creates a formatted "bootable" floppy disk that can start your computer system and store compressed files. For example, to create a "dblboot" disk in drive A, you would enter the following command:

```
DBLBOOT A:
```

Note: DblBoot only works with high-density drives (1.44 Meg 3½″ or 1.2 Meg 5¼″ disks).

Defrag. When space is readily available, files are saved in their entirety in one disk area. However, over time, as you save and delete files, contiguous file areas are replaced by a quilt-like, fragmented pattern of used and unused disk space. Portions of files and free disk space may be scattered throughout the disk. This fragmentation into bits and pieces of files and free space significantly increases the time it takes to save and retrieve disk files.

A defragmentation utility, such as DOS's **Defrag**, rearranges and consolidates the free disk space, significantly improving the speed with which files are accessed. The command to invoke Defrag is

```
DEFRAG C:
```

(*Note:* Other defragmentation programs also consolidate files as well, thus increasing the efficiency even further.)

Backup. DOS's backup utility lets you quickly copy files on your hard disk onto one or more floppy disks for safekeeping. Backup lets you perform full or partial backups, but unlike more sophisticated utilities, it cannot save file backups to a tape drive. The command for Backup is

```
BACKUP
```

Other DOS utilities let you optimize available memory, protect your system from viruses, and modify your keyboard or screen to accommodate special needs. These utilities include MemMaker, VSAFE, AccessDOS, and related programs.

System Utilities

MemMaker. *MemMaker* is an automatic program that optimizes the use of your computer's memory. When invoked, MemMaker examines memory-resident programs and device drivers and changes your setup program to make the best use of your computer's memory. This action can free up additional RAM space by as much as 100K over older DOS memory managers. The command to invoke MemMaker is

MEMMAKER

Note: to cancel MemMaker changes, you can type
MEMMAKER /UNDO

VSAFE.   *VSAFE* is an antivirus utility that continuously monitors your computer memory and disks for viruses and displays a warning message when it finds one. The command to invoke VSAFE is

VSAFE

Note: To remove VSAFE from memory, type
VSAFE /U

AccessDOS.   *AccessDOS* is a collection of DOS programs that can modify the screen and keyboard to accommodate persons with hearing and motion disabilities. Such programs includes "StickyKeys" and "ToggleKeys," which lock in Shift, Alt, and Ctrl keys, allowing you to use one finger when typing; "MouseKeys," which uses the keyboard to simulate a mouse; and "ShowSounds," which alters the screen display to indicate various sound cues. Related programs allow you to adjust the response sensitivity of the keyboard and, using DVORAK.SYS, reconfigure the standard keyboard layout to an alternate Dvorak (or "simplified") keyboard design. The command to invoke the AccessDOS menu is

ADOS

which can be typed at the DOS prompt or placed into an AUTOEXEC.BAT file to automatically invoke it when you boot your computer.

Summary

- Hierarchical directories, which allow related files to be grouped together for easy access, are useful for managing files on disks with large storage capacities.
- When files are arranged in a hierarchical structure, the main directory, located at the top, is known as the root directory. Subdirectories are those subordinate directories beneath it, into which it is subdivided. First-level subdirectories are typically set aside for DOS files, applications software files, and language translators. The TREE command allows you to view the interrelationship of subdirectories in the hierarchy.
- The MD (make directory) command allows you to make a new subdirectory within the hierarchy. Once a subdirectory exists, it can be referenced in DOS commands by name (as in *DIR \DOS*) or changed to the active directory (made the default) with the CD (change directory) command.
- An empty subdirectory can be removed with the RD (remove directory) command.
- The DOS TREE command creates a listing of the entire directory hierarchy for easy reference. Adding the modifier /F will also include the filenames contained in each subdirectory.
- PROMPT is an internal command that allows you to modify the standard DOS prompt to display more information, such as the active subdirectory name.
- PATH is an internal command that creates a command search path through selected disk drives and subdirectories. It tells DOS which subdirectories should be searched, and in what order, to find appropriate command files.
- A batch file is a text file that contains a series of DOS commands. A batch file allows you to perform a set of tasks by invoking a one-word command.

You can create a batch file using the COPY CON command.

- TYPE is an internal command that allows you to view any text file. Text files can also be edited by using the DOS EDLIN command, the full-screen editor, or an ASCII word processor.

- Changes to the standard DOS boot process can also be made by using CONFIG.SYS and AUTOEXEC.BAT files. CONFIG.SYS is a text file of commands that changes the standard DOS configuration of buffers and files. You can also add device drivers that let DOS recognize additional devices that are not usually part of the computer. AUTOEXEC.BAT is a special batch file that is automatically run by DOS when it boots up. Any batch file can be used by renaming it AUTOEXEC.BAT.

- DOS uses three symbols for redirecting output and input. The "greater than" symbol (>) redirects output; the "less than" symbol (<) redirects the source of input; the vertical line symbol (¦), also known as a pipe, connects two commands together, using the output of the first command as the input for the next.

- A DOS filter is a command that modifies input in some way. DOS offers three types of filters: MORE, which displays a screenful of information at a time; SORT, which alphabetizes a file according to a specified column; and FIND, which allows you to search for a specific set of characters in a file.

- A warm boot is a process by which DOS can be restarted without turning off the power. It is achieved by pressing and holding the Ctrl and Alt keys, then pressing the Del key and releasing all three.

Shown in parentheses are the page numbers on which key terms are boldfaced.

Key Terms

AUTOEXEC.BAT (DOS49)	Defrag (DOS57)	Pipe (DOS51)
Batch file (DOS45)	DoubleSpace (DOS57)	PROMPT (DOS42)
CD or CHDIR (Change Directory) (DOS41)	EDLIN (DOS47)	RD or RMDIR (Remove Directory) (DOS42)
	Filter (DOS53)	
	FIND (DOS54)	
	MD or MKDIR (Make Directory) (DOS37)	Root directory (DOS36)
CONFIG.SYS (DOS48)		SORT (DOS54)
COPY CON (DOS45)		Subdirectory (DOS36)
DblBoot (DOS57)	MORE (DOS53)	TREE (DOS38)
Device driver (DOS48)	PATH (DOS44)	TYPE (DOS47)

Quiz

True/False

1. Hierarchical disk files can only be used on larger-capacity drives.

2. Subdirectories can have as many subordinate directories as you desire.

3. When using subdirectories, most of the useful applications programs should be kept in the root directory for easy access.

4. The commands to create, change, and remove subdirectories are all internal DOS commands.

5. Directory listings produced with the DIR command identify subdirectories with the characters "<SUB>."

6. Subdirectories cannot be removed if they have files in them.

7. Typing *PROMPT* and pressing the Enter key will return the DOS prompt to its standard form.

8. DOS's PATH command tells the operating system which subdirectories should be searched to find a command file.

9. All batch files must end with the extension .BAT.

10. The DOS EDLIN line editor is better for editing text files than a standard word processor.

Multiple Choice

11. What is another name for the main directory of a disk?
    a. Root directory
    b. Subdirectory
    c. Directory #1
    d. Hard disk

12. Which one of the following commands is used to create a new subdirectory?
    a. CD
    b. RD
    c. COPY CON
    d. MD

13. The DOS command called _____ displays each subdirectory and shows its relationship to the root directory.
    a. PATH
    b. TREE
    c. PROMPT
    d. MKDIR

14. Which one of the following DOS commands will make the root directory the active directory?
    a. CD \
    b. CD <ROOT>
    c. MD \ROOT
    d. ACTIVE = ROOT

15. Which directory can be removed with the RD command?
    a. The root directory
    b. A subdirectory with an empty subordinate subdirectory
    c. A subdirectory with only one text file
    d. None of these directories can be removed

16. Which one of the following prompts might appear on your screen if you had used the PROMPT PG command?
    a. A>
    b. B:PG =
    c. B:\DOS>
    d. 11-01-91:B:ROOT>

17. Which one of the following commands would instruct DOS to search for command files in the subdirectories DOS and WP?
    a. PATH \DOS;\WP
    b. PROMPT DOS + WP
    c. PATH \DOS\WP
    d. SRCH:DOS>WP

18. Which one of the following techniques *cannot* be used to create a new batch file?
    a. A word processor that writes ASCII text files
    b. The COPY CON command
    c. The EDLIN line editor
    d. The TYPE command

19. Which one of the following files will be run automatically when you boot DOS?
    a. AUTOEXEC.BAT
    b. CONFIG.BAT
    c. START.BAT
    d. BOOTUP.BAT
20. A vertical bar (¦) symbol is known as a(n)
    a. output redirect symbol.
    b. input redirect symbol.
    c. filter.
    d. pipe.

Matching

Select the term that best matches each phrase below:

a. Batch file   g. Subdirectory
b. Root directory   h. Warm boot
c. COPY CON   i. CD
d. TYPE   j. Filter
e. EDLIN   k. Pipe
f. Device driver   l. MORE

21. A file that contains one or more commands that DOS executes at one time
22. A program that lets DOS recognize hardware that is not part of the computer itself
23. An external DOS command that reads input, modifies it in some way, and then outputs it
24. A symbol that connects two DOS commands together allowing the output from one command to be used as input for another command
25. A directory that is subordinate to another directory
26. The DOS line editor
27. An internal DOS command that displays the contents of a specified text file
28. An internal DOS command that changes the active directory of the specified or default drive
29. A DOS command that displays the contents of a file one screenful at a time
30. A DOS command that places keyboard entries into a text file

Answers

True/False: 1. F; 2. T; 3. F; 4. T; 5. F; 6. T; 7. T; 8. T; 9. T; 10. F
Multiple Choice: 11. a; 12. d; 13. b; 14. a; 15. d; 16. c; 17. a; 18. d; 19. a; 20. d
Matching: 21. a; 22. f; 23. j; 24. k; 25. g; 26. e; 27. d; 28. i; 29. l; 30. c

Exercises

I. Operations

Provide the DOS command required to do each of the operations shown below. For each operation, assume a system with dual-diskette drives, A and B, and assume the DOS disk is in the default drive, A. You may want to verify each of your commands by trying each on your computer system.

1. Make a subdirectory called WORD and a subdirectory called DOS on the disk in Drive B (requires two steps).
2. Make a subdirectory named TEXT that is subordinate to WORD created in Exercise 1.
3. Copy the file SORT.EXE from the default disk to the TEXT subdirectory created in Exercise 2.
4. List the directory of the WORD subdirectory.
5. Produce a list of all the subdirectories on Drive B.
6. Change the active directory to WORD on Drive B.
7. Remove the TEXT subdirectory (requires two steps).
8. Change the DOS prompt to show the active subdirectory followed by a ">" (output) symbol.
9. Create a path that will search the DOS and WORD subdirectories (in that order) for command files.
10. Create a batch file named GO that will produce a directory of Drive B's root directory (three steps).
11. List the GO batch file's contents.

II. Commands

Describe fully, using as few words as possible in each case, what is accomplished by each of the DOS commands given below. Assume that each exercise part is independent of any previous parts. Be aware that some commands may result in error messages; where this is the case, respond "Error message" and state the reason for the message. Assume that the computer system contains dual-diskette drives, A and B; also assume that the disk in Drive A is the default disk and contains DOS's external commands, and that the disk in Drive B already contains subdirectories named DOS and WP.

1. MD B:\UTILITY\LIST
2. CD B:\DOS
3. PATH A:\;B:\WP
4. RD B:\UTILITY
5. ERASE A:\WP*.NOV
6. TREE B:
7. COPY CON B:BEGIN.BAT
8. PROMPT TBPG
9. DIR ¦ SORT /R ¦ MORE
10. DIR>B:/WP/LIST.TXT
11. FIND "EXE" LIST.TXT

III. Applications

Perform the following operations using your computer system. You will need a DOS disk and one additional blank disk to complete this exercise (it can be the one you have been using as long as you don't mind erasing the files). In a few words, describe how you accomplished each operation, and its result.

1. Boot your computer and format the disk in Drive B with the FORMAT /S command.
2. Create two subdirectories on Drive B named DOS and SAMPLES.

3. Create a subdirectory named OTHERS subordinate to the SAMPLES subdirectory.

4. Copy all files on Drive A that start with *S* and have an .EXE extension to the DOS subdirectory on Drive B.

5. Using COPY CON, create a batch file named LIST that will list all the subdirectories on Drive B.

6. Using COPY CON, create an AUTOEXEC.BAT file that will set the prompt to show the active subdirectory and create a search path through the DOS subdirectory.

7. Sort the directory of Drive A in alphabetical order by DATE and send the output to a file called SORTED.TXT on Drive B.

8. List the directory of Drive A on the screen, sorted by filename, and displayed one screen at a time.

DOS 6.0 Feature and
Operation Reference

DOS Keys

Special keys used by DOS are described next. For the specific location of these keys, check your particular keyboard.

Alt `Alt`

Usually used in combination with other keys, the Alt key typically is held down when striking another key.

Arrow Keys `→` `←` `↑` `↓`

In some situations, can be used to move the cursor, one character or one menu selection at a time, in the direction indicated by the arrow. When using DOS interactively in the command mode, the left arrow key works like the Backspace key.

Backspace `← Backspace`

Erases characters to the left of the cursor position.

Break `Break`

Stops a running program.

Caps Lock `Caps Lock`

Used to keep the Shift key active temporarily so that all characters being typed in are uppercase.

Ctrl `Ctrl`

Usually used in combination with other keys, the Ctrl key is typically held down when striking another key. Note:

- **Ctrl+Numlock** freezes the display; pressing **Ctrl+S** or any other key restarts the display.
- **Ctrl+PrtSc** sends lines to both the screen and printer; pressing **Ctrl+PrtSc** again disables this feature.

- Ctrl + C stops the execution of a program; Ctrl + Break does the same thing.
- Ctrl + Alt + Del causes a warm boot (system restart).

Del (Delete) `Del`

In certain situations, erases characters at the cursor position; in other situations, pressing Del has no effect on the current operation.

Enter `↵` or `Enter ↵`

Serves two principal functions: (1) When creating a batch file in DOS, used to enter a return at the end of each command line. (2) When using DOS interactively, used to enter a DOS command.

Esc (Escape) `Esc`

In certain situations, lets you abort an operation; in other situations, the Esc key has no effect on the current operation.

Function Keys `F1` `F2` `F3` . . .

Used to execute preprogrammed DOS routines in some versions of DOS. The F1 function key, for instance, usually repeats the last command one keystroke at a time.

Ins (Insert) `Ins`

In certain situations, lets you insert characters at the cursor position; in other situations, the Ins key has no effect on the current operation.

NumLock `NumLock`

Used to activate the numeric keypad that is on the right side of most keyboards. NumLock works as a toggle key; hitting it once activates the keypad, and hitting it again deactivates the keypad.

Pause `Pause`

Halts the scrolling of display output until another key is depressed.

Pg Up and Pg Dn (Page Up and Page Down) `Pg Up` and `Pg Dn`

Used to scroll one page backward (up) and forward (down).

PrtSc (Print Screen) `PrtSc`

Used in combination with the Shift key to send the contents of the current display screen to the printer.

Shift `↑` or `↑ Shift`

Serves two principal functions: (1) Works like the Shift key on a typewriter; when it is held down and a letter or number key is struck, an uppercase letter or the symbol assigned to the number key is produced. (2) Used in combination with another key; when the Shift key is held down and the other key is struck, a DOS command is invoked; for instance, Shift + PrtSc sends the contents of the display screen to the printer.

Tab `↤↦` or `Tab ↬`

Used to reach a preset Tab stop or a choice in the DOS shell program.

DOS Device Names

The device names listed next are reserved words for special input or output devices.

The Name . . .	Is Used to Identify . . .
COMx	The serial communications port(s)
LPTx or PRN	The parallel printer port(s) (PRN used for LPT1)
CON	The keyboard
NUL	The "do nothing" device

Summary of Common DOS Features

Following is a brief summary, with examples, showing how to use some of DOS's most popular features. In this summary

1. The following conventions apply to disk drives:

Hard-Disk System

Invoke internal commands at C:\> (the system prompt) and external commands at C:\DOS> (the DOS subdirectory prompt).

Dual-Diskette System

Invoke all commands at A>. For external commands, the DOS disk must be in Drive A.

If no disk drive is specified, assume that the feature or command works the same on dual-diskette systems as it does on hard-disk systems.

2. The syntax examples contain general terms such as filename.ext, command name, and directory name within angle brackets (<>). When you issue the commands shown in the examples, you must enter the *actual* filenames, extensions, etc. The entry [path] in the examples signifies that identifying a path to a file may also be necessary. Do not type in any of the brackets when typing in the appropriate filename, path, etc.

AUTOEXEC. BAT File

The special batch file that is executed when DOS is booted. Normally, AUTOEXEC.BAT is used to do such tasks as establish a path to subdirectories, personalize the system prompt, and start up an applications package when the system is booted. AUTOEXEC.BAT must reside on the root directory of the boot disk.

You can use the COPY CON command, EDIT, or EDLIN to create an AUTOEXEC.BAT file. To see how to do this with COPY CON, refer to the example provided with the COPY CON command. If the file in Step 1 of that example were given the name AUTOEXEC.BAT instead of RUNWP.BAT, you would have an AUTOEXEC.BAT file that would start you in WordPerfect as soon as you turned your computer system on.

Some of the DOS commands and batch-file subcommands commonly used in AUTOEXEC.BAT files are named and described next:

Command	Purpose in AUTOEXEC.BAT File
CD	Changes to the directory where you would like to begin your work
DATE	Uses the computer system's internal clock to establish the date
DIR	Displays the root directory when the computer system is booted up
ECHO	Enables you to include a message, which is displayed when the computer system is booted up
PATH	Specifies the path DOS will invoke when the computer system is booted up and also the path that will be active when you begin to type in commands
PROMPT	Allows you to customize the system prompt
TIME	Uses the computer system's internal clock to establish the time of day

Batch Files

A batch file is an ASCII text file that contains DOS commands and/or special batch subcommands. DOS executes the commands in a batch file as though each of them were separately entered at the DOS prompt. All batch files have the extension .BAT.

The batch subcommands are the following:

Subcommand	Action
CALL	Temporarily interrupts one batch file to process another
ECHO	Displays a message on the screen; also, can turn on/off the displaying of batch commands as these commands are invoked
FOR...IN...DO	Allows loops to be created in a batch file
GOTO <label>	Unconditionally transfers to the line after a specified label in a batch file
IF	Enables a command to be executed only under certain conditions
PAUSE	Stops processing and waits for the operator to press a key
REM	Enables comments—which can be displayed if the echo is on—into a batch file
SHIFT	Lets you change the position of replaceable parameters

CHDIR (CD) Command

Internal command that moves you from one directory or subdirectory to another in the default drive.

Type **CD \<directory name>** ↵   *or*   **CD <directory name>** ↵

Note the following:

- **CD \LOTUS** will move you to the LOTUS directory, regardless of where you were when this command was executed
- **CD JILL** will move you to a directory named JILL, provided that JILL is immediately subordinate to your current directory

CHKDSK Command

External command that displays a status report on a disk.

Hard-Disk System	**Dual-Diskette System**
With your data diskette in Drive A,	With your data diskette in Drive B,
Type **CHKDSK A:** ↵	Type **CHKDSK B:** ↵

CLS Command

Internal command used to erase the display screen.

Type **CLS** ↵

CONFIG. SYS File

Special ASCII text file that DOS reads during booting to establish such things as the maximum number of files that can be used at one time, the number of file buffers and stacks to be put into use, communications with nonstandard system devices (such as a mouse), and a number of other system directives.

Following is a list of DOS subcommands (system directives) used by CONFIG.SYS:

Directive	Action Taken
BREAK	Enables the Ctrl + Break sequence to be recognized during disk operations (in addition to the time when DOS is reading from the keyboard)
BUFFERS	Sets the number of disk buffers used by DOS
COUNTRY	Lets DOS switch to time, date, currency, and case conventions used in a specific country
DEVICE	Installs the specified device driver
DEVICEHIGH	Loads drivers into the upper memory area
DOS	Enables DOS to maintain a link to and/or to load part of itself into the upper memory area
DRIVEPARM	Sets parameters for a physical disk drive when you start DOS
FCBS	Allows you to specify the number of file control blocks that can be open concurrently and, also, files that DOS cannot automatically close
FILES	Allows you to specify the number of files that DOS can have open at one time
INSTALL	Installs certain memory-resident programs
LASTDRIVE	Establishes the highest disk drive in the computer system
REM	Allows comments to be entered into a CONFIG.SYS file
SHELL	Tells DOS which command processor is to be used and the location of the processor
STACKS	Allows you to specify the number and size of data stacks
SWITCHES	Disables extended keyboard functions

When you are planning to install a new applications software package, the documentation included with it should specify acceptable settings of CONFIG.SYS directives. To see that these settings are met, use the TYPE command to list

CONFIG.SYS. CONFIG.SYS files can be established or edited with the COPY CON command and with EDIT or EDLIN.

Internal command that allows you to copy one or more files.

**COPY
Command**

Hard-Disk System	**Dual-Diskette System**
The target disk should be in Drive A.	The source disk goes in Drive A and the target disk in Drive B.
To copy one file,	To copy one file,
Type **COPY** <filename.ext> **A:** ↵	Type **COPY** <filename.ext> **B:** ↵
To copy all files with the same extension,	To copy all files with the same extension,
Type **COPY** *.<ext> **A:** ↵	Type **COPY** *.<ext> **B:** ↵
To copy all files with the same filename but different extensions,	To copy all files with the same filename but different extensions,
Type **COPY** <filename>.* **A:** ↵	Type **COPY** <filename>.* **B:** ↵
To copy all files,	To copy all files,
Type **COPY** *.* **A:** ↵	Type **COPY** *.* **B:** ↵

Popular version of the COPY command that enables an ASCII text file to be created at the keyboard. The created file can be a batch file, configuration file, or any other sort of ASCII file.

**COPY CON
Command**

Type **COPY CON [path]** <filename.ext> ↵

To create, for instance, a three-line batch file that changes the current directory to the WordPerfect directory (WP51) and starts WordPerfect, follow the steps below:

1. Type **COPY CON C:\DOS\RUNWP.BAT**

Note that RUNWP.BAT will be the name of the batch file you create. Your keystrokes will be "copied" to it and the file will be stored in the DOS directory (DOS).

2. Press ↵

The cursor will drop to the next line without any prompt displayed.

3. Type **C:** and press ↵

The cursor will drop to the next line.

4. Type **CD \WP51** and press ↵

The cursor will drop to the next line.

5. Type **WP** and press ↵

The cursor will drop to the next line.

6. Press the **F6** function key or the **Ctrl** + **Z** key combination, to indicate the end of the file.

DOS will respond that one file has been copied.

7. Press ↵

8. Use the TYPE command to inspect the file's contents

DIR Command

Internal command that displays names of files on a disk.

To see the default drive directory,

    Type **DIR** ↵

To see the default drive directory one page at a time,

    Type **DIR/P** ↵

To see a directory of filenames across the width of the screen,

    Type **DIR/W** ↵

To see a directory of Drive B,

    Type **DIR B:** ↵

To search within all directories for a given file,

    Type **DIR** <filename> **/s**

DISKCOPY Command

External command that erases all files on the target disk and formats it before copying the contents of the source disk onto the target disk.

Hard-Disk System

Starting at C:\DOS>,

    Type **DISKCOPY A: A:** ↵

and follow the screen prompts.

Dual-Diskette System

With your DOS disk in Drive A,

    Type **DISKCOPY A: B:** ↵

and follow the screen prompts.

ERASE Command

Internal command that permanently erases one or more files from a disk. Be sure you are at the prompt corresponding to the directory containing the files to be erased.

To erase one file,

    Type **ERASE** <filename.ext> ↵

To erase all files with the same extension,

    Type **ERASE *.**<ext> ↵

To erase all files with the same filename,

    Type **ERASE** <filename>**.*** ↵

To erase all files listed on the directory,

    Type **ERASE *.*** ↵

To erase the contents of Drive B while logged onto Drive A,

    Type **ERASE B:*.*** ↵

External command that prepares a new diskette for use or erases what was on a disk used before.

FORMAT Command

Hard-Disk System

With your unformatted diskette in Drive A or B, type (respectively) either

FORMAT A: ↵ or

FORMAT B: ↵

and follow the screen prompts.

Dual-Diskette System

With your unformatted data diskette in Drive B,

Type **FORMAT B:** ↵

and follow the screen prompts.

Preparing Bootable Diskettes. To format diskettes so that you can boot directly from them, use a /S switch after the disk-drive indicator. For instance, to prepare the diskette in Drive B as a bootable diskette,

Type **FORMAT B:/S** ↵

Formatting Double-Density Diskettes in High-Density Drives. The FORMAT command must be supplemented with special switches when you want to format a double-density (lower-density) diskette in a high-density drive. Follow the rules below.

- $5\frac{1}{4}$-*inch diskettes:* To format a 360-kilobyte diskette in a 1.2 megabyte drive, use the /F:360 switch. For example, if Drive A is 1.2 megabytes and you are formatting a 360-kilobyte diskette there,

   Type **FORMAT A: /F:360** ↵

- $3\frac{1}{2}$-*inch diskettes:* To format a 720-kilobyte diskette in a 1.44-megabyte drive, use the /F:720 switch. For example, if Drive B is 1.44 megabytes and you are formatting a 720-kilobyte diskette there,

   Type **FORMAT B: /F:720** ↵

External command that provides online information about DOS commands. To get information on a specific topic, follow the instructions below:

HELP Command

If you are at the command prompt and wish a list of all DOS commands along with a brief description of them,

Type **HELP** ↵

If you are at the command prompt and need help on a specific command,

Type **HELP <command name>** ↵

If you are at the opening screen in the DOS shell program and wish to access general information about the Help feature,

1. Press **Alt** + **H**

2. Press the highlighted letter corresponding to the Help category you want on the pull-down menu

If you are at the opening screen in the DOS shell program and wish to access help information about a specific command,

1. Press **Alt** to select the menu bar

DOS

2. Use the right- and left-arrow keys on the keyboard, or click the mouse, to move to the menu that contains the command you want help on

3. Use the up- and down-arrow keys on the keyboard, or click the mouse, to move to the specific command you want help on

4. Press **F1**

If you are in a dialog box in the DOS shell program or in a mode that allows context-sensitive help (i.e., help with whatever you are doing at the moment),

1. Select the help button or the command button relating to feature with which you need help, either by using the keyboard or by clicking the mouse

2. Press **F1**

Help is usually provided through either a Help window or a Help pull-down menu, the features of which are described next:

Help Window

Feature	Description
Help text	Gives help, with references to related topics displayed in a different shade or color
Scroll bar	Enables you to scroll to additional help text that is outside the current window
Close button	Returns to the DOS shell program
Back button	Displays the previous help screen, if it exists
Keys button	Gives help with keys and key sequences used by the DOS shell program
Index button	Accesses the alphabetical listing of help topics
Help button	Describes how to use the help system

Help Pull-down Menu

Option	Description
Index	Accesses the alphabetical listing of help topics
Keyboard	Gives help with keys and key sequences used by the DOS shell program
Shell basics	Provides a tutorial on the DOS shell
Commands	Gives DOS shell commands (menu choices) organized by main-menu topics, with context-sensitive help available
Procedures	Provides instructions for using the DOS shell
Using Help	Describes how to use the help system
About shell	Displays the version of the current DOS shell and, also, copyright information

**MKDIR
(MD)
Command**

Internal command that creates a new subdirectory on the default drive. Be sure you are at the prompt corresponding to the drive or directory where the new subdirectory will be located. Then

Type **MD** **\<directory name>** ↵ or **MD** **<directory name>** ↵

Note the following:

- **MD   JACK** enables you to create a directory called JACK subordinate to the current directory.
- **MD   \WP51** points you to the root directory (through the initial slash) and creates a subdirectory called WP51 under it.

External command that lets you change DOS's prompting message from A>, B>, or C> to something more informative.

> Type **PROMPT** <string>   ↵

**PROMPT
Command**

The string you type in will generally consist of the dollar sign ($) and one of the characters listed in Figure DOS2–6 (see page DOS43).

Internal command that removes a directory or subdirectory once all files in it have been erased. At the system prompt,

> Type **RD**   \<directory   name>   ↵   or **RD**   <directory   name>   ↵

**RMDIR
(RD)
Command**

Note that:

- **RD FRED** removes a subdirectory called FRED.

(FRED must be empty of all files before you can remove it.)

Internal command that changes the name of a file. Be sure you are at the prompt of the directory containing the file to be renamed.

> Type **REN** <old filename.ext   new filename.ext>   ↵

**RENAME
(REN)
Command**

Note that:

- **REN   DICK   JOHN** changes the name of a file called DICK to JOHN.

The shell program, which provides a graphical interface to access and execute DOS commands, first became available in Version 4.0 of DOS. In Version 5.0, the shell program was enhanced considerably with a Windows-like look. Assuming the shell program is on the hard disk and you are accessing it from the hard disk,

> Type **DOSSHELL**   ↵

**Shell
Program**

The procedures you will have to follow at this point depend greatly on both what you want to do and whether you are using a mouse or a keyboard.

External command that displays the names of all directories on a drive and, optionally, the names of all files within those directories.

> Type **TREE**   ↵   or **TREE/F**   ↵

**TREE
Command**

Note that:

- **TREE** displays the names of directories only
- **TREE/F** displays the names of both directories and the files within them.

TYPE Command

Internal command that enables you to display the contents of a file.

>   Type **TYPE** <filename.ext> ↵

Normally, TYPE is used to display ASCII text files. While it can also be used on non-ASCII (program) files, strange-looking characters are likely to be substituted in the listed output where non-ASCII characters would normally appear. Note that:

- **TYPE AUTOEXEC.BAT** will display the contents of the AUTOEXEC.BAT file
- **TYPE CONFIG.SYS** will display the contents of the CONFIG.SYS file

UNDELETE Command

External command that lets you restore one or more files previously marked for deletion with the ERASE or DELETE commands. UNDELETE works only for files in unremoved directories that have not been overwritten. For optimum results, you should use this command *immediately* after you've made an inadvertent deletion, before you've written any more files to disk. If you are not using DOS's Mirror Tracking feature, switch to the drive and directory in which you wish to undelete files and

>   Type **UNDELETE** <filename.ext> ↵

Note that:

- **UNDELETE FRED** allows you to restore a previously deleted file named FRED from the default drive.
- **UNDELETE ∗.BAT** allows you to restore all files with a .BAT extension. DOS will prompt for a yes or no response on each recoverable .BAT file, asking you whether you want it undeleted or not. If you want to undelete a file, answer Y to the prompt and type in the first letter of the file's name, to replace the question mark DOS is displaying in that position in the name.

UNFORMAT Command

External command that lets you unformat (reconstruct) an accidentally reformatted hard disk or diskette, to recover any files lost during the reformat. As with UNDELETE, this command works optimally if you discover the inadvertent erasure immediately, before you have written anything new to the disk, and if you use the Mirror Tracking feature. At the command prompt, to unformat a diskette,

1. Depending on the drive on which you will be mounting the disk to be unformatted, type **UNFORMAT A:** ↵ or **UNFORMAT B:** ↵

2. When the prompt appears onscreen, insert the diskette to be unformatted and press ↵

VER Command

Internal command that displays the DOS version in use.

>   Type **VER** ↵

Some of the most noteworthy versions of DOS are listed in the following table:

MS-DOS Version / Release	Description / Principal Changes
1.0	Original version of DOS
2.0	Permits multiple directories, enabling DOS to be conveniently used with a hard disk

MS-DOS Version / Release	Description / Principal Changes
3.0	Allows high-density 5¼-inch diskettes, RAM disk, and volume names
3.1	Adds networking features
3.2	Extends DOS to include 3½-inch drives
3.3	Allows high-density 3½-inch diskettes
4.0	Adds a shell (menu) feature
5.0	Introduces a Windows-like shell interface, a vastly improved online Help feature, a full-screen editor, the UNDELETE and UNFORMAT commands, and extended-memory features
6.0	Improves memory management and adds utilities for file compression, disk defragmentation, virus check, and backup.

XCOPY Command

External command that copies files (except hidden and system files) and directories, including subdirectories. This command lets you copy all the files in a directory, including the files in its subdirectories.

Type **XCOPY <directory> destination <options>**

<directory>	Specifies the location and names of the files to copy and must include either a drive or a path.
destination	Specifies the destination of the files to be copied. *Destination* can include a drive letter and a colon, a directory, a filename, or a combination.
<options>	
/ a	Copies source files that have their archive file attributes set. This switch does not modify the archive file attribute of the source file.
/ m	Copies source files that have their archive file attributes set. Unlike the /a switch, the /m switch turns off archive file attributes in the files specified in *source*. For information about how to set the archive file attribute, see the attrib command.
/ d:*date*	Copies only source files modified on or after a specified date. The format of *date* depends on the country setting used.
/ p	Prompts to confirm whether you want to create each destination file.
/ s	Copies directories and subdirectories, unless they are empty. If this switch is omitted, XCOPY works within a single directory.
/ e	Copies any subdirectories, even if they are empty. (You must use the /s switch with this switch.)
/ v	Verifies each file as it is written to the destination file.
/ w	Displays a message and waits for a response before starting to copy files.

If you omit *destination,* the XCOPY command copies the files to the current directory. If *destination* does not contain an existing directory and does not end with a backslash (\), XCOPY prompts you. You can then press *F* if you want the file(s) to be copied to a file. Press *D* if you want the file(s) to be copied to a directory.

XCOPY versus DISKCOPY. If you have a disk that contains files in subdirectories and you want to copy it to a disk that has a different format, use the XCOPY command. In general, use XCOPY unless you need a complete disk image copy. Use DISKCOPY to make copies of system disks or to make exact copies to similar-sized disks.

Quick Reference to DOS Commands

Following is a list of DOS commands along with brief descriptions of them. Note that subcommands, such as those available with batch and configuration (CONFIG.SYS) files, are not listed here; instead, refer to the appropriate materials in earlier parts of the appendix.

Command	Description
APPEND	Searches directories on specified disks for nonbatch, nonprogram files
ASSIGN	Assigns requests for one disk drive to another disk drive
ATTRIB	Makes a file read only
BACKUP	Makes backup copies of hard-disk files and places them onto diskettes
BASICA	Used to summon BASIC in early versions of DOS
CHCP	Displays the code page (font) used by DOS
CHDIR (CD)	Changes the current directory
CHKDSK	Displays a report showing how a disk is being utilized
CLS	Clears the display screen
COMMAND	Starts a second copy of the command interpreter, COMMAND.COM
COMP	Compares two files to see if they are identical
COPY	Copies the contents of a file into another file; can also be used to concatenate two or more files and to send the output from one hardware device to another device
CTTY	Lets you change the device from which you enter commands
DATE	Used to display or change the system date
DEBUG	Allows you to debug and test executable files
DEL	Deletes a file from the disk
DIR	Displays names of files and subdirectories belonging to a disk directory or subdirectory
DISKCOMP	Compares two disks to see if their contents are identical
DISKCOPY	Formats a target diskette and copies the contents of a source diskette onto it

DOS

Command	Description
DOSKEY	Creates DOS macros
DOSSHELL	Summons DOS's menu interface
EDIT	Starts the full-screen editor
EDLIN	Summons DOS's line editor, EDLIN
EMM386	Enables or disables expanded-memory support
ERASE	Erases one or more files
EXE2BIN	Converts executable (EXE) files to binary format
EXIT	Leaves COMMAND.COM and returns to the program that invoked it (if one exists)
EXPAND	Expands a compressed DOS file
FASTOPEN	Stores directory information in RAM, for rapid access of files
FC	Compares two disk files and displays differences
FDISK	Configures a hard disk for use
FIND	Searches a file for a particular string of characters
FOR	Runs a specified command for each file in a set of files
FORMAT	Makes a disk ready for use
GRAFTABL	Tells DOS to display special graphics characters
GRAPHICS	Enables DOS to print graphics characters
HELP	Provides online help for features and commands
JOIN	Produces a single directory structure from the directories of two disk drives
KEYBXXX	Changes the keyboard layout to match layouts of keyboards used in different countries
LABEL	Assigns, modifies, or deletes the volume label on a disk
LOADHIGH	Loads a program into the upper memory area
MEM	Displays the amount of used and unused RAM, allocated and free RAM areas, and the names of all programs currently in the system
MIRROR	Keeps track of files for unformatting and undeleting purposes
MKDIR (MD)	Creates a subdirectory
MODE	Used to control line width and line spacing on printers, number of characters per line and colors on a display device, and such things as parity and transmission rates on serial ports
MORE	Used to set the display to pause after each screen page of multiscreen outputs
NLSFUNC	Used for country-specific applications

(continued)

Command	Description
PATH	Tells DOS to search a specified area on disk if a program not in the current directory needs to be executed
PRINT	Used to set up a print queue containing the names of up to 32 files to be printed
PROMPT	Used to change the system prompt
QBASIC	Used to summon BASIC
RECOVER	Recovers a file from a disk with damaged sectors or from a disk with a damaged directory
REN	Renames a file
REPLACE	Replaces disk files with files of the same name on another disk; also copies files from one disk to another
RESTORE	Restores backup files
RMDIR (RD)	Removes a subdirectory
SET	Sets or indicates the system environment
SETVER	Sets the DOS version number under which programs are designed to run
SHARE	Provides file and record locking
SORT	Reads lines from the standard input device, sorts them ascendingly or descendingly, and then sends them to the standard output device
SUBST	Lets you partition the disk, thereby setting up directories as if they were separate disks
SYS	Copies DOS's hidden system files to a specified disk
TIME	Used to set the system clock
TREE	Displays the path to and contents of each subdirectory on disk
TYPE	Lists the contents of a file
UNDELETE	Allows previously erased files to be retrieved
UNFORMAT	Allows the previous contents of formatted disks to be recovered
VER	Displays the number of the DOS version in use
VOL	Displays the disk's volume label, if it exists
XCOPY	Copies specific files from one or more subdirectories

EDIT

EDIT, an external DOS command, is the *full-screen editor* available with DOS Version 5.0 and 6.0.

EDIT can be invoked either from the command prompt or from the DOS shell program.

To invoke EDIT from the command prompt,

  Type **EDIT [path]<filename.ext>** **↵**

To invoke EDIT from the DOS shell program,

1. Select *Editor* from the *Main* group in the program list by using either the keyboard or mouse

2. When prompted, type **[path]<filename.ext>**

3. If on a keyboard, type **↵** ; otherwise, click the mouse

Keys used in EDIT fall into three categories: basic keystrokes, cursor-movement and scrolling keystrokes, and editing keystrokes, as described in the following tables.

Basic Keystrokes

Keystroke(s)	Description
Alt	Activates the menu bar, allowing you to select commands off of it with a keyboard or mouse
F1	Accesses the online Help feature. Topics between the ◄ and ► symbols can be accessed. Choose topics by clicking them with a mouse or, with a keyboard, by using **Tab** or **Shift** + **Tab** followed by **↵** . Use the **Esc** key to leave the Help feature.
F6	Toggles between help and editing screens while a help screen is active
Esc	Abandons the current window or dialog box without making a selection

Cursor-Movement and Scrolling Keystrokes

Keystroke(s)	Description
Mouse click	Moves cursor to next command or option
↑ **↓** **←** **→**	Moves one character or one line at a time
Ctrl + **←**	Moves left one word
Ctrl + **→**	Moves right one word
Home	Moves to beginning of line
End	Moves to end of line
Pg Up	Moves forward a screen

(continued)

Keystroke(s)	Description
Pg Dn	Moves backward a screen
Ctrl + Enter	Moves to start of next line
Ctrl + Q E	Moves to top of screen
Ctrl + Q X	Moves to bottom of screen
Ctrl + Home	Moves to top of file
Ctrl + End	Moves to bottom of file
Ctrl + ↑	Scrolls up one line
Ctrl + ↓	Scrolls down one line
Ctrl + Pg Up	Scrolls to the right one screen
Ctrl + Pg Dn	Scrolls to the left one screen
Home	Moves all the way to the left
End	Moves all the way to the right
Ctrl + Home	Moves to the top of a document
Ctrl + End	Moves to the end of a document

Editing Keystrokes

Keystroke(s)	Description
← Backspace	Deletes character to left of cursor position
Delete	Deletes character at the cursor position
Ctrl + T	Deletes from cursor to the end of word
Insert	Switches between Insert and Overwrite modes
Ctrl + Y	Deletes entire line
Ctrl + Q Y	Deletes from cursor position to end of line

Moving, Copying, and Deleting Text

To move, copy, or delete text, you first need to highlight it onscreen through a process called "blocking."

Blocking Text.   To block text with the mouse,

1.   Point to the first character in the text you want selected
2.   Drag the mouse pointer to the last character you want selected
3.   Release the mouse button

If you want to unblock or reblock the text, click the mouse anywhere on the Edit screen.

To block text with the keyboard,

1. Move cursor to the first character of text you want selected
2. With the Shift key depressed, use the arrow keys to move cursor to the last character in the block
3. Release the Shift and arrow keys

To abort the selection, press any one of the arrow keys.

Moving Text.   To move the currently selected text block,

1. Select *Cut* from the *Edit* menu. The blocked text is removed and temporarily stored in a memory buffer.
2. Move the cursor to where you want to move text
3. Select *Paste* from the *Edit* menu

Copying Text.   To copy the currently selected text block,

1. Select *Copy* from the *Edit* menu
2. Move the cursor to the location where the text will be copied
3. Select *Paste* from the *Edit* menu

Deleting Text.   To delete the currently selected text block,

Press **Del**

To print all or part of an edited file,

1. If you want to print only part of a file, select that part
2. Choose *Print* from the *File* menu
3. If prompted, select either *Selected Text Only* or *Complete Document*
4. Select *OK*

Printing a File

Use the File menu to select one of the choices in the following table.

Saving and Exiting

Choice	Description
New	Saves the current file and clears the screen
Open	Saves the current file and lets you access a new file
Saves	Saves the current file and continues displaying it on the screen
Save As	Saves the current file under a new name, leaving the old file intact
Exit	Saves the current file and exits to the command prompt or Shell program

To return to the command prompt or shell, saving or abandoning your edited file in the process,

Exiting

1. Select *Exit* from the *File* menu
2. Select *Yes* to save the file or *No* to abandon it without saving

DOS

EDLIN

EDLIN, an external DOS command, is a *line editor* available with DOS. You can use it to create AUTOEXEC.BAT files, CONFIG.SYS files, or any other ASCII files.

Type **EDLIN** <filename.ext> ↵

Here is a list of available EDLIN commands (DOS subcommands).

Command	Description	Function
A	Append lines	Reads portions of a large file into memory on an as-needed basis
C	Copy lines	Copies lines in a file
D	Delete lines	Deletes lines from a file
E	End edit	Terminates EDLIN and saves the file you have been working on
I	Insert lines	Inserts new lines in a file
L	List lines	Displays onscreen all or some of the lines of a file
M	Move lines	Moves lines within a file
P	Page	Lists the contents of a file a screen page at a time
Q	Quit edit	Terminates EDLIN without saving the file you have been working on
R	Replace text	Replaces all occurrences of a string of text, in a range of lines, with a different string
S	Search text	Searches a file for a specified text string
T	Transfer lines	Transfers the contents of one file into another file
W	Write lines	Writes a specified number of lines onto disk

Some special keystrokes that are available in EDLIN follow.

Key	Function
F3	Copies all lines from the keyboard buffer onto a new line
F5	Copies all characters in the current line into the keyboard buffer; these characters can be transferred to another line through the F3 key
F6	Acts as a toggle switch between the Insert mode and the Overwrite mode; in other words, pressing the F6 key once lets you insert characters at the cursor position, while pressing the F6 key again lets you type over the character at the cursor position
Del	Erases characters to the right of the cursor position
Esc	Causes the computer system to ignore the current line

EDLIN uses its own prompt character (*) and automatically supplies line numbers as you are entering lines of a file. Be sure to hit the Enter key after typing in each EDLIN line and after typing in each EDLIN command. The following examples show a number of useful EDLIN commands:

- **I** is the command you enter to begin typing in lines of an EDLIN file, when you get the first * prompt. EDLIN will respond to this command with "1:*", prompting you to type in the first line of the file.
- **5I** enables a line to be inserted at the existing line 5 position.
- **1,5,L** lists lines 1 through 5 of an EDLIN file.
- **E** saves a file to the file name you declared when signing onto EDLIN and, also, ends an EDLIN session.
- **Q** abandons changes and ends an EDLIN session.
- **1,5,D** deletes lines 1 through 5 of an EDLIN file.

Common Extensions

Shown here are both special extensions used by DOS and special extensions used by popular DOS-based applications software packages.

Extension	Common Use
ASC	ASCII text file
ASM	Assembler source file
AUX	Auxiliary file
BAK	Backup file
BAS	BASIC program file
BAT	Batch file
BIN	Binary program file
C	C source file
CBL	COBOL source file
COM	DOS command file
CPI	Display screen file
DAT	Data file
DBF	Database file (dBASE)
DCT	Dictionary file
DIF	Data interchange format file
DOC	Document (text) file
DRV	Device driver file
EXE	Executable program file
FNT	Font file
FRM	Report form file (dBASE)
HLP	Help file

(continued)

Extension	Common Use
MEU	Menu file
MOS	Mouse driver file
MSG	Message file
NDX	Index file (dBASE)
OBJ	Object program file
PAS	Pascal source file
PIC	Graph file (1-2-3)
PRN	Print file
SYS	System or device driver file
TXT	Text (document) file
WK1	Worksheet file (1-2-3)
WKS	Another extension for worksheet files (1-2-3)

Glossary

AUTOEXEC.BAT. The batch file that is executed automatically when DOS is started. (DOS49)

Batch file. A file, with an extension of .BAT, containing one or more commands that DOS executes at one time. (DOS45)

Booting. The process of getting a computer system ready to use by reading certain command files into RAM. (DOS6)

Change Directory (CD or CHDIR). An internal DOS command that changes the active directory of the specified or default drive. (DOS41)

CHKDSK. An external DOS command (short for CHecKDiSK) that analyzes a disk's directory and File Allocation Table and produces a report indicating available space on the disk and in RAM. (DOS27)

CLS. An internal DOS command that clears the screen and redisplays the DOS prompt. (DOS28)

COMP. An external DOS command that compares the contents of two files to see if they are exactly alike. (DOS27)

CONFIG.SYS. A text file of commands that changes the standard DOS configuration. (DOS48)

COPY. An internal DOS command that makes a duplicate copy of a file. (DOS19)

COPY CON. A variation of the COPY command that places keyboard entries into a text file. (DOS45)

DATE. An internal DOS command that enables you to view or change the system date. (DOS28)

DblBoot. A data-compression command that creates a formatted "bootable" floppy disk to start a computer system and store compressed files. (DOS57)

Default drive. The disk drive to which the operating system (or active applications program) is currently pointing. (DOS8)

Defrag. A utility that rearranges and consolidates free disk space, significantly improving file access time. (DOS57)

Device driver. A program that lets DOS recognize devices that are not part of the computer itself. (DOS48)

DIR. An internal DOS command that displays the names of files on a disk. (DOS17)

DISKCOMP. An external DOS command that verifies if the contents of two disks are exactly alike. (DOS28)

DISKCOPY. An external DOS command that copies the contents of an entire disk onto another disk. (DOS24)

DoubleSpace. A data-compression program that reduces the space occupied by most files on a hard disk to as little as half their original size. (DOS57)

EDLIN. An internal DOS command that invokes a DOS line editor, which can be used to create new text files or modify existing ones. (DOS47)

ERASE. An internal DOS command that removes a file from a disk's directory. Also called DEL. (DOS25)

External command. A DOS command that is not loaded into RAM when the computer is started up. (DOS11)

Filter. An external DOS command that reads input, modifies it in some way, and then outputs it. (DOS53)

FIND. A DOS filter that searches for a specific series of characters (or text "string") within a file. (DOS54)

FORMAT. An external DOS command that prepares a disk for use. (DOS11)

Internal command. A DOS command that is loaded into RAM when the computer is started up. (DOS11)

LABEL. An internal DOS command that allows you to create, change, or delete the volume label of a specified disk. (DOS28)

Make Directory (MD or MKDIR). An internal DOS command that creates a new subdirectory on the specified disk. (DOS37)

MORE. A DOS filter that displays the contents of a file one screenful at a time. (DOS53)

PATH. An internal DOS command that causes specified subdirectories to be searched for command or batch files. (DOS44)

Pipe. A symbol (¦) that connects two DOS commands together, allowing the output from one command to be used as input for another command. (DOS51)

PROMPT. An external DOS command that allows you to create a new system prompt. (DOS42)

Remove Directory (RD or RMDIR). An internal DOS command that removes an empty subdirectory on the specified disk. (DOS42)

REN. An internal DOS command (short for RENAME) that allows you to change the filename (including extension) of any file. (DOS24)

Root directory. The main directory, or highest directory in a hierarchy. (DOS36)

SORT. A DOS filter that alphabetizes a file according to a character in a specified column. (DOS54)

Subdirectory. A directory that is subordinate to another directory. (DOS36)

SYS. An external DOS command that transfers DOS files to a previously formatted disk. (DOS16)

TIME. An internal DOS command that enables you to view or change the system time. (DOS28)

TREE. An external DOS command that displays all of the subdirectory paths that exist on the specified drive. (DOS38)

TYPE. An internal DOS command that displays the contents of a specified text file. (DOS47)

VER. An internal DOS command that displays the current DOS version number. (DOS28)

VOL. An internal DOS command that displays the volume label of a specified disk. (DOS28)

Warm boot. A procedure by which a computer can be restarted quickly by skipping the usual memory checks. (DOS6)

Wildcard. A character that acts as a stand-in for other characters in a filename. (DOS9)

XCOPY. An external DOS command that copies files and directories, including subdirectories. (DOS23)

DOS

Index

MICROSOFT WINDOWS 95

EDWARD G. MARTIN

CHARLES S. PARKER

CHARLES E. KEE

This manual contains numerous features that help you master the material quickly and reinforce your learning:

- *A Table of Contents.* A list of the manual's contents appears on the first page of the manual. Each chapter starts with an *outline,* a list of learning *objectives,* and an *overview* that summarizes the skills you will learn.

- *Bold Key Terms.* Important terms appear in bold type as they are introduced. They are also conveniently listed at the end of each chapter, with page references for further review.

- *Color as a Learning Tool.* In this manual, color has been used to help you work through each chapter. Each step is numbered in green for easy identification. Within each step, text or commands that you should type appear in orange. Single keys to be pressed are shown in yellow boxes. For example,

   1 Type WIN and press ↵

- *Step-by-Step Mouse Approach.* This manual stresses the mouse approach. Each action is numbered consecutively in green to make it easy to locate and follow. Where appropriate, a mouse shortcut (toolbar icon) is shown in the left margin; a keyboard shortcut may be shown in brackets at the right, as follows:

   1 Click Edit, Cut   [Ctrl + X]

As your skills increase, the "click this item" approach slowly gives way to a less-detailed list of goals and operations so that you do not mindlessly follow steps, but truly master software skills.

- *Screen Figures.* Full-color annotated screens provide overviews of operations that let you monitor your work as you progress through the tutorial.

- *Tips.* Each chapter contains numerous short tips in bold type at strategic points to provide hints, warnings, or insights. Read these carefully.

- *Checkpoints.* At the end of each major section is a list of checkpoints, highlighted in red, which you can use to test your mastery of the material. Do not proceed further unless you can perform the checkpoint tasks.

- *Summary and Quiz.* At the end of each chapter is a bulleted summary of the chapter's content and a 30-question quiz with true/false, multiple-choice, and matching questions.

- *Exercises.* Each chapter ends with two sets of written exercises (Operations and Commands) and six guided hands-on computer applications that measure and reinforce mastery of the chapter's concepts and skills. Each pair of applications present problems relating to school, personal, and business use.

- *Mastery Cases.* The final page of each chapter presents three unguided cases that allow you to demonstrate your personal mastery of the chapter material.

- *A Note about the Manual's Organization.* The topics in this manual are arranged in order of increasing difficulty. Chapters 1 and 2 present beginning and intermediate techniques and should be completed in sequence, for each skill builds upon the previous one. However, Chapter 3 includes several *independent* modules that present advanced skills. These modules may be followed in any order or omitted, as time and interest allow.

- *End-of-Manual Material.* The manual also provides a comprehensive reference *appendix* that summarizes commands and provides alphabetical listings of critical operations, a *glossary* that defines all key terms (with page references), and an *index* to all important topics.

WHAT'S NEW FOR MICROSOFT WINDOWS 95

1. *Simpler Look:* Only two major components to the main Windows 95 screen—a taskbar (bottom of screen) and the desktop (area above taskbar).

2. *Launching Programs:* Programs can be easily launched (started) from the Windows *Start* menu. This menu is accessible through the taskbar.

3. *Closing Windows:* A Close button, resembling an "X," has been added to every Window's title bar. This feature allows for quick closing of a window (exiting) by mouse.

4. *File and Folder Names:* File (program or document) and folder (groups of files) names are no longer restricted to eight characters plus an optional three-character extension. These names can contain up to 255 characters.

5. *Easier Multitasking:* The taskbar can be used to quickly switch between running programs.

6. *File Management:* Windows offers two programs for file management: My Computer displays the parts of a computer in a window, and Explorer displays the parts of a computer in a tree form. Files can be copied or cut and pasted in the same way as other selected (marked) data in the Windows environment.

MICROSOFT WINDOWS 95

1

THE WINDOWS ENVIRONMENT

OUTLINE

OBJECTIVES

After completing this chapter, you will be able to

1 Explain the difference between a character-based and a graphical-user-interface (GUI) environment.

2 Describe the procedures to start and shut down Windows.

3 Describe the components of the Windows screen.

4 Operate common Windows features including launching and closing programs and using window components.

5 Operate more than one program at a time—multitasking.

6 Describe how to access on-line help and use dialog boxes.

7 Explain the operations of other *Start* menu commands.

OVERVIEW

This chapter introduces you to the basics of Microsoft Windows 95—a *graphical user interface,* or *GUI* (pronounced "gooey"), operating environment that uses symbols (pictures) and menus instead of typewritten commands. You will learn how to start and shut down Windows 95, read the Windows 95 screen, operate common Windows features, use basic document management techniques, use multiple programs (multitasking), use the on-line help feature, and operate other options of the *Start* menu.

Although you can sit at a microcomputer and try each action presented in the tutorials, it is best to read the text first and examine the screens in preparation for the hands-on sessions and as a review. This text assumes that you have a mouse. However, keyboard actions are presented where available.

As you operate Windows, the items on your Windows screen may differ from the figures presented in this module. What you see depends on how Windows was set up on your system. However, many of Windows' key components, such as the taskbar, *Start* menu, and *Close* button, operate the same way.

Each set of tutorials is followed by a "Checkpoint"—a set of questions or tasks that quickly tests your mastery of the skills presented in that section. Do not proceed to the next section if you cannot successfully answer the Checkpoint questions. Review the material and try again.

GETTING STARTED

Embarking on any new learning experience is both exhilarating and frightening. This is especially true (and perhaps mysterious) when you are using technology. Some experiences may frustrate you, especially when your commands seem to be ignored or misunderstood. Remember, however, that the computer is only a tool that responds to *your* instructions.

Today, a **graphical user interface,** or **GUI** (pronounced "gooey"), operating system can simplify communication with your computer by using common symbols (called **icons**) and menus instead of typewritten commands. To begin a program, you simply select its symbol and name from a menu instead of typing its name. It is similar to when a company displays a picture of a phone instead of using the word "phone" to identify a phone booth. The GUI operating system presented in this text is called **Microsoft Windows 95.**

In the Windows environment, much of your work is done in rectangular boxes called windows. A **window** may contain a **program** (set of computer instructions) or **document** (a file with data). It is also used to request or give information about a task or feature. **Data** may include text and objects. **Objects** are graphic images (pictures or symbols) that may include text. Icons and windows are also considered objects.

The Windows environment also offers a variety of other features that are normally unavailable in a character-based environment (one that requires the use of typewritten commands). These features include the ability to operate several programs at once (called *multitasking*) and to easily and quickly share or link (dynamically connect) data among programs.

Although Windows provides a dynamic GUI operating environment, it requires more processing time than a character-based environment. If you are operating Windows on a less than state-of-the-art computer system, the time it takes to process your information may be intolerably slow.

Having said all this, relax. Normally, you cannot hurt the computer, nor can it hurt you. Do not be afraid to experiment with commands and techniques as you gain confidence in how they are used. As the old adage says, practice makes perfect.

HANDLING DISKS AND HARDWARE

Like automobiles, microcomputers can provide reliable service for years if they are used and maintained properly. Careful handling of your hardware and disks can significantly extend their life and reduce maintenance costs and down time. **Hardware** is any physical computer equipment. **Disks** are storage media that can be used to hold computer generated files. A **file** may contain a program or document. A *program,* as mentioned earlier, is simply a set of instructions. A *document* is a file that contains data. It is similar to paper documents. Files may also be organized into folders on a disk or other storage media. A **folder** is a group of related files.

When operating your computer system, avoid such obvious risks as hitting the hardware (such as banging on the keyboard). You should also keep the work environment clean.

To complete this tutorial, you will need a blank disk and a hard disk or network system that contains Windows 95. This text assumes that your computer hardware is configured with at least one disk drive (called Drive A) and a hard-disk drive (called Drive C). If you have a second drive, it is typically labeled as Drive B, and a CD ROM drive is identified as Drive D. Your actual configuration may differ.

As you read the rest of this chapter, pay particular attention to the number of steps in each section and follow them while sitting at your computer. This module refers to Windows 95 as simply "Windows."

STARTING WINDOWS

The procedure to starting Windows on a system with a hard-disk drive is easy. Simply turn on your computer system (called **booting up**) and wait for the Windows screen to appear as in Figure WIN1-1. Your screen may differ slightly.

FIGURE WIN1-1   ■   THE WINDOWS SCREEN

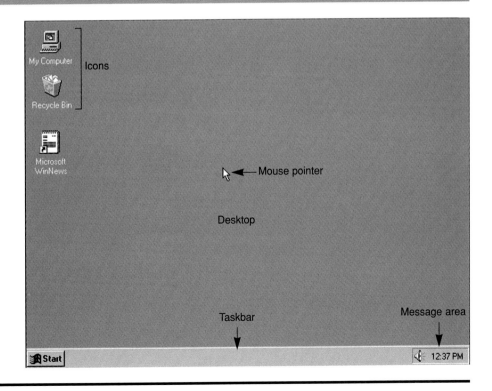

USING A NETWORK. Windows may be available to you through a local network. In this case, Windows is kept on the hard disk of another computer that is shared by many users. So many network configurations are used today that it is difficult to predict which one you will use. Check with your instructor or network administrator for specific instructions. In general, if you use a Windows 95 network, you start your system the same way as you do when using a hard-disk drive system. If you are using a network in which Windows 95 is available through a network menu, in general, you might do the following:

STEPS

1 Boot the network operating system (perhaps with your own disk)

2 Type any command needed to access the network menu

In many networks, you do this by typing **LAN** and pressing the Enter key

3 Select (or type) the appropriate command on your screen to access Windows

4 Go to Step 3 in the following section—"Using a Hard-Disk Drive"

USING A HARD-DISK DRIVE. This text assumes that Windows is on your hard disk (Drive C). To start Windows,

STEPS

1 Turn on your system unit

2 Turn on the monitor's separate power switch, if necessary

> Tip: If you programmed Windows to start in MS-DOS mode, at the C:\ prompt, simply type WIN and press Enter.

3 Wait for the Windows screen

As Windows is booting up, you may see a variety of self-tests being performed. A screen briefly appears with the caption "Microsoft Windows 95" and finally the Windows screen as in Figure WIN1-1 appears. If a "Welcome to Windows 95" screen appears in the center of your screen,

4 Press Esc or Alt + F4 or click the *Close* button to remove the "Welcome to Windows 95" screen

The "Welcome to Windows 95" screen is a **dialog box** (a window that requests or gives information). It provides a different tip on using Windows each time you start the program. You may also get information about what is new in this version of Windows.

> **Tip:** Clicking the *Show this Welcome Screen next time you start Windows* check box at the bottom of the dialog box and then clicking the *Close* button will remove the *Welcome to Windows 95* dialog box from the opening screen.

THE WINDOWS SCREEN

Your screen should now resemble Figure WIN1-1. (Note: The contents of your screen may differ depending on how it was programmed.) The **Windows screen** has two primary parts: the taskbar and the desktop. The **taskbar** is the bar at the bottom of the screen with a *Start* button on its left side. The **desktop** is the large area above the taskbar. Occupying the upper left side of the desktop are several icons, starting with *My Computer.*

Another object that should currently appear on your screen is a small graphic resembling an arrow. This is called the **mouse pointer** or **pointer.** You control its movements by using a **pointing device.** The most common pointing device is a **mouse.** Other pointing devices include a trackball, pointing stick, track pad, or electronic pen. These pointing devices are more commonly used with portable computers.

THE TASKBAR.   As you will soon see, the taskbar's **Start button** (left side) can be used to access the *Start* menu (the Windows main menu) by mouse. You can use the **Start menu** to start programs, find documents, adjust system settings, open a document (file), access help, or shut down Windows. Each option on the *Start* menu is listed with its corresponding icon to its left.

The taskbar can also be used to switch quickly between opened (running) programs or other windows by mouse. As you open each item, a corresponding button appears on the taskbar. These buttons will be used later in the "Basic Multitasking" section to switch among open programs.

The button on the right side of the taskbar displays the system time and other messages. These messages are generally displayed as icons. For instance, the taskbar in Figure WIN1-1 displays an icon of a speaker indicating that the system has sound features. If you are using a portable computer on battery power, an icon displaying the battery level would appear. The display on your taskbar may differ.

THE DESKTOP.   The desktop is the electronic version of the top of an office desk. Objects that may occupy the desktop include icons and windows. Remember, icons are symbols that represent a program, document, or other features. The icons on the desktop are similar to a closed book or notepad. If opened, their contents are viewed through windows (rectangular boxes) on the desktop. All programs and documents are displayed through windows on the desktop. Later, you will practice moving and resizing icons and windows on the desktop.

MOUSE AND KEYBOARD OPERATIONS

Two common input devices used today are the mouse and the keyboard. An *input device* is a piece of equipment (hardware) that allows you to communicate with a computer. This text assumes that you have both a mouse and a keyboard.

In Windows, the primary input device for accessing *commands* is a mouse or other pointing device. As such, most command steps presented in this manual refer to mouse operations. Keyboard commands, where available as *shortcut keys,* are presented in brackets [ ] to the right of a mouse command. For example (do not invoke this command!),

---

STEPS

1 Click the *Start* button on the taskbar for the *Start* menu   [**Ctrl** + **Esc**]

(Note also that, where available, an icon is placed in the left margin of a command as a visual aid.)

To invoke this command you either use the mouse instructions on the left or the keys in brackets on the right.

Shortcut keys provide quick keyboard access to specific commands. They may involve pressing a function key alone or in conjunction with the Ctrl, Alt, or Shift keys. **Function keys** are labeled F1 through F12, and they may be located at the extreme left of your keyboard or across the top in one horizontal row. The Ctrl, Alt, or Shift keys may also be used in conjunction with other keys.

Windows also offers a feature called **MouseKeys** to invoke the common mouse actions by keyboard. The procedures to activate this feature are discussed under the "MouseKeys" portion of this section.

In the following exercises, you will practice basic mouse techniques as summarized in Figure WIN1-2a. You will also learn how to turn on the MouseKeys feature if you desire to use the keyboard to invoke the same mouse actions. MouseKey commands are summarized in Figure WIN1-2b.

POINTING.   Often, the mouse pointer resembles a small arrow on your screen. You control its movements by using a pointing device. In Windows, the mouse pointer may appear in the forms displayed in Figure WIN1-2c. A mouse or other pointing device generally has at least two buttons-left and right. You can use a mouse to perform several actions. The most basic is pointing. This involves moving your mouse on a flat surface, which moves the mouse pointer on your screen to a desired item or area. If you are using a pointing device other than a mouse, refer to its manual for operating instructions.

To **point** (move) your mouse pointer:

STEPS

1 Slowly move your mouse on a flat surface or mouse pad (a small rubber pad) and notice the direction in which the mouse moves on your screen

Note: If you run out of space, simply lift your mouse, place it in the original position, and start again.

FIGURE WIN1-2 ■ MOUSE POINTERS AND ACTIONS

(a) Common mouse actions.
(b) Mouse actions by
keyboard.

Mouse Action	Description
Pointing	Moving the mouse, and thus the mouse pointer, to the desired item.
Clicking	Pressing and quickly releasing the left mouse button.
Right-Clicking	Pressing and quickly releasing the right mouse button.
Dragging	Pressing and holding the left mouse button while moving the mouse to the desired location with the object pointed to.
Dropping	Releasing the mouse, and thus releasing the object pointed to after dragging.
Double-Clicking	Rapidly pressing and releasing the left mouse button twice.

(a)

In order to use the numeric keypad for mouse actions, the *Use MouseKeys* feature and NumLock must be on. When on, a Mouse icon will appear in the message area of the taskbar. Double-clicking this icon will open the Accessibility Options Properties dialog box for adjusting or turning off the *Use MouseKey* features.

Mouse Icon Appearance	Operation	Numeric KeyPad Keys
	Horizontally, Vertically (1)	[←], [→], [↑], [↓]
	Diagonally (1)	[Home], [End], [PgUp], [PgDn]
	Click	[5]
	Double-Click	[+]
	Switch to Right Click (2)	[−], [5] or [+]
	Switch to Both Click (2)	[*], [5] or [+]
	Switch Back to Normal (Left) Click	[/]
	Drag Turn On Mouse Button Hold Down	[Ins] (Do Not Hold)
	Drag Mouse (1)	[←], [→], [↑], [↓], [Home], [End], [PgUp], [PgDn]
	Turn Off Mouse Button Hold Down	[Del] (Do Not Hold)

(b)

(1) Pressing and holding the Ctrl key with these keys will speed up the pointer movement. Pressing and holding the Shift key with these keys will slow down the pointer movement.

(2) When on, pressing the [5] key will invoke their action.

continued

FIGURE WIN1-2 ■ *continued*

(c) Common mouse pointers in Windows.

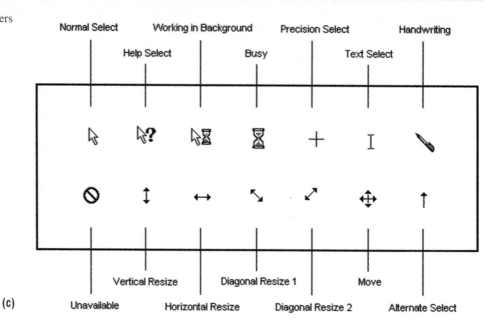

(c)

2 Point to the *My Computer* icon at the top left corner of your desktop

3 Slowly point to the *Start* button at the left side of the taskbar and wait

FIGURE WIN1-3 ■ **POINTING AND CLICKING**

(a) Pointing to a button in the Windows environment often displays its function. (b) Pointing and clicking the *Start* button opens the *Start* menu. (c) Pointing to a menu item followed by a "▶" at its right opens a submenu.

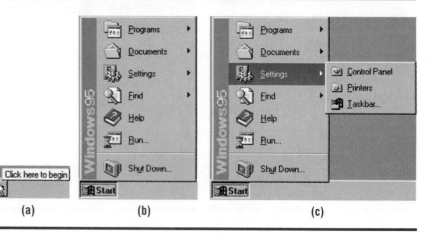

The caption "Click here to begin" should briefly appear as in Figure WIN1-3a. Many buttons in the Windows environment offer brief descriptions when you point to them.

CLICKING.   The second most common mouse action is **clicking.** This involves pointing to an item and then rapidly pressing and releasing the left mouse button.

STEPS

1   Click the *Start* button (point to the *Start button* and then rapidly press and release your left mouse button)   [Ctrl + Esc]

The *Start* menu should appear as in Figure WIN1-3b. As mentioned earlier, this is the main menu in Windows. Although the *Start* menu's operations are discussed later, use it now to further practice mouse operations. Note also that each option is listed with a corresponding icon to its left and that each option has an underlined letter. For example, the *Help* option has an icon of a book with a question mark and the letter "H" is underlined. You can tap the underlined letter to access the option by keyboard.

As you proceed with the next exercise, watch the mouse pointer as you move it within a menu. It moves with a selection highlight to each item you point to. In addition, pointing to menu items with a "▶" to its far right opens a submenu. Try this:

2   Slowly point to *Settings* and notice a submenu as in Figure WIN1-3c   [S]

Although you can select a submenu item by pointing to and then clicking it, you will practice this later. Now, to close the *Start* menu without selecting anything,

3   Click an open space on the desktop to close the menu without selecting anything
[Esc twice]

A menu item without a "▶" to its far right starts a feature or opens a window. For now, keep the *Start* menu opened as you proceed to the next step. Here you will practice invoking a direct command from the *Start* menu:

4   Click the *Start* button   [Ctrl + Esc]

5   Point to *Help*

As you move your mouse pointer, notice again that the selection highlight moves with it to *Help*.

6   Click *Help* to open the *Help* dialog box   [H]

Remember, to click, rapidly press and release your left mouse button.

The *Help* dialog box should now appear on your screen. Remember, a *dialog* box is a window that either provides or requests information. For example, the *Help* dialog box provides information on a desired topic. Dialog box operations will be discussed in detail later.

To close the dialog box,

> **7** Click the *Cancel* button at the bottom right of the box　　　**[Esc]**

RIGHT-CLICKING. Pointing to an item and clicking your *right mouse button,* or **right-clicking,** generally results in opening its *Shortcut* menu. A **Shortcut menu** contains common commands that you can invoke on the related item. For example,

STEPS

> **1** Right-click a blank area of the desktop for its *Shortcut* menu

The desktop's *Shortcut* menu as in Figure WIN1-4a, should now appear. To select a menu item, you can either click (left mouse button) it or press its underlined letter. Menu items that appear in a lighter color are not currently available. For now, to close *Shortcut* menu without selecting a command,

> **2** Click (left mouse button) anywhere outside the *Shortcut* menu　　　**[Esc]**

You can also close a *Shortcut* menu by opening another item or another *Shortcut* menu. Try opening these *Shortcut* menus,

> **3** Right-click an open area of the taskbar for its *Shortcut* menu as in Figure WIN1-4b

> **4** Right-click the *Start* button for its *Shortcut* menu as in Figure WIN1-4c

> **5** Right-click the *My Computer* icon for its *Shortcut* menu as in Figure WIN1-4d

> **6** Click (left mouse button) anywhere outside the *Shortcut* menu to close it without selecting a command　　　**[Esc]**

FIGURE WIN1-4 ■ *SHORTCUT* MENUS

Pointing to certain items in the Windows environment and clicking your right mouse button will open a *Shortcut* menu.
(a) The desktop *Shortcut* menu. (b) The taskbar *Shortcut* menu. (c) The *Start* button *Shortcut* menu.
(d) The *My Computer* icon *Shortcut* menu.

(a)

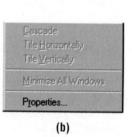

(b)

(c)

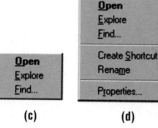

(d)

Different *Shortcut* menus are available for many items in the Windows environment. In some cases, different *Shortcut* menus are available for each part of an item. For example, in Steps 3 and 4, you received two different *Shortcut* menus from clicking your right mouse button on the two different areas of the taskbar.

DRAGGING AND DROPPING.   The next mouse action you will try is called *dragging* and *dropping*. This action is often used to move or copy icons, windows, or other objects. **Dragging** involves pointing to a desired object and then pressing and holding your left mouse button while moving your mouse and the object to a new location. **Dropping** involves releasing your mouse and thus releasing the object after dragging it to a new location. Try this:

STEPS

1 **Drag the *My Computer* icon from the top left corner to the center of your screen (point to and then press and hold your left mouse button down while moving the pointer and the *My Computer* icon to the center of your screen)**

2 **Drop the *My Computer* icon (release your mouse and thus the *My Computer* icon)**

> **Tip: Pressing and holding the Ctrl key while dragging and dropping an object will copy the object in the new location.**

Your screen should resemble Figure WIN1-5a. (Please note that parts of your screen may differ.)

DOUBLE-CLICKING.   Another commonly used mouse action is **double-clicking.** This involves first pointing to an item and then rapidly pressing and releasing your left mouse button twice. Double-clicking an icon on your screen resizes it to a window. Double-clicking also has a variety of other uses that will be discussed as needed.

Before beginning the next exercise, notice that the *My Computer* icon is a different color than the other icons on the desktop. This indicates that it is the **active (or current) icon.** Keyboard commands will generally affect this icon. For example (do not invoke), if you press the Enter key, the icon would open to a window. To open the *My Computer* icon to a window by mouse requires double-clicking it. Try this:

STEPS

1 **Double-click the *My Computer* icon (Rapidly press and release your left mouse button twice.)**
The *My Computer* icon now resizes to a Window as in Figure WIN1-5b. (The contents of your window may differ.) To close it,

FIGURE WIN1-5   ■   **DRAGGING AND DROPPING, AND DOUBLE-CLICKING**

(a) Dragging and dropping
the *My Computer* icon (or
any object) will move it.
(b) Double-clicking an icon
resizes it to a window.
(The content of your winow
may differ.)

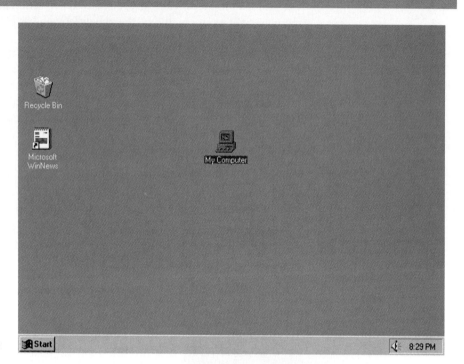

(a)

(b)

   2 Click the *Close* button (the button with an "X" in it) at the top right of the window.
[**Alt** + **F4**]

The "X" button is referred to as the **Close button.** It is available on most windows
and is a shortcut to closing a window. It closes any window, and thus the program, document, or other feature encased in it.

3 Drag and drop the *My Computer* icon to its original position.

(Remember, point to the icon, press and hold the left mouse button while moving the pointer and icon to the top left corner of the desktop, and then release your mouse.)

MOUSEKEYS.   Although many commands can be invoked by shortcut keys, Windows offers a feature called *MouseKeys,* which enables you to use the numeric keypad to invoke the common mouse actions. These actions include clicking, right-clicking, double-clicking, and dragging and dropping. *If you do not intend to use MouseKeys to invoke mouse actions or if the feature is not available, skip this section.* Check with your instructor before activating this feature.

To use MouseKeys, you will need to turn on the *Use MouseKeys* feature. This feature is part of the Accessibility Properties, which can be accessed through the Control Panel. (Note: The Accessibility feature must be installed on your system.)

STEPS

■ **1**   Click the *Start* button   [**Ctrl** + **Esc**]

■ **2**   Point to *Settings* for its submenu

■ **3**   Click *Control Panel* for its window

■ **4**   Double-click the *Accessibility Options* icon for its dialog box

■ **5**   Click the *Mouse* tab

■ **6**   Click the *Use MouseKeys* check box

A "✓" should now appear in the *Use MouseKeys* checkbox. If it does not, click again.

■ **7**   Click the *OK* button to exit the dialog box

■ **8**   Click the *Close* button of the Control Panel window (at top right corner)

When the MouseKeys feature is on, a mouse icon appears in the message area of the taskbar. The numeric keypad (NumLock = on) can be used to invoke mouse actions by using the instructions in Figure SS1-2b. When this feature is on, the numeric keypad cannot be used for number entry.

SHUTTING DOWN WINDOWS

The **shut down** command of the *Start* menu is used to exit Windows. Try this:

STEPS

■ **1**   Click the *Start* button for the *Start* menu   [**Ctrl** + **Esc**]

■ **2**   Click *Shut Down* for its dialog box   [**U**]

As described in Figure WIN1-6, your *Shut Down Windows* dialog box has several options. Although you may have a few other options, the options in Figure WIN1-6 should be available.

3 **Click the _Yes_ button to accept the default option of shutting down the computer.**

The mouse point briefly turns into an hourglass, and then a "Please wait…" screen briefly appears. Finally, a screen appears with the captions "It is now safe to turn off your computer."

4 **You can now shut off the power switches to your computer system**

☑ **CHECKPOINT**

✓ Describe the difference between a character-based environment and a graphical-user-interface environment.
✓ What is Windows?
✓ Describe the procedures to start and shut down Windows.
✓ What is the taskbar and desktop?
✓ Describe the following basic mouse actions: point, click, right-click, drag and drop, and double-click.

COMMON WINDOWS FEATURES

Windows provides a wealth of common features to make operating different programs easier. For example, most programs in Windows can be launched and closed the same way. **Launching** is the Windows term for starting a program. *Closing* as described earlier, is the process of closing a window and thus the program, document, or other Windows feature that is encased in it. All programs and documents are displayed in windows (rectangular boxes)

FIGURE WIN1-6 ■ THE *SHUT DOWN WINDOWS* DIALOG BOX

The *Shut Down Windows* dialog box. (The options in your dialog box may differ.)

Shuts down the operating system and then restarts it

Shuts down the operating system and then restarts it in the MS-DOS mode.

Shut Down Windows

Are you sure you want to:

◉ Shut down the computer? ◄——— Shuts down the operating system
○ Restart the computer?
○ Restart the computer in MS-DOS mode?

Yes   No   Help

that have common components. The operations of these components will be discussed in detail shortly. **WordPad,** a simple word processor, will now be used to help you learn about these common features. WordPad is a standard accessory program that comes with Windows.

1 Boot up your computer (turn your system on)

2 Start Windows (if needed)

3 If needed, click the *Cancel* button or press Esc to remove the "Windows Welcome" screen

LAUNCHING A PROGRAM

The most common way to launch a program in Windows is to use the *Start* menu. Although only WordPad is used to demonstrate this, the steps to launch other programs are similar. As you perform each step, take special note of the structure of the Windows main menu system.

Now, to launch WordPad (or any program):

1 Click the Start button (taskbar) for the *Start* menu   [Ctrl + Esc]
(Remember, to click, first point to the *Start* button and then rapidly press and release your left mouse button.)

2 Point to *Programs* for its submenu   [P]

Your *Programs* submenu should now appear on your screen similar to Figure WIN1-7. (The contents of your *Programs* submenu may differ.) As with the *Start* menu, each item in the *Programs* submenu is listed with its corresponding icon at its left. An item with a "▶" to its far right opens to another submenu. In the *Programs* submenu, these items are called **program groups.** They are logical groupings of programs and files into folders by category for easier visual access. Remember, a *folder* is a group of related files.

Individual programs not grouped into a folder in the *Programs* submenu or any other menu are available for direct access. For example, the MS-DOS prompt or Windows Explorer are programs that can be launched directly from the *Programs* sub-menu.

To open the *Accessories* group submenu as in Figure WIN1-8,

3 Point to *Accessories* for its submenu   [A , ↓ if needed, →]

The *Accessories* program group menu displays several subprogram groups and accessories programs. For example, the *Games* or *System Tools* options are subprogram groups that open to their own submenus. Like the *Programs* submenu, items not followed by a

FIGURE WIN1-7 ■ THE *PROGRAMS* SUBMENU

Pointing to and clicking the *Start* button, and then pointing to *Programs* opens its submenu.

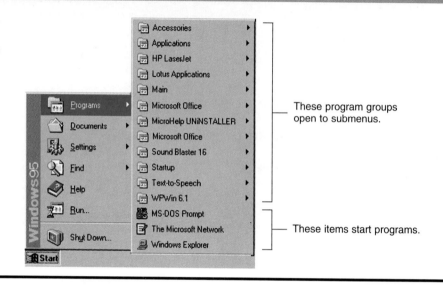

These program groups open to submenus.

These items start programs.

"▶" to their far right are programs that can be accessed directly from the *Accessories* submenu-for example, WordPad (a simple word processor), Calculator (an on-line calculator), and so on.

4 Click *WordPad* to launch it

[Arrow keys, ↵]

FIGURE WIN1-8 ■ THE *ACCESSORIES* SUBMENU

Pointing to the *Accessories* group opens its submenu.

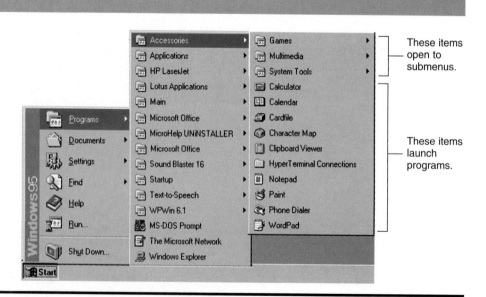

These items open to submenus.

These items launch programs.

A brief copyright message appears and is quickly replaced by the WordPad window. The size of WordPad's window when it first appears on the desktop depends on its size when last used. It may appear as a window that occupies less than the entire desktop similar to Figure WIN1-9a (the position of the window may differ on your screen). It may also appear as a window that occupies the entire desktop (when this happens, it is said that the window is **maximized**) as in Figure WIN1-9b. A maximized window is one that is enlarged to its maximum size. Sometimes a window's maximum size may be less than the entire desktop space. If your WordPad window is maximized, do the following to reduce its size for this exercise:

5 If needed, press Alt + Spacebar , R

At this point examine your taskbar. A button titled "Document - WordPad" has been automatically added. Remember, as you open each program, file, or other item in Windows, a corresponding button appears on the taskbar. You can use these buttons to switch to a desired opened item. This will be further discussed later.

As demonstrated earlier with the *My Computer* icon, a program or file may also be launched (or opened) by double-clicking its icon. This method requires the program or file's icon to be available on the desktop or in a window. Procedures to create icons for programs and files are discussed later.

TYPES OF WINDOWS

As mentioned earlier, a *window* is a rectangular box that may contain a program, document, or dialog box. A window that contains a program is called a **program window.** Each program window may contain only one program. For example, the WordPad window contains only that program. Program windows also occupy the desktop.

Programs that allow you to work with multiple documents at the same time use *document windows* to display each document. A **document window** is a window within a program window. It occupies the interior space (called the **workspace**) of its program window. It may contain text and objects. Many popular programs do allow for multiple document windows.

> **Note:** Programs used in this manual generally allow you to work with only one document at a time. As such, the document occupies most or all of the program's workspace.

Dialog boxes, as mentioned earlier, are windows that request or give information. Dialog box operations are discussed in detail in "The Help Feature" section.

TITLE BAR

A window's *title bar* contains its name. The **title bar** is the first row in any window. For example, in Figure WIN1-9a, the title "Document - WordPad" is currently displayed in WordPad's title bar. A program or document window's title bar generally has several standard features. As in Figure WIN1-10a and b, they include (from left to right) the program or document's icon, name, two window resizing buttons, and a *Close* button. The resizing buttons that appear on a title bar depend on its window's size. For example,

(a) When you first start a program, it may appear as a window less than the size of the entire desktop.

(b) It may also appear maximized (covering the entire desktop).

(a)

(b)

FIGURE WIN1-10 ■ TITLE BARS

(a) Title bar of a less than maximized window.
(b) Title bar of a maximized window.
(c) Description of title bar parts.
Note: Title bar parts are described in Figure WIN1-10C.

① ②   ③④⑥

Document - WordPad

(a)

① ②   ③⑤⑥

Document - WordPad

(b)

WIN

Part #	Part	Description
1	Icon	An icon that identifies the program or document. Clicking this icon opens a control-menu. Double-clicking it closes the program.
2	Name Section	The section that identifies the window. Double-clicking this section resizes the window. Right-clicking this section opens the window's control-menu.
3	Minimize Button	A resizing button that normally appears on all program and document windows. Clicking this button reduces the window to its taskbar button. Minimized windows run on less system memory and do not need to be restarted to be used.
4	Maximize Button	A resizing button that appears only on a program or document window that is not maximized. Clicking this button enlarges a window to its maximum size. Once the window is maximized, this button is replaced by a Restore button.
5	Restore Button	A resizing button that appears only on a window that is maximized. Clicking this button restores a window to its previous size. Once the window is reduced, this button is replaced by a Maximize button.
6	Close Button	Appears on all windows. Clicking this button closes the window.

(c)

a less than maximized window's title bar has a *Maximize* button. A maximized window's title bar as in Figure WIN1-10b has a *Restore* button. The functions of each of these items is discussed next.

ICON.   Each program (or document) in the Windows environment is automatically assigned an icon to represent it. These icons may appear to the left of the item's name in the *Start* menu's submenu system and in the title bar of a window. Clicking this icon on the left side of a title bar opens a **control-menu.** This menu contains commands that can be used to move, resize, or close a window. Try this:

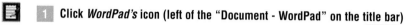

1 Click *WordPad's* icon (left of the "Document - WordPad" on the title bar)

[**Alt** + **Spacebar**]

The window's control-menu, as in Figure WIN1-11, should now appear. At this point, you can select a command from the menu by either clicking the command or pressing its underlined letter. For now, to close the menu without selecting a command,

2 Click any area outside of the menu

[**Esc**]

You can also open Window's control-menu by right-clicking anywhere on the title bar.

> **Tip:** Although not illustrated, document windows also have control-menus. To open a document window's control-menu, click its document icon or press the Alt + – (minus) keys. The position of a document window's icon differs depending on the window's size. For example, a maximized document window's icon appears at the left end of its program's menu bar. This is because it shares its title bar with its program. Other times it appears at the left end of its title bar, as with a program window.

> **Note:** Shortcut keys presented in brackets to the right of a mouse command use the window's control-menu to demonstrate resizing and moving a window.

NAME SECTION. In addition to identifying a window, the name section of a title bar can also be used to resize or move the window. To resize the window using its title bar,

---

FIGURE WIN1-11 ■ **CONTROL-MENU**

Clicking a program or document icon on a title bar opens its control-menu.

WIN

Document - WordPad   **1** **Point anywhere on the caption "Document - WordPad" on the title bar**

[**Alt** + **Spacebar**]

2 **Double-click it (Remember, to double-click, rapidly press and release your mouse twice.)**

[**X**]

Your WordPad window should now be maximized on your screen as in Figure WIN1-9b. Now, to use the title bar to return it to its original size (that is, to **restore** it):

3 **Double-click the name portion of the title bar**   [**Alt** + **Spacebar** , **R**]

Your WordPad window should now be restored to its original size as in Figure WIN1-9a.

To move a window using its title bar,

4 **Point to the name section of the WordPad title bar**   [**Alt** + **Spacebar**]

5 **Drag it to the top of your screen**   [**M** , ↑ **to top of screen**]

(Remember, to drag, press, and hold your left mouse button while moving the mouse pointer and the object, in this case the WordPad window, to its new location.)

Notice that only an outline of the window moves with the mouse pointer. The window itself will move after you drop its outline in the new location.

6 **Drop the window's outline (release your mouse)**   [↵]

As you will see later, the ability to resize or move a window is helpful when using multiple windows. For now,

7 **Move the WordPad window back to its original position by dragging and dropping its title bar**   [**Alt** + **Spacebar** , **M** , ↓ **as needed**, ↵]

Again, your screen should resemble Figure WIN1-9a.

RESIZING BUTTONS.   **Resizing buttons** provide a quick way to change the size of a window. Three types of resizing buttons exist: minimize, maximize, and restore. Only one or two resizing buttons appear at a time on the right side of the title bar.

As in Figure WIN1-10, the **Minimize button** resembles a square box with a dash in it. Clicking this button will reduce the window to its taskbar button. Try this:

1 **Click WordPad's** *Minimize* **button**   [**Alt** + **Spacebar** , **N**]

Note that after Step 2, the WordPad window shrinks to its button on the taskbar as in Figure WIN1-12. The button is also no longer depressed. When a window is minimized

Clicking a window's minimize button reduces it to its taskbar button.

it operates using less system memory. This is helpful when using more than one program at a time. A minimized window also allows you to switch to that program quickly without having to relaunch it. For example, to restore WordPad to its former size,

 2 Click the *Document - WordPad* button on the taskbar   [**Alt** + **Tab**]

As in Figure WIN1-10, the **Maximize button** resembles a square box with a smaller square box in it. As mentioned earlier, maximizing a window enlarges it to its maximum size. Try this:

3 Click WordPad's *Maximize* button   [**Alt** + **Spacebar** , **X**]

Your WordPad window should now fill your screen, as in Figure WIN1-9b. Note that the *Maximize* button has now been replaced by a *Restore* button. The **Restore button** only appears on the title bar when a window is maximized. It can be used to resize a window to its previous size. Try this:

4 Click WordPad's *Restore* button   [**Alt** + **Spacebar** , **R**]

Your WordPad window again should resemble Figure WIN1-9a. Note that the *Restore* button has been replaced by a *Maximize* button.

CLOSE BUTTON.   As mentioned earlier, the *Close* button resembles an "X" and can normally be found on the right end of a window's title bar. This button is available on all windows. It is the quickest way to close the window.

STEPS

1 Click the *Close* button   [**Alt** + **F4**]

Alternative window closing techniques are discussed later.

MENU BAR

Only program windows have menu bars. The menu bar is located just below the window's title bar, as in Figure WIN1-13. A **menu bar** provides mouse and keyboard access to a program's features through *pull-down menus*. A **pull-down menu** is one that drops down from its menu selection. Certain pull-down menus are standard on

FIGURE WIN1-13 ■ MENU BAR

(a) Only program
windows have menu bars
below their title bars. The
menu bar allows mouse
and keyboard access to a
program's features by
pull-down menus.
(b) A summary of menu
bar operations.

(a)

	Mouse Actions	**Keyboard Actions**
Open Pull-Down Menu	Point to and click menu bar item	Press [Alt] + [Underlined letter of menu bar item]
Select a Menu Item	Point to and click the item	Press the item's underlined letter or use arrow keys to move selection highlight to item and press Enter
Description of Menu Item's Function	Open menu and then point to item	Use arrow keys to move selection highlight to item

(b)

WIN

most windows programs, such as, the *File, Edit,* and *Help* menus. Although these pull-down menus have the same name in different programs, their options may differ. You will now take a closer look at how to operate a menu bar.

STEPS

1 Launch the WordPad program (Remember, click the *Start* button, point to *Programs, Accessories, WordPad,* and then click.)

2 Click WordPad's *Maximize* button to enlarge it to a full screen (if needed)

[**Alt** + **Spacebar** , **X**]

> Note: A maximized window makes it visually easier to operate its components. You can however, operate the same components in a smaller screen.

This manual will refer to a pull-down menu as simply a *menu.*

USING MENUS. Menus from the menu bar can be opened by clicking the desired menu bar item or pressing the Alt key and the underlined letter of the menu bar item. Try this to open the *Help* menu:

1 Click *Help* for its menu (Remember, point to and click *Help* or press **Alt** + **H** .)

The *Help* menu should appear as in Figure WIN1-14a. The *Help* menu of any program window provides general and specific help on operating the program. To select an option by mouse, simply click it; to select an option by keyboard, press the item's underlined letter. You can also use the arrow keys to move the highlight to the desired item and press Enter. Note that the Alt key is used with an underlined letter only when opening a menu. Try this:

2 Click *About WordPad*   [**A**]

This command opens an *About* dialog box, which displays information about the current program. This information may include the program's version, serial number, ownership, and system resources. All windows programs have an *About* dialog box that can be accessed through its *Help* menu. To close the dialog box,

3 Click the *OK* button   [**Esc**]

Now, to open the *File* menu,

4 Click *File*   [**Alt** + **F**]

FIGURE WIN1-14 ■ COMMON MENUS

Most menu bars have *Help, File,* and *Edit* menus.
(a) The *Help* menu provides access to a program's on-line help.
(b) The *File* menu provides access to basic file management commands.
(c) The *Edit* menu provides access to a variety of document editing commands.

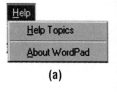

(a)

(b)

Edit	
Undo	Ctrl+Z
Cut	Ctrl+X
Copy	Ctrl+C
Paste	Ctrl+V
Paste Special...	
Paste Link	
Clear	Del
Select All	Ctrl+A
Find...	Ctrl+F
Find Next	F3
Replace...	Ctrl+H
Links...	
Object Properties...	Alt+Enter
Object	

(c)

The *File* menu should now appear as in Figure WIN1-14b. This menu has file management commands that you can use to save or open (retrieve) files from disk or other storage media. A *file* may contain a program or document. (Remember, a program is simply a set of instructions and a document may contain data or objects.) These procedures will be discussed later. Again, to select a menu item, simply click it; to select an item by keyboard, press the underlined letter. For now, to close a menu without selecting a command,

5 **Click anywhere outside the menu**   [**Alt**]

Another common menu is the *Edit* menu. This menu generally provides commands to undo your last action, copy, move, or link (dynamically connect) a selection. A **selection** is data marked for editing or other operations. Data selection techniques and *Edit* menu operations are discussed in detail later. To open the *Edit* menu as in Figure WIN1-14c,

6 **Click *Edit***   [**Alt** + **E**]

Leave this menu opened as you continue to the next steps.

Once one menu is opened, you can quickly move to another menu by pointing. Try this:

7 **Point to Insert**   [→]

8 **Point to Format**   [→]

9 **Point to Help**   [→]

10 **Click anywhere outside the menu to close it**   [**Alt**]

MENU COMMANDS.   Many programs display a brief description of a menu command when pointed to. The location of this description is often in the program's status bar (generally at the bottom of the window) or its title bar. Try this to get a brief description of the *Save As* command in the *File* menu.

STEPS

1 **Click *File* for its menu**   [**Alt** + **F**]

2 **Point to (but do not click) *Save As***   [↓ three times]

The message "Saves the active document with a new name." appears in WordPad's status bar as in Figure WIN1-15.

3 **Click anywhere outside the *File* menu to close it**   [**Alt**]

FIGURE WIN1-15 ■ COMMAND DESCRIPTION

Pointing to a menu item will display a description of its function in the status bar.

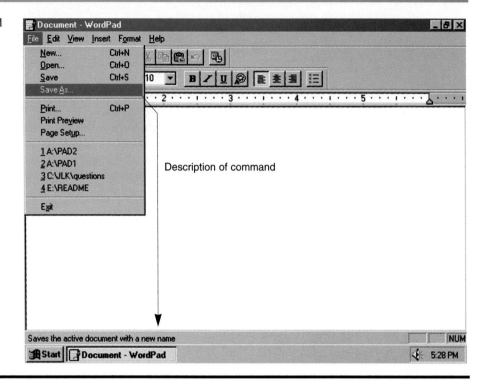

Description of command

MENU INDICATORS

Menus throughout the Windows environment use standard Windows indicators or conventions. Earlier, when you used the *Start* menu, items with a " ▶ " at their far right open to a submenu and items with no notation invoke a command directly. This is true for any menu in the Windows environment. WordPad's *File* menu will now be used to illustrate other menu indicators.

STEPS

1 Click *File*   [**Alt** + **F**]

The *File* menu should appear again as in Figure WIN1-16a. (Your *File* menu may differ slightly.) Menu items with neither a triangle pointer " ▶ " at their extreme right (not shown in Figure WIN1-16a) nor an ellipsis (…), such as *Save,* invoke a command directly. If shortcut keys can be used to invoke a menu directly, they are displayed at the extreme right of the item. For example, the Shortcut keys Ctrl + S appear to the far right of the command Save.

Figure WIN1-16b lists standard windows menu indicators.

FIGURE WIN1-16 ■ MENU INDICATORS

(a) Menus in the Windows environment use menu indicators that are standard. (b) A summary of menu indicators.

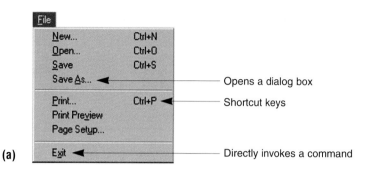

(a)

Opens a dialog box

Shortcut keys

Directly invokes a command

Menu Items with	Description
Ellipsis (…)	Opens to a dialog box or another window.
▶ at far right	Opens to a submenu.
No notation	Invokes a command or other feature.
Keys at far right	Short key(s) to invoke the menu item by keyboard.
✔ to left of item	A toggle (on/off) feature that has been turned on.
Dimmed (or not visible)	A menu item not currently available.

(b)

2   **Click anywhere outside the menu to close it**   [**Alt**]

COMMAND BUTTONS AND DROP-DOWN BOXES

Many Windows programs offer a variety of command buttons and drop-down boxes for quick mouse access to program features. A **command button,** when clicked, directly accesses a feature in a program or window. Earlier, you learned how to operate several *window command buttons* such as the Minimize, Maximize, Restore, and Close buttons. Here you will examine a few command buttons that directly access WordPad's program features.

A **drop-down box** is a rectangular box with a "▼" button on its right side. In your WordPad window, the box that contains the caption "Times New Roman" is a drop-down box. Clicking the "▼" button of a drop-down box opens a list of available options.

Most programs group command buttons and drop-down buttons into sets with related functions. As in Figure WIN1-17a, WordPad has two sets of command buttons beneath its menu bar. The first set is called the toolbar and the second is called the format bar. The format bar also contains two drop-down boxes. The **toolbar** contains buttons that affect basic file management and editing. The buttons and drop-down boxes on the **format bar** can be used to change the text appearance and alignment. Programs may use different terminology for these bars.

FIGURE WIN1-17 ■ COMMAND BUTTONS AND DROP-DOWN BOXES

(a) Many programs have bars with command buttons and drop-down boxes. WordPad's bars are called the toolbar and format bar.

(b) Pointing to a button will display a caption of its function.

(c) Pointing to a drop-down box will display a caption of its function.

(d) Clicking the ▼ button of a drop-down box opens its drop-down list.

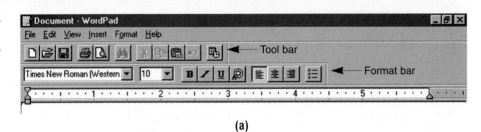

(a)

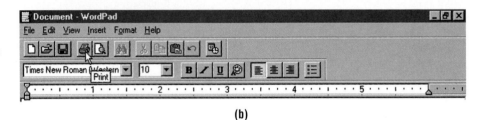

(b)

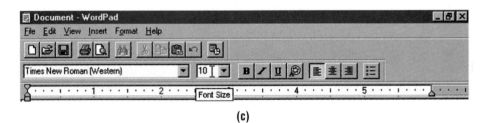

(c)

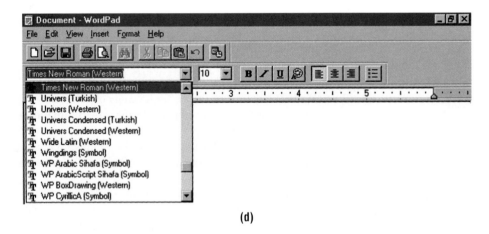

(d)

When you point to most buttons and drop-down boxes in the Windows environment, their titles will appear. A brief description of their function also appears in the status bar or title bar. Try this:

1 **Point to the *Print* button (toolbar) and wait a moment**

The caption "Print" appears on your screen and its function appears in the status bar as in Figure WIN1-17b.

2 **Point to the drop-down box that contains "10" (format bar)**

The caption "Font Size" appears as in Figure WIN1-17c. A **font** is a type style. **Font size** is the size of the current font measured in points (approximately ½ inch per point). Now, to open a drop-down menu:

3 **Click the ▼ button of the *Font* drop-down box (format bar) for the *Font* drop-down list**

A *Font* drop-down list should appear as in Figure WIN1-17d. The contents of your list may differ, depending on the fonts installed in your system. Now, to close the drop-down list without selecting an option,

4 **Click anywhere outside the drop-down list**   **[Esc]**

Actual operations of program command buttons and drop-down boxes will be discussed later.

SHORTCUT MENUS

Earlier, under the "Mouse Operations" section, you practiced opening *Shortcut* menus by pointing to an object and clicking your right mouse button. In most windows (program, document, or dialog box), pointing to certain areas and right-clicking will also open a *Shortcut* menu. These menus provide quick access to commands related to the area clicked. Try this:

1 **Right-click a blank area within WordPad's workspace (the large interior space of the window)** (Remember, to right-click, point to and then rapidly press and release your right mouse button.)

A *Shortcut* menu as in Figure WIN1-18a appears. To select a *Shortcut* menu option, simply click it or press its underlined letter. For now, try to open another *Shortcut* menu as follows:

2 **Right-click the "10" in the *Font Size* drop-down box (format bar) for its *Shortcut* menu**

The *Shortcut* menu as in Figure WIN1-18b now appears.

3 **Click anywhere outside the *Shortcut* menu to close it**   **[Esc]**

FIGURE WIN1-18 ■ *SHORTCUT* MENUS

(a) Pointing to WordPad's workspace and clicking the right mouse button will open this *Shortcut* menu.
(b) Pointing to a drop-down box on the format bar and clicking the right mouse button will open this *Shortcut* menu.

(a)   (b)

WORKSPACE

As mentioned earlier, a window's *workspace* is its large interior space. A program window's workspace may contain one or more documents. This depends on the program. For example, WordPad only allows one document to occupy its workspace at a time.

FIGURE WIN1-19 ■ **CREATING A DOCUMENT**

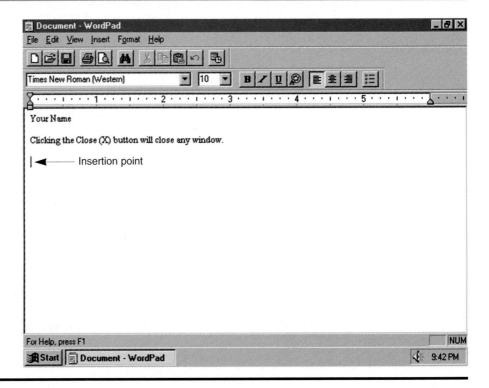

Programs such as Microsoft Word and Excel allow multiple documents to occupy their program windows' workspaces. A document window also has a workspace that may contain data or graphical images.

Currently, as in Figure WIN1-19, there is a vertical blinking line called the insertion point in WordPad's workspace. The **insertion point** is simply a placeholder. It indicates where the next character you enter will appear. The insertion point appears in any window or box that allows character entry.

To close WordPad,

STEPS

 　1　 **Click WordPad's *Close* button**　　　　　　　　　　　　　　**[Alt + F4]**

 　　Tip: Double-clicking WordPad's program icon (located at the left end of the title bar) will also close the program quickly.

☑ **CHECKPOINT**

✓　Open WordPad, maximize it, and then restore it.
✓　Open WordPad's *Help* menu and then close it
✓　Describe the standard menu indicators used in the Windows environment.
✓　Open the *Font Size* drop-down box (format bar) and then close it.
✓　Close WordPad.

BASIC DOCUMENT MANAGEMENT

Many Windows programs are used to create documents that may contain text and graphic images (pictures). A *document* is simply an electronic file created with a program. When using any program to create a document, it is important to learn the basic document management commands. These commands include saving to and then opening (retrieving) from a disk, and printing a hard copy on paper.

In this section, you will create a simple document with text in WordPad as in FigureWIN1-19. You will also save, print, and open (retrieve) this document. Detailed operating instructions for other WordPad features are discussed in Chapter 3.

STEPS

　1　 **If needed, start Windows and remove the "Welcome" screen**

　2　 **Launch WordPad (Accessories group)**

▣ 3 If needed, click WordPad's *Maximize* button to enlarge it to a full screen

[Alt + Spacebar , X]

USING THE DEFAULT DOCUMENT

Most programs are launched with a blank new document in their workspace. This is called the **default document.** It is like a clean sheet of paper.

To enter data into WordPad's workspace, simply type using your keyboard. If you make a mistake, use the Backspace or Delete keys to erase the incorrect data. Try this:

STEPS

1 Type your name

2 Press ↵ twice

3 Type Clicking the Close (X) button will close any window.

4 Press ↵ twice

The workspace in your WordPad should resemble Figure WIN1-19.

SAVING A DOCUMENT

In most programs, the *File* menu offers two options for saving a document. These options are *Save* and *Save As.* Invoking the **Save** command on a previously saved document will resave it under its original name. Invoking it on an unsaved document opens the *Save As* dialog box for assigning a filename. Invoking the **Save As** command allows you to save the current document under a different name and warns you if the name has already been used. This feature is helpful when updating documents because it allows you to save the updated version under a new name, thus keeping the original under its old name.

FILENAMES.   Before saving any document, you must assign it a **filename.** Filenames are used to identify a document or program. If you are using DOS-based or pre-Windows 95 programs, you are restricted to filenames of up to 8 characters with a 3-character optional extension. The programs that come with Windows 95 can accept filenames of up to 255 characters.

SAVING.   As mentioned earlier, when invoked on an unsaved document, both the Save and Save As command will open the *Save As* dialog box. Try this:

> **1** Insert your data disk into Drive A

 2 Click *File, Save*   [**Ctrl** + **S**]

A *Save As* dialog box should appear similar to Figure WIN1-20a. (Your dialog box's contents may differ.) Most *Save As* dialog boxes have similar features. These features are identified in Figure WIN1-20a and described in WIN1-20c. Note that the word "Document" in the *Filename* text box is highlighted. At this point you can type a filename in this text box, which will type over the highlighted text. To save this document as PAD1,

> **3** Type **PAD1** in the Filename text box

You can also set default drive at this point before saving. The **default drive** is the drive that your program is currently pointing to. In this case, it is your hard or network drive. Because you will be saving the documents you create on your data disk in Drive A, you must first set the program to Drive A. Do this by using the *Save in* drop-down box. Note that you only need to set the default drive once during a work session. It will remain the default drive until you change it or close the program.

 4 Click the "▼" button of the *Save in* drop-down box

🖫 3½ Floppy (A:) **5** Click the *3½ Floppy (A:)* drive icon

> **Tip:** Instead of using the *Save in* drop-down box in Steps 4 and 5, you could also type the drive letter and a colon with the filename (for example, A:PAD1) in Step 3 to set the default drive for the current session.

If your disk was not formatted, you will receive a dialog box that asks if you would like to format now. Before performing Steps 6 through 9 to format, check with your instructor. If your disk is already formatted, skip Steps 6 through 9.

> **6** Click the *Yes* button for the *Format* dialog box

> **7** Click the *Full* option

> **8** Click *Start* button to begin formatting your disk

> **9** Click the *Close* button and then the next *Close* button

Formatting prepares a disk for use on your computer. Every new disk that is not preformatted must be formatted (organized for your computer) before you can store anything on it. Formatting sets up the disk's directory and file allocation table and divides

FIGURE WIN1-20   ■   SAVING AND OPENING DOCUMENTS

(a) The *Save As* dialog box.
(b) The *Open* dialog box.
(c) Descriptions of dialog box components.

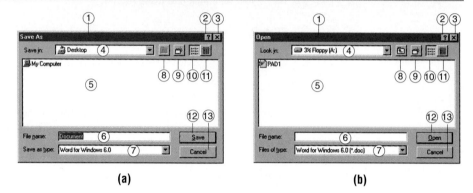

(a)   (b)

	Item	Description
1	Title bar	Identifies the dialog box. Right-click for control-menu. Drag to move dialog box.
2	"?" (Help) button	Click to change to help pointer and then click item for help on its operation.
3	"X" (Close) button	Click to close the dialog box.
4	Save in/Look in box	A drop-down box that is used to set the default drive and directory.
5	Files list box	A list box that displays the files in the default directory.
6	File name box	A text box that is used to enter a file's name.
7	Save as type/Files of type	A drop-down box that can be used to save a document in a specific file type or open a document of a specific file type.
8	Up One Level button	Click to display file structure up one level in the Files List box.
9	Create a New Folder button	Click to create a new folder.
10	List button	Click to list the content of the default directory in the Files List box without details. This is the default display.
11	Details button	Click to display file details in the Files List box.
12	Save/Open button	Click to save or open a document.
13	Cancel button	Click to cancel the dialog box.

(c)

the disk into addressable storage locations. It will also check for defective tracks on the disk and seal them off from further use.

Caution: A disk that was previously formatted can be reformatted; however, the process will delete the disk's files and set up a new blank directory.

WIN

To save the document,

10 **Click the _Save_ button**

Now, try the *Save* command again. As you invoke the command this time, the *Save As* dialog box does not appear. This is because the file has already been assigned a filename. Also note that the message "Saving file, Please Wait." briefly appears at the bottom of the WordPad window and your mouse pointer briefly appears as an hourglass.

 11 **Click _File_, _Save_**   [**Ctrl** + **S**]

Your document has been resaved under its previous name.

PRINTING A DOCUMENT

Most *File* menus have a **Print** command that allows you to print a hard copy of the current document or desired selection on paper. This command, of course, requires you to have a printer that is connected and configured for your system. Each program may offer different printing options; however, most programs allow you to specify the number of copies. To print your PAD1 document,

STEPS

1 **Turn on your printer (be sure that it has paper)**

 2 **Click _File_, _Print_ for the _Print_ dialog box**   [**Ctrl** + **P**]

3 **Click the _OK_ button**   [⏎]

Your printer should now produce a hard copy of PAD1.

CREATING A NEW DOCUMENT

The **New** command (*File* menu) will clear a window's workspace so that you can begin a new document.

STEPS

 1 **Click _File_, _New_**   [**Ctrl** + **N**]

A *New* dialog box appears with several format options. Note that some programs do not offer this dialog box. To select the default format,

2 **Click the _OK_ button**   [⏎]

Your WordPad workspace should now be blank.

If you created a new document, but forgot to save it and invoked the New command, a dialog box will appear asking if you would like to save it. This dialog box will also appear if you invoke the New command on a modified document that was not resaved.

> Tip: Invoking the New command in a program that allows *multiple documents* in its workspace will open a new document window. This window will be placed on top of other opened document windows. These programs generally have a Close command in their *File* menus, which allows you to close the document windows that you are not currently using. Clicking a document window's *Close* button will also close it. Closing documents or programs not in use will free some of your system's memory. This will allow your system to operate more efficiently.

OPENING A DOCUMENT

The **Open** command (*File* menu) retrieves a saved document from a disk and places it into a window. Opening a document can be done by typing its filename or selecting it from a list. Only the latter is discussed here. Try this to open PAD1:

STEPS

1 Click *File, Open* for the *Open* dialog box   [**Ctrl** + **O**]

The *Open* dialog box should again appear as in Figure WIN1-20b. As described in Figure 1-20c, this dialog box has features and operations similar to those in the *Save As* dialog box. At this point you can also set the default drive if needed. For example, click the "▼" button of the *Look in* drop-down box and then click the *3½ Floppy (A:)* drive icon.

2 Click *PAD1* in the *Files* list box

3 Click the *Open* button   [↵]

> Tip: You can also double-click a document's name in the *Files* list box instead of Steps 2 and 3 to open it.

4 Click *File, New, OK* to clear your workspace

> Tip: Programs that allow multiple documents in their workspace will require clicking *File, Close* or pressing [Ctrl] + [F4] to clear your workspace before Step 4. Some programs automatically open a new document when you invoke the Close command (*File* menu). In this case, skip Step 4.

Note also that in most programs, the *File* menu lists the last few documents used. To open one, simply click it.

☑ CHECKPOINT

Note: You may want to save your Checkpoint files on another disk. Figures in this manual will not display check point files.

✓ Launch WordPad and create your own letterhead.
✓ Save the document as LETTERHEAD. (Be sure to set your default drive to A, if needed.)
✓ Use the New command to clear WordPad's workspace and then close the program.
✓ Launch WordPad again and open your LETTERHEAD document.
✓ Resave your LETTERHEAD document and then close the program.

BASIC MULTITASKING

Multitasking is the ability to work with two or more programs at the same time. As seen earlier, you can launch more than one program during a work session in Windows. You can also quickly switch to an opened program by clicking its button on the taskbar. Here you will learn how to manipulate program windows on the desktop, custom resize them, and share data between them.

LAUNCHING MULTIPLE PROGRAMS

In Windows, you may launch as many programs as your system's memory can handle. The procedures to launch more that one program are the same as those for launching a single program. Just repeat the procedure until each program you desire is launched. To practice launching more than one program in a session, launch WordPad, open your PAD1 document, and then launch Notepad.

STEPS

1 If needed, start Windows and remove the "Welcome" screen

 2 Click the *Start* button   [Ctrl + Esc]

3 Point to *Programs* for its submenu

4 Point to *Accessories* for its submenu

5 Click *WordPad*

6 Click *File, Open* for its dialog box   [Ctrl + O]

7 Click the "▼" button of the *Look in* drop-down box

 🖙 3½ Floppy (A:) 8 Click *3½ Floppy (A:)* drive icon

9 Click *PAD1* and then the *Open* button

10 **Launch Notepad (Accessories group)**

At this point there should be two program windows on the desktop with corresponding buttons on the taskbar. The size of each window may vary.

You should note several other things at this point. Windows automatically added a button for each program opened on the taskbar. The button that is currently depressed—in this case, Notepad—is the **active window.** On the desktop, generally, only one program window, dialog box, or icon can be active at a time. The active window or icon is the one on which you are currently working. It is also the window or icon that will accept most keyboard commands. Note also that the active window's title bar (top row of window), is in a darker color than that of other open windows.

SWITCHING BETWEEN PROGRAMS

To switch back to WordPad as the active window using its taskbar button,

---

| Pad1 - WordPad | **1** Click the *PAD1-WordPad* button on the taskbar | **[Alt + Tab]** |

> **Tip:** You can also switch between windows by clicking any area of the desired window, if visible. Remember, Windows allows you to open as many programs, documents, or dialog boxes as your system's memory can handle. Again, as you open each program or dialog box, a button is added to the taskbar. You can use these buttons to switch to a desired program or another window.

STANDARD WINDOW DISPLAYS

The ability to rearrange multiple windows makes them visually easier to work with. Windows has several standard multiple window displays: Cascade, Tile Horizontally, Tile Vertically, and Minimize All Windows. The **Cascade** display makes multiple windows of equal size overlap each other, as in Figure WIN1-21a. The **Tile** display places multiple windows beside each other, either horizontally (FigureWIN1-21b) or vertically (Figure WIN1-21c). The **Minimize All Windows** command reduces all windows to their taskbar button, as in Figure WIN1-21d.

CASCADING WINDOWS.   To cascade the program windows on the desktop,

---

1 Point to the space between the Notepad and *System time* button (or any space between buttons) on the taskbar similar to Figure WIN1-22

2 Right-click it for the *Shortcut* menu in Figure WIN1-22b

FIGURE WIN1-21 ■ **STANDARD WINDOWS DISPLAYS**

(a) Cascaded windows.
(b) Tiled horizontally
windows.

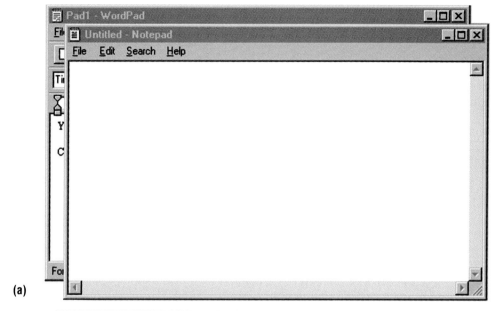

(a)

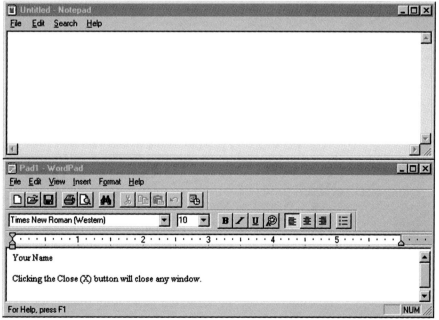

(b)

continued

3 Click *Cascade*

Your windows should appear as in Figure WIN1-21a. To switch to a window, simply click its taskbar button or click anywhere on the desired window.

FIGURE WIN1-21 ■ *continued*

(c) Tiled vertically windows.
(d) Minimized all windows.

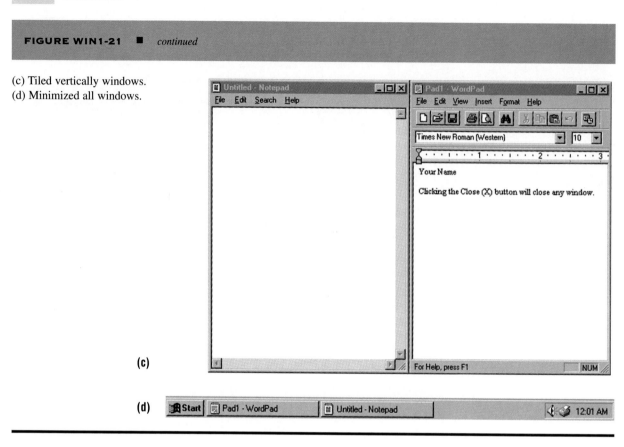

(c)

(d)

Tip: As you perform each display command, note that an Undo Cascade command appears on the *Shortcut* menu to undo your last display command.

FIGURE WIN1-22 ■ OPENING THE TASKBAR'S *SHORTCUT* MENU

(a) Position your pointer on
an open area of the taskbar.
(b) Right-click to open the
taskbar's *Shortcut* menu.

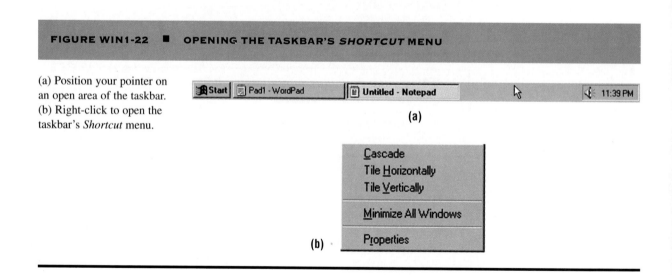

(a)

(b)

TILING WINDOWS.   To tile the windows horizontally and then vertically,

STEPS

1   Right-click the space between the Notepad and *System time* button (or any space between buttons) on the taskbar for the *Shortcut* menu

2   Click *Tile Horizontally*

Your windows should now appear as in Figure WIN1-21b. Again, to switch to a window, simply click its taskbar button or click anywhere on the desired window. Now, to change the display to tile vertically,

3   Right-click the space between the Notepad and *System time* button (or any space between buttons) on the taskbar for the *Shortcut* menu

4   Click *Tile Vertically*

Your windows should now appear as in Figure WIN1-21c.

MINIMIZING ALL WINDOWS.   To minimize all window in the desktop,

STEPS

1   Right click the space between the Notepad and *System time* button for the *Shortcut* menu

2   Click *Minimize All Windows*

All windows in the desktop are now minimized as in Figure WIN1-21d.

3   Right click the space between the Notepad and *System time* button (or any space between buttons) on the taskbar for the *Shortcut* menu

4   Click *Undo Minimize All*

5   Close each program on the desktop (If needed, drag the window's title bar to reposition the window so that its *Close* button is displayed.)

Tip: You can also use the *Shortcut* menu for displaying windows to change the properties of the taskbar. This will be discussed in later chapters.

CUSTOM WINDOW DISPLAYS

Most program and document windows can be resized to meet a user's need. To custom resize a window, simply drag and drop one of its window walls. Try this:

1 Launch WordPad

2 Right-click an open space on the taskbar for the *Shortcut* menu

3 Click *Cascade*

When the Cascade command is invoked with only a single window on the desktop, it resizes the window to a medium size window. This is done to make the next exercise visually easier.

4 Drag the window's title bar to move it to the center of the desktop

5 Slowly point to the right wall until your mouse pointer resembles that in Figure 1-23a

6 Drag this wall to the left until you have reached the last character of the title bar's name and then drop the wall there (release your mouse)

Your window should resemble Figure WIN1-23b.

SHARING DATA

In the Windows environment you can easily share data within the same document or between documents of the same or different programs. Remember, data may include text and objects. Sharing includes copying, moving or linking information. **Copying** is the process of duplicating data in a new location. **Moving** involves relocating data. **Linking** creates a special connection between data in different documents. The documents can be

---

FIGURE WIN1-23 ■ CUSTOM RESIZING A WINDOW

(a) Dragging a window's wall or corner will resize the window.
(b) The resized window.

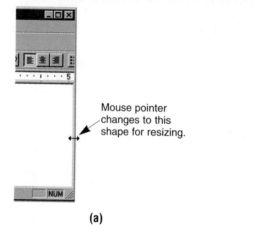

Mouse pointer changes to this shape for resizing.

(a)

(b)

from the same program or from different programs. Linking techniques are demonstrated later.

The exercises in this section provides an overview of sharing data among documents of different programs. Detailed operating instructions for sharing data within the same document and documents of other programs are provided in Chapter 3 of this manual.

STEPS

1 If needed, start Windows and remove the "Welcome" screen

2 Launch WordPad and open the PAD1 document (if needed, set the default drive to A)

3 Maximize WordPad

4 Launch Notepad

Pad1 - WordPad **5** Switch to WordPad (click its taskbar button)

SELECTING.   Selecting is a process of marking data for editing. Selected data is called a *selection.* The selection process from one program to another may differ. Generally, however, to select text in a word processing program, simply drag your mouse pointer over the desired text. With the keyboard, press and hold the Shift key while using the arrow keys. In a graphics program, you normally have to first pick a selection tool, then drag your mouse pointer around the object. Selection techniques are discussed as they relate to an operation.

COPYING DATA.   The commands to copy a selection are called Copy and Paste (*Edit* menu). The **Copy** command duplicates the selection onto Windows **Clipboard.** This program temporarily holds a selection for future pasting. The **Paste** command involves placing a selection from Clipboard to a desired location. This location can be within the same document or another document. The other document can be a different program's document. In the next exercises, you will copy some data from your PAD1 document to a Notepad document. **Notepad** is a program that allows you to create or edit text-only files.

Try to copy the sentence "Clicking the Close (X) button will close any window." from the PAD1 document (WordPad) to the default Notepad document as in Figure WIN1-24.

STEPS

1 Use your arrow keys to move to the beginning of "Clicking the Close (X) button will close any window." as in Figure WIN1-25a

FIGURE WIN1-24 ■ COPYING DATA

Data can be copied from one program to another.

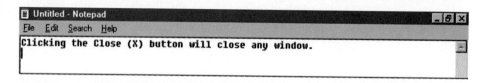

2 Slowly point to the left of the "C" in "Clicking" and wait for your pointer to change to a right pointing arrow as in Figure WIN1-25b

3 Click to select the entire line (you can also drag across to select the line) as in Figure WIN1-25c

FIGURE WIN1-25 ■ SELECTING DATA

(a) Move your insertion point to the beginning of the selection.
(b) Point to the left of "Clicking."
(c) Click to select the entire sentence.

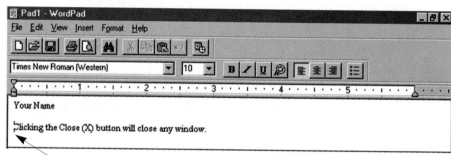

(a)

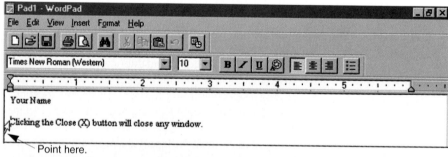

(b)

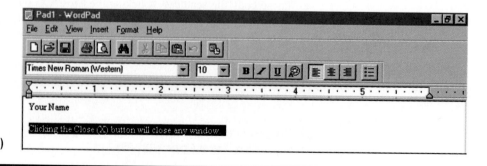

(c)

WIN

Tip: To select by keyboard, press and hold your Shift key while using your arrow keys.

4 Click *Edit, Copy* to copy the selection to the Clipboard   [**Ctrl** + **C**]

 Untitled - Notepad

5 Click the *Untitled-Notepad* button on the taskbar to switch to it   [**Alt** + **Tab**]

6 Click *Edit, Paste* to paste the selection   [**Ctrl** + **V**]

Your screen should resemble WIN1-24. The Paste command will place the selection at the insertion point. Now save the Notepad document as NOTE1 and then close it.

7 Click *File, Save*   [**Ctrl** + **S**]

Remember, since this is the first time that your are saving the document, the Save command will open the *Save As* dialog box before saving.

8 Type **NOTE1**

Now change the default drive to A before saving.

9 Click the ▼ button of the *Save in* drop-down box

3½ Floppy (A:)   **10** Click the *3½ Floppy (A:)* drive icon

11 Click the *Save* button   [↵]

Your document has now been saved as NOTE1. Notice that the caption NOTE1 appears in Notepad's title bar.

12 Click Notepad's *Close* button to close the program   [**Alt** + **F4**]

13 Close WordPad without saving   [**Alt** + **F4**]

MOVING DATA.   To move a selection, use the same commands as with copying; however, instead of clicking *Edit, Copy* (or pressing Ctrl + C) in Step 4 earlier, click *Edit, Cut* (or press Ctrl + X). The **Cut** command moves a selection from a document to the Clipboard for future pasting.

ALTERNATIVE WINDOW CLOSING TECHNIQUES

Until now, you have been using a window's *Close* button (or the Alt+F4 shortcut keys) to exit a program. Other techniques to close a program window include using its **File** menu or control-menu, or its program icon. Each one of these techniques will be demonstrated.

1 Launch WordPad, Paint, and then Notepad

2 Cascade the windows (remember to use the taskbar *Shortcut* menu)

To close Notepad using its *File* menu,

3 Click *File*   [**Alt** + **F**]

4 Click *Exit*   [**X**]

To close Paint using its control-menu,

5 Point anywhere on Paint's title bar and click your right mouse button
[**Alt** + **Spacebar**]

> **Tip:** You can also click (left mouse button) the program's icon on the title bar to open the control-menu.

6 Click *Close*   [**C**]

To close WordPad using its program icon,

7 Point to WordPad's program icon to the left of "Document - WordPad" on the title bar

8 Double-click WordPad's program icon

A summary of closing techniques displayed in Figure WIN1-26.

☑ CHECKPOINT

✓ Launch WordPad and NotePad.
✓ Cascade and then tile the windows. Next, switch to WordPad.
✓ Open your LETTERHEAD document and copy your letterhead to the default NotePad document.
✓ Save the NotePad document as NOTEHEAD.
✓ Close each program using a different closing technique.

THE HELP FEATURE

Windows offers an extensive main on-line help feature. Many dialog boxes and program windows also have help features. Procedures to access these help features are discussed next.

FIGURE WIN1-26 ■ ALTERNATIVE PROGRAM CLOSING TECHNIQUES

Method	By Mouse	By Keyboard
Shortcut	Click *Close (X)* button or double-click program icon (title bar)	Press [Alt] + [F4]
Control-Menu	Click program icon (title bar) or right-click title bar and then click *Close*	Press [Alt] + [Spacebar], [C]
File Menu	Click *File, Exit*	Press [Alt] + [F], [X]

WIN

USING WINDOWS MAIN HELP

Windows Main Help can be opened through the *Start* menu.

STEPS

   1 **Start Windows and remove the "Welcome" screen (if needed)**

   2 **Click the *Start* button**   **[Ctrl + Esc]**

   3 **Click *Help***   **[H]**

The *Help Topics: Windows Help* dialog box should appear. This dialog box has three tabs: Contents, Index, and Find. A **tab** is a section of a dialog box, similar to tabs used in a manual file system. The *Contents* tab lets you access help topics by category. The *Index* tab allows you to access help topics by typing a word or phrase, or by selecting from a list. The *Find* tab allows you to search for all help topics related to a specific word or phrase. Only the *Index* tab is demonstrated here. See the appendix for instructions on using the other tabs.

> **Note: The techniques used in this section to operate and select help features are common to most dialog boxes and windows.**

REQUESTING HELP BY TYPING.   The *Index* tab can be used to search for help by either typing the desired topic's name or selecting it from the index's list. To request help on the filenames by typing,

STEPS

Index   **1** **Click the *Index* tab (if needed)**

Your dialog box should resemble Figure WIN1-27a. The insertion point should now be in the text box just below "1. Type the first few letters of the word you're looking for." As you type each letter in the next steps, watch the *Index* list box.

2 **Type** **f**

A selection highlight appears in the lower list box and scrolls (moves) to "Faster ways to work with Windows." This is the first topic that starts with an "f."

3 **Type** **ilenames**

Now, as in Figure WIN1-27b, the selection highlight moves to "filenames." This topic also has a variety of subtopics listed below it. To select the subtopic "about longer filenames,"

4 **Double-click** *about longer filenames*   [↓ , ↵]

FIGURE WIN1-27 ■ **REQUESTING HELP**

(a) The Help *Index* tab.
(b) Typing a topic's name or clicking the topic in the list box will select it.
(c) Help on long filenames.

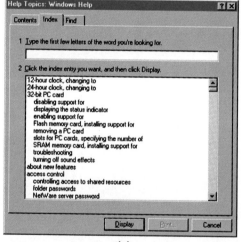

(a)

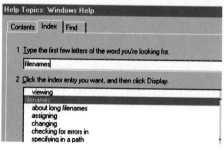

(b)

(c)

A Help window appears with the topic "A new look and feel" and a list of topics. To receive help on "Longer filenames,"

 5   Click *Longer filenames*

A window displaying help on longer filenames appears as in Figure WIN 1-27c. Now to close both windows,

6   Click the *Close* button of the *What's New* window   [**Alt** + **F4**]

7   Click the Close button of the Windows Help window   [**Alt** + **F4**]

REQUESTING HELP BY SELECTING. To access help on longer filenames by selecting from the *Index* list box,

STEPS

 1   Click the *Start* button for the *Start* menu   [**Ctrl** + **Esc**]

2   Click *Help* for its dialog box

 3   Click the *Index* tab, if needed

Again, your dialog box should resemble Figure WIN1-27a. Items listed in a list box are normally displayed in numeric and then alphabetical order. This list box has a scroll bar on its right wall. A **scroll bar** allows you to move (scroll) vertically or horizontally through a list box or window's contents by mouse. Clicking the arrow button on either end of a scroll bar or dragging the small box (called the *scroll box*) on the scroll bar will quickly move through the contents of a list box or window. Scroll bars generally appear in a list box or window when its contents is larger than its display area. They may appear either on the list box or window's right and/or bottom wall. Try this to locate the topic "filenames" in the *Index* list box:

Scroll box ⟶ 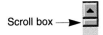 **4**   Point to the scroll box just beneath the up arrow scroll button

5   Slowly drag the scroll box down until topics that begin with the letter "f" appear in the list box

6   Click either arrow scroll button until "filenames" appears

Note that the selection highlight does not move from its position when using the scroll bar. To move the selection highlight to "filenames,"

7   Double-click *about long filenames* in the list box

8   Click *Long filenames*

A window displaying help on long filenames appears as in Figure WIN 1-27c. Leave these windows open as you proceed to the next section.

> **Tip:** To scroll to a desired item quickly, type the item's first letter and then use the scroll bar to locate the item.

PRINTING HELP INFORMATION.   Help topics can be printed by using a *Short-cut* menu. To print the information on the *Long filenames,*

STEPS

1 Turn on your printer

2 Right-click anywhere within the *What's New* Help window for its *Shortcut* menu

3 Click *Print Topic* for the *Print* dialog box

4 Click *OK*

[X] **5** Click the *What's New* window's *Close* button

At this point you can return to the *Help Topics: Windows Help* dialog box by clicking the *Help Topics* button (do not click) or exit help. To exit help,

[X] **6** Click Windows Help's *Close* button

> **Tip:** To copy a help topic to the Clipboard for pasting into a program, click *Copy* instead of *Print Topic* in Step 3.

GETTING HELP WITHIN A DIALOG BOX

Many dialog boxes have a [?] button to the left of the *Close* button that can be used to access help on a specific area of a dialog box. Try this:

STEPS

 1 Click the *Start* button for the *Start* menu

2 Click *Help* for its dialog box

Find   **3** Click the *Find* tab

?   **4** Click the [?] button (left of the *Close* button)

Your mouse pointer changes to an arrow with a question mark. Pointing to and clicking a desired area of the dialog box will open a caption box describing the area's operations. For example,

5 Click the text box below the caption "1. Type the word(s) you want to find"

A caption box appears with a brief description of the text box's operation as in Figure WIN1-28.

6 Click anywhere outside the caption box to close it

X   **7** Click the dialog box's *Close* button

> **Tip:** In general, to access help in dialog boxes that do not have a help [?] button, simply press [F1].

GETTING HELP WITHIN A PROGRAM WINDOW

Most Windows programs have a *Help* menu that can be accessed through its menu bar. You can also press F1 to access a program's main help. Although each program's help features may differ, their general dialog box and window operations are similar to the Windows main help. In addition, most programs offer both general and specific help. You may want to try the Help feature in a few different programs to get a feel for its operations.

FIGURE WIN1-28 ■ DIALOG BOX HELP

Clicking the *Help* button and then a desired item on a dialog box will display a caption on its operation.

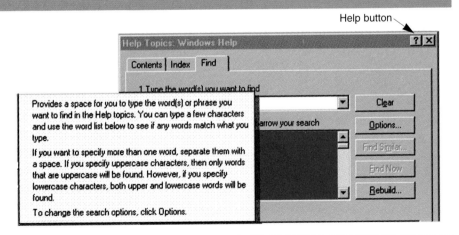

CHECKPOINT

✓ Access Windows main *Help* dialog box.
✓ Use the *Index* tab to search for help on "dialog boxes, using."
✓ Print the information on dialog boxes.
✓ Close the Help window.
✓ How can you access help on a specific dialog box component operation?

OTHER START MENU COMMANDS

The *Start* menu, as in Figure WIN1-29, offers several other commands in addition to Programs and Help. These commands include Documents, Settings, Find, and Run. The first three open submenus and the Run command opens a dialog box. The operation of each option is discussed next.

DOCUMENTS MENU

The **Documents menu** can be used to open any of the last 15 documents used with its related program. To use the *Documents* menu,

 1 Click the *Start* button

[Ctrl + Esc]

FIGURE WIN1-29 ■ START MENU COMMANDS

2 Point to *Documents* to open its submenu

3 Click any document listed to open it

Windows will now open the document you selected and its related program.

 4 Click the program window's *Close* button

> Tip: To clear the Documents menu, click the *Start* button, point to *Settings*, click *Taskbar*, the *Start Menu Programs* tab, the *Clear* button, OK.

SETTINGS MENU

The **Settings menu** contains commands to launch the Control Panel program, Printers program, and open the *Taskbar Properties* dialog box. Each of these items will be discussed next.

CONTROL PANEL.   The **Control Panel** program can be used to change the settings of your computer. Many of these settings are automatically set when Windows was installed on your system. However, sometimes these settings may require adjustment (for example, when adding new hardware or changing the system's time).

STEPS

 1 Click the *Start* button   [**Ctrl** + **Esc**]

2 Point to *Settings* to open its submenu

3 Click *Control Panel*

The Control Panel window should appear similar to Figure WIN1-30. (Your Control Panel contents may differ.) At this point you can access any of its items by clicking the item, clicking *File,* and then *Open.* Try this to open the *Date/Time* dialog box as in Figure WIN1-31,

 4 Click the *Date/Time* icon

5 Click *File* (on the menu bar), *Open*   [↵]

This dialog box has two tabs: *Date & Time* and *Time Zone.* The *Date & Time* tab is used to set the system date and time. The *Time Zone* tab is used to set your own time zone. For now,

---

FIGURE WIN1-30 ■ THE CONTROL PANEL

The Control Panel can be
used to adjust the computer's
settings.

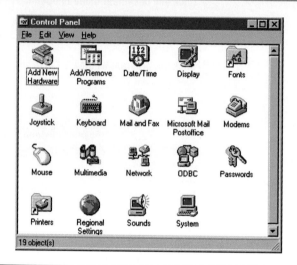

---

6 Click the *Cancel* button to return to the Control Panel window [**Esc**]

7 Click the Control Panel's *Close* button [**Alt** + **F4**]

FIGURE WIN1-31 ■ THE DATE/TIME PROPERTIES DIALOG BOX

This dialog box can be used
to adjust the system's date
and time.

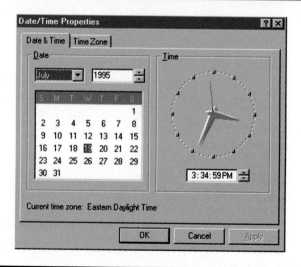

> **Tip: Instead of Steps 4 and 5, you can double-click an icon to open it.**

PRINTERS.   **Printers** is a program that displays the current printers installed on your system. You can use this window to add another printer or open a window displaying the activity of a printer.

TASKBAR.   The Taskbar command opens a **Taskbar Properties dialog box.** This dialog box can be used to change the taskbar's display settings and add or remove programs from the *Programs* menu. The operations of this dialog box will be examined in detail later.

FIND MENU

The **Find menu** opens to a menu that displays at least the command *Files or Folders.* This command is used to locate files or folders within your system quickly. A *folder* is a set of related files. Its operation will be discussed in Chapter 2.

RUN DIALOG BOX

The **Run dialog box** as in Figure WIN1-32, allows you to launch a program, or to open a folder or document by typing its command line. This dialog box is often used to install new programs. To open the *Run* dialog box,

STEPS

1 Click the *Start* button   [Ctrl + Esc]

2 Click *Run* for its dialog box

The *Run* dialog box should appear as in Figure WIN1-32. The Browse feature of this dialog box is helpful to locate files. Try this:

3 If needed, insert your data disk

4 Click the *Browse* button for its dialog box

As in Figure WIN1-32, the *Browse* dialog box resembles an *Open* dialog box. In fact, its components operate the same way. For now, close all windows and shut down Windows.

5 Click the *Browse* dialog box's *Close* button

6 Click the *Run* dialog box's *Close* button

7 Click the *Start* button and then *Shut Down*

FIGURE WIN1-32 ■ **THE RUN COMMAND**

(a) Clicking the Run
command (*Start* menu) opens
its dialog box.
(b) Clicking the *Browse*
button opens a dialog box
that can be used to look in a
particular directory of a disk.

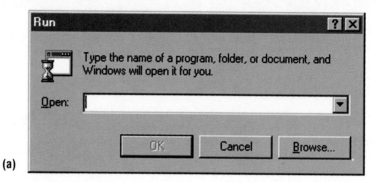

(a)

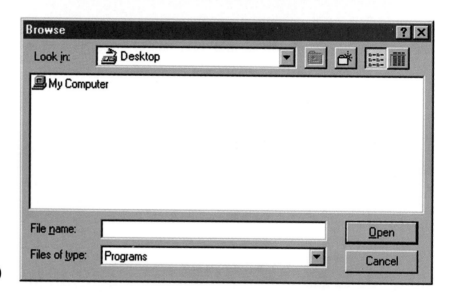

(b)

☑ CHECKPOINT

✓ What does the Document command of the *Start* menu allow you to do?
✓ Which *Setting* menu command can be used to change system settings?
✓ Which dialog box can be used to add new programs to the taskbar?
✓ How do you access it?
✓ Describe the function(s) of the Run command.
✓ For what reason is the Find command (*Start* menu) used?

SUMMARY

■ Windows is a graphical user interface, or GUI (pronounced "gooey"), operating system that simplifies communication with your computer by using common symbols
(called icons) and menus instead of typewritten commands.

■ A window is a rectangular box that may contain a program (set of computer instructions) called a program window or document (a file with data, information, or graphics) called a document window. It may also be used to request or give information about a task or feature called a dialog box.

■ Booting up is the process of starting Windows on a system with a hard-disk drive. This generally involves turning on your computer system and waiting for the Windows screen.

■ The Windows screen has two main parts: the taskbar (bottom of screen) and the desktop (large area above the taskbar). The desktop also has several icons, starting with the *My Computer* icon. Icons are small graphical images or symbols (pictures) that may represent programs, documents, and other features.

■ The mouse pointer, or pointer, is a small graphical image resembling an arrow on the screen. You control it by using a pointing device such as a mouse (most common), trackball, pointing stick, track pad, or electronic pen.

■ Pointing involves moving the mouse pointer on your screen to a desired item. Clicking involves pointing to a desired item and then rapidly pressing and releasing your left mouse button. Clicking will invoke an item's feature. Right-clicking involves pointing to a desired item and then pressing and releasing the right mouse button. Right-clicking will open an item's *Shortcut* menu.

■ Dragging and dropping can be used to move or copy icons, windows, or other objects. Dragging involves pointing to a desired object and then pressing and holding the left mouse button while moving the mouse and the object to a new location. Dropping involves releasing the mouse and thus the object after dragging it to a new location.

■ Double-clicking (pointing to and then rapidly pressing and releasing the left mouse button twice) is generally used to open an icon directly to a window or other feature.

■ Shortcut keys provide a quick way to invoke certain commands by pressing a function key alone or in conjunction with the Ctrl, Alt, or Shift keys. The Ctrl, Alt, and Shift keys may also be used in conjunction with other keys.

■ Clicking the taskbar's *Start* button (left side) or pressing Ctrl + Esc will open the Windows main menu called the *Start* menu. It is used to start programs, find documents, adjust system settings, find a document (file), access help, or shut down Windows. Each option on the *Start* menu is listed with its corresponding icon to its left.

■ To shut down (exit) Windows, click the *Start* button, *Sh<u>u</u>t Down,* and then the *<u>Y</u>es* button.

■ *Launching* is the Windows term for starting a program. The *Programs* menu of the *Start* menu is normally used to launch a program. It contains a list of program groups and certain primary programs. Program groups open to submenus. They are logical groupings of programs and files into categories for easier visual access.

■ Closing is the process of closing a window and thus exiting the program, document, or other Windows feature that is encased in it. To close any window, click its *Close* button (a button with an "X" at the right end of the title bar).

■ The title bar is the first row in any window and is used to identify the window. It can be used to resize, move, or close a window. It may include the program or document's icon, name, two window resizing buttons, and a *Close* button. The title bars in dialog boxes may include a *Help* (?) button instead of resizing buttons.

■ A menu bar provides mouse and keyboard access to a program's features through pull-down menus. Only program windows can have a menu bar. Most Windows programs have *File, Edit,* and *Help* menus. To open a pull-down menu from a

WIN

bar, click the desired menu bar item or press the Alt key and the underlined letter of the menu bar item.

■ Standard Windows menu indicators include (1) items with a "▶" open a submenu, (2) no notation directly invokes a command, (3) items with an ellipsis (...) open another window, and (4) dimmed items are currently not available.

■ A command button directly accesses a program or window's feature when clicked. Command buttons that can be used to manipulate a window are located on the title bar. They include the program or document icon, *Minimize, Maximize, Restore,* and *Close* buttons. Command buttons that activate a program feature are generally grouped in functional sets below the menu bar. These sets are often called a toolbar or format bar.

■ A drop-down box resembles a one-line rectangular box that has a "▼" button on its right side. They may be found with command button sets or in dialog boxes. Clicking the "▼" button of a drop-down box opens a drop-down list of available options.

■ Basic document management includes procedures to use the default document to create documents with data and objects and then save, print, and open those documents. It also includes using the New command to clear the current workspace for a new document. These commands are generally located in a program's file menu.

■ Filenames are used to identify a document or program and can have up to 255 characters.

■ Formatting prepares a disk for use on the computer. Every new disk that is not pre-formatted must be formatted (organized for your computer system) before you can store anything on it. Formatting sets up the disk's directory and file allocation table and divides the disk into addressable storage locations. It also checks for defective tracks on the disk and seals them off from further use.

■ Multitasking is the computer's ability to work with two or more programs at the same time. For each program launched, a corresponding button is added to the taskbar. To switch to a program, click its taskbar button.

■ The active window is the one currently in use. Its title bar is highlighted and taskbar button depressed. Most keyboard commands affect the active window.

■ The ability to rearrange the display of multiple windows makes them visually easier to work with. Standard multiple window displays available through the taskbar's *Shortcut* menu include Cascade (overlapping each other), Tile Horizontally (on top of each other), Tile Vertically (next to each other), and Minimize All Windows (reduced to the taskbar button). You can also custom resize a window by dragging one of its walls or corners.

■ Information can be easily copied, moved, or linked within the same document or among documents of the same or different programs. These commands are located in the *Edit* menu and include *Copy, Cut, Paste,* and *Paste Link.* The Copy command duplicates a selection (marked data or objects) onto the Clipboard (a temporary holding program) for future pasting. The Cut command moves the selection to the Clipboard. The Paste command copies a selection from the Clipboard to a desired location.

■ Windows main *Help* dialog box can be opened through the *Start* menu. It has three tabs: Contents, Index, and Find. A tab is a section of a dialog box, similar to tabs used in a manual file system. The *Contents* tab lets you access help topics by category. The *Index* tab allows you to access help topics by typing a word or phrase or selecting from a list. The *Find* tab allows you to search for all help topics related to a specific word or phrase.

■   To get help on a specific operation of a dialog box, click the [?] button (title bar) and then the desired item or press F1. To get help in a program window, click *Help* for the *Help* menu and then click the desired help item or press F1.

■   Other *Start* menu commands include Documents (opens to a menu that can be used to open any of the last 15 documents used), Settings (opens to a menu that can be used to open the Control Panel window, Printers window, and *Taskbar Properties* dialog box), Find (used to locate files or folders quickly), and Run (used to open a program, folder, or document by typing its command line). The Run command is often used to install new programs.

KEY TERMS

Active (or current) icon (WIN11)
Active window (WIN38)
Booting up (WIN3)
Cascade (WIN38)
Clicking (WIN9)
Clipboard (WIN43)
Close button (WIN12)
Command button (WIN27)
Control Panel (WIN53)
Control-menu (WIN20)
Copy (WIN43)
Copying (WIN42)
Cut (WIN45)
Data (WIN2)
Default document (WIN32)
Default drive (WIN33)
Desktop (WIN5)
Dialog box (WIN5)
Disks (WIN3)
Document (WIN2)
Document window (WIN17)
Documents menu (WIN52)
Double-clicking (WIN11)
Dragging (WIN11)
Drop-down box (WIN27)
Dropping (WIN11)
File (WIN3)
Filename (WIN32)
Find menu (WIN55)
Folder (WIN3)
Font (WIN29)

Font size (WIN29)
Format bar (WIN27)
Formatting (WIN33)
Function keys (WIN6)
Graphical user interface, or GUI (WIN2)
Hardware (WIN2)
Icons (WIN2)
Insertion point (WIN31)
Launching (WIN14)
Linking (WIN42)
Maximize button (WIN22)
Maximized (WIN17)
Menu bar (WIN22)
Microsoft Windows 95 (WIN2)
Minimize all windows (WIN38)
Minimize button (WIN21)
Mouse (WIN5)
Mouse pointer (WIN5)
MouseKeys (WIN6)
Moving (WIN42)
Multitasking (WIN37)
New (WIN35)
Notepad (WIN43)
Objects (WIN2)
Open (WIN36)
Paste (WIN43)
Pointer (WIN5)
Pointing (WIN6)
Pointing device (WIN5)
Print (WIN35)
Printers (WIN55)

Program (WIN2)
Program groups (WIN15)
Program window (WIN17)
Pull-down menu (WIN22)
Resizing buttons (WIN21)
Restore (WIN21)
Restore button (WIN22)
Right-click (WIN10)
Run dialog box (WIN55)
Save (WIN32)
Save as (WIN32)
Scroll bar (WIN49)
Selection (WIN25)
Settings menu (WIN53)
Shortcut keys (WIN6)
Shortcut menu (WIN10)
Shut down (WIN13)
Start button (WIN5)
Start menu (WIN5)
Tab (WIN47)
Taskbar (WIN5)
Taskbar properties dialog box (WIN55)
Tile (WIN38)
Title bar (WIN17)
Toolbar (WIN27)
Window (WIN2)
Windows screen (WIN5)
WordPad (WIN15)
Workspace (WIN17)

WIN

QUIZ

TRUE/FALSE

____ 1. A graphical user interface operating system uses symbols and menus instead of typewritten commands.

____ 2. Launching is the process of starting a program.

____ 3. Double-clicking an object opens its *Shortcut* menu.

____ 4. The desktop is the interior space of a window.

____ 5. Pressing the **Ctrl** + **Esc** keys opens the *Start* menu.

____ 6. The *File* menu in most programs contains commands to save, open, or print a document.

____ 7. Only program windows have a *Close* button.

____ 8. Pressing the **Alt** + **F4** keys will close a program window.

____ 9. Multitasking is the computer's ability to work with more than one program at the same time.

____ 10. The *Run* dialog box can be used to install programs.

MULTIPLE CHOICE

____ 11. The bar at the bottom of the Windows screen is called the
    a. Status bar
    b. Menu bar
    c. Taskbar
    d. Desktop

____ 12. The main portion of the Windows screen is called the
    a. Desktop
    b. Workspace
    c. Taskbar
    d. Title bar

____ 13. All of the following are mouse actions except
    a. Point
    b. Click
    c. Press
    d. Right Click

____ 14. A program window's title bar has all of the following except
    a. Name section
    b. Resizing buttons
    c. *Close* button
    d. *Help* button

____ 15. A program window can be closed by all of the following except
    a. Press **Alt** + **F4**
    b. Click *File, Close*
    c. Click the *Close* button
    d. Click *File, Exit*

___ 16. To open an item's *Shortcut* menu,
    a. Click *File, Shortcut*
    b. Click *Start, Shortcut*
    c. Right Click the item
    d. Press **Alt** + **S**

___ 17. Dragging a corner of a nonmaximized window will _____ it.
    a. resize
    b. move
    c. cascade
    d. tile

___ 18. The process of marking data for editing is called
    a. Copying
    b. Coloring
    c. Selecting
    d. Right Clicking

___ 19. Clicking the ? button of a dialog box will
    a. Close it
    b. Open its menu
    c. Start its function
    d. Access help

___ 20. The Copy command places a copy of a selection in the _____ for future pasting.
    a. Desktop
    b. Clipboard
    c. taskbar
    d. dialog box

MATCHING

Select the lettered item from the figure that best matches each phrase below.

___ 21. Controlled by a pointing device.
___ 22. Clicking this item opens the Windows main menu.
___ 23. Right clicking this item will open a *Shortcut* menu with the Cascade command.
___ 24. Clicking this item will open a menu with document Saving, Opening, and Printing commands.
___ 25. Clicking this item will open a control-menu.
___ 26. Dragging this item will move a window.
___ 27. Clicking this item maximizes a window.
___ 28. Clicking this item will close a window.
___ 29. Pressing **Ctrl** + **Esc** will open this menu.
___ 30. Clicking this item will open a menu with Copying, Cutting, and Pasting commands.

ANSWERS

True/False: 1. T; 2. T; 3. F; 4. F; 5. T; 6. T; 7. F; 8. T; 9. T; 10. T
Multiple Choice: 11. c; 12. a; 13. c; 14. d; 15. b; 16. c; 17. a; 18. c; 19; d; 20. b
Matching: 21. k; 22. l; 23. m; 24. f; 25. b; 26. c; 27. d; 28. i; 29. j; 30. e

FIGURE WIN1-33 ■ CHAPTER 1 MATCHING FIGURE

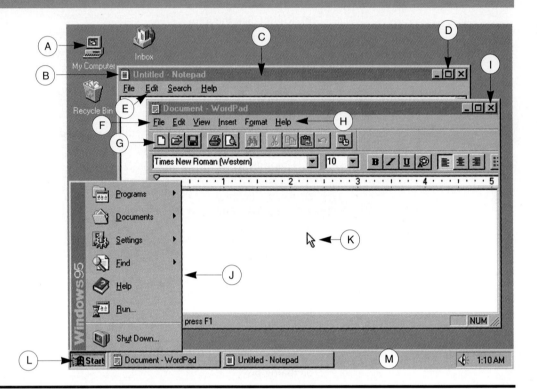

EXERCISE

I. OPERATIONS

Provide the Windows commands to do each of the following operations. For each operation, assume a hard-disk system with a disk in Drive A. You may want to verify each command by trying it on your computer.

1. Start Windows and open the *Start* menu.
2. Launch the WordPad and Notepad programs.
3. Vertically tile and then cascade the windows.
4. Switch to WordPad and maximize it.
5. Type the second item from the chapter's summary.
6. Save this file as SUMMARY1.
7. Select the entire paragraph and copy it to the Clipboard.
8. Switch to Notepad and maximize it.
9. Paste the paragraph into Notepad's default document and save it as SUMMARY2.
10. Close all windows and then shut down Windows.

II. COMMANDS

Describe fully, using as few words as possible, what command is initiated, or what is accomplished, in Windows by the actions described below. Assume that each exercise part is independent of any previous parts.

1. Pressing **Ctrl** + **Esc** keys.

2. Clicking the *Start* button.

3. Pointing to a *Start* menu item that has a "▶" at its right.

4. Double-clicking a program window's title bar.

5. Pressing the **Alt** + **F4** keys when using a program.

6. Clicking the "X" button of a window.

7. Pointing to a WordPad toolbar button.

8. Clicking a program's taskbar button.

9. Pressing the **Ctrl** + **X** keys on a selection.

10. Pressing the **Ctrl** + **V** keys.

III. APPLICATIONS

Perform the following operations, briefly tell how you accomplished each operation, and describe its results.

APPLICATION 1: GETTING STARTED

1. Boot your computer and start Windows.

2. Point to the *Start* button on the taskbar and wait for its caption.

3. Click the *Start* button for the *Start* menu.

4. Point to <u>Programs</u> for its submenu.

5. Point to *Accessories* for its submenu.

6. Click *WordPad* to launch it.

7. Click WordPad's *Close* button.

8. Drag and drop the *Recycle Bin* icon in the center of the desktop.

9. Double-click the *Recycle Bin* icon to launch it.

10. Click the Recycle Bin's *Close* button.

11. Shut down Windows.

APPLICATION 2: COMMON WINDOWS FEATURES

1. Boot your computer and start Windows.

2. Launch WordPad.

3. Use the *WordPad* control-menu to minimize it. (Hint: Click its icon on the title bar or right click the tile bar.)

4. Resize the WordPad to a window and then maximize it.

5. Point to a few of the toolbar and format bar buttons for their titles.

6. Use the keyboard to open the *Edit* menu and then move the highlight to a few of the commands and review their descriptions as they display on the status bar.

7. Close the menu without selecting a command.

8. Open the toolbar's *Shortcut* menu and then close it.

9. Close WordPad.

10. Shut down Windows.

APPLICATION 3: BASIC DOCUMENT MANAGEMENT

1. Boot your computer and start Windows.

2. Start WordPad.

3. Type your name.

4. Save the document as MYNAME.

5. Use the new command (*File* menu) to clear the workspace an open a new document.

6. Open MYNAME.

7. Type your address below your name (use two lines).

8. Resave the document as MYNAME.

9. Print the MYNAME document.

10. Close WordPad and the shut down Windows.

APPLICATION 4: BASIC MULTITASKING

1. Boot your computer and start Windows.

2. Launch WordPad and Notepad.

3. Switch to WordPad and open the MYNAME document created in Application 3.

4. Select the data in the MYNAME document.

5. Use the Copy command to copy the selection to the Clipboard.

6. Switch to Notepad.

7. Use the Paste command to place the selection in the default Notepad document.

8. Tile horizontally and then cascade the windows.

9. Minimize all windows.

10. Close all windows and shut down Windows.

APPLICATION 5: THE HELP FEATURE

1. Boot your computer and start Windows.

2. Open the main *Help* dialog box.

3. Click the *Index* tab.

4. Use the *Index* list to access help on multitasking.

5. Print the contents of the Help window.

6. Click the *Find* tab.

7. Locate topics related to windows.

8. Close all Help windows.

9. Launch Paint and use its *Help* menu to access help on toolbox.

10. Close any windows and shut down Windows.

APPLICATION 6: OTHER START MENU COMMANDS

1. Boot your computer and start Windows.

2. Use the *Documents* menu to open your last document (or any document).

3. Close the window.

4. Use the *Settings* menu to launch the Control Panel.

5. Examine the settings options in the Control Panel window.

6. Close the window.

7. Use the *Find* menu to locate the PAD1 file on your disk.

8. Close the window.

9. Open the *Run* dialog box and browse through the contents of your data disk.

10. Close any opened window and shut down Windows.

MASTERY CASES

The following mastery cases allow you to demonstrate how much you have learned about this software. Each case describes a fictitious problem or need that can be solved using the skills that you have learned in this chapter. Although minimum acceptable outcomes are specified, you are expected and encouraged to design your own response (files, data, lists) in ways that display your personal mastery of the software. Feel free to show off your skills. Use real data from your own experience in your solution, although you may also fabricate data if needed.

These mastery cases allow you to display your ability to

- Start and shut down Windows.
- Use common windows features.
- Operate basic document management commands.
- Perform basic multitasking operations.
- Use on-line help.

CASE 1:   USING WINDOWS AT SCHOOL

You have been asked to prepare a small presentation describing the common components of a window. Use WordPad to prepare a list of common window parts and their operations. Save the document and print it. Close the program and shut down Windows.

CASE 2:   USING WINDOWS AT HOME

Members of your home have asked you to prepare instructions on how to launch a program and access on-line help. Use WordPad to prepare these instructions. Save the document and print it. Close the program and shut down Windows.

CASE 3: USING WINDOWS AT WORK

You have been asked to prepare a small presentation on the benefits of multitasking. Use WordPad to create a document listing a few benefits of multitasking and save the document. Next, launch Notepad and copy the data from your WordPad document to it. Save and print the Notepad document. Close both programs and shut down Windows.

2

MANAGING YOUR COMPUTER

OBJECTIVES

After completing this chapter, you will be able to

1. Describe how to launch and use My Computer to view and find your computer's components.
2. Explain how your computer stores programs and documents.
3. Use My Computer for formatting a disk and performing disk diagnostics.
4. Create folders and documents using My Computer and Folder windows.
5. Rename a file and open or print multiple files.
6. Copy, move, and create *Shortcut* icons for single and multiple files.
7. Use the Undo command and recycle bin.
8. Change properties of various components of your system.
9. Launch and operate Windows Explorer.

OVERVIEW

This chapter introduces a variety of techniques to help you to better manage your computer. It focuses on using My Computer, a program that allows you to view and manage every part of your computer. First, you will review how to launch My Computer. You will then learn how your computer stores files, as well as how to format and diagnose a disk, look in a folder (group of files),

create new folders, and open, rename, and print single and multiple files or folders. You will also practice single and multiple file sharing and removing techniques that include copying, moving, creating shortcuts, deleting, and recycling.

Next, you will learn how to control your computer environment by changing an item's properties (characteristics), changing the computer's default settings, and managing your printing.

This chapter concludes with a look at Windows Explorer, another program that you can use to manage your computer. In Explorer, folders and other components of your system are listed in a hierarchal tree. Selecting (marking) a folder (or other item) on the tree will display its contents (files and folders). Commands used with the My Computer program are also available through Explorer.

UNDERSTANDING MY COMPUTER

My Computer is a program that can be used to browse (view) and access all of the components of your computer. You can also use it to access features that will help you manage your files and control your computer settings and printing. As you will soon see, system components are displayed as icons in My Computer's workspace.

LAUNCHING MY COMPUTER

As demonstrated in Chapter 1, the My Computer program is normally launched directly from the desktop, not the *Start* menu. To launch the My Computer program,

STEPS

1 Double-click the *My Computer* icon at the top left corner of the desktop

To resize the window to resemble the Figure WIN2-1,

2 Right-click an empty area of the taskbar for its *Shortcut* menu

3 Click *Cascade*

Your My Computer window should resemble Figure WIN2-1 (the contents of your window may differ).

Although you can work with a window in a variety of sizes and places on the desktop, it is recommended that you resize your window(s) as indicated in the tutorials. This will make it easier to relate them to the corresponding figures.

The My Computer window contains a variety of common Windows features, including a title bar (with a *Program* icon, resizing buttons, and a *Close* button), a menu bar, workspace, and status bar. These items operate the same as in other program windows. Currently occupying its workspace are several drive icons, the *Control Panel* folder and the *Printers* folder.

STORING PROGRAMS AND DOCUMENTS

Before learning how to use My Computer, you should understand how your computer stores programs and documents. Storage media includes disks (hard disk and 3½″ or 5¼″

Double-clicking a *Drive* or *Folder* icon will open its Folder window.

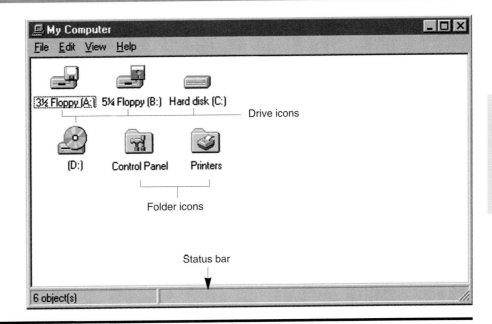

disks), CD-ROM (a special disk that has *read only memory*), tape, and system memory (RAM or ROM). This text assumes that you are using a hard disk and a 3½″ disk for data. (Note: Windows often refers to 3½″ or 5¼″ disks as floppies.) In addition, any disk can be assigned a **label** (name). Disk labeling is discussed in the "Changing Properties" section of this chapter.

FILES AND FOLDERS.   A *file* is a program or document that is saved on a disk or other storage media. Files are represented by icons and titles (filenames). The number of files that can be stored on a particular storage media depends on its capacity.

A *folder* is a group of related files. Folders may also contain other folders called **subfolders.** In Windows, a disk (or other storage media) is considered a folder. In this manual, the disk will be referred to as the *main folder.* In pre-Windows 95 systems, a folder was called a *directory* and a subfolder was called a *subdirectory.* The main folder was called the *root (or main) directory.*

Note: Throughout this manual, file operations often relate to both files and folders.

FILE AND FOLDER NAMES.   As mentioned earlier, filenames are used to identify documents or programs. Folder names are used to identify groups of files. If you are using DOS-based or pre-Windows 95 programs, you are restricted to filenames with up to 8 characters and an optional 3-character extension. The programs that come with Windows 95 can accept filenames of up to 255 characters.

STORAGE TERMINOLOGY. Your computer defines the storage volume of a disk in terms of bytes. A **byte** is equivalent to one alphanumeric character (A–Z, 0–9, and so forth). A kilobyte (KB) is one thousand bytes, a megabyte (MB) is one million bytes, and a gigabyte (GB) is one billion bytes.

DRIVES. A **drive** is a device that reads and/or writes to a storage medium (such as a disk or CD-ROM). As displayed in the My Computer window (Figure WIN2-1), drive icons and letter titles are used to identify each drive in your system. The letter C is normally used to represent the hard drive, the letters A and B represent disk drives, and the letter D is generally used for a CD-ROM. Other letters may be used to identify a network. Your actual configurations may differ.

DISK OPERATIONS

My Computer can be used to perform some basic disk operations including formatting and diagnosing a disk. *Formatting* prepares a disk for use on your computer. Disk diagnostics features can examine a disk for a variety of problems and repair them.

FORMATTING. Every new disk that is not preformatted must be formatted (organized for your computer) before you can store anything on it. Formatting sets up the disk's folder and file allocation table and divides the disk into addressable storage locations. It will also check for defective tracks on the disk and seal them off from further use. A disk that has been previously formatted can be reformatted. This will, however, delete the disk's files and set up a new blank main folder.

The data disk that you are currently using is already formatted and should not be reformatted. (Remember, reformatting will erase the entire contents of your disk.) Disk formatting procedures and options have been provided in Figure WIN2-2. Use them only as needed.

> **Tip:** When first saving a document on an unformatted disk, Windows will ask if you desire to format the disk.

DISK DIAGNOSTICS. Windows offers several disk diagnostic tools to locate and repair a variety of disk problems. These tools are accessible through the *Disk Properties* dialog box and should only be used when needed. See the "Changing Properties" section of this chapter for information on accessing these tools.

FINDING A FILE

The **Find** feature can be used to locate any file in a folder. (Remember, a disk is considered a main folder.) Once located, you can open the file from the lower section of the *Find* dialog box.

FIGURE WIN2-2 ■ FORMATTING A DISK

(a) Procedures to format a disk.
(b) The *Format* dialog box.

Procedures to Format a Disk

Caution: Formatting a disk will erase all of its contents!

1. Launch My Computer

By *Shortcut* Menu

2. Right-click the *3½ Floppy (A:)* drive icon for its *Shortcut* menu
3. Click *Format* for its dialog box

By *File* Menu

2. Click the *3½ Floppy (A:)* drive icon to select it
3. Click *File, Format* for its dialog box

At this point you can select any of the options of the dialog box as indicated in Figure WIN2-2b. In general,

Reformat a Formatted Disk

4. Click *Start* to perform a quick format (the default setting)

Format a New Unformatted Disk

4. Click a *Full* option and then *Start*

A *Format Results* dialog box will appear when the formatting process is completed. This dialog box provides information about the disk. To remove it and return to the *Format* dialog box,

5. Click *Close* (*Format Results* dialog box)

You can now either format another disk by removing the current disk, inserting a new one, and repeating Steps 4 and 5, or you can exit the dialog box. To exit,

6. Click *Close* (*Format* dialog box)

(a)

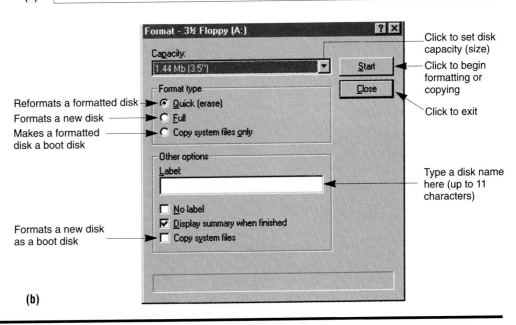

(b)

INITIAL SEARCH. To locate the NOTE1 file in the main folder of your data disk,

1 Insert your data disk into Drive A

BY *SHORTCUT* MENU

2 Right-click the *3½ Floppy (A:)* drive icon

3 Click (left mouse button) *Find* for its dialog box

BY *FILE* MENU

2 Click the *3½ Floppy (A:)* drive icon

3 Click *File, Find*

The *Find* dialog box should appear as in Figure WIN2-3a. To search for the NOTE1 document,

---

FIGURE WIN2-3 ■ THE *FIND* DIALOG BOX

(a) The *Find* dialog box can be accessed from a *Shortcut* menu or the *File* menu.
(b) The Search results appear at the bottom of the dialog box.

Type the desired file name here

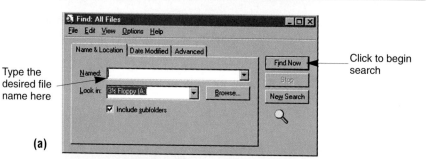

Click to begin search

(a)

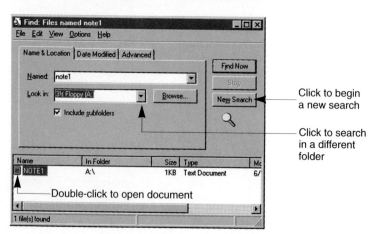

Click to begin a new search

Click to search in a different folder

Double-click to open document

(b)

4 **Type** **NOTE1** **in the** *Find* **text box**

5 **Click the** *Find Now* **button**

The results of your search will appear at the bottom of the dialog box as in Figure WIN2-3b. To access the file,

 6 **Double-click** *NOTE1*   [↵]

Your NOTE1 document now appears on your screen in Notepad.

7 **Close Notepad**   [**Alt** + **F4**]

NEW SEARCH.   To perform another search using the *Find* dialog box you need to first click the *New Search* button. The command will remove the results of the previous search prior to your entering a new find request. Try this to locate the PAD1 file on your data disk:

1 **Click the** *New Search* **button**

 2 **Click the "▼" button of the** *Look in* **drop-down box**

 3 **Click** *3½ Floppy (A:)* **in the** *Look in* **drop-down list**

4 **Click the** *Named* **drop-down box to place the insertion point there**

(Remember, the insertion point is a vertical blinking line that indicates when the next character you type will appear.)

 **5** **Type** **PAD1** **in the** *Find* **text box**

6 **Click the** *Find Now* **button**   [↵]

The results of your search should appear at the bottom of the dialog box. If desired, you can now open the document by double-clicking it. For now,

 7 **Close the** *Find* **dialog box**

LOOKING IN A FOLDER

The *Drive* and *Folder* icons can be used to open Folder windows. **Folder windows** display the contents of a disk (or other storage media) or folders within the disk. Remember, a disk is also considered a folder and will be referred to as the *main folder.*

FOLDER DISPLAY OPTIONS.   The My Computer program offers two ways to browse through folders: separate windows for each folder (the default) or a single window that changes to display each folder that is opened. The text assumes that your system is set to the default browse option. Try this to open the Folder window that displays your data disk's main contents:

STEPS

1. If needed, insert your data disk into Drive A

2. Double-click the *3½ Floppy (A:)* drive icon

3. If needed, click the *Maximize* button of the 3½ Floppy (A:) window

A 3½ Floppy (A:) window should appear maximized as in Figure WIN2-4a. (The contents of your window may differ.) As you will shortly see, Folder windows can also perform a variety of file management operations.
   To check the browse settings of My Computer,

4. Click *View, Options* for its dialog box

Folder |
5. If needed, click the *Folder* tab

6. If the *Browse folders using a separate window for each folder* option is selected (black dot in option circle), click the *Cancel* button and skip Step 7

7. If the *Browse folders using a separate window for each folder* option is not selected, click it, and then click *OK*

Tip: When viewing folders through a single window that changes to display each folder that is opened, you can click the *Up One Level* (see left margin for button) toolbar button to go back one level. The Toolbar must, of course, be on.

TOOLBAR.   Like other Windows programs, many menu commands can be accessed through a toolbar. Currently, the My Computer toolbar may not be displayed in your window. If needed, to display the toolbar,

STEPS

1. Click *View, Toolbar*

FIGURE WIN2-4 ■ THE 3½″ FLOPPY (A:) WINDOW

(a) The 3½″ floppy (A:) window is the main folder window of your data disk. (b) Clicking *View, Toolbar* will turn on/off the toolbar. This toolbar is the same for all folder windows, the My Computer window, and the Explorer window. Pointing to a toolbar button displays its title.

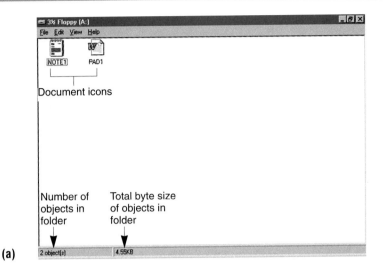

(a)

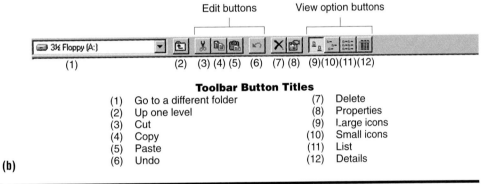

(b)

Toolbar Button Titles			
(1)	Go to a different folder	(7)	Delete
(2)	Up one level	(8)	Properties
(3)	Cut	(9)	Large icons
(4)	Copy	(10)	Small icons
(5)	Paste	(11)	List
(6)	Undo	(12)	Details

A toolbar similar to Figure WIN2-4b should appear below your menu bar. The Toolbar command (*View* menu) can be used to turn on/off any folder window's toolbar. This toolbar contains the same features in the My Computer window, Folder windows, and the Explorer window. As with many buttons and drop-down boxes in the Windows environment, pointing to a toolbar item will display its title.

THE STATUS BAR.   The status bar (bottom of window) displays the number of objects (*drive, file,* and *folder* icons) in the workspace and the amount of bytes that those objects occupy on the disk. (The objects and bytes information in your window may differ.) All items in a folder or the My Computer window are referred to as *objects.* The status bar is also used for other messages when using this program. For example, if you open a pull-down menu and point to any of its choices, a brief description of its function will appear in the status bar. Try this:

> **1** Click _View_ for its drop-down menu   [**Alt** + **V**]

> **2** Point to (do not click) _Details_   [Do not press **D** ; use arrow keys]

The message "Displays information about each item in the window." appears in the status bar.

As you use this program or any other program that has a status bar, you will find its brief messages helpful.

VIEWING OPTIONS

The workspace in a Folder window (or My Computer window) can be adjusted to display the icons in a smaller size, in a list, and with more or less detail. These _View_ options are available through the _View_ menu or toolbar.

> **1** If needed, click _View, Toolbar_ to turn it on

As with many buttons and drop-down boxes in the Windows environment, pointing to a toolbar item will display its title. For example,

> **2** Point to the last toolbar button on the right and wait (do not click)

The title "Details" should appear.

> **3** Either click the _Details_ toolbar button or click _View, Details_ (_Menu_ bar)

Your Folder window should now display detailed information on each object similar to Figure WIN2-5a. A _Details bar_ appears below the toolbar. Each object's name, size, type, and date and time last modified or created is displayed below this button bar.

Any _Details bar_ buttons can be used to switch the display order from ascending to descending (or vice versa) by clicking the button's title. For example,

Name

> **4** Click the _Name_ button on the Details bar

Your objects are now displayed in a reverse alphabetical order by name. To return the display to the original ascending order,

> **5** Click the _Name_ button again

The _Size_ button will reverse the order of the display by object size, the _Type_ button by object document type, and the _Modified_ button by object date and time.

Now try a few other view options:

FIGURE WIN2-5 ■ VIEW OPTIONS

(a) The *Details view* option displays each object's name, size, type, and date and time created or last modified.
(b) The *List view* option lists objects in vertical columns.
(c) The *Small Icons view* option displays objects as small icons in horizontal rows.
(d) The *Large Icons view* option (the default) displays objects as large icons in horizontal rows.

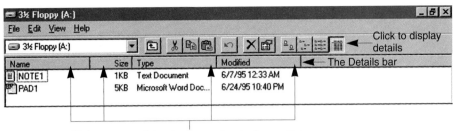

Click to reverse list order (ascending to descending or vice versa) by clicking the button's title.

(a)

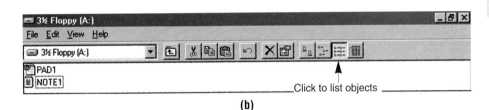

Click to list objects

(b)

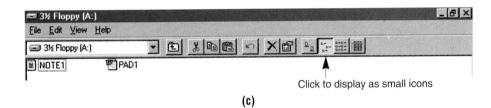

Click to display as small icons

(c)

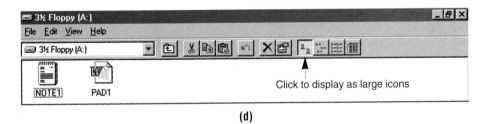

Click to display as large icons

(d)

 6 Click **View, List** to list objects vertically as small icons as in Figure WIN2-5b

 7 Click **View, Small Icons** to display objects as small icons horizontally as in Figure WIN2-5c

 8 Click **View, Large Icons** to return objects to their original size as in Figure WIN2-5d

View menu options are listed and described in Figure WIN2-6. More advanced *View* options such as *Folder browsing* options, displaying hidden files and MS-DOS file extensions, and file association settings can be controlled by using the *Options* dialog box. Refer to the dialog box's on-line help for these operations.

WIN

FIGURE WIN2-6 ■ THE *VIEW* MENU

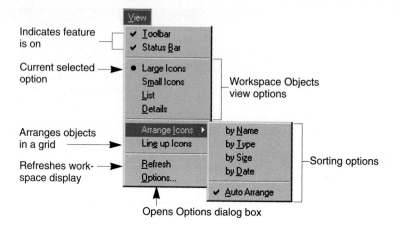

Indicates feature is on

Current selected option

Workspace Objects view options

Arranges objects in a grid

Refreshes workspace display

Sorting options

Opens Options dialog box

|X| 9 **Close the 3½ Floppy window**

|X| 10 **Close the My Computer window**

☑ **CHECKPOINT**

✓ Launch My Computer and describe the components of its workspace.
✓ Open a window displaying the contents of your hard-disk drive or network drive.
✓ Turn on the toolbar and change the display to show all details.
✓ Describe the meaning of the details of the first object in the window.
✓ Reset the display to large icons and close the drive and My Computer windows.

MANAGING YOUR FILES

My Computer can be used to perform a variety of file management tasks. **File management** involves organizing and maintaining files (including folders) within your computer environment. This section explores some of the fundamental file management commands. First, you will learn how to create new folders in the main folder and then within other folders. This allows you to group your documents into subgroups (subfolders) within the same disk. Next, you will examine and apply single and multiple selection techniques to open files and folders from a Folder window. You will then practice several object-renaming techniques and print a selection.

STEPS

1 **Start Windows and remove the "Welcome" window if necessary**

2 **Launch My Computer**

3 **Insert your data disk into Drive A if needed**

4 **Double-click the *3½ Floppy (A:)* drive icon**

5 **Click the *Maximize* button of the *3½Floppy (A:)***

FOLDERS

Folders are used to group files. A *Folder* icon is used to represent each folder created on a disk. Double-clicking a *Drive* icon in the My Computer window opens a Folder window that displays the main contents of the disk in its drive. (Remember, this text also refers to this folder as the *main folder*.)

Folders can also be created within folders. Double-clicking a folder within a Folder window displays its contents in another Folder window.

CREATING A NEW FOLDER.   To create the folders *Database, WIN 95, Word Processing,* and *Spreadsheets* as in Figure WIN2-7:

1 **Click *File* for its menu as in Figure WIN2-8a**

This *File* menu appears when no objects are selected (marked) in the window.

2 **Point to *New* for its submenu and then click *Folder***

A new folder appears in the 3½ Floppy window. Note that its title is highlighted, indicating that whatever you enter next will type over the text in the highlighted area.

3 **Type** Database **and then press** ↵

4 **Click *File* for its menu as in Figure WIN2-8b**

Tip: If desired, pressing an arrow key when text is highlighted (selected) will remove the highlight.

FIGURE WIN2-7 ■ CREATING FOLDERS

You can use the *File* menu or the workspace *Shortcut* menu to create new folders.

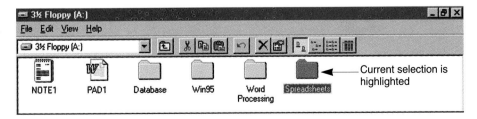

Current selection is highlighted

FIGURE WIN2-8 ■ *FILE* **MENUS AND** *WORKSPACE SHORTCUT* **MENU**

(a) The *File* menu when no objects are selected.
(b) The *File* menu when at least one object is selected.
(c) The *Workspace Shortcut* menu.

(a)

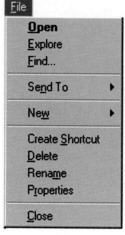

(b)

(c)

This *File* menu appears when at least one object is selected in the window's workspace. It offers a few more commands that you can invoke on the selected object(s). Currently, the *Database* folder is selected (notice that its title and icon are highlighted).

5 **Point to *New*, and then click *Folder* to create another new folder**

6 **Type** WIN 95 **and then press** ↵

Now try using a *Shortcut* menu to create the next folder.

7 **Right-click an empty area of the 3½ Floppy window's workspace for its *Shortcut* menu as in Figure WIN2-8c**

8 **Point to *New*, and then click *Folder* to create another new folder**

9 **Type** Word Processing **and then press** ↵

10 **Create the *Spreadsheets* folder using either the *File* menu or a *Shortcut* menu**

These new *Folder* icons should now occupy the workspace of the 3½ Floppy window similar to Figure WIN2-7. Again, your workspace may differ depending on the objects you have on your disk.

FOLDERS WITHIN FOLDERS.   To create a subfolder (folder within a folder), first open the folder that you would like to contain the subfolder. Opening a folder displays its contents in a window. You will now create the folders *Roster* and *Consult* within the *Database* folder as in Figure WIN2-9a.

FIGURE WIN2-9 ■ CREATING FOLDERS WITHIN FOLDERS

(a) and (b) To create a folder within a folder, first open the folder that is to contain the subfolder(s) and then use the *File* menu or *Shortcut* menu to create the subfolders.

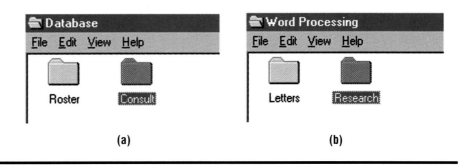

(a)   (b)

WIN

Database

1 **Double-click the *Database* folder**

> **Tip: You can also open a folder by clicking it and then clicking *File*, *Open* or by right-clicking it and then clicking *Open*.**

2 **Click the *Maximize* button of the Database window**

The Database window opens with a blank workspace. This window operates the same way as any other Folder window.

3 **Click *File*, point to *New*, and then click *Folder***

4 **Type Roster and then press ↵**

Now use the workspace *Shortcut* menu to create the folder *Consult.*

5 **Right-click an empty area of the Database window's workspace for its *Shortcut* menu**

6 **Point to *New* and then click *Folder***

7 **Type Consult and then press ↵**

The new folders in the Database window should now resemble Figure WIN2-9a.

8 **Close the Database window**

Next, you will create the folders *Letters* and *Research* in the Word Processing folder as in Figure WIN2-9b.

Word
Processing

9 Double-click the *Word Processing* folder and then maximize it

10 Create the folders *Letters* and *Research* within the Word Processing folder

11 Close the Word Processing window

Before continuing, rearrange the objects in alphabetical order by name.

12 Click *View*, point to *Arrange Icon* for its submenu

The *Arrange Icon* submenu has a variety of sorting options. For now,

13 Click *by Name* to rearrange icons in alphabetical order

Note that Windows displays folder icons first.

DOCUMENT APPROACH

To create a new saved document without first launching its program, use the *New* submenu that you just used to create folders. (Note: The related program or document type must be listed in the submenu.) Try this to create a new text (Notepad) document:

STEPS

BY *SHORTCUT* MENU

1 Right-click an empty area of the work-space for its *Shortcut* menu

2 Point to *New* and then click *Text Document*

BY *FILE* MENU

1 Click *File*

A *New Text Document* icon appears in the 3½ Floppy window workspace. This document is already saved, however, it is blank. To name this document NOTE2 and then open it,

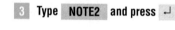

3 Type NOTE2 and press ↵

NOTE2

4 Double-click the *NOTE2* icon

Note that text documents generally open in the Notepad program. Next you will enter the following text and then save and close the document.

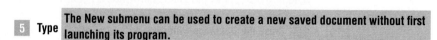

5 Type The New submenu can be used to create a new saved document without first launching its program.

6 Click *File*, *Save*

7 Close the Notepad window

SELECTING MULTIPLE FILES

Selecting, as defined earlier, is the process of marking items. Once marked, you can invoke a variety of commands on them. Remember, file selection techniques apply to both files and folders. To select a file, simply click it. To select additional files, press and hold the Ctrl key while clicking each additional file (or other objects). You may also select files in a block. A **block** is a set of contiguous files (or other objects). To select a block of files, click the first file and then press and hold the Shift key while clicking the last file in the block. A block can be selected alone or with other selected files. Figure WIN2-10 summarizes object selection techniques used in the next section.

> Tip: Clicking *Edit, Invert Selection* reverses the items selected with those that are not. Clicking *Edit, Select All* or press Ctrl + A selects all files in a window.

OPENING FILES

In general, a document created and saved with a Window program is automatically **associated** (has a special connection) to its program. As such, you directly open such documents

FIGURE WIN2-10 ■ OBJECT SELECTION TECHNIQUES

(a) Selecting one object.
(b) Selecting a group of objects.
(c) Selecting a block of objects.

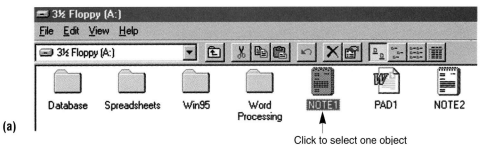

(a)

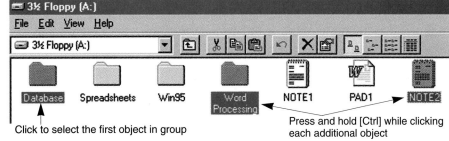

(b)

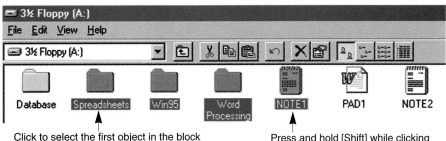

(c)

(along with their programs) from a Folder window without first launching their programs. This method provides quicker access to your document if you know the folder in which it was stored. The open techniques discussed in this section can be applied to single or multiple files (a group or block). Files include documents, programs, and folders. Like opening a folder, opening a document or launching a program involves double-clicking its icon or using its *Shortcut* menu or the *File* menu. To open (or launch) folders or multiple documents and programs, select their icons and then click <u>*File*</u>, <u>*Open*</u> (from the menu bar).

SINGLE FILE.   The quickest way to open any object in a window is to double-click it. However, you can also use the object's *Shortcut* menu or the *File* menu. To open the NOTE1 document using either of these techniques:

STEPS

NOTE1

BY *SHORTCUT* MENU

1 **Right click *NOTE1***

2 **Click *Open***

BY *FILE* MENU

1 **Click the *NOTE1* icon to select it as in Figure WIN2-10a**

2 **Click *File*, *Open***

Your NOTE1 document now appears in the Notepad window (its program).

 3 **Close Notepad**

GROUP OF FILES.   To open (or launch) a group of files at once, first select the group and then use the Open command of the *File* menu. Try this to open the *Database* folder, *Word Processing* folder, and NOTE2 document.

STEPS

Database

1 **Click the *Database* folder (the first object in the group)**

2 **Press and hold** Ctrl **while clicking the *Word Processing* folder icon and then the *NOTE2* file icon**

Your selected group should resemble Figure WIN2-10b.

 3 **Click *File*, *Open* to open the objects**   [↵]

All three objects are now open.

 4 **Close the Database, Word Processing, and NOTE2 (Notepad) windows**

BLOCK OF FILES.   Like opening a group of files, opening a block of files involves first selecting the block and then clicking *File, Open.* To open the *Spreadsheet, Win95, Word Processing* folders, and NOTE1 document:

Spreadsheets

1 Click the *Spreadsheets* folder icon

2 Press and hold   Shift   while clicking the *NOTE1* icon

Your block selection should resemble Figure WIN2-10c. Now, to open the objects,

3 Click *File, Open*   [↵]

All four objects should now be open on your screen.

4 Close all windows except the My Computer and 3½ Floppy windows

RENAMING FILES

Any file or folder can be easily renamed using the same techniques. You can use an object's *Shortcut* menu or *File* menu to rename it. When using the *File* menu, you must first select the object. Try this to rename the *Spreadsheets* folder to *Worksheets:*

BY *SHORTCUT* MENU	BY *FILE* MENU
Spreadsheets **1** Right-click the *Spreadsheets* folder icon for its *Shortcut* menu	**1** Click the *Spreadsheets* folder icon to se-lect it
2 Click *Rename*	**2** Click *File, Rename*

Note that the folder's title is now highlighted (selected). The first alphanumeric character you type will delete the old title.

3 Type   Worksheets   and then press ↵

A more direct technique to rename an object is to click its title after it has been selected. Try this to change the *Win95* folder to *Windows 95:*

Win95

4 Click the *Win95* folder icon to select it

5 Click the *Win95* title

The folder's title is now selected and ready to be changed.

WIN

FIGURE WIN2-11 ■ RENAMING FILES

The *Spreadsheet* and *Win95* folders have been renamed *Worksheet* and *Windows 95*, respectively.

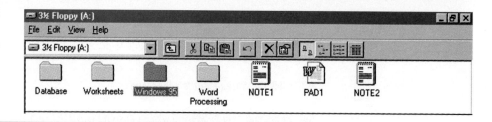

6 Type   Windows 95   and then press ↵

The icons in your 3½ Floppy window should resemble Figure WIN2-11.

PRINTING FILES

Document files can be printed using a Folder window. Simply select the desired file icon(s) and then invoke the print command from the *File* menu. Try this to print the NOTE1 and NOTE2 documents:

STEPS

1 Turn on your printer

NOTE1

2 Click the *NOTE1* file icon to select it

3 Press and hold   Ctrl   while clicking the *NOTE2* document to select it

4 Click *File*, *Print*

As you wait, Windows first opens each document with its program, prints them, and then closes the document and its program.

To print a single document, it is generally quicker to use its *Shortcut* menu. For example, to print the NOTE2 document,

STEPS

NOTE2

1 Right click the *NOTE2* icon for its *Shortcut* menu

2 Click *Print*

3 Close all windows

☑ CHECKPOINT

  ✓ Launch My Computer and open the 3½ Floppy window.
  ✓ Print the NOTE1 document.
  ✓ Create a folder with your name on it.
  ✓ Open the folder and create two more folders named *Computers* and *Accounting*.
  ✓ Rename the *Accounting* folder *Art*. Close all windows.

SHARING AND REMOVING YOUR FILES

Sharing files involves copying or moving documents, programs, and folders within the same folder or between folders. Remember, *copying* is the process of duplicating a selection into a new location and *moving* relocates it there. In Windows, you can also create an icon (called a **Shortcut icon**) that has a link (special connection) to the original file or folder. This allows you to open the original document or folder or to launch the original program from the desktop or another folder.

    After practicing sharing techniques you will learn how to use the Undo command to undo your last action, and the Delete command to remove unwanted files. You will then learn about Windows **Recycle Bin,** a program that stores references to files deleted from other places on your hard disk and desktop.

STEPS

1 **If needed, start Windows and remove the "Welcome" screen**

2 **Launch My Computer**

3 **Insert your data disk into Drive A**

4 **Double-click the *3½ Floppy (A:)* drive icon for its Folder window**

5 **If needed, maximize the window and turn on the toolbar (*View*, *Toolbar*)**

6 **Click *View*, point to *Arrange Icons*, and then click *by Name* to sort by name**

COPYING AND MOVING

The exercises in this section explore a variety of techniques used to copy or move files and folders. They include using the Copy, Cut, and Paste commands of the *Edit* menu or *Shortcut* menus as well as drag and drop techniques. The folder from which a selection is copied or cut (moved) will be called the *source folder*. The folder in which it is

FIGURE WIN2-12 ■ **SHARING FILES SUMMARY**

The following techniques assume that you have already launched My Computer and your source folder is opened.

With the Same Folder

Edit Menu	Drag and Drop
1. Select objects 2. Click *Edit, Cut* (to move), or *Copy* 3. Click *Edit, Paste*	1. Select the objects 2. Press and hold [Ctrl] while dragging and dropping the selection to copy it to a new location in the workspace (or simply drag and drop to move)

Between Folders in the Same Disk

Edit Menu	Drag and Drop
1. Select objects 2. Click *Edit, Cut* (to move), or *Copy* 3. Double-click the destination folder icon to open it 4. Click *Edit, Paste*	1. Open the destination folder window 2. Right-click an empty area of the taskbar for its *Shortcut* menu, and then click *Minimize All Windows* 3. Click the taskbar buttons of the source and destination folder windows 4. Right-click an empty area of the taskbar, and then click *Tile Vertically* 5. Select the objects 6. Press and hold [Ctrl] while dragging and dropping the selection from its source to its destination folder to copy (or simply drag and drop to move)

Between Folders of Different Disks

Edit Menu	Drag and Drop
1. Select objects 2. Click *Edit, Cut* (to move), or *Copy* 3. Click the *My Computer* taskbar button to switch to it 4. Open the destination folder 5. Click *Edit, Paste*	1. Click the *My Computer* taskbar button to switch to it 2. Open destination folder window 3. Right-click an empty area of the taskbar for its *Shortcut* menu, and then click *Minimize All Windows* 4. Click the taskbar buttons of the source and destination folder windows 5. Right-click an empty area of the taskbar, and then click *Tile Vertically* 6. Select objects 7. Drag and drop the selection from its source to its destination folder to copy (or press and hold [Alt] while dragging and dropping to move)

pasted (placed) in will be called the *destination folder*. Figure WIN2-12 presents a summary of sharing techniques. You should try all the techniques and then use the one that feels most comfortable to you.

WITHIN THE SAME FOLDER.   To copy or move a selection of files (and folders) within the same folder, simply copy it to the Clipboard and then paste it into your destination folder. When copying or moving within the same folder, the source and destination folders are the same.

To create a copy of the NOTE1 document on the same disk as in Figure WIN2-13,

NOTE1

1   Click the *NOTE1* icon to select it

2   Click *Edit, Copy*   [**Ctrl** + **C**]

(To move the selection, click *Cut* (or **Ctrl** + **X**), instead of *Copy* (or **Ctrl** + **C**) in Step 2.) The selection is now copied to the Clipboard for future pasting. (The Cut command moves the selection onto the Clipboard.) To paste (copy the selection from the Clipboard) it within the workspace of the 3½ Floppy window,

3   Click *Edit, Paste*   [**Ctrl** + **V**]

A document icon appears titled *Copy of NOTE1*, as in Figure WIN2-13. At this point you can rename the copy if desired.

BETWEEN FOLDERS.   A selection of files can also be copied or moved to another folder using the Copy and Paste commands. The folder can be within the same disk or in another disk. The only difference is that the destination folder is on another disk. Only copying or moving files between folders on the same disk is demonstrated. See Figure WIN2-12 for procedures to share files between folders of different disks.

To copy the *Windows 95* folder, NOTE1, and PAD1 documents to the *Letters* folder within the *Word Processing* folder as in Figure WIN2-14:

Windows 95

1   Click the *Windows 95* folder to select it

FIGURE WIN2-13 ■ COPYING WITHIN THE SAME FOLDER

When copying within the same folder, Windows adds the words "Copy of" before the copied file's name.

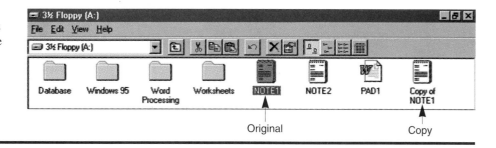

These objects have been copied from the main folder to the Letters subfolder.

---

2 Press and hold ☐Ctrl☐ while clicking the *NOTE1* and then the *PAD1* icons to select them

(Remember, pressing and holding the Ctrl key while clicking allows you to select additional icons.)

 3 Click *Edit, Copy*

 (To move the selection, click *Cut* (or ☐Ctrl☐ + ☐X☐), instead of *Copy* (or ☐Ctrl☐ + ☐C☐) in Step 2.)

Word
Processing
4 Double-click the *Word Processing* folder to open its window

5 If desired, click *View, Toolbar*

BY *SHORTCUT* MENU   **BY *EDIT* MENU**

Letters
6 Right-click the *Letters* folder for its *Shortcut* menu

7 Click *Paste*

6 Double-click the *Letters* folder to open its window

The folder must be open to paste by the *Edit* menu. Menu bar or Toolbar commands normally only affect the current window.

7 Click *Edit, Paste*   [☐Ctrl☐ + ☐V☐]

The selection is now copied to the Letters directory. If you used the *Shortcut* menu to paste, you will need to perform Step 8 to view the copies in the *Letters* folder.

Letters
8 If needed, double-click the *Letters* folder to open it

The contents of your Letters window should resemble Figure WIN2-14 (your window size may differ). Note that the selection has been copied with its original name. Windows uses the original file or folder name when copying to a different folder.

 9 **Close the Letters and Word Processing windows**

BY DRAGGING AND DROPPING.   Drag and drop techniques involve copying or moving a selection by moving your pointer (with the selection) to a new location, sometimes with the use of other keys. In the next exercise you will copy a block of objects from your main folder (the 3½ Floppy window) to the *Consult* folder using the drag and drop technique. Remember, a *block* is a contiguous set of selected objects. The block you will copy to the *Consult* folder begins with the *Worksheets* folder icon and ends with the *NOTE1* file icon. When copied, it should appear in the Consult folder window as in Figure WIN2-15:

STEPS

1 **Open your 3½ Floppy window, if needed**

2 **Double-click the *Database* folder icon**

Database

Note that the source folder and destination folder windows must be in view to use the drag and drop technique. To display only the 3½ Floppy (source folder) and Database (destination folder) windows without closing the My Computer window,

3 **Right-click an empty space in the taskbar for its *Shortcut* menu (use the space between the *Database* taskbar button and the time message area)**

4 **Click *Minimize All Windows* to reduce them to their taskbar buttons**

FIGURE WIN2-15 ■ DRAGGING AND DROPPING

These objects were copied from the main folder by pressing and holding the Ctrl key while dragging and dropping.

Remember, minimized windows are still running, but at a minimum state. This allows you to access them quickly without relaunching or opening. It also conserves system memory (RAM), which will make your system operate more efficiently. Now open only the 3½ Floppy and Database windows and then horizontally tile them as in Figure WIN2-16.

5 Click the *3½ Floppy (A:)* taskbar button to open its window

🖳 3½ Floppy (A:)

6 Click the *Database* taskbar button to open its window

🖳 Database

7 Right-click an empty area of the taskbar for its *Shortcut* menu and then click *Tile Horizontally*

Your screen should resemble Figure WIN2-16. Both source and destination are in view.

Worksheets

8 Click the *Worksheets* folder icon (the first object in the block)

9 Press and hold **Shift** while clicking the *NOTE1* icon (the last object in the block)

(To select large objects in a block, they must be displayed horizontally.)

10 Point to any object in the selection

FIGURE WIN2-16 ■ TILING SOURCE AND DESTINATION FOLDERS

The taskbar *Shortcut* menu can be used to tile the source and destination folders to better view them in drag and drop sharing operations.

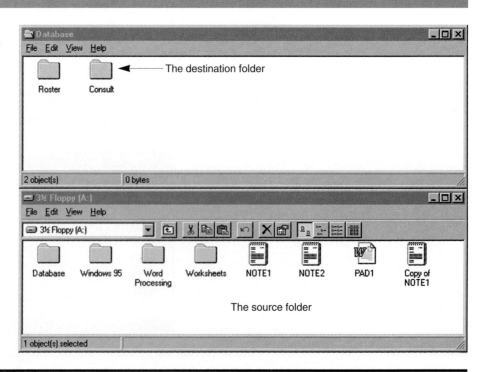

11 **Press and hold** **Ctrl** **while dragging the selection to the** *Consult* **folder icon**

(To move instead of copy, do not press and hold the Ctrl key while dragging in Step 11.)

Consult

12 **Drop the selection into the** *Consult* **folder icon**

13 **Double-click the** *Consult* **folder icon to display its content as in Figure WIN2-15.**

☒ **14** **Close all windows**

COPYING AN ENTIRE DISK.   The *Copy Disk* dialog box (Figure WIN2-17) can be used to copy the contents of an entire disk to another disk. It is accessible through the **Copy Disk** command of the *My Computer* file menu (after selecting the desired drive icon) or the desired drive icon's *Shortcut* menu. When using this command, the Copy from disk must be the same size and capacity as the Copy to disk. For example, if the original disk is a 3½″ 1.44MB disk, the Copy to disk must also be a 3½″ 1.44MB disk.

SENDING FILES.   The **Send to** submenu, as in Figure WIN2-18, can be used to copy a selection to another disk, fax, or electronic mail. To use this feature, simply select the items that you desire to send, click *File,* point to *Send to,* and click the desired destination option. The Send to menu can be customized to include destinations other than the default options. It is also available through *Shortcut* menus. Refer to your on-line help for these procedures.

CREATING A SHORTCUT

A *Shortcut icon* can be created that has a dynamic link to its original document, program, or folder. This link allows you to use the *Shortcut* icon to open (launch) the file or folder it represents from any folder or the desktop.

FIGURE WIN2-17 ■ THE *COPY DISK* **DIALOG BOX**

The *Copy Disk* dialog box can be used to copy the entire contents of one disk to another of the same capacity.

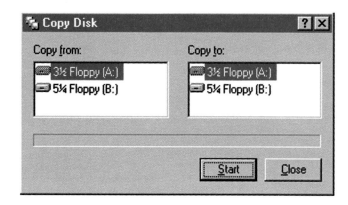

FIGURE WIN2-18 ■ **THE *SEND TO* SUBMENU**

The *Send to* menu is
available in the *File* menu
after a selection is made. It
can be used to send the
selection to any of its listed
destinations.

PLACING SHORTCUTS IN A FOLDER. To create shortcut icons for the *Windows 95* folder, place the *Copy of NOTE1* documents in the Worksheets folder as in Figure WIN2-19:

STEPS

1 **Launch My Computer**

2 **Insert your data disk and double-click the *3½ Floppy (A:)* drive icon**

Windows 95

3 **Click the *Windows 95* folder icon to select it**

4 **Press and hold Ctrl while clicking the *Copy of NOTE1* file icon to select it**

5 **Click *Edit, Copy*** [Ctrl + C]

FIGURE WIN2-19 ■ **CREATING SHORTCUTS**

To create a shortcut icon, use
the Copy and then the Paste
Shortcut commands.

Worksheets

6 Double-click the *Worksheets* folder to open it

7 Click *Edit, Paste Shortcut*

8 Click *View*, point to *Arrange Icons*, and then click by *Name*

Shortcut icons now appear in the Worksheets folder window as in Figure WIN2-19. You can use these icons to open the folder or files they represent from the Worksheet folder. Try this:

9 Double-click the *Copy of NOTE1* Shortcut icon to open it

10 Close the Copy of NOTE1 (Notepad) and Worksheets folder windows

WIN

PLACING SHORTCUTS ON THE DESKTOP.   If you are on a network, your system may not allow you to create a shortcut on the desktop. Check with your instructor before proceeding with the next steps.

To create a shortcut for the *Windows 95* folder on the desktop as in Figure WIN2-20,

STEPS

Windows 95

1 Click *Windows 95* to select it

2 Click *Edit, Copy*   **[Ctrl + C]**

3 Right-click an empty area of the taskbar for its *Shortcut* menu

4 Click *Minimize All Windows* for a better view of the desktop

5 Right click the area to the right of the *My Computer* icon (or any desired area) on the desktop

FIGURE WIN2-20 ■ CREATING A SHORTCUT ON THE DESKTOP

Once an object is copied to the Clipboard, it can also be pasted as a shortcut on the desktop. Simply right-click an empty area of the desktop and then click *Paste Shortcut.*

6 **Click** *Paste Shortcut*

Your *Shortcut* icons should now appear on your desktop (selected) similar to Figure WIN2-20. (The actual positions of your *Shortcut* icons may differ.) At this point, you can double-click the *Shortcut* icon to open its linked folder (or file). Unless deleted, *Shortcut* icons will appear on your desktop each time you start Windows. For now, to delete the *Shortcut* icon for the *Windows 95* folder:

7 **If needed, select the** *Windows 95* **folder's** *Shortcut* **icon on the desktop**

8 **Press**   **Delete**

9 **Click** *Yes*

> **Note: File deletion is discussed further under the "Deleting and Recycling" section of this chapter.**

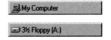

10 **Click the** *My Computer* **icon and then the** *3½ Floppy* **taskbar buttons to resize them to a window**

USING UNDO

Most Windows programs provide an **Undo** command that can be used to undo your last action. The My Computer program also provides an undo command. Try this:

STEPS

1 **Switch to the 3½ Floppy window (Click its title bar or any open area of the window.)**

2 **Copy the PAD1 document into the same window**

(Remember, right-click PAD1, click *Copy,* and then click *Edit, Paste.*) A copy of your PAD1 document now appears. To undo this action,

3 **Click** *Edit, Undo Copy*   [**Ctrl** + **Z**]

A *Confirm File Delete* dialog box appears asking "Are you sure you want to delete 'Copy of PAD1'?" For now,

4 **Click** *Yes*

The Undo command deletes the copy of PAD1.
    The Undo command is a handy tool, but it is limited as to the types of actions it will undo.

DELETING AND RECYCLING

Any selection in Windows can be deleted. The **Delete** command removes a selection from its current place and can be invoked from the *File* menu or an object's *Shortcut* menu. As seen earlier, you can also invoke the Delete command by simply pressing the Delete key. When deleting a selection from your hard disk or network disk, the file's reference is normally relocated to the *Recycle Bin* (a Windows program that stores file references as a result of invoking the Delete command) without actually deleting the file. Once there, you can either permanently delete the selection or restore it. Deleting a *Shortcut* icon will not affect the original file.

DELETING SELECTIONS   The process of deleting a selection from a data disk and hard disk is the same. Try this:

STEPS

1 **Select the *Windows 95* folder, *Worksheets* folder, and *Copy of NOTE1* file icons**

(Remember to press and hold the Ctrl key when selecting each additional icon.)

2 **Click *File, Delete***   [**Delete**]

A dialog box appears asking you to confirm the deletion. To delete these objects,

3 **Click *Yes***

Your 3½ Floppy window should appear as in Figure WIN2-21.

 4 **Close all windows**

> **Tip:** Deleting icons from the desktop requires using the Delete key or its *Shortcut* menu.

RECYCLING.   Selections deleted from a hard disk are removed from their folder, the desktop, or other location and relocated to the Recycle Bin. Once there, you can either

FIGURE WIN2-21 ■ DELETING FILES

The *Windows 95* folder, *Worksheets* folder, and *Copy of NOTE1* file icons have been deleted from the main folder.

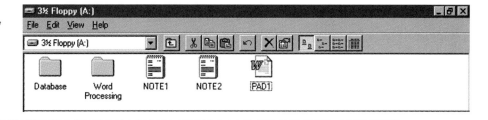

restore or permanently delete the files. See the Recycle Bin operations listed in Figure WIN2-22.

DELETED, BUT GONE FOREVER? A final note about deleting. When you delete a file, Windows does not really remove it from the disk. It simply replaces the first character in its filename with a special initial character. This character tells the system to ignore the file and use its space allocation, even though the file is still physically left on the disk. Although its name does not appear in a folder, the file's contents are not written over until another file is saved on the disk. This opens the possibility of *undeleting* files (even those deleted from the Recycle Bin). As long as you have not copied or saved another file on the disk, Windows has a utility program called Undelete to help you identify the deleted files and put them back in their original folders—in effect *undeleting* them. The Undelete (MWUNDEL) program is located in the Applications group on the *Programs* menu. Refer to your on-line help to use this program.

☑ **CHECKPOINT**

✓ Describe the different techniques that can be used to copy or move files.
✓ Launch My Computer and open the main folder window of your data disk.
✓ Copy all your files and folders into the folder with your name (created in the previous checkpoint.)

FIGURE WIN2-22 ■ RECYCLE BIN OPERATIONS

When invoking the Delete command to remove a file(s) from your hard-disk folder, the selection's reference is moved from its current position to the Recycle Bin. At this point, you can either restore or permanently delete the file(s) from the Recycle Bin.	
Restoring Files	**Deleting Files from the Recycle Bin**
1. If Needed, minimize all windows 2. Double-click the *Recycle Bin* icon 3. Select the desired file(s) to restore 4. Click *File, Restore* 5. Close the *Recycle Bin*	1. If needed, minimize all windows 2. Double-click the *Recycle Bin* icon 3. Select the desired file(s) to delete 4. Click *File, Delete*

Emptying the Recycle Bin

Because each file deleted from your hard-disk folder is automatically moved to the Recycle Bin, the quantity of files stored there can grow over time if not deleted. The Empty Recycle Bin command can be used to delete the bin's entire contents.

1. If needed, minimize all windows
2. Right-click the *Recycle Bin* icon
3. Click *Empty Recycle Bin*

Note: When deleting a folder from your hard-disk folder, the files deleted within the folder are listed individually in the Recycle Bin.

✓ Create a *Shortcut* icon for the folder with your name in your main folder and then close My Computer.
✓ Describe the Recycle Bin.

CONTROLLING YOUR ENVIRONMENT

You can adjust the default settings of most items in your Windows environment. **Default settings** are the normal settings of your environment. An item's **properties** include the way information and other attributes (characteristics) are displayed or set. The Change Properties command can alter most objects' default characteristics. The **Control Panel** contains tools to set various parts of your system, including adding and removing hardware drivers (programs that help a piece of hardware communicate with your computer), screen displays, fonts, and so forth. These tools are also in the form of *Properties* dialog boxes. Another folder that can be accessed through My Computer is called **Printers.** This folder allows you to add a new printer, switch printers (if you have installed more than one printer), and check and control the status of your current print jobs.

> **Tip:** As seen in Chapter 1, you can also use the *Settings* submenu (*Start* menu) to access the Control Panel, Printers program, and *Taskbar Properties* dialog box.

CHANGING PROPERTIES

You can view and adjust almost any object's properties in Windows. The quickest way to open an object's *Properties* dialog box is to right click it and then click *Properties*. To better understand this topic, you will examine a disk's properties, file and folder properties, and the taskbar and *Start* menu properties.

DISK PROPERTIES.   To examine the properties of a disk,

STEPS

1   **Start Windows and remove the "Welcome" screen if necessary**

2   **Launch My Computer**

3   **Insert your data disk into Drive A if needed**

4   **Right-click the *3½ Floppy* drive icon and then click *Properties***

A *3½ Floppy (A:) Properties* dialog box similar to Figure WIN2-23a should appear. It displays the name, type of disk, used and free space in bytes, and total capacity of the disk (your dialog box may differ). At this point you can change the label (name) of the disk. Try this:

5 In the *Label* text box type your last name (maximum of 11 characters without spaces)

6 Click the *Apply* button

The *Apply* button invokes your latest adjustment and keeps the dialog box open, whereas the *OK* button invokes your latest adjustments and exits the dialog box.

A *Disk's Properties* dialog box also offers a variety of diagnostic tools in its *Tools* tab. For example,

7 Click the *Tools* tab

The *Tools* tab should appear as in Figure WIN2-23b. Examine the options presented in the tab. At this point, you can launch any of these diagnostic programs by clicking their respective buttons. These diagnostic programs should be used as needed. For now,

8 Click the *Cancel* button to exit the dialog box

FILE AND FOLDER PROPERTIES. File and folder properties are similar. To illustrate their *Properties* dialog boxes,

STEPS

1 Double-click the *3½ Floppy (A:)* drive icon

FIGURE WIN2-23 ■ **THE *3½ FLOPPY (A:) PROPERTIES* DIALOG BOX**

(a) The *General* tab can be used to name (label) a disk. It also provides used/free space and total disk capacity information.
(b) The *Tools* tab can be used to launch diagnostic and backup programs.

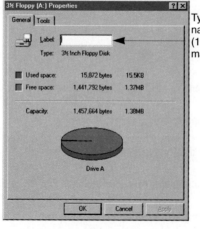

Type here to name disk (11 character maximum)

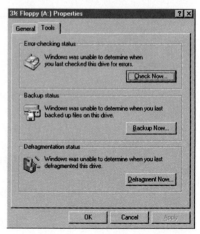

(a)

(b)

Word
Processing

2 Right-click the *Word Processing* folder and then click *Properties*

Your dialog box should appear similar to Figure WIN2-24a.

3 Click the *Cancel* button

NOTE1

4 Right-click the *NOTE1* icon and then click *Properties*

Your dialog box should appear as in Figure WIN2-24b. Note that the information in both dialog boxes (refer to Figures WIN2-24a and 24b) are similar. In addition, you may change the attributes of the folder or file to Read-only, Hidden, Archive, or System (if available). The *Read-only* check box will protect a folder or file from being written on. The *Hidden* check box will hide the folder or file from the current Folder window display. The *Archive* check box will provide a backup of the folder or file, and the *System* check box will save the file as a systems file. Clicking an empty check box places a "✓" in it, indicating that the feature is on. Clicking it again will turn the feature off.

5 5. Close all windows

TASKBAR AND START MENU PROPERTIES.   The *Taskbar Properties* dialog box can be used to change the properties of the taskbar and the *Start Menu Programs* menu.

STEPS

1 Right-click an empty area of the taskbar and then click *Properties*

FIGURE WIN2-24 ■ *FOLDERS* AND *FILE PROPERTIES* DIALOG BOXES

(a) The *Word Processing Folder Properties* dialog box.
(b) The *NOTE1 File Properties* dialog box.

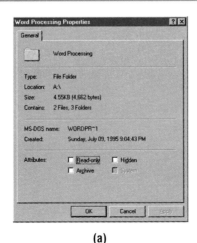

(a)   (b)

Your *Taskbar Properties* dialog box should appear as in Figure WIN2-25a. It has two tabs: *Taskbar Options* and *Start Menu Programs.* As with any check box a "✓" in the box indicates that a feature is on. For example, the *Always on top* and *Show Clock* check boxes each have "✓". These are the default settings. To turn a feature on or off, simply click its check box.

2 **Click the *Start Menu Programs* tab**

As in Figure WIN2-25b, you can use this tab to add, remove, or edit programs from the *Programs* menu of the *Start* menu. If you desire, you can use this tab to customize your *Programs* menu. You can also use this tab to clear the contents of the *Documents* submenu. Remember, the *Documents* submenu lists the last 15 documents you worked on. For now,

3 **Click *Cancel* to exit the dialog box**

RESIZING AND MOVING THE TASKBAR. The taskbar can be enlarged to display Window Taskbar buttons in two rows. To enlarge it, point to its top border until the pointer appears as a double-headed arrow, and then drag up. To resize the taskbar to its original size, drag the top border down. To move the taskbar, simply point to an open area along the bar, and then drag and drop it into its new location.

USING THE CONTROL PANEL

The Control Panel is a program that can be used to change the settings on your computer. It operates similarly to any Folder window. To launch the Control Panel as in Figure WIN2-26,

---

FIGURE WIN2-25 ■ **THE TASKBAR PROPERTIES**

(a) The *Taskbar Options* tab can be used to change the appearance of the taskbar.
(b) The *Start Menu Programs* tab can be used to add, remove, or edit the *Programs* submenu. It can also be used to clear the *Documents* submenu.

Indicates features are on (the default)

Indicates features are off

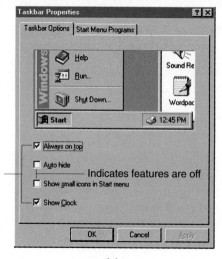

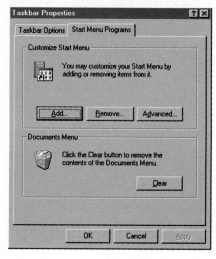

(a)   (b)

STEPS

1 **Launch My Computer**

Control Panel

2 **Double-click the** *Control Panel* **folder icon**

3 **If desired, click** *View, Toolbar* **to turn the toolbar on**

4 **Click the** *Maximize* **button of the Control Panel window**

> **Tip: The Control Panel can also be opened by clicking the** *Start* **button, pointing to** *Settings*, **and then clicking** *Control Panel*.

The *Control Panel* folder should appear as in Figure WIN2-26. Most icons in this window open to other windows that allow you to set the feature that you desire.

To better understand changing system settings, the following exercises provide procedures to change your system's date and time, alter its screen display, and add new hardware.

CHANGING DATE AND TIME.   To change your system's date and time,

STEPS

1 **Double-click the** *Date/Time* **icon**

FIGURE WIN2-26 ■ THE CONTROL PANEL

The Control Panel can be used to adjust the settings on a system.

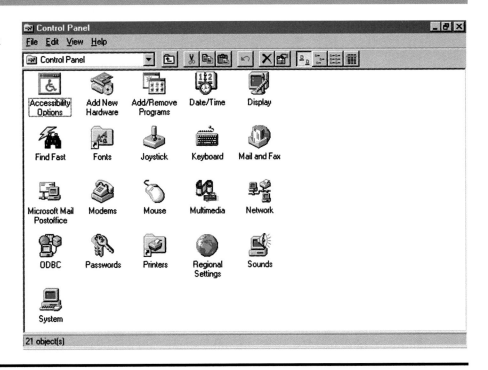

The *Date/Time Properties* dialog box should appear as in Figure WIN2-27. Your date and time will differ. This dialog box can be used to adjust your system's date and time if needed. For now,

2 **Click the *Cancel* button**

> **Tip: To access this dialog box quickly, double-click the time message at the right side of the taskbar.**

DISPLAY OPTIONS. Four screen display properties can be set through the *Display Properties* dialog box. They include Background, Screen Saver, Appearance, and Settings. Background changes involve placing or replacing an image as the background screen of your desktop. Screen savers help prevent the "burning in" of a frequently used program's image on your monitor's screen. Appearance changes involve setting the color of items displayed in Windows. Settings choices pertain to the quality of the color and resolution of all displays in Windows. Each property has its own tab in the *Display Properties* dialog box. Only the *Background* tab is demonstrated next. Other tabs operate similarly. If you are operating your own computer, you may desire to use this dialog box to customize your screen displays. Check with your instructor before performing the next step.

STEPS

Display

1 **Double-click the *Display* icon**

Your dialog box should appear similar to Figure WIN2-28. The *Background* tab allows you to place a pattern or wallpaper as the background display of your desktop. Note that the default setting is "None." Your settings may differ.

FIGURE WIN2-27 ■ THE *DATE/TIME PROPERTIES* DIALOG BOX

This dialog box is used to adjust the system's date and time.

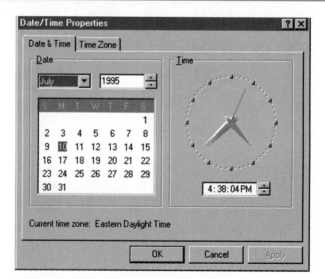

Like all tabs in this dialog box, the top portion displays a sample of the current setting section and the bottom portion contains the options to change the current settings. If this is your own computer, you can use the Background tab to change the desktop's appearance. Try this:

2 If needed, click *None* in the *Pattern* list box

3 Click *Arches* (or any other desired wallpaper) in the *Wallpaper* list box

Depending on your display settings (below the *Browse* button), a picture of an arch (the Center display option, which is the default), as in Figure WIN2-29a, or a full screen of arches (the Tile display option), as in Figure WIN2-29b, should appear in the display area (top portion) of the tab. If you selected a different wallpaper in Step 3, its picture should be displayed. You can place any of the available patterns or wallpaper as your desktop's background or even create your own. For now, cancel your selection:

4 Click the *Cancel* button to return to previous settings

ADDING NEW HARDWARE.   In the spirit of "plug and play," which is a move to simplify new hardware installation, Windows has developed the *New Hardware* wizard. A **wizard** is a program that helps make complicated tasks easier. **Plug and play** is the idea of simply plugging new hardware into your system and playing with (using) it immediately. Although Windows does not provide a 100 percent Plug-and-Play environment, the New Hardware wizard will make the installation of many hardware components simpler.

FIGURE WIN2-28 ■ THE *DISPLAY PROPERTIES* DIALOG BOX

This dialog box can be used to set the background screen, turn the Screen Saver program on and off, and set the Screen Saver program.

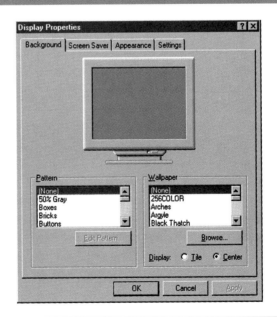

FIGURE WIN2-29 ■ **CHANGING BACKGROUND DISPLAYS**

(a) The Center Arches wallpaper display as it will appear on your desktop background if the *OK* or *Apply* button is clicked. (b) The Tile Arches wallpaper display will fill the desktop background if selected and applied.

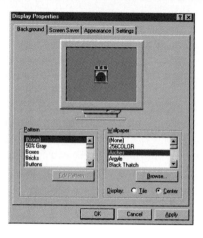

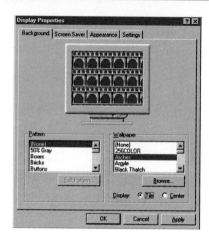

(a)

(b)

To use the New Hardware wizard, simply install your hardware with the power off, and then start Windows, launch My Computer, open the Control Panel, and then open the *Add New Hardware* icon. Next follow the New Hardware wizard instructions to complete the installation process.

USING PRINTERS

The *Printers* program is used to add a new printer to your system, switch the default printer, or view or control the status of current print jobs. A print job is simply documents sent to your printer to be printed. Windows allows you to send several print jobs to your printer. Although they are printed in the order sent, you can use the Printers program to change this.

STEPS

1 Close the Control Panel and launch My Computer, if needed

Printers

2 Double-click the *Printers* folder icon

> **Tip:** The *Printers* folder can also be opened by clicking the *Start* button, pointing to *Settings*, and then clicking *Printers*.

A Printers window should appear similar to Figure WIN2-30a. The printers available in your system may differ. Your window should also include an *Add Printer* icon, which can be used to launch the Add Printer wizard. This wizard helps you install a new printer into Windows after you have connected to your system. To see the status of your current print jobs,

3 Double-click your printer's icon

A window similar to Figure WIN2-30b should appear for your printer. The title bar displays the name of your printer. If you were printing any documents, they would first appear

FIGURE WIN2-30 ■ **THE *PRINTERS* FOLDER**

(a) The *Printers* folder can be used to add a new printer, set the default printer, or open a Printer's status window.

(b) The Printer's status window displays current print jobs and can also be used to control the jobs.

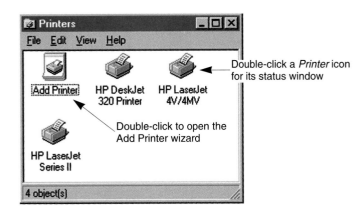

(a)

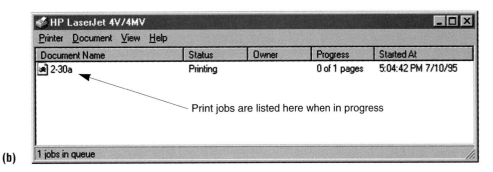

(b)

WIN

here. If you have several print jobs to process, they would be listed in this window with their current print status. Refer to your on-line help to learn more about operating this window. For now,

 4 **Close all windows**

 CHECKPOINT

✓ Define properties and default settings.
✓ Copy any document within your data disk and rename it as **Read Only.**
✓ Change the properties of the Read Only file to *Read Only.*
✓ Describe how to add a program to your *Start* menu
✓ Describe some of the settings that can be changed using the Control Panel.

UNDERSTANDING EXPLORER

Windows Explorer is another program that you can use to manage your computer. The components of your system are listed in a hierarchal tree. Selecting a folder (or other item) from the tree on the left side of the window will display its contents on the right side. Commands used with the My Computer program are also available through Explorer.

LAUNCHING EXPLORER

You can launch Explorer using the *Start* menu. Under this method, Explorer will open with its default display, which should be your hard disk. You can also launch Explorer from the My Computer (or a folder) window using a *Shortcut* menu, the *File* menu, or the toolbar. This method will directly display the contents of a desired disk or other folder.

The following exercises demonstrate both methods to launch Explorer.

BY THE *START* MENU.   When launching Explorer by using the *Start* menu, it will open with your hard disk selected on the left and its contents displayed on the right. This is the default view.

STEPS

1 Click the *Start* button   [**Ctrl** + **Esc**]

2 Point to *Programs* and then click *Windows Explorer*

Explorer should display the contents of your hard-disk drive (or default disk drive).

 3 Close Explorer

BY MY COMPUTER.   To launch Explorer by using My Computer,

STEPS

1 Right-click My Computer for its *Shortcut* menu

2 Click *Explore*

The Explorer window should now appear on your desktop.

 3 Close Explorer

Now, to launch Explorer through My Computer displaying the contents of your data disk,

STEPS

1 Launch My Computer and insert your data disk into Drive A, if needed

BY *SHORTCUT* MENU	BY *FILE* MENU

2 Right-click the *3½ Floppy (A:)* icon for its *Shortcut* menu

2 Click the *3½ Floppy (A:)* icon to select it

3 Click *Explore*

3 Click *File, Explore*

4 If needed, click the *Maximize* button   [**Alt** + **Spacebar** , **X**]

> **Note:** Although it is not necessary to maximize the Explorer window, a maximized window is visually easier to work with.

5 If desired, click *View, Toolbar* to turn it on

6 If needed, click *View, Details* to display file details.

As in Figure WIN2-31, Explore opens with the *3½ Floppy (A:)* icon selected on its left side and the listing of its contents on its right. Note that Explorer and My Computer have

FIGURE WIN2-31 ■ **WINDOWS EXPLORER**

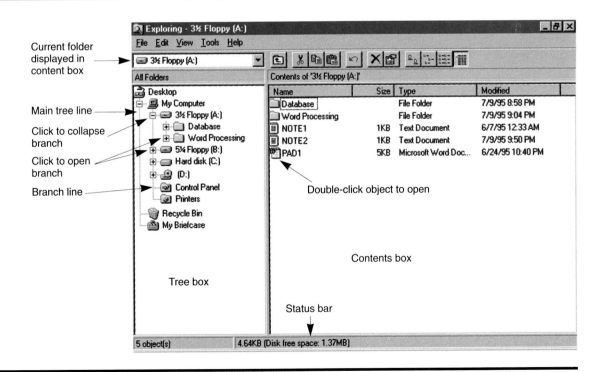

WIN

the same menu bar and toolbar. See Figure WIN2-4 for a description of its toolbar components.

Your Explorer window should resemble Figure WIN2-31. Leave this window open as you continue to the next section.

OPERATING EXPLORER

Explorer's commands operate similar to those of My Computer, however, the information in its workspace is displayed differently. As in Figure WIN2-31, the left side of the workspace displays a vertical hierarchical tree of all your system's components. This side will be referred to as the *Tree box*. The right side of the screen displays the contents of the item selected in the Tree box and will be referred to as the *Contents box*. It is similar to the workspace of a folder window. Items in both boxes are listed in alphabetical order.

VIEWING A TREE. The Tree box (left side of Explorer's workspace), as mentioned earlier, displays all your system's components in a vertical tree starting with the desktop icon on top. The left most vertical tree line is the **main tree line** and displays all items that appear on the desktop, including My Computer and the Recycle Bin. All lines extending from the main tree are called **branches.**

The *Go to a different folder* drop-down box (left side of toolbar) identifies the current folder selection—3½ Floppy (A:). Its contents are displayed in the Contents box (right side of window).

To select a different item on the tree, simply click it. Try this to select the desktop,

---

STEPS

 Desktop   **1**   Click the *Desktop* icon in the Tree box

The *Desktop* icon now appears highlighted in the tree and its contents appear in the right side of the window. Now, select the Control Panel,

Control Panel   **2**   Click the *Control Panel* icon

The *Control Panel* icon is now highlighted and its contents displayed in the contents box.

> **Tip:** You can also use the *Go to a different folder* drop-down box to select an item on the tree.

The Home key will quickly move the selection highlight to the beginning of any list in a list box and the End key will move the selection to the end of the list. Try this,

3   Press   Home   to select the desktop

4   Press   End   to select the last item on the tree

3½ Floppy (A:)   **5**   Click the *3½ Floppy (A:)* icon to select it

Your Explorer window should again appear similar to Figure WIN 2-31. This time the *3½ Floppy (A:)* icon is highlighted. Note that when you originally launched Explorer, it displayed the 3½ Floppy (A:) without its icon being highlighted. This is because Explorer launches with a dotted selection rectangle (see the *Database* icon in the figure) on the first item in the Contents box.

EXPANDING AND COLLAPSING BRANCHES.   The " + " icon to the left of any icon in the Tree box indicates that the item can be expanded to display a tree branch of folder(s) below it. Clicking a + icon expands the current tree.

STEPS

⊞ ▢ Database   **1   Click the + icon to the left of the *Database* folder icon**

The *Database* folder icon now branches to display the folders it contains and the +
changes to a − as in Figure WIN2-32a. Note that its subfolder, Consult, also has subfolders. To display its subfolders as in Figure 2-32b,

⊞ ▢ Consult   **2   Click the + icon to the left of the *Consult* folder icon**

To collapse the branches and return the display to Figure WIN2-31,

⊟ ▢ Database   **3   Click the − icon to the left of the *Database* folder icon**

FILE MANAGEMENT.   You can perform all commands discussed under the "Managing Your Files" and "Sharing and Removing Your Files" sections of this chapter using Explorer. Instead of selecting files from a Folder window, you select them from the Contents box. Once selected, you can use the *File* menu to open, rename, or print them.

FIGURE WIN2-32 ■ EXPANDING BRANCHES

(a) Clicking a [+] icon to the left of a *Folder* icon expands its branch by one level.
(b) All branches of the database folder have been expanded.

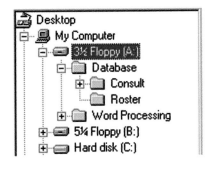

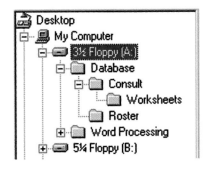

(a)   (b)

The Copy or Cut commands (*Edit* or *Shortcut* menu) can also be applied to any selection in Explorer's Contents box. The main difference between Explorer and My Computer is that you may need to scroll through your tree to locate the destination folder before invoking the Paste command. (Remember, in My Computer, you simply open the destination folder and click *Edit, Paste,* or right-click it and then click *Paste.*) The possible need to scroll to the destination folder makes the drag and drop sharing technique more cumbersome.

CONTROLLING THE ENVIRONMENT. Just as with My Computer, to change an object's properties in Explorer, simply invoke the Change Properties command from the item's *Shortcut* menu or *File* menu. To use Control Panel and Printers programs from Explorer, simply click its icon in the Tree box and then double-click the desired feature's icon in the Contents box.

VIEW OPTIONS. Explorer has view options similar to those of My Computer. You can access them by using the *View* menu or toolbar buttons. Icons can also be sorted as desired by using the *Arrange icons* submenu (*View* menu).

Before continuing to Chapter 3, complete the following steps to delete all folders (and any folders within them) that you created on your data disk for the exercises in this chapter. These folders include *Database* and *Word Processing:*

STEPS

🖴 3½ Floppy (A:) **1** If needed, click *3½ Floppy (A:)* drive icon in the Tree box

📁 Database **2** Click the *Database* folder in the Contents box

3 Press and hold **Ctrl** while clicking the *Word Processing* folder icon

4 Click *File, Delete, Yes*

If you are using the Word Processing modules of the Mastering Today's Software series, you will need to create a folder called XWP: The *XWP* folder is also needed to perform the Application 1 problem at the end of this chapter.

5 Click *File* and then point to *New*

6 Click *Folder*

7 Type **XWP** and press ↵

☒ **8** Close all windows

9 Shut down Windows

☑ **CHECKPOINT**

✓ What is Explorer?
✓ Launch Explorer and select the Control Panel from the Tree box (left side).

✓ Select the *3½ Floppy (A:)* drive icon in the Tree box, use the Contents box to open NOTE1 and PAD1, and then close them.
✓ Copy PAD1 within the same main folder and then rename it PAD2.
✓ Delete PAD2 and then close Explorer.

SUMMARY

- My Computer is a program that can browse (view) and access all of the components of a computer system, manage files, and control computer settings and printing. It is normally launched by double-clicking its icon on the desktop. Its workspace is usually occupied by several drive icons, the *Control Panel* folder, and *Printers* folder.

- Storage media includes disks (hard disk and 3½″ or 5¼″ disks), CD-ROM (a special disk that has *read only memory*), tape, and system memory (RAM or ROM). This text assumes that you are using a hard disk and a 3½″ disk for data.

- A *file* is a program or document that is saved on a disk or other storage media and is represented in Windows by icons and titles (filenames). The number of files that can be stored on a particular storage media depends on its capacity.

- A *folder* is a group of related files. Subfolders are folders within folders. A disk (or other storage media) is also considered a folder and is referred to as the *main folder.*

- Filenames identify a document or program. Folder names identify a group of files. They can have up to 255 characters.

- A byte is equivalent to one alphanumeric character (A–Z, 0–9, and so forth). A kilobyte (KB) is one thousand bytes, a megabyte (MB) is one million bytes, and a gigabyte (GB) is one billion bytes.

- A drive is a device that reads and/or writes to a storage medium (such as a disk or a CD-ROM). In My Computer, drive icons and letter titles are used to identify each drive in the system. The letter *C* normally represents the hard drive; the letters *A* and *B* represent the disk drives, and the letter *D* generally identifies the CD-ROM. Other letters may be used to identify a network.

- *Formatting* prepares a disk for use on the computer. It sets up the disk's folder and file allocation table and divides the disk into addressable storage locations. It also checks for defective tracks on the disk and seals them off from further use.

- The Find feature can be used to locate any file in a folder and then open it.

- Drive and folder icons can be used to open Folder windows that display their contents.

- The My Computer program offers two ways to browse through folders: separate windows for each folder (the default) or a single window that changes to display each folder that is opened. These settings are changed through the *Options* dialog box (*View* menu).

- The My Computer and Folder windows status bar (at the bottom of the window) displays the number of objects (drive, file, or folder icons) in the workspace and the amount of bytes that those objects occupy on the disk. All items in a folder or the My Computer window are referred to as *objects*. The status bar is also able to display other messages when using this program.

- The workspace in a Folder window (or My Computer window) can be adjusted to display the icons in a smaller size, in a list, and with more or less detail by using the *View* menu or toolbar buttons. The sort order of objects can also be changed using the *View* menu.

WIN

- More advanced *View* options such as folder browsing choices, displaying hidden files, and MS-DOS file extensions and file association settings can be controlled by using the *Options* dialog box.
- File management involves organizing and maintaining files (including folders) within the computer environment.
- Double-clicking a *Drive* icon in the My Computer window opens a Folder window that displays the main contents of the disk in its drive. Double-clicking a folder within a Folder window displays its contents in another Folder window.
- The Folder command of the *New* submenu (*File* menu) can be used to create a new folder or subfolder.
- A new saved document can be created without first launching its program by clicking the desired file type in the *New* submenu (*File* menu).
- Selecting is the process of marking items. To select a file, click it. To select additional files, press and hold the Ctrl key while clicking each additional file (or other objects). Files may also be selected in a block. A block is a set of contiguous files (or other objects). To select a block of files, click the first file and then press and hold the Shift key while clicking the last file in the block. A block can be selected alone or with other selected files.
- Most documents created and saved with Windows programs are automatically associated (have a special connection) to their program and can be opened from a Folder window without first launching their individual programs. Files include documents, programs, and folders. To open (or launch) folders or multiple documents and programs, select their icons and then click *File, Open* (menu bar).
- Any file or folder can be easily renamed by using an object's *Shortcut* menu or *File* menu.
- To print document files from a Folder window, select the desired file icon(s) and then invoke the Print command from the *File* menu.
- Sharing files involves copying or moving documents, programs, and folders within the same folder or between folders.
- A *Shortcut* icon has a link (special connection) to the original file or folder and can be used to open the original document or folder or to launch the original program from the desktop or another folder. To create a *Shortcut* icon use the Copy and Paste Shortcut commands of the *Edit* menu.
- The Undo command (**Ctrl** + **Z**) is available in most programs and will undo your last action.
- Copy and move techniques include using the Copy, Cut (to move), and Paste commands of the *Edit* menu or *Shortcut* menus as well as drag and drop techniques. The folder from which a selection is copied or cut (moved) from is called the *source folder.* The folder to which it is pasted (placed) is called the *destination folder.*
- When copying within the same folder, the source and destination folders are the same. Windows automatically adds the words *"Copy of"* to the copy's title.
- Files or folders copied between folders are assigned their original names.
- Drag and drop techniques involve copying or moving a selection by pressing and holding the left mouse button while moving the pointer with the selection to a new location, sometimes with the use of other keys. The source folder and destination folder windows must be in view to use the drag and drop technique.
- The *Copy Disk* dialog box copies the contents of an entire disk to another disk. It is accessible through Copy Disk command of the My Computer *File* menu (after you have selected the desired drive icon) or the desired drive icon's *Shortcut* menu.

- The *Send* submenu (*File* menu) copies a selection to another disk, fax, or electronic mail.

- The Delete command removes a selection from its current place and is invoked from the *File* menu, an object's *Shortcut* menu, or by pressing the Delete key. When deleting a selection from your hard disk or network disk, the file's reference is normally relocated to the Recycle Bin (a Windows program that stores file references as a result of invoking the delete command) without actually deleting the file. Once there, you can either permanently delete the selection or restore it. Deleting a *Short* icon will not affect the original file.

- Default settings are the normal settings of your environment. Properties include the way information and other attributes (characteristics) of an item are displayed or set. The Change Properties command alters any object's default characteristics.

- The Control Panel contains tools to set various parts of a system, including adding and removing hardware drivers (programs that help a piece of hardware communicate with the computer), screen displays, fonts, and so forth.

- The Printer program is used to add a new printer, switch printers (if more than one printer is installed), and check and control the status of current print jobs.

- A wizard is a program that helps make complicated tasks easier. Plug and play is the idea of simply plugging new hardware into your system and playing with (using) it immediately.

- Windows Explorer is another program that can be used to for managing a computer. The system components are listed in a hierarchal tree. Selecting a folder (or other item) from the tree on the left side will display its contents on the right side, which is similar to a Folder window. Commands used with the My Computer program are also available through Explorer.

KEY TERMS

Associated (WIN83)	File management (WIN78)	Recycle Bin (WIN87)
Block (WIN83)	Find (WIN70)	Send to (WIN93)
Branches (WIN110)	Folder windows (WIN73)	Sharing files (WIN87)
Byte (WIN70)	Label (WIN69)	Shortcut icon (WIN87)
Control Panel (WIN99)	Main tree line (WIN110)	Subfolders (WIN69)
Copy disk (WIN93)	My Computer (WIN68)	Undo (WIN96)
Default settings (WIN99)	Plug and play (WIN105)	Windows Explorer
Delete (WIN97)	Printers (WIN99)	(WIN107)
Drive (WIN70)	Properties (WIN99)	Wizard (WIN105)

QUIZ

TRUE/FALSE

____ 1. Both My Computer and Windows Explorer are programs that have file management features.

____ 2. My Computer is normally launched from the *Start* menu

____ 3. The status bar of the 3½ Floppy (A:) window displays disk storage information.

___ 4. A folder may only contain document and program files.
___ 5. Folder windows can be used to perform file management operations.
___ 6. The Shift key must be used to select a group of files by mouse.
___ 7. Sharing files involves copying or moving files.
___ 8. The Settings program is used to change the default settings of your system.
___ 9. Deleting a file from your data disk (3½″ disk) moves it to the Recycle Bin.
___ 10. Explorer displays the hierarchy of your system in a tree.

MULTIPLE CHOICE

___ 11. A folder may include all of the following except
   a. A taskbar
   b. Other folders
   c. The *Program* file icon
   d. The *Document* file icon

___ 12. Double-clicking a drive icon will
   a. Start the drive wizard
   b. Reformat the disk
   c. Open the main folder window of a disk or other storage media
   d. Launch My Computer

___ 13. A group of related files is a
   a. Folder
   b. File
   c. Window
   d. Drive

___ 14. A device that reads and/or writes to a disk is called a
   a. Folder
   b. File
   c. Window
   d. Drive

___ 15. Which item(s) of a Folder window can be used to create a new folder?
   a. Toolbar
   b. *File* menu
   c. *Edit* menu
   d. *Folder* menu

___ 16. A set of contiguous files is a(n)
   a. Icon
   b. Block
   c. Menu
   d. Toolbar

___ 17. Before performing any file management commands on a file, you must
   a. Format it
   b. Recycle it
   c. Rename it
   d. Select it

___ 18. Dragging and dropping a selection between folders will ____ the selection.
   a. move
   b. open
   c. copy
   d. recycle

___ 19. Which of the following contains features to change the settings of your computer?

    a. Printers

    b. *Shortcut* menu

    c. Toolbar

    d. Control Panel

___ 20. An icon that can be used to open a file or folder stored in a different folder is a

    a. *Shortcut* icon

    b. *Smart* icon

    c. *Toolbar* button

    d. *File* icon

MATCHING

Select the lettered item from the figure that best matches each phrase below.

___ 21. Double-click this icon to open a Folder window displaying your hard disk's main folder.

___ 22. Click this button to display the details of all objects listed in the window.

___ 23. Use this menu to sort the objects in the window's workspace.

___ 24. Use this menu to move or copy a selection.

___ 25. This icon is created by using a command in the *New* submenu.

FIGURE WIN2-33 ■ MATCHING FIGURE

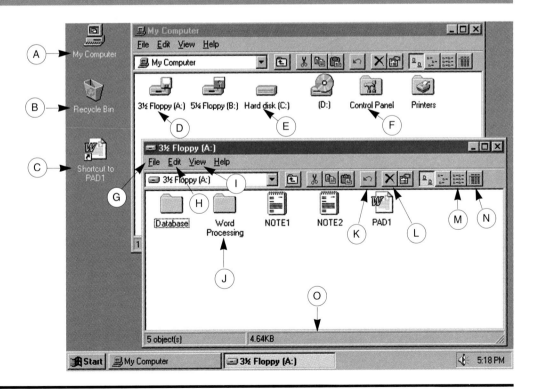

___ 26. This icon has a link to the file it represents.
___ 27. Click this button to undo your last action
___ 28. May hold items deleted from your hard disk.
___ 29. Can be used to change the settings of your computer.
___ 30. A bar used to display information about the contents of a window.

ANSWERS

True/False: 1. T; 2. F; 3. T; 4. F; 5. T; 6. F; 7. T; 8. F; 9. F; 10. T
Multiple Choice: 11. a; 12. c; 13. a; 14. d; 15. b; 16. b; 17. d; 18. c; 19. d; 20. a
Matching: 21. e; 22. n; 23. i; 24. h; 25. j; 26. c; 27. k; 28. b; 29. f; 30. o

EXERCISE

I. OPERATIONS

Provide the Windows commands necessary to complete each of the following operations. For each operation, assume a hard-disk system with a disk in Drive A. You may want to verify each command by trying it on your computer.

1. Launch My Computer.

2. Insert your data disk and open its main folder window.

3. Create a folder called WORD and then a subfolder within it called TEXT on your data disk.

4. Open the *Text* folder window and create a text document with the title OPERATIONS.

5. Open the OPERATIONS document, type in your name, and resave it.

6. Copy the icon for the OPERATIONS file to your data disk's main folder.

7. Rename the copy of the OPERATIONS file to SHARING

8. Create a *Shortcut* icon for the SHARING file in the *Text* folder.

9. Close My Computer and then launch Explorer to view your data disk.

10. Expand all branches of the *Word* folder and then collapse them. Close Explorer.

II. COMMANDS

Describe fully, using as few words as possible, what command is initiated or what is accomplished in Windows by the actions described below. Assume that each exercise part is independent of any previous parts.

1. Double-clicking the *My Computer* icon.

2. Double-clicking the *3½ Floppy (A:)* drive icon after inserting your data disk into Drive A.

3. Right-clicking an object in a Folder window.

4. Clicking the first object in a Folder window and then pressing and holding the Shift key while clicking the last object in the folder.

5. Dragging and dropping a selection from one folder to another.

6. Pressing the Delete key on a selection of files in your *Hard-disk* folder.

7. Clicking the right most toolbar button in a Folder window.

8. Right clicking the *My Computer* icon and then clicking *Explore.*

9. Clicking a *Shortcut* icon.

10. Clicking a − icon in the Tree box of Explorer.

WIN

III. APPLICATIONS

Perform the following operations, briefly tell how you accomplished each operation, and describe its results.

APPLICATION 1: UNDERSTANDING MY COMPUTER

1. Start Windows and launch My Computer.

2. If needed, use the steps on page WIN112 to create the *XWP* folder.

3. Use the Find feature to search for the NOTE1 file on your data disk.

4. Perform a new search to locate the *XWP* folder.

5. Open the *XWP* folder and then close it.

6. Open the main folder window of your data disk.

7. Turn on the toolbar and then use it to change the display to show file details.

8. Change the display back to large icons.

9. Close the 3½ Floppy window.

10. Close the My Computer window.

11. Shut down Windows.

APPLICATION 2: MANAGING YOUR FILES

1. Start Windows and launch My Computer.

2. Insert your data disk and open its main Folder window.

3. Create two folders named PERSONAL and BUSINESS.

4. Open the *Personal* folder and create two subfolders named CHECKING and SAVINGS.

5. Open the *Business* folder and create subfolders for SALES and PURCHASES.

6. Close the *Business* and *Personal* folder windows.

7. Create two text documents named ACCT #101 and INVOICES in the main folder.

8. Select and then open the ACCT#101 and INVOICES documents together.

9. Type **1/1/XX Balance $1,000** in the ACCT#101 document and then resave and close it.

10. Type **INV#354 Windows $5,000** in the INVOICES document and then resave and close it.

11. Select and print the ACCT #101 and INVOICES documents from the Folder window.

12. Close all windows and shut down Windows.

APPLICATION 3: SHARING YOUR FILES: COPYING AND MOVING

This problem requires first completing Application 2.

1. Start Windows and launch My Computer.

2. Insert your data disk and open its main Folder window.

3. Open the *Business* and *Personal* folders.

4. Minimize all windows and then open only the 3½ Floppy (A:) and Business windows.

5. Tile the windows horizontally and then move the INVOICES file from the *3½ Floppy (A:)* folder to the *Sales* subfolder in the *Business* folder.

6. Open the *Sales* subfolder and copy the INVOICES file to the *Purchase* folder.

7. Rename the INVOICES file in the *Purchase* folder to ORDERS.

8. Close the *Sales, Purchase,* and then *Business* folder windows.

9. Using similar techniques, move the ACCT #101 file to the *Checking* subfolder of the *Personal* folder, and then copy it to the *Savings* subfolder and rename as ACCT #202.

10. Close all windows and then shut down Windows.

APPLICATION 4: ADVANCE SHARING TECHNIQUES

This problem requires first completing Application 3.

1. Start Windows and launch My Computer.

2. Insert your data disk and open its main Folder window.

3. Open the *Business* folder and then the *Sales* subfolder.

4. Copy the INVOICES file three times within the Sales folder window.

5. Rename the files as INVOICE1, INVOICE2, INVOICE3, and INVOICE4.

6. Select and copy INVOICE1, INVOICE3, and INVOICE4 to the *Savings* folder.

7. In the *Savings* folder, rename the files BONDS, MUTUAL FUNDS, and MONEY MARKET.

8. Delete the ACCT #202 file in the *Savings* folder.

9. Create a *Shortcut* icon to open the MONEY MARKET file from the main folder window.

10. Open the MONEY MARKET file using its *Shortcut* icon and then close it.

11. Delete the MONEY MARKET file shortcut.

12. Close all windows and shut down Windows.

APPLICATION 5: CONTROLLING YOUR ENVIRONMENT

1. Start Windows and launch My Computer.

2. Insert your data disk and open the disk's properties.

3. Change the label of the disk to MY DISK.

4. Open the main folder for your data disk.

5. Change the properties for the PAD1 file to read-only.

6. Open the *Taskbar Properties* dialog box, clear your *Documents* menu contents, and then close it.

7. Open the Control Panel and examine, but do not change, the system's date and time.

8. Use the *Display* dialog box to add wallpaper of your choice to your desktop's background.

9. Use the *Display* dialog box to turn on or change your screen saver.

10. Close all windows and shut down Windows.

APPLICATION 6: OPERATING WINDOWS EXPLORER

This problem requires first completing Application 4.

1. Start Windows, launch My Computer, and insert your data disk.

2. Launch Windows Explorer to display the contents of the 3½ Floppy (A:) drive.

3. Expand all branches of the *Business* and *Personal* folders.

4. Create another folder in the *Business* folder called INVENTORY. (Hint: First select the *Business* folder in the tree and then use the *File* menu.)

5. Copy INVOICE2 and INVOICE4 from the *Sales* folder to the *Inventory* folder and then rename them ITEM1 and ITEM2.

6. Open the ITEM1 and ITEM2 documents using Explorer and then close them.

7. Select the *Checking* folder in the tree and create two new folders called NOW and REGULAR.

8. Expand the new branches of the *Checking* folder.

9. Collapse all branches in your *3½ Floppy (A:)* folder.

10. Close all windows and shut down Windows.

MASTERY CASES

The following mastery cases allow you to demonstrate how much you have learned about this software. Each case describes a fictitious problem or need that can be solved using the skills that you have learned in this chapter. Although minimum acceptable outcomes are specified, you are expected and encouraged to design your own response (files, data, lists) in ways that display your personal mastery of the software. Feel free to show off your skills. Use real data from your own experience in your solution, although you may also fabricate data if needed.

These mastery cases allow you to display your ability to

- Launch My Computer and Windows Explorer.
- Use My Computer to browse in folders.
- Perform a variety of file management techniques.
- Share and remove files.
- Control your computer environment.

CASE 1. USING WINDOWS AT SCHOOL

You have been asked to create a folder for each class that you are taking this semester. Create two text documents in one of the new folders, naming them REPORT 1 and REPORT 2. Copy those files to each new folder. Rename the REPORT 2 files to HOMEWORK 2. Close all windows and shut down Windows.

CASE 2. USING WINDOWS AT HOME

You have just installed Windows on your computer and desire to customize your screen display. Use the Control Panel and *Taskbar Properties* dialog box to accomplish this. Also select and turn on a desired screen saver. Close all windows and shut down Windows. (This case requires your own computer or the ability to change settings on the system that you are using. Check with your instructor before doing this case.)

CASE 3. USING WINDOWS AT WORK

You have been assigned to organize the customer files in your office. Create folders for five customers. Next, create two subfolders within one of the customer folders and name them *Receivables* and *Sales*. Create two text documents in the *Sales* folder and copy them to the *Sales* folders of the other customers. Launch Explorer and open all the branches of your data disk. Create a *Shortcut* icon for the *Sales* folder of one of the customers and place it in the main folder. Use the *Shortcut* icon to open the folder. Close all windows and shut down Windows.

3

OTHER WINDOWS FEATURES

OBJECTIVES

After completing this chapter, you will be able to

1 Use the editing features of WordPad (a word processing program).
2 Create and edit objects and text with Paint (a graphics program).
3 Perform object linking and embedding operations, including editing a linked or embedded object.

4 Use Windows accessibility options to adjust keyboard, display, sound, and mouse controls to individual preference.
5 Describe other Windows Accessories programs and communication features.

OVERVIEW

This chapter provides tutorials on using WordPad (a word processor) and Paint (a graphics program). It also examines how to share information between programs by using object linking or embedding techniques and the communication features of Windows.

The chapter concludes with an overall look at operating other Windows programs, including accessibility options, accessories, and communications software.

WORDPAD

WordPad is a simple word processing program that can help you create and edit documents. Both text and objects (graphic) images may be placed into a WordPad document. Only text entry and editing are discussed in this section. For object linking, embedding, and editing, see the "Linking and Embedding" section of this chapter.

WordPad allows you to edit (change) the content, text appearance, and format (layout) of your document. Content changes include inserting, deleting, modifying, copying, and moving text in your document. **Text appearance** changes include alterations to font type, style (regular, bold, or italic), and size. **Layout (format)** changes concern the way text is arranged in a document—for example, changing margin or tab settings.

GETTING STARTED

As demonstrated earlier, commands to launch and close WordPad (or any program), create, save, open, and print a document are common for most Windows programs. Although these commands are reviewed as needed in the following exercises, you should review the "Basic Document Management" section in Chapter 1 before continuing.

LAUNCHING WORDPAD.   Like most Windows programs, WordPad can be launched from the *Start* menu.

STEPS

1 Click the *Start* button   [**Ctrl** + **Esc**]

2 Point to *Programs* and then *Accessories* for its submenu

3 Click *WordPad* to launch it

4 If needed, click WordPad's *Maximize* button to maximize it [**Alt** + **Spacebar** , **X**]

Your WordPad window should resemble Figure WIN3-1.

> **Tip: Remember, as illustrated in the "Document Approach" section in Chapter 2, you can also create and name a new document for any program in a Folder window.**

THE WORDPAD WINDOW.   As identified in Figure WIN3-1, the WordPad window has a variety of common Windows features including a title bar (with program icon, program and document name, resizing buttons, and a close button), menu bar, toolbars (including a Format bar), workspace, and status bar. The operation of each component

FIGURE WIN3-1 ■ WORDPAD

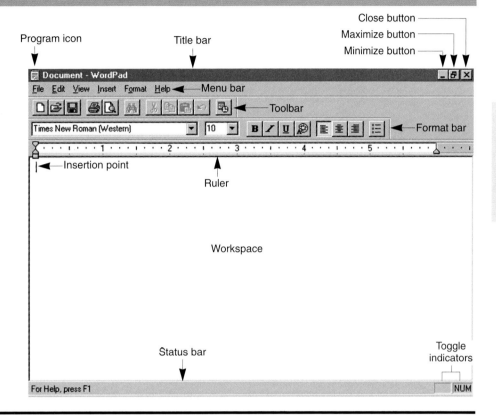

WIN

will be discussed as needed. WordPad also opens with a ruler just below its toolbars. This feature will be used later to set margins and adjust tab settings.

ENTERING TEXT.   As seen earlier, the average Windows program opens with a new blank document in its workspace. This is called the *default document.* You will now use WordPad's default document to create the document in Figure WIN3-2.

FIGURE WIN3-2 ■ ENTERING TEXT

```
Your Name↵
↵
Windows is a graphical user interface (GUI) that uses pictures instead of typewritten commands to help
you communicate with your computer. It is like using a picture of a cigarette in place of a written "No
Smoking" sign. |
```

As you enter text, do not press the Enter (or Return) key unless indicated. Unlike a typewriter, pressing the Enter key is *not* required at the end of each line. Text automatically flows to the next line as you type. This word processing feature is called **wordwrap.**

In a word processor, the Enter key produces a line break at the point where it is pressed. A **line break** ends a line before it reaches the right margin. It also moves the insertion point to the beginning of the next line. Line breaks are generally needed at the end of a paragraph, each line of an address, a salutation, or to skip a line.

Create a short document by entering text as follows:

STEPS

1 Type your name

2 Press ↵ three times

(Remember, do not press the Enter key as you type the following paragraph. Word-Pad's wordwrapping feature will automatically flow your text to the next line.)

3 Type the paragraph shown in Figure WIN3-2

> **Tip:** If you make a mistake while typing, press the Backspace key to remove the error and type the correct text.

DOCUMENT MANAGEMENT. Basic document management commands include saving to disk, clearing the workspace, opening, and printing.

As demonstrated earlier, you can use the Save or Save As command to save a document. Invoking the Save command on a new document will open the *Save As* dialog box so that you can assign the document a filename. Remember, Windows 95 programs can accept filenames with up to 255 characters. Try this:

STEPS

 1 Click *File, Save*   [**Ctrl** + **S**]

2 In the Filename box, type **1WORDPAD**

If needed, use Steps 3 and 4 to set the default drive to Drive A.

 3 Click the "▼" button of the *Save in* drop-down box for its list

 3½ Floppy (A:)   4 Click *3½ Floppy (A:)* to set the default drive to Drive A

5 Click the *Save* button   [↵]

> **Tip:** Instead of Steps 3 and 4, you can change the default drive by typing A:\ before 1WORDPAD (for example, type [A:\1WORDPAD]) in Step 2. Also, if your data disk is not formatted, Windows will ask you whether you want to format it.

Your mouse pointer briefly changes to an image of a time bottle indicating " Please Wait" and the message "Saving File. Please wait." appears in the status bar (at the bottom of the window).

Invoking the Save command on a document previously saved will resave it under its original name. Try this:

6   Click *File*, *Save*   [**Ctrl** + **S**]

Later, you will use the Save As command to save a revised copy of the document under another name. For now, clear your workspace for a new document.

7   Click *File*, *New*, *OK*   [**Ctrl** + **N** , ↵]

> **Note:** WordPad and many other programs offer several document types for a new document. If available, you can generally select the document type before clicking *OK* in Step 7.

Your workspace is now blank and ready for a new document. At this point you can create a new document. For now, however, you will practice opening the 1WORDPAD document. Remember, *opening* a document retrieves it from a disk.

8   Click *File*, *Open*   [**Ctrl** + **O**]

9   Type **1WORDPAD** in the Filename box or click it in the list box

10   Click the *Open* button

Your 1WORDPAD document should again occupy WordPad's workspace.

> **Tip:** The *Save As* and *Open* dialog box can also be used for a variety of file management tasks similar to operating a Folder window. For example, to perform file management commands on a specific file, right click it in the *Files* list box for its *Shortcut* menu. This menu contains the same commands if the file had been right-clicked in a Folder window. Right-clicking a blank area of the *Files* list box will also open the same *Shortcut* menu as in a Folder window. See Chapter 2 for instructions on how to use these *Shortcut* menus.

Now, to print preview and then print the document:

11   Click *File*, *Print Preview* to view the full page

The Print Preview feature displays a full page view of your document as it will appear when printed. This allows you to view text alignment and other format settings. You can zoom in to view different portions of your document by pointing and clicking the desired area. For now, to close the Print Preview feature, return to the document and then print it:

12 **Click the _Close_ button on the toolbar**

13 **Turn on your printer**

 14 **Click _File, Print, OK_**   [**Ctrl** + **P** , **↵**]

Basic document management commands are summarized in Figure WIN3-3.

CLOSING WORDPAD. As practiced earlier, WordPad (or any other program) can be closed by any method listed in Figure WIN1-26 in Chapter 1. Remember, closing exits the program. For now, to close WordPad,

STEP

 1 **Click WordPad's _Close_ button**   [**Alt** + **F4**]

INSERTING NEW TEXT

WordPad allows you to insert (add) new text to material previously typed. Once inserted, WordPad automatically reformats the document. Practice inserting the new text shown in Figure WIN3-4a:

STEPS

1 **Launch WordPad**

2 **If needed, click its _Maximize_ button**

 3 **Click _File, Open_ for its dialog box**   [**Ctrl** + **O**]

If needed, do Steps 4 and 5 to set the default drive to Drive A.

 4 **Click the "▼" button of the _Look in_ drop-down box for its list**

💾 3½ Floppy (A:) 5 **Click _3½ Floppy (A:)_ to set the default drive to Drive A**

 6 **Click the _File name_ box and type** `1WORDPAD` **or click it in the list box**

7 **Click the _Open_ button**

FIGURE WIN3-3 ■ COMMON OPERATIONS

	Operation	Menu	Shortcut Keys
	Saving a Document to a disk[1]		
	With the Same Name	Click _File_, _Save_	Ctrl + S
	With a New Name	Click _File_, Save _As_	Alt + F, A
	Opening a Document from a Disk	Click _File_, _Open_	Ctrl + O
	Printing a Document		
	To paper	Click _File_, _Print_	Ctrl + P
	To the screen	Click _File_, _Print Preview_	Alt + F, V
	Creating a New Document[2]	Click _File_, _New_	Ctrl + N

[1]When saving a document for the first time, both the Save and Save As commands will open the _Save As_ dialog box for entering the document's name. All other times, the Save command will re-save a document under its original name and the Save As command will open the _Save As_ dialog box. This offers you the option to save a revised document under a new name.

[2]In a program that allows only one document in its workspace—such as WordPad, Paint, and Notepad—the New command clears the program's workspace of a previous document so that you can create a new document. With a program that allows for multiple documents in its workspace, the New command opens a new document window over the current one. Refer to your specific program's on-line help to determine the maximum number of documents that can be opened and other document format options that may be available using the New command.

Tip: Double-clicking 1WORDPAD in place of Steps 6 and 7 will also open the document.

Again your document should resemble Figure WIN3-2. Now you are ready to insert new text.

8 **Move the insertion point to just before "instead"**
(To move the insertion point by mouse, simply click the desired position. With the keyboard, use the arrow keys.)

FIGURE WIN3-4 ■ **ENTERING TEXT**

```
Your Name                                     and menus ─┐
                                                         │
                                                         ▼
Windows is a graphical user interface (GUI) that uses pictures instead of typewritten commands to help
you communicate with your computer. It is like using a picture of a cigarette₍in place of a written "No
Smoking" sign.                                           ▲
                            with a red slash through it ─┘
```

(a) Inserting new text into a document.

```
Your Name
M/D/YY   ◄──────────  Click Insert, Date and Time, OK

Windows is a graphical user interface (GUI) that uses pictures and menus instead of typewritten commands
to help you communicate with your computer. It is like using a picture of a cigarette with a red slash
through it in place of a written "No Smoking" sign.
```

(b) The WordPad document with new text inserted.

---

9 **Type** **and menus**

Notice that the words to the right of your insertion point have moved over to make room for the new words.

10 **Press** **Spacebar** to separate "menus" and "instead"

11 **Move your insertion point before the "i" in "in" on the second line**

12 **Type** **with a red slash through it**

13 **Press** **Spacebar**

WordPad also has a feature that allows you to insert the system's date and time. Try this to insert your system's date (which should normally be the current date):

14 **Move to the line below your name**

15 **Click** *Insert, Date and Time, OK*

Note that the default date format is mm/dd/yy. You can select a different format before clicking *OK* in Step 15.

Your document should resemble Figure WIN3-4b. To save this revised document as 2WORDPAD,

16 **Click** *File, Save As* **for its dialog box**

17 **Type** **2WORDPAD** **in the Filename box**

18 **Click the _Save_ button**   [⏎]

Your revised document has now been saved as 2WORDPAD. Your original document, 1WORDPAD remains unmodified on your disk.

SELECTING TEXT

Selecting text involves marking (highlighting) it for editing. A selection of text is simply a contiguous segment of text. Text must be selected in order for you to perform appearance and format changes on it.

Mouse and keyboard selection techniques are summarized in Figure WIN3-5a. Some of these selection techniques will be demonstrated in the exercises to follow. WordPad's mouse selection area is illustrated in Figure 3-5b.

To cancel a selection by mouse, simply click the selection. With the keyboard, press any arrow key.

WIN

FIGURE WIN3-5 ■ SPECIAL SELECTION TECHNIQUES

(a) Summary of special selection techniques.
(b) The selection area of a WordPad document and mouse pointer. When using a mouse, you must first point to the selection area. This area is located on the left margin of the document. Notice that the mouse pointer will change to a right-slanted arrow.

Selecting a(n)	By Mouse	By Keyboard
Line	Point to the line from the selection area and click.	Move the insertion point to the beginning of the line and press the Shift and End keys.
Paragraph	Point to any line of the paragraph from the selection area and double-click	Move the insertion point to the first line of the paragraph and then press and hold the Shift key while pressing the Arrow key to the last line of the paragraph.
Entire document	Point to any part of the document from the selection area and then press and hold the Ctrl key while clicking.	Move the insertion point to the beginning of the document and then press the Ctrl, Shift, and End keys together.
Block of lines	Point to the first line of the block from the selection area and click. Point to the last line of the block from the selection area and then press and hold the Shift key while clicking.	Move the insertion point to the first line of the block and then press and hold the Shift key while pressing the Arrow key to the last line of the block.

(a)

(b)

DELETING TEXT

Deleting text involves removing it from your document. When you delete text in a Word-Pad document, the remaining text automatically reformats. As mentioned earlier, to delete single characters to the left, press the Backspace key. To delete individual characters to the right, press the Delete key. To delete a selection (block) of text, use either the Clear command (*Edit* menu) or the Delete key.

Only a selection deletion is illustrated next. Try using the Backspace and Delete keys for individual character deletions on your own.

Delete the entire second line of your paragraph, beginning with "to" by doing the following:

STEPS

BY MOUSE

1   Slowly point to the beginning of the second line from the left margin as in Figure WIN3-5b (your pointer should be pointing right)

2   Click to select the line

BY KEYBOARD

1   Move the insertion point to the beginning of the second line

2   Press   **Shift**   +   **End**   to select the line

3   Click *Edit, Clear*   [**Delete**   ]

The second line of your paragraph should now be deleted and the remaining text reformatted.

> **Tip:** To delete an entire paragraph, use the select command in Figure WIN3-5a and then click *Edit, Clear* or press the Delete key.

UNDOING AN ACTION

Many Windows programs contain an *Undo* command which you can invoke through the *Edit* menu, toolbar, or Shortcut keys. This command undoes your last action. To undo your deletion,

---

STEPS

   1   Click *Edit, Undo*   [**Ctrl**   +   **Z**   ]

2   Click the selection to remove the highlight   [Any arrow key]

CHANGING TEXT APPEARANCE

If your printer has the capability, you can change the overall type face (**font**), style, and size of your text to improve the appearance of your document. You can also add strike-out and underline effects or change text color. All text appearance changes may be made prior to or after typing text.

In the following sections, you will type new text with a different font and then make other text enhancements to your document. Use Figure WIN3-6 as a guide.

FONT CHANGES.   Windows comes with several Truetype (TT) fonts that can be accessed by using the Format bar or the *Font* dialog box (*Format* menu). In the next exercise, you will change the font to Arial and font size to 14 points and then type in new text. (Note: A *point* is a typesetting unit of measure equivalent to about ½ of an inch.)

WIN

STEPS

1   Open the 2WORDPAD document

2   Press **Ctrl** + **End** to move to the end of the document

3   Press ↵ twice to skip two lines

BY FORMAT BAR	**BY *FONT* DIALOG BOX**
4 Click the "▼" button of the *Font* drop-down box (left side of Format bar) for its list as in Figure WIN3-7a (Your system's fonts may differ.)	4 Click *Format, Font* for its dialog box as in Figure WIN3-7b (Your system's fonts may differ.)

FIGURE WIN3-6 ■ TEXT ENHANCEMENTS

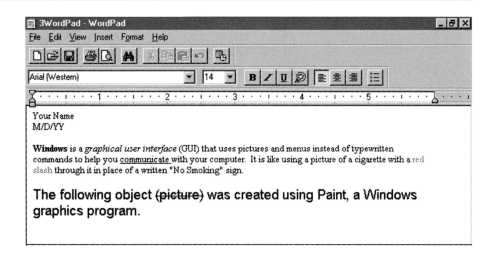

FIGURE WIN3-7 ■ CHANGING FONTS

(a) The *Font* drop-down list (Format bar) can be used to select an available font (typeface).

(b) The *Font* dialog box (*Format* menu) can also be used to select a font.

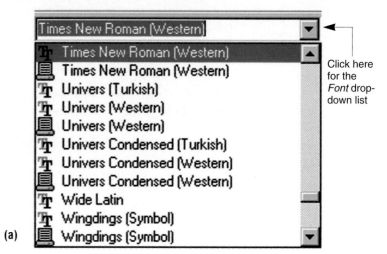

(a)

(b)

---

5 **Press** **A** **to move the selection highlight to the beginning of the list**

Tip: Pressing a letter in a list will move the selection highlight to the first item beginning with that letter in the list.

BY FORMAT BAR

6 If needed, click the ▼ button of the *Font* drop-down list's scroll bar until *Arial* is visible

7 Click *Arial* to select it

8 Click the ▼ button of the *Font Size* drop-down box (Format bar)

9 Click *14* for font size

BY *FONT* DIALOG BOX

6 If needed, click the ▼ button of the *Font* list box's scroll bar until *Arial* is visible

7 Click *Arial* to select it

8 Click *14* in the *Size* list box

9 Click *OK*

10 Type The following object (picture) was created using Paint, a Windows graphics program.

The font change is in effect from the point of change forward.

11 Save your document as 3WORDPAD *(File, Save As)*

OTHER TEXT ENHANCEMENTS.   As mentioned earlier, you can also change font style (which includes bolding or italicizing text), strikeout, underline, and change the color of text. Again, as you perform the exercises in this section use Figure WIN3-6.

Two ways to emphasis text is to bold or italicize it. **Bolding** darkens text, whereas **italicizing** slants text. Try this:

STEPS

1 Move the insertion point before "Windows" in the first paragraph (Either click it or use the arrow keys.)

2 Select the word *"Windows"*

Remember, either drag across the text with your mouse or press and hold the **Shift** key while pressing the → key.

Tip: Double-clicking a word will select it quickly.

B

3 Click *Format, Font, Bold* (in the *Font Style* list box), *OK*   [**Ctrl** + **B**]

Now, italicize "graphical user interface":

4 Select *"graphical user interface"*

5 Click *Format, Font, Italic* (in the *Font Style* list box), *OK*   [**Ctrl** + **I**]

You can also emphasize text by underlining or striking it out (putting a line through it). Do the following to underline "communicate" and strikeout:

6 Select *"communicate"* from the second line of your paragraph

7 Click *Format, Font,* the *Underline* check box, *OK*   [**Ctrl** + **U**]

8 Select *"(picture)"* in the last sentence

9 Click *Format, Font,* the *Strikeout* check box, *OK*

WordPad has options to change text color for further emphasis. Do not do Steps 10 and 11 if you do not have a color monitor or printer.

10 Select *"red slash"* at the end of the second line of the first paragraph

11 Click *Format, Font,* the "▼" button of the *Color* drop-down box, *Red, OK*

12 Press any arrow key to unselect

Compare your document to Figure WIN3-6.

13 Resave this document as 3WORDPAD

14 Print the document and then open a new document

CHANGING TEXT LAYOUT

Layout (format) refers to the format of text in a paragraph or in an entire document. It includes indentation, alignment, bullet style, and tab changes. You can make layout changes using the *Format* menu, ruler, or toolbars.

INDENTATION. In WordPad, **indentation** relates to the way a paragraph is indented or set from the left or right margin. You can also set the indentation for just the first line of a paragraph. Use the ruler or *Paragraph* dialog box (*Format* menu) for indentation changes. In the next exercises, you will indent only the first line of the first paragraph and then change the indentation of the second paragraph as in Figure WIN3-8.

STEPS

1 Open the 3WORDPAD document

2 Move the insertion point before the "W" in "Windows" in the first paragraph

FIGURE WIN3-8 ■ CHANGING TEXT LAYOUT

Your Name
M/D/YY

Windows is a *graphical user interface* (GUI) that uses pictures and menus instead of typewritten commands to help you communicate with your computer. It is like using a picture of a cigarette with a red slash through it in place of a written "No Smoking" sign.

**The following object (picture)
was created using Paint, a
Windows graphics program.**

WIN

3 Click *Format, Paragraph* for its dialog box

4 Double-click the *First line* text box to highlight its contents

5 Type **.5** and then click *OK*

The first line of your first paragraph should now be indented as in Figure WIN3-9a.

> Tip: Instead of performing Steps 3 through 5, you can drag the First Line Indent marker from the top left of the ruler to its current position above the .5″ marker (See Figure WIN3-9a).

6 Move the insertion point before "The" in the second paragraph

7 Click *Format, Paragraph* for its dialog box

8 Type **1.5** in the Left text box and then press **Tab**

9 Type **2** in the Right text box and then click *OK*

> Tip: Instead of Steps 7 through 9 you can drag the Left and Right Margin Indent markers on the ruler to the desired settings.

The entire second paragraph is now indented 1.5" from the left margin and 2" from the right margin as in Figure WIN3-9b. Note again that the corresponding markers on the ruler have also moved.

FIGURE WIN3-9 ■ INDENTATION ADJUSTMENTS

(a) You can indent the first line of a paragraph by dragging the First Line Indent marker on the ruler or by using the *Paragraph* dialog box (*Format* menu).
(b) You can indent the left or right margins of a paragraph by dragging their respective markers on the ruler or by using the *Paragraph* dialog box (*Format* menu).

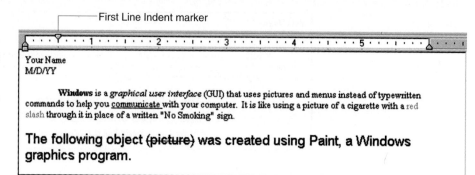

(a)

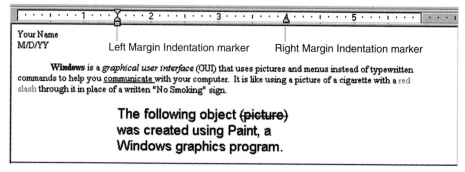

(b)

Tip: To indent an entire document before typing, open a new document, use the *Paragraph* dialog box or ruler to set the indentation and then begin typing. To indent an entire document after typing, click *Edit, Select All* (or press [Ctrl] + [A]) and then use the *Paragraph* dialog box or ruler to set the indentation.

10 Save this document as 4WORDPAD

11 Print the document

ALIGNMENT CHANGES. **Alignment** is how text aligns against a margin. The default alignment of WordPad and many word processors is *left*. Left aligned text has a *ragged right edge* as in Figure WIN3-10a. WordPad offers three alignment settings: left, center, and right. The next exercise will demonstrate the latter two alignments using the first paragraph of your 3WORDPAD document.

FIGURE WIN3-10 ■ ALIGNING TEXT

(a) Left aligned paragraph (the default).
(b) Center aligned paragraph.
(c) Right aligned paragraph.

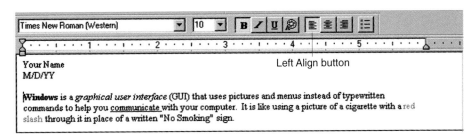

(a)

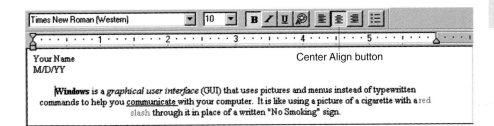

(b)

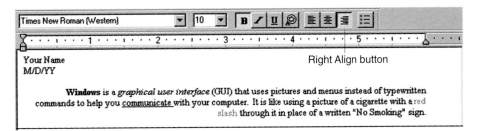

(c)

STEPS

1 Open the 3WORDPAD document

2 Move the insertion point before the "W" in "Windows" in the first paragraph

 3 Click the *Center Align Format bar* button

Your text is now center aligned as in Figure WIN3-10b.

4 Click the *Right Align Format bar* button

WIN

Your text in now right aligned as in Figure WIN3-10c.

5   Click the *Left Aligned Format bar* button

Your paragraph is now back to left aligned.

6   Click *File, New, OK, No* for a new document without saving the current one

BULLET STYLE.   WordPad has a **bullet style** format that automatically inserts a bullet at the beginning of each line after pressing the Enter key. Try this to create the document in Figure WIN3-11:

STEPS

1   On a new document, type   New Features of Windows 95 include

2   Press ↵ twice

3   Click *Format, Bullet Style* to turn it on

4   Press   Ctrl   +   B   to turn on the bold feature

5   Type   Start Button   and then press   Spacebar

6   Press   Ctrl   +   B   to turn off the bold feature

7   Type   for quickly launching a program and accessing other features.

8   Press ↵ to move to the next bullet

Tip: To delete an unwanted bullet, press the Backspace key.

FIGURE WIN3-11 ■ BULLET STYLE FORMAT

Bullet Style button

New Features of Windows 95 include:

- **Start Button** for quickly launching a program and accessing other features.
- **Taskbar** for easy switching between opened programs.
- **My Computer** for managing the components of your computer.
- **Close Button** for quickly exiting a window.

9 Repeat Steps 4 through 8 for the remaining three bullets using Figure WIN3-11 as a guide (Be sure to press Enter after typing the last bullet. You must add a blank bullet before turning off the feature.)

10 Click *Format, Bullet Style* to turn it off

11 Save this document as 5WORDPAD

12 Print the document

TAB CHANGES.   **Tabs** are used to place text in specific positions on a line. These positions are called *tab stops*. WordPad's default tab stops are preset at one-half inch apart. As seen earlier, pressing the Tab key before beginning a paragraph will start your text one-half inch from the left margin. You can customize tab positions so that pressing the Tab key once will move you to a desired location. You can change tab stops using the ruler or *Tab* dialog box (*Format* menu). To create the document in Figure WIN3-12 using different tab stop settings:

STEPS

1 Click *File, New, OK,* (if needed, *No*) for a new document   [Ctrl + N , ↵ , N]

2 Click the *Center Align* button (Format bar)

3 Press   Ctrl   +   B   to turn on the bold feature

4 Type   Standard Shortcut Keys

FIGURE WIN3-12   ■   CHANGING TAB SETTINGS

Clicking the ruler will place a Tab marker at the location clicked. Tab markers can also be set using the *Tab* dialog box (*Format* menu).

Standard Shortcut Keys

Open the Start Menu	Ctrl+Esc
Close a Program	Alt+F4
Create a New Document	Ctrl+N
Save a Document	Ctrl+S
Open a Saved Document	Ctrl+O
Print a Document	Ctrl+P
Undo the Last Action	Ctrl+Z
Copy a Selection	Ctrl+C
Cut a Selection	Ctrl+X
Paste a Selection	Ctrl+V
Select All	Ctrl+A
Help	F1

B

5 Press **Ctrl** + **B** to turn off the bold feature

6 Press ↵ twice and then click the *Left Align* button (Format bar)

Now to set tab stops at the one-inch and four-and-a-half-inch marks:

BY RULER

7 Point beneath the one-inch mark on the ruler

8 Click beneath the one-inch mark on the ruler (an "L" appears)

9 Click beneath the four-and-a-half-inch mark on the ruler

BY *FORMAT* MENU

7 Click *Format, Tabs* for its dialog box

8 Type **1** and click the *Set* button to set the first tab stop

9 Type **4.5**, click the *Set* button to set the second tab and then click *OK*

10 Press **Tab** to move to the one-inch tab mark

11 Type **Open the Start Menu**

12 Press **Tab** to move the four-inch tab mark

13 Type **Ctrl + Esc** and then press ↵

(Remember, you are typing the Shortcut keys, not pressing them.)

14 Type in the rest of the Shortcut keys listed in Figure WIN3-12 using the same techniques as illustrated in Steps 10 through 13

15 Save this document as 6WORDPAD

16 Print the document

17 Click *File, New, OK* to clear the workspace   [**Ctrl** + **N** , ↵]

MOVING AND COPYING A SELECTION

As mentioned earlier, WordPad can accept text and objects (graphic images). These items can be selected and moved or copied within a document (or to another file). *Moving* involves changing a selection's location. *Copying* involves duplicating a selection in another location. The difference between moving and copying is that moving removes (cuts) a selection from its original position, but copying leaves the original unchanged.

Because procedures for moving and copying are similar, only moving commands are illustrated next. To move the first sentence of the first paragraph to the end of the document as in Figure WIN3-13:

FIGURE WIN3-13 ■ MOVING A SELECTION

The first sentence of the first paragraph has been moved to the end of the document using the Cut and Paste commands (*Edit* menu).

> Your Name
> M/D/YY
>
> It is like using a picture of a cigarette with a red slash through it in place of a written "No Smoking" sign.
>
> ## The following object (picture) was created using Paint, a Windows graphics program.
>
> Windows is a *graphical user interface* (GUI) that uses pictures and menus instead of typewritten commands to help you communicate with your computer.

WIN

STEPS

1 Open the 3WORDPAD document

2 Select the sentence beginning with "Windows" (include the space after the period)

3 Click *Edit, Cut* to move the selection to the Clipboard   [**Ctrl** + **X**]

(To copy instead of cut, Click *Edit, Copy* or press **Ctrl** + **C** , for Step 3)

Remember, the Clipboard is a Windows program that temporarily holds copied or cut selections for future pasting.

4 Move your insertion point to the end of the document   [**Ctrl** + **End**]

5 Press ↵ twice

6 Click *Edit, Paste*   [**Ctrl** + **V**]

Remember, the Paste command places a selection from the Clipboard into a desired location. Your document should resemble Figure WIN3-13.

7 Close WordPad without saving this document

8 If desired, shut down Windows

Tip: You can also move a selection by dragging and dropping it.

☑ CHECKPOINT

✓ Launch WordPad and type the first paragraph in this module.
✓ Change the font (including style and size) of some of the text in the paragraph.
✓ Underline, strikeout, boldface, and italicize some of the text in the paragraph.

✓ Center align the paragraph.
✓ Copy the last sentence to the beginning of the paragraph and then close WordPad without saving the document.

PAINT

Paint is a graphics program that you can use to create and save color images (pictures). It can also be used for editing graphic images created with other programs and for editing and saving screen captures. *Screen captures* are similar to what would result if you took a photograph of your current screen.

GETTING STARTED

Like WordPad, commands to launch and close Paint, save, open, print, and create a new document are common for most Windows programs. Although these commands are reviewed as needed in the following exercises, you should review the "Basic Document Management" section in Chapter 1 before continuing.

As with most graphics programs, Paint uses the mouse pointer as its drawing tool in its workspace. Drawing tool selection and operation techniques are discussed later.

LAUNCHING PAINT.   Like most Windows programs, Paint can be launched from the *Start* menu.

STEPS

1 Click the *Start* button   [**Ctrl** + **Esc**]

2 Point to *Programs* and then *Accessories* for its submenu

3 Click *Paint* to launch it

4 If needed, click Paint's *Maximize* button to maximize it   [**Alt** + **Spacebar** , **X**]

5 If needed, click *View, Status Bar* to turn it on

Your Paint window should resemble Figure WIN3-14.

> **Tip:** Remember, as illustrated in Chapter 2 "Document Approach," you can also create and name a new document for any program in a Folder window.

MOUSE ACTIONS BY KEYBOARD.   Freehand drawing with a mouse is generally easier than with a keyboard. Drawing with a keyboard, however, allows you to be more accurate in moving the mouse pointer. Before drawing in Paint with a keyboard,

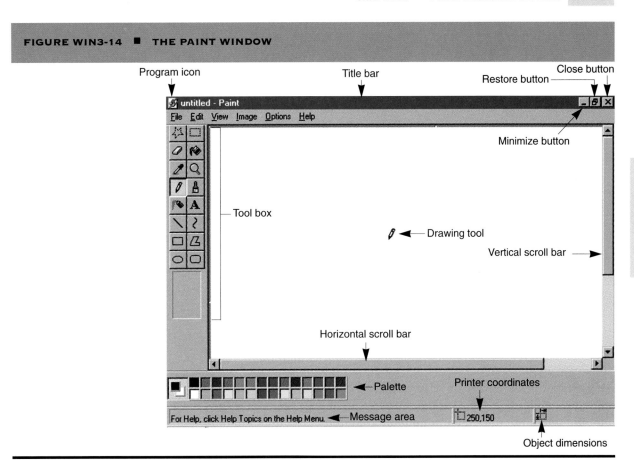

you will need to turn on the Use MouseKeys feature. This feature is part of the Accessibility Properties feature, which can be accessed through the Control Panel. If you desire to use the MouseKeys, see the "Mouse and Keyboard Operations" section in Chapter 1 and Figure WIN1-2b.

THE PAINT WINDOW.   As identified in Figure WIN3-14, the Paint window has a variety of common Windows features including a title bar (with program icon, program and document name, resizing buttons, and a close button), menu bar, workspace, and status bar. Each component operation is discussed as needed. Paint also opens with a tool box at the left side of its workspace and a palette just above the status bar. When the mouse pointer is in the workspace, it becomes the selected drawing tool. In this case, it is a pencil—the default drawing tool. This feature will be used shortly to select a drawing tool and color.

STATUS BAR.   As identified at the bottom of Figure WIN3-14, the status bar has three sections: a messages area (left side), pointer coordinates (position), and object dimensions (right side). The pointer coordinates area displays the horizonal (x-axis) and vertical (y-axis) coordinates of your pointer in Paint's drawing area (workspace). This is expressed in terms of pixels. A **pixel** is equivalent to one small dot. All objects drawn with your computer are composed of pixels.

1 **Move your pointer around the drawing area until you are at the coordinates 100, 150 (horizontal or x=100, vertical or y=150)**

2 **Move your pointer to the coordinates 400, 100**

The width × height dimensions of an object in pixels appear at the far right end of the status bar when drawing. As a guide, both the pointer coordinates and width × height dimension pixels are supplied in the exercises to follow.

DOCUMENT MANAGEMENT. Basic document management commands include saving to disk, clearing the workspace, opening, and printing. These commands are reviewed throughout the exercises in this section and are common to most Windows programs. See Figure WIN3-3 in the WordPad section for a summary.

CLOSING PAINT. As with all programs, Paint can be closed by any of the methods listed in Figure WIN1-26 in Chapter 1. Remember, closing exits the program. For now, to close Paint,

 1 **Click Paint's *Close* button**   [**Alt** + **F4**]

SELECTING A DRAWING TOOL

A **drawing tool** is the instrument that you use to create a drawing. Selecting a drawing tool involves not only selecting the tool itself but also selecting its drawing width or fill style and its color. These items are normally selected from Paint's tool box and palette.

When you first launch Paint, the default drawing tool is a pencil. To draw with the pencil or any drawing tool, simply drag it. This will be demonstrated shortly.

The selections in the next exercises are required for the object that you will draw in the following section.

1 **Launch *Paint***

 2 **If needed, click Paint's *Maximize* button to maximize it**   [**Alt** + **Spacebar** , **X**]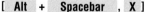

3 **If needed, click *View*, *Status Bar* to turn it on**

SELECTING A TOOL. The **tool box,** as in Figure WIN3-15a, provides a variety of tools that can be used to create a drawing. Remember, the pointer becomes the selected drawing tool when in the workspace (drawing area). Procedures for tool selection are the same for each tool. Many tools offer options as to drawing width, shape, opaqueness, and fill style. If available for a tool, these options appear at the bottom of the tool box when the tool is selected. To see some of these options and practice selecting different tools, select the Line and then Ellipse tools.

> **Tip:** Pointing to many buttons in the Windows environment without clicking will display their titles.

To select the Line tool,

STEPS

1   Click the *Line* tool box button

Note that a variety of line widths appear below the tool buttons in the tool box as in Figure WIN3-15b. The default line width setting is the thinnest width. *The drawing width selected for the line or curve tool becomes the drawing width for any other tool selected afterward.* For the first drawing exercise in the next section, select the widest drawing width now:

2   Click the *Thickest* drawing width in the tool box (bottom width)

FIGURE WIN3-15 ■ SELECTING A DRAWING TOOL

(a) The tool box provides a variety of drawing tools. To select a tool, simply click its button. The lower portion of the tool box displays a tool's options (if any).
(b) Selecting the Line or Curve tool will display these drawing width options at the bottom of the dialog box.
(c) The Ellipse, Rectangle, Polygon, and Rounded Rectangle tools offer these fill style options when selected.

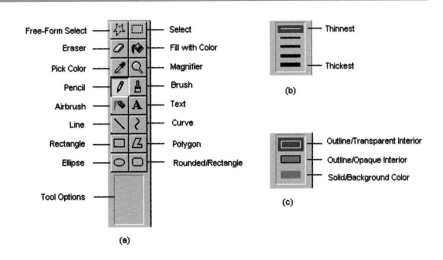

WIN

Tip: Drawing width options also appear when the Curve tool is selected.

To select the Ellipse tool:

3 **Click the *Ellipse* tool**

As in Figure WIN3-15c, three fill style options appear at the bottom of the tool box: outline with a transparent interior, outline with an opaque interior, and solid with the background color. This tool can be used to draw ellipses or perfect circles. Wait until you are ready to complete the first drawing exercises in the next section before making this selection.

Tip: Fill styles are also available when using the Rectangle, Polygon, and Round Rectangle tools.

SELECTING A PALETTE COLOR. The **palette,** as in Figure WIN3-16, has a Select Colors box and a Paint Palette. The **Select Colors box** displays the currently selected foreground (black) and background colors (white). The color used by a tool when drawing is the foreground color. The background color is the drawing area's color. The **drawing area** is the workspace of Paint's window, which is like a piece of canvas or paper.

This text assumes that you are using a color monitor and that your palette has a variety of colors. If you have a black-and-white monitor, just pick a different pattern from the palette when performing the next exercises.

To select another foreground color, simply click the desired color in the palette. For example, to select red,

---

FIGURE WIN3-16 ■ **THE PALETTE**

Clicking a color in the paint palette will select the foreground color, which is used by the selected drawing tool. Right-clicking a color in the paint palette will select the background color.

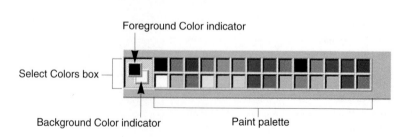

WIN

STEP

1 Click the *Red* palette box

Note that the foreground color in the Select Colors box is now red. Leave this selection for the first drawing exercise.

> **Tip: To change the background color, right-click the desired color.**

DRAWING OBJECTS

Once you have selected a drawing tool, width, and color, you are ready to draw an object. An *object* is a picture that may include a graphic image or text. For example, the *My Computer* icon on the desktop is an object that includes a picture of a computer and the title "My Computer." To learn how to use Paint's features, you will create the "No Smoking" symbol in Figure WIN3-17. As you draw, take special note of the techniques that are used to draw each part of this picture. This text assumes that you have completed the previous section "Selecting a Drawing Tool."

DRAWING A SHAPE.   In this section you will use the Ellipse, Line, and Rounded Rectangle tools to draw a "don't" symbol (circle with a slash) and a cigarette. Horizontal and vertical (x, y) pointer position coordinates and width × height object dimensions are provided for drawing each shape. You do not have to be exactly at each set of coordinates or dimensions for the shapes that you create next. They are provided only as a guide.

To draw a red circle as in Figure WIN3-18a:

STEPS

1 Point to the position 30, 160 (horizontal, vertical)

FIGURE WIN3-17 ■   A DRAWING OF A "NO SMOKING" SYMBOL

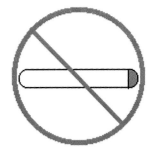

2 Press and hold **Shift** while dragging diagonally southeast to the dimensions 140 × 140 (width × height) and then release your mouse.

Holding the Shift key while dragging creates a perfect circle instead of an ellipse. Your circle should resemble Figure WIN3-18a.

> **Tip:** If you make a mistake, click *Edit, Undo* to undo your last action.

To save this drawing as 1PAINT:

 3 Click *File, Save*

4 Type **1PAINT** in the Filename text box

 5 Click the "▼" button of the *Save as type* drop-down box and then click *16 Color Bitmap*

The default file type is 256 Color Bitmap. Although this is the highest quality file, it requires a lot of disk space when saved. The exercises in this manual will use 16 Color Bitmap to conserve disk space.

 6 If needed, click the "▼" button of the *Save in* drop-down box and then click *3½ Floppy (A:)* to change the default drive to Drive A

7 Click the *Save* button

To draw a line across the circle as in Figure WIN3-18b:

 8 Click the *Line* tool on the tool box

FIGURE WIN3-18 ■ DRAWING SHAPES

(a) To draw a circle, press and hold the Shift key while dragging the Ellipse tool diagonally.
(b) To draw a straight line, press and hold the Shift key while dragging the Line tool.
(c) The Rounded/Rectangle, Line, and Fill With Color tools were used to create this picture of a cigarette.

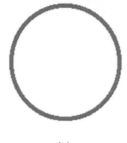

(a)   (b)   (c)

9 Move to position 50, 182

10 Press and hold Shift while dragging southeast diagonally to the dimensions 95 × 95 and then release your mouse (As with drawing a circle, holding the Shift key while dragging the Line tool will draw a perfect line.)

Your "don't" symbol should resemble Figure WIN3-18b.

11 Resave your drawing as 1PAINT

Now to draw a cigarette as in Figure WIN3-18c.

12 Click the thinnest line width in the bottom section of the tool box

13 Click the *Rounded Rectangle* tool to select it

14 Click the color *Black* in the palette

15 Move to position 245, 220

16 Without releasing your mouse until the shape is completed, drag down to the dimensions 1 × 20, and then drag right horizontally to the dimensions 125 × 20

17 Release your mouse

18 Click the *Line* tool again

19 Move your pointer to position 358, 220

20 Press and hold Shift while dragging down vertically to the dimensions 1 × 20 and then release your mouse

Your cigarette drawing should resemble Figure WIN3-18c. Unlike the figure, the tip of your cigarette should be blank.

21 Resave the document as 1PAINT

FILLING IN AN AREA.   The Fill with Color tool can be used to *fill in* an area with a color or pattern. In the next exercise, you will use the Fill with Color tool to fill in the tip of the cigarette with gray and the open space of the drawing area with yellow.

STEPS

1 If needed, open the 1PAINT document

2 Click the *Fill with Color* tool to select it

3 Click the color *Gray* in the palette

4 Move the *Fill with Color* tool within the cigarette tip and then click it to fill

5 Resave the drawing as 1PAINT

Now, to fill in the drawing area with yellow,

6 Click the color *Yellow* in the palette

7 Point to any open space in the drawing area and click

The area around your "don't" symbol and cigarette are now yellow. Continue to the next section without saving, keeping the screen as is.

UNDOING.   Like other Windows programs, Paint has an undo command that will undo your last action. *Undo* does not work if you have resaved your document or selected another drawing tool.
To undo the yellow fill,

1 Click *Edit*, *Undo*   [**Ctrl**   +   **Z**   ]

The yellow now disappears from your drawing area.

2 Click *File*, *New*, *No* to clear your drawing area   [**Ctrl**   +   **N** ,   **N**   ]

MOVING AND COPYING OBJECTS

When drawing, the ability to move or copy an object can save time and help create other objects. For instance, in the next exercise you will move the "don't" symbol over the cigarette to create a "No Smoking" symbol.
The process of moving or copying a selection in Paint is the same as in WordPad. However, as you will soon see, the selection procedure is different.
Remember, moving a selection involves changing its location. Copying a selection involves duplicating it in another location. The difference between moving and copying is that moving removes (cuts) the selection from its original position.

SELECTING AN OBJECT.   To select an object in Paint, you must use either the *Select* or the *Free-Form Select* tool. The **Select tool** is used to select an object with a dashed rectangular box. The **Free-Form Select tool** is used to custom or precision select an object with a dash line by its contour. Only selecting with the Select tool is demonstrated next:

1 Open the 1PAINT document

2 Click the *Select tool* (top right tool)

3 Move your pointer to position 15, 150 and click

4 Drag diagonally southeast to the dimensions 165 × 165 and then release your mouse

Your "don't" symbol should now be selected with a rectangular dashed box. If it is not fully selected, repeat Steps 3 and 4 and adjust your coordinates and dimensions as needed.

> **Tip:** To select an object with the Free-Form Select tool, simply drag your mouse around the object.

Once an object is selected, it can be moved or copied within the drawing area or to another document. Because these procedures are similar, only moving techniques are demonstrated next:

5 Click *Edit, Cut* to move the selection to the Clipboard   [**Ctrl** + **X**]

(To copy instead of cut, click *Edit, Copy* or press **Ctrl** + **C** in Step 5.)

Remember, the Clipboard is a program that temporarily holds a cut or copied selection for future pasting.

6 Click *Edit, Paste*   [**Ctrl** + **V**]

Your selection now appears at the top left corner of the drawing area. At this point, it can be moved to any position within the drawing area by dragging and dropping.

7 Point anywhere within the rectangular selected area

8 Drag and then drop the "don't" symbol (red circle with a slash) over the cigarette as in Figure WIN3-19

9 Click anywhere outside the selection area to deselect

Your "No Smoking" symbol should resemble Figure WIN3-17.

10 Resave this drawing as 1PAINT

> **Tip:** A quick way to move a selected object around the drawing area is to drag it. To copy using this technique, you must hold the Ctrl key while dragging.

WIN

FIGURE WIN3-19 ■ SELECTING AN OBJECT

To select an object, click the Select tool and drag diagonally across the object. The selected object will appear with a dashed line around it. The dots on the dashed line are handles that can be dragged to resize the selection.

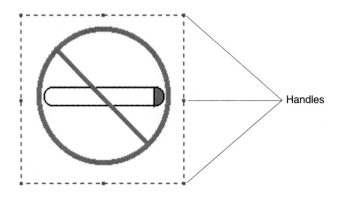

Handles

INSERTING TEXT

The **Text tool,** denoted by "A," allows you to place text into your drawing. As with other tools, you may select its color by using the palette. In addition, a **Text toolbar** is available when using the Text tool for other text appearance changes including font, font size, and style changes.

To add the caption "NO SMOKING" above the "No Smoking" symbol in your 1PAINT document as in Figure WIN3-20,

STEPS

1 **If needed, open the 1PAINT document**

FIGURE WIN3-20 ■ THE COMPLETED "NO SMOKING" SIGN

NO SMOKING

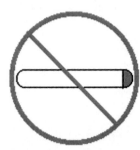

2 **Click the *Text* tool in the tool box**

You must now define the *text area,* as in Figure WIN3-21a. This is the area where your text will appear in the document:

3 **Move to the position 235, 110 and click**

4 **Without releasing your mouse button, drag right horizontally to the 145 × 1 width and height and then drag down vertically to 145 × 35 as in Figure WIN3-21a**

5 **Release your mouse button**

6 **If needed, click *View, Text Toolbar* (Font toolbar) to turn it on**

7 **Click the "▼" button of the *Font* drop-down box (Text toolbar)**

8 **Use the vertical scroll bar of the *Font* drop-down list to locate *Times New Roman* and click it**

9 **Click the "▼" button of the *Font Size* drop-down box and then click *14* for font size**

10 **Click the *Bold* button**

FIGURE WIN3-21 ■ INSERTING TEXT

(a) To insert text, click the *Text* tool and then drag to define the text area.
(b) Clicking *View, Text Toolbar* after defining the text area turns on this toolbar.

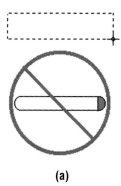

(a)

(b)

WIN

The selections in your Text (Font) toolbar should resemble Figure WIN3-21b.

 Click the *Text Entry* box to move the insertion point there

 Type   NO SMOKING

13 **Click outside of the *Text Entry* box to deselect it**

14 **If needed, to better center the "NO SMOKING" text above the "No Smoking" symbol, click the *Select tool,* select the "NO SMOKING" text, and then drag and drop it as needed.**

Your completed "No Smoking" sign should resemble Figure WIN3-20.

15 **Resave this drawing as 1PAINT**

16 **Click *File, Print, OK* to print your 1PAINT document (If you do not have a color printer, your image will print with gray tones.)** **[Ctrl + P , ↵]**

17 **Close Paint**

CAPTURING A SCREEN

Screen capturing is the process of taking a picture of your current screen. To capture a screen, simply press the *Print Screen* button on the keyboard. This copies the current image of your screen to the Clipboard for future pasting. Pasting this image to Paint allows you to edit, save, and print it.

> **Tip: A screen capture can be pasted to any program that accepts it.**

Try this to capture a screen of the Paint window with your 1PAINT document opened.

STEPS

1 **Launch and maximize your Paint window**

2 **Open the 1PAINT document**

3 **Press   Print Screen   and wait a few seconds**

4 **Click *File, New* and if needed, *No* to clear the workspace**

5 **Click *Edit, Paste*** **[Ctrl + V]**

An image of the screen similar to Figure WIN3-22 appears selected in Paint's drawing area. You can now edit and save this image. For now, exit Paint without saving:

 6 **Click Paint's *Close* button, *No***

7 **If desired, shut down Windows**

FIGURE WIN3-22 ■ SCREEN CAPTURING

Pressing the Print Screen key copies the image of the current screen to the Clipboard. Clicking *Edit, Paste* places the image into Paint for editing, saving, and printing.

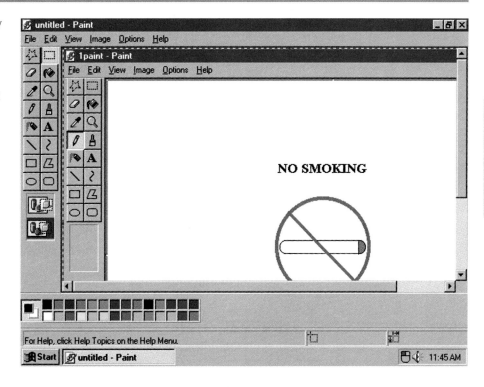

Tip: To screen capture just the active window, press [Alt] + [Print Screen].

 CHECKPOINT

✓ Launch Paint
✓ Draw a happy face with any line size and color you desire and save it as FACE.
✓ Copy the face image created in the previous checkpoint and change its expression to a sad face.
✓ Insert the text "Happy" above the happy face image and "Sad" above the other image.
✓ Resave the document as FACE and close Paint.

LINKING AND EMBEDDING

Earlier you learned how to copy and move information both between and within programs. Here you will explore two other techniques to share information between documents of different programs: linking and embedding.

In linking and embedding, an **object** is a set of information. The document with the original information is called the **source file.** The document receiving the information is called the **container file** or **compound document.**

The term **OLE** (short for "Object Linking and Embedding") refers to transferring information from one program to another as an object. When you OLE an object, it retains its source file's display format in the container file. For example, if you OLE a selection from Paint into a WordPad document, it will appear in Paint's format. This will be demonstrated shortly.

Objects may also be linked or embedded into a container file in formats that may differ from their source. Format options may differ for different programs. Only OLE (objects linked or embedded as objects) operations are demonstrated here. You may want to try the other format options on your own.

LINKING

Linking establishes an ongoing connection between the source file that provides the object and the container file that receives it. The object remains stored in the source file. The copy of the object in the container file is automatically updated whenever the source file's object is changed. For example, if a Paint object is linked with WordPad, changes in the Paint object will appear in the WordPad document.

EMBEDDING

Embedding inserts an object from the source file into a container file. The object then becomes part of the container file. Any changes in the source file do not appear in the embedded object.

You can, of course, change information in the embedded object. An embedded object is edited by using its source program without changing the source file. You might, for example, embed information from a Paint document into a WordPad document and then change only the information in the container file (WordPad document).

Because linking and embedding operations are similar, only an embedding operation is demonstrated next. Linking commands are supplied in brackets "[ ]" where different.

EMBEDDING AN OBJECT.   The following exercise embeds the "NO SMOKING" sign in the 1PAINT document into the 3WORDPAD document. Remember, embedding an object simply inserts it into the container file with the ability to edit the object using the source program. The following procedure assumes that you created the 3WORDPAD and 1PAINT documents from the previous modules in this chapter:

1 Start your computer and Windows

2 Launch Paint and open the 1PAINT document

3 If needed, click *View, Status Bar* to turn it on

4 Click the *Select* tool

5 Move your pointer to position 215, 100 (horizontal, vertical)

6 Drag the pointer diagonally southeast to position 210, 210 to select your drawing

7 Click *Edit*, *Copy* to copy the selection to the Clipboard   [Ctrl + C]

Note: You must start with the source file to create a link.

Remember, the Copy command copies a selection to the Clipboard, a program that temporarily holds the selection for future pasting, embedding, or paste linking into another location. Now you will use the *Paste Special* dialog box to embed your object into the 3WORDPAD document.

8 Launch WordPad, maximize it (if needed) and open the 3WORDPAD document

9 Press Ctrl + End to move to the bottom of the document

10 Press ↵ twice to skip two lines.

11 Click *Edit*, *Paste Special* for its dialog box as in Figure WIN3-23

This dialog box lets you either paste (the default), which embeds an object, or paste link (if available). Several format options, if available, are listed in the *As* list box of the dialog box. To paste as an embedded bitmap object,

FIGURE WIN3-23 ■ THE PASTE SPECIAL DIALOG BOX

This dialog box is used for embedding or linking objects.

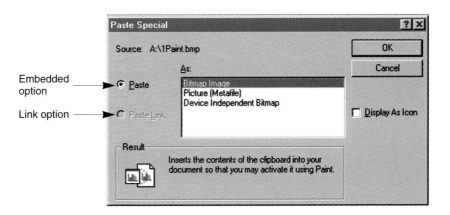

12   **Click *OK***

(To paste link instead of embed, click the *Paste Link* option (if available), then click OK for Step 12.)

The 1PAINT image appears in the WordPad document as in Figure WIN3-24. It is also currently selected and can be moved by dragging it, or it can be resized by dragging one of its handles.

13   **Click outside the embedded object to deselect it.**

14   **Save this document as 1EMBED**

EDITING AN EMBEDDED OBJECT.   To edit an embedded (or linked) object in its source program,

STEPS

1   **Double-click the embedded (or linked) object in WordPad**

The object is now displayed in its source program within the WordPad document as in Figure WIN3-24b. Note also the Paint's menu bar, tool box, palette, and status bar also appear in the WordPad window. This allows you to edit the object in Paint.

2   **Use the Rectangle tool to draw a rectangular box around the "NO SMOKING" text as in Figure WIN3-25**

3   **Click outside the object's window to deselect it**

4   **Resave your embedded document as 1EMBED and print it**

> **Tip: Some programs, upon saving the edited container file, give you the option to change the source file.**

Your printed document now appears as in Figure WIN3-25. Because this object is embedded, only the container file was changed. Embedded objects are stored with the container file. Changes in the source file are not typically reflected in the container file. Complete the following steps to see that your source file has been unchanged.

> **Tip: If this object were linked, the changes would be automatically reflected in the source and container files. Linked information is stored with the source file.**

5   **Click the *1Paint-Paint* taskbar button to switch back to Paint**

FIGURE WIN3-24 ■   EMBEDDING AN OBJECT

(a) This object has been embedded from the 1PAINT document.
(b) Double-clicking an embedded object allows you to edit it in its source program without changing its source file.

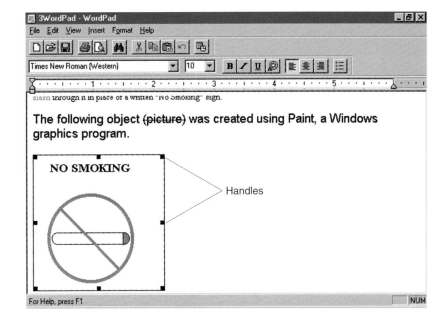

(a)

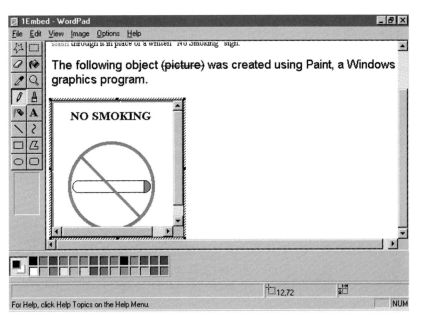

(b)

Examine the source document and note that the changes made in the 1EMBED document are not reflected there.

 6   Close Paint and WordPad

FIGURE WIN3-25 ■ **THE PRINTED COMPLETED DOCUMENT**

Your Name
M/D/YY

Windows is a *graphical user interface* (GUI) that uses pictures and menus instead of typewritten commands to help you communicate with your computer. It is like using a picture of a cigarette with a red slash through it in place of a written "No Smoking" sign.

The following object (picture) was created using Paint, a Windows graphics program.

NO SMOKING

---

7 **Shut down Windows**

> **Tip:** If the object were linked and you later made changes to the linked Paint document while the WordPad document was not opened, the changes would appear the next time you opened it. Of course, this will only happen if both source and container files and programs are available in the same system.

> **Tip:** To link or embed an entire document (file), use the Object command of the *Insert* menu. You can also use this command to embed a new object into a container file. For example, you can create a worksheet in Word using Excel. Once the new object is embedded, you can also link it. See your on-line instructions for details.

☑ CHECKPOINT

✓ Launch Paint and open the FACE document created in the Paint Checkpoint and resave it with the name SERVER.
✓ Select and copy the images to the Clipboard.
✓ Launch WordPad, type your name, and then save the document as CONTAINER.

✓ Embed the images from the Clipboard to the CONTAINER file beneath your name.
✓ Edit the embedded object from the CONTAINER document, adding a few things to the images and resave.

OTHER WINDOWS PROGRAMS

Windows comes with a variety of programs. To use many of these programs, you must first install them on your system. This section provides an overview of some of these programs and their key features. Check with your instructor before trying to access any of them.

STEP

1 Start Windows

ACCESSIBILITY OPTIONS

Windows **accessibility options** allows you to adjust keyboard, display, sound, and mouse controls based on individual preference. You can access the accessibility options through the Control Panel. Try this:

STEPS

 1 Click the *Start* button   [**Ctrl** + **Esc**]

2 Point to *Settings* for its submenu and then click *Control Panel*

 3 Double-click the *Accessibility Options* icon

As in Figure WIN3-26, the *Accessibility Options* dialog box has five tabs: Keyboard, Sound, Display, Mouse, and General. Each tab clearly defines its option.

4 Examine the Keyboard tab options

5 Click each of the other tabs to see their options

If you are working on your own system, you may want to select some of the options offered in the *Accessibility Options* dialog box. If you are on a network or other system, check with your instructor before making any changes.

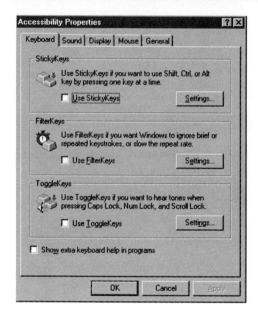

ACCESSORIES

The Windows **Accessories** group includes a variety of programs that can help you perform daily tasks. You have already worked with at least three of these programs, namely, Notepad, WordPad, and Paint. Figure WIN3-27 summarizes the Accessories programs. (Note: Your system's programs may vary.)

COMMUNICATIONS

Windows comes with a variety of **communications programs** that can be used for connecting to other computers, on-line services, electronic mail, and fax operations. Microsoft also has its own on-line service called Microsoft Network. **Electronic mail** allows users to send and receive electronic documents through a network or other forms of communication. Many of these programs require a modem, fax/modem, and/or network. See Figure WIN3-28 for a summary of these programs and their requirements.

A very popular source of on-line information service is the **Internet,** a group of international computer networks communicating by phone lines. It provides a variety of services including *electronic mail,* news, research information, and games.

You can use Windows Dial-Up Network to connect to the Internet or Microsoft Network. Both features require a modem and Microsoft Network also requires that you have Microsoft Exchange and have signed up as a user. See your on-line Help window for more information on accessing the Internet.

FIGURE WIN3-27 ■ WINDOWS ACCESSORIES

Accessory Program	Function
Calculator	On-line Calculator.
Calendar	For daily scheduling.
Cardfile	For creating electronic index cards.
Character Map	For inserting symbols and characters in a document.
Clipboard Viewer	For viewing the contents of Windows Clipboard.
Desktop Wallpaper	For inserting background images (pictures in the desktop background.
Document Templates	For creating new documents for your most common programs.
Games	Includes several games such as Solitaire, Minesweeper, Hearts, and FreeCell.
Mouse Pointers	For changing the size of your mouse pointer.
Notepad	For creating and editing text-only files.
Net Watcher	For monitoring your network.
Online User Guide	Windows 95 User Guide.
Paint	For creating, editing, and saving color images.
Quick View	For viewing a document without opening it.
Screen Savers	For preventing damage to your screen by displaying moving images while it is idle.
System Monitor	Monitor system performance.
System Resource Meter	For viewing system resource levels.
Windows 95 Tour	On-line tutorial for operating Windows 95.
WinPopup	For sending or receiving messages on a network.
WordPad	For creating simple documents.

STEPS

1 Close any open window

2 Shut down Windows

☑ CHECKPOINT

✓ What is available through the Windows accessibility options?
✓ Launch Calendar (Accessories group) and enter your class schedule for the current week. Save this file as SCHEDULE and then close the program.

FIGURE WIN3-28 ■ WINDOWS COMMUNICATION PROGRAMS

Program Group	Description
Dial-up Network	For connecting to other computers by modem.
Direct Cable Connection	For connecting to other computers by parallel or serial cable.
Hyper Terminal	For connecting to on-line services and other computers by modem.
Phone Dialer	For dialing a phone through a modem.
Microsoft Exchange	For managing and integrating electronic mail, MAPI, and other messaging programs. (Requires a network and/or modem.)
Microsoft Mail Services	For accessing Microsoft Mail Post Offices. (Requires a network and/or modem.)
Microsoft Fax Services	For sending and receiving faxes. (Requires a fax/modem.)
Microsoft Fax Viewer	For viewing Microsoft Fax images. (Requires a fax/modem.)
Microsoft Network	Microsoft's on-line service. (Requires Microsoft Exchange and a modem.)
Multilanguage Support	For creating documents in other languages.
Multimedia	For using CD-ROM drives and sound cards to play sound and videos.

✓ Launch Cardfile and create index cards for five or more of your friends and family members. Include each person's name, address, and telephone number. Save this file as PHONE and then close the program.

✓ Describe a few communications programs that come with Windows.

✓ What is the Clipboard Viewer and how can you access it?

SUMMARY

■ *WordPad* is a simple word processing program that can create and edit computer documents with text and objects (graphic) images.

■ Content changes include inserting, deleting, modifying, copying, and moving text in the document.

■ Text appearance changes include alterations to font type, style (regular, bold, or italic), and size.

■ Layout (format) changes concern the way text is arranged in a document, such as changes to the margin or tab settings.

■ Pressing the Enter key when using WordPad is *not* required at the end of each line. Text automatically flows to the next line as you type, which is called wordwrapping.

■ The Enter key produces a line break at the point where it is pressed ending a line before it reaches the right margin. It also moves the insertion point to the beginning of the next line. Line breaks are generally needed at the end of a paragraph, each line of an address, a salutation, or to skip a line.

- Selecting text involves marking (highlighting) it for editing. A selection of text is simply a contiguous segment of text. Text must be selected to perform appearance and format changes on it.

- Deleting text involves removing it from a document. When you delete text in a *Word-Pad* document, the remaining text automatically reformats.

- Paint is a graphics program that can create and save color images (pictures). It can also edit graphic images created with other programs as well as edit and save screen captures.

- Screen capturing is similar to taking a photograph of your current screen.

- Paint uses the mouse pointer as its drawing tool in its workspace. In addition to common Windows features, Paint also has a tool box at the left side of its workspace and a palette at the bottom of its window.

- Paint's status bar has three sections: a messages area (left side), pointer coordinates, and object dimensions in pixels (right side). All objects drawn with a computer are composed of pixels (small dots).

- In linking and embedding, an object is a set of information. The document with the original information is called the source file. The document receiving the information is called the container file or compound document.

- Object Linking and Embedding (OLE) refers to transferring information from one program to another as an object.

- Linking establishes an ongoing connection between the source file that provides the object and the container file that receives it. The object remains stored in the source file. The copy of the object in the container file is automatically updated whenever the source file's object is changed.

- Embedding inserts an object from the source file into a container file. The object then becomes part of the container file. Any changes in the source file do not appear in the embedded object.

- Accessibility options allow you to adjust keyboard, display, sound, and mouse controls based on individual preference.

- The Windows Accessories group includes a variety of programs that are helpful in performing daily tasks and are listed in Figure WIN3-27.

- Windows Communication programs can be used for connecting to other computers, on-line services, electronic mail, and fax operations. Microsoft also has its own on-line service called Microsoft Network. Many of these programs require a modem, fax/modem, and/or network.

KEYTERMS

Accessibility options (WIN163)
Accessories (WIN164)
Alignment (WIN138)
Bolding (WIN135)
Bullet style (WIN140)
Communications programs (WIN164)
Container file or compound document (WIN158)
Drawing area (WIN148)
Drawing tool (WIN146)
Electronic mail (WIN164)

Embedding (WIN158)
Font (WIN133)
Free-Form Select tool (WIN152)
Indentation (WIN136)
Internet (WIN164)
Italicizing (WIN135)
Layout (format) (WIN124)
Line break (WIN126)
Linking (WIN158)
Object (WIN158)
OLE (WIN158)
Paint (WIN144)
Palette (WIN148)

Pixel (WIN145)
Screen capturing (WIN156)
Select Colors box (WIN148)
Select tool (WIN152)
Source file (WIN158)
Tabs (WIN141)
Text appearance (WIN124)
Text tool (WIN154)
Text toolbar (WIN154)
Tool box (WIN146)
Wordwrap (WIN126)

QUIZ

TRUE/FALSE

____ 1. Most Windows programs can be launched from the *Start* menu.
____ 2. Only text can be placed into a WordPad document.
____ 3. Selecting text or an object involves marking it for editing.
____ 4. Only the Open and *Save As* dialog boxes can be used for file management.
____ 5. WordPad's ruler can be used for text appearance changes.
____ 6. Paint can be used to create color drawings with text and objects.
____ 7. The Cut command will move any selection to the Windows Clipboard for future pasting.
____ 8. Changes in a linked source file do not affect the container file.
____ 9. Double-clicking an embedded object will allow you to edit using its source program.
____ 10. Communications programs can only be used with a modem.

MULTIPLE CHOICE

____ 11. All of the following can be used to open a saved document except,
    a. Clicking *Open, File*
    b. Using My Computer
    c. Pressing **Ctrl** + **O**
    d. Clicking *File, Open*

____ 12. Which command will clear the workspace of WordPad, Paint, or Notepad?
    a. Clear
    b. New
    c. Exit
    d. Delete

____ 13. Which graphical WordPad feature can be used to set indentation by mouse?
    a. Toolbar
    b. *Edit* menu
    c. Ruler
    d. Indent bar

____ 14. The Copy command will copy a selection to
    a. Windows Clipboard
    b. A new location in the same document
    c. A new location in another document
    d. Paint

____ 15. To select a drawing tool in Paint
    a. Double-click its button in the tool box
    b. Click its button in the tool box
    c. Select it from the *Tools* menu
    d. Click its button in the palette

____ 16. To select the background color
    a. Click the color in the tool box
    b. Click the color in the palette
    c. Click the color in the *Color* menu
    d. Right-click the color in the palette

___ 17. The term OLE is short for
    a. Object Line and Edit
    b. Object Linking and Embedding
    c. Opening Linking and Embedding
    d. Opening Layout and Edit

___ 18. In an embedding operation the embedded object is stored in the
    a. Source file
    b. Original document
    c. Container file
    d. Source program

___ 19. In a linking operation the linked object is stored in the
    a. Source file
    b. Original document
    c. Container file
    d. Source program

___ 20. To edit a linked or embedded object from the container document
    a. Click *Edit, Linked, or Embedded*
    b. Click the *OLE* toolbar button
    c. Double-click the linked or embedded object
    d. Click *Edit, Paste Special*

FIGURE WIN3-29 ■ MATCHING

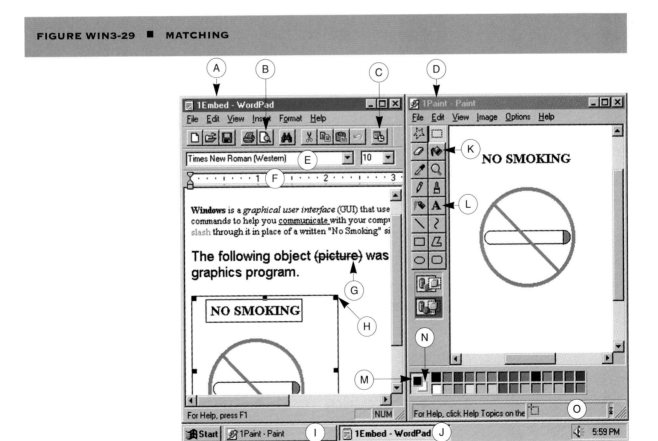

MATCHING

Select the lettered item from the figure on page WIN169 that best matches each phrase below.

___ 21. Indicates the active program.
___ 22. Dragging this item will resize the object.
___ 23. The selected foreground color.
___ 24. Can be used to adjust margins and tab settings by mouse.
___ 25. Used to insert text into a drawing.
___ 26. Can be used to insert the system date.
___ 27. The container document's name in an embedding operation.
___ 28. An effect created with the *Font* dialog box.
___ 29. The area where pointer coordinates are displayed when drawing an object.
___ 30. Used to fill an area with color.

ANSWERS

True/False: 1. T; 2. F; 3. T; 4. F; 5. F; 6. T; 7. T; 8. F; 9. T; 10. F
Multiple Choice: 11. a; 12. b; 13. c; 14. a; 15. b; 16. d; 17. b; 18. c; 19. a; 20. c
Matching: 21. j or a; 22. h; 23. m; 24. f; 25. l; 26. c; 27. a; 28. g; 29. o; 30. k

EXERCISE

I. OPERATIONS

Provide the commands to do each of the following operations. For each operation, assume a hard-disk system with a disk in Drive A. You may want to verify each command by trying it on your computer.

1. Launch WordPad and Paint and switch back to WordPad.
2. Type your name, address, and phone number on three separate lines.
3. Change the font type, size, and style of your name.
4. Center your name, address, and phone number
5. Save this WordPad document as MYLETTER.
6. Switch to Paint, draw a star, and fill it in with yellow.
7. Save the Paint document as STAR.
8. Embed the star from your Paint document into the WordPad document.
9. Edit the star from your WordPad document by adding a circle around it.
10. Resave the MYLETTER document and close all programs.

II. COMMANDS

Describe fully, using as few words as possible, what command is initiated or what is accomplished in Windows by the actions described below. Assume that each exercise part is independent of any previous parts.

1. Pressing **Ctrl** + **O** .

2. Pressing **Ctrl** + **S** .

3. Pressing **Ctrl** + **A** .

4. Clicking WordPad's ruler.

5. Double-clicking a linked object in the container file.

6. Using the Paste Special command.

7. Turning on the MouseKeys in the *Accessibility Properties* dialog box.

8. Pressing **Print Screen** .

9. Pressing and holding the Shift key while dragging the Line tool in Paint.

10. Dragging the handle of a selected object.

III. APPLICATIONS

Perform the following operations, briefly tell how you accomplished each operation, and describe its results.

APPLICATION 1: USING WORDPAD

1. Start Windows and launch WordPad.

2. Maximize the WordPad window.

3. Type the paragraphs in the box that follows. Be sure to include text appearance and layout changes.

4. Save this document as OLE.

5. Close WordPad and shut down Windows.

Your Name

Object Linking and Embedding (OLE) is a technique of transferring information from one program to another as an object. An <u>object</u> is a set of information. The document with the original information is the *source file*. The document receiving the information is the *container file*.

Linking establishes an ongoing <u>connection</u> between the source file that provides the object and the container file that receives it. The object *remains* stored in the source file. Whenever the object is changed in the source file, its copy in the container file is automatically updated.

Embedding *inserts* an object from the source file into a container file. Embedded objects can be edited from the container document using its source program. Changes to the object in the container file normally *do not* affect the source file.

APPLICATION 2: USING PAINT

1. Start Windows and launch Paint.

2. Maximize the Paint window and turn on the status bar.

3. Click the Ellipse tool.

4. Draw the head of a male stick figure (make sure you leave enough room for the body).

5. Click the Line tool.

6. Draw the body of the stick figure.

7. Save this drawing as FIGURE.

8. Print the FIGURE document.

9. Close Paint and shut down Windows

APPLICATION 3: USING A SCREEN CAPTURE

1. Start Windows and launch Paint.

2. Press **Print Screen** to capture your current screen.

3. Select the tool box from the screen capture of the Paint Window.

4. Cut the selection to the Clipboard.

5. Clear your Paint workspace.

6. Paste the selection (tool box) into the new Paint document.

7. Move it to the center of the drawing area.

8. Label the tool box. (Use Figure WIN3-15 as a guide.)

9. Save this as TOOLBOX and print it.

10. Close Paint and shut down Windows.

APPLICATION 4: EMBEDDING AN OBJECT
(Complete Applications 1, 2, and 3 before proceeding with this problem.)

1. Start Windows, launch WordPad, and open the OLE document created in Application 1.

2. Launch Paint and open the FIGURE document created in Application 2.

3. Maximize both windows.

4. Embed the stick figure from the FIGURE Paint document into the OLE WordPad document.

5. Save the revised OLE document as COUPLE.

6. Double-click the stick figure object in the COUPLE document to edit it.

7. Draw another stick figure.

8. Resave the document as COUPLE.

9. Print the COUPLE document.

10. Close all programs and shut down Windows.

APPLICATION 5: USING MOUSEKEYS

Note: Although using the Windows MouseKeys feature is helpful in creating precision drawings, it can be used with any operations in place of a mouse. The accessibility options must be installed on to your system to do this problem.)

1. Start Windows and launch Paint.

2. Turn on the MouseKeys. (For instructions, see the "Mouse and Keyboard Operations" section and Figure WIN1-2 in Chapter 1.)

3. Try to draw your favorite icon using the keyboard.

4. Save the document as MYICON.

5. Print the document.

6. Close Paint and shut down Windows.

APPLICATION 6: USING OTHER WINDOWS PROGRAMS

1. Start Windows and launch Cardfile.

2. Use the following steps to create five index cards for four family members or friends and yourself. Include each person's name, address, and phone number.
    a. Click _Edit, Index_ for its dialog box.
    b. Type last name, first name, (for example, Kee, Charles)
    c. Click _OK_
    d. Type first and last names (for example, Charles Kee) and press [↵]
    e. Type address and phone number on separate lines
    f. Click _Card, Add_
    g. Repeat Steps b through e for each new card.

3. Save this file as ADDRESSBOOK.

4. Launch WordPad and maximize its window.

5. Switch to Cardfile.

6. Click the Index (top portion of index card) to select your own card.

7. Select and copy only your name and address to the Clipboard.

8. Switch to WordPad and paste your selection there.

9. Save the WordPad document MYADDRESS and print it.

10. Close all programs and shut down Windows.

MASTERY CASES

The following mastery cases allows you to demonstrate how much you have learned about this software. Each case describes a fictitious problem or need that can be solved using the skills that you have learned in this chapter. Although minimum acceptable outcomes are specified, you are expected and encouraged to design your own response (files, data, lists) in ways that display your personal mastery of the software. Feel free to show off your skills. Use real data from your own experience in your solution, although you may also fabricate data if needed.

These mastery cases allow you to display your ability to

- Launch WordPad and Paint.
- Make text appearance and layout changes to WordPad documents.
- Create objects in Paint.
- Embed objects from Paint documents into WordPad documents.
- Edit embedded objects.

CASE 1: USING WINDOWS AT SCHOOL

You have been asked to create a graphical guide to help your classmates learn some of the key components of the Windows screen. Arrange your Windows screen as you see fit. Screen capture it into Paint and save it. Now, use Paint to add labels, boxes, arrows, and any other objects you feel will help other students. Print and then resave the document. Close all windows and shut down Windows.

CASE 2: USING WINDOWS AT HOME

You have been asked to create a family tree and place it in a letter to your parent(s). Use Paint to draw and label the tree. Save and print this document. Next, prepare a short WordPad document addressed to your parent(s) explaining that you used Windows Paint to create the family tree. Change the fonts and layout as you feel necessary. Embed the family tree from your Paint document into your WordPad document. Save and print it. Now, edit the embedded object to include each person's place of birth. Resave and print it. Close all windows and shut down Windows.

CASE 3: USING WINDOWS AT WORK

Your are in the real estate business and need to create a flyer that announces the sale of a building. Use WorddPad to create this flyer and be sure that it has your company's name and a description of the property being sold, including its address and selling price. Use different fonts and other text enhancements to make your flyer more appealing. Next, using Paint, draw a picture of a house and embed it into your flyer. Now, add a "For Sale" sign to the embedded object. Save all documents and print only the flyer. Close all windows and shut down Windows.

MICROSOFT WINDOWS 95
FEATURES AND OPERATION REFERENCE

MOUSE OPERATIONS

A mouse (or other pointing device) allows you to control a mouse pointer (graphical image). As you move your mouse, the mouse pointer moves in a similar fashion on your screen. Common mouse pointer images and commands are summarized on Figure WIN1-2a and b in Chapter 1.

COMMON MOUSE ACTIONS

POINT. Pointing involves moving the mouse pointer on the screen by moving your mouse on a flat surface. When pointing in a menu, the selection highlight moves with the pointer to the desired item. Pointing to an item with a "▶" at its far right will open its submenu.

CLICK. Clicking involves quickly pressing and releasing your left mouse button.

DOUBLE-CLICK. Double-clicking involves quickly pressing and releasing your left mouse button twice.

DRAG. Dragging involves pressing and holding the left mouse button while moving the mouse pointer to a new location. Dragging can be used to select (mark by highlighting) text. Dragging can also be used in moving and copying operations called *dragging and dropping.*

DRAG AND DROP. Dragging and dropping can be used to move or copy a selection by mouse. Dropping is releasing your mouse button and the selection after dragging. To move or copy a selection using drag and drop:

	Moving	Copying
Within the Same File	Drag and drop	Press and hold Ctrl while dragging and dropping
Between Files	Press and hold Alt key while dragging and dropping	Drag and drop

RIGHT-CLICK. Right-clicking involves quickly pressing and releasing your right mouse button.

SELECT. Selecting is the process of marking (highlighting) text or other objects in order to edit, move, copy, open, print, or delete the item. Selecting text by mouse generally involves dragging your pointer over it. Selecting an object or menu item generally involves clicking it. Graphic programs, such as Paint, require special selection techniques that involve first selecting a Selection tool and then dragging your mouse pointer.

KEYBOARD OPERATIONS

Windows and many Windows programs can also be operated by keyboard. Keys that provide quick access to commands are called *Shortcut keys*. Shortcut keys are generally available with most Windows programs. Many also follow Windows standard Shortcut keys structure. For example, pressing `Alt` + `F4` will exit any program or dialog box. Keys used to perform mouse actions such as clicking, right-clicking, double-clicking, and dragging and dropping are called *MouseKeys*. Windows Accessibility Options must be installed on your system to use MouseKeys.

Other keyboard options available with the Accessibility Options include StickyKeys, FilterKeys, and ToggleKeys. *StickyKeys* allows you to use the Alt, Ctrl, or Shift keys by pressing each key one at a time. *FilterKeys* is an option that instructs Windows to ignore repeated keystrokes. *ToggleKeys* provides a sound when the Num Lock, Caps Lock, or Scroll Lock is pressed.

COMMON SHORTCUT KEYS

ALT. Pressed alone, the Alt key activates the selection highlight on a program window's menu bar. Once activated, the highlight can open a pull-down menu by either pressing its underlined letter or using the arrow keys and then the Enter key. If used with other keys, press and hold the Alt key while tapping the other key(s).

- `Alt` + `F4` exits any Windows program or dialog box.
- `Alt` + `Spacebar` opens a program window or dialog box's control-menu.
- `Alt` + `–` opens a document window's control-menu.
- `Alt` + `Tab` switches to the last active program when operating multiple programs.
- `Alt` + `Esc` switches to the next running program when operating multiple programs.
- `Alt` + `Print Screen` copies an image of the active window to Windows for future pasting.

ARROW KEYS. The arrow keys can be used with other keys or alone. When used with the Shift key, they expand a selection in the direction of the arrow. When used alone, an arrow key

- Moves the selection highlight in the direction of the arrow in a menu, list box, or drop-down box.
- Moves the insertion point in the direction of the arrow in a document or text box.

BACKSPACE.   The Backspace key erases single characters to the left of the insertion point.

CAPS LOCK.   The Caps Lock key keeps the Shift key active so that characters can be typed in uppercase.

CTRL.   The Ctrl key is generally used with other keys to invoke a command.

- **Ctrl** + **Alt** + **Delete**   exits the current program if it stops responding to the system. It is also used to reboot the computer.
- **Ctrl** + **B**   turns the bold feature on or off.
- **Ctrl** + **C**   copies a selection to Windows Clipboard for future pasting.
- **Ctrl** + **Esc**   opens the *Start* menu.
- **Ctrl** + **F4**   closes the active document window.
- **Ctrl** + **F6**   switches the active document window when using multiple document windows.
- **Ctrl** + **I**   turns the italic feature on or off.
- **Ctrl** + **N**   opens a new document.
- **Ctrl** + **O**   opens a document.
- **Ctrl** + **P**   prints a document.
- **Ctrl** + **S**   saves a document to disk.
- **Ctrl** + **U**   turns the underline feature on or off.
- **Ctrl** + **V**   pastes the contents of Windows Clipboard to a desired location.
- **Ctrl** + **X**   cuts a section from its position and moves it to Windows Clipboard for future pasting.
- **Ctrl** + **Z**   undoes the last action.

DELETE.   The delete key erases the following:

- Single character to the right of the insertion point when editing data.
- A selection.

END.

- Moves the insertion point to the end of a line when editing data.
- Moves the selection highlight to the last item in a menu, list, or drop-down box.

ENTER.   This key invokes a selected command from a menu or dialog box.

ESC.   This key cancels a menu or dialog box.

FUNCTION KEYS.   The function keys, numbered **F1** through **F12**, are used alone, or in combination with the **Alt**, **Ctrl**, and **Shift** keys, to invoke commands. Except for the **F1** key, which is generally used to invoke on-line help, each program often defines the use of the function keys differently.

HOME.

- Moves the insertion point to the beginning of the line of data in a document, text box, or drop-down box.
- Moves the selection highlight to the beginning of a list in a menu, list box, or drop-down box.

INSERT.   In certain situations, the Insert key allows you to insert characters at the insertion point, called a *typeover,* when editing data in a document, text box, or drop-down box.

NUM LOCK.   This toggle (on/off) key activates the keypad that is on the right side of most keyboards. Pressing the Num Lock key either turns the keypad on or off.

PAGE UP AND PAGE DOWN.   This key moves your screen diplay one screen page up or one down.

PRINT SCREEN (PRTSC).   This key captures an image of a screen to Windows Clipboard for future pasting.

SHIFT.   This key works similar to the Shift key on a typewriter. When you hold it down and then press a letter or number, an uppercase letter or symbol assigned to a number key is produced. Other common commands invoked with the Shift key include:

- **Shift** + **Arrow key** expands the selection highlight in the direction of the arrow.
- **Shift** + **Tab** moves the insertion point or the selection highlight (or dotted rectangle) back one choice in a dialog box.
- **Shift** + **End** expands the selection highlight to the end of a line.

TAB.   This key moves the insertion point or dotted selection rectangle to the next option in a dialog box.

MOUSE ACTIONS BY KEYBOARD—MOUSEKEYS

MouseKeys is a feature of Windows Accessibility Options that you can access through the Control Panel. It allows you to use the numeric keypad to invoke mouse actions such as clicking, right-clicking, double-clicking, and dragging and dropping. To use any accessibility options, the program must first be installed on your system. This can be checked through Windows Add/Remove Programs feature.

CHECKING FOR THE ACCESSIBILITY OPTIONS FEATURE.   If the *Accessibility Options* icon appears in the Control Panel, then it has been installed on your system and is ready for use. To check,

---

STEPS

1 Click the *Start* button   [**Ctrl** **+** **Esc**]

2 Point to *Settings*

3 Click *Control Panel*

4 Examine the Control Panel window for the *Accessibility Options* icon

If the *Accessibility Options* icon does not appear and you have the Windows 95 CD-ROM (you must also have a CD-ROM drive) or setup disks, go to the Installing Accessibility Options section for installation procedures. If you want to turn on the MouseKey option, see the Turning On/Off MouseKeys section. To exit the Control Panel,

5 Click the Control Panel's *Close* button

INSTALLING ACCESSIBILITY OPTIONS.   The accessibility options can be installed using the *Add/Remove Programs* dialog box.

STEPS

1 Click the *Start* button   [**Ctrl** **+** **Esc**]

2 Point to *Settings*

3 Click *Control Panel*

4 Double-click the *Add/Remove Programs* icon

5 Click the *Windows Setup* tab

6 Click the *Accessibility Options* check box

7 Click the *Apply* button

8 Insert the Windows 95 CD-ROM or appropriate disk as requested on the screen

9 Click the *OK* button

TURNING MOUSEKEYS ON OR OFF. The MouseKeys feature can be turned on or off using the *Mouse* tab of the *Accessibility Properties* dialog box. When the MouseKeys feature is on, you can use the numeric keypad to invoke mouse actions. To turn on/off the MouseKeys feature,

STEPS

1 Click the *Start* button   [**Ctrl** + **Esc**]

2 Point to *Settings* for its submenu

3 Click *Control Panel* for its window

4 Double-click the *Accessibility Options* icon for its dialog box

5 Click the *Mouse* tab

6 Click the *Use MouseKeys* check box

7 Click the *OK* button to exit the dialog box

8 Click the *Close* button of the Control Panel window

When the MouseKeys feature is on, a *mouse* icon appears in the message area of the taskbar. Double-clicking this icon also opens the *Accessibility Properties* dialog box.

USING MOUSEKEYS. When the MouseKeys feature is on, you can control the mouse pointer movement by using the numeric keypad. See Figure WIN1-2d in Chapter 1 for this type of operation.

SUMMARY OF COMMON WINDOWS FEATURES

As in Figure WIN1-1 of Chapter 1, the Windows screen has two main components: a taskbar (which appears at the bottom of the screen) and the desktop (which is the large area above the taskbar). The taskbar has a *Start* button on its left and a message area displaying the system's time (and other messages) on its right. The desktop has several icons (small pictures) on it, including *My Computer* and the *Recycle Bin*. The following is summary of common Windows operations.

ADDING NEW HARDWARE

Windows provides a *New Hardware wizard* (a *wizard* is a program that helps make complicated tasks easier) to help you install new hardware.

STEPS

1   Turn off power

2   Install the new hardware

   3   Click the *Start* button   [Ctrl   +   Esc   ]

4   Point to *Settings* and then click *Control Panel*

5   Double-click the *Add New Hardware* icon for the New Hardware wizard

6   Follow the wizard's instructions

ADDING, REMOVING, AND CONTROLLING PRINTERS

The Printers program can be used to add a new printer to your system, switch the default printer, or view or control the status of current print jobs. A print job is simply documents sent to your printer to be printed. Windows allows you to send several print jobs to your printer. Although they are printed in the order sent, you can use Printers to change this order.

LAUNCHING PRINTERS.   To launch the Printers program,

STEPS

   1   Click the *Start* button   [Ctrl   +   Esc   ]

2   Point to *Settings* and then click *Control Panel*

   3   Double-click the *Printers* folder icon for its window

Printers

ADDING A NEW PRINTER. To add a new printer,

STEPS

1 Launch the Printers program

2 Double-click the *Add Printer* icon in the Printers window

3 Follow the Add Printer wizard

REMOVING A PRINTER. To remove a printer,

STEPS

1 Launch the Printers program

2 Click the desired printer icon to be removed

3 Press Delete

4 Click *Yes*

CONTROLLING A CURRENT PRINT JOB(S). To see the status or control your current print jobs immediately after invoking the print command,

STEPS

1 Double-click the *Printers* icon in the message area of the status bar

The title bar of your printer's window should display the name of your printer. If you were printing any documents, it would first appear here. If you have several print jobs, they would be listed in this window with their current print status.

2 Select the print job(s) for editing

3 Invoke the desired edit command

For example, if you desired to delete selected print jobs, simply press the Delete key in Step 3. You can also open your printer's window by double-clicking its icon in the Printers window.

ADDING OR REMOVING PROGRAMS

To add/remove programs from Windows,

STEPS

1 Click the *Start* button   [**Ctrl** + **Esc**]

2 Point to *Settings* and then click *Control Panel*

3 Double-click the *Add/Remove Programs* for its *Properties* dialog box

You can also add or remove Windows setup programs by using this dialog box.

ARRANGING ICONS ON THE DESKTOP

To sort icons by name, type, size, or date or to turn the *Auto Arrange* option on or off,

STEPS

1 Right-click an empty area of the desktop for its *Shortcut* menu

2 Click *Arrange Icons* for its submenu

3 Click the desired arrangement option

To line up icons on the desktop,

STEPS

1 Right-click an empty area of the desktop for its *Shortcut* menu

2 Click *Line up Icons*

CASCADING WINDOWS ON THE DESKTOP

STEPS

1 Right-click an empty area of the taskbar for its *Shortcut* menu

2 Click *Cascade*

CHANGING DATE AND TIME

To change your system's date and time,

STEPS

1 Double-click the *Date/Time* icon

2 Make desired adjustments

3 Click *OK*

To access this dialog box quickly, double-click the time message at the right side of the taskbar.

CHANGING DISPLAY OPTIONS

You can set four screen display properties through the *Display Properties* dialog box. They include Background, Screen Saver, Appearance, and Settings. Background changes involve placing or replacing an image as the background screen of your desktop. Screen Savers help prevent the image of a frequently used program from "burning in" on your monitor's screen. Appearance changes involve setting the color of items displayed in Windows. Settings options vary the quality of the color and resolution of all displays in Windows. Each property has its own tab in the *Display Properties* dialog box.

STEPS

1 Open the Control Panel

Display

2 Double-click the *Display* icon

3 Click the desired tab

4 Make the desired changes

5 Click *OK*

CONTROL PANEL

The Control Panel is a program that can be used to change the settings on your computer. It operates similarly to any folder window. To launch the Control Panel as in Figure WIN2-26,

STEPS

1 Launch My Computer

Control Panel

2 Double-click the *Control Panel* folder icon

3 If desired, click *View, Toolbar* to turn the toolbar on

4 Click the *Maximize* button of the Control Panel window

Most icons in this window open to other windows that allow you to set the desired feature.

To view a description of an icon in the Control Panel in the status bar,

5 Click the desired icon

To access an icon's features,

6 Double-click the desired icon

You can also click the *Start* button, point to *Settings,* and then click *Control Panel* in place of Steps 1 and 2.

CREATING A NEW DOCUMENT ICON ON THE DESKTOP

STEPS

1 Right-click an empty area of the desktop for its *Shortcut* menu

2 Click *New* for its submenu

3 Click the desired document type

4 Type the document's name and then press ↵

5 Drag the document icon to its desired position on the desktop

CREATING A NEW FOLDER ICON

To create a new folder icon on the desktop,

STEPS

1 Right-click an empty area of the desktop for its *Shortcut* menu

2 Click *New* and then *Folder*

3 Type the folder's name and then press ↵

4 Drag the folder icon to its desired position on the desktop

CREATING A NEW *SHORTCUT* ICON

Shortcut icons provide quick access to a program or document.

1 Right-click an empty area of the desktop for its *Shortcut* menu

2 Click *New* and then *Shortcut* for the *Create Shortcut* dialog box

3 Type in the desired command line or click the *Browse* button and select from its dialog box

4 When back in the *Create Shortcut* dialog box, click the *Next* button

5 If desired, type in a name for the *Shortcut* icon, and then click the *Finished*, or *Next* button (whichever appears)

If no icon is associated with the shortcut, a *Select Icon* dialog box will appear. If so

6 Click a desired icon and then click the *Finished* button

7 Drag the *Shortcut* icon to its desired position on the desktop

DISPLAYING THE TITLE OF A COMMAND BUTTON

A command button invokes its feature when clicked. In general, to display the title of a command button,

1 Point to the desired button and wait for its title to appear

2 Point away from the button to remove the title

HELP

To access Windows main Help feature,

1 Click the *Start* button

2 Click *Help* for its dialog box

[Ctrl + Esc]

3 Click the desired tab

LAUNCHING A PROGRAM

To launch any program using the *Start* menu,

STEPS

1 Click the *Start* button   [Ctrl   +   Esc   ]

2 Point to *Programs* for its submenu

3 If needed, point to the desired program group (folder)

4 Click the desired program to launch it

LAUNCHING OR OPENING ICONS ON THE DESKTOP

STEPS

1 Double-click the desired icon

MINIMIZING ALL WINDOWS ON THE DESKTOP

STEPS

1 Right-click an empty area of the taskbar for its *Shortcut* menu

2 Click *Minimize All Windows*

PASTING TO THE DESKTOP

To paste the contents of Windows Clipboard to the desktop,

STEPS

1 Right-click an empty area of the desktop for its *Shortcut* menu

2 Click _Paste_

PASTING A _SHORTCUT_ ICON TO THE DESKTOP

To paste the contents of Windows Clipboard to the desktop as a _Shortcut_ icon,

STEPS

1 Right-click an empty area of the desktop for its _Shortcut_ menu

2 Click _Paste Shortcut_

PROPERTIES OF THE DESKTOP

STEPS

1 Right-click an empty area of the desktop for its _Shortcut_ menu

2 Click _Properties_ for the _Display Properties_ dialog box

PROPERTIES OF AN OBJECT

To change the properties of an object (drive, program, or document icon),

STEPS

1 Right-click the object for its _Shortcut_ menu

2 Click _Properties_ for its _Properties_ dialog box

PROPERTIES OF THE TASKBAR

To access Taskbar properties by _Shortcut_ menu,

STEPS

1 Right-click an empty area of the taskbar for its _Shortcut_ menu

2 Click _Properties_

To access taskbar properties by *Start* menu

1 **Click the *Start* button**   [**Ctrl** + **Esc**]

2 **Point to _Settings_ for its submenu**

3 **Click _Taskbar_**

RUN

You can use the Windows *Run* dialog box to launch or open a desired program or document by typing its command line. Use it also to install new software from a CD-ROM or disks.

1 **Click the *Start* button**   [**Ctrl** + **Esc**]

2 **Click _Run_ for its dialog box**

3 **Type in the desired command line or click the _Browse_ button to use its dialog box to select**

4 **Click _OK_**

SHORTCUT MENU

To open any object's (including an icon's) *Shortcut* menu,

1 **Right-click the object**

To open the desktop's *Shortcut* menu,

1 **Right-click an empty area of the desktop**

To open the taskbar's *Shortcut* menu,

STEPS

> **1** Right-click an empty area of the taskbar

SHUTTING DOWN

Shutting down Windows exits the operating system. Other *Shut Down* options are generally available upon invoking the command. These options are displayed in the *Shut Down Windows* dialog box as in Figure WIN1-6. To shut down Windows,

---

STEPS

> **1** Click the *Start* button   [**Ctrl** + **Esc**]

> **2** Click *Shut Down* for its dialog box as in Figure WIN1-6

> **3** Click the *Yes* button

> **4** Wait for Windows to prompt you with "It's now safe to turn off your computer."

> **5** Turn off your computer

START MENU

To open the *Start* menu, Windows' main menu system,

STEPS

> **1** Click the *Start* button   [**Ctrl** + **Esc**]

Items on the *Start* menu (or any menu) with a "▶" to the far right open to a submenu. To select "▶" items from a menu,

> **2** Point to the item with a "▶" to the far right   [Underlined letter or use arrow keys]

To select other items from the *Start* menu,

> **3** Click the desired item   [Underlined letter or use arrow keys]

To exit the *Start* menu (or any menu) without selecting,

> **4** Click outside of the menu   [**Esc**]

See Figures WIN1-7 and WIN1-8 in Chapter 1 for examples of the *Start* menu.

SWITCHING BETWEEN RUNNING PROGRAMS

To switch between running programs by taskbar,

STEPS

1 Click the desired program's taskbar button

To switch between running programs by keyboard,

STEPS

1 Press **Alt** + **Tab** until you locate the desired program

To switch between running programs where the desired program window is visible on the desktop,

STEPS

1 Click any area of the desired program window to switch to it

TASKBAR *SHORTCUT* MENU

STEPS

1 Right-click an empty area of the taskbar

2 Click the desired choice

TILING WINDOWS ON THE DESKTOP

STEPS

1 Right-click an empty area of the taskbar for its *Shortcut* menu

2 Click either *Tile Horizontally* or *Tile Vertically*

TIME AND DATE DIALOG BOX

STEPS

1 Double-click the time message on the taskbar

2 Adjust settings as desired

3 Click the *OK* button

SUMMARY OF COMMON WINDOW FEATURES

Most windows (programs, documents, or dialog boxes) have a variety of common Windows features. These features include

- *Title bar* with the program's icon at its left, the program's name in its center, and two resizing buttons and a *Close* button on its right. It is located at the top of a window. See Figure WIN1-10 in Chapter 1.
- A *menu bar* is available only on Program windows. It is located just below the title bar, providing mouse or keyboard access to a program's features through pull-down menus.
- A *toolbar* is a set of command buttons and drop-down boxes that provides mouse access to a program's features. It is normally located below the menu bar.
- A *workspace* is the large interior space within a window.
- A *status bar* is a line of information, generally located at the bottom of a program window.

CLOSING A WINDOW

Closing a window exits it. To close by using the *Close* button (the "X" button on the right side of the title bar)

STEPS

☒   **1** Click the *Close* button   [**Alt** + **F4** for program windows and dialog boxes]

                                            [**Ctrl** + **F4** for document windows]

To close a window by program or document icon (located on the left side of the title bar):

STEPS

1 Double-click the program or document icon

To close a window by control menu,

1 **Either click the program or document icon or right-click the title bar for the window's control menu**

2 **Click _Close_**   [**Alt** + **Spacebar** for program windows,
                                               Alt + **−** for document windows]

CONTROL MENU

Use a window's *control menu* to resize, move, or close the window. To open any window's control menu,

1 **Right-click the title bar**

2 **Click the desired item**

You can also open a program or document window's control menu by clicking its icon.

MAXIMIZING A WINDOW

To maximize (enlarge a window to its maximum size),

1 **Click the _Maximize_ button on the right side of the window's title bar**
                    [**Alt** + **Spacebar** , **X** for program windows and dialog boxes,
                                               Alt + **−** , **X** for document windows]

MENU BAR OPERATIONS

To open a pull-down menu,

1 **Click the desired menu bar item**   [**Alt** + Underlined letter of menu bar item]

To obtain a description of a pull-down menu item's function in the status bar,

2 Point to (do not click) the desired item   [Arrow keys]

To select an item from a pull-down menu,

3 Click it   [Underlined letter]

MINIMIZING A WINDOW

To minimize a program window,

STEPS

1 Click the *Minimize* button on the right side of a program window's title bar

[Alt + Spacebar , N]

For a document window,

STEPS

1 Click the *Minimize* button on the right side of the menu bar   [Alt + - , N]

RESTORING A WINDOW

To resize a maximized program window (one at its largest size) to a smaller window using the Restore command,

STEPS

1 Click the *Restore* button on the right side of a program window's title bar

[Alt + Spacebar , R]

For a document window,

STEPS

1 Click the *Restore* button on the right side of the menu bar   [Alt + – , R]

TOOLBARS

If available, Toolbars provide a set(s) of buttons and drop-down boxes that you can use to access a program's features by mouse.

TURNING A TOOLBAR ON OR OFF. If a toolbar is not turned on (displayed below the menu bar) by default, you must use the *View* menu to turn it on. In general, to turn a toolbar on or off,

STEPS

1 Click *View* for the *View* menu, and then *Toolbars*

2 Click the desired toolbar (if available)

3 Repeat Steps 1 and 2 if needed to turn additional toolbars on or off

USING A TOOLBAR. Like most buttons in the Windows environment, you can point to a toolbar button for its title or click it to invoke its feature.

To receive a toolbar button's title in a caption and a description of its function in the status bar,

STEPS

1 Point to (do not click) the desired toolbar button and wait

To remove the title caption and description message,

2 Point away from the button

To invoke a command by toolbar,

STEPS

1 Click the desired toolbar button

SUMMARY OF COMMON FILE AND EDIT COMMANDS

The techniques to invoke many basic file and edit commands are the same for most Windows programs. They include File commands to save, open, close, or print a document. Edit commands include selecting, copying, moving, pasting, and undoing. These commands are available with most Windows programs and are summarized next.

CLOSING A DOCUMENT

Closing a document removes it from system memory. You should invoke this command whenever a document is not being used to free up system memory. To close a document,

 1 Click *File, Close*   [**Ctrl** + **F4**]

COPYING A SELECTION

The Copy command duplicates a selection to Windows Clipboard, a temporary holding area. The Paste command copies the current contents of the Clipboard to a desired location. The location can be within the same document or in another document of the same or a different program.

1 Select the desired item or items

 2 Click *Edit, Copy* to copy the selection to the Clipboard   [**Ctrl** + **C**]

3 Move to the desired destination

 4 Click *Edit, Paste*   [**Ctrl** + **V**]

MOVING A SELECTION

The Cut command moves a selection from its current position to Windows Clipboard, a temporary holding area. The Paste command copies the current contents of the Clipboard to a desired location. The location can be within the same document or in another document of the same or a different program.

1 Select the desired item or items

 2 Click *Edit, Cut* to move the selection to the Clipboard   [**Ctrl** + **X**]

3 Move to the desired destination

 4 Click *Edit, Paste*   [**Ctrl** + **V**]

OBJECT LINKING AND EMBEDDING

An *object* is a set of information. Object linking and embedding (OLE) is the transferring of information from one program to another as an object. The *source file* (document) contains the original object and the *container file* or *compound document* contains the copy.

Objects may also be linked or embedded into a container file in the same format or in a format that differs from its source. Format options may differ for different programs.

LINKING AN OBJECT.   *Linking* establishes an ongoing connection between the source file that provides the object and the container file that receives it. The object remains stored in the source file. The copy of the object in the container file is automatically updated whenever the source file's object is changed.

STEPS

1   Launch the source program and open (or create) the source file

2   Select the object to be linked

3   Click *Edit, Copy*   [Ctrl + C]

4   If needed, launch the container program and open (or create) the container file

5   If needed, switch to the container file

6   Move to the position where you want the linked object to appear

7   Click *Edit, Paste Special* for its dialog box

8   Click the *Link* option

9   If desired, click a format

10   Click *OK*

EMBEDDING AN OBJECT.   *Embedding* inserts an object from the source file into a container file. The object then becomes part of the container file. Any changes in the source file do not appear in the embedded object. To embed an object,

STEPS

1   Perform Steps 1 through 7 for linking an object

2 If needed, click the *Paste* option

3 If desired, click a format

4 Click *OK*

EDITING A LINKED OR EMBEDDED OBJECT.   To edit a linked or embedded object in the container file,

STEPS

1 Double-click the object

If the object was linked, the source file and its program will appear (if running). Changes to the source file will automatically be reflected in the container file. If the object was embedded, the source program will appear in the container file. Edit changes will only affect the container file.

2 Edit the object

3 Click anywhere outside the object to turn off the edit mode

4 Save the document(s) (if linked, both source and container files must be resaved)

OPENING A DOCUMENT

STEPS

1 Click *File, Open* for its dialog box   [**Ctrl** + **O**]

2 If needed, change the default drive using the *Look in* drop-down box

3 Type in the desired file's name in the *File name* text box or click it in the *Files* list box

4 Click the *Open* button

PRINTING A DOCUMENT

STEPS

1 Click *File, Print* for its dialog box   [**Ctrl** + **P**]

2   Select the desired print options

3   Click *OK*

SAVING A DOCUMENT

The *File* menu available in most programs offers two options for saving a document: Save and Save As. Invoking the Save command on a previously saved document will re-save it under its original name. Invoking the Save As command allows you to save the current document under a different name and will warn you if the name is the same as another file. This is helpful when updating documents because it allows you to save the updated version under a new name, thus keeping the original under its old name. Both the Save and Save As commands open the *Save As* dialog box when invoked on an unsaved document. This allows you to assign the document a filename. Filenames can have up to 255 characters.

To save a document for the first time,

STEPS

1   Click *File*, *Save* (or *File*, *Save As*) for the *Save As* dialog box   [Ctrl   +   S   ]

2   If needed, change the default drive using the *Save in* drop-down box

3   Type in the desired file's name in the *File name* text box or click it in the *Files* list box

4   Click the *Save* button

To resave a document under its previous name without confirmation,

STEPS

1   Click *File*, *Save* for its dialog box   [Ctrl   +   S   ]

To resave a document under its previous name with confirmation,

STEPS

1   Click *File*, *Save As* for its dialog box

2   Click the *Save* button

3   Click the *Replace* button

To resave a document under a new name,

STEPS

1 Click *File, Save As* for its dialog box

2 If needed, change the default drive using the *Save in* drop-down box

3 Type in the desired file's name in the *File name* text box

4 Click the *Save* button

UNDOING THE LAST ACTION

STEPS

 1 Click *Edit, Undo*   [Ctrl + Z]

SUMMARY OF COMMON MY COMPUTER AND EXPLORER FEATURES

My Computer and *Explorer* are programs that allow you to view and manage every part of your computer. My Computer displays the components of your system as icons in its workspace and uses separate windows to display the contents of those items. Explorer uses a single window to list the components of your system (left side) and display the contents of a selected component (right side). Explorer also lists your system's components in a hierarchical tree. Both programs have the same menu bar and toolbar options and their status bar displays similar information.

Generally, before using any My Computer or Explorer feature, you should launch the program.

LAUNCHING MY COMPUTER

The My Computer program is normally launched directly from the desktop, not the *Start* menu. To launch the My Computer program,

STEPS

 1 Double-click the *My Computer* icon at the top left corner of the desktop

The My Computer window contains a variety of common Windows features, including a title bar (with a program icon, resizing buttons, and a *Close* button), a menu bar, workspace, and status bar. These items operate the same as in other Program windows. Its workspace is normally occupied by several drive icons, the *Control Panel* folder, and *Printers* folder.

LAUNCHING EXPLORER

The way Explorer is launched determines its workspace's display. For example, if you launch Explorer using the *Start* menu, it will open with its default display which should be your hard disk. You can also launch Explorer from the My Computer (or a folder) window using a *Shortcut* menu, the *File* menu, or the toolbar. This method directly displays the contents of a desired disk or other folder.

LAUNCHING BY THE *START* MENU.   To launch Explorer by using the *Start* menu,

---

STEPS

1 Click the *Start* button   [**Ctrl** + **Esc**]

2 Point to *Programs* and then click *Windows Explorer*

Explorer now opens with your hard disk selected on the left and its contents displayed on the right. This is the default view.

LAUNCHING BY MY COMPUTER.   To launch Explorer by using My Computer,

---

STEPS

1 Right-click My Computer for its *Shortcut* menu

2 Click *Explore*

The Explorer window should now appear on your desktop

LAUNCHING BY *SHORTCUT* MENU OR *FILE* MENU.   To launch Explorer by *Shortcut* or *File* menu

---

STEPS

1 Launch My Computer and, if needed, open the desired drive window

BY *SHORTCUT* MENU

2 Right-click the desired *Drive* or *Folder* icon for its *Shortcut* menu

3 Click *Explore*

BY *FILE* MENU

2 Click the desired *Drive* or *Folder* icon to select it

3 Click *File, Explore*

Explorer now opens with the desired *Drive* or *Folder icon* selected on its left and the its contents displayed on the right.

Explorer commands operate similar to My Computer commands; however, the information in its workspace is displayed differently. The left side of the workspace displays a vertical hierarchical tree of all your system's components. This side will be referred to as the *tree box*. The right side of the screen displays the contents of the item selected in the tree box and will be referred to as the *Contents box*. It is similar to the workspace of a folder window. Items in both boxes are listed in alphabetical order.

The following techniques can be applied to My Computer or Explorer unless otherwise noted. The techniques can be invoked only after either one of the programs has been launched.

COPYING OBJECTS

Copying is the process of duplicating a selection into a new location. The folder from which a selection is copied is called the *source folder*. The folder to which it is pasted (placed) is called the *destination folder*. A summary of copying techniques is presented in Figure WIN2-12.

COPYING BY *EDIT* MENU.   To copy a selection of files (and folders),

STEPS

1 Open the source folder's window

2 Select the objects to be copied

3 Click *Edit, Copy*   [**Ctrl** + **C**]

4 Move to the destination folder

5 Click *Edit, Paste*   [**Ctrl** + **V**]

COPYING BY DRAGGING AND DROPPING.   Drag and drop techniques involve copying a selection by moving your pointer with the selection to a new location, sometimes with the use of the Ctrl key.

To copy a selection within the same folder or to another folder within the same disk,

1 Open the source folder

2 If needed, open the destination folder, tile the folder windows, and then switch back to the source folder

3 Select the desired objects in the source window

4 Press and hold Ctrl while dragging the selection to the desired destination

5 Drop the selection in the desired location (release the mouse)

To copy a selection to a folder in another disk, use the previous steps; however, do not press and hold the Ctrl key when performing Step 4.

COPYING AN ENTIRE DISK.   Use the *Copy Disk* dialog box (Figure WIN2-17) to copy the contents of an entire disk to another disk. It is accessible through Copy Disk command of the *My Computer* file menu (after selecting the desired drive icon) or the desired drive icon's *Shortcut* menu. When using this command, the *Copy from* disk must be the same as the *Copy to* disk.

CREATING A DOCUMENT

You can create a new saved document without first launching its program by using the *New* submenu, which you just used to create folders. (Note: The related program or document type must be listed in the submenu.) Try this to create a new text (Notepad) document:

BY *SHORTCUT* MENU   **BY *FILE* MENU**

1 Right-click an empty area of the work-   1 Click *File*
   space for its *Shortcut* menu

2 Point to *New* and then click the desired document type

3 Type the document's name and then press ↵

CREATING A SHORTCUT ICON

A *Shortcut* icon can be created with a dynamic link to its original document, program, or folder. This link allows you to use the *Shortcut* icon to open/launch the file or folder it represents from any folder or the desktop.

To place *Shortcut* icons in a folder,

1. Select the object(s) for the *Shortcut* icon

2. Click *Edit, Copy*   [**Ctrl** + **C**]

3. Move to the destination (open the destination folder if needed)

4. Click *Edit, Paste Shortcut*

To place *Shortcut* icons on the desktop,

1. Select the object(s) for the *Shortcut* icon

2. Click *Edit, Copy*   [**Ctrl** + **C**]

3. Right-click an empty area of the taskbar for its *Shortcut* menu

4. Click *Minimize All Windows* for a better view of the desktop

5. Right-click the area to the right of the *My Computer* icon (or any desired empty area) on the desktop

6. Click *Paste Shortcut*

DELETING

Any selection in Windows can be deleted. The *Delete* command removes a selection from its current place and can be invoked from the *File* menu or an object's *Shortcut* menu.
The process of deleting a selection from a data disk and hard disk is the same.

1. Select the objects to be deleted

2. Click *File, Delete*   [**Delete**]

A dialog box appears asking you to confirm the deletion. To delete these objects,

3. Click *Yes*

FINDING A FILE

Use the Find feature to locate any file in a folder. Once located, you can open the file from the lower section of the *Find* dialog box.

INITIAL SEARCH.   To locate a desired file,

STEPS

1   If needed, insert the desired disk or CD-ROM into the appropriate drive

BY *SHORTCUT* MENU

2   Right-click the desired drive icon

3   Click *Find* for its dialog box

BY *FILE* MENU

2   Click the desired drive icon

3   Click *File, Find* for its dialog box

4   Type the desired filename in the *Find* text box

5   Click the *Find Now* button   [↵]

The results of your search will appear at the bottom of the dialog box.

To access the file from the bottom of the *Find* dialog box,

6   Double-click it

NEW SEARCH.   To perform another search using the *Find* dialog box

STEPS

1   Click the *New Search* button

The command will remove the results of the previous search prior to your entering a new find request.

2   If desired, use the *Look in* drop-down box to select a drive

3   Click the *Name* drop-down box to place the insertion point there

4   Type in the desired filename in the *Find* text box

5   Click the *Find Now* button   [↵]

The results of your search should appear at the bottom on the dialog box. If desired, you can now open the document by double-clicking it.

FOLDERS

Folders are used to group files. A *Folder* icon is used to represent each folder created on a disk. *Drive* and *Folder* icons can be used to open Folder windows. *Folder windows* display the contents of a disk (or other storage media) or folders within the disk. Remember, a disk is also considered a folder and will be referred to as the *main folder.*

OPENING A FOLDER (OR DRIVE).   To open a folder (or drive) in My Computer or a Folder window,

STEPS

1 Double-click the desired *Drive* or *Folder* icon to display its contents in another window

In Explorer, clicking an icon on the hierarchical tree (left side) will display its contents on the right side of the window.

CREATING A NEW FOLDER.   To create the folders,

STEPS

1 Click *File* for its menu as in Figure WIN2-8a

This *File* menu appears when no objects are selected (marked) in the window.

2 Point to *New* for its submenu and then click *Folder*

FOLDERS WITHIN FOLDERS.   To create a subfolder (a folder within a folder), first open the folder where you desire the subfolder to be placed, and then use Steps 1 and 2 for creating a new folder.

FOLDER DISPLAY OPTIONS.   The My Computer program offers two ways to browse through folders: separate windows for each folder (the default) or a single window that changes to display each folder that is opened. To check or change the browse settings of My Computer,

STEPS

1 Click *View, Options* for its dialog box

2 If needed, click the *Folder* tab

3 If the *Browse folders using a separate window for each folder* option is selected (a black dot will appear in the option circle), click the *Cancel* button

4 If the *Browse folders using a separate window for each folder* option is not selected, click it, and then click *OK*

When viewing folders through a single window that changes to display each open folder, you can click the *Up One Level* (see the left margin for the button) toolbar button to go back one level. The toolbar must, of course, be on.

SELECTING MULTIPLE FILES (OBJECTS)

Selecting is the process of marking items. Once marked you can invoke a variety of commands on an item. Refer to Figure WIN2-10 for a summary of object selection techniques.

SINGLE OBJECT. To select a single object,

STEPS

1 Click the object

GROUP OF OBJECTS. To select a group of objects (several objects),

STEPS

1 Click the first object of the group

2 Press and hold **Ctrl** while clicking each additional object

BLOCK OF OBJECTS. To select a block (a set of contiguous objects),

STEPS

1 Click the first object in the block

2 Press and hold **Shift** while clicking the last file in the block

A block can be selected alone or with other selected files.

REVERSE A SELECTION. To reverse a selection of files,

1 Click *Edit, Invert Selection* to reverse the items selected with those that are not

SELECT ALL. To select all files in a window,

1 Click *Edit, Select All*   [**Ctrl** + **A**]

OPENING FILES

Most documents created and saved with Windows programs are automatically *associated* (have a special connection) with their program. As such, they can be directly opened (with their program) from a Folder window without first launching their programs. If you know the folder your document was stored on, this method provides quicker access to it.

SINGLE FILE. The quickest way to open any object in a window is to double-click it. However, you can also use the object's *Shortcut* menu or the *File* menu.

BY *SHORTCUT* MENU	**BY FILE MENU**
1 Right-click the desired *File* icon	1 Click the desired *File* icon to select it
2 Click *Open*	2 Click *File, Open* [↵]

GROUP OF FILES. To open (or launch) a group of files at once, first select the group and then use the Open command of the *File* menu.

1 Click the first object in the group

2 Press and hold **Ctrl** while clicking each additional object of the group

3 Click *File*, *Open* to open the objects   [↵]

BLOCK OF FILES.   Like opening a group of files, opening a block of files involves first selecting the block and then clicking *File*, *Open.*

STEPS

1 Click the first object in the block

2 Press and hold **Shift** while clicking the last object of the block

3 Click *File*, *Open*

PRINTING FILES

To print document files from a Folder window,

STEPS

1 Turn on your printer

2 Select the desired files

3 Click *File*, *Print*

To print a single document using its *Shortcut* menu,

STEPS

1 Right-click the *File* icon for its *Shortcut* menu

2 Click *Print*

RECYCLE BIN

Selections deleted from a hard disk are removed from their folders, the desktop, or other locations and relocated to the Recycle Bin. Once there, you can either restore or permanently delete the files. See Figure WIN2-22 in Chapter 2 for Recycle Bin operations.

RENAMING FILES

You can easily rename any file or folder using the same techniques.
To rename an object by *Shortcut* or *File* menu,

STEPS

1　If needed, open the desired Folder window

BY *SHORTCUT* MENU

2　Right-click the object's icon for its *Short-cut* menu

3　Click *Rename*

BY *FILE* MENU

2　Click the object's icon to select it

3　Click *File, Rename*

4　Type a desired filename and then press ↵

To rename an object by clicking its title after it has been selected,

---

STEPS

1　If needed, click the object's icon to select it

2　Click the object's title

The folder's title is now selected and ready to be changed.

3　Type in the new name and then press ↵

SENDING FILES

Use the *Send* submenu to copy a selection to another disk, fax, or electronic mail.

STEPS

1　Select the items that you desire to send

2　Click *File,* point to *Send To* for its submenu

3　Click the desired destination option

The *Send To* menu can be customized to include destinations other than the default options. It is also available through *Shortcut* menus. Refer to your on-line help for these procedures.

TOOLBAR

Like other Windows programs, many menu commands can be accessed from a toolbar. The My Computer, Folder, and Explorer windows have the same toolbar as in Figure WIN2-4. To turn the toolbar on or off,

STEPS

1 Click *View, Toolbar*

As with many buttons and drop down boxes in the Windows environment, pointing to a toolbar item displays its title.

VIEWING OPTIONS

The Workspace in the My Computer window, Folder Window, or the right side of the Explorer window can be adjusted to display the icons in a smaller size, in a list, and with more or less detail. These view options are available through the *View* menu or toolbar. *View* menu options are listed and described in Figure WIN2-6 of Chapter 2.

STEPS

1 If needed, click *View, Toolbar* to turn it on

2 Click *View, Details* to display detailed information on each object

A *Details bar* now appears below the toolbar. Each object's name, size, type, and date and time last modified or created is displayed below this button bar. You can switch the display order from ascending to descending (or vice versa) by using any *Details* bar button's title. Other *View* options include the following:

3 Click *View, List* to list objects vertically as small icons

4 Click *View, Small Icons* to display objects as small icons horizontally

5 Click *View, Large Icons* to return objects to the default size

More advanced *View* options such as folder browsing, choices, displaying hidden files, and MS-DOS file extensions and file association settings can be controlled by using the *Options* dialog box. Refer to the dialog box's on-line help for these operations.

VIEWING OPTIONS—EXPLORER'S TREE DISPLAY

The left side of the Explorer window displays all the components of your system in a vertical tree starting with the *Desktop* icon on top. The left-most vertical tree line is the *main tree line* and it displays all items that appear on the desktop including My Computer and the Recycling Bin. All lines extending from the main tree are called *branches*.

The *Go to a different folder* drop-down box (left side of toolbar) identifies the current folder selection. Its contents are displayed in the *Contents* box (right side of window).

SELECTING AN ICON ON THE TREE.   To select a different item quickly,

STEPS

1 Click the desired icon on the tree

The selected icon now appears highlighted in the tree and its contents appear in the right side of the window.

GO TO TOP OF TREE.   To go to the top of the tree (the desktop),

STEPS

1 Press Home

GO TO END OF TREE.   To go to the end of the tree,

STEPS

1 Press End

EXPAND BRANCHES.   The "+" icon to the left of any icon in the tree box indicates that the item can be expanded to display a tree branch of folder(s) below it. To expand a branch of a tree to display folders that are within a folder,

STEPS

1 Click its + icon to left of the desired icon on the tree

COLLAPSE BRANCHES.   A "–" to the left of a folder on a tree indicates that its branches are displayed. To collapse the branches,

1 Click the – icon to the left of the desired icon on the tree

UNDOING THE LAST ACTION

1 Click *Edit, Undo*   [**Ctrl**   +   **Z**   ]

SUMMARY OF DIALOG BOX FEATURES

A *dialog box* is a window that requests or gives information. A Dialog Box window operates similar to a program window; however, it cannot be resized. A dialog box has a title bar that displays its name, a *Help (?)* button, and a *Close* button. It also has a control menu (right-click the title bar to open).

Dialog boxes may also have *tabs,* which are different parts of a dialog box.

USING DIALOG BOX OPTIONS

To access Windows on-line help in using dialog box options,

1 Click the *Start* button   [**Ctrl**   +   **Esc**   ]

2 Click *Help*

3 Click the *Index* tab

4 Type   **DIALOG BOXES, USING**   or click it in the list box

5 Click the *Display* button

6 Click *The Basics* in the *Topics Found* dialog box

7 Click the *Display* button

8 Click the *Using dialog boxes* button

Your Windows Help window should appear as in Figure WINA-1. Dialog boxes may have one or more of these components. To learn how to operate them, simply click the desired component on the screen. When you are done,

 9 Click the *Close* button of the window

PARTS OF A DIALOG BOX

Most parts of a dialog box are identified in Figure WINA-1. These and other dialog box components are described next.

CHECK BOX.   A square box identified by its title to the right. A "✓" or "X" indicates that the option has been selected. More than one check box can be selected at a time.

COMMAND BUTTON.   A command button directly invokes the item it represents when clicked.

DROP-DOWN BOX.   A drop-down box initially appears as a single line box with a "▼" button on its right. Clicking the "▼" button opens a drop-down list. Some drop-down boxes allow text entry for selecting.

FIGURE WINA-1 ■ OPERATING DIALOG BOX OPTIONS

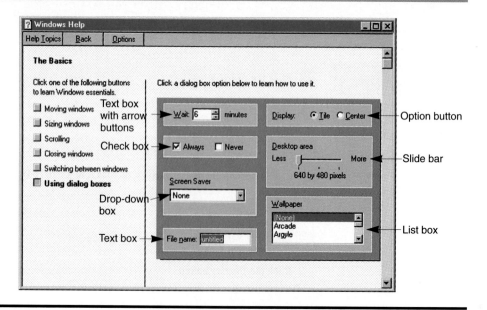

GROUP BOX.   A group box is an area of a dialog box that contains related option buttons or check boxes.

INFORMATION BOX.   An information box generally displays information about a current dialog box selection.

LIST BOX.   A list box presents available options in alphabetical order.

OPTION BUTTON.   An *Option* button is a small circle with its title to the right. When occupied by a "•" (dot), it indicates that the option is selected. Only one option can be selected in a group.

TAB.   A tab identifies a section of a dialog box. Clicking a tab will display that section's format.

TEXT BOX.   A text box allows text entry to communicate with the computer.

QUICK REFERENCE TO WORDPAD FEATURES

WordPad is a simple word processing program that you can use to create and edit documents with text and objects (graphic images). The following is a quick reference to Word-Pad's features). When invoking menu commands by mouse, simply click the item(s). With the keyboard, press the Alt key and the underlined letter of the menu bar item and then the underlined letter of the menu item. Otherwise perform the actions as indicated.

Feature	Commands	Shortcut Keys
Alignment Changes		
Left	*Left Align Format bar* button	Ctrl + L
Center	*Center Align Format bar* button	Ctrl + E
Right	*Right Align Format* bar button	Ctrl + R
Bold On/Off	*Bold Format bar* button	Ctrl + B
Bullet Style	*Format, Bullet Style*	
Copy a Selection		
From Source	*Edit, Copy*	Ctrl + C
To Destination	*Edit, Paste*	Ctrl + V

Feature	Commands	Shortcut Keys
Date and Time (insert)	*Insert, Date and Time*	
Delete a Selection	*Edit, Clear*	Delete
Deleting One Character		
Left		Backspace
Right		Delete
Edit a Selected Object	*Edit, Object* or double-click object if embedded or linked	
Embed an Object	*Edit, Paste Special, OK*	
Find a Text String		
Find Dialog Box	*Edit, Find*	Ctrl + F
Next Find	*Edit, Find Next*	F3
Font Changes	*Format, Font*	
Format Bar Off/On	*View, Format Bar*	
Indentation Changes	*Format, Paragraph*	
Link an Object	*Edit, Paste Special, Link, OK*	
Move a Selection		
From Source	*Edit, Cut*	Ctrl + X
To Destination	*Edit, Paste*	Ctrl + V
New Document	*File, New*	Ctrl + N
Object Properties (Edit)	*Edit, Properties*	Alt + ↵
Open a File	*File, Open*	Ctrl + O
Page Setup	*File, Page Setup*	
Print	*File, Print*	Ctrl + P
Print Preview	*File, Print Preview*	
Replace a Text String	*Edit, Replace*	Ctrl + H
Ruler Bar Off/On	*View, Ruler*	
Save a Document	*File, Save*	Ctrl + S
Save As Dialog Box	*File, Save As*	
Select		
All	*Edit, Select All*	Ctrl + A
Text	Drag across text	Shift + Arrow key
Object	Click object	
Status Bar Off/On	*View, Status Bar*	
Tab Settings	*Format, Tabs*	
Toolbar Off/On	*View, Toolbar*	
Underline	Underline *Format bar* button	Ctrl + U
Undo	*Edit, Undo*	Ctrl + Z

QUICK REFERENCE TO PAINT FEATURES

Paint is a graphics program that can be used to create, open, edit, and save color images (pictures). You can also use it to edit graphic images created with other programs and to edit and save screen captures. The following is a quick reference to Paint's features. When invoking menu commands by mouse, simply click the item(s). With the keyboard, press the Alt key and the underlined letter of the menu bar item and then the underlined letter of the menu item. Otherwise perform the actions as indicated.

Feature	Commands	Shortcut Keys
Attributes of Document (width, height, unit of measure, and color)	*Image, Attributes*	Ctrl + E
Clear Image	*Image, Clear Image*	Ctrl + Shift + N
Color		
Background	Right-click the desired color in the palette	
Foreground	Click the desired color in the palette	
Color Box Off/On	*View, Color Box*	Ctrl + A
Copy a Selection		
From Source	*Edit, Copy*	Ctrl + C
To Destination	*Edit, Paste*	Ctrl + V
Copy a Selection to a File	*Edit, Copy To*	
Delete a Selection	*Edit, Clear Selection*	Delete
Display Options		
Normal Size	*View, Zoom, Normal Size*	Ctrl + PgUp
Large Size	*View, Zoom, Large Size*	Ctrl + PgDn
Custom	*View, Zoom, Custom*	
Full Window	*View, View Bitmap*	Ctrl + F
Draw Opaque	*Options, Draw Opaque*	
Drawing Tool	Click the desired tool in the tool box	
Flip/Rotate	*Image, Flip/Rotate*	Ctrl + R
Invert Colors	*Image, Invert Colors*	Ctrl + I
Move a Selection		
From Source	*Edit, Cut*	Ctrl + X
To Destination	*Edit, Paste*	Ctrl + V
New Document	*File, New*	Ctrl + N
Open a File	*File, Open*	Ctrl + O
Page Setup	*File, Page Setup*	
Palette Colors		
Edit	*Options, Edit Colors*	
Retrieve Saved Colors	*Options, Get Colors*	
Save	*Options, Save Colors*	
Paste an Object from a File	*Edit, Paste From*	
Print	*File, Print*	Ctrl + P
Print Preview	*File, Print Preview*	

Feature	Commands	Shortcut Keys
Repeat a Command	*Edit, Repeat*	F4
Select		
Object	*Select tool,* Drag diagonally across object	
All	*Edit, Select All*	Ctrl + L
Send a Document	*File, Send*	
Set as Wallpaper on Desktop		
Tiled	*File, Set As Wallpaper (Tiled)*	
Centered	*File, Set As Wallpaper (Centered)*	
Stretch/Skew	*Image, Stretch/Skew*	Ctrl + W
Text Toolbar On/Off	*View, Text Toolbar*	
Tool Box Off/On	*View, Tool Box*	Ctrl + T
Undo	*Edit, Undo*	Ctrl + Z

GLOSSARY

Accessibility options. A feature that allows you to adjust keyboard, display, sound, and mouse controls based on individual preference. It is accessible through the Control Panel. (WIN163)

Accessories. A group of programs that can help you perform daily tasks. They include Notepad, WordPad, Paint, and a variety of other programs. (WIN164)

Active (current) icon. The icon that is currently highlighted on your screen. Keyboard commands will affect this icon. (WIN11)

Active window. The window within which you are currently working. Its title bar is highlighted and taskbar button depressed. It accepts most keyboard commands. (WIN38)

Alignment. The way text aligns against a margin. The default alignment of WordPad and many word processors is left. Left aligned text has a ragged right edge. Other common alignment settings include center and right (ragged left edge). (WIN138)

Associated. A special connection between a document and its program that allows the document to be open in its program from a menu, My Computer, Explorer, and other parts of Windows. (WIN83)

Block. A set of contiguous files (or other objects or text). (WIN83)

Bolding. A command that darkens text for emphasis. (WIN135)

Booting up. The process of turning on your computer system. (WIN3)

Bullet style. A WordPad format feature that automatically inserts a bullet at the beginning of each line. (WIN140)

Byte. A binary unit of measure equivalent to one alphanumeric character (A–Z, 0–9, and so forth). A kilobyte (KB) is one thousand bytes, a megabyte (MB) is one million bytes, and a gigabyte is one billion bytes. (WIN70)

Cascade. A standard multiple-windows display that presents the windows overlapping each other. (WIN38)

Clicking. Rapidly pressing and releasing a mouse button (normally the left button). (WIN9)

Clipboard. A Windows program that temporarily holds a selection for future pasting. Data is copied or moved there by using the Copy or Cut commands of a program's *Edit* menu. (WIN43)

***Close* button.** An "X" button, located on the top right corner of most windows. Clicking it will close the window. (WIN12)

***Command* button.** Any button that when clicked directly accesses a program or window's feature. (WIN27)

Communications programs. Programs that can be used for connecting to other computers, on-line services, electronic mail, and fax operations. Windows comes with a variety of these programs. (WIN164)

Container file or compound document. The document receiving the information in a linking or embedding operation. (WIN158)

Control-menu. Clicking a window's Program or Document icon (left of the window name on the title bar) or right-clicking anywhere on the title bar will open its control menu. This menu contains commands to resize, move, or close a window. (WIN20)

Control Panel. A Windows feature that contains a variety of tools to set various parts of your system. These tools are also in the form of *Properties* dialog boxes. (WIN53)

Copy. The command that copies a selection to Windows Clipboard for future pasting. It can be accessed through the *Edit* menu, *Shortcut* menu, or *Toolbar* button (if available). (WIN43)

Copy disk. A command used to copy the entire contents of a disk to another disk of the same capacity. It is accessible through the My Computer *File* menu (after selecting the desired *Drive* icon) or the desired *Drive* icon's *Shortcut* menu. (WIN93)

Copying. The process of duplicating data to a new location. (WIN42)

Cut. The command that moves a selection from a document to the Clipboard for future pasting. It can be accessed through the *Edit* menu, *Shortcut* menu, or *Toolbar* button (if available). (WIN45)

Data. Text and graphic images (pictures) called objects. (WIN2)

Default document. The new blank document that appears in a program's workspace when it is launched. (WIN32)

Default drive. The drive to which a program is currently pointing. Files can be saved and opened from the disk or other storage media in this drive. (WIN33)

Default settings. The normal settings of your environment. (WIN99)

Delete. A command that removes a selection from its current place. It can be invoked from the *File* menu or an object's *Shortcut* menu. (WIN97)

Desktop. The large area above the taskbar in the Windows screen. Occupying the upper left side of the desktop are several icons, starting with the *My Computer* icon. (WIN5)

Dialog box. A window that either provides or requests information. (WIN5)

Disks. Storage media that can be used to hold computer-generated files. (WIN3)

Document. A file with data. (WIN2)

Document window. A window that contains a document. Document windows occupy a Program window's workspace. (WIN17)

Documents menu. A submenu of the *Start* menu that can be used to open any of the last 15 documents used with its program. (WIN52)

Double-clicking. Rapidly clicking your left mouse button twice. (WIN11)

Dragging. Pressing and holding your left mouse button while moving your mouse and the object to which it is pointing. (WIN11)

Drawing area. The workspace of Paint's window, which is like a piece of canvas or paper. (WIN148)

Drawing tool. The mouse pointer when in Paint's drawing area. It is used to create a drawing. (WIN146)

Drive. A device that reads or writes to a storage medium (such as a disk or CD-ROM). (WIN70)

Drop-down box. A one-line rectangular box that has a "▼" button on its right side. Clicking that button will open a drop-down list. (WIN27)

Dropping. Releasing your mouse and thus the object to which it is pointing after it has been dragged. (WIN11)

Electronic mail. A feature that allows you to send and receive electronic documents through a network or other forms of communication. (WIN164)

Embedding. The process of inserting an object from a source file into a container file. The object then becomes part of the container file. Any changes in the source file do not appear in the embedded object. The embedded object in the container file

can be edited using its source program without changing the source document. (WIN158)

File. A storage unit that may contain a program or document. (WIN3)

File management. The process of organizing and maintaining files (including folders) within your computer environment. (WIN78)

Filename. A name assigned to a document or program to identify it. A filename can have up to 255 characters. (WIN32)

Find. A feature that can be used to locate any file in a folder in your system. It is accessible through the *Start* menu, a drive, file, or folders *Shortcut* menu, or the *File* menu of the My Computer, Folder, or Explorer windows. (WIN70)

Find Menu. A submenu that can be used to locate files or folders within your system quickly. (WIN55)

Folder. A folder is a set of related files. (WIN3)

Folder windows. A window that displays the contents of a disk (or other storage media) or folders within the disk. (WIN73)

Font. A character type style. (WIN29)

Font size. The point size of the current font. A point is a typesetting unit of measure equivalent to $\frac{1}{72}$ inch. (WIN29)

Format bar. A set of command buttons and drop-down boxes that can be used to access features related to changing the appearance and alignment of a WordPad document's text. (WIN27)

Formatting. The process of preparing a disk for use on a computer. Formatting sets up the disk's directory and file allocation table and divides the disk into addressable storage locations. It also checks for defective tracks on the disk and seals them off from further use. (WIN33)

Function keys. Keys that are labeled F1–F12 on your keyboard. They may be located at the extreme left of your keyboard or across the top in one horizontal row. (WIN6)

Graphical user interface (GUI). Pronounced "gooey," this is any operating system that simplifies communication with a computer by using common symbols (called icons) and menus instead of typewritten commands. (WIN2)

Hardware. Any physical computer equipment. (WIN2)

Icons. Small graphical images or symbols used to represent a program, document, or other feature in the Windows environment. (WIN2)

Indentation. The way a paragraph is indented or set from the left or right margin. (WIN136)

Insertion point. A vertical blinking line that indicates where the next character you type will appear. The insertion point appears in any window or box that allows character entry. (WIN31)

Internet. A group of international computer networks communicating by phone lines. It provides a variety of services including electronic mail, news, research information, and games. (WIN164)

Italicizing. A command that slants text for emphasis. (WIN135)

Launching. Starting a program. (WIN14)

Layout (format). Changes that concern the way text is arranged in a document—for example, changing margin or tab settings. (WIN124)

Line break. A line break ends a line before it reaches the right margin. It is created by pressing the Enter key. It also moves the insertion point to the beginning of the next line. Line breaks are generally needed at the end of a paragraph, each line of an address, a salutation, or to skip a line. (WIN126)

Linking. A special feature that establishes an ongoing connection between the source file that provides the object and the container file that receives it. The object remains stored in the source file. The copy of the object in the container file is automatically updated whenever the source file's object is changed. (WIN42)

Maximize button. A resizing button resembling a small rectangular box. It is located to the right of the *Minimize* button on the title bar. Clicking it will enlarge a window to its maximum size. (WIN22)

Maximized. A window that is enlarged to its maximum size. (WIN17)

Menu bar. A feature available only in program windows. It provides mouse and keyboard access to a program's features through drop-down menus. The Menu bar is located just below a window's title bar. (WIN22)

Microsoft Windows 95. A Graphical User Interface operating system. (WIN2)

Minimize all windows. A multiple windows display that reduces all windows on the desktop to their taskbar buttons. (WIN38)

Minimize button. A resizing button that reduces a window to its taskbar button. (WIN21)

Mouse. A common pointing device used to control a mouse pointer (a small graphical image often in the form of an arrow) on your screen. (WIN5)

Mouse pointer or pointer. A small graphical image, often in the shape of an arrow, whose movements are controlled by a using a pointing device. It can be used to select features. (WIN5)

Moving. The process of relocating data. (WIN42)

Multitasking. The ability to work with two or more programs at the same time. (WIN37)

My Computer. A program that can be used to browse (view) and manage all of the components of your computer. (WIN68)

New. The *File* menu command that will clear a program window's workspace so that you can begin a new document. For programs that allow multiple documents, this command will open a new document window. (WIN35)

Notepad. A Windows Accessories program that can be used to create or edit text only files. (WIN43)

Object. In general, an object in Windows includes any icon, window, or set of information (linking and embedding). (WIN158)

Objects. Any graphical image (picture or symbol). They include icons and windows. (WIN2)

OLE. Short for "object linking and embedding," OLE refers to transferring information from one program to another as an object. (WIN158)

Open. A *File* menu command that can be used to retrieve a saved document from a disk. (WIN36)

Palette. Used to select foreground and background colors when using Windows Paint, a graphics program. The *Select Colors* box displays the currently selected foreground and background colors. The color used by a tool when drawing is the foreground color. The background color is the drawing area's color. (WIN148)

Paste. The *Edit* menu command that places a selection from the Clipboard to a desired location. (WIN43)

Pixels. Dots that make up a computer-generated picture or character. (WIN145)

Plug and play. The idea of simply plugging new hardware into your system and playing with (using) it immediately. (WIN105)

Pointing. A mouse action that involves moving your mouse on a flat surface, and thus moving the mouse pointer on your screen to a desired item or area. (WIN6)

Pointing device. A device used to control a mouse pointer (small graphical image often in the form of an arrow) on your screen. Pointing devices may include a mouse, trackball, trackpoint (pointing stick), track pad, or electronic pen. (WIN5)

Print. The *File* menu command that produces a hard copy of a document on paper. (WIN35)

Printers. A folder that can be accessed through My Computer or the *Settings* submenu (*Start* menu). It is used for adding a printer, switching printers (if you have installed more than one printer), and checking and controlling the status of current print jobs. (WIN55)

Printers. A Windows program that can be used to view the current printers installed and their activity.

Program. A set of computer instructions. (WIN2)

Program groups. Logical groupings of programs and files by categories on the *Programs* submenu for easier visual access. (WIN15)

Program window. A window that contains a program. Program windows occupy the desktop. (WIN17)

Properties. The way information and other attributes (characteristics) of an item are displayed or set. The Change Properties command can be used to alter any object's default characteristics. (WIN99)

Pull-down menu. A menu that drops down from its menu bar selection. (WIN22)

Recycle Bin. A program that stores references to files deleted from other places on your hard disk and desktop. (WIN87)

Resizing buttons. Located on the title bar, clicking a resizing button will quickly resize a window. Resizing buttons include *Minimize, Maximize,* and *Restore* button. (WIN21)

Restore. A window resizing command that reduces a maximized window to its previous size. (WIN21)

Restore button. A resizing button that appears on the right side of a window's title bar when a window is maximized. Clicking it will resize a window to its previous size. (WIN22)

Right-clicking. Pointing to an object and pressing and releasing the right mouse button. (WIN10)

Run dialog box. A dialog box accessed through the *Start* menu. It can be used to launch programs, or open folders or documents by typing its command line. It is often used to install new programs. (WIN55)

Save. A command that can be used to save a document for the first time and re-save a previously saved document under its original name without confirmation. (WIN32)

Save as. A command that opens the *Save As* dialog box for saving. It allows you to save an updated document under a different name, thereby keeping the original document under its old name. (WIN32)

Screen capturing. The process of taking a picture of the current screen by pressing the Print Screen key. This copies the current image of the screen to the Clipboard for future pasting. (WIN156)

Select colors box. A section of the palette in Windows Paint program that displays the currently selected foreground and background colors. (WIN148)

Selection. Data marked for editing. (WIN25)

Send to. A submenu that can be used to copy a selection to another disk, fax, or electronic mail. (WIN93)

Settings menu. A submenu of the *Start* menu that can be used to launch the Control Panel window, Printers window, and open the *Taskbar Properties* dialog box. (WIN53)

Sharing files. Copying or moving documents, programs, and folders within the same folder or between folders. (WIN87)

Shortcut icon. An icon created with a link (special connection) to the original file or folder. It allows you to open the original document or folder or to launch the original program from the desktop or another folder. (WIN87)

Shortcut keys. Keys that provide quick keyboard access to specific commands. They may involve pressing a function key alone or in conjunction with the Ctrl, Alt, or Shift keys. The Ctrl, Alt, or Shift keys may also be used in conjunction with other keys. (WIN6)

Shortcut menu. A menu that contains common commands that can be invoked on the related item. Right-clicking will open an item's *Shortcut* menu, if available. (WIN10)

Shut down. The *Start* menu command that can be used to exit Windows. (WIN13)

Source file. The document with the original information in a linking or embedding operation. (WIN158)

Start button. Located on the left side of the taskbar, the *Start* button can be used to open the Windows *Start* menu (main menu) by mouse. (WIN5)

Start menu. The Windows main menu. It can be used to start programs, find documents, adjust system settings, find a document (file), access help, or shut down Windows. It can be opened by clicking the *Start* button on the taskbar or pressing the Ctrl + Esc keys. Each option on the *Start* menu is listed with its corresponding icon to its left. (WIN5)

Subfolder. A folder within a folder. (WIN69)

Tab. A section of a dialog box, similar to tabs used in a manual filing system. (WIN47)

Tabs. A word processing feature used to place text in specific positions on a line. (WIN141)

Taskbar. The bar at the bottom of the Windows screen with a *Start* button on its left side. It is used to start programs and switch between running programs. (WIN5)

Taskbar Properties dialog box. A dialog box used to change the taskbar's display settings and add or remove programs from the *Programs* menu. (WIN55)

Text appearance. Changes to the physical appearance of text. It includes font type, style (regular, bold, italic), and size. (WIN124)

Tile. A standard multiple windows display that presents the windows next to each other either horizontally or vertically. (WIN38)

Title bar. The top row of a window. It identifies the window's name. It can also be used to resize or close a window. (WIN17)

Tool box. A Windows Paint feature that provides a variety of tools for creating a drawing. (WIN146)

Toolbar. A set of command buttons that relate to basic file management and editing commands in WordPad. (WIN27)

Undo. A command that can be used to undo your last action. It is available in many Windows programs. (WIN96)

Window. A rectangular box that may contain a *program* (a set of computer instructions) or *document* (a file with data, information, and/or graphics). It also is used to request or give information about a task or feature. (WIN2)

Windows Explorer. A program that can be used for managing your computer. The components of a system are listed in a hierarchical tree on the left side of the window. Selecting a folder (or other item) from the tree will display its contents on the right side. (WIN107)

Windows screen. The main screen of Windows 95. It has two primary parts: the taskbar and the desktop. (WIN5)

Wizard. A program that helps make a complicated task easier. (WIN105)

WordPad. A simple word processing program that comes with Windows. (WIN15)

Wordwrap. A word processing feature that automatically flows text to the next line as you type. (WIN126)

Workspace. The large interior space of a window. (WIN17)

INDEX

MICROSOFT WORD 7.0
FOR WINDOWS 95

EDWARD G. MARTIN
CHARLES S. PARKER

This manual contains numerous features that help you master the material quickly and reinforce your learning:

- *A Table of Contents.* A list of the manual's contents appears on the first page of the manual. Each chapter starts with an *outline,* a list of learning *objectives,* and an *overview* that summarizes the skills you will learn.

- *Bold Key Terms.* Important terms appear in bold type as they are introduced. They are also conveniently listed at the end of each chapter, with page references for further review.

- *Color as a Learning Tool.* In this manual, color has been used to help you work through each chapter. Each step is numbered in green for easy identification. Within each step, text or commands that you should type appear in orange. Single keys to be pressed are shown in yellow boxes. For example,

- *Step-by-Step Mouse Approach.* This manual stresses the mouse approach. Each action is numbered consecutively in green to make it easy to locate and follow. Where appropriate, a mouse shortcut (toolbar icon) is shown in the left margin; a keyboard shortcut may be shown in brackets at the right, as follows:

As your skills increase, the "click this item" approach slowly gives way to a less-detailed list of goals and operations so that you do not mindlessly follow steps, but truly master software skills.

- *Screen Figures.* Full-color annotated screens provide overviews of operations that let you monitor your work as you progress through the tutorial.

- *Tips.* Each chapter contains numerous short tips in bold type at strategic points to provide hints, warnings, or insights. Read these carefully.

- *Checkpoints.* At the end of each major section is a list of checkpoints, highlighted in red, which you can use to test your mastery of the material. Do not proceed further unless you can perform the checkpoint tasks.

- *Summary and Quiz.* At the end of each chapter is a bulleted summary of the chapter's content and a 30-question quiz with true/false, multiple-choice, and matching questions.

- *Exercises.* Each chapter ends with two sets of written exercises (Operations and Commands) and six guided hands-on computer applications that measure and reinforce mastery of the chapter's concepts and skills. Each pair of applications present problems relating to school, personal, and business use.

- *Mastery Cases.* The final page of each chapter presents three unguided cases that allow you to demonstrate your personal mastery of the chapter material.

- *A Note about the Manual's Organization.* The topics in this manual are arranged in order of increasing difficulty. Chapters 1 and 2 present beginning and intermediate techniques and should be completed in sequence, for each skill builds upon the previous one. However, Chapter 3 includes several *independent* modules that present advanced skills. These modules may be followed in any order or omitted, as time and interest allow.

- *End-of-Manual Material.* The manual also provides a comprehensive reference *appendix* that summarizes commands and provides alphabetical listings of critical operations, a *glossary* that defines all key terms (with page references), and an *index* to all important topics.

WHAT'S NEW IN MICROSOFT WORD 7.0 FOR WINDOWS 95

1. *Address Book:* A database that provides easy access to contact information that you use often.

2. *AutoFormat:* Documents can be automatically formatted.

3. *Enhanced AutoCorrect:* Word can apply borders, headings, fractions, and list formatting while you type.

4. *Highlighter:* A new text enhancement tool that lets you emphasize key statements in your document.

5. *Internet Assistant:* Create documents to share on the World Wide Web.

6. *Spell It:* In addition to the Speller, this online feature checks spelling as you enter text, underlining potentially misspelled words, and displaying alternative spellings.

MICROSOFT WORD 7.0
FOR WINDOWS 95

1

WORD PROCESSING BASICS:
CREATING A DOCUMENT

WP

OBJECTIVES

After completing this chapter, you will be able to

1 Explain the general capabilities of a word processing program.
2 Describe the procedures to launch and exit Word.
3 Explain the various components of the Word window and how to alter their appearance.
4 Explain the use of wordwrap.

5 Contrast the difference between the insert and overtype modes.
6 Enter text onto the document window and save it as a file.
7 Close a document, open a document, and prepare a printed copy.

OVERVIEW

This chapter introduces the concept of word processing by presenting the basic techniques for using Word 7.0 for Windows 95, a well-known word processing package. First, you will learn how to start Word, how to interpret its screen, and how to enter text. Then, you will learn how to save and open documents, edit them to correct mistakes or improve content, and print them. You will also learn how to exit the program correctly.

WORD PROCESSING

Word processing is the use of computer technology to create, manipulate, save, and print text materials such as letters, memos, manuscripts, and other documents. Most word processing packages on the market offer the same basic capabilities. If you learn one, you will know what to expect from most others, even if the commands are different.

The instructions presented in this section pertain to Word for Windows 95 Version 7.0. Word for Windows 95 is a program based on a *graphical user interface,* or *GUI* (pronounced "gooey"), which uses symbols and menus instead of typewritten commands to help you communicate with the computer. It is like using a picture of a cigarette with a slash through it in place of a written "No Smoking" sign. Communication with the computer using a GUI becomes more universal. Many of the symbols and operations have become standard throughout the industry. The GUI environment that Word operates in is called *Microsoft Windows 95.* GUI symbols are called **icons.**

Word is also a *What-You-See-Is-What-You-Get,* or *WYSIWYG* (pronounced "wizzy-wig"), word processor. This feature allows you to work in a screen that resembles your final printed page. For example, if you use a type enhancement, like *italic,* or place a graphic in your document, your screen will show these items as they will appear on the final printed page.

You can invoke Word's capabilities by mouse or keyboard. This text presents mouse actions as the primary approach. Where appropriate, shortcut keystrokes are shown in the right margin.

When operating Word for Windows 95, it is highly recommended that you use the mouse to invoke commands. This approach is visually easier and sometimes quicker than the keyboard. If you do not have a mouse, obviously you must use the keyboard.

GETTING STARTED

Before you begin, be certain you have all the necessary tools: a hard disk or network that contains Windows 95, Word for Windows 95, and a formatted disk on which you will store the documents you create. This text assumes that you will be using Word on a hard-disk drive, although directions for networks are included.

LAUNCHING WINDOWS 95

Before starting any Windows 95 application, you must first launch Windows. In the Windows environment, you work in rectangular boxes called *windows.* A window may contain an application or a document. A window may also request or provide information (in which case, the window is called a **dialog box**).

As you proceed through the chapter, take note of the steps provided in each section and follow them while sitting at your computer. This module will refer to Windows 95 as simply "Windows."

USING A HARD-DISK DRIVE.   This text assumes that the Windows and Word programs are on your hard disk, which is identified as Drive C. To start Windows:

STEPS

1 **Turn on your computer to boot the operating system.**

Windows should start automatically. A "Starting Windows 95" message may appear. If your system boots to a menu, go to Step 3 in the next section, on using a network. If a C:\> prompt appears on your screen,

2 **Type WIN and press ↵ (This key may also be labeled "Enter" or "Return")**

> **Note: Throughout this module, text or commands that you should type will be shown in an orange box.**

You should now be at the Windows 95 desktop as in Figure WP1-1. (The actual contents of your window may differ.)

WP

FIGURE WP1-1 ■   THE WINDOWS 95 DESKTOP

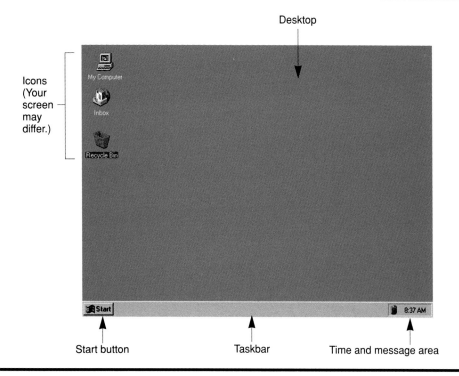

Desktop

Icons
(Your
screen
may
differ.)

Start button   Taskbar   Time and message area

3   If a "Welcome to Windows 95" dialog box appears, click the *Close* button or press   **Esc**

4   Insert your data disk into Drive A (or Drive B)

USING A NETWORK.   Word may be available to you through a local area network. In this case, Word is kept on the hard-disk drive of another computer that is shared by many users. To use Word, you must access the program from your own microcomputer. So many network configurations are in use today that it is difficult to predict which one you will use. Check with your instructor for exact directions. In general, however, to start Word,

STEPS

1   Boot the network operating system (perhaps with your own disk)

2   Type any command needed to get the network menu

In many networks, this is done by typing   **LAN**   and pressing the   **↵**   key.

3   Make sure your data disk is in Drive A (or Drive B)

4   Select (or type) the appropriate command on your screen to access Windows 95

MOUSE AND KEYBOARD OPERATIONS

Skip this section if you are already familiar with using a mouse and keyboard.

USING A MOUSE.   A *mouse* is an input device that allows you to control a **mouse pointer** (graphical image) on your screen and select program features. Currently, it appears as a small arrow. As you move your mouse on a flat surface, the mouse pointer moves on your screen in a similar fashion. In Word, the mouse pointer may appear in the forms displayed in Figure WP1-2. *Pointing* means moving the mouse. To *point* your mouse,

STEPS

1   Slowly move your mouse on a flat surface or mouse pad (a small rubber pad) and notice the direction that the mouse pointer moves on your screen. If you run out of space, simply lift your mouse and replace it.

2   Point to the *Start* button in the taskbar (use the tip of the arrow to point)

3   Point to the *My Computer* icon (at the upper left)

Clicking involves quickly pressing and releasing the left mouse button. This action will normally select the item at which the mouse pointer is positioned. Try this:

FIGURE WP1-2 ■ MOUSE POINTERS AND ACTIONS

(a) Common mouse pointers.
(b) Common mouse actions.

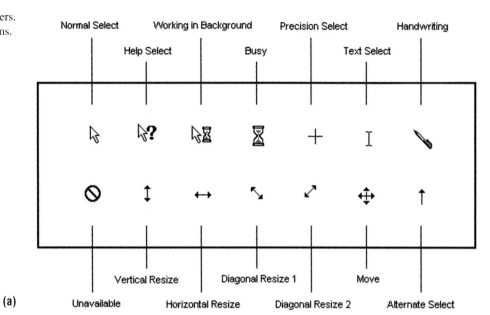

(a)

(b)

Mouse Action	Description
Pointing	Moving the mouse, and thus the mouse pointer, to the desired item.
Clicking	Pressing and quickly releasing the left mouse button.
Right-clicking	Pressing and releasing the right mouse button.
Double-clicking	Rapidly pressing and releasing the left mouse button twice.
Dropping	Releasing the mouse and thus the object pointed to, after dragging.
Dragging	Pressing and holding the left mouse button, while moving the mouse to the desired location.

4 Click *Start* to see its menu

5 Click anywhere in the desktop to close the menu for now

Another basic mouse action is called **double-clicking.** Double-clicking involves quickly pressing and releasing the left mouse button *twice*. To practice double-clicking,

6 Point to the *My Computer* icon and double-click the icon

Note: If a window does not appear, you may not be clicking quickly enough. Double-click the icon again.

WP

7 **Now click the "X" (Close) button at the upper right of this window**

Many Windows applications also support a feature called *drag and drop*. This feature allows you to use a mouse to move a selection (text or object) from one place to another. This feature will be illustrated later.

The common mouse actions are summarized in Figure WP1-2b.

USING A KEYBOARD.   At times, Windows features may also be accessed by keyboard. Keystrokes required to operate Word's menu system are discussed under the section "The Menu Bar" (later in this chapter).

Most applications also provide special keystrokes called **shortcut keys.** Shortcut keys provide quick access to certain commands. Shortcut keys require you to press a function key, either alone or in combination with the Ctrl, Alt, and/or Shift keys (a listing of shortcut keys can be found in the appendix). For example, to close windows using its shortcut key:

STEPS

1 **Press** **Alt** + **F4** **(Hold the Alt key, press the F4 key, and then release both keys)**

2 **Press** **N** **to cancel the command**

This manual presents its tutorials using the mouse approach. Where appropriate, keyboard shortcuts will be shown in brackets at the right of the step.

LAUNCHING WORD

The procedure to start, or launch, Word is the same as for any Windows application. Note that the Word program icon is usually found in the Microsoft Office program group.

STEPS

 1 **Click the *Start* button to access its menu**   **[** **Ctrl** + **Esc** **]**

2 **Point to the *Programs* item in the list**

Note that the letter "P" is underlined. This indicates that you can press **P** if you want to select it. If the Word icon appears in this list, skip Step 3.

3 **Point to the *Microsoft Office* item in the menu that appears to the right.**

Note that if the Word program is located in a group other than Microsoft Office, use the proper group in place of Office.

To start Word using its icon,

 4 **Point to the *Microsoft Word* item** [→]

5 **Click the *Microsoft Word* item** [↵]

> Note: You can also start Word through the Microsoft Office Shortcut toolbar. First, click the *Microsoft Office* icon and then click the *W* icon in the Office toolbar.

A Word copyright screen may appear briefly but is quickly replaced by the Word window as in Figure WP1-3.

6 **If a "Tip of the Day" toolbar appears, click the *Tip Wizard* button to close it.**

UNDERSTANDING WORD

You should now be looking at the Word window as shown in Figure WP1-3. This is the main application window that appears each time you start the program. Occupying its workspace is a new document window into which text and pictures (graphics) may be placed.

> Note: When you want to leave Word, for now, press Alt + F, X, and then N. You can then launch Word again to continue.

THE WORD WINDOW

There is only one Word window. However, depending on your available memory, up to nine individual document windows may be opened.

The Word window has several standard Windows features as well as features unique to Word. Examine your screen, as you read the following brief summary of these features and their operations.

TITLE BAR.   All windows have a title bar located across the top. The **title bar** identifies the name of the window, in this case, Microsoft Word. It can also be used to resize or move the window. This is useful when using more than one program. Try this:

STEPS

1 **Point anywhere within the Title bar**

FIGURE WP1-3 ■ **THE WORD WINDOW**

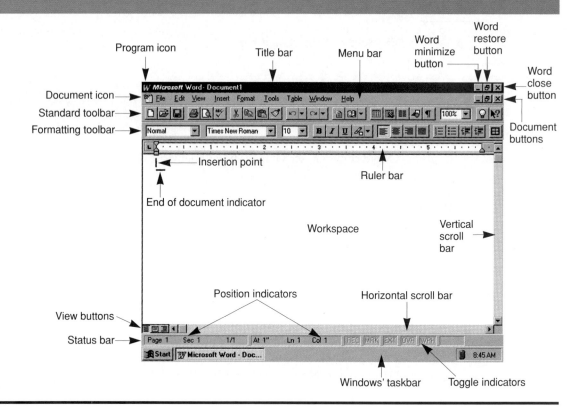

| 2 | **Double-click it**

The Word window should now appear as a smaller, independent window on your screen.
To *maximize* or return the window to a full screen,

| 3 | **Point to and double-click the Title bar again**

MENU BAR.   Word's menu bar is located directly below its title bar. Only application
windows have a menu bar. A **menu bar** provides access to the applications commands
through pull-down menus. A **pull-down menu** provides a list of commands related to
the menu bar item. Menu bar operations are described in "The Menu Bar" section.

TOOLBARS.   Two toolbars are normally located below the menu bar. A **toolbar** is a
Word feature that provides quick access to frequently used features by mouse. A *button*
is a box that may contain a picture or words representing a command. Clicking it will invoke the command. For example, clicking the disk button will access Word's Save feature. Word provides eight different toolbars that offer mouse shortcuts. The *Standard*
and *Formatting* toolbars appear by default. The formatting toolbar also indicates the

FIGURE WP1-4 ■ *SHORTCUT* MENUS

Word *Shortcut* menus provide quick access to specific Word features. To open a *Shortcut* menu, click the right mouse button or press Shift + F10.

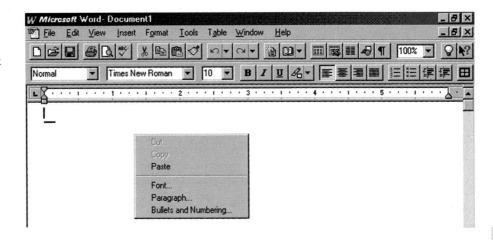

current font (character) style being used at the insertion point. For example, the current character style that you are using is called Times New Roman 10pt (pt = point size). A point is a typesetting measurement of height equal to about $\frac{1}{72}$ of an inch. It is Word's default font. Methods to change fonts are addressed in Chapter 2.

> **Tip: Toolbar buttons are shown in the margin where appropriate.**

RESIZING BUTTONS. Like all application windows, the Word window has two resizing buttons located at its upper right corner. Clicking a **resizing button** will quickly resize the window. Three types of resizing buttons are available.

- A *Minimize button* reduces the window to a button on the task bar.
- A *Restore button* reduces a maximized (full screen) window to a smaller window. The restore button appears only when a window is maximized.
- A *Maximize button* resizes the window to a full screen. The *Maximize* button appears only when a window is less than full screen.

Try this:

STEPS

1 **Point to Word's *Restore* button**

2 **Click the button**

Your Word window should appear as a smaller window. Note also that the *Restore* button has been replaced by a *Maximize* button. Now, resize the window back to a full screen as follows:

WP

3 Point to and click the Word window *Maximize* button

Your Word window should appear again as in Figure WP1-3.

Document window resizing buttons operate the same way and are discussed in the "Understanding a Document Window" section.

CLOSE BUTTON.   At the extreme right of the resizing buttons is the Word Window's Close button. Clicking this button once will exit word, closing the window.

RULER BAR.   Beneath the toolbars is a **ruler bar** that visually displays the document's current margin and tab settings. By default, the ruler bar appears when you start Word. If you have no ruler bar (as in Figure WP1-3), display it now as follows:

STEPS

1 Click *View*

Note that you can also press   **Alt** + **V**   (the underlined letter).

2 Click *Ruler*

You could also press   **R** .

The Ruler bar is discussed later in the chapter.

WORKSPACE.   All windows have a **workspace.** It is the interior space of the window. Currently, the Word window workspace is fully occupied by a single document window but it can contain up to nine document windows at a time. A document window's workspace is discussed in "The Document Window" section of this chapter.

STATUS BAR.   Located at the bottom of the Word window, the **status bar** displays information about the document currently in use and the insertion point's location. It is discussed in detail in "The Status Bar" section.

SHORTCUT MENUS.   **Shortcut menus** provide quick access to specific Word features. A *Shortcut* menu is opened by pointing to certain areas of the Word window and clicking the right mouse button.

Try this:

STEPS

1 Point to an open space in the center of the document window's workspace

2 Right-click the mouse (click the right mouse button)

A *Shortcut* menu should appear as in Figure WP1-4.

3 Point to and click (left button) outside of the *Shortcut* menu to close it

PROGRAM ICON.   As with all application windows, the *Word window Program* icon is located in its upper left corner. It resembles a letter W. As seen earlier, a **program icon** can be used to close a window by double-clicking it. It can also be used to open a control-menu by mouse. A **control-menu** may contain commands to resize, move, and close the window. In addition, some control-menus contain a command to switch to another running application or document.

> **Tip:** *Minimize, Restore,* and *Maximize* commands can be accessed with the keyboard through the control-menu. Operation of the Word window's Program icon and buttons are discussed in the appendix.

THE MENU BAR

Word's menu bar gives you access to most of the program's features through pull-down menus. When a menu bar item is selected, a *pull-down menu* is opened providing a related list of commands. This module will refer to a pull-down menu simply as a "menu."

> **Note:** *Click = point to and click* from this point on. In many cases, you can also use the keyboard to invoke mouse menu commands. Remember to press Alt plus the underlined letter to select a menu bar item, or the underlined letter alone to select from a pull-down menu. Mouse toolbar shortcuts are shown in the margin.

OPENING AND CLOSING A MENU.   Try this to open the *File* menu,

---

STEPS

1 Click *File*   [**Alt** + **F**]

The *File* menu opens as in Figure WP1-5. Note that opening a menu by keyboard requires pressing the Alt key and the underlined letter (mnemonic) of a menu bar item.
    Now, do the following to close the menu:

2 Click any open space outside the menu   [**Alt** , **Esc** , **Esc**]

SELECTING A MENU ITEM.   Once a menu is open, simply click the desired menu item or press its underlined letter. Try this to open the *File* menu and then select *Exit* to exit Word:

STEPS

1 Click *File* for the *File* menu

2 Click *Exit*

You should now have exited Word and returned to the Windows desktop. To restart Word,

FIGURE WP1-5 ■ OPENING A PULL-DOWN MENU

(a) To open a pull-down menu, point to and click a desired menu bar item or press the Alt key and the underlined letter of the menu bar item.

(b) Menu conventions (indicators).

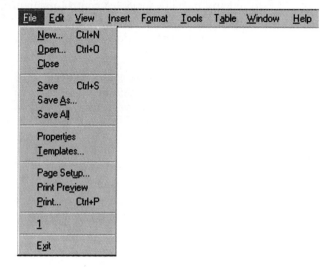

(a)

Menu Items with	Explanation
No notation	Invoke a command or other feature
Keys at far right	Shortcut key(s) for invoking the menu item by keyboard
Dimmed (or not visible) characters	Menu item is not currently available
Ellipsis (…)	Opens to a dialog box or another window
Dot (or check) on the left side	A feature that is activated

(b)

[W] Microsoft Word   [3] **Double-click the Word icon**   [↵]

Tip: Another keyboard method to open a menu is to first press the Alt key to turn on the highlight. (The Alt key is a toggle [on/off] switch that activates or deactivates the highlight bar.) Once turned on, the highlight bar can be moved to a menu bar item by pressing an arrow key. Pressing the Enter key will then open its menu. Next, press the down arrow key to move the highlight to the desired menu item and press the Enter key to select it.

Note: Menu bar commands presented in the mouse approach can also be accessed by keyboard.

MENU INDICATORS

Word uses standard Windows menu conventions in its menu system. These conventions apply to all types of menus—pull-down menus, control menus, and *Shortcut* menus. The *File* menu will be used to help you understand these menu conventions.

 1 **Click *File***

The *File* menu should appear again as in Figure WP1-5a.

As seen in the last section, menu items without an ellipsis (…), such as *Exit*, directly invoke a command.

If a shortcut key(s) can be used to directly invoke a menu item, it is displayed at its extreme right. For example, the shortcut keys "Ctrl+P" are displayed to the right of *Print*.

Menu items with an ellipsis (...) open a dialog box or another window. A *dialog box* requests or provides information to help you perform a task. Try opening the *Save As* dialog box as follows:

2 **Click *Save As* for its dialog box**

You will later use the *Save As* dialog box to save documents you create in Word. For now, to exit the dialog box:

3 **Click the *Cancel* button**

> **Tip: The Esc key can be used to cancel a menu or dialog box display.**

A summary of menu conventions is listed in Figure WP1-5b.

THE DOCUMENT WINDOW

The *document* (or *file*) *window* is an area of your screen that resembles a portion of a clean sheet of paper. When you start Word, it opens with a new document window that automatically occupies the Word window's entire workspace.

As in Figure WP1-3, the work area of the document window is currently blank except for an **insertion point** (usually represented by a blinking vertical line) at the upper left corner. The insertion point is simply a placeholder; it shows where the next keystroke you type into your document will appear. A horizontal bar currently beneath the insertion point shows the end of your document.

Document windows have several standard features as well as features unique to Word. Each of these window features displays information or does specific tasks. The location of some of these features depends on the size of the document window. For instance, the document window on your screen shares its title bar with Word's title bar. This is true whenever a document window is maximized. As in Figure WP1-3, the title bar's caption "Document1" next to "Microsoft Word" is the current document's name.

In addition, a maximized document window's icon and *Restore* button occupy the left and right ends of the menu bar.

WP

As you will see later, a document window that is less than maximized has its own title bar and resizing buttons (which allows you to minimize and maximize).

Some of the following features may be included in the Word document window. (Use Figure WP1-3 and your screen to locate each feature as you read.)

 SCROLL BARS. **Scroll bars** can be used to quickly scroll (move) through a document with a mouse. Scroll bars are at the right wall (vertical scroll bar) and at the bottom wall (horizontal scroll bar) of a document window. When maximized, the bottom wall of a document window is just above the status bar.

Scroll bars only work when there is text or an object inside the window. Clicking the arrow button at either end of the scroll bar will scroll through an existing document moving in the direction of the arrow. Dragging the small square box (called *scroll box*) along the scroll bar will also scroll through an existing document.

> **Tip: Scroll bars do not move the insertion point. After scrolling to a desired position of your document, you must point to and click that position to move the insertion point there.**

 PAGE VIEW BUTTONS. The three **page view buttons** to the left of the horizontal scroll bar allow you to use the mouse to change the page view from *Normal view* to *Page Layout view* or *Outline view*. (More on these views later.)

THE STATUS BAR

As in Figure WP1-6, the status bar, located at the bottom of the Word window, provides information about visible text, modes selected for text entry, and the insertion point's current location. You will now learn about the various components of the status bar more fully. Examine your screen and identify each component as it is discussed.

PAGE 1. The **Page message** shows the document page on which the insertion point is currently located. As you move the insertion point onto a new page or return to a previous one, the Page message will change appropriately. It is not always easy to judge

FIGURE WP1-6 ■ THE WORD STATUS BAR

The Word status bar is located at the bottom of the Word window. It provides information related to the document displayed on screen.

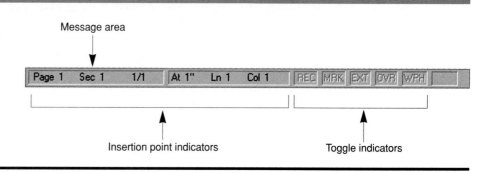

page position by looking at the insertion point alone. When you start creating multi-page documents, you will greatly appreciate the page indicator.

SEC 1.   The **Section message** shows the current document section. Each section can contain different formatting options.

1/1.   The numbers that follow the Section message indicate the actual page count and total pages in the document. Currently, 1/1 indicates that you are on page 1 of a 1-page document.

AT 1″.   The **At message** displays the vertical position of the insertion point within the current page. This position is expressed in inches, as in 2″ (which means two inches down from the page top). The At message changes each time you begin a new line or move back through your document.

LN 1.   The **Line message** displays the insertion point's vertical position expressed in text lines, as in 1, which indicates the first line. Like the At message, the Line message changes as you move vertically. Try this:

STEPS

1 Press ↵ three times to move the insertion point down three lines

Notice how the At message now reads **1.50″** and the Ln message reads **4.**

2 Press Backspace three times to move back to the original position

The At and Ln messages have returned to their original settings.

COL 1.   The **Column message** shows the current horizontal character position of the insertion point from the left margin. As you type, the Col message changes appropriately. Try this:

STEPS

1 Type your name

Notice how the Col message changed to show your current typing position.

2 Press ↵

Notice that the insertion point returned to the left margin and that the Col message again displays *1.*

TIME.   The time appears next on the status bar.

MODE INDICATORS.   The remaining space on the status bar is reserved for *mode indicators* for macro recording (REC), revision marking (MRK), extended text selection (EXT), overtype/insert (OVR), and WordPerfect help (WPH). Dimmed indicators are "off." Double-clicking an indicator will turn it on or off. More on mode indicators later.

Examine the screen shown in Figure WP1-7. Notice that it indicates that the insertion point in Document2 (see title bar) is on Page 2, which is the second of five pages, 1.5″ or four lines from the top, and six characters from the left margin. Notice also that the overtype toggle is on.

> Note: Word also uses its status bar to display help prompts. A help prompt provides information about a button or other window objects as you point to them. Help prompts also appear when pointing to a menu item.

For example,

STEPS

1 Point to the *Print* button on the toolbar, but do not click it.

The message "Prints the active document using the current defaults" appears in the status bar and a "Print" title appears beneath the button.

FIGURE WP1-7 ■ THE TITLE BAR AND STATUS BAR

The Word title bar indicates that the active document window is "Document2." The status bar shows that the overtype mode is "on" and the insertion point is positioned in Page 2, 1.5 inches from the top of the page.

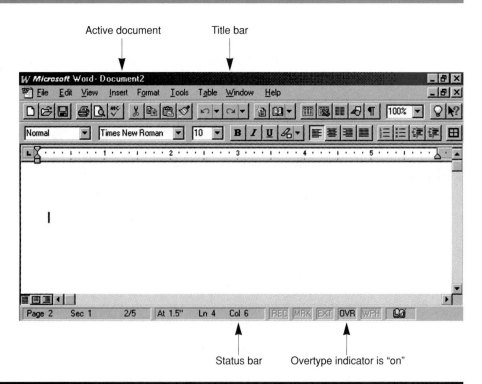

Learning how to read the status bar and its subtle messages will significantly enhance the ease with which you use Word in the future.

THE HELP FEATURE

Word's on-line help includes general and specific help windows, a search feature, examples, demos, and reference information. Most dialog boxes also have a *Help* button that will access a Help window related to its operation.

USING THE HELP WINDOW.   Word's Help window provides a built-in reference for every Word command. To initiate this Help feature:

STEPS

1   Click *Help* and then *Microsoft Word Help Topics*   [**F1**]

A *Help Topics* dialog box will appear.

2   If needed, click the *Contents* tab located just below the Help Topics title bar. You may simply click the desired topic and then click *Open,* or double-click the topic to view it.

To close the *Help* dialog box:

 3   Click the *Help* dialog box Close button on its title bar or click *Cancel*   [**Alt** + **F4**]

USING THE INDEX FEATURE.   The *Index tab* can be used to search for help on a specific topic. For example, to search for help on Word's Undo feature,

STEPS

1   Click *Help* and then *Microsoft Word Help Topics*

2   Click the *Index* tab

A screen similar to Figure WP1-8 will appear.

3   Type Undo

4   Click the *Display* button to list related topics in alphabetical order as in Figure WP1-9

5   Click *Undo mistakes* in the list to select it

6   Click the *Display* button

An explanation will appear.

Now to exit the *Help* dialog box,

 7   Click the Close button in the title bar   [**Alt** + **F4**]

WP

FIGURE WP1-8 ■ **THE WORD HELP WINDOW**

Command tabs ➡

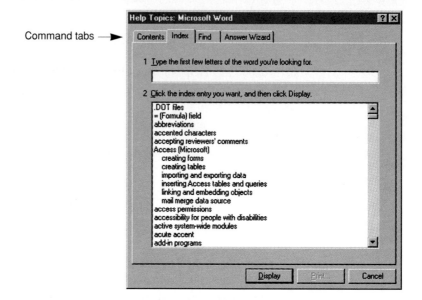

INSERTION POINT MOVEMENTS

The insertion point can be moved by mouse or keyboard through text—anywhere from the beginning to the end of your document. However, it cannot be moved beyond the last

FIGURE WP1-9 ■ **THE *TOPICS FOUND* DIALOG BOX**

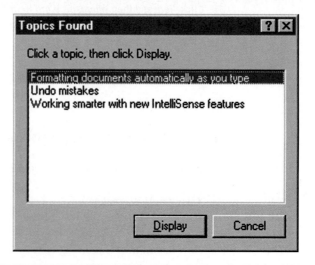

character of your document. Because both mouse and keyboard techniques are quite different, they will be shown separately. Do the following to prepare for the exercises in this section:

1 If needed, launch Word to obtain a blank document window

2 Type the sentences shown in Figure WP1-10

Do not press the Enter key until the very end, as indicated. Do not worry about where each line of text ends on your screen.

MOVING THE INSERTION POINT BY MOUSE.   To move the insertion point by mouse, simply point to the desired location and click. Try this to move to each of the locations:

1 Click the "T" in "This" at the beginning of the text (Remember, click = point to and click), and then move the mouse pointer away from the "T" to see the insertion point's new position

2 Click the "a" in the first "and" on the second line, and then move the mouse pointer away from the "a"

3 Click anywhere below the last line of text

Note that the insertion point moves to the end of your document—the horizontal end of document marker.

To move the insertion point around a large document, click the scroll bar buttons (or drag the scroll box) to move to the desired location. Next, click the desired location to move the insertion point there.

MOVING THE INSERTION POINT BY KEYBOARD.   Several different keys can be used to move the insertion point. These keys include the arrow keys, Home, End, Pg

FIGURE WP1-10 ■ USING INSERTION POINT CONTROL KEYS

Type this text. Do not press the Enter key until the end (as shown by the paragraph symbol).

This is an example of moving the insertion point within a document using the arrow keys by themselves and in combination with the Ctrl and Home keys. Two other keys, Pg Up and Pg Dn, also move the insertion point around the document.¶

Up, or Pg Dn. The arrow keys will move the insertion point a single character at a time (left, right, up, or down) through the text. The keys can also be used with the Ctrl and Alt keys to produce additional insertion point movements. Figure WP1-11 lists several insertion point movement keystrokes. Use the keyboard to try some insertion point movements on the typed paragraph.

STEPS

1 Press **Ctrl** + **Home** to move the insertion point to the beginning of the text

2 Press ↓ to move down one line

3 Press → to move one character to the right

4 Press **Ctrl** + → to move one word to the right

5 Press **End** to move to the end of the line

6 Press **Ctrl** + **End** to move to the end of the document

FIGURE WP1-11 ■ INSERTION POINT MOVEMENTS

To Move the Insertion Point...	Press These Keys:
One character left	←
One character right	→
One word left	Ctrl + ←
One word right	Ctrl + →
To left side of screen	Home
To right side of screen	End
One line up	↑
One line down	↓
To top of screen	Pg Up
To bottom of screen	Pg Dn
To previous page	Alt + Pg Up
To next page	Alt + Pg Dn
One paragraph up	Ctrl + ↑
One paragraph down	Ctrl + ↓
To beginning of document	Ctrl + Home
To end of document	Ctrl + End

> **7** **Press** →

Note that the insertion point does not move and a warning "beep" may sound. Remember that you cannot move beyond the end of the document.

Get the idea? Try a few insertion point movements on your own. Although you do not need them all now, these movements will become more useful to you as your documents grow longer.

☑ CHECKPOINT

✓ Launch Word and get to the Word screen.
✓ What is the meaning of the status bar message "Page 3 At 1″ Ln 1 Col 1"?
✓ Access the Help window, then close it.
✓ Type a few sentences and then move the insertion point using the first ten keystrokes in Figure WP1-11.
✓ Exit from Word *without* saving the document.

THE BASICS: SAVING, OPENING, AND EXITING

Before you begin to type and edit, you should understand how to save and open your files for use, and how to exit Word. Once you know these procedures, whenever you want to stop, you can first save your work on disk and then exit the program. (You may also want to mark the spot where you stopped in this text.) Then, when you return, you can boot your computer, launch Word, open your document, find your place in the text, and continue from where you left off.

STEPS

> **1** **Launch Word if needed, or select *File*, *Close*, *No*, *File*, *New*, ↵ to start a fresh document**

Now, enter this brief sentence on your screen:

> **2** **Type   This is a sample of typing.**

> **3** **Press ↵**

Although this is a small amount of typing, it is, nonetheless, a document, and can be used to practice the basic techniques of saving, opening, and exiting.

SAVING A DOCUMENT TO DISK

Because documents you create with this module will be saved to your data disk, it is wise to change the default drive to A (or B) before saving your document. Make sure that you have placed your disk into the appropriate disk drive. To open the *Save As* dialog box, set your default drive and then save your document with the name **EXAMPLE**, do the following:

WP

1   **Click _File_ and then _Save As_**

Because this is the first time you are saving this document, the _Save As_ dialog box should appear as in Figure WP1-12. (Note: The contents of your dialog box may differ from the figure.) In addition to saving a document, you can use this dialog box for changing the default drive, default directory, and the format in which a document will be saved (as you will soon see).

FIGURE WP1-12   ■   THE _SAVE AS_ DIALOG BOX

(a) Components of the _Save As_ dialog box.
(b) Changing the Save in disk drive to A and entering the filename "EXAMPLE."

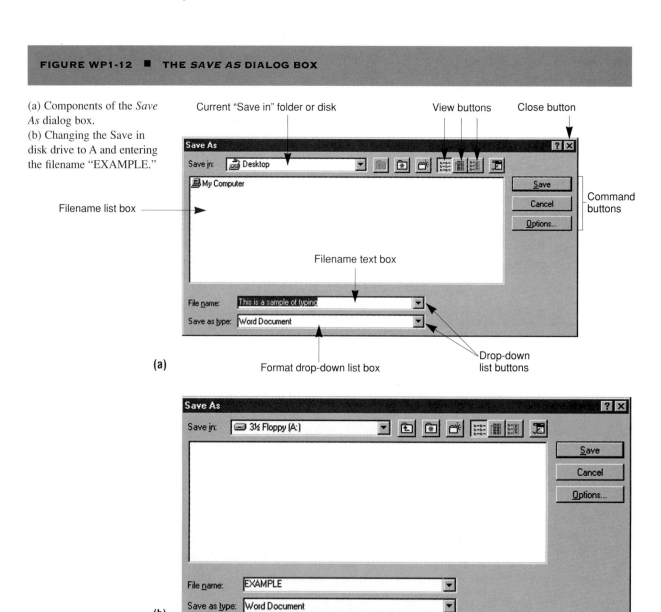

(a)

(b)

Like all dialog boxes, the *Save As* dialog box has a variety of standard Windows options. To select an option by mouse, simply click it. With the keyboard, press the Alt key and the underlined letter of the option. Dialog box options may include the following:

- *Text boxes.* A box in which text can be typed (such as the *File name* text box).
- *List boxes.* A box that alphabetically lists options available for selection (such as the *File name* list box).
- *Drop-down boxes.* An area that appears as a single line box with a $\downarrow$ button at its right side (such as the *Save in* drop-down box). Selecting this button opens a list with available choices. The current selection is highlighted.
- *Check boxes.* A small square box next to an option. Selecting an empty check box places a "✔" in it. This indicates that the feature is on.
- *Option buttons.* A small circle next to an option that operates the same way a check box does. A selected *Option* button contains a black dot in it. Only one *Option* button can be selected in a group. (Note: the *Save As* dialog box does not have *Check* or *Option buttons.*)
- *Command buttons.* Selecting a *Command* button will invoke the command it represents (such as the *Save* button).

2 If you have not done so already, insert your data disk into Drive A or B

⬛ **3** Click the button of the *Save in* drop-down box for the *Drives* list

💾 3½ Floppy (A:)   **4** Click the 3½ Floppy (A:) drive icon to change the default drive to A (or select B)

5 Double-click the *File name* text box to move the highlight there (if only the insertion point appears in the text box, double-click it again to highlight its contents)

6 Type   **EXAMPLE**   (the name of your document) and delete any additional characters

If all went well, your *Save As* dialog box should resemble WP1-12b. (The contents of your boxes may differ.) Note the following changes in the dialog box:

- The current path is now A: (or B:). The path is the location on a disk or other storage media to which files will be saved or from which files will be opened.
- The filename "EXAMPLE" appears in the *File name* text box.

To save your document,

7 Click the *Save* button   [↵]

> **Tip:** You can also select dialog box options by pressing the Tab key to move the highlight to a desired option and then pressing the Enter key.

Your default drive for saving and opening documents is now set. You will not need to reset the default drive again as long as you stay in Word. When you save (or open) a document now, it will be stored on (or fetched from) your data disk.

Tip: You must redesignate the desired "look in" drive whenever you restart Word.

Even if you do not change the default drive, you can still save and open documents, but you will have to include a disk identifier in front of the document's name (as in A:EX-AMPLE) each time you save it, to ensure that the data disk is used. It is simpler to change the default drive before saving or opening. It is also safer—you will not run the risk of mistakenly saving your documents onto your program disk.

The drive light will flash briefly as the document is being saved. When the process is finished, the drive and document name (Example) should appear in the title bar, next to "Microsoft Word," as in Figure WP1-13. Although you may not see it in your file lists, Word automatically adds the filename extension ".doc" to documents that you create and save in it. This extension associates (connects) the document with the Word application. You can now continue working on your document.

"SAVE AS" VERSUS "SAVE".   Once you have saved your document, you can easily save it again as you work by selecting the *File-Save* command. The document will immediately be saved to your disk with the same name, automatically replacing the old file. For example,

STEPS

1 Click *File* and then *Save*

The file has been saved again. Any changes you have made in your document have been safely copied to your disk.

FIGURE WP1-13 ■   A SAVED DOCUMENT

Once a document has been saved (or opened), its document name will appear in the title bar.

Document name

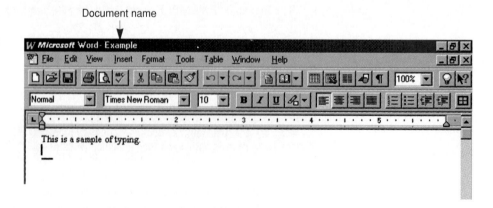

At times, however, you may want to save a document with a different name than its current one so you don't erase the old file. To accomplish this, you must use the Save As command when you save the file instead of *Save*. Try this:

2   **Click** <u>*File*</u> **and then** *Save* <u>*As*</u>

The *Save As* dialog box appears as before. Note that the current name "EXAMPLE" automatically appears in the *File name* box. If you wanted to change the name, you could type a new one in its place and select *OK,* or press the Enter key. You could also identify a new drive, subdirectory, or file type, if needed.

In this example, however, you can cancel the command as follows:

3   **Click** *Cancel*   **[Esc]**

Remember, use the Save command as you work to save the current document immediately with the same name. Use the Save As command to change a document's name, location, or file type. Both techniques will save—it's your choice.

> **Tip:** When you save a document for the first time, the Save command will open a *Save As* dialog box so that you can name the document.

The Save or Save As command—which copies (or "backs up") the current version of your document from primary memory to disk—should be used frequently as you work. In this way, if you lose power for any reason, a recent copy of your document will be available on your disk.

CLOSING A DOCUMENT

There are times when you will want to close the document window of an old document before you start a new one. Try this:

STEPS

1   **Click** <u>*File*</u> **and then** <u>*Close*</u>   **[Ctrl + F4]**

If you have already saved your document, the window will disappear. If not, a dialog box will appear asking "Do you want to save changes?" If this happens,

2   **Click the** <u>*No*</u> **button**

3   **You can exit from Word now (by pressing** **Alt** **+** **F4** **,** **X** **,** **N** **) or continue on to the next section**

Note that you could have saved the document by selecting the <u>*Yes*</u> button.

WP

This will close the current document. If you did not close your document window, each new document window you open would be placed on top of the preceding window in Word's workspace. Remember, depending on your system's memory, you may open up to nine documents in the workspace. Get into the habit of always closing one document *before* opening another document unless you intend to work on several documents at a time. Multiple document operations are discussed in Chapter 3.

> **Tip:** A quick way to close a document (or any other) window is to double-click its *Program* icon.

STARTING A NEW DOCUMENT WINDOW

When Word is first launched, a new document window appears on the screen, awaiting your text entry. At times, you may want to open a new, or blank, window on your own. For example, to open a new document window now,

1 Click *File* and then *New* [**Ctrl** + **N**]

> **Tip:** If you use the *New* icon, the program will bypass the *New* dialog box and move directly to a new default document.

A *New* dialog box appears, offering several document styles for your use. Although you should explore these styles after you master Word's basics, for now, select the "Normal" style:

2 Click *OK* [↵]

A new document window appears on your screen. For now, close the window you have just opened.

3 Click *File* and then *Close* [**Ctrl** + **F4**]

OPENING A DOCUMENT

Once you have saved a document to disk, it is available for viewing, typing, editing, or printing. In fact, you need not finish working on a document all at once. In normal practice, you can type a portion of a document, save it, and exit from Word. Later on, you can return to continue where you had stopped by merely *opening* an old document for use. **Opening** a document copies a previously saved file from your disk into a new document window in Word, as if you had retyped it yourself. To prepare for these exercises, do the following:

1   If needed, start your computer and launch the Word program

2   Close the current document window

In Word, you have two ways to open a document from the *Open* dialog box: type its name or select it from a list.

TYPING A DOCUMENT'S NAME.   If you know a document's name, the most direct way to open it is to click the Open button (toolbar) or use   **Ctrl** + **O** . (*Note:* If you have just launched Word, make sure to set the default drive appropriately.) Try this:

1   Click *File* and then *Open* for the *Open* dialog box   [**Ctrl** + **O**]

You should see an *Open* dialog box similar to Figure WP1-14. Note that only document files appear in the *File name* list. The *Open* dialog box can be used to open a saved document, change the default drive, and change the default directory. It operates much like the *Save As* dialog box.

If your default drive is correct (check the "Look in" text box), go to Step 4. If not, do Steps 2 and 3 to change it to Drive A (or B as appropriate).

FIGURE WP1-14 ■ THE *OPEN* DIALOG BOX

Components of the *Open* dialog box.

Active drive or folder (Look in)

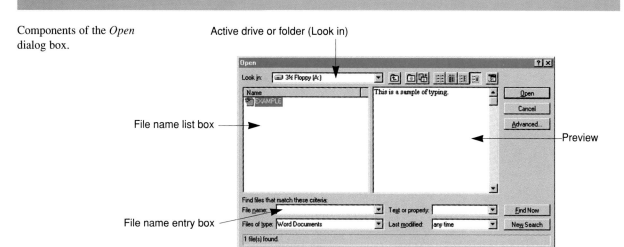

File name list box

File name entry box

Preview

⬛ 3½ Floppy (A:)

2   Click the button of the *Look in* drop-down box and then click the *3½ Floppy A:* (or *B:*) drive icon to change the default drive

3   Double-click the *File name* text box to highlight its contents

4   Type   **EXAMPLE**

5   Click *Open*

The document is opened. If your screen shows a *File not found* dialog box, then either you spelled the filename incorrectly (now or when you saved it) or you did not set your default drive correctly. If you were not successful in opening the document, click the *OK* button (or press the Enter key) to exit the *Error* dialog box, check for these mistakes, and try again.

SELECTING A DOCUMENT FROM A LIST.   If you do not remember the name of a document, or forget its exact spelling, you may prefer this second technique. In this procedure, you use the *Files* list box of the *Open* dialog box to select the one you want. Try this:

STEPS

1   Click *File* and then *Close* to close your document   [**Ctrl** + **F4**]

2   Click *File* and then *Open* for the *Open* dialog box   [**Ctrl** + **O**]

Your screen should resemble Figure WP1-14, displaying all the document files on your disk (your screen may have more files than shown in the figure).

3   Click *example* from the *File name* list box to move the highlight to it   [**Tab** , ↓]

4   Click the *Open* button   [↵]

> Tip: To quickly open the file by mouse, replace Steps 3 and 4 by double-clicking "example" in the *Files* list box.

If all went well, your document should now appear on the screen. Practice the Save As and Open routines a few times; then use them as needed.

> Tip: Once a document has been saved, you can also open it directly in Windows 95 by clicking *Start*, pointing to *Documents,* and then clicking the filename. This action will launch Word and open the document.

EXITING WORD AND SHUTTING DOWN WINDOWS

Now that you have experienced the basics of Word, you should also learn how to exit from the program when you are finished. There are several ways to exit the Word window. Earlier, the example in "The Menu Bar" section illustrated closing the window using menu bar selections.

Here, you will learn how to exit Word and then shut down Windows. As you exit Word, you will be offered another chance to save any unsaved or modified document(s) in its workspace. To exit Word using its *Program* icon:

STEPS

 1 Click Word's *Program* icon for its control-menu   [**Alt** + **Spacebar**]

2 Click *Close* to exit Word

If your screen responds with a dialog box saying "Do you want to save changes to EXAMPLE?" your document was modified and not resaved. At this point, you may select the *Yes* button (to resave), the *No* button (to close and not resave), or the *Cancel* button. Because you have already saved this document, you should answer *No*, as follows:

3 Click the *No* button

> **Tip:** A quick way to exit Word is to double-click its program icon or press Alt + F4.

If all went well, you should be in Windows. To shut down Windows:

4 Click the *Start* button

5 Click *Shut Down*

6 Click the *Yes* button to shut down Windows

Remember, you can also use the Exit command of the *File* menu to exit Word. To do so by mouse, click *File* and then *Exit* in the application's window. With the keyboard, press the **Alt** + **F** keys and then the **X** key.

In general, the Save command is used for copying a document from time to time as you work on it—a safety precaution. The Close Application routine can be used to save your document when you are finished and want to exit Word entirely.

If you're stopping for now, simply shut off your computer (unless your lab follows a different procedure—check first).

☑ CHECKPOINT

✓   Launch Word; set the default drive appropriately.

WP

✓   Type your name on the first line and your class underneath it. Save this document with the name EXAMPLE (replace the old file).

✓   Close the open document.

✓   Use the *Open* dialog box to open the EXAMPLE document.

✓   Exit Word and shut down Windows.

CREATING A DOCUMENT

As you have seen, entering text into Word is similar to using a typewriter, with a few notable exceptions. The most important is the use (or, more appropriately, nonuse) of the Enter key. To prepare for these exercises,

STEPS

1   **Start Windows and then launch Word if needed**

2   **Insert your data disk into Drive A (or B)**

CHANGING THE DISPLAY

The Word screen is an extremely useful guide to the insertion point's position and text appearance. However, you may want to adjust some screen settings to suit your particular needs. Two common changes include adjusting the screen view mode and turning on the ruler bar. These display changes may help you access commands more quickly and visualize your work more clearly.

VIEW MODES.   Word offers five basic view modes, which can be invoked through the *View* menu choice: Normal, Page Layout, Outline, Master Document, and Full Screen. Of these, the first two are of interest to the beginner.

■   **Normal view** is Word's default. It provides a WYSIWYG ("What-You-See-Is-What-You-Get") screen that displays a simplified view of your document. It omits most page settings from the screen. Generally, the normal view mode is the best all-purpose screen to use for text entry, editing, and formatting. This mode will be used throughout this module except in the sections that contain format changes that require another mode to see (for example, headers).

■   **Page Layout view** is a full-featured WYSIWYG mode that presents the document exactly as it will appear when printed. All text, graphics, page, and formatting settings are displayed, such as margins, footnotes, headers and footers, and page numbers. It is useful for checking final placement of objects on each document page, but runs slightly slower than normal view.

■   *Outline view* "collapses" the document so that only its major headings are displayed. This is useful when you work on outlines or want to organize your document.

- *Master Document view* allows you to manage a large document by creating separate files (called *subdocuments*) and then combining them as if they were one.
- *Full Screen view* maximizes the space available for your document by removing all toolbars, rulers, and menus. You must then access commands through their short-cut keys until you exit the full screen view. If you switch to full screen mode, you must exit it by pressing [Alt] + [V] and then [U] for "F<u>u</u>ll screen."

This exercise will change the view from Normal to Page Layout and then back again so that you may learn the procedure to use as you see fit. To change to the Page Layout view, do the following:

STEPS

  1 Click <u>*V*</u>*iew*, <u>*P*</u>*age Layout* or click the *Page Layout* view button on the status bar

Your screen should resemble Figure WP1-15a. Note that a page edge is now evident at the top, and a vertical ruler bar now appears at the left of the window. To return to the Normal view, do the following:

  2 Click <u>*V*</u>*iew*, <u>*N*</u>*ormal* or click on the *Normal* view button on the status bar

Use the View menu item to switch among different views as needed.

THE RULER BAR.   Some users prefer to have a visual indication of margins and tabs on the screen as they work (as shown in Figure WP1-15b). This indicator is called the *ruler bar.* The straight gray edges at the 0-inch and 6-inch markers indicate the positions of the left and right margins. The triangular symbols at the margins indicate indent settings. The tick marks below the inch line show default tab positions. If the ruler bar does not appear on your screen, you can activate it as follows:

STEPS

1 Click <u>*V*</u>*iew*

2 Click <u>*R*</u>*uler* to display a ruler bar

The ruler bar becomes part of the document window to which it is attached. It can be de-activated by the same commands listed above.

You may leave the ruler bar on your screen as long as you want. To remove it, repeat Steps 1 and 2.

AUTOCORRECT

Before you enter text, you should understand Word's automatic spell checker, **Auto-Correct**—a feature that checks your spelling as you enter each word. Try this brief example:

WP

FIGURE WP1-15 ■ **PAGE DISPLAY CHANGES**

(a) The Page Layout view.
(b) The Ruler bar.

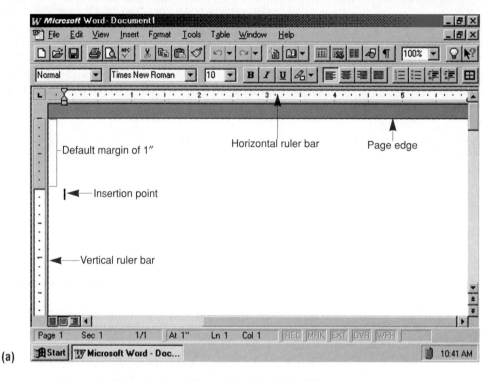

(a)

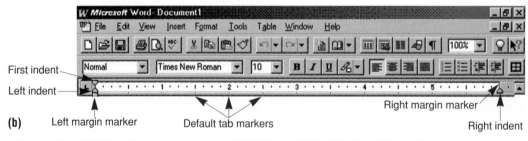

(b)

STEPS

1. Type   **helllo**   (type *three* "l"s)

2. Press   **Spacebar**   to indicate the end of the word

AutoCorrect now attempts to match the word you've typed to its list of acceptable words. If it finds a match, no change occurs on your screen. In this example, however, Auto-Correct cannot match the word. As shown in Figure WP1-16, it underlines "helllo" with a red wavy line, indicating that "helllo" is a potential misspelling. A *Tip Wizard* box may also appear, displaying the message "Click the right mouse button...."

FIGURE WP1-16 ▪ THE AUTOCORRECT FEATURE

(a) The potentially misspelled word is underlined with a red, wavy line.
(b) Right-click the word to access the AutoCorrect *Shortcut* menu.

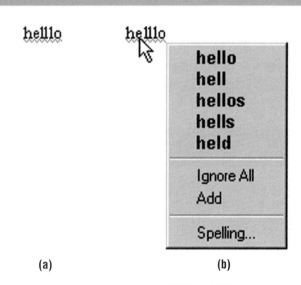

(a)   (b)

Tip: AutoCorrect should be active by default. If it is not, you can click the *Tools, Options, Spelling* tab, then click the *Automatic Spell Checking* check box, and the *OK* button to activate it.

3 If a *Tip Wizard* box appeared, close it by clicking the *Tip Wizard* icon

To correct a misspelling, you can simply press **Backspace** and retype the word correctly or let AutoCorrect suggest the correct spelling as follows:

4 Right-click the mouse (press the right mouse button)

A menu displays a set of suggested words with proper spellings.

5 Click *Hello* in the list to make the change

Feel free to use the AutoCorrect feature as you work in this manual to detect spelling errors and correct them as you enter text.

THE ENTER KEY

On a typewriter, the Enter (or Return) key is pressed at the end of each line. This is known in word processing as a **hard return.** A hard return moves the insertion point to the next line—creating a "line break" at the point where the Enter key was pressed.

Word processing programs, however, do not require hard returns to move to the next line. Instead, when text reaches the right margin, it will wrap automatically to the next line as you continue typing. This action, called **wordwrap,** automatically inserts a **soft return** at the end of each line. If you later add or delete text, or change margins, Word will reformat your document by shifting these soft returns to new locations. Hard returns, on the other hand, cannot be moved by the Word program.

Thus, the only time you must press the Enter key is when you want to end a line *before* it reaches the right margin, as in the case of an address line, a salutation, the end of a paragraph, or to skip a line. Until you get used to this, a paragraph symbol (¶) will be used in this chapter (as seen in Figure WP1-17) to remind you when to press the Enter key.

FIGURE WP1-17 ■ THE SAMPLE1 DOCUMENT

Remember to press the Enter key only when you see a paragraph symbol. Your margins may cause some words to wordwrap differently than shown here.

(Type today's date here)¶
¶
¶
Mr. Phil D. Basket¶
People Against Littering¶
2000 Environment Boulevard, Suite 999¶
Seattle, WA 98101¶
¶
Dear Mr. Basket:¶
¶
Thank you for your letter regarding Shrub-Garb products. Our company takes pride in being the first to develop a garbage disposal product that is not only completely biodegradable, but environmentally pleasing as well.¶
¶
As you know, our Shrub-Garb brand garbage bags are made to resemble bushes and shrubs that are native to each geographic area in the United States. On garbage day, there are no unsightly plastic containers to mar your view, but rather a collection of green "shrubs" growing around your house. As you add more garbage, the shrubs just get larger.¶
¶
Our garbage bags come in five sizes, ranging from the tiny "Azalea" to our very popular "Sequoia" model for large families. We even have red, gold, and white varieties for those locales that experience seasonal color changes in the fall and winter months.¶
¶
Enclosed please find our 19XX Price List. We look forward to your order and appreciate your interest in Shrub-Garb. If I can be of further assistance, do not hesitate to contact me.¶
¶
Sincerely,¶
¶
¶
¶
(Type your name here)¶
Regional Sales Manager¶

Create a letter by entering text as follows:

1   Launch Word (or close any open document and then start a new document window)

Remember: Press the Enter key *only* when you see the paragraph symbol (¶) in the figure.

2   Type the letter shown in Figure WP1-17

When typing with a proportionally spaced typeface, the default in Word, leave one space after a period. When typing in a monospaced typeface, such as Courier, it is customary to leave two spaces.

> **Tip: If you make a mistake while typing, press the Backspace key to remove the error, and retype the correct text. AutoCorrect may mark your typing error with red, wavy underscores. Leave them alone for now.**

3   Save this document as SAMPLE1 (remember to change the *Look in* drive to A: or B: as appropriate)

4   Close the document

☑ CHECKPOINT

✓   Describe the different Word View modes.
✓   Describe how to switch between modes.
✓   Activate the ruler bar. Where are default tabs set?
✓   Open EXAMPLE. Insert two lines at the bottom of the document and type your class and today's date.
✓   Save the document again, and then exit Word.

EDITING A DOCUMENT

Typing in Word is relatively easy as long as you allow the program to wordwrap for you as you type. Otherwise, text entry is much like that on a typewriter.

The true power of Word, however, lies in its ability to help you *edit,* or change, the content or appearance of your document. Perhaps you need to correct typing mistakes, or want to modify a first draft. Whatever the reason, Word (like most word processing programs) allows you total editing flexibility to add, delete, modify, or move words in your document. You can add new text, type over existing text, or delete old text. The following exercises examine all three techniques. If SAMPLE1 is not on your screen,

WP

> **1** Launch Word or close any open document
>
> **2** Open the SAMPLE1 document (change to the proper drive if needed)

USING THE ZOOM MODE

At times, you may find that the text or graphics displayed in the document window is inappropriate for your use. It may be too large to see your work area comfortably or too small to read easily. Whenever this occurs, you can use Word's Zoom feature. **Zoom** lets you adjust the magnification of the display without affecting the document itself or how it will appear when printed.

The current magnification, 100% by default, is displayed in the *Zoom* indicator box on the right side of the standard toolbar (see Figure WP1-3 if needed). You can change this setting by typing a new magnification or selecting a preset one from a *Zoom* list. For example, you will now adjust the zoom to 125% of its normal size as follows:

 1 Click the *Zoom* control box on the toolbar

> **2** Type **125** in the box
>
> **3** Press ↵ to accept

The text displayed on the screen will increase to 125%. You may type any magnification or reduction you desire.

 Tip: To select a preset zoom by mouse, click the down arrow to the right of the *Zoom* indicator box and then click the desired size. With the keyboard, press Alt + V, Z, use the down arrow to move to the desired size, and then press the Enter key.

> **4** Using the technique in Steps 1–3, reset the zoom to 100%

Note: Although this module displays all figures at 100% zoom, you may set the *Zoom* indicator box to any comfortable percentage.

ADDING NEW TEXT

There are many ways to add new text to your document. You can move or copy text from another document into your current document (as you will see later). You can also type text directly from the keyboard. When typing, you can have the new text combine with existing screen text, or you can replace it. You do this by selecting the insert mode or the overtype mode before you begin to add text.

THE INSERT MODE.   Unlike typewriters, word processing programs allow you to add, or insert, text into material that is already in your document. Word is normally set to insert. As you type, the **insert mode** ensures that existing screen text will move over to make room for the new characters. Before you attempt to insert, you should always check to see that the insert toggle is on. To check, glance at the right side of the status bar. If "OVR" is dimmed, then the insert mode is on. However, if the "OVR" indicator appears, then the program is in overtype mode and *is not* ready to insert. To see this, try the following:

STEPS

1 **Double-click *OVR* in the status bar**   [**Insert**   ]

Notice that "OVR" appears in the status bar, as in Figure WP1-18.

2 **Double-click *OVR* in the status bar**   [**Insert**   ]

"OVR" is no longer displayed. Double-clicking *OVR* on the status bar or pressing the Insert key "toggles" the insert mode on and off as needed. Make sure that the insert mode is on before continuing.

You will now practice the three inserts shown in Figure WP1-19. Try the first insert carefully as follows:

To move the insertion point to the first insert position—the "l" in "letter" on the first line of the first paragraph:

3 **Click the "l" in "letter"**   [→]

Your insertion point should now be directly to the left of the "l," as shown in Figure WP1-20a.

4 **Type recent**

FIGURE WP1-18 ■ THE INSERT MODE

If "OVR" appears in the status bar, Word is not in the insert mode.

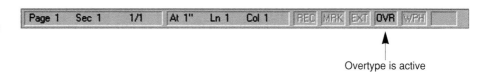

Overtype is active

FIGURE WP1-19 ■ INSERT EXERCISE

These two words and one phrase are about to be placed in your document.

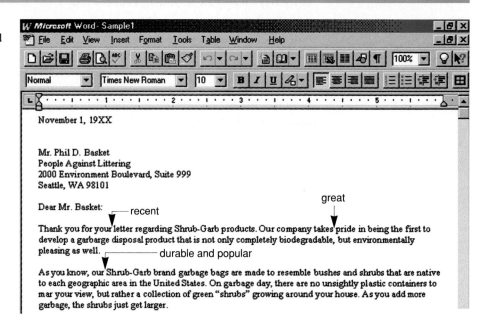

Your text should now resemble Figure WP1-20b. Notice that the words to the right of your insertion point have moved over to make room for the new word. Words may even move beyond the right margin, depending upon what has been inserted. This will be fixed in a moment.

FIGURE WP1-20 ■ INSERTING TEXT

(a) The insertion point is positioned where new text will be entered.
(b) The new word has pushed the old text to the right to make room.

(a)

Dear Mr. Basket: ———— Insertion point is here

Thank you for your letter regarding Shrub-Garb products. Our company takes pride in being the first to develop a garbarge disposal product that is not only completely biodegradable, but environmentally pleasing as well.

(b)

Dear Mr. Basket:

Thank you for your recent letter regarding Shrub-Garb products. Our company takes pride in being the first to develop a garbarge disposal product that is not only completely biodegradable, but environmental pleasing as well.

> **5** **Press** **Spacebar** **to separate "recent" and "letter"**

Notice that the wordwrap feature automatically *reformats* the paragraph to fit within the margins again.

Do not press the Enter key when the insert is completed. It will only break the line in the middle (as in Figure WP1-21a). If you ever do this by mistake, simply press the Backspace key to erase the extra keystroke and return the line to normal (as in Figure WP1-21b).

Now, repeat this procedure for the second and third inserts shown in Figure WP1-19 as follows:

> **6** **Move to the "p" in "pride" in the first paragraph**

> **7** **Type** **great** **and press** **Spacebar**

> **8** **Move to the "S" in "Shrub-Garb" on the first line of the second paragraph**

> **9** **Type** **durable and popular** **and press** **Spacebar**

Your screen should now resemble Figure WP1-22.

> **10** **Save this document again as SAMPLE1**

Tip: To quickly resave a document without changing its name by mouse, click the *Save* button on the toolbar.

FIGURE WP1-21 ■ FIXING A MISPLACED ENTER

(a) Pressing the Enter key will break your line in the wrong place.
(b) Pressing the Backspace key will remove the keystroke and fix the line.

Dear Mr. Basket: ——— The Enter key was pressed here

Thank you for your recent
letter regarding Shrub-Garb products. Our company takes pride in being the first to develop a garbage disposal product that is not only completely biodegradable, but environmentally pleasing as well.

(a)

Dear Mr. Basket:

Thank you for your recent letter regarding Shrub-Garb products. Our company takes pride in being the first to develop a garbage disposal product that is not only completely biodegradable, but environmentally pleasing as well.

(b)

FIGURE WP1-22 ■ THE SAMPLE1 DOCUMENT WITH ALL THREE INSERTS

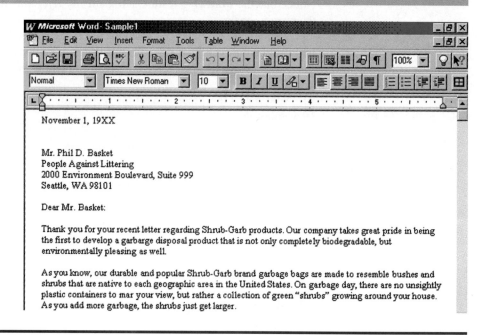

THE OVERTYPE MODE. At times you will simply want to replace text. Perhaps you transposed (reversed) letters or want to replace an old word with a new one. In these situations, it may be easier to switch to the overtype mode. In the **overtype mode**, new text replaces old text character for character in the document. When the insert mode is toggled on, the overtype mode is off (and vice versa). As you have seen, the Insert key toggles between the insert and overtype modes. The following exercises provide some practice with the overtype mode. Figure WP1-23 displays the changes you will make.

If the "OVR" indicator is active on your status bar, go to Step 2.

STEPS

   1   Double-click *OVR* in the status bar to toggle on the overtype mode.   [**Insert**]

   2   Move the insertion point to the first "9" in "Suite 999" (The insertion point will appear to the left of the first "9")

   3   Type   **876**

Notice how the new text *types over* the old, replacing it character for character. As with Insert, do not press the Enter key when you are finished. Try one more:

   4   Move to the "f" in "five" in the third paragraph (Remember, the insertion point will appear just to the left of the "f")

These two changes are about to replace text in your document using the overtype technique.

Mr. Phil D. Basket
People Against Littering
2000 Environment Boulevard, Suite 999 ◄— 876
Seattle, WA 98101

Dear Mr. Basket:

Thank you for your recent letter regarding Shrub-Garb products. Our company takes great pride in being the first to develop a garbarge disposal product that is not only completely biodegradable, but environmentally pleasing as well.

As you know, our durable and popular Shrub-Garb brand garbage bags are made to resemble bushes and shrubs that are native to each geographic area in the United States. On garbage day, there are no unsightly plastic containers to mar your view, but rather a collection of green "shrubs" growing around your house. As you add more garbage, the shrubs just get larger.
                                                            ◄— four
Our garbage bags come in five sizes, ranging from the tiny "Azalea" to our very popular "Sequoia" model for large families. We even have red, gold, and white varieties for those locales that experience seasonal color changes in the fall and winter months.

WP

5 Type four

Overtype is a straightforward way to replace text—with the OVR indicator active on the status bar, simply type the replacement characters.

6 Resave this document as SAMPLE1

7 Double-click *OVR* in the status bar to turn off the overtype toggle   [Insert]

DELETING TEXT

You may also want to remove, or *delete*, text from your document. As Figure WP1-24 shows, you can delete one character at a time, or as many pages as you like. You will now use some simple techniques to remove the words marked in Figure WP1-25.

USING THE DELETE KEY.   The **Delete key** deletes a character at the insertion point position. Each time you press the Delete key, one character is deleted and any text to its right moves left to fill in the gap. Try this:

STEPS

1 Use the mouse or the arrow keys to move the insertion point before the comma after "Boulevard" in the third line of the address

2 Press Delete

FIGURE WP1-24 ■ WORD DELETE COMMANDS

To Delete...	Press these Keys:
One character to the left of the insertion point	Backspace
One character at the insertion point	Delete
One word at the insertion point	Ctrl + Delete
One word to the left of the insertion point	Ctrl + Backspace
Text that has been selected	Backspace or Delete

Notice that the comma has been deleted and the text "Suite 876" has moved left.

3 Press   Delete   ten times to delete "Suite 876"

Use the Delete key to remove the word "completely" on the second line of the first paragraph as follows:

4 Move the insertion point to the "c" in the word "completely"

5 Press   Delete   until you have deleted the word and the space after it

FIGURE WP1-25 ■ DELETING EXERCISE

These five text blocks are about to be deleted in your document using various delete commands.

Mr. Phil D. Basket
People Against Littering
2000 Environment Boulevard, Suite 876
Seattle, WA 98101

Dear Mr. Basket:

Thank you for your recent letter regarding Shrub-Garb products. Our company takes great pride in being the first to develop a garbarge disposal product that is not only completely biodegradable, but environmentally pleasing as well.

As you know, our durable and popular Shrub-Garb brand garbage bags are made to resemble bushes and shrubs that are native to each geographic area in the United States. On garbage day, there are no unsightly plastic containers to mar your view, but rather a collection of green "shrubs" growing around your house. As you add more garbage, the shrubs just get larger.

Our garbage bags come in four sizes, ranging from the tiny "Azalea" to our very popular "Sequoia" model for large families. We even have red, gold, and white varieties for those locales that experience seasonal color changes in the fall and winter months.

USING THE BACKSPACE KEY.   The **Backspace key** deletes a character *to the left* of the insertion point as it moves the insertion point one space to the left. Try using the Backspace key to remove the word "brand" in the first line of the second paragraph as follows:

STEPS

1 Move the insertion point before the letter "g" in the word "garbage" in the first line of the second paragraph (*after* the word you want to delete)

2 Press   **Backspace**

Notice that the space before the "g" has been deleted and the word "garbage" has moved left.

3 Press   **Backspace**   five times to delete "brand"

Use the Backspace key to remove the word "growing" *and the space* on the fourth line of the second paragraph as follows:

4 Move the insertion point to the "a" in the word "around"

5 Press   **Backspace**   until you have deleted the space and the word "growing"

DELETING WORDS WITH CTRL + BACKSPACE.   You can delete one character at a time with the Delete or Backspace keys. You can also delete an entire word, one at a time (and the space that precedes it), by combining keystrokes. To do this, position your insertion point after the word to be deleted, hold the Ctrl key, press the Backspace key, and then release both. Try deleting the phrase "in the fall and winter months" using this technique as follows:

STEPS

1 Move the insertion point to the period after "winter months" on the last line of the third paragraph

2 Press   **Ctrl**   +   **Backspace**

Notice that the word "months" *and the space before it* are gone.

3 Hold   **Ctrl**   and press   **Backspace**   five more times to delete the previous five words

4 Resave the document as SAMPLE1

OTHER DELETE TECHNIQUES.   Word offers other ways to delete text quickly. Although you will not use them now, you may want to examine these on your own. For

WP

example, pressing Ctrl + Delete will delete the word that follows the insertion point. In the next chapter, you will also learn how to delete large areas of text easily.

"UNDELETING" TEXT.   The **Undo** command can be invoked through Word's menu bar or by pressing the Ctrl + Z keys. This will restore text that you deleted by mistake. Try this:

STEPS

  1 Click _Edit_ and then _Undo_   [**Ctrl** + **Z**]

> **Note: The command that follows the word "Undo" in the menu depends on your most recent action.**

Notice that the text you deleted most recently appears on the screen highlighted for easy recognition. You could keep invoking Undo to restore previous changes in text, formatting, or other actions. For now,

  2 Click the _Edit_ and then _Redo_ to redo the deletion.   [**Ctrl** + **Y**]

Use the Undo command whenever you need to retrieve text that was inadvertently removed. You can also restore other text changes as well.

BASIC FORMAT ENHANCEMENTS

It is easy to make formatting changes to enhance, or emphasize, portions of text. You may want to center headings or bold or underline text. These formatting features can be specified either before or after text is typed. In this chapter, you will practice three format enhancements—center, bold, and underline—_before_ typing text. The next chapter will examine enhancements to text that has already been typed.

CENTERING.   Headings or titles are often centered. The **Center** feature leaves equal margins on both sides of a line of text. The following exercise demonstrates how to request centering before typing the text to be centered. You will place the heading shown in Figure WP1-26 at the beginning of your document.

STEPS

1 Launch Word and open SAMPLE1 (or press **Ctrl** + **Home** to move to the beginning of the document)

2 Make sure that Word is in the Insert mode

Remember, "OVR" should _not_ be active in the status bar.

FIGURE WP1-26 ■ CENTERING EXERCISE

The heading is about to be placed at the beginning of your document automatically centered by the program.

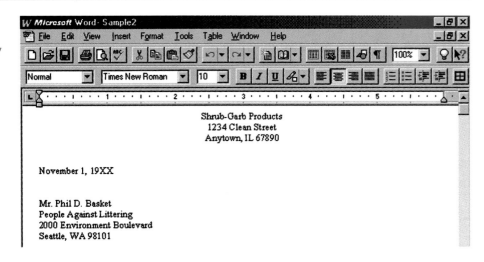

 3 If "OVR" appears, press **Insert** (or double-click OVR)

Now, create some blank lines at the beginning of your document as follows:

4 Press ↵ twice

5 Press ↑ twice to return to the top

6 Click the *Center* button on the toolbar   [**Ctrl** + **E**]

> Tip: You could also click *Format, Paragraph*, then click the Alignment list arrow and select *Centered, OK*, but this is cumbersome.

Notice how the insertion point moves to the center of the line.

7 Type   **Shrub-Garb Products**   and press ↵

The text has been centered automatically. Note how the insertion point remains centered. Because the centering feature is still active, you need only type the next lines as follows:

8 Type   **1234 Clean Street**   and press ↵

9 Type   **Anytown, IL 67890**   and press ↵

Now, shut off the centering feature as follows:

WP

10 Click the *Align Left* button on the toolbar   [**Ctrl** + **L**]

The insertion point returns to the left margin as expected.

11 Save the document with a new name of SAMPLE2 (use Save As)

UNDERLINING.   The **Underline** feature—which lets you place an underscore beneath text—is another text enhancement. Unlike a typewriter, Word can underline as you type. It is simply a matter of turning the underline toggle on before you type, and then off when you are finished. The following exercise demonstrates this technique. You will place the sentence shown in Figure WP1-27 at the end of your document.

STEPS

1 Open SAMPLE2 if needed

2 Move to the end of your document   [**Ctrl** + **End**]

3 Press ↵ to create a blank line

4 Type   P.S. All of us at Shrub-Garb

(Make sure you press the Space bar after the word "Garb" to separate it from the next word.) You are now ready to "toggle on" the underlining feature.

U

5 Click the *Underline* toolbar button to toggle the Underline feature on   [**Ctrl** + **U**]

Notice how the *Underline* button on the toolbar is depressed, indicating that the Underline toggle is on.

6 Type   greatly appreciate

Note how these words appear underlined on your screen.

U

7 Click the *Underline* button on the toolbar to toggle the Underline feature *off* [**Ctrl** + **U**]

The *Underline* button has returned to normal, showing that Underline is no longer active.

FIGURE WP1-27 ■ UNDERLINING EXERCISE

The following sentence with underlined text is about to be added to the end of your document.

P.S. All of us at Shrub-Garb <u>greatly appreciate</u> your concern.

8 Type a space and `your concern.`

The line on your screen should resemble Figure WP1-27.

9 Resave the document as SAMPLE2

BOLDING. **Bold**, or boldface, is a text enhancement that emphasizes text by making it darker when it is printed. Like underlining, bolding is easily achieved by turning the Bold toggle on before you type and off when you are done. In this exercise, you will place the sentence shown in Figure WP1-28 at the end of your document.

STEPS

1 Open SAMPLE2 if needed

2 Move to the end of your document

Your insertion point should be at the end of the sentence after the word "concern."

3 Press `Spacebar` to start a new sentence

4 Type `We have enclosed a`

(Make sure you press the Spacebar after the word "a" to separate it from the next word.) You are now ready to "toggle on" the Bolding feature.

B **5** Click the *Bold* button on the toolbar to toggle Bold *on*   [`Ctrl` + `B`]

Notice how the *Bold* button is depressed on the toolbar. As with the Underline feature, this indicates that the Bold toggle is on.

6 Type `discount coupon`

The words will appear bold on your screen.

B **7** Click the *Bold* button on the toolbar to toggle Bold *off*   [`Ctrl` + `B`]

FIGURE WP1-28 ■ BOLDING EXERCISE

The following sentence with bold text is about to be added to the end of your document.

> P.S. All of us at Shrub-Garb <u>greatly appreciate</u> your concern. We have enclosed a **discount coupon** for your use.

The button has returned to normal to show that the Bold feature is no longer active.

8 Press   **Spacebar**   and type   **for your use.**

9 Press ↵

The sentence on your screen should now resemble Figure WP1-28.

10 Resave this document as SAMPLE2

Your final screen document should resemble the printed version shown in Figure WP1-29. Note that you will not see all of the document on your screen at once. Press the Ctrl + Home keys to view the top of your document and the Ctrl + End keys to view the bottom.

HIGHLIGHTING. You can use Word's **Highlight** feature to mark important text blocks for review. Although highlighted text can be printed (if a light color is used), the Highlight feature is routinely used to identify text for later editing directly on the screen. This exercise will demonstrate the highlight techniques of marking, finding, and removing. Assume you want to highlight the text block "durable and popular" in the second paragraph of your document.

STEPS

1 Open SAMPLE2 if needed

2 Click the *Highlight* button on the toolbar

3 Select the text block: Click to the immediate left of the "d" in "durable" and then drag the mouse to the immediate right of the "r" in "popular"

4 Release the mouse to highlight the text block

The text will be marked by a yellow background (the default setting) as if you had drawn a highlighter pen over it. You could continue to mark text, but in this example, proceed as follows:

5 Click the *Highlight* button again to turn off further highlighting

When you want to review the marked text, you can simply look for highlights in the document, or use the Find command as follows:

6 Click the beginning of the document

7 Click *Edit, Find*   [**Ctrl** + **F**]

8 In the *Find* dialog box, click the *Format* button, click *Highlight* and then click the *Find Next* button

9 When done, click the *Cancel* button

FIGURE WP1-29 ■ THE PRINTED DOCUMENT

This is how the "final" document appears when printed with all insertions, overtypes, deletions, and underlined and bold text. Note: Your margins may differ.

Shrub-Garb Products
1234 Clean Street
Anytown, IL 67890

Today's date

Mr. Phil D. Basket
People Against Littering
2000 Environment Boulevard
Seattle, WA 98101

Dear Mr. Basket:

Thank you for your letter regarding Shrub-Garb products. Our company takes great pride in being the first to develop a garbage disposal product that is not only biodegradable, but environmentally pleasing as well.

As you know, our durable and popular Shrub-Garb garbage bags are made to resemble bushes and shrubs that are native to each geographic area in the United States. On garbage day, there are no unsightly plastic containers to mar your view, but rather a collection of green "shrubs" around your house. As you add more garbage, the shrubs just get larger.

Our garbage bags come in four sizes, ranging from the tiny "Azalea" to our very popular "Sequoia" model for large families. We even have red, gold, and white varieties for those locales that experience seasonal color changes.

Enclosed please find our 19XX Price List. We look forward to your order and appreciate your interest in Shrub-Garb. If I can be of further assistance, do not hesitate to contact me.

Sincerely,

Your name
Regional Sales Manager

P.S. All of us at Shrub-Garb <u>greatly appreciate</u> your concern. We have enclosed a **discount coupon** for your use.

When you no longer need highlight, you can remove it as follows:

10 **Click the *Highlight* button**

11 Click the down arrow to the right of the *Highlight* button to access the highlight color

12 Click *none*

13 Repeat Steps 3–5 to select the text block and turn off the *Highlight* button

14 Return the highlight color to yellow before using the *Highlight* feature again in the future

☑   CHECKPOINT

✓   Open the EXAMPLE document. Insert a blank line under the date. Center and type the heading "Adding New Text."

✓   Indent (press Tab) a new paragraph; type the first paragraph of "Adding New Text" from page WP36 into your document.

✓   Save the amended file using the same filename.

✓   Delete the parentheses and the words within them from the paragraph you have just typed.

✓   Underline the word "document" where it appears two times in the paragraph. Bold-face the heading. Save the file again.

PRINTING A DOCUMENT

The ultimate destination of most documents is paper. Although you work with documents on the screen, and save documents on disk for editing and future use, your goal is usually to produce a printed copy of the finished document.

Word has several commands for printing. You will examine the most common techniques in this exercise; later chapters will present others. Before you print, verify that

STEPS

1 Your computer is connected to a printer

2 The printer is turned on

3 The paper is correctly aligned in the printer

Now, you are ready to print.

4 Open SAMPLE2 if it is not on your screen

PRINTING A FULL DOCUMENT

The most frequently used Print command is the one that prints your full document (all of its pages). This is done as follows:

1   **Click** *File* **and then** *Print* **for the** *Print* **dialog box**   [**Ctrl** + **P**]

A *Print* dialog box appears as in Figure WP1-30. Note that the *All* option is highlighted in the Page range box.

2   **Click** *OK* **to print the full document**   [↵]

You will be returned to your document as it is printing. Compare the printed version with Figure WP1-29.

PRINTING ONE PAGE

At times you will want to make a correction to one page but will not need to reprint the entire document. Instead, you can print a single page as follows:

1   **Position the insertion point on the desired page**

(In this example, there is only one page.)

FIGURE WP1-30 ■ THE *PRINT* **DIALOG BOX**

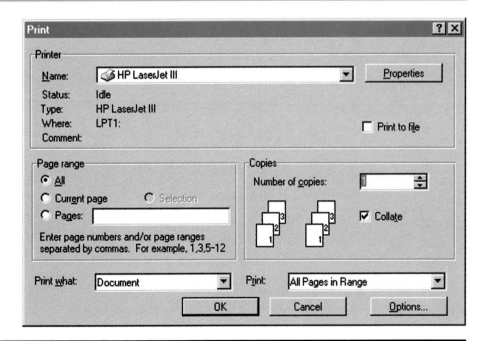

2 Verify that the printer is ready (on, on-line, with paper aligned)

 3 Click *File* and then *Print*   [**Ctrl** + **P**]

4 Click *Current Page*   [↓]

5 Click the *OK* button   [↵]

The single page will print. In the current one-page document, there is no difference between printing the full document and printing one page.

☑ CHECKPOINT

✓ Open the SAMPLE1 document.
✓ Use the Save command to save your document.
✓ Print the entire SAMPLE1 document.
✓ Using the Current Page feature, print only Page 1 of SAMPLE1 (there is only one page).
✓ Exit Word.

SUMMARY

■ Word processing is the use of computer technology to create, manipulate, save, and print text materials such as letters, reports, and other documents. Most word processing packages offer the same basic capabilities.

■ The Word work screen displays an insertion point, showing the current typing position, a menu bar, toolbars, and a status bar, which includes messages regarding the position of the insertion point and the condition of various toggles.

■ The At and Ln messages indicate the vertical position of the insertion point within the current page. The Col message shows the current horizontal position of the insertion point.

■ The status bar normally displays the overtype mode status and other toggle indicators.

■ Word offers five view modes. Of these, Page Layout view is a full-featured WYSIWYG screen that looks exactly as it will when printed. Word's default Normal view is a WYSIWYG screen that displays the main contents of your document (no footers, footnotes, headers, page numbers, or several other formatting features).

■ A Ruler bar can be added to the document window to provide a visual indication of margins and tab settings.

■ To move the insertion point by mouse, point to the desired location and click. The arrow, Home, End, Pg Up, or Pg Dn keys can be used alone or with other keys to move the insertion point. The arrow keys, alone, move the insertion point one character in any direction.

■ Entering text in Word is like typing on a typewriter, except that the Enter key should be used only to leave blank lines or end paragraphs. It places a hard return in the document, which ends the line and moves the insertion point to the next line.

■ Wordwrap occurs when the text that you are entering reaches the right margin. A soft return is automatically added to the text to move the next word onto the next line.

■ The Save As and Save commands copy the current version of your document to disk. The Open command copies a file from disk back into the document window.

- Word can be set to function in the insert mode or overtype mode. When Word is in the insert mode, existing text on the screen is moved to the right to make room for new text that is entered. When the insert toggle is off, the overtype mode allows new text to replace old text on the screen character for character. The OVR indicator appears on the screen to show that the overtype mode is active.
- Text can be deleted using the Delete key or the Backspace key. The Delete key removes characters at the insertion point and adjusts the remaining characters on the right to fill in. The Backspace key moves the insertion point to the left and deletes any character there. Ctrl + Backspace deletes one word at a time.
- Text can be enhanced through centering, underlining, and bolding. Centering leaves equal margins on both sides of the text; underlining places an underscore beneath characters; bolding prints characters darker.
- The ultimate destination of most documents is paper, in the form of a printed copy. Word allows you to print the full document or selected pages.
- Some of the commands that were presented in this chapter include the following:

Command	Mouse Approach	Keyboard Approach
Undo	*Edit, Undo*	
Help	*Help, Contents*	F1
Close	*File, Close* or double-click document window's *icon*	Ctrl + F4
Ruler	*View, Ruler*	Alt + V, then R
Save	*File, Save As* or *Save*	Alt + F, then A, or Ctrl + S
Open	*File, Open* or *Open File* button	Ctrl + O
Insert/Overtype	Double-click *OVR*	Insert
Center	*Center* button	Ctrl + E
Underline	*Underline* button	Ctrl + U
Bold	*Bold* button	Ctrl + B
Print	*Print* button	Ctrl + P
Exit	*File, Exit* or double-click Word's program icon	Alt + F4

KEY TERMS

Shown in parentheses are the page numbers on which key terms are boldfaced.

At message (WP15)
AutoCorrect (WP31)
Backspace key (WP43)
Bold (WP47)
Center (WP44)
Clicking (W4)
Column message (WP15)
Control-menu (WP11)
Delete key (WP41)
Dialog box (WP2)
Double-clicking (WP5)
Hard return (WP33)
Help prompt (WP16)
Highlight (WP48)
Icon (WP2)

Insert mode (WP37)
Insertion point (WP13)
Line message (WP15)
Menu bar (WP8)
Mouse pointer (WP4)
Normal view(WP30)
Opening (WP26)
Overtype mode (WP40)
Page Layout view (WP30)
Page message (WP14)
Page view buttons (WP14)
Program icon (WP11)
Pull-down menu (WP8)
Resizing button (WP9)
Ruler bar (WP10)

Shortcut keys (WP6)
Shortcut menu (WP10)
Section message (WP15)
Scroll bars (WP14)
Soft return (WP34)
Status bar (WP10)
Title bar (WP7)
Toolbar (WP8)
Underline (WP46)
Undo (WP44)
Word processing (WP2)
Wordwrap (WP34)
Workspace (WP10)
Zoom (WP36)

WP

QUIZ

TRUE/FALSE

____ 1. To start Word by mouse, double-click its icon in the appropriate submenu of the *Start* menu.

____ 2. The Ruler bar provides information about the current location of the insertion point.

____ 3. The message "Col 12" indicates the vertical position of the insertion point.

____ 4. Word displays the current line and position in inches.

____ 5. The Status bar is a visual indication of margins and tabs.

____ 6. Pressing the Enter key produces a hard return.

____ 7. The Insert key is used to switch between the insert and overtype modes.

____ 8. The insert mode is on if you can see a font message in the lower left corner of the screen.

____ 9. If you know your document's name, you can open it by pressing Alt + O.

____ 10. The Close command of the *File* menu will close the current document.

MULTIPLE CHOICE

____ 11. Which screen component does not normally appear when Word is started?
   a. Document name
   b. Insertion point
   c. Ruler bar
   d. Position indicator

____ 12. What feature of Word for Windows 95 displays a screen that resembles the final printed page?
   a. Graphical-user-interface (GUI)
   b. What-You-See-Is-What-You-Get (WYSIWYG)
   c. Print screen
   d. VGA monitor

____ 13. Which key(s) is used to invoke the Undo feature?
   a. Delete
   b. Alt + U
   c. Ctrl + Z
   d. End

____ 14. Which save document feature allows you to rename a file before saving?
   a. Save
   b. Open File
   c. Save File
   d. Save As

____ 15. A document window may be closed by all of the following except:
   a. Double-clicking its *Program* icon.
   b. Clicking *File* and then *Exit*
   c. Pressing Ctrl + F4
   d. Clicking *File* and then *Close*

____ 16. You need not press the Enter key when you reach the right margin because of the _____ feature.
   a. wordwrap

    b. hard return
    c. overtype
    d. insert

___ 17. Which key deletes text at the insertion point and then moves text from the *right* of the insertion point to fill in?

    a. Backspace
    b. Esc
    c. Overtype
    d. Delete

___ 18. Which dialog box contains an option to change the default drive?

    a. *Save As* dialog box
    b. *Print* dialog box
    c. *Close* dialog box
    d. *Drive* dialog box

___ 19. The *Print* dialog box can be opened by selecting or pressing

    a. *Print* or P
    b. *File, Print* or Ctrl + P
    c. *Print* or Shift + P
    d. *File, Print* or P

___ 20. The Word window can be exited by all of the following except

    a. Double-clicking its program icon.
    b. Selecting *File* and then *Exit*
    c. Selecting *Close* from its control-menu
    d. Selecting *File* and then *Close*

MATCHING

Select the lettered item from the figure on the next page that best matches each phrase below.

___ 21. This standard Windows feature can be used to resize the document window to a smaller window by mouse (only).

___ 22. This Word feature can be used to change view mode by mouse (only).

___ 23. This section identifies a window.

___ 24. This Word feature provides quick access by mouse to several frequently used file, text appearance, text layout, and text editing features.

___ 25. This Word feature provides quick access to frequently used features such as File and Print commands.

___ 26. A graphical display of left and right margin positions and tab positions.

___ 27. This standard Windows application feature provides access to the program's features through pull-down menus.

___ 28. This standard Windows feature can be used to resize the application (Word) window by mouse (only).

___ 29. This standard Windows feature opens the application's control-menu.

___ 30. This feature allows you to quickly move (scroll) horizontally through a document by mouse.

ANSWERS

True/False: 1. T; 2. F; 3. F; 4. T; 5. F; 6. T; 7. T; 8. F; 9. F; 10. T
Multiple Choice: 11. a; 12. b; 13. c; 14. d; 15. b; 16. a; 17. d; 18. a; 19. d; 20. d
Matching: 21. j; 22. k; 23. a; 24. e; 25. d; 26. f; 27. h; 28. i; 29. b; 30. l

WP

FIGURE WP1-A ■ MATCHING FIGURE

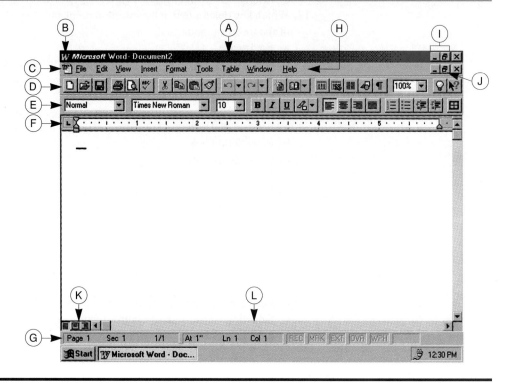

EXERCISES

I. OPERATIONS

On a separate piece of paper, provide the Word command sequences required to do each of the following operations. For each operation, assume a hard-disk system with a disk in Drive A. You may wish to verify each command by trying it on your computer system.

1. Start Windows and then launch the Word program.

2. Add the Ruler bar to your document window.

3. Switch to Page Layout view mode.

4. Center the words "MASTERING BUSINESS SOFTWARE."

5. Insert two blank lines.

6. Add the word "PRODUCTIVITY" after the word "BUSINESS" in Exercise 4.

7. Type the word "underlined" underlined and the word "bold" bold.

8. Use the *Open file* dialog box to change the default drive to Drive A.

9. Save this document as EXWP1-1.

10. Close the document window.

11. Open the document named EXWP1-1.

12. Save the document as EXWP1-2.

13. Exit the Word program.

II. COMMANDS

Describe clearly what command is initiated or what is accomplished in Word by the actions described below. Assume that each exercise part is independent of any previous parts.

1. Pressing the Ctrl + P keys

2. Pressing the Ctrl + F4 keys

3. Pressing the Ctrl + E keys

4. Pressing the Backspace key

5. Double-clicking "OVR" on the status bar

6. Pressing the F1 key

7. Pressing the Enter key

8. Pressing the Alt + V then N keys

9. Clicking the toolbar button labeled "B"

10. Clicking the toolbar button labeled "U"

III. APPLICATIONS

Perform the following operations using your computer system. You will need a hard drive or network with Windows and Word on it. You will also need one additional disk to store the results of this exercise. In a few words, tell how you accomplished each operation and describe its result. *Note:* Of the six application exercises, each pair relates to school, home, and business respectively.

APPLICATION 1: LETTER OF INQUIRY

1. Boot your computer; start Windows and launch the Word program.

2. Type the following letter. Make sure you underline and boldface as shown. Don't worry if the lines of text do not wrap exactly as shown in the sample. Instead, let wordwrap take effect to control your line breaks within paragraphs.

3. Save this letter as WORK1-1A, changing the default drive as needed.

4. Print a copy of the letter on your printer.

5. Close the document window.

6. Open the WORK1-1A document from your data disk.

7. Make the following changes to your letter:
   a. Add a line and the words "Admissions Office" under "Ms. May I. Komin."
   b. Delete the word "currently" in line 2.
   c. Change the word "investigating" to "considering."
   d. At the end of the first paragraph, add the sentence: "I have chosen the Southwest due to the variety of sand textures and colors available for my sculpture."

8. Save the modified letter as WORK1-1B.

9. Print a copy of the modified letter.

Your name
Your address
Your city, state zip

Today's date

Ms. May I. Komin
University of Greater Las Yackos
Las Yackos, AR 54321

Dear Ms. Komin:

I am a senior at Pilemore College and plan to graduate in June with a degree in **Sand Castle Sculpting.** I am currently investigating a few graduate schools in the Southwest where I may continue my education toward a Masters degree in Fine Arts.

Would you please send me your University of Greater Las Yackos (U.G.L.Y.) catalog, application forms, and other pertinent information for my review. I am especially interested in <u>work-study programs</u> and <u>available scholarships</u>.

Sincerely,

Your name

10. Close the document and then exit the program.

APPLICATION 2: RESEARCH PROJECT

1. Boot your computer; start Windows and launch the Word program.

2. Type the following proposal. Make sure you underline and boldface as shown. Don't worry if the lines of text do not wrap exactly as shown in the sample. Instead, let wordwrap take effect to control your line breaks within paragraphs.

3. Save this proposal as WORK1-2A, changing the default drive if needed.

4. Print a copy of the proposal on your printer.

5. Close the document window.

6. Open the WORK1-2A document from your data disk.

7. Make the following changes to your proposal:
   a. Before "The final list..." in the last line, add the following sentence: "I planned to also include a discussion of weaknesses in these texts, but my initial review has discovered <u>none.</u>"
   b. Delete the book written by Martin and Burstein.
   c. Change the words "ten years" in the first sentence to "century."

8. Save the modified proposal as WORK1-2B.

Your name
Your class
Today's date

PROPOSAL FOR COLLEGE RESEARCH

For my term research project, I propose to evaluate the best computer books of the past ten years and summarize their strengths in readability, technical accuracy, and comprehensiveness. My preliminary investigation has revealed the following titles for use in this project:

Martin, E., and Burstein, J. Computer Systems Fundamentals. Chicago: Dryden Press, 1990.

Martin, E., and Parker, C. Mastering Today's Software. (First and Second Editions), Fort Worth, The Dryden Press, 1992–1995.

Martin, E., ed. Productivity Software Guides. Fort Worth: The Dryden Press, 1994–1995.

Martin, E. Productivity Software Guides (for WordPerfect, Quattro, and Paradox). Fort Worth: The Dryden Press, 1994–1995.

Parker, C. Computers and Their Applications. (First and Second Editions). Fort Worth: The Dryden Press, 1988–1991.

Parker, C. Productivity Software Guides. (First through Fourth Editions). Fort Worth: The Dryden Press, 1984–1993.

Parker C. Understanding Computers and Information Processing: Today and Tomorrow (First through Fifth Editions). Fort Worth: The Dryden Press, 1984–1995.

The final list may include additional titles by these (and other) authors.

9. Print a copy of the modified proposal.

10. Close the document and then exit the program.

APPLICATION 3: LETTER OF COMPLAINT

1. Boot your computer; start Windows and launch the Word program.

2. Type the following letter. Make sure you underline and boldface as shown. Don't worry if the lines of text do not wrap exactly as shown in the sample. Instead, let wordwrap take effect to control your line breaks within paragraphs.

3. Save this letter as WORK1-3A.

4. Print a copy of the letter on your printer.

5. Close the document window.

6. Open the WORK1-3A document from your data disk.

7. Make the following changes to your letter:

Your name
Your address
Your city, state zip

Today's date

Mr. William M. Plenty
Customer Relations
Pencils by Mail Corporation
#2 Graphite Road
Yellow Wood, NY 11001

Dear Mr. Plenty:

Last month, I ordered <u>ten (10) dozen</u> of your special <u>one-foot</u> pencils. Instead, your company sent me **one dozen ten-foot** pencils by mistake! It is almost impossible to climb through my front door since the pencils take up a lot of room.

Since your company clearly made the mistake, would you please ship me my correct order immediately by overnight express and then send a truck, and a few strong workers, to pick up these pencils and remove them from my front hall.

Sincerely,

Your name

a. Add the words "Vice President" followed by a comma to the left of "Customer Relations" on the second line of the address.
b. Delete the word "clearly" in the first line of the second paragraph. Then, delete the words "would you" on the same line.
c. Change the word "Sincerely" to "Disappointedly yours."
d. After the second paragraph, add the sentence: "If this exchange is impossible, how about sending some giant reams of ruled paper and a large sharpener?"

8. Save the modified letter as WORK1-3B.

9. Print a copy of the modified letter.

10. Close the document and then exit the program.

APPLICATION 4: VIDEO LIST

1. Boot your computer; start Windows and launch the Word program.

2. Type the following list of a video collection. Center the heading and make sure you underline and boldface as shown. Press Tab as needed to move to each column, and

WP

STAR TREK NEXT GENERATION VIDEO COLLECTION

TAPE	COUNTER	EPISODE	STAR DATE
A[Tab]	0000[Tab]	Encounter at Farpoint[2 Tabs]	41153.7
A	1200	Where No One Has Gone Before	41263.1
A	2350	11001001	41365.9
A	3100	The Neutron Tone	41986.0
A	4000	Tin Man	43779.3
A	4850	Darmok	45047.2
B	0000	A Matter of Time	45349.1
B	1150	Violations	45429.3
B	2325	Power Play	45571.2
B	3990	Cause or Effect	45652.1
B	4765	I, Borg	45845.2
C	0000	The Inner Light	45944.1
C	1250	Realm of Fear	46041.1
C	3125	A Fistful of Datas	46271.5
C	2465	Ship in a Bottle	46424.1
C	4870	Lessons	46693.1
D	0000	The Chase	46731.5
D	1175	Parallels	47391.2
D	2290	Inheritance	47410.2
D	2700	Data Shuts Off	47500.0
D	3010	Thine Own Self	47611.2
D	4025	Masks	47615.2
D	4755	Journey's End	47751.2

press the Enter key at the end of each row to return to the next line. Once you've typed the first line, tab as needed to align data in each succeeding row.

3. Save this list as WORK1-4A.

4. Print a copy of the list on your printer.

5. Close the document window.

6. Open the WORK1-4A document from your data disk.

7. Make the following changes to your list:
   a. Add the following lines and entries: B, 3005, Ethics, 45587.3; and C, 4100, Face of the Enemy, 46519.1.
   b. Delete the entry: D, 2700, Data Shuts Off, 47500.0.
   c. Change A, 3100 to read "The Neutral Zone" and B, 3990 to read "Cause and Effect."

8. Save the modified list as WORK1-4B.

9. Print a copy of the modified list.

10. Close the document and then exit the program.

APPLICATION 5: JOB INQUIRY LETTER

1. Boot your computer, launch the Word program, and (if needed) set the default to the drive that contains your data disk.

2. Type the following letter. Make sure you center, underline, and boldface as shown. Don't worry if the lines of text do not wrap exactly as shown in the sample. Instead, let wordwrap take effect to control your line breaks within paragraphs.

3. Save this letter as WORK1-5A.

4. Print a copy of the letter.

5. Close the document.

6. Open the WORK1-5A document from your data disk.

7. Make the following changes to the second paragraph:
   a. Add the words "off cliffs" after "jumped."
   b. Delete the word "enclosed."
   c. Change the word "falling" to "plummeting."
   d. After the last word, "you," add the sentence "Fortunately, I landed in water both times, which gives me some related experience to the job being offered by your firm."

8. Save this modified letter as WORK1-5B.

Hugh Ken Hierme
123–456 Job Search Lane
New Job, CA 98765

(Type today's date here)

Anita Worker
Mar-Park Consulting Services
7546 Pleasant Beach Avenue
San Dinmyshoos, CA 98766

Dear Ms. Worker:

In response to your advertisement in yesterday's <u>Employment Times</u>, enclosed please find my resume in application for the position of **cliff diver.**

Although I haven't jumped professionally, I am sure that my enclosed history of falling off the Golden Gate Bridge, and the <u>Eiffel Tower</u>, will be of interest to you.

I will be available for a job interview as soon as my **splints** and **body cast** are removed. I look forward to hearing from you at your earliest convenience.

Sincerely,

9. Print a copy of this new letter.

10. Close the document and exit the program.

APPLICATION 6: EMPLOYER RESPONSE LETTER

1. Boot your computer, launch the Word program, and (if needed) set the default to the drive that contains your data disk.

2. Type the following letter. Make sure you underline and boldface as shown. Don't worry if the lines of text do not wrap exactly as shown in the sample. Instead, let wordwrap take effect to control your line breaks within paragraphs.

3. Save this letter as WORK1-6A.

4. Print a copy of the letter.

Mar-Park Consulting Services
7546 Pleasant Beach Avenue
San Dinmyshoos, CA 98766

(Type today's date here)

Mr. Hugh Hierme
123-456 Job Search Lane
New Job, CA 98765

Dear Mr. Hierme:

Thank you for your response to our advertisement in the <u>Employment Times</u>, for the position of **cliff diver.** We have had more than 400 inquiries from well-qualified applicants.

Your experience falling off the Golden Gate Bridge and the Eiffel Tower is of interest to us for two reasons: it displays your willingness to travel and shows that you have no fear of extreme heights.

We would like to schedule an interview with you for next week and will arrange to send a limousine to bring you, and your **body cast,** to our offices. Please call my secretary at **1-800-JUMPNOW** to arrange a time that is convenient. I look forward to meeting you.

Sincerely,

Anita Worker
Human Resources Director

WP

5. Close the document.

6. Open the WORK1-6A document from your data disk.

7. Make the following changes to the second paragraph:
   a. Add the word "great" before "interest."
   b. Delete the word "extreme."
   c. Change the word "falling" to "plunging."
   d. After the last word, "heights," add the sentence "We would be interested in learning about any bungee jumping or parachuting that you may have done as well. A copy of your current health plan would also be of interest."

8. Save this modified letter as WORK1-6B.

9. Print a copy of this new letter.

10. Close the document and exit the program.

MASTERY CASES

The following mastery cases allow you to demonstrate how much you have learned about this software. Each case describes a fictitious problem or need that can be solved using the skills you have learned in this chapter. Although minimum acceptable outcomes are specified, you are expected and encouraged to design your response (files, data, lists) in ways that display your personal mastery of the software. Feel free to show off your skills. Use real data from your own experience in your solution, although you may also fabricate data if needed.

These mastery cases allow you to display your ability to

- Launch the program.
- Enter text into a document.
- Save the document on disk.
- Edit the text with insert or overtype.
- Add basic text enhancements.
- Print the document.

CASE 1: CREATING A LETTER

Your instructor has asked you to review the strengths and weaknesses of your computer course. Write a letter in proper form (you may use the form shown in Application 6), addressed to your instructor, critiquing the course and this book. Be sure to center your heading and use boldface and underlining where appropriate. The letter should contain at least three paragraphs. Save and print the letter.

CASE 2: CREATING A RÉSUMÉ

You have decided to apply for a part-time job. Prepare a one-page résumé that presents your educational background, work and volunteer experience, and other appropriate information. Use any acceptable format (check with your instructor or librarian), and make use of the tab key, underline, and boldface as needed. Save and print the résumé.

CASE 3: CREATING A MEMORANDUM

Your boss would like you to demonstrate how Word can benefit your coworkers. Write a memo, in proper business form, inviting the secretarial staff to attend a one-hour meeting at a date and time you specify. Explain briefly in the memo why Word is useful and why attendance is important. Save and print the memo.

2

EXPANDING WORD PROCESSING: ENHANCING DOCUMENT APPEARANCE

WP

OBJECTIVES

After completing this chapter, you will be able to

1 Use the *Open* dialog box to list and manage files
2 Describe the purpose of the Show/Hide feature and use it to locate and delete text enhancement codes
3 Explain the use of the Select feature to move, copy, delete, or enhance text selections
4 Describe how to change layout parameters such as margins, tabs, line spacing, alignment, and paragraph indentation

5 Describe how to search for text strings or replace text with new text throughout the document
6 Describe how to change text attributes including changing font settings and adjusting text appearance
7 Use the auxiliary tools—Spelling Check, Thesaurus, and Grammar Check—to modify words in your document

OVERVIEW

This chapter extends your use of word processing by presenting additional techniques to help you understand the screen and modify text. First, you will learn to use the *Open* dialog box to manipulate disk files. Then, you will examine the hidden codes embedded in your document with the Show/Hide feature.

The Select feature expands your ability to move or adjust large areas of text quickly. You will then learn how to modify layout parameters, including margins, tabs, spacing, and justification. The chapter then presents find and replace techniques for changing text. After this, you will learn how to change text attributes including changing font settings and adjusting text appearance and size. Finally, the chapter examines three auxiliary programs—the Spelling, Thesaurus, and Grammar programs—which can locate potential errors and improve the vocabulary and grammar used in your document.

USING THE *OPEN* DIALOG BOX

Word offers a number of useful file management commands that let you manage your files without having to return to Windows. File management commands include file copying, deleting, printing, and renaming. You can access these commands through the *Open* dialog box.

STEPS

1 First, boot your computer and Windows

2 You can now launch Word as you did in Chapter 1

Now that you are in Word, there are three ways to access the *Open* dialog box. You can open it directly using the menu commands *File, Open File,* you can click the *Open* toolbar icon, or you can use the Ctrl + O shortcut keys.

 3 Click *File* and then *Open*   [**Ctrl** + **I**]

4 If needed, change the default drive to A: (or B:) by clicking the drop-down arrow in the *Look in* box, and clicking the appropriate drive

An *Open* dialog box should appear as shown in Figure WP2-1. In this box, you can change the file search parameters in the File name box and specify the type of file on which to carry out the search. At the moment, the search is set to find all Word documents (those with "doc" extensions).

UNDERSTANDING THE *OPEN* DIALOG BOX

An *Open* dialog box should now appear (although your file list may differ). Examine its components as you read about them in the following paragraphs.

THE *NAME* BOX.   The left portion of the dialog box includes a Name box that displays the selected files that match the search criterion. In this example, all Word documents on your data disk should be listed. If the list was extensive, you could use the scroll bar to see additional filenames.

FIGURE WP2-1 ■ THE *OPEN* DIALOG BOX

File search settings can be
specified in this dialog box.

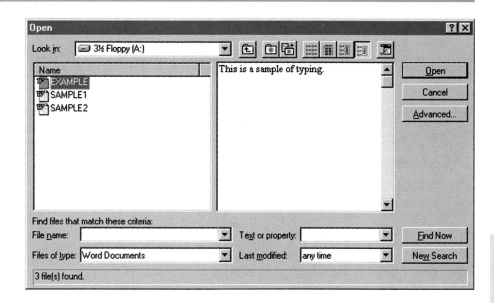

THE *PREVIEW* BOX. If Preview is active, the right side of the dialog box will display an image of the file highlighted in the *Name* box. The *Preview* box lets you view the contents of a file without having to open it.

THE *VIEW* BUTTONS. Above the *Preview* box, the *View* buttons (as shown in Figure WP2-2) allow you to choose one of four displays appearing on the upper right portion of the screen. You may select from among List, Details, Properties, or Preview.

THE *FIND NOW* BUTTON. The *Find Now* button, when selected, generates a new list of files that match your search criteria.

FIGURE WP2-2 ■ THE *VIEW* BUTTONS

List   Properties

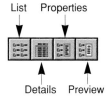

Details   Preview

THE *OPEN* BUTTON.   The *Open* button opens the highlighted file into a new window.

THE *CANCEL* BUTTON.   The *Cancel* button removes the *Open* dialog box from the screen.

You will now learn how to operate some of the file commands and how to view files using the features in the *Open* dialog box.

SELECTING A FILE.   Generally, a file should be selected (marked) before invoking any other file management command or activating the view feature. File selection can be made by highlighting a filename in the Name box. For example, to select the file SAMPLE1, use one of the following methods:

STEPS

---

1 Point to *SAMPLE1* in the Name box   [**Tab**]

2 Click *SAMPLE1*   [↓]

Note that the preview of the SAMPLE1 document appears on the screen. This file selection process can be used to select any file from the *Listed Files* box. Multiple file selections can also be made. Multiple file techniques will be discussed later. The various View commands will now be applied to the SAMPLE1 file.

USING THE *VIEW* BUTTONS

The *View* buttons allow you to obtain information about the documents stored on your disk. For example,

---

STEPS

---

1 Click the *List* view button

As shown in Figure WP2-3a, the name box displays a list of all filenames that meet the current search criteria. (Extensive file lists will appear in multiple columns.)

2 Click the *Details* view button

The name box now expands to display filenames in the left column, with details about their size, file type, and modification date to their right, as in Figure WP2-3b.

3 Click the *Properties* view button

As shown in Figure WP2-3c, information about the highlighted file is displayed to the right of the *Name* box.

4 Click the *Preview* view button (the default)

FIGURE WP2-3 ■ USING THE *VIEW* BUTTONS

(a) List view
(b) Details view
(c) Properties view
(d) Preview view

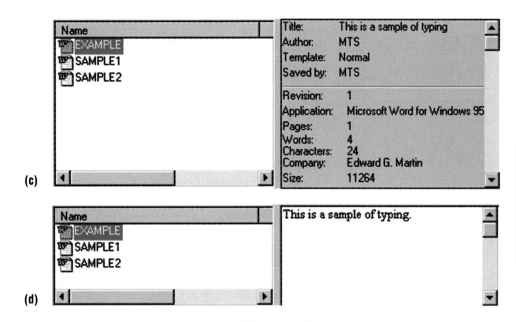

The contents of the highlighted file are displayed in a separate box, as shown in Figure WP2-3d. This view is useful for previewing a file prior to opening it.

> **Tip:** You may leave the *Open* dialog box in any view. The setting will remain until you switch to another view.

SETTING SEARCH CRITERIA

By default, only Word documents are listed in the *Name* box. However, you can adjust the list to display specific filenames, file types, or dates of preparation. This is especially important when disks contain hundred of files. You may also want to find files that contain specific text. The following exercises briefly demonstrate these techniques.

SEARCHING BY FILENAME.   To restrict the search to a specific set of filenames, type the desired pattern in the *File name* entry box. For example, to list all files that begin with an "S," do the following:

1   Click the *File name* entry box at the lower left   [**Alt** + **N**]

2   Type **S**

3   Click the *Find Now* button   [**Alt** + **F**]

The list now displays only those filenames that begin with the letter "S." You may further define your search by using a *wildcard,* which can represent one character (?) or a
series of characters (*). Figure WP2-4 displays a few wildcard examples.

4   To return to the default setting, click the *New Search* button   [**Alt** + **W**]

Your list should now display all the Word files on your disk, because the default settings were reset.

SEARCHING BY FILE TYPE.   To search for a different file type, change the "Files
of type" entry. For example, to display all files, perform the following steps:

1   Click the drop-down button in the *Files of type* entry box   [**Alt** + **T**]

A list of available file types appears, as shown in Figure WP2-5b. If needed, use the
scroll bar or arrows keys to display the desired file type. For now,

FIGURE WP2-4 ■ FILENAME SEARCH USING WILDCARDS

To Search for	Use This Wildcard	Examples	
A single character	?	c?t	Finds names like "cat," "cot," and "cut"
		c?t?	Finds names like "cite," "city," and "cute"
A string of characters	*	n*	Finds names that begin with "n"
		n*r	Finds names like "nor," "never," and "november"
		*ber	Finds names like "september," "october," "november," and "december"
Initial characters	Use characters	n	Finds names that begin with "n"
		nov	Finds names that begin with "nov"

FIGURE WP2-5 ■ SEARCHING BY FILE TYPE

(a) Click the drop-down button to initiate a change of file type.
(b) Click the desired type from the drop-down list.

(a)

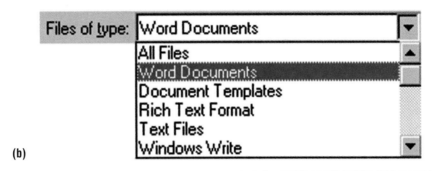

(b)

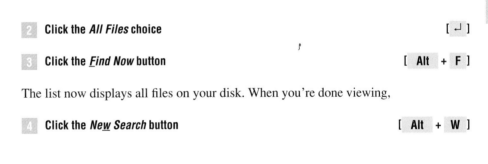

2   **Click the *All Files* choice**   [↵]

3   **Click the *Find Now* button**   [**Alt** + **F**]

The list now displays all files on your disk. When you're done viewing,

4   **Click the *New Search* button**   [**Alt** + **W**]

SEARCHING BY TEXT.   You can also list documents that contain a specific word or phrase. For example, to locate files that contain the word "greatly," perform the following steps:

STEPS

1   **Click the *Text* or *Property* entry box**   [**Alt** + **X**]

2   **Type   greatly   as in Figure WP2-6**

3   **Click the *Find Now* button**   [**Alt** + **F**]

Only those files that contain the search word will be displayed.

4   **Click the *New Search* button**   [**Alt** + **W**]

FIGURE WP2-6 ■ SEARCHING FOR TEXT

Enter search word here

Find files that match these criteria:

File name: [   ] [▼]   Te_xt or property: |greatly   [▼]   [Find Now]

Files of type: |Word Documents [▼]   Last modified: |any time   [▼]   [New Search]

0 file(s) found.

SEARCHING BY LAST MODIFIED DATE.   At times, you may want to view files based on the date you last modified their contents. For example, to locate files that were last modified "today," perform the following steps:

STEPS

1   Click the *Last Modified* entry box   [**Alt** + **M**]

The option list that appears allows you to specify files that were modified *any time, today, last week, this week, last month,* or *this month.* If needed, you can use the scroll bar or arrows keys to move to the desired choice. For now,

2   Click *today* (or move to it and press ↵)

3   Click the *Find Now* button   [**Alt** + **F**]

The list now displays those files that were modified today. When you have finished examining the list,

4   Clear the search (click *New Search*)

Tip: You can combine any of these searches techniques to further restrict your list. Simply identify the desired search settings and then click *Find Now.*

5   Close the *Open* dialog box (use *Cancel*)

MANAGING FILES

You can also use the *Open* dialog box to perform simple file management, such as copying, renaming, deleting, or printing files. The following exercises demonstrate these techniques. To prepare,

1 Access the *Open* dialog box   [**Ctrl** + **O**]

2 If needed, change the "Look In" entry to your disk

> **Tip:** You can use the standard Windows techniques of Shift + click to select a group of files—or Ctrl + click to select multiple files—before invoking one of the following file management commands. The command will then operate on all the files selected.

COPYING A FILE.   To duplicate a file, such as SAMPLE1, perform these steps:

1 Right-click SAMPLE1 in the *File* list (Remember: To right-click, point to the SAMPLE1 filename and click the right mouse button)

A *Shortcut* menu will appear. If you pressed the left mouse button by mistake, simply repeat Step 1.

2 Click *Copy* in the *Shortcut* menu

Although you will not see it, the file has been copied to the Windows Clipboard and is now available for pasting elsewhere.

3 Right-click anywhere in the blank area of the *File name* box

Another *Shortcut* menu appears.

4 Click *Paste* in the *Shortcut* menu

A new filename, COPY OF SAMPLE1, appears in the list. You have copied the file successfully.

RENAMING A FILE.   You can modify the name of any file without affecting its contents. To change the name of a file, such as COPY OF SAMPLE1, perform these steps:

1 Click COPY OF SAMPLE1 in the *File* list

A rectangle appears around the filename. Now simply type the new name as follows:

2 Type **TEST** and press ↵

The renamed file appears alphabetically.

DELETING A FILE.   To remove a file, such as TEST, perform these steps:

`STEPS`

1 Right-click TEST in the *File* list to access its *Shortcut* menu (point to TEST and click the right mouse button)

2 Click *Delete* in the *Shortcut* menu

A *Confirm File Delete* dialog box will appear.

3 Click *Yes* to delete the file

The file's name is removed from the list. If you delete a file on a hard disk by mistake, you can always retrieve it from the Recycle Bin by following standard Windows procedures.

> **Tip: You can also delete a file by pointing to the filename in the list and pressing the Delete key.**

PRINTING A FILE.   To print a file, such as SAMPLE1, perform these steps:

`STEPS`

1 Right-click SAMPLE1 in the *File* list

2 Click *Print* in the *Shortcut* menu

A *Print* dialog box will appear. Although you could continue with the print routine, in this example, cancel as follows:

3 Click *Cancel* to end the print routine

☑ **CHECKPOINT**

  ✓ Use the *Open* dialog box to view SAMPLE1.
  ✓ Copy SAMPLE1 to SILLY (copy and rename).
  ✓ Find the file size of SAMPLE2.
  ✓ List all Word documents that contain the word "garbage."
  ✓ Exit the *Open* dialog box.

UNDERSTANDING HIDDEN CODES

Before tackling format changes, you should understand the hidden codes that determine your document's appearance. Word does not normally display formatting codes but "hides" them within your document. These codes are generated every time you issue commands for such effects as hard return, tab, and space. Understanding the placement of these codes, and how to remove them, is essential, and you must learn to recognize and locate them in your document. Word's Show/Hide feature makes it easy by displaying these hidden codes.

Although you may invoke the Show/Hide command at any point in a document, this exercise requires that you be at the start of SAMPLE2, so prepare your computer as follows (*Note:* Unless otherwise indicated, figures displaying documents are in Normal view mode. Although it is not necessary to work in this mode, your system may operate more efficiently.):

STEPS

1 **Switch to Normal view mode, if necessary**   [**Alt** + **V** , **N**]

2 **Open SAMPLE2 if it is not on your screen**

3 **Move to the start of the document if needed**

DISPLAYING HIDDEN CODES

To initiate the Hidden Codes feature as shown in Figure WP2-7, the easiest approach is to click the *Show/Hide* toolbar button. However, you can also use menus as follows:

STEPS

1 **Click *Tools* and then *Options***

2 **Click the *"View"* tab if needed**   [→]

3 **Click *All* at the bottom center of the menu**

4 **Click the *OK* button**   [↵]

Your document window should now resemble Figure WP2-7. Some of the hidden codes are now evident. Spaces appear as dots between words, and hard returns (places where you pressed the Enter key) appear as paragraph symbols. *Note:* If your document had tabs, they would appear as right-pointing arrows.

You may show or hide hidden codes on your screen as you prefer. It will not affect any work that you do. At times, it may be easier to see where you have placed hard returns, spaces, and tabs, especially when you attempt to delete them. For now,

FIGURE WP2-07 ■ REVEALING HIDDEN CODES

When the Show/Hide command is invoked, codes are revealed for hard returns (¶) and spaces (·). Tabs will appear as arrows (→).

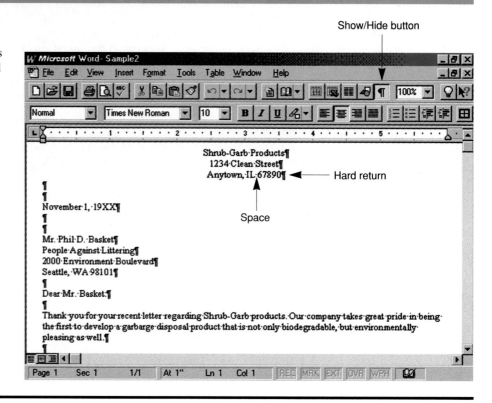

5 To "hide" the codes once again, repeat Steps 1-4.

> Tip: Use the *Show/Hide* button to display hidden codes quickly. You can leave hidden codes on your screen as you work. Insert, delete, or modify text as you normally would.

DELETING TEXT ENHANCEMENTS

With hidden codes displayed, it is easier to locate and remove unwanted codes, such as extra spaces and hard returns. Any code displayed can be deleted by positioning the insertion point appropriately and then pressing the Delete or Backspace key, just as you would to delete "normal" text. However, text enhancements, such as centering, underlining, and bolding, must be removed by adding new commands that supersede them.

Try the following exercises:

STEPS

1 Move to the start of your document (Ctrl + Home)

For example, to remove the "centered" attribute of the first text line and return it to aligned left, it is easiest to click the *Align Left* toolbar button. However, you can also use menus as follows:

2 Click *Format* and then *Paragraph*

3 Click the *Indents and Spacing* tab if needed   [**Alt** + **I**]

 4 Click the *Alignment* drop-down button

5 Click *Left*   [→]

6 Click the *OK* button   [↵]

The first heading line is no longer centered. You can now repeat the procedure as follows:

7 Move to the second heading line and change its alignment from center to left using Steps 2–6.

8 Change the third heading line to left align as well.

Now, try a similar technique to remove a bold text enhancement.

9 Move to the d in "discount" near the end of your document as in Figure WP2-8a.

FIGURE WP2-8 ■ REMOVING A TEXT ENHANCEMENT

(a) Move the insertion point as shown.
(b) The insertion point is positioned at the start of the bold enhancement.

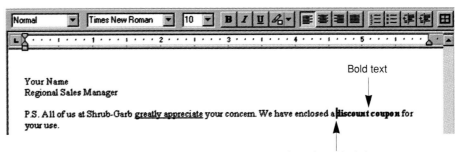
(a)

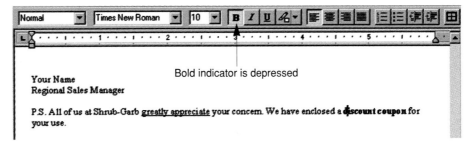
(b)

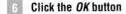

You must now position the insertion point at the start of the bold enhancement. If the *Bold* toolbar button is depressed on your screen, skip Step 10.

10   **Press → once to move past the d.**

The *Bold* toolbar button should now be depressed, showing the start of the bold enhancement, as shown in Figure WP2-8b. You can now remove the bold enhancement as follows:

B   It is easiest to click the *Bold* toolbar button. However, you can also use menus as follows:

11   **Click *Format* and then *Font***

12   **Click the *Font* tab if needed**   [**Alt** + **N**]

13   **Click *Regular* in the *Font Style* box**

14   **Click the *OK* button**   [↵]

The bold enhancement has been removed from the first word.

15   **Now remove the bold enhancement from the word "coupon" using the procedure in Steps 9–14. Find the start of the bold enhancement and then remove it.**

(Remember that it is much easier to simply click the *Bold* toolbar button after Step 9.)

16   **Save this amended document as SAMPLE3**

Underlining can be removed in a similar manner. Find the start of the underlining enhancement (look for the depressed *Underline* toolbar button) and then click the button to remove it. You can also access the *Font* menu (Steps 11–12) and then use the *Underline* box to change "single" to "none." Try this on your own but do not save the document again.

17   **Close the SAMPLE3 document window.**

☑ **CHECKPOINT**
   ✓   On a new document window, type a few sentences, including some centered, bold, and underlined words. Print the page.
   ✓   Locate and delete the centered text enhancements.
   ✓   Locate and delete the bold and underline enhancements.
   ✓   Print the page.
   ✓   Close the document without saving.

THE SELECT FEATURE

The **Select** feature allows you to edit or format complete words, sentences, paragraphs, or entire documents at one time. A *selection* is a segment of contiguous text. It can be as small as one letter or as large as a document. The following exercises let you experiment with Select commands for moving, copying, deleting, formatting, and saving. To prepare for these exercises,

STEPS

1 **Launch Word or close any open document windows**

2 **Open the SAMPLE2 document**

IDENTIFYING A SELECTION

Identifying a selection is a three-step process: (1) move to the start of the selection, (2) turn on the *Select* feature, and then (3) move to the end of the selection. Try this:

STEPS

1 **Move your insertion point to the "M" in "Mr. Phil D. Basket." As shown in Figure WP2-9a, your insertion point should appear before the "M"**

2 **Double-click the "EXT" section of the status bar turn on the Select mode   [F8]**

> **Tip: If a *Help for WordPerfect Users* dialog box appears when you press F8, click the *Close* button, then turn the feature off by clicking *Tools, Options, General tab,* the *Help for WordPerfect Users* checkbox (second from top), Navigation keys checkbox (third from top), OK.**

The word "EXT" appears in darker typeface on the right side of the status bar, showing that the Extend feature is active.

FIGURE WP2-9 ■ USING THE SELECT COMMANDS

(a) The insertion point is positioned at the start of a text selection.
(b) Moving the insertion point after double-clicking the Select area of the status bar, or after pressing F8, highlights the desired selection.

November 1, 19XX
——————— Insertion point is here
▼
Mr. Phil D. Basket
People Against Littering
2000 Environment Boulevard
Seattle, WA 98101

(a)

November 1, 19XX
——————— Selected text is highlighted
▼
Mr. Phil D. Basket
People Against Littering
2000 Environment Boulevard
Seattle, WA 98101

(b)

3 **Press → eight times**

This positions your insertion point past the word "Phil," as in Figure WP2-9b, with the selection of text highlighted on your screen. You have successfully identified a selection (or block) of text.

4 **Press ← eight times to move back to the "M"**

Notice that the highlight shrinks as you move back. You may change the amount of text included in a selection by moving the insertion point until you are satisfied. In fact, you can mark selections with any insertion point movement you know. For example, to highlight the entire line,

5 **Press ↓**

If you change your mind, just turn off the Select mode as follows:

6 **Double-click "EXT" on the status bar to turn off the Select mode, then click anywhere to remove highlight** **[Esc]**

Tip: To select text by mouse do one of the following:	
For selection of a...	**Use this mouse action:**
Block of text	Drag mouse over text
Word	Double-click word
Paragraph	Triple-click anywhere in the paragraph
Line	Point to line from left margin and click
Several lines	Point to first line from left margin and drag down

Once a selection has been identified, you can then invoke other commands that will affect the entire selection. The following exercises demonstrate various commands that work with text selections.

MOVING A SELECTION

A *selection move* is a process that lets you identify a text selection and move it anywhere in a document (or into another file). In this exercise, you will move Phil's name beneath the name of the company in the address. The Cut and Paste commands used to move selections originated from the scissors-and-rubber-cement days of precomputer editing.

STEPS

1 **Open SAMPLE2 if it is not on your screen**

Now identify the entire name line as a selection:

2 **Move to the "M" in "Mr. Phil D. Basket"**

3 **Double-click the "EXT" section of the status bar** **[F8]**

4 **Press** ↓

The line is highlighted as a selection as in Figure WP2-10a. Now, invoke the Cut command as follows:

5 **Click _Edit_ and then _Cut_ to cut the selection** [**Ctrl** + **X**]

At this point, the selection disappears from the screen. In effect, you have "cut" the selection from your document and placed it into a temporary holding area. It is not lost, but merely awaiting your command to "paste" it back in.

6 **Press** ↓ **to go to the next line**

7 **Click _Edit_ and then _Paste_ to paste the selection in its new location** [**Ctrl** + **V**]

The selection is now in its new location, as in Figure WP2-10b.

8 **Save this document as SAMPLE4**

COPYING A SELECTION

A _selection copy_ is a process that lets you identify a text selection and duplicate it anywhere in the document (or in another file). It is identical to move except that the original selection stays where it is. To perform a selection copy, follow the same steps as for a selection move, but click _Copy_ instead of _Cut_ or press the Ctrl + C keys instead of the Ctrl + X keys in Step 5 above. For example,

STEPS

1 **Open SAMPLE4 if it is not on your screen**

2 **Move the insertion point before the "M" in "Mr. Phil D. Basket"**

3 **Turn on the Select mode**

FIGURE WP2-10 ■ THE SELECT COMMAND

(a) The selected text.
(b) The selection has been pasted back into the document.

November 1, 19XX

Selected text is highlighted

Mr. Phil D. Basket
People Against Littering
2000 Environment Boulevard
Seattle, WA 98101

(a)

November 1, 19XX

Text has been moved

People Against Littering
Mr. Phil D. Basket ◄
2000 Environment Boulevard
Seattle, WA 98101

(b)

WP

4 Press **End** to select the "Mr. Phil D. Basket" line

Note that the End key will move the highlight to the end of a line of text.

5 Click *Edit* and then *Copy* to copy [**Ctrl** + **C**]

This time the selection does not disappear from your screen.

6 Press ↑ to move the insertion point to the "People Against Littering" line

7 Click *Edit* and then *Paste* to paste the selection [**Ctrl** + **V**]

The selection is copied, as in Figure WP2-11.

8 Save this document again as SAMPLE4

> **Tip:** You can also select text by dragging the mouse or holding Shift and pressing an arrow key.

MOVING OR COPYING "STANDARD" SELECTIONS

More often than not, your text selection may be a "standard" size—a complete sentence, paragraph, or a page. If so, Word provides an easy way to move or copy it. In this case, the keyboard (F8) approach is most useful. Try this example:

STEPS

1 Open SAMPLE4 if it is not on your screen

2 Move the insertion point anywhere in the first sentence of the first paragraph

3 Press **F8** three times

Notice how the entire sentence is highlighted, as in Figure WP2-12. The rest of the procedure is the same as you've already learned. For now,

FIGURE WP2-11 ■ COPYING A SELECTION

November 1, 19XX

Mr. Phil D. Basket ◄——— Selection is copied here
People Against Littering
Mr. Phil D. Basket
2000 Environment Boulevard
Seattle, WA 98101

FIGURE WP2-12 ■ IDENTIFYING STANDARD TEXT SELECTIONS

Moving to a sentence and pressing F8 three times will quickly select it.

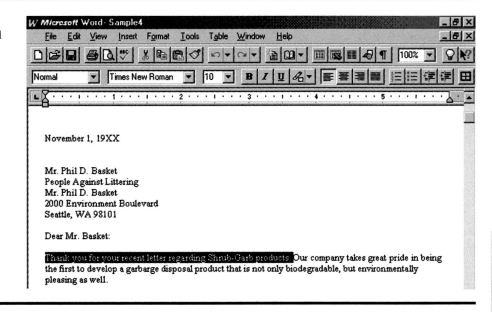

4 Press **Shift** + **F8** three times to reduce the selection

5 Press **Esc** to shut off the Select mode, then click mouse or press arrow key

This leaves the sentence in the same place for now. You can use this technique to move, copy, or even delete entire sentences, paragraphs, or pages.

> **Tip: Pressing F8 repeatedly increases the selection to word, sentence, paragraph, and page.**

DELETING A SELECTION

A *selection deletion* is a process that lets you identify a selection of text and remove it. It is similar to a selection move except that the selection is simply cut from the document; it is not pasted back. Try this exercise:

STEPS

1 Open SAMPLE4 if it is not on your screen

To select the *second* "Mr. Phil D. Basket" line as in Figure WP2-13a,

2 Move to the start of the selection

3 Turn on the Select mode

WP

FIGURE WP2-13 ■ DELETING A SELECTION

(a) The selection is marked.
(b) The selection is deleted.

November 1, 19XX

Mr. Phil D. Basket
People Against Littering
Mr. Phil D. Basket
2000 Environment Boulevard
Seattle, WA 98101

(a)

November 1, 19XX

Mr. Phil D. Basket
People Against Littering
2000 Environment Boulevard
Seattle, WA 98101

(b)

---

4 Press **End** to select the line

5 Press **Delete** to remove selection

The selection is deleted, as in Figure WP2-13b. As with any other deleted text, if you make a mistake in selection deletions, you can always use the Edit, Undo feature to restore your cut.

SELECTION ENHANCEMENTS

Selection enhancement is a process that lets you identify a selection of text and change its formatting. Perhaps you want to underline or bold text, or center an existing heading. First,

STEPS

1 Close any open document without saving

2 Open SAMPLE3

The following exercises demonstrate each of these techniques.

CENTER. This document's heading is no longer centered. You can use the Select command to center it once again.

STEPS

1 If necessary, move the insertion point to the "S" in "Shrub-Garb"

2 Turn on the Select mode

3 Press ↓ three times

The entire heading is now identified as the selection. Here's a quick way to center:

4 **Click the *Center* toolbar button**   [**Ctrl** + **E**]

5 **Turn off the Select mode and remove the highlight (click or move)**

The selection is centered.

6 **Save the document as SAMPLE5**

UNDERLINE AND BOLD.   Selection enhancements to make text underlined or boldfaced are performed in a similar manner—just identify the selection and invoke the enhancement. For example,

STEPS

1 **Open SAMPLE5 if needed**

2 **Move to the "e" in "environmentally" in the last sentence of the first paragraph (Note that the insertion point should appear before the "e")**

3 **Select "environmentally pleasing"**

4 **Click the *Underline* button on the toolbar**   [**Ctrl** + **U**]

5 **Turn off the Select mode and remove the highlight**

To bold a selection, click the *Bold* button on the toolbar or press the Ctrl + B keys in place of Step 4 above.

UPPERCASE AND LOWERCASE.   If you want to change all the letters in a selection to uppercase or lowercase form without having to retype them, you can use Word's Change Case feature. Try this:

STEPS

1 **Open SAMPLE5 if needed**

2 **Move to the "S" in "Shrub-Garb" in the heading**

3 **Turn on the Select mode**

4 **Press** **End**

5 **Click *Format* and then *Change Case***

A *Change Case* dialog box appears as in Figure WP2-14, offering five case types:

FIGURE WP2-14 ■ THE *CHANGE CASE* DIALOG BOX

You can make one of five types of adjustments to selected text by clicking the appropriate line or moving to it.

Explanation:

Capitalizes first word in sentence ——————————
Sets all characters to lowercase ——————————
Sets all characters to uppercase ——————————
Capitalizes each word ——————————
Sets all uppercase to lowercase —————————— and all lowercase to uppercase

Dialog box:

Change Case   ? X

○ Sentence case.
○ lowercase
◉ UPPERCASE
○ Title Case
○ tOGGLE cASE

OK
Cancel

---

6   **Click *UPPERCASE* and then *OK***

7   **Click anywhere to turn off the Select mode**   [↓]

The text has been changed accordingly.

8   **Resave as SAMPLE5**

9   **Close all document windows**

SAVING A SELECTION

Sometimes you may want to save a selection of text so that you can recall it for later use. In the SAMPLE5 document, assume that you want to save the second paragraph (the one that starts with "As you know...").

STEPS

1   **Open SAMPLE5 if needed**

2   **Move the insertion point to the first character in the second paragraph—the "A" in "As"**

3   **Select the entire paragraph and the line beneath it**

Your screen should resemble Figure WP2-15.

You can now copy the selection to the Windows Clipboard and then save it separately as follows:

4   **Click *Edit* and then *Copy***   [**Ctrl** + **C**]

FIGURE WP2-15 ■ SAVING A SELECTED TEXT BLOCK

The text block has been specified and appears highlighted.

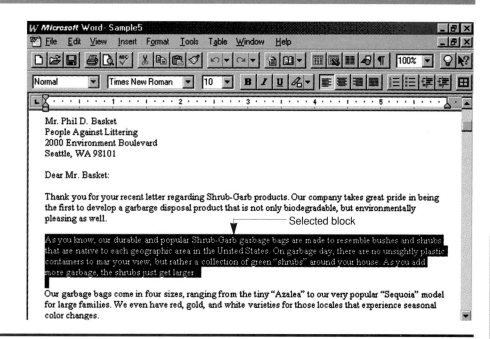

Selected block

---

5 Click *File* and then *Close*

6 Create a new document (*File, New, OK*)

7 Click *Edit* and then *Paste*   [**Ctrl** + **V**]

The selection returns to the new screen. You can now save it as a new document as follows:

8 Save the document as GARBAGE (use *File, Save* or **Ctrl** + **S**)

9 Close the document

The selected text block is now saved as GARBAGE.DOC and is available for use.

RETRIEVING A SELECTION

Stored text selections can be opened just like any other disk file.

1 Use *File* and then *Open* to open the GARBAGE document   [**Ctrl** + **O**]

As expected, the paragraph appears on your screen, available for use.

WP

You can also add any text block selection to another document by copying from the first document, opening the desired "target" document, and then pasting it back in, as you have already learned. For now,

2 **Close the document window**

☑ CHECKPOINT

- ✓ Open the SAMPLE3 document.
- ✓ Using Select, underline the first sentence.
- ✓ Set the last sentence to all uppercase.
- ✓ Delete the middle paragraph.
- ✓ Close, but do *not* save the document.

CHANGING LAYOUT FORMAT

Word includes commands that let you control the final layout of your document. **Layout** refers to the appearance of text on the page—the combination of print and white space. Until now, you have been using Word's default settings for such layout settings as margins, tabs, line spacing, and alignment.

You will now create a short document that will include a number of these layout features. Remember that all layout changes, like other formatting adjustments, take effect *at the insertion point* and affect all following text until another format change is made. *Note:* Layout changes in existing text will affect the paragraph in which the change is made. In addition, since Word is a WYSIWYG program, layout changes should appear on your screen as they would appear in your final printout. To begin:

STEPS

1 **Launch Word if needed or close any open document**

2 **Start a new document**

3 **The ruler bar should appear. If not, activate it by clicking _View_ and then _Ruler_**

As described earlier, the ruler bar provides you with visual margin and tab indicators. As you will see later, these indicators can be dragged and dropped to change their current position.

MARGINS

The default margins are set at 1.25 inches on both the left and right sides of the document. Often, you may want to make margins larger or smaller. You can use the *Page Setup* dialog box to set the document's margins or you can adjust margins anywhere within a document with the ruler bar. You'll try both here. First, you'll change the left and right margins to 1.5 inches and 2 inches respectively.

SETTING MARGINS WITH PAGE SETUP.   To set a document's margins through the *Page Setup* dialog box, do the following:

■ Click *File* and then *Page Setup*

■ If needed, click the *Margins* tab   [Alt + M]

A *Page Setup* dialog box appears as in Figure WP2-16a. The current margin settings appear at the left; a page preview is shown in the center. The *Apply To* drop-down list allows you to set margins for the "Entire document" (default) or from "This point forward." You can now adjust the margins as follows:

■ Click the *Left margin* entry box

■ Delete the current entry

FIGURE WP2-16 ■ ADJUSTING MARGINS

(a) The *Page Setup* dialog box allows you to change margins and other page settings.
(b) The Ruler bar reflects the new settings.

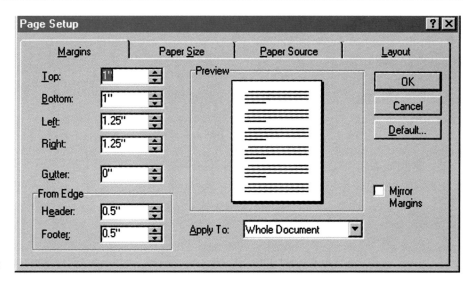

(a)

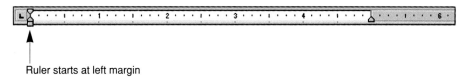

Ruler starts at left margin

(b)

5 Type **1.5**

6 Click the *Right margin* entry box

7 Delete the current entry and type **2**

8 Click the *OK* button   [↵]

The document screen will now return, ready to use the new margins. Note that the ruler bar has been adjusted to show the available horizontal typing space, now five inches, as in Figure WP2-16b.

To see the effect of the new margins,

9 Type the document shown in Figure WP2-17

Remember to press the Tab key at the beginning of each paragraph, but do *not* press the Enter key until you reach the end of each paragraph, as shown. Note that the Tab key indents the first line of a paragraph.

10 Save this document as LAYOUT1

SETTING MARGINS WITH THE RULER BAR.   You can also change the margins whenever you want by moving the insertion point to the desired position and setting margins with the mouse. This can be done before you type or after text has been entered. The paragraph following the change will be reformatted automatically to conform to the new margins. For example,

---

FIGURE WP2-17 ■ MARGIN PRACTICE DOCUMENT

NOTE: Press **Tab** when you see [Tab] and ↵ when you see ¶.

Word Publishing¶
¶
[Tab]   It is clear that the current distinctions made among word processing, desktop publishing, and presentation graphics programs will soon die out. It is likely that all three will merge into one "word publishing" software package including sophisticated text entry, editing, layout, and graphics capabilities.
[Tab]   Yet, the increased power offered by such programs places more emphasis on the artistic training and skills of potential users. We must remember that, like an artist's brush, these programs can just as easily produce junk as masterpieces. It is still the human who must creatively apply these tools and be held accountable for the end product. The ease afforded by technology does not eliminate our responsibility for its use--in fact, it places higher demands on our skills and vigilance.¶
¶
Source: Martin/Burstein. COMPUTER SYSTEMS FUNDAMENTALS, The Dryden Press, 1990.¶

1 **Move to the start of Paragraph 2 (click it or use the arrow keys)**

First, examine the ruler bar as shown in Figure WP2-18a. Recall that the left margin is set at 1.5 inches. You will now use the Ruler bar to reset the margin to 2 inches, one-half inch further to the right from its current position.

2 **Point to the rectangular marker at the Ruler bar's left margin, as shown in Figure WP2-18b**

3 **Click and then drag the marker one-half inch to its right**

4 **Release the mouse button**

> **Tip: You can also select a text block and then invoke the Ruler bar margin change for the entire block.**

The second paragraph assumes the new margins as in Figure WP2-19. Examine the new margins that take effect in Paragraph 2.

5 **Save the document as LAYOUT2**

RESETTING MARGINS.   To return paragraph margins to the previous setting, simply repeat Steps 2–4, but move the ruler bar marker to the desired setting (in this case, one-half inch to the left).

> **Tip: You can adjust the right margin using the same procedure by pointing to the right margin's triangular pointer.**

WP

FIGURE WP2-18 ■ USING THE RULER BAR

(a) The Ruler bar currently shows 5″ between the left and right margins.
(b) Drag the left margin rectangular mark ½″ to the right and release.

(a)

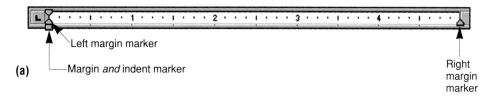

Left margin marker

Margin *and* indent marker

Right margin marker

(b)

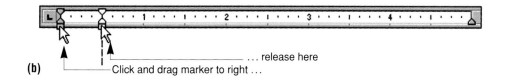

... release here

Click and drag marker to right ...

FIGURE WP2-19 ■ **USING THE NEW MARGINS**

The selected paragraph adjusts to the new margins shown in the Ruler bar.

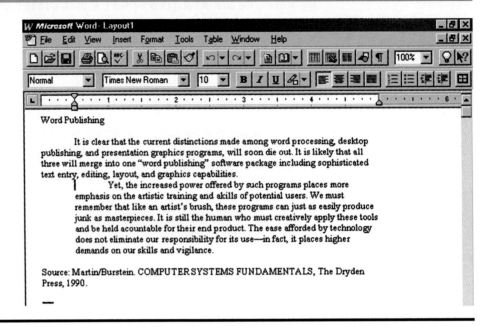

SPACING

The default setting for line spacing is single spacing. This can be changed easily using a procedure similar to that for changing margins. Spacing can be changed for each paragraph or text blocks (selection). For example, double space your document as follows:

STEPS

1. Close all open documents and then open LAYOUT1

2. Move to the beginning of the first paragraph (click or use arrow keys)

SPACING A PARAGRAPH.   Although the mouse is usually more direct, it is easier to change paragraph spacing by keyboard. Of course, you may use either approach. To double-space the paragraph, do the following:

3. Click *Format* and then *Paragraph*   [**Ctrl** + **2**]

4. Click the *Indents and Spacing* tab if needed

5. Click the *Line Spacing* drop-down arrow

6. Click *Double* and then the *OK* button

The first paragraph is now double-spaced. As you can see, the keyboard approach is much quicker and is recommended.

SPACING A SELECTED TEXT BLOCK.   Invoking a spacing change affects only the paragraph that contains the insertion point. You can also change the spacing of any selected text block by selecting the text before invoking the spacing command as follows:

STEPS

1 Move the insertion point to the start of the first paragraph if it's not already there.

2 Select all the remaining text as shown in Figure WP2-20.

3 Press   **Ctrl** + **2** (or use the mouse approach)

4 Turn off text selection (Remember? Click outside the text block or press an arrow key to remove highlight)

The text block is now double-spaced.

5 Save the document as LAYOUT3

FIGURE WP2-20 ■ SPACING A SELECTED TEXT BLOCK

The selected block will be double-spaced.

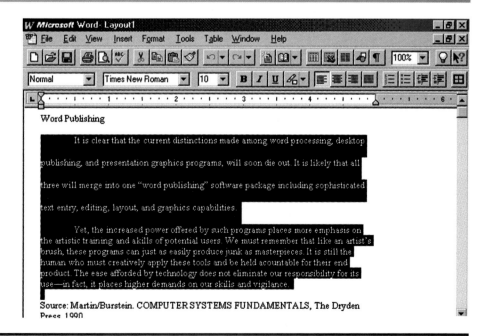

> **Tip:** Ctrl + 1 sets single space, Ctrl + 2 sets double space, and Ctrl + 5 sets spacing to 1½ lines.

RESETTING SPACING.   To return a paragraph or text block to single spacing, simply repeat the spacing procedure but use Ctrl + 1 instead of Ctrl + 2. For example,

STEPS

1. Use Steps 1–4 in the previous exercise, but use **Ctrl** + **1** in Step 3, to return the entire document to single-spacing

2. Close the document *without* saving it

ALIGNMENT

Alignment arranges words neatly at the margin. In Word, documents can have four different alignment settings: *left* margin only, *right* margin only, *justified* (both margins aligned), or *center* (neither margin aligned). As shown in Figure WP2-21 the two most popular options are *left* and *justified*. In **justified text,** Word places extra spaces between words to ensure that the last letter of each line aligns with the lines above it at both margins when the document is printed.

   Margins that are not aligned are ragged—they do not have added spaces and, as in normal typing, may not line up at the margin edge. Thus, left alignment (also called *ragged-right*) leaves a ragged right edge; justified leaves no ragged edges at all. The default setting for Word is left aligned text.

CHANGING ALIGNMENT.   Of course, text alignment can be changed easily, much like spacing. Do the following:

FIGURE WP2-21 ■ ALIGNMENT

(a) Left-aligned text.
(b) Justified text.

> This paragraph sample displays an example of left-aligned text in Word. The left margin is aligned, but the right margin is left "ragged." Extra spaces are not inserted between words by the program, but are left as if typed on a typewriter. Left-aligned text is also known as "ragged right."

(a)

> This paragraph sample displays an example of justified text in Word. Notice that the left and right margins are both aligned. Extra spaces are inserted automatically as needed between words by the program to ensure that the last letter of each line aligns neatly with the text above it.

(b)

1 Close all documents and open **LAYOUT1**

2 Move the insertion point to the beginning of the document

3 Select the entire document (try *Edit, Select All*)   [**Ctrl** + **A**]

Note that alignment is typically set at the start of your document so that the entire document is consistent.

 4 Click the *Justify* button on the toolbar   [**Ctrl** + **J**]

> Note: Use the toolbar buttons or keys shown in Figure WP2-22 to select other alignments.

5 Shut off the Select Text mode (click, move, or Shift + F8, Esc)

Your screen should now resemble Figure WP2-23, with the entire document justified (aligned at both margins).

6 Save the document as **LAYOUT4**

7 Close the document window

You can use this procedure to set any alignment anywhere within your document.

PARAGRAPH INDENT

At times, you may want to create an itemized list similar to that shown in Figure WP2-24. Pressing the Tab key indents only the first line of each item, but it will not indent

---

FIGURE WP2-22 ■ ALIGNMENT OPTIONS

To Set Alignment to	By Mouse	By Keyboard
Left-aligned		Ctrl + L
Centered		Ctrl + E
Right-aligned		Ctrl + R
Justified		Ctrl + J

WP

FIGURE WP2-23 ■ JUSTIFIED TEXT

The alignment of the selected text has been set to "justified."

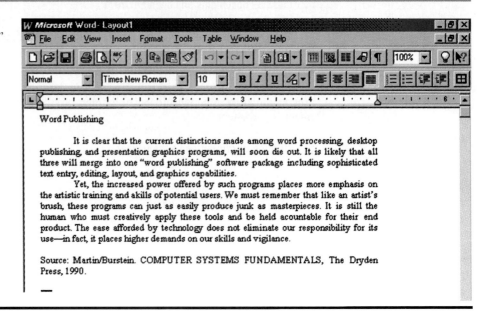

the entire paragraph as shown. Word provides a number of Indent commands for this purpose. As shown in Figure WP2-25, the *Formatting* toolbar includes four buttons related to indenting text, namely, *numbered list, bullet list, increase indent,* and *decrease indent* buttons. **Indent** lets you indent an entire paragraph without changing the margins. Try this example, using Figure WP2-24 as a guide:

FIGURE WP2-24 ■ PARAGRAPH INDENT PRACTICE DOCUMENT

The following criteria should be used when considering new applicants for job openings in your department:

1. The qualified applicant should possess skills in fundamental microcomputer concepts and terminology.
2. The qualified applicant should possess at least a two-year degree in computer science, business, or a related field. An official college transcript will be required before a final decision can be made.
3. He or she should have a working knowledge of basic DOS techniques on an IBM-compatible or Apple Macintosh microcomputer, as well as experience with word processing and spreadsheet applications. The applicant may be required to demonstrate stated skills on our equipment.
4. He or she should have excellent written and oral communication skills.

FIGURE WP2-25 ■ PARAGRAPH INDENT BUTTONS ON THE FORMATTING TOOLBAR

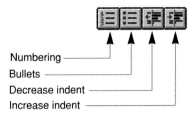

Numbering
Bullets
Decrease indent
Increase indent

STEPS

1 Close any open documents

2 Open a new document (remember to select "Normal" template)

3 Type the first sentence of the text in Figure WP2-24

4 Press ↵ twice after "department:"

Now, invoke the numbered list as follows:

5 Click the *Numbering* button on the toolbar

The insertion point moves to the first tab, and a number "1" automatically appears.

6 Type the sentence after "1." from Figure WP2-24

Notice that the second line of the sentence does not return to the left margin, but is automatically indented.

7 Press ↵ after typing "terminology."

The Enter key adds a hard return and also a second number in the list.

8 Continue to type the remaining items in the list (omitting their numbers) and press ↵ after each complete item

9 When the list is complete, repeat Step 5 to turn off the Numbered List Indent feature

10 Save this document as LAYOUT5

Tip: Use the *Bullets* button (or press Alt + O, N, B) to create bulleted lists.

TABS

Tabs are used to place text in specific positions on each line, typically every half inch. Each time you depress the Tab key, the insertion point moves a half inch to the right.

At times, you may want to remove some tab settings so that pressing the Tab key once would send you directly to a desired location. You may also need to adjust positions of the tabs, or want to change the type of tab available.

Five key options are available for tab settings:

Left Align	Text is aligned at the tab stop
Center	Text is centered over the tab stop
Right Align	Text is right-aligned at the tab stop
Decimal Align	Text is aligned on a decimal point at the tab stop
Bar	A vertical line is inserted through the selected paragraph at the tab stop

These tabs can also be set with a *dot leader* that fills the space up to the tab with a line of dots, dashes, or a solid line. This is useful in such lists as a table of contents, where the eye must move across the line to find a corresponding number.

In Word, tabs are measured relative to the left margin. For example, if the left margin is 1½″, then a **relative tab** of ½″ is one-half inch to its right, or a total of two inches from the page edge.

For practice, you will erase the current default tabs, and then place two tab settings into the document, to prepare for the table shown in Figure WP2-26.

STEPS

1 **Close any open document**

2 **Start a new document window**

3 **Type the first paragraph of Figure WP2-26**

4 **Press ↵ twice after the word "positions:"**

In general, tabs can be changed by menu or through the ruler bar. First, you will use the menu technique to understand the process.

FIGURE WP2-26 ■ TAB PRACTICE DOCUMENT

At pressent, we have the following job openings. Applicants displaying the criteria stated in the job description should be given priority in placement for these positions:

Data Entry	7.50/hr
Word Assistant	10.50
Excel Assistant	11.25
Senior Programmer	15.75
Systems Analyst	25.35

5 **Click _Format_ and then _Tabs_**

A _Tabs_ dialog box appears as shown in Figure WP2-27. Existing tab stops are displayed at the left. Currently, there are no tab stops set. The default tab setting of . 5″ appears in the center. Alignment and leader settings can be adjusted in the middle of the dialog box.

Notice that default tabs are active only to the right of set tab stops. That is, any tab stops you specify will supersede (or have priority over) default tabs to their left. Thus, you do not need to alter default tabs for now. Instead, just proceed to specify new tab stop locations as follows:

6 **In the _Tab Stop Position_ entry box, type 1.5 and then press the ↵ key**

Your Ruler bar should resemble Figure WP2-28a. An "L" marker (for "Left-align tab") appears on the ruler bar at 1½ inches from the left margin. Note, too, that the default "tick" marks are no longer active to the left of the new tab stop. You can now set the second desired tab as follows:

7 **Click _Format_ and then _Tabs_**

8 **Type 5 in the _Tab Stop Position_ entry box but _do not_ press ↵**

This specifies a tab to be set five inches from the left margin. You can now change some tab parameters as follows:

9 **Click the _Decimal_ option in the Alignment box**

10 **Click the #2 (Dot) _Leader_ option in the leader box**   [**Alt** + **2**]

WP

FIGURE WP2-27 ■ **THE _TABS_ DIALOG BOX**

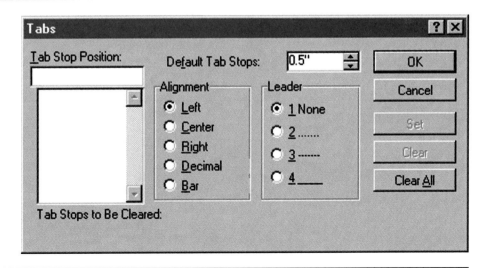

FIGURE WP2-28 ■ **SETTING TABS**

(a) The Ruler bar displays
the set tab stop.
(b) Setting a decimal tab with
dot leader at 5″.

(a)

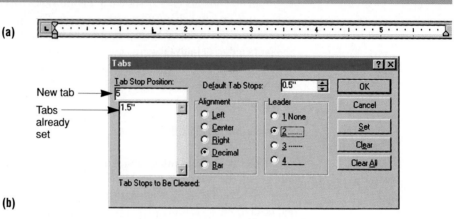

New tab

Tabs
already
set

(b)

Your screen should resemble Figure WP2-28b. Although you could continue to set
tabs, you can accept this tab and close the dialog box now as follows:

11 **Click the _Set_ button**

12 **Click the _OK_ button**

Your Ruler bar should now resemble Figure WP2-29a. Word uses the symbols shown
in Figure WP2-29b to indicate the five basic tab stops that can be set on the ruler
bar. At present, there is a left tab at 1½ inches from the left margin and a decimal tab
at 5 inches.

Once tabs have been set, you can proceed to type and see the effect immediately.
Using Figure WP2-26 as a guide:

FIGURE WP2-29 ■ **DISPLAYING TABS ON THE RULER BAR**

(a) The new tabs are
displayed.
(b) The five basic tab stop
symbols.

(a)

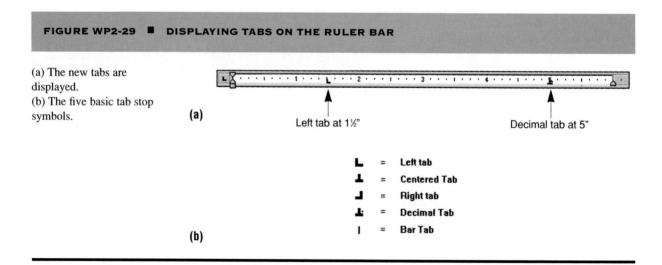

Left tab at 1½"

Decimal tab at 5"

L	=	**Left tab**
⊥	=	**Centered Tab**
⅃	=	**Right tab**
⊥	=	**Decimal Tab**
I	=	**Bar Tab**

(b)

13 Press **Tab** once to move to the first tab column

14 Type **Data Entry**

15 Press **Tab** again to get to the second tab column

16 Type **7.50/hour** and press ↵

Your screen should now resemble Figure WP2-30. Text is left-aligned at 1.5″ from the left margin. The second column has dot leaders and its decimal point is 5″ from the left margin.

17 Enter the remaining lines in the table, pressing **Tab** before each column and ↵ at the end of the line

The completed screen should resemble Figure WP2-26. Note how the decimal points align.

18 Save this document as LAYOUT6

Tabs can be set anywhere in the document. See the appendix or Word's on-line help for further Tab setting operations.

ADJUSTING TABS WITH THE RULER BAR.   Although you can use the *Tabs* dialog box to create or remove all types of tabs, you can also set some types of tabs, and delete them, directly on the Ruler bar. Before you leave this document, if you have a mouse, you can practice this technique as follows:

STEPS

1 Open the LAYOUT6 document if needed

You would now place the insertion point wherever you want the new ruler bar to take effect. In this case,

FIGURE WP2-30 ■ USING THE NEW TAB SETTINGS

Note the dot leader between the first and second tab stops.

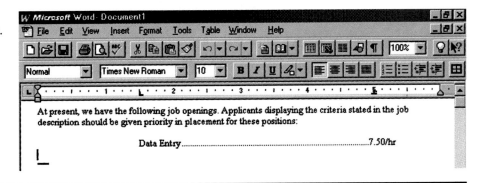

WP

2   **Move to the end of the document (use** **Ctrl** **+** **End** **)**

Now, try setting a new left-align tab stop at 1 inch as follows:

3   **Point to the 1″ mark on the ruler bar as in Figure WP2-31a**

4   **Click the mouse button to set the tab**

Word places an "L" symbol on the ruler bar at the 1″ mark as shown in Figure WP2-31b. Remember that the "L" stands for "Left-aligned tab."

To *delete* an existing tab stop, such as the one at 1½ inches, do the following:

5   **Point to the tab symbol to be deleted, in this case, the "L" at 1½″**

6   **Press and hold the left mouse button and drag the symbol anywhere *below* the ruler bar, as shown in Figure WP2-31c**

7   **Release the mouse button; the tab is gone**

Although left-align tabs are the most common, you may, at times, want to use a different type of tab, such as a center tab. This can also be done with the Ruler bar as follows:

8   **Point to the "L" symbol button at the extreme left of the ruler bar, as shown in Figure WP2-31d**

9   **Click the symbol to change it from "left-align" to "center"**

> **Tip:** Each time you click the symbol button, the tab symbol cycles to the next basic symbol, namely, left-align, center, right-align, decimal, and then back to left-align. You simply stop at the one you want to use.

FIGURE WP2-31 ■ ADJUSTING TABS WITH THE RULER BAR

(a) Point to the new location.
(b) Click to set the tab stop.
(c) Drag a tab off the Ruler bar to delete it.
(d) The tab symbol button can be clicked to change the tab type.
(e) Press the Alt key while clicking to display ruler measurements.

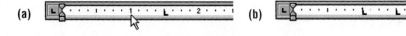

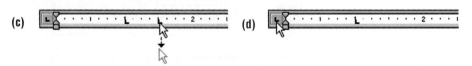

`10` **Now place the tab at the 2″ mark (point and click as before)**

A center tab marker now appears on the bar. You can place any one of the four tab types with this approach. If you need to position tabs more precisely, you can add one more techniques:

`11` **Point to the "L" marker at 1″**

`12` **Depress and hold   Alt   while pressing the left mouse button**

As long as you continue to hold both buttons, the Ruler bar will display exact inch measurements from your tab to the left and right margins, as shown in Figure WP2-31e. You could now move the pointer to the exact desired position. For now,

`13` **Release both buttons to return to the "normal" Ruler bar**

> **Tip: This exact-measurement ruler bar technique can also be used when setting left or right margins.**

`14` **Press ↑ and ↓ to scroll through your document**

Note how the ruler bar changes to reflect the settings at various points in the text.

`15` **Save the document again as LAYOUT6**

`16` **Close the document window**

☑ **CHECKPOINT**

✓   On a new document window, set alignment to *Justified* and both margins to 2″. Type a paragraph of your choice.
✓   Beneath the paragraph, reset tabs as follows: a left-align tab at 3″ and a right-align tab with dot leader at 5″.
✓   Type a price list of five items.
✓   Beneath the list, type a paragraph using the paragraph indent feature.
✓   Save as LAYOUT7. Close the document.

GLOBAL EDITING

Most word processing programs let you locate specific selections of text and, if you want, replace them with others. In word processing, a "selection" of text is called a **text string**—a collection of contiguous characters or words. Such strings may be a few characters long or consist of several neighboring words. The following exercises provide some insight into finding or replacing these strings. First, create a practice document as follows:

WP

1   Launch Word or close any open documents and open a new one

2   Type the text shown in Figure WP2-32

3   Save the document as FIND1

FIND

The **Find** feature allows you to specify a text string, or series of keystrokes, and have the program locate each occurrence of the string in your document. This exercise allows you to search for the word "data" in your document:

1   Move the insertion point to the beginning of the document

> Tip: Searches start at the current insertion point. Moving to the beginning of your document ensures that the entire text will be searched.

2   Click *Edit* and then *Find* for the *Find* dialog box   [**Ctrl** + **F**]

3   Type   **data**   (lowercase)

4   Click the *Find Next* button   [↵]

The program will locate the first occurrence of the word "data" and highlight it.

Note that entering a search string will locate *all* occurrences of the string, even if some of its letters are uppercase (as in "Data" or "DATA"). If you want the search to be restricted to exact matches only ("Data" will only locate "Data"), click the *Match Case* checkbox or press Alt + C.

FIGURE WP2-32 ■   FIND AND REPLACE PRACTICE DOCUMENT

> Data and information are not the same. Data are the raw facts that you input into a computer system. Information, on the other hand, is the result of processing data into a more useful form.
>
> Decisions are never made on data, but rather on the information that can be produced by manipulating the data in a way that helps solve a problem. For example, you can organize data, sort data, select from data, perform math on data, group data, and summarize data.

5 Click the *Find Next* button   [↵]

You could repeat Step 5 to find every occurrence of "data," or stop whenever you want. Note that the insertion point will remain at the most recent match. You can also search *backward* through a file (always from the current insertion point). In this case, to initiate a backward search.

6 Click the *Search* drop-down arrow   [Alt + S]

7 Click *Up* to select it   [↑]

8 Click the *Find Next* button   [↵]

The highlight moves to the previous match.

9 Click the *Cancel* button to close the *Find* dialog box and click to clear last item found [Esc]

> **Tip:** If you can't think of a particular word when typing a document, type zzz (or something similar) as a placemarker and continue. Later, you can search for the zzz's and then type in the words you want in their place.

REPLACE

The **Replace** feature lets you locate a specific text string, or series of keystrokes, and replace it with another string. The new string need not be the same length as the one it replaces. This exercise replaces the word "data" in your document with the word "porcupines":

1 Open FIND1 if needed

2 Move to the beginning of the document

Like Find, Replace starts at the current insertion point.

3 Click *Edit* and then *Replace* for the *Replace* dialog box   [Ctrl + H]

The *Replace* dialog box appears as in Figure WP2-33.

> **Tip:** The previous search string always reappears when you issue a new Find or Replace command.

4 Type data (unless it already appears on screen)

5 Press Tab

FIGURE WP2-33 ■ **THE *REPLACE* DIALOG BOX**

The insertion point moves to the *Replace With* text box.

6 **Type** **porcupines**

7 **Switch the *Search* drop-down list to "All" if needed (click and select)**

Tip: You can use the *Format* or *Special* buttons to identify other codes in the *Search* or *Replace* boxes.

8 **Click the *Replace All* button**

A message appears acknowledging the replacements.

9 **Click the *OK* button to continue**

10 **Click the *Close* button to exit the dialog box**

The program has located and replaced *all* occurrences of the word "data," as in Figure WP2-34. Of course, replacing text is not as simple as it appears. You have to be concerned with the agreement of verbs, vowels, and gender in any changes you produce. You must also watch out for text strings that are part of larger words. For example, replacing "in" with "out" could create words like "outner," "woutdow," and "thout." In

FIGURE WP2-34 ■ REPLACING TEXT

The string "data" has been replaced with "porcupines."

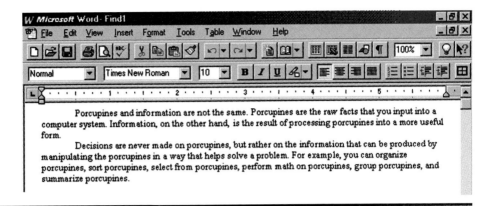

these cases, you can activate the *Whole Words Only* option or search for a whole word like " in " (surrounded by a space on either side to make sure it's a separate word) and replace it with " out " (also surrounded by spaces).

11 **Save this document as FIND2**

You may also select the *Replace* button. This lets you control which strings are replaced and which are not. As the program locates each matching string, it will stop. You can then respond selecting the *Replace Next,* or the *Cancel* button to stop the rest of the routine.

Change *every other* "porcupine" to "hamster" using the replace technique as follows:

12 **Move to the start of the FIND2 document**

13 **Click *Edit* and then *Replace***   [**Ctrl** + **H**]

14 **Type   porcupine   and press   Tab**

15 **Type   hamster**

16 **Click the *Replace* button**

The program stops at the first "porcupine."

Tip: You can click the dialog box's title bar and drag it to a more convenient location.

17 **Click the *Replace* button again to change it to "hamster"**

The program now moves to the next "porcupine."

18 **Click the *Find Next* button to leave "porcupine" and find the next "porcupine"**

19 Repeat Steps 16–18 to move through the entire document, replacing every other match

20 If you reach the end of the document, press ↵ or click *OK* to continue

21 Close the *Replace* dialog box

22 Close the document *without* saving

> **Tip:** You can always use the Undo command (*Edit* menu) to undo your last replace-
> ment(s).

☑ CHECKPOINT

✓ Type Steps 13–18 in the replace procedure onto a new document window.
✓ Replace all "press" with "tap."
✓ Use the *Replace* button to replace the second "tap" with "depress."
✓ Save as FIND3.
✓ Close the document.

CHANGING TEXT ATTRIBUTES

Until now, you have been using the default Word text, modifying it slightly to create enhanced bold or underlined characters. However, if your printer has the capability, you can change the overall typestyle and also enhance text appearance and size to great-ly improve the look of your document.

To prepare for this exercise,

STEPS

1 Launch Word or close any open document

2 Open the LAYOUT2 document

(If you do not have this document, or want to practice, type only the first paragraph of text as in Figure WP2-17, then skip to Step 5.)

3 Position the insertion point at the left margin at the beginning of the second paragraph (to the left of "Yet")

4 Delete the rest of the text on the page

Your screen should resemble the first paragraph of Figure WP2-17. This small amount of text is sufficient to demonstrate the techniques that affect text appearance.

5   **Save the document as FONT1**

SELECTING FONTS

A *font* is a style of type. The initial font is the typestyle in which Word prints normal text. Typically, Word uses a font called "Times New Roman 10 pt" (pt=point size) as an initial font, although any font and size can be used (if it is available to Word and your printer can produce it). A *point* is a typesetting measurement of height equal to about ½ of an inch.

Fonts can be changed within a document. In addition, the default font may be changed for a single document or for all new documents created with a specific printer. See the appendix to change the default font.

CHANGING A FONT WITHIN A DOCUMENT.   Like other Word commands, font changes take effect at the current insertion point and determine the style of text that follows. Assume that you want to change the font from the beginning of the paragraph forward. To change text that is already typed, you must use the select technique.

WP

STEPS

1   **Move the insertion point before the "I" in "It" at the beginning of the paragraph**

2   **Select the entire paragraph (drag the mouse, use   Shift   +   →   , or press   F8   four times)**

3   **Click *Format*, and then *Font* for the *Font* dialog box**

A *Font* dialog box appears as in Figure WP2-35. Font (typeface), style, size, appearance, and a variety of other font changes can be invoked from this box. It opens with the font currently being used at the insertion point highlighted in its *Font* list box. In this case it is the initial font. (The contents of your *Font* list box may differ.)

The *Font* list box is used to select a different typeface. The font selected determines the overall typestyle from the insertion point forward (or until it is changed)—all other text enhancements (in size and appearance) simply provide variations. To select the font face "Arial,"

4   **Drag the scroll box on the vertical scroll bar up until the font *Arial* is in view [PgUp   ]**

5   **Click *Arial* to select it   [↓]**

Note: The box at the lower right always displays a sample of the current font selection.

FIGURE WP2-35 ■ THE *FONT* DIALOG BOX

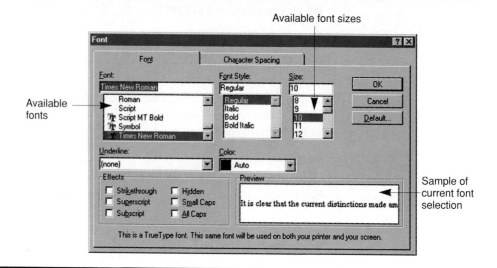

Available font sizes

Available fonts

Sample of current font selection

Fonts typically offer character widths that are either proportionally spaced or a fixed size. The widths of proportionally spaced characters (such as those in this book) vary depending on the letter; an "i" is much narrower than an "m." However, fixed-size text characters all have the same width; an "i" occupies the same width as an "m."

Font size can be changed just as easily. Available point sizes appear in the *Size* drop-down list. (*Note:* The default point size "10" currently appears in the *Size* text box prior to your change.) To change the point size to 14:

6   Scroll if needed and then click *14* in the *Size* list box

7   Click the *OK* button

The text style of the characters displayed on the screen line is now adjusted to reflect your new font choice. In addition, the font indicator on the toolbar now displays the active font.

8   Turn off the select mode (click the mouse, or press an arrow key)

9   Print the document.

Figure WP2-36 displays the printed document with the font change.

10   Save the document as FONT2

> **Tip:** You can also use the Formatting toolbar to change font and size. Simply click the drop-down list arrow and select as needed. By keyboard, use Ctrl + Shift + F for font, or Ctrl + Shift + P for point size. Then select with arrows and the Enter key.

FIGURE WP2-36 ■ PRINTED DOCUMENT WITH FONT CHANGE

Word Publishing

It is clear that the current distinctions made among word processing, desktop publishing, and presentation graphics programs, will soon die out. It is likely that all three will merge into one "word publishing" software package including sophisticated text entry, editing, layout, and graphics capabilities.

REMOVING FONT SETTINGS.   As with other text enhancements, font settings can be changed by selecting the desired text and specifying another font.

ADJUSTING TEXT APPEARANCE

You can also modify the appearance of any text, using procedures similar to underlining or boldfacing. The following exercises examine two techniques: adjusting the appearance of text that already exists in your document and adjusting appearance of new text as it is entered.

ADJUSTING THE APPEARANCE OF EXISTING TEXT.   Most often, you will want to change the appearance of text that you have already entered into your document. This is easily done, as you might expect, with the Select mode. For example, you will now change the appearance of the title "Word Publishing" in the FONT1 document.

STEPS

1 On a clean screen, open FONT1

2 Select the words "Word Publishing"

Remember, to activate the select mode by mouse, simply drag the mouse over "Word Publishing." With the keyboard, use Shift + the right arrow key to select "Word Publishing."

3 Click *Format* and then *Font* for the *Font* dialog box

The *Effects group* box of the *Font* dialog box lists six enhancement selections (samples of each [except the Hidden selection] appear in Figure WP2-37). You now select the enhancement you want to use. For example, to set the title in small capital letters,

FIGURE WP2-37 ■ A TEXT SAMPLER

(a) Effects.
(b) Styles.
(c) Underlines.

~~Strikethrough~~	Regular	Single Underline
Superscript	*Italic*	Double Underline
SMALL CAPS	***Bold Italic***	Dotted Underline
(a)	(b)	(c)

---

4 Click *S<u>m</u>all Caps* in the *Effects group* box

5 Click the *OK* button

6 Turn off the Select mode (by pressing an arrow key or clicking any open area)

Using a similar technique, you will now try double underlining:

7 Select the words "will soon die out" in the first sentence

8 Open the *Font* dialog box (select *F<u>o</u>rmat, <u>F</u>ont* as before)

9 Click the *Underline* drop-down arrow

10 Click *Double*

11 Click the *OK* button

12 Turn off the Select mode (click or move)

13 Save this document as FONT3

ADJUSTING THE APPEARANCE OF NEW TEXT. Using a technique similar to boldfacing or underlining, you can also adjust text appearance as you type. In this case, you invoke the text change, type the text, and then return to normal text. For example, you will now type some italicized bold text at the end of the document.

STEPS

1 Open FONT3 if needed

2 Move to the end of the document (**Ctrl** + **End**)

3 Press ↵ to leave an extra blank line

4 Click *Format* and then *Font* for the *Font* dialog box

5 Click *Bold Italic* in the *Font Style* box

6 Click the *OK* button

Note that the insertion point itself appears in bold italic.

7 Type   **This is bold and italicized text.**

Tip: You can also click the *Bold* and *Italic* toolbar buttons on the Formatting toolbar.

The new text will appear bold and italicized. You must now return the appearance set-ting to normal so that additional text will not be affected.

8 Open the *Font* dialog box

9 Click *Regular* in the *Font Style* box

10 Click the *OK* button

Tip: You can also click the *Bold* and *Italic* toolbar buttons to turn off each enhancement.

11 Resave this document as FONT3

☑ CHECKPOINT

✓ Open a document of your choice or type a few sentences.
✓ Change the initial document font to a different style and size. Save the document as TEXT1.
✓ Open TEXT1. Change the text appearance of the first sentence to italic.
✓ Change the size of the second sentence to 8 pt.
✓ Save the document as TEXT2.

USING AUXILIARY TOOLS

Word offers several useful auxiliary programs—a spelling checker, a thesaurus, and a grammar checker. These programs are not part of the main word processor but can be in-voked on command through the *Tools* menu or the standard toolbar.

WP

SPELLING CHECK

Word's **spelling check** enables you to check each word in your document for correct spelling. It is especially useful if you are a poor speller or typist, because the spelling checker will identify most typographical errors and misspelled words.

To prepare for this exercise, do the following:

STEPS

1 Launch Word or close any open document

2 In a new document window, type the text in Figure WP2-38

Make sure to type all six errors as they appear in the figure. Although you would not deliberately make these errors, they will allow you to practice some spelling check techniques. Note that the AutoCorrect feature has underlined the potential errors with red, wavy lines.

3 Save the document as WPSPELL1

4 Move to the start of the document

 5 Click *Tools* and then *Spelling*   [**F7**]

After a few moments, the *Spelling* dialog box appears, as shown in Figure WP2-39.

Word will now check each word in your document against its list. The first word that does not appear in its list will be highlighted, as shown in Figure WP2-39. The box displays some suggested spellings in its *Change To* and *Suggestions* list box—one of which may be the spelling you desire.

The *Spelling* command buttons will perform the following functions (Remember, to select a button by mouse, click it. With the keyboard, press the Alt key and the underline letter of the button's command.):

Command Button	Function
Change	Replaces the highlighted word in the document with the word in the *Change To* text box. To change the word in the *Change To* text box to a different word from the *Suggestions* list box, click the desired word or press the Down arrow key to move the highlight to the desired word.
Change All	Changes all occurrences of the word to the new word.
Ignore	Skips the highlighted word once without correcting it. The program will highlight this word again if it appears later in the document.

FIGURE WP2-38 ■ **SPELLING PRACTICE DOCUMENT (WITH SIX ERRORS)**

Make sure you type these six errors: exmaple, speling, typ, am am, prakticing, learnhow

This is an exmaple of word's speling check tool. I don't really typ this poorly. I am am only prakticing so that I can learnhow to use it.

FIGURE WP2-39 ■ THE SPELLING CHECK WINDOW

The spelling check has located a misspelled word and offers suggestions for change.

Word highlighted in document

Suggestions

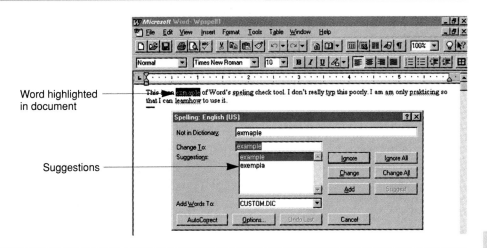

Command Button	Function
Ignore All	Skips the highlighted word now and for the remainder of the document. This is usually chosen for proper names that are not contained in the list.
Add	Adds a word to spelling check's word list. This is useful for words that are used often. You should not attempt to add words to the list if you are not using your own computer system.
Suggest	List word suggestions in the *Suggestions* list box.

Examine Figure WP2-39. Notice that "exmaple" is highlighted at the top of the screen and that the correct spelling, "example," is listed in the *Change To* box.

6 **Click the *Change* button to replace with "example"**

The next incorrect word, "speling," is highlighted. The program offers a half-dozen or so alternatives in its *Suggestions* list box. The correct choice happens to appear in the *Change To* box. If it didn't, you could click the desired word or press the arrow keys to move to it. For now,

7 **Click the *Change* button to replace and move to the next misspelling**

The word "typ" is now highlighted, but the desired spelling is *not* in the *Change To* box. To select it,

8 **Click *type* in the *Suggestions* list box to select it**   [**Tab** , ↓]

9 **Click the *Change* button**   [↵]

Your screen should now resemble Figure WP2-40. Here is a different probable error—two words in a row spelled exactly the same, without any punctuation between them. The spelling check can identify a common typing error—repeated words.

WP

FIGURE WP2-40 ■ IDENTIFYING A REPEATED WORD

The spelling check has found a repeated word.

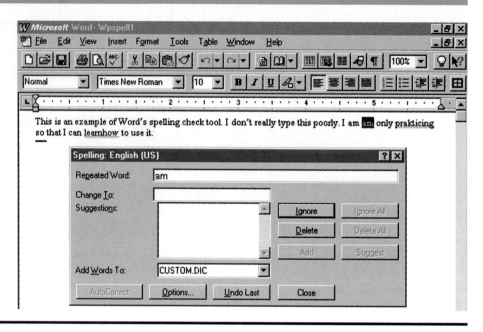

10 Click the *Delete* button to delete one *am*

11 Click the *Change* button to replace with *practicing*

Your screen should now resemble Figure WP2-41, highlighting "learnhow." This is clearly a typographical error. To fix it,

12 Press ← to move the insertion point before the "h" in "how" in the *Change To* text box

13 Press Spacebar to separate the words

14 Click the *Change* button   [↵]

Finding no more incorrect words, a "complete" message now appears.

15 Click the *OK* button to leave the spelling check   [↵]

16 Save the corrected document as WPSPELL2

The spelling check is a useful auxiliary to word processing, but it is not infallible. It will find most mistakes, but it will not look for capitalization, nor will it find words that are spelled correctly *but used wrong,* as in "Eye herd ewe wore hear" instead of "I heard you were here." *You* are still responsible for checking your own documents for proper usage, spelling, and grammar.

FIGURE WP2-41 ■ **EDITING AN ERROR**

The spelling check also allows you to edit the text if you want to correct a typographical error.

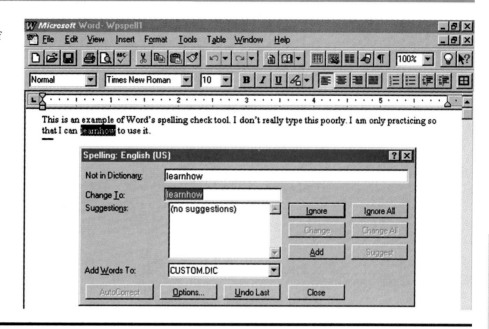

THESAURUS

An electronic **thesaurus** suggests synonyms—words with similar meaning—to the one at the current insertion point. Some programs also list antonyms—words with opposite meaning—as well. A thesaurus operates much like a spelling check, but allows you to examine different nuances or (as the thesaurus itself suggests) different hints, shades, and subtleties of meaning. In this way, it enhances your vocabulary and allows you to express your thoughts more precisely (or should we say accurately, exactly, or directly). To prepare for this exercise, do the following:

STEPS

1 Launch Word or close any open document

2 Open a new document window

3 Type the sentence, Too many cooks spoil the broth.

You will now use this well-known quote to examine the Thesaurus feature.

4 Place the insertion point on the word "many"

To open the Thesaurus dialog box,

5 Click *Tools* and then *Thesaurus*   [**Shift**   +   **F7**   ]

After a few moments, the thesaurus will present a dialog box resembling Figure WP2-42. Notice that the thesaurus displays the highlighted word in two places: in the document and in the *Looked Up* text box. Procedures for word selection and replacement are described next.

Try some of the following Thesaurus commands. Examine Figure WP2-42. To select and replace with the word "myriad" from the thesaurus.

STEPS

1 Point to *myriad* in the *Synonym* list box   [**Alt** + **S**]

2 Click *myriad* to select it   [**↓**]

3 Click the *Replace* button   [**Alt** + **R**]

The word "many" is replaced by "myriad" on the screen. Now, use the thesaurus to replace "cooks."

4 Move the insertion point to *cooks*

5 Click *Tools* and then *Thesaurus*   [**Shift** + **F7**]

No synonyms are suggested for "cooks" other than "cook." At this point, you can try examining related words as follows:

6 Double-click *Related Words* in the *Meanings* list box   [**↵**]

FIGURE WP2-42 ■ THE THESAURUS WINDOW

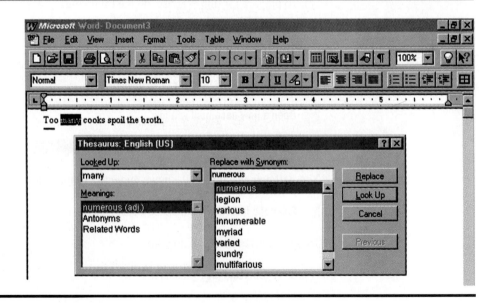

You can now select "Chef" from the synonym list as follows:

7   **Repeat Steps 1-3, this time replacing "cooks" with "chef"**

8   **Type an** **s** **onto "chef" in the document**

9   **Move insertion point to "spoil"**

10   **Invoke the thesaurus**

11   **Click *wreck***

12   **Click the *Replace* button**

13   **Change the word "broth" on your own**

14   **Close the document *without* saving it**

The sentence might now read, "Too numerous chefs wreck the consommé." Obviously, a thesaurus can be overused, but it can also offer helpful suggestions when you want your vocabulary to be precise.

Explore the techniques you have learned in this chapter. Create a few documents, change margins, tabs, and spacing, and try out the intricacies of the spelling check and thesaurus until you are satisfied with your mastery of each.

GRAMMAR CHECK

Word also includes a **grammar check**—an auxiliary program that checks for grammatical errors in your writing. To prepare for this exercise,

STEPS

1   **Launch Word or close any open document**

2   **Open a new document window if needed**

Type the following sentence with all its mistakes, exactly as it appears:

3   **Type**   **is the best things in lif free.**

Be sure to type "is" without a capital, misspell "life" (without the "e"), and place a period at the end of the sentence instead of a question mark. This is enough text to demonstrate the basic operation of the grammar checker.

4   **Save this document as GRAMMAR1**

> **Tip:** It is a good idea to save documents before changing them with spelling check, thesaurus, or grammar check. You may want to return to the original in the future.

WP

To start the grammar check,

5 Click _Tools_ and then _Grammar_

A *Spelling Check* dialog box should appear. The grammar check has highlighted the first writing problem, "lif," and has invoked the spelling check to allow you to fix it. As you normally would in the *Spelling Check* dialog box,

6 Change "lif" to "life"

Your screen should now resemble Figure WP2-43. The *Grammar Check* dialog box has identified a lack of subject-verb agreement as the next problem; that is, you have mixed plural and singular references. The program offers two suggestions: either change "is" to "are" or change "things" to "thing." Before solving this problem, let's look at some of the options offered in the *Grammar Check* dialog box:

- The *Help* button invokes a Help window. After reading it, you will have to close the window to continue.
- *Ignore* lets you ignore the suggestion and move to the next error.
- *Next Sentence* skips the current sentence entirely and continues at the start of the next sentence.
- *Change* lets you implement the suggested correction.
- *Ignore Rule* tells the program to stop checking for this type of error in the document (very dangerous to shut off).
- *Explain* presents you with an explanation of the error. After reading it, you will have to close the resultant dialog box to continue.

FIGURE WP2-43 ■ THE *GRAMMAR CHECK* DIALOG BOX

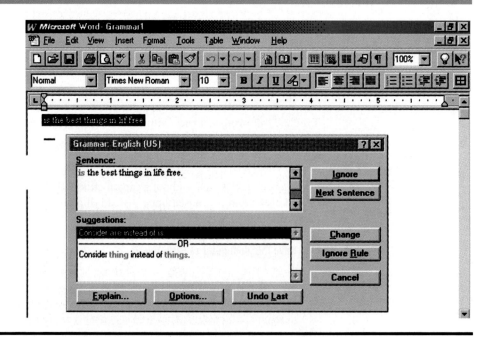

- *Options* allows you to adjust the type of writing style you want to check.
- *Undo Last* cancels the last grammar change you made.
- *Cancel* exits the grammar check.

For now,

7 Click *Change* (or press **Alt** + **C**) to accept the first suggestion

The next problem is capitalization.

8 Click *Change* (or press **Alt** + **C**) to accept changing "are" to "Are"

When the document is completely checked, a set of readability statistics appears on the screen. It is interesting to examine the word count and other statistics about your document. When you are done,

9 Click the *OK* button, or press ↵ to return to your document

10 Save the corrected document as GRAMMAR2

11 Close the GRAMMAR2 document and exit Word (if desired)

Feel free to explore grammar check's features on your own.

☑ CHECKPOINT

- ✓ Type a paragraph with at least ten spelling or typographical errors; save it as WPSPELL3.
- ✓ Use spelling check to correct all the errors, and save the corrected version as WPSPELL4.
- ✓ Use the thesaurus to change at least ten words to their synonyms; save as WPSPELL5. Close the document.
- ✓ Create a sentence with three grammatical errors and then use grammar check to correct them.
- ✓ Save as WPGRAM1.

SUMMARY

- The *Find File* dialog box offers a number of useful file management commands, including *Copy, Delete, Print, Create Directory, Preview,* and *Open.*
- The Show/Hide feature displays normally hidden codes in the current document. This feature can be used to locate and delete unwanted formatting or text enhancements.
- Word commands and enhancements take effect at the insertion point where they were issued.
- A text selection is a segment of contiguous text. Select commands can be used to move, copy, delete, or enhance text selections. Text enhancements include centering, bolding, underlining, and shifting to uppercase and lowercase letters.
- Layout refers to the arrangement of text and white space on a page. Layout changes include margins, tabs, spacing, alignment, and paragraph indent.
- Alignment neatly arranges words at a margin. The most popular alignment options are left and fully justified. Margins that are not aligned are called *ragged.*

- Tabs are used to position text in specific locations on each line. Tabs can be set an absolute distance from the left margin, left, center, right, decimal, or bar.
- The Indent feature allows an entire paragraph to be indented without changing the margins elsewhere in a document.
- The Find feature locates each occurrence of a specific text string in a document. The Replace feature adds the ability to replace each found text string with another one.
- A font change refers to a change in type style. Text appearance and size changes can also be made to improve the look of a document.
- Auxiliary tools include spelling check, thesaurus, and grammar check. The spelling check identifies words that might be misspelled. Thesaurus suggests synonyms for words selected by the user. The grammar check identifies grammar errors and suggests corrections for a selection of text or the entire document.

KEY TERMS

Shown in parentheses are the page numbers on which key terms are boldfaced.

Alignment (WP96)	Relative tab (WP100)	Tab (WP100)
Find (WP106)	Replace (WP107)	Text string (WP105)
Grammar check (WP121)	Select (WP80)	Thesaurus (WP119)
Indent (WP98)	Selection enhancement	
Justified text (WP96)	(WP86)	
Layout (WP90)	Spelling check (WP116)	

QUIZ

TRUE/FALSE

___ 1. The *Open* dialog box is invoked by typing **OPEN**.
___ 2. The Save in box is found in the *Open* dialog box.
___ 3. The grammar check suggests synonyms for words selected by the user.
___ 4. In the Show/Hide screen, a dot indicates a tab.
___ 5. Text enhancements can be canceled by specifying a new enhancement in the same place.
___ 6. Text selections are identified on the screen through the use of highlighted text.
___ 7. A selection enhancement is used to change the format of text that is about to be typed on the screen.
___ 8. Word can change selections of text to uppercase and lowercase letters.
___ 9. The default setting for line spacing is single spacing.
___ 10. Indenting an entire paragraph is invoked with the Tab key.

MULTIPLE CHOICE

___ 11. Which command allows a file to be viewed without opening it?
    a. Zoom
    b. Copy
    c. Select
    d. Preview

___ 12. The Show/Hide feature can reveal all but which one of the following?
    a. Hard returns
    b. Tabs
    c. Soft returns
    d. Spaces

___ 13. A segment of contiguous text is called a
    a. Selection
    b. Hidden code
    c. Document
    d. Highlight

___ 14. "Cut and Paste" is the word processing function that _____ a selection.
    a. copies
    b. deletes
    c. selects
    d. moves

___ 15. When a selection is highlighted on the screen, invoking the Save As command will do which of the following?
    a. Save the highlighted selection to disk
    b. Open a selection from disk
    c. Save the entire document to disk
    d. Produce an error message

___ 16. Which one of these is *not* an alignment setting in Word?
    a. Left align
    b. Mid align
    c. Justify
    d. Right align

___ 17. The left-align style is also known as
    a. Ragged left
    b. Ragged right
    c. Left indented
    d. Completely justified

___ 18. Which type of tabs are measured with reference to the left page *edge?*
    a. Left-aligned tabs
    b. Decimal tabs
    c. Right-aligned tabs
    d. None of these

___ 19. A collection of characters specified in a Find or Replace function is called a
    a. Revealed code
    b. Layout feature
    c. Dot leader
    d. Text string

___ 20. Which of the following series of words will be considered to be entirely correct by the spelling check?
    a. I went to to the store.
    b. He soar The plain fly in thee ski.
    c. She heard a loudnoise.
    d. We waited for the airplain to land.

MATCHING

Select the lettered item from Figure WP2-A that best matches each phrase below:

FIGURE WP2-A ■ MATCHING EXERCISE

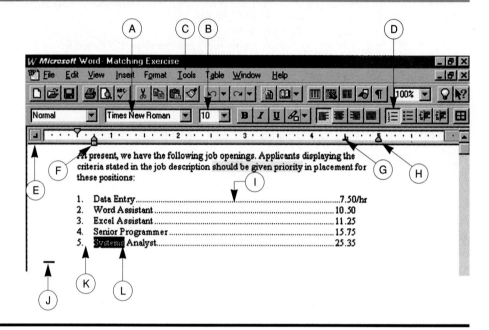

___ 21. Clicking this item invokes a numbered list.
___ 22. This item indicates, and can modify, the right margin setting.
___ 23. This feature is caused by tabbing to a dot leader tab stop.
___ 24. This is displayed when you press [F8] twice or double-click.
___ 25. A graphic feature that indicates the end of a document.
___ 26. This section indicates the current font setting.
___ 27. This section changes the type of tab stop to be set.
___ 28. This item indicates the position of a decimal tab.
___ 29. This can be used to invoke the spelling check or thesaurus.
___ 30. This feature will change both the left margin and indent markers.

ANSWERS

True/False: 1. F; 2. T; 3. F; 4. T; 5. T; 6. T; 7. F; 8. T; 9. T; 10. F
Multiple Choice: 11. d; 12. c; 13. a; 14. d; 15. a; 16. b; 17. b; 18. d; 19. d; 20. b
Matching: 21. d; 22. h; 23. i; 24.1; 25. j; 26. a; 27. e; 28. g; 29. c; 30. f

EXERCISES

I. OPERATIONS

Provide the Word actions required to do each of the following operations. For each operation, assume a system with a hard disk and a disk in Drive A. Further assume that the default drive has been set to Drive A earlier, and that a file called NOTES1 is on the data disk. If you want to verify each command, type a few words in Word and then save it as a document called NOTES1 on your disk before you begin to answer these questions.

1. See a list of files using the *Open* dialog box for the disk in Drive A.

2. Copy the NOTES1 file to a file called NOTES2.DOC.

3. Copy the NOTES2 file to TESTNOTE.DOC.

4. Delete the TESTNOTE.DOC file.

5. Open the NOTES1 file onto the work screen.

6. Activate the Show/Hide screen, and then exit it.

7. Underline any text with the Select Underline command.

8. Move the underlined text to the bottom of your document.

9. Remove the underlining from the text.

10. Change the spacing of the entire document to double-spaced.

11. Change the margins to Left 2″ and Right 1.5″.

12. Print the document.

13. Save the document as NOTES1.

14. Exit Word.

II. COMMANDS

Describe clearly what command is initiated or what is accomplished in Word by the actions described below. Assume that each exercise part is independent of any previous parts.

1. Highlighting a filename in the *Open* dialog box

2. Clicking the toolbar button that displays a paragraph symbol (¶)

3. Pressing the F8 key or double-clicking "EXT"

4. Clicking the "scissors" toolbar button or pressing the Ctrl + X keys

5. Dragging the rectangular ruler marker 1″ to the right

6. Pressing the Ctrl + 2 keys

7. Clicking the even-lined toolbar button or pressing the Ctrl + J keys

8. Clicking the numbered toolbar button or pressing the Alt + O and N, Alt + N keys

9. Clicking the leftmost portion of the ruler bar

10. Clicking the toolbar button that displays "ABC" and a checkmark, or pressing the F7 key

III. APPLICATIONS

Perform the following operations using your computer system. You will need a hard drive or network with Word on it. You will also need your data disk for retrieval and for storing the results of this exercise. In a few words, tell how you accomplished each operation and describe its result. Save the document after each operation is completed so that you can always return to these exercises later. *Note:* Of the six application exercises, each pair relates to school, home, and business respectively.

APPLICATION 1: ADJUSTING THE LETTER OF INQUIRY

1. Boot your computer; start Windows and launch the Word program.

2. Open the WORK1-1A document you prepared in Chapter 1, or type it now by following Application 1, Exercise 2 in the previous chapter. If you just typed the document, save it now as WORK1-1A, changing the default drive as needed.

3. Use the *Open* dialog box to copy this document to a file called WORK2-1.DOC on your disk.

4. Fully justify the entire document.

5. Remove the bold enhancement from "Sand Castle Sculpting" in the first paragraph so that the text appears in normal typeface.

6. Use the Select mode ("EXT") to move the first paragraph beneath the second paragraph. Fix the spacing between the paragraphs if needed.

7. Use the bulleted list technique to bullet each paragraph at the left margin and indent each paragraph one tab stop after the bullet.

8. Using the Select mode, change "Sand Castle Sculpting" to all uppercase letters.

9. Move to the start of the first paragraph and change the line spacing to double-spacing for the first paragraph only.

10. Change the margins for the entire letter to Left = 1″ and Right = 1″.

11. Change the first tab stop to .8″ after the left margin.

12. Change the entire document to Arrus BT font with a type size of 12 points (or use another font and size if these are not available).

13. Use the thesaurus tool to change the following words in the letter to their synonyms: *investigating, pertinent, especially.*

14. Use the spelling check and grammar check tools to check your work. Make any appropriate changes.

15. Resave the modified document as WORK2-1.DOC, print a copy of it, and then close the document window.

APPLICATION 2: ADJUSTING THE RESEARCH PROJECT PROPOSAL

1. Boot your computer; start Windows and launch the Word program.

2. Open the WORK1-2A document you prepared in Chapter 1, or type it now by following Application 2, Exercise 2 in the previous chapter. If you just typed the document, save it now as WORK1-2A, changing the default drive as needed.

3. Use the *Open* dialog box to copy this document to a file called WORK2-2.DOC on your disk.

4. Replace all occurrences of "E." with "Edward." and all occurrences of "C." with "Charles."

5. Remove the bold enhancement from the centered title at the top of the page so that the text appears in normal typeface.

6. Use the Select mode ("EXT") to move the three bottom entries written by Parker to the top of the list. Fix the spacing after the top three entries if needed.

7. Use the numbered list technique to number each entry at the left margin and indent each entry one tab stop in after the number.

8. Using the Select mode, change the title to initial capital letters only so it reads "Proposal for Course Research."

9. Double space the first paragraph only.

10. Change the margins for the entry list only (after the first paragraph) to Left = 2″ and Right = 2″.

11. At the point where you changed margins in Exercise 10, change the first tab stop to .75″ after the left margin.

12. Change the three lines of text at the top left of the document to Bookman Old Style with a type size of 16 points. (Use another font and size if these are not available.)

13. Use the thesaurus tool to change the following words to their synonyms: *best, summarize, comprehensiveness.*

14. Use the spelling check and grammar check tools to check your work. Make any appropriate changes.

15. Resave the modified document as WORK2-2, print a copy of it, and then close the document window.

APPLICATION 3: ADJUSTING THE LETTER OF COMPLAINT

1. Boot your computer; start Windows and launch the Word program.

2. Open the WORK1-3A document you prepared in Chapter 1, or type it now by following Application 3, Exercise 2 in the previous chapter. If you just typed the document, save it now as WORK1-3A, changing the default drive as needed.

3. Use the *Open* dialog box to copy this document to a file called WORK2-3.DOC on your disk.

4. Set only the first paragraph to fully justified alignment.

5. Remove the underline enhancements from the text in the first paragraph so that the text appears in normal typeface.

6. Use the Select mode ("EXT") to move the address line "Customer Relations" beneath the "Pencils by Mail Corporation" line.

7. Use the numbered list technique to number each paragraph in the body of the letter at the left margin and indent each paragraph one tab stop in after the number.

8. Using the Select mode, change "Pencils by Mail Corporation" in the address and "one dozen ten-foot pencils" in the first paragraph to all uppercase letters.

9. Move to the start of the first paragraph and change the line spacing to double spacing for only the two paragraphs in the body of the letter.

10. Change the margins for the entire letter to Left = 1″ and Right = 1.5″.

11. At the same point you adjusted the margins in Exercise 10, change the first tab stop to .4″ after the left margin.

12. Change the entire document to Century Gothic font with a type size of 11 points. (Use another font and size if these are not available.)

13. Use the thesaurus tool to change a few words of your choice in the letter to their synonyms.

14. Use the spelling check and grammar check tools to check your work. Make any appropriate changes.

15. Resave the modified document as WORK2-3, print a copy of it, and then close the document window.

APPLICATION 4: ADJUSTING THE VIDEO LIST

1. Boot your computer; start Windows and launch the Word program.

2. Open the WORK1-4A document you prepared in Chapter 1, or type it now by following Application 4, Exercise 2 in the previous chapter. If you just typed the document, save it now as WORK1-4A, changing the default drive as needed.

3. Use the *Open* dialog box to copy this document to a file called WORK2-4.DOC on your disk.

4. Use the Replace command to change tape volumes of "B" to "E." Do not change any other occurrence of the letter "B."

5. Remove the bold enhancement from the title so that the text appears in normal typeface.

6. Use the Select mode ("EXT") to move the text block containing all six entries for TAPE "A" to the bottom of the list.

7. Use the numbered list technique to number each entry at the left margin and indent each paragraph one tab stop in after the number.

8. Using the Select mode, change *all* the entries to uppercase letters.

9. Move to the start of the first entry and change the line spacing to one and one-half spacing for the rest of the document.

10. Change the margins for the entire letter to Left = .5″ and Right = .5″.

11. At the same position as the margin change in Exercise 10, change the first tab stop to .6″ after the left margin.

12. Change the centered title at the top of the document to Desdemona font with a type size of 14 points. (Use another font and size if these are not available.)

13. Use the thesaurus tool to change a few words of your choice in the letter to their synonyms.

14. Use the spelling check tool to check your work. Make any appropriate changes.

15. Resave the modified document as WORK2-4, print a copy of it, and then close the document window.

APPLICATION 5: ADJUSTING THE JOB INQUIRY LETTER

1. Boot your computer; start Windows and launch the Word program.

2. Open the WORK1-5A document you prepared in Chapter 1, or type it now by following Application 5, Exercise 2 in the previous chapter. If you just typed the document, save it now as WORK1-5A, changing the default drive as needed.

3. Use the *Open* dialog box to copy this document to a file called WORK2-5.DOC on your disk.

4. Set the alignment of the text in the body of the letter to justified.

5. Remove the bold enhancement from the text in the third paragraph so that the text appears in normal typeface.

6. Use the Select mode ("EXT") to move the second paragraph beneath the third paragraph. Fix the spacing between the paragraphs if needed.

7. Use the numbered list technique to number each paragraph at the left margin and indent each paragraph one tab stop in after the number.

8. Using the Select mode, change "Mar-Park Consulting Services" to all uppercase letters.

9. Move to the start of the first paragraph and change the line spacing to double spacing for the rest of the document.

10. Change the margins for the entire letter to Left = 1.5″ and Right = 1.5″.

11. Change the first tab stop to 1″ after the left margin.

12. Change the three lines of centered text at the top of the document to a different font of your choice with a type size of 16 points. (Use another point size if 16 is not available.)

13. Use the thesaurus tool to change a few words of your choice in the letter to their synonyms.

14. Use the spelling check and grammar check tools to check your work. Make any appropriate changes.

15. Resave the modified document as WORK2-5, print a copy of it, and then close the document window.

APPLICATION 6: ADJUSTING THE EMPLOYER RESPONSE LETTER

1. Boot your computer; start Windows and launch the Word program.

2. Open the WORK1-6A document you prepared in Chapter 1, or type it now by following Application 6, Exercise 2 in the previous chapter. If you just typed the document, save it now as WORK1-6A, changing the default drive as needed.

3. Use the *Open* dialog box to copy this document to a file called WORK2-6.DOC on your disk.

4. Replace all occurrences of "We" with "I" in the document.

5. Remove the bold enhancement from "cliff diver" and the underline enhancement from "Eiffel Tower" so that the text appears in normal typeface.

6. Use the Select mode ("EXT") to delete the second paragraph entirely. Fix the spacing between the paragraphs if needed.

7. Use the bulleted list technique to add bullets to each of the two remaining paragraphs and indent each paragraph one tab stop in after the bullet.

8. Using the Select mode, change "Employment Times" in the first paragraph to all uppercase letters.

9. Move to the start of the first paragraph and change the line spacing to double spacing for the rest of the document.

10. Change the margins for the entire letter to Left = 2″ and Right = 2″.

11. Change the first tab stop to .6″ after the left margin.

12. Change the top three lines of address to Playbill font with a type size of 20. (Use another font and size if these are not available.)

13. Use the thesaurus tool to change the following words to their synonyms in the document: response, inquiries, convenient.

14. Use the spelling check and grammar check tools to check your work. Make any appropriate changes.

15. Resave the modified document as WORK2-6, print a copy of it, and then close the document window.

MASTERY CASES

The following mastery cases allow you to demonstrate how much you have learned about this software. Each case describes a fictitious problem or need that can be solved using the skills you have learned in this chapter. Although minimum acceptable outcomes are specified, you are expected and encouraged to design your response (files, data, lists) in ways that display your personal mastery of the software. Feel free to show off your skills. Use real data from your own experience in your solution, although you may also fabricate data if needed.

These mastery cases allow you to display your ability to

- Use the Open feature to copy documents.
- Use the Select feature to modify existing text.
- Adjust margins and tabs.
- Change text font and size attributes.
- Use auxiliary tools to check spelling and grammar.

CASE 1: REVISING A LETTER

Your instructor has returned the letter you wrote in Chapter 1 and has asked you to present your critique in a numbered list, rather than letter form. Adjust margins and tabs appropriately and redo the letter as required. Change the font and size for best effect. Make sure spelling and grammar are perfect before saving it as a new document. Print the new list.

CASE 2: REVISING A RÉSUMÉ

Redo the one-page résumé you created in Chapter 1 to make use of more effective font styles and sizes. Add bullets to each item in any list. Check your spelling before you save and print it as a new document.

CASE 3: REVISING A MEMORANDUM

Revise the memo you created in Chapter 1 into an 8½" x 11" poster to remind staff of the meeting. Select larger and more appropriate fonts and margins. Move text into a bulleted outline form to attract attention. Center important times and dates for emphasis. Save as a new document and print the poster.

WP

3

ADVANCED WORD PROCESSING: MULTIPAGES, MULTIDOCUMENTS, AUTOMATION, GRAPHICS, AND SHARING FILES

OUTLINE

OVERVIEW

PREPARING FOR THIS CHAPTER

MODULE 1: MANAGING MULTIPAGE
   DOCUMENTS
Soft Page Breaks
Hard Page Breaks
Headers and Footers
Page Numbering
Page Jumps

MODULE 2: WORKING WITH MULTI-
   DOCUMENT WINDOWS
Switching Between Document
   Windows
Arranging Document Windows
Resizing a Document Window

MODULE 3: MERGING FILES
Identifying the Basic Merge
   Documents
Creating the Main Document
Editing the Data Source
Merge—Combining the Files

MODULE 4: AUTOMATING COMMANDS
   WITH MACROS
Creating a Macro
Invoking a Macro
Editing a Macro

MODULE 5: FOOTNOTES AND
   ENDNOTES
Creating a Footnote
The *Note Options* Dialog Box
Editing a Footnote
Deleting a Footnote

MODULE 6: ORGANIZING DATA WITH
   OUTLINES AND SORTS
Preparing an Outline
Editing the Outline
Modifying the Outline Format
Sorting

MODULE 7: GRAPHICS AND TABLES
Borders and Horizontal Lines
Creating Tables in Word
Adding Graphics Boxes

MODULE 8: SHARING INFORMATION
   AMONG PROGRAMS
Exporting and Importing
Exporting Files from Word
Importing Files into Word
Linking Data from Other Office
   Applications

OBJECTIVES

After completing the modules in this chapter, you will be able to do any or all of the following:

1 Demonstrate techniques for managing multipage documents, including page breaks, page numbering, and page jumps.

2 Create and modify headers, footers, and page numbers.

3 Work with multidocuments.

4 Create and merge main documents and data sources to create individualized letters.

5 Explain the purpose of macros and describe the procedures for creating, editing, and invoking them.

6 Create and modify text outlines and sorting.

7 Draw lines and boxes using the graphics and table features and add graphic figures and captions to text.

8 Export files from and import files into Word.

OVERVIEW

This chapter provides an advanced set of word processing techniques, including managing larger documents, using multiple documents simultaneously, merging files, creating outlines, automating commands, using tables and graphics, and sharing files. Each procedure is presented as a separate module that can be studied independently.

Using files available on disk, and others created by you, the chapter first examines features related to multipage documents, such as automatic headers, footers, and page numbering. Techniques for using multiple documents are presented next, including copying between files and merging. Creating, using, and editing macros are introduced next, followed by procedures for managing footnotes and outlines. The chapter concludes with the advanced word processing procedures involved in creating tables, combining text and graphics, and sharing files.

PREPARING FOR THIS CHAPTER

This text includes a separate data disk that contains files for use with this chapter. These files reduce the amount of keystroking you must do. If you do not have this disk (or want extra practice), you can create the files yourself.

The files must first be copied to your data disk so they will be available for use. Check with your instructor or lab technician for the proper technique for your system. For example, if the files are already stored on your LAN, you may be able to copy them directly to your disk (in this case, follow your lab's instructions). If you have two disk drives, you can copy the files from the Dryden File disk (B:\WORD*.*) directly to your data disk (A:). If you have only one disk drive and a hard-disk drive, you will have to copy the files using the technique that follows, summarized in Figure WP3-1.

STEPS

1 Start Windows if needed

First, you must copy the files from the Dryden File disk's Word subdirectory to your hard-disk drive as follows:

2 Double-click the *My Computer* group icon to open its window

3 Put the Dryden file disk in Drive A

4 In the *My Computer* window, double-click the *3½ floppy (A:)* icon

5 In the 3½ Floppy (A:) window, click the *Word* folder icon

6 Click *Edit, Copy*   [**Ctrl** + **C**]

FIGURE WP3-1 ■ PREPARING THE FILES FOR USE

(a) Click the *Word* folder in Drive A.
(b) Select *Edit, Select All* in the *Word* folder.

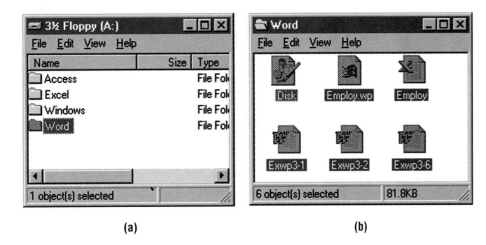

(a)   (b)

You have now told Windows to copy the contents of Drive A's *Word* folder. You can now specify into which drive it should be copied.

7 On the taskbar, click the *My Computer* button to reopen its window

8 In the My Computer window, double-click the *Drive C* icon to open its window

9 In the Drive C window's menu bar, click *Edit, Paste*   [**Ctrl** + **V**]

The files are now copied into a new *Word* folder on Drive C, which appears within the Drive C window. You can now transfer the files onto your own data disk.

10 Remove the Dryden disk and place your disk in Drive A.

11 In the Drive C window, double-click the *Word* folder to open its window.

12 In the *Word* folder's menu bar, select *Edit, Select All*   [**Ctrl** + **A**]

13 In the same menu, select *Edit, Copy*   [**Ctrl** + **C**]

14 On the taskbar, click the *3½ Floppy (A:)* button to reopen its window

15 Press **F5** to "refresh" the contents of the window and return to its root directory

16 In the *3½ Floppy (A:) window* menu, click *Edit, Paste*   [**Ctrl** + **V**]

The files have been copied onto your disk's root directory and are now available for use. You no longer need the *Word* folder in Drive C and could remove it or leave it alone as follows:

WP

17 If you want to remove the *Word* folder from Drive C, perform the following steps:

    a.   On the taskbar, click the *Drive C* button to reopen its window

    b.   Click the *Word* folder icon to select it

    c.   Press   Delete

    d.   Click "Yes" to send the *Word* folder and its contents to the recycle bin

18 Press Alt + F4 four times to close all the open windows (or click the "close" button at the upper right of each open window, but this takes longer)

19 Click anywhere in the desktop to deselect the *My Computer* icon.

MODULE 1: MANAGING MULTIPAGE DOCUMENTS

Word's basic commands are sufficient for preparing short documents, such as letters and memos. As documents become larger, however, you can call upon advanced features to help you move around the file and manage the final output. Such features include page breaks, headers and footers, page numbering, and insertion point movements.

A two-page document (EXWP3-1) has been prepared for your use. Open the document as follows:

STEPS

1 Boot your computer and start Windows

2 Launch Word

3 Open the EXWP3-1 document on Drive A (or B)

> **Tip:** By default, Word lists only those files whose extension is "DOC." If you want to see all of the files on your disk, you must first change the "Files of Type" drop-down list to *All Files (*.*)*. You can do this by clicking its drop-down arrow and then clicking *All Files (*.*)*, or by pressing Alt + T and moving the highlight to it.

Note that the font used in the EXWP3-1 document is Courier New 10 pt.

If you do not have EXWP3-1 available (or want the practice), change the document font, set all margins to 1 inch, type the text shown in Figure WP3-2 and then save it as EXWP3-1. It's a good idea to adjust the Zoom control to "Page Width" to see the entire width of each line of text.

FIGURE WP3-2 ■ THE EXWP3-1 DOCUMENT

(a) First half of the EXWP3-1 document to be opened or typed.

REPORT DEADLINES

Andrea sat nervously in front of the microcomputer screen. She stretched her fingers over the keyboard while Elissa Roberts, manager of Freddy Johnson's travel Agency, looked on. Andrea had skipped lunch to finish this work, stopping only when the stiffness in her neck and fingers forced her to take a break. This was her first big assignment since completing the word processing course at Oakridge University. She could have used more practice with the word processor--especially on this keyboard, which differed from the one she used at school. Her fingers kept pressing the wrong key for SHIFT, forcing her to backspace and retype more often than usual. If only she were better acquainted with the layout, she'd be fine. But there was no time for that now. Andrea knew that time was short, and excuses wouldn't help. The job simply had to be completed.

Andrea had arrived at work earlier that morning to learn that an important meeting had been moved up, well ahead of schedule. With only hours left before the meeting, Andrea had been asked to put her word processing training to the test--a typewriter was clearly too slow for all the work that had to be done. After four hours of straight typing, she was tired, but could not let Elissa down.

After her brief rest, Andrea searched through the filenames on disk and retrieved the first ten pages of the proposal she had saved a few minutes ago. Even though she was under intense pressure, her training had taught her to constantly make backup copies of her work for safekeeping. She couldn't afford to lose any part of this report if something unforeseen happened to the computer.

"There's still so much to do," she thought. "Even if I can read Freddy's handwritten notes, the current margins and spacing are all wrong, the paragraphs must be changed around, the itinerary is incomplete, the typing errors must be corrected." Not being the best speller, she also dreaded the editing that would follow after the rest of the report had been typed. But there was no turning back. The meeting could not be postponed, and the report must be ready. Andrea began to type.

Elissa joined Andrea a few minutes later. She began deciphering Freddy's handwriting and dictating it to Andrea. Andrea didn't stop to fix mistakes, but just typed it into the word processor as quickly as possible.

(continued)

(a)

4 To set the Zoom control, click the toolbar's Zoom drop-down arrow and then select the *Page Width* zoom   [**Alt** + **V** , **Z**]

Before continuing, save this document as follows:

5 Click *File, Save As*

FIGURE WP3-2 ■ **THE EXWP3-1 DOCUMENT (CONTINUED)**

(b) Second half of document.

When she finished the rough draft, Andrea printed out the itinerary portion and brought it to Elissa for review. She made sure to print it triple-spaced, leaving more than enough room for written additions. While Elissa filled in the missing data, Andrea went back to the computer and started the built-in spelling checker. As each error appeared on the screen, she corrected it herself or selected one of the computer's correct spelling choices. Elissa returned with the completed itinerary that Andrea used to fill in the missing sections of the document.

Now it was time for "clean up." Andrea ran her punctuation and style program. It found a few run-on sentences, some missing punctuation, and a repeated word. Andrea corrected these flaws quickly. Next, she printed a double-spaced draft of the entire document on her dot-matrix printer and made copies on the photocopier. Freddy, Elissa, and Andrea got together to review their copies for style and content. Freddy felt that the word "fantastic" was overused and would have negative results at the meeting. Elissa didn't like the order of paragraphs on page 20. Andrea spotted an error, "we hope you enjoy your tip," that the speller could not pick up. Andrea made note of the changes.

Retrieving the document once more, Andrea located each appropriate page and altered the document to match her notes. She moved the paragraphs around, deleted a few sentences, and used the on-line thesaurus to replace "fantastic" with "fabulous," "fanciful," "marvelous," and just plain "great." She almost forgot to change "tip" to "trip."

Now, after a quick command to change the left margin to allow space for a binder, and adding headers and page numbers. Andrea was ready to print. She saved the document on disk and took it into Elissa's office where the laser printer was located. A few commands later and the report was being printed, letter-perfect, at twelve pages a minute. Within three minutes, it was done.

Andrea ran to the photocopier, made ten copies, and inserted them into presentation binders. Five minutes after the meeting started, Andrea walked in with a stack of impressive reports--one for each participant. Then she calmly walked out and collapsed at her desk!

(b)

6 Type the filename   EXWP3-1

Check that the *Save as type* box displays "Word Document." If it does, continue with Step 9. If it does not, change it as follows:

7 Click the *Save as type* drop-down arrow   [**Alt** + **T**]

8 Scroll up to *Word Document* and click it.   [↑]

9 Click the *Save* button   [↵]

The EXWP3-1 document is now saved in Word format.

SOFT PAGE BREAKS

Just as Word inserts soft returns each time you reach the right margin, it also creates **soft page breaks** each time you reach the end of a text page. These breaks are shown by a line extending across the width of the screen. They are *soft* because, like soft returns, they are not locked into one particular spot but change their location as you edit your document. Move to the first soft page break as follows:

STEPS

1 Press   **Ctrl** + **Alt** + **Pg Dn**   to move to Page 2

2 Press **↑** once

> **Tip:** Pressing Ctrl + Alt + Pg Dn moves down one page. Use Ctrl + Alt + Pg Up to move up one page.

Your screen should now resemble Figure WP3-3. The insertion point is positioned on the last line of the page. The soft page break is shown by the dotted line beneath your insertion point.

3 Press **↓** once

You should now be on the first line of Page 2, directly beneath the soft page break. Note that the page indicator reflects this on the status bar.

   If you were to change the text in some way (add text, delete text, adjust margins, or set line spacing, for example), the soft page break would automatically relocate to the proper position. Try this:

4 Press   **Ctrl** + **Home**   to move to the beginning of the document

5 Select the entire document (click and drag the mouse to the end or press **F8** five times)

6 Press   **Ctrl** + **2**   to set double-spacing

FIGURE WP3-3 ■ **A SOFT PAGE BREAK**

A soft page break is placed automatically by Word and is shown with a single dotted line across the page.

Soft page break

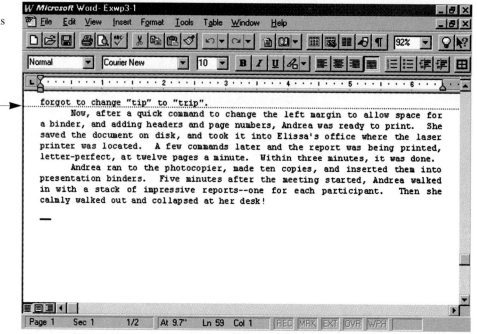

7   Move to the first line of Page 2 (use **Pg Up** or **Pg Dn** as needed). Note that the soft page break has changed its position

8   Save this document as EXWP3-1A, making sure to change the file type to "Word Document" before saving if needed

Tip: You cannot remove or adjust soft page breaks. They are placed automatically by the program and will be moved or eliminated as you make changes in your document.

HARD PAGE BREAKS

At times you will want to force a page break before reaching the physical end of the page. Perhaps you want to separate a title page from the rest of a document, or make sure a report section starts on a new page. You can do this by clicking *Insert* and then *Break* (the mouse approach) or by pressing Ctrl + Enter (the keyboard approach) to insert a hard page break, which appears as a dotted line extending across the screen, labeled "Page Break." Like a hard return, a **hard page break** remains fixed at a specific location in the text. It does not change its location unless you change it.

CREATING HARD PAGE BREAKS. Try creating the following hard page break:

STEPS

1 **Close any open documents**

2 **Open EXWP3-1A**

3 **Move your insertion point to Ln 2 (At 1.3″) of Page 1**

This is just below the title. Your screen should resemble Figure WP3-4a.

> **Tip:** You can remove the red, wavy lines of AutoCorrect by pointing to any marked word, right-clicking, and then clicking the *Ignore All* menu option.

4 **Click *Insert* and then *Break***   [**Ctrl** + ↵]

WP

FIGURE WP3-4 ■ CREATING A HARD PAGE BREAK

(a) Place the insertion point where you want the page to end.
(b) Click *Insert* and then *Break* or just press *Ctrl + Enter* to create a hard page break (shown by a dotted line and the words "Page Break").
(Note: Your screen may display red, wavy lines of AutoCorrect. Disregard them for now.)

(a)

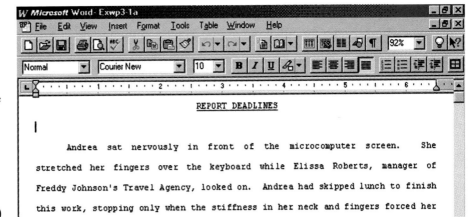

Hard page break →

(b)

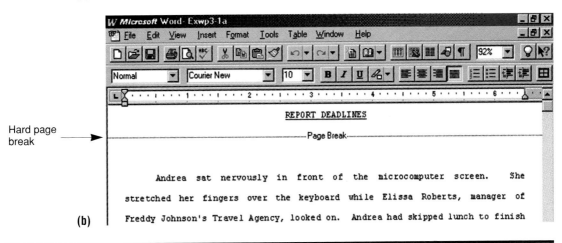

5 Choose *Page Break* and then click the *OK* button

As shown in Figure WP3-4b, a hard page break has been inserted. Page 1 now contains only the title, whereas Page 2 starts the story. No matter how you adjust your text, this page break will remain between the title and the first paragraph of your document (unless you remove it).

REMOVING HARD PAGE BREAKS. Hard page breaks are removed like any other text—with the Delete or Backspace key. Because the line clearly indicates the location of the hard page break on the screen, it is easy to do. You have two choices: either place the insertion point on the line below the hard page break and press the Backspace key, or place the insertion point on the line itself and press the Delete key. Try this:

STEPS

1 Press ↑ to position the insertion point on Pg 1 Ln 2 (the line itself)

2 Press **Delete** to remove the hard page break

(You could have also placed the insertion point on the first line of Page 2 and pressed the Backspace key.) Try inserting and deleting a few hard page breaks for practice.

3 Close the document without saving

HEADERS AND FOOTERS

Headers and **footers** are lines of text that usually appear on every page of a multipage document. They contain descriptive information such as a document title or a chapter name. In a long letter, they might indicate a topic and date. Headers, the more common variety, are used at the top of the document, whereas footers appear at the bottom.

Word allows up to two headers and footers (for odd or even pages), but only one to a page. A header or footer is usually positioned one inch from the top (or bottom) of the page, with one blank line between it and the main text. The remaining space is used for your document.

CREATING A HEADER. The following exercise creates a header for the EXWP3-1 document (a footer can be created in a similar fashion).

STEPS

1 Launch Word and open the EXWP3-1 document

Usually you do not place a header (or footer) on a document's first page. You must, therefore, position your insertion point on the page where the header will begin.

2 Press **Ctrl** + **Alt** + **Pg Dn** to move to Page 2 or scroll there

3 Click *View* and then *Header and Footer*

A number of things happen to your screen, as shown in Figure WP3-5a. The view changes to Page Layout, a rectangle labeled "Header" and enclosed by a dashed-line appears at the top of the page, and a *Header and Footer* toolbox is displayed. Figure WP3-5b displays the buttons included in the toolbox. The dashed line, which does not print in your final document, provides an entry area for the header text.

> **Tip:** If needed, the toolbox can be moved to a more convenient screen location by clicking its title bar and dragging it elsewhere.

4 If a footer rectangle appears instead, click the *Switch Between Header and Footer* button in the toolbox   ↑

You must now tell Word to start the header on the current page, otherwise it will appear on the first page as well. To do this,

FIGURE WP3-5 ■ CREATING A HEADER

WP

(a) Click *View* and *Header* (or press Alt + V, H) to invoke the *Header and Footer* toolbox.
(b) The *Toolbar* buttons.

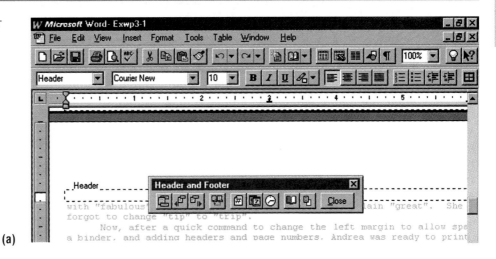

(a)

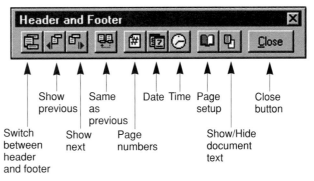

(b)

5   Click *File* and then *Page Setup* (or just click the *Page Setup* button in the toolbox)

A *Page Setup* dialog box appears as shown in Figure WP3-6a. To set the header so that it does not appear on the first page,

6   Click the *Different First Page* check box   [**Alt** **+** **F**]

7   Click the *OK* button   [↵]

8   Type   **Word Processing**

9   Press ↵ as in Figure WP3-6b

FIGURE WP3-6 ■ THE *PAGE SETUP* DIALOG BOX

(a) Selecting Different First Page ensures that the header will start on page 2.
(b) The header has been typed with a blank line beneath it to separate it from the text.

Select
this box

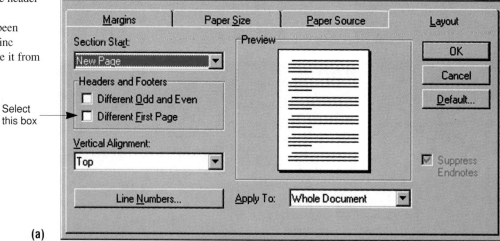

(a)

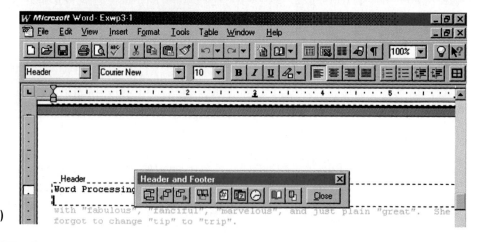

(b)

10 **Click the *Close* button**   **[Alt + V , H]**

Note that pressing the Enter key in Step 9 leaves an extra blank line between the header and the text. You could press Enter again to leave two lines if desired.

Use the Page Layout view to see the header as follows:

 11 **Click *View*, *Page Layout* (or click the *Page Layout* button on the status bar)**

Your screen should resemble Figure WP3-7. If you press the Ctrl + Alt + Pg Up keys to move to Page 1, you should see no header.

12 **Save the document as EXWP3-1B (switch file type to "Word Document" if needed before saving)**

The procedure to create a footer is identical, except that you select *Footer* before Step 4.

> **Tip:** Headers and footers reduce the number of text lines that can be printed on each page. This may cause text to "spill over" onto a new page. Therefore, use Page Layout view or Print Preview to check proper text layout before printing.

 13 **Switch to *Normal View* (click button or click *View*, *Normal*)**

EDITING A HEADER.   A header or footer can be modified with almost the same procedure that created it. For example, to change the header "Word Processing" to "Word Processing Assignment," follow these steps:

FIGURE WP3-7 ■ THE COMPLETED HEADER

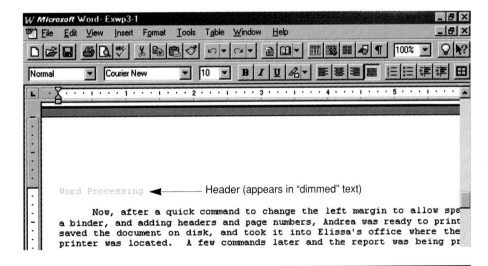

Header (appears in "dimmed" text)

STEPS

1 Click _View_ and then _Header and Footer_

> **Tip: If you are in the Page Layout view, you can access the header by double-click-ing the dimmed header area.**

The insertion point will move to the header area. Drag the Header and Footer dialog box out of the way if needed.

2 Move to the end of "Word Processing" (but before the next line)

3 Press Spacebar and type Assignment

4 Click the _Close_ button   [**Alt** + **Shift** + **C**]

The insertion point is now back in the main text and in Normal view. Editing a footer is identical, except that you select Footer before Step 2.

DELETING A HEADER.   Headers and footers can be deleted if you no longer need them in your document. The approach is the same as deleting any text—move to the appropriate page, then find and delete the header text.
  To do this,

STEPS

1 Click _View_ and then _Header and Footer_

2 Switch to the header if needed

3 Use Delete or Backspace to remove the header text

4 Close the header (click _Close_)   [**Alt** + **V** , **H**]

The header will not appear in your document.

5 Close the document window without saving these changes

PAGE NUMBERING

When you are typing a multipage document, you may want to include page numbers. As with headers, page numbers typically start on Page 2, leaving the first page un-numbered.
  The following exercises will allow you to number pages in your document, position the number on the page, and modify the numbering scheme.

POSITIONING.   Creating page numbers is simply a matter of telling the program where you want them to appear.

STEPS

1 Close any open document and then open the EXWP3-1 document

Now move your insertion point to the page where numbering will begin.

2 Press   Ctrl   +   Alt   +   Pg Dn   to move to Page 2

3 Click *Insert* and then *Page Numbers* for its dialog box

A *Page Numbers* dialog box appears as in Figure WP3-8a. The dialog box's position button currently indicates that page numbers will appear at the bottom right. You can position numbers at the top (header) or bottom (footer) of each page. You can also align them at the left, center, or right of the page, or place them inside or outside the margins. Try the following exercise to readjust the current setting to the top of the page:

4 Click the *Show Number on First Page* check box to turn off this feature   [Alt + S]

WP

FIGURE WP3-8 ■ THE *PAGE NUMBERS* DIALOG BOX

(a) By default, page numbers are set to the bottom right corner.
(b) The numbers have been moved to the top.

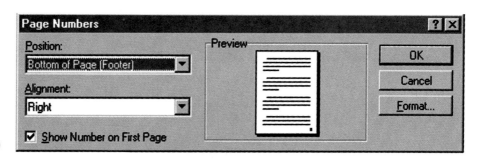

(a)

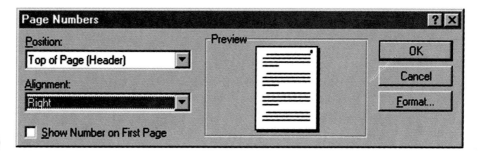

(b)

▼   **5** Click the *Position* drop-down arrow   [**Alt** + **P**]

6 Click *Top of Page (Header)*   [↓]

Note that the preview image reflects the new page number location.

▼   **7** Click the *Alignment* drop-down arrow

From this list, you can change the horizontal alignment of the number. For now, leave it "Right" as follows:

▼   **8** Click the *Alignment* drop-down arrow to close the list as in Figure WP3-8b   [**Tab**]

9 Click the *OK* button to accept and exit the dialog box   [↵]

10 Save this document as EXWP3-1C

If you switch to Page Layout view or print the document, you will see the page number repositioned at the top right of Page 2.

> **Tip:** Page numbers can also be included within a header or footer. Move the insertion point to the position in the header where a page number is desired and then click the *Page Numbers* button.

RENUMBERING.   At times, a document's physical page number may not be the number you want to use. For example, if the first two pages of a report are a title page and table of contents, you may want numbering to start with the *third* page shown as Page 1, not Page 3. A minor change can accomplish this easily. To see the effect, first open the document EXWP3-2 as follows:

STEPS

1 Launch Word or close any open document

2 Open the EXWP3-2 document

> **Note:** If you do not have EXWP3-2, create it now by opening EXWP3-1 and modify it by following the instructions listed in Figure WP3-9.

Once the document is opened, your screen may appear blank. This is because you are viewing the top of the cover page.

3 Save as EXWP3-2—a Word document

4 Switch to Page Layout view if it is not set already

If EXWP3-2 is not available, open EXWP3-1 and follow these instructions to create the EXWP3-2 document.

To create EXWP3-2 from EXWP3-1:
1. At start of document, change line spacing to 2, and the initial font to Courier New 10.
2. Delete the title line.
3. Press the Enter key ten times.
4. Center the heading "Thoughts about Word Processing"
5. Create a hard page break.
6. Create page numbers on the top right.
7. Insert the following two paragraphs at the beginning of the new page:
   (Note: Your text may wordwrap differently)

   According to Charles Parker, "word processing is the use of computer technology to create, manipulate, and print text materials." These materials include such items as letters, memos, legal contracts, article manuscripts, and other documents. As Parker explains it, word processing saves so much time that most people stop using their typewriters once they learn word processing.

   The following story, written by Edward Martin, demonstrates why word processing is so valuable to a typical office. The story, reprinted here with permission of the author, begins as follows:

8. Add this closing paragraph at the end:

   Clearly, this story demonstrates that word processing can greatly benefit normal typing tasks. It can even make the impossible possible. Even though this is impressive, it would appear that this is only the beginning. If word processing is combined with special graphics software and additional computer equipment, it can create a desktop publishing system--"a microcomputer-based publishing system that lets you combine page elements such as text, art, and photos, thus creating attractive-looking documents that look like they came off a printer's press." But that is another story.

WP

5 **Press** `Ctrl` + `Alt` + `Pg Dn` **to go to the top of Page 2**

6 **Set the zoom to Page Width of 75%**

Your screen should resemble Figure WP3-10. Notice that Page 2 is *numbered* as Page 2! Because this document has a cover page, which should not be numbered, you must renumber the pages. To renumber the document starting with Page 2, so that it will begin as Page 1:

7 **Click _I_nsert and then *Page N_u_mbers* for the *Page Numbers* dialog box**

8 **Click the _F_ormat button for the *Page Number Format* dialog box**

FIGURE WP3-10 ■ CHANGING PAGE NUMBERS

The first text page of the document will be numbered as Page 2 and should be changed.

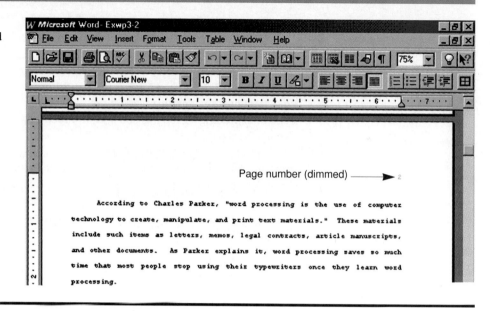

9 Click the *Start At* button at the bottom

A "1" appears in the Start At text entry line. You could type a new number, but for now,

10 Click the *OK* button and then click the *Close* button   [↵ twice]

As in the top right of your document, the page counter has been set to 1.

11 Close the document without saving it

Page number locations (Position) and page numbering are usually set at the same time.

> **Tip:** You can remove page numbers as you did a header. Select *View, Header* and *Footer,* then move to the number and delete it.

PAGE JUMPS

Normal insertion point controls let you move easily on one page, but they can become tedious when working on a larger document. Word offers a few features to move around multipage documents easily. By mouse, you can click the *Page Up* or *Page Down* buttons at the bottom of the vertical scroll bar in Page Layout view to scroll one page at a time in either direction. (Scrolling does not move the insertion point, only the viewing area of the document.) With the keyboard, you can press Ctrl + Alt + Pg Up or Ctrl + Alt + Pg Dn to move one page at a time in either direction. Better yet, the

Go To command quickly relocates the insertion point on any page you name. In effect, it "jumps" directly to that page. Try this:

☐ 1   **Launch Word or close any open document and then open EXWP3-2**

☐ 2   **Click *Edit* and then *Go To* for its dialog box**   [**Ctrl** + **G**]

☐ 3   **Type** **3** **to select the third page**

☐ 4   **Press ↵ to go to Page 3**

> **Tip:** By changing the Go to **W**hat selection, you can move to other Word items, such as lines or footnotes.

The insertion point is repositioned at the start of Page 3.

☐ 5   **Close the Go To box (select *Close* or press** **Esc** **)**

☐ 6   **Close the document without saving**

☑ CHECKPOINT

✓   Close any open document and open EXWP3-1. Add a footer that places the words "Check Point" at the lower left.

✓   Change the page numbering to appear in the bottom center of each page.

✓   Renumber Page 1 to start as Page 10.

✓   Save the document as WPCHECK1.

✓   Print it, and then close the document.

MODULE 2: WORKING WITH MULTIDOCUMENT WINDOWS

A powerful tool (and challenge) is the capability to work with multidocuments simultaneously. Although this technique allows you to move freely between documents as if they were one, it also places demands on your ability to keep track of where you are and what you are doing. The following exercises allow you to practice working with two documents. Note that Word allows you to open up to nine documents in its workspace.

WP

SWITCHING BETWEEN DOCUMENT WINDOWS

Using multidocuments is a fairly straightforward procedure. First, you type (or open) a document normally. Then, you start a new document window and type a second document or simply open a second document. From then on, you move back and forth between the documents as needed. The key to understanding where you are at any given time is to watch the title bar for the document's name. In the following exercise, you will create two short documents, copy a paragraph from one into the other, and then save the completed document.

ENTERING DOCUMENT 1.   The first task is to open or create a new document. In this example, you will create a short document as follows:

STEPS

1   **Launch Word (or close all documents and start a new one) and switch to Normal view if needed**

Note: If you start Word, your documents will be numbered 1 and 2 as in this exercise. If you are already in Word, your two documents may have different identification numbers.

2   **Type the text shown in Figure WP3-11a**

FIGURE WP3-11 ■ ENTERING THE DOCUMENTS

(a) Type the text in Part a into Document 1 and save it as EXWP3-3a.
(b) Type the text in Part b into Document 2 and save it as EXWP3-3b.
(Note: Press the Enter key whenever you see the paragraph [¶] symbol.)

(a) Text for Document 1:

This sample illustrates how easily text can be copied from one document into another by switching between two documents in Word. For example, this paragraph is part of the first document. It was typed into the Document 1 window and then saved as EXWP3-3a.¶

¶

This paragraph was also typed into the first document. If you were to print out a copy of EXWP3-3a, you would only see these two paragraphs.¶

¶

(b) Text for Document 2:

This paragraph was typed into the Document 2 window and saved as EXWP3-3b. If you were to print out a copy of EXWP3-3b, you would only see this paragraph.¶

¶

Remember to press the Enter key only when you reach each paragraph symbol (¶) in the figure.

3 Save this document as EXWP3-3A

ENTERING DOCUMENT 2.   To create a second document, you must start a new document window as follows:

STEPS

1 Click *File* and then *New*   [**Ctrl** + **N**]

2 Click the *OK* button to accept a Blank document template   [**↵**]

Note that "Document 2" appears on the title bar.

3 Type the text shown in Figure WP3-11b (pressing the Enter key as shown)

4 Save this document as EXWP3-3b

You now have two documents in memory at the same time. To switch back and forth between documents, as shown in Figure WP3-12, try this:

5 Click *Window* and then *1 EXWP3-3A* to switch   [**Ctrl** + **F6**]

6 Click *Window* and then *2 EXWP3-3B* to switch back   [**Ctrl** + **F6**]

MANIPULATING TEXT IN MULTIPLE DOCUMENTS.   You can now manipulate text between the two documents almost as easily as you do within one.

In normal use, you may choose to keep document EXWP3-3b simply as a reference as you work on document EXWP3-3a, switching to it whenever necessary. You can also scroll each document independently to move to particular locations within each.

However, a more important reason for using multidocuments is the capability of copying (or moving) text from one document into the other. In this exercise, you will copy the paragraph in EXWP3-3b and place it after the first paragraph in EXWP3-3a.

STEPS

1 Switch your screen to document EXWP3-3b if needed

Now select the paragraph for copying as follows:

2 Move the insertion point to the start of the paragraph, as shown in Figure WP3-13a

3 Point anywhere in the paragraph

FIGURE WP3-12 ■ SWITCHING BETWEEN DOCUMENT WINDOWS

(a) and (b) Clicking *Window* and then selecting a document or pressing Ctrl + F6 allows you to switch between documents in memory.

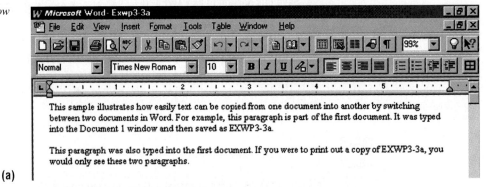

(a)

(b)

---

4 Triple-click the left mouse button to select the paragraph or double-click the "EXT" indicator on the status bar and then click the end of the paragraph [**F8** , ↓ twice]

 5 Click *Edit* and then *Copy* to copy (or click the *Copy* toolbar button) [**Ctrl** + **C**]

This procedure has been identical to the normal copy routine up to this point. Because the "target" for the paragraph is in document EXWP3-3a, you must now switch to that document and complete the copy as follows:

6 Click *Window* and then *1 EXWP3-3A* [**Ctrl** + **F6**]

7 Move the insertion point to the beginning of the second paragraph

 8 Click *Edit* and then *Paste* to complete the copy [**Ctrl** + **V**]

9 Press ↵ to create a blank line

Your screen should now resemble Figure WP3-13b, with the paragraph from EXWP3-3b copied into EXWP3-3a.

SAVING. Now that you have copied successfully, save the new document as EXWP3-3c (as you would save any document).

FIGURE WP3-13 ■ COPYING BETWEEN DOCUMENTS

(a) The insertion point is at the start of the first paragraph in document EXWP3-3b.
(b) The selection has been copied into the middle of document EXWP3-3a.

Insertion point is here ——

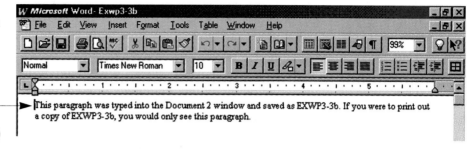

(a)

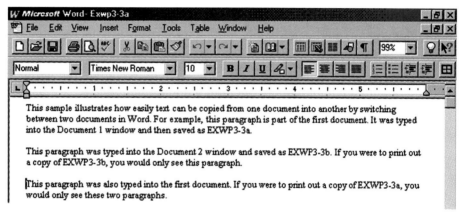

(b)

STEPS

1 Invoke the *Save As* command

2 Type **EXWP3-3c**

3 Press ↵

CLOSING THE SECOND DOCUMENT.   You no longer need EXWP3-3b in the computer's main memory, so close it as follows (remember that it is already saved on your disk as EXWP3-3b):

STEPS

1 Click *Window* and then *2 EXWP3-3B*   [**Ctrl** + **F6**]

 2 Click the *Close* button of the EXWP3-3B window or select *File, Close* (be careful to click the *Close* button of the *document, not* Word)   [**Ctrl** + **F4**]

3 If needed, click the *No* button to answer to "Save changes to EXWP3-3B?"

You will now be returned to the document EXWP3-3c. Each time you want to add text from another document, simply repeat the procedure.

ARRANGING DOCUMENT WINDOWS

Until now, you have been viewing multiple documents on separate screens. It is also possible to display several documents on one screen at the same time. Word's **Arrange All** option arranges document windows one above the other in Word's workspace. This is equivalent to Window's Tile command. Try the following exercise to display documents EXWP3-3a and EXWP3-3b on one screen.

STEPS

1 Close any open document

2 Open EXWP3-3a

3 Open EXWP3-3b

> **Tip:** To open both documents with one command, click the first, Ctrl + click the second, and then click the *Open* button.

At present, you can see only EXWP3-3b on the screen.

4 Click *Window* for the *Window* menu

5 Click *Arrange All*

As in Figure WP3-14, the document windows are arranged one above the other in the workspace. To switch the active document window press Ctrl + F6, or simply click the title bar (or any open area) of the document window you desire. (Remember, the active window has a highlighted title bar.) You could now perform copy or cut and paste actions more easily.
   To close both documents:

6 Click each document window's *Close* button   [**Ctrl** + **F4** twice]

RESIZING A DOCUMENT WINDOW

Document windows can be resized within Word's workspace. Standard window resizing commands include Restore (resize to a previous size or smaller window), Minimize (shrink to an icon or taskbar button), and Maximize (enlarge to maximum size). Window resizing is useful when working with more than one window. In this situation, you can

FIGURE WP3-14 ■ ARRANGING DOCUMENT WINDOWS

Arranging document windows displays them one above the other. The active window's title bar is highlighted and displays a *Document* icon to the left.

Active window

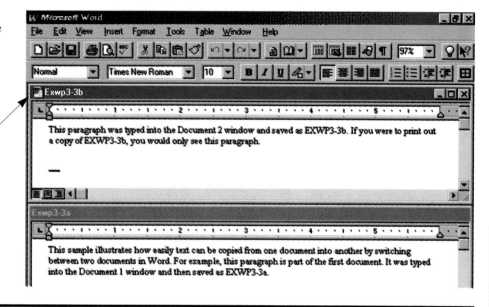

resize a window to display only the work that you need. A window may also be custom resized to a desired size. When resizing by keyboard, you must use the window's control-menu.

STANDARD WINDOW RESIZING.   Try the following exercises to resize the EXWP3-3a document window:

1　Close any document window

2　Open EXWP3-3a

3　If the document appears in its own window (as in Figure WP3-15a) click its *Maximize* button   [**Ctrl** + **F10**]

4　Point to the document window's *Restore* button on the right side of the menu bar
                                                                                   [**Alt** + **–**]

5　Click the document window's *Restore* button to reduce the window   [**R**]

The EXWP3-3a window should appear as a smaller window within Word's workspace similar to Figure WP3-15a. Note that the window now has its own title bar and two resizing buttons (top right).

FIGURE WP3-15 ■   RESIZING A WINDOW

(a) The Restore command will reduce a window to a smaller size.
(b) The window has been minimized to an *Icon* button.

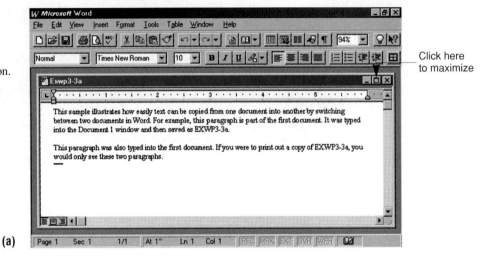

Click here to maximize

(a)

(b)

---

6 **Click the *Minimize* button to reduce the window to an *Icon* button**   [**Alt** + **—** , **N**]

The EXWP3-3a document now appears as an *Icon* button at the bottom left of Word's workspace as in Figure WP3-15b. To return the document to its maximum size,

7 **Click the *Document* icon's *Maximize* button**   [**Alt** + **A**]

> **Tip: Double-clicking the title bar of any nonmaximized window or pressing Ctrl + F10 will also resize the window.**

8 **Close the window *without* saving it**

CUSTOM WINDOW RESIZING.   Windows may also be custom resized to any desired size. Try the following to custom resize the EXWP3-3a window as in Figure WP3-16:

STEPS

1 **Open EXWP3-3a**

FIGURE WP3-16 ■ CUSTOM RESIZING

Custom resizing results in a smaller document image.

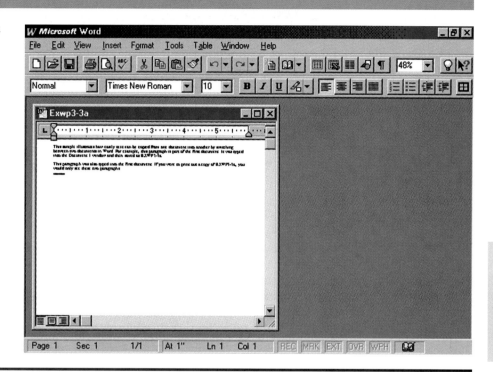

WP

2	Click the document window's *Restore* button	[**Ctrl** + **F5** , **R**]
3	Point slowly to the right window wall until the pointer changes to a horizontal pointer with an arrow on each side	[**Ctrl** + **F8** , **S**]
4	Drag the right wall's outline to just after the 3" mark on the ruler bar	[→]
5	Release the mouse button to complete the resizing	[← , ↵]

The EXWP3-3a window should appear as Figure WP3-16. Note that if the text is too small to see, you could always use the Zoom feature to increase its size.

6 Close the EXWP3-3a document

Note that resizing adjustments are not saved with the document.

> **Tip:** You can quickly resize a window's bottom and side walls by slowly pointing to a lower corner until the pointer changes to a diagonal pointer with an arrow at each end. Next drag the corner to the desired size and release the mouse. Custom-resizing techniques can only be applied to less than maximized windows.

CHECKPOINT

✓ Open a new document window.
✓ Open EXWP3-1. Copy the first and last paragraphs into the new document window.
✓ Save this document as WPCHECK2.
✓ Show both document windows on the screen.
✓ Close both documents

MODULE 3: MERGING FILES

Merge is a process by which information from two sources is combined to produce a third document. This is extremely useful in creating customized letters. In this procedure, a standard form letter can be altered for each customer to include the customer's specific name, address, and so forth.

An easy way to merge is to create a form letter *without* any customer identification. Then, when you need a new letter, open the form and type in the new name and address. Although useful for a few letters, this gets fairly tedious for a long list.

A better method uses two separate files: a main document and a data source. The **main document** contains text (such as a form letter) and instructions for merging. The **data source** contains the specific data to be merged into the main document (such as a list of names and addresses). The following exercise creates both files and then merges them to produce individualized letters.

IDENTIFYING THE BASIC MERGE DOCUMENTS

In this exercise, you will identify the two basic documents you will need to perform the merge.

1 **Close any open document and then open a new document window (maximize the window if needed)**

2 **Click *Tools* and then *Mail Merge***

A *Mail Merge Helper* dialog box appears as shown in Figure WP3-17. This dialog box leads you through the merge process. You must first identify the documents that you will use, starting with the main document as follows:

3 **Click the *Create* button under the Main Document heading (Item #1)**

4 **From the drop-down list, click *Form Letters***

5 **Click the *Active Window* button**

The main document has been identified. You can now concentrate on the data source that will be used in the merge.

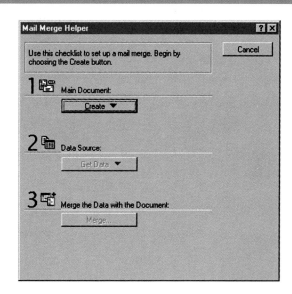

WP

6 Click the *Get Data* button under the Data Source heading (Item #2)

7 From the drop-down list, click *Create Data Source*

A *Create Data Source* dialog box appears as in Figure WP3-18a. You can now identify the data you will want to collect in the data source that will ultimately appear in the main document. In this procedure, you specify the field names that will be placed in the *header row*—the first row of the data source.

The Field Names in Header Row lists the fields that are typically used in a data source. You can use this list as is, add fields that do not appear, or remove fields that are not needed. For example, to remove the "Job Title" field,

8 Click *Job Title*   [Alt + N , ↓]

9 Click the *Remove Field Name* button

10 Using the procedure in Steps 8–9, remove these additional six fields from the list: City, State, PostalCode, Country, HomePhone, and WorkPhone

You can add fields to the header list as well. For example, to add an "Item" field, do the following:

11 Click the *Field Name* entry box

12 Press Delete to remove the current entry

13 Type Item

FIGURE WP3-18 ■ CREATING A DATA SOURCE

(a) Suggested fields appear in the Field Names in Header Row list.
(b) The list has been edited by adding and removing fields.

(a)

(b)

14 Click the *Add Field Name* button

15 Using the procedure in Steps 11–14, add a new field name for *Price*

Your screen should resemble Figure WP3-18b. Note that the Title field has scrolled up to make room for the new fields. Although it is still part of the header row, it does not appear on the list. You can always scroll the list as needed to see all the fields.

<table>
<tr><td>16</td><td>Click the OK button to accept the list</td><td>[Tab to OK, ↵]</td></tr>
</table>

A *Save as Data Source* dialog box appears. It is identical to the familiar *Save As* dialog box.

<table>
<tr><td>17</td><td>Save the file on your disk as DATA1 (switch the Save in drive if needed, type DATA1 and then press ↵)</td></tr>
</table>

The source document has now been identified.

CREATING THE MAIN DOCUMENT

Now that you have identified the main document and data source files, you can either place data into the data source or create the main document's form letter. In this exercise, you will create the main document as follows:

STEPS

1   Click the *Edit Main Document* button

The blank document window appears on your screen. Note that it has an added MailMerge toolbar that simplifies the creation process. Your goal is to create the form shown in Figure WP3-19.

WP

We Sell Anything, Inc.
1001 Knights Road
Mobius Strip, NM 12345

November 1, 19XX

«Title» «FirstName» «LastName»
«Company»
«Address1»
«Address2»

Dear «Title» «LastName»:

Thank you for your recent letter inquiring about our product, «Item». The current price is «Price», plus appropriate tax. We would be happy to fill your order upon receipt of a «Company» purchase order or check.

Sincerely,

Martin Parker
Sales Manager

> **Tip:** To remove AutoCorrect's red, wavy lines, point to a word with red, wavy lines, right-click, and then click *Ignore All*.

This form starts with a centered heading and date, and then places markers for six data fields: Title, FirstName, LastName, Company, Address1, and Address2. The salutation includes markers for Title and LastName, while the paragraph includes markers for Item, Price, and Company. When this form letter is merged with the data source, these field markers will be replaced with the actual data. Create this main document as follows:

2 Type the three centered heading lines as shown at the top of Figure WP3-19, pressing ↵ after each

3 Press ↵ to insert a blank line (skip a line)

4 Type today's date and skip another line

You are now positioned correctly to insert the first field marker, Title. To insert the marker, do the following:

Insert Merge Field

5 Click the *Insert Merge Field* button on the MailMerge toolbar   [**Alt** + **Shift** + **F**]

A drop-down list of available fields appears as in Figure WP3-20a.

6 Click *Title* to select it   [↓ , ↵]

A field marker called "<<Title>>" (enclosed in double arrow brackets) appears in the document, showing where the Title data will appear when the form is merged. You can now continue with the form. Use this technique for inserting any field: position the insertion point in the form and then insert the field marker.

7 Press   **Spacebar**   to leave a space between words

FIGURE WP3-20 ■ INSERTING FIELD MARKERS INTO THE MAIN DOCUMENT

(a) Clicking the *Insert Merge Field* button opens a drop-down field list.
(b) Pressing Alt + Shift + F opens an *Insert Merge Field* dialog box.

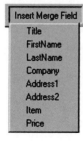

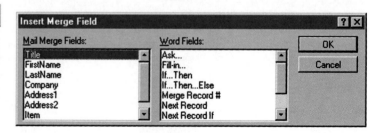

(a)   (b)

8 Using Steps 5–6, insert a field marker for *FirstName*

9 Press   Spacebar

10 Insert the *LastName* field marker

11 Press ⏎ to move to the next line

Compare your screen to the top of Figure WP3-19. Using it as a reference, continue as follows:

12 Insert the *Company* field marker and press ⏎

13 Insert the *Address1* field marker and press ⏎

14 Insert the *Address2* field marker and press ⏎ twice to insert a blank line

15 Type   Dear   and press   Spacebar

16 Insert the *Title* field marker, leave a space, and then insert the *LastName* field marker

17 Type   :   (a colon) and press ⏎

18 Press ⏎ to skip a line

19 Type the rest of the letter as in Figure WP3-19

As you type, enter the fields ITEM, PRICE, and COMPANY when you reach them, and continue with the correct punctuation after each. If you make a mistake, backspace and repeat the procedure. Use the text select technique to delete any misplaced field markers.

SAVING THE FILE.   Main documents are saved with the standard Save As command. They can be opened and modified like any other text file.

STEPS

1 Save this file as FORM1

2 Close the document or continue

EDITING THE DATA SOURCE

With the main document safely on disk, you can now concentrate on the data source to merge with it. In this exercise, you will create two data records. In real applications, of course, your data list might contain hundreds of entries—but the procedure would be the same. Fortunately, Word automates much of this for you.

STEPS

1 Open the FORM1 document if it is not already on the screen

2 Click *Tools* and then *Mail Merge*

3 Click the *Data Source Edit* button (in item #2)   [**Alt** + **D**]

4 Click *Data: A:\DATA1*   [↵]

A data form appears as shown in Figure WP3-21. This form will hold the data for one record. The fields you created appear at the left. The insertion point awaits your first entry in the center. Using the record shown in Figure WP3-22a as a guide, you can now enter data for the first record as follows:

5 Type **Mr.** in the *Title* text box

6 Press ↵ to accept the data and move to the next field

7 Type **John** in the *FirstName* text box and press ↵

8 Continue to enter the data shown in Figure WP3-22a, pressing ↵ after typing each entry

Tip: If you make a mistake, use the Shift + Tab keys to return to your error. You can then correct it, press the Enter key, and then tab forward to where you left off.

FIGURE WP3-21 ■ *THE DATA FORM DIALOG BOX*

Each screen holds the data for one record.

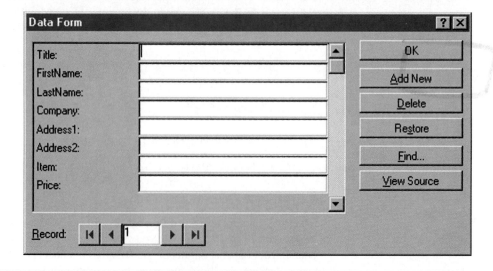

FIGURE WP3-22 ■ ENTERING DATA

(a) Record 1.
(b) Record 2.

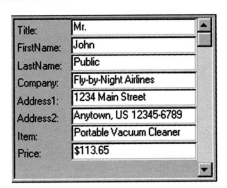

Record: 1

(a)

Record: 2

(b)

After entering the price data, a new blank record form will appear on your screen, and the record counter at the lower left will display a "2." You can now continue with the second record.

9 **Enter the data for the second record as shown in Figure WP3-22b, pressing ↵ after typing each entry**

When the third blank record form appears,

10 **Click the *OK* button to accept the data**

11 **If you want to stop for now, close the FORM1 document**

MERGE—COMBINING THE FILES

Once the files for main document and data source have been created, they can be combined to form individual letters. Of course, you can modify either one before merging them together. The following exercise demonstrates the merge technique.

1 **Open the FORM1 document if it is not already on the screen**

PREVIEWING A MAIL MERGE.   If you use a mouse, you can preview the effects of a proposed merge before actually invoking the merge command. This allows you to examine the documents for errors before actually combining them. To preview a mail merge,

WP

2 **Click the _View Merged Data_ button on the Mail Merge toolbar**

The field markers in the main document are replaced with the data from the first record, as shown in Figure WP3-23a. Note that the text is adjusted automatically to conform to the size of each field of data. To see the next record,

---

FIGURE WP3-23 ■ PREVIEWING THE MERGED DOCUMENTS

(a) The first letter contains the data for Record 1.
(b) Record 2's data appear in the second letter.

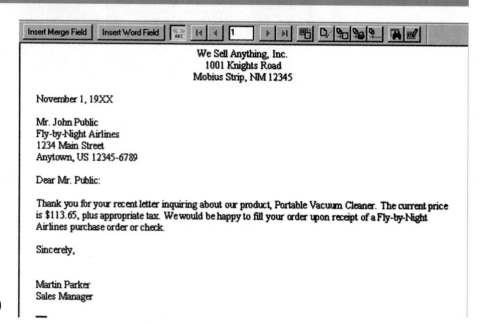

(a)

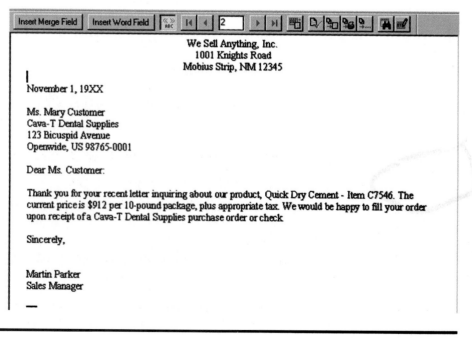

(b)

3 Click the *Next Record* button on the Mail Merge toolbar

The data from the second record appears as in Figure WP3-23b. To return to the main document form,

4 Repeat Step 2 to toggle off the *View Merged Data* feature

MERGING THE FILES. To actually merge the main document with the data source, do the following:

1 Click *Tools* and then *Mail Merge,* or simply click the *Merge to New Document* button on the Mail Merge toolbar

2 Click the *Merge* button in Item #3

A *Merge* dialog box will appear. To continue,

3 Click *Merge*

A new document window, entitled *"FormLetters1,"* appears with both letters. The merged document will include a new page for each record that was contained in the data source file. Scroll through the document and compare its contents to the letters shown in Figure WP3-23. This document can now be treated as any other file. You can edit it, save it, or print it as needed. Of course, you can also regenerate it by invoking the merge command again in the future. For now,

4 Save the document as MERGE1

5 Close the document window

☑ CHECKPOINT

✓ Identify a main document named WPCHECK3.
✓ Create a data source file named WPCHECK4 with fields for FIRSTNAME, LAST-NAME, and PHONE.
✓ Enter data in the data source file for three records, each containing a name and phone number.
✓ Merge WPCHECK4 into WPCHECK3 and print the results.
✓ Close the resultant merge file without saving it.

MODULE 4: AUTOMATING COMMANDS WITH MACROS

After using Word for a while, you may identify several tasks that you perform on a regular basis. Perhaps you type a company heading each time you start a letter, or you copy and print each file you use. Instead of repeating a complicated set of mouse actions or keystrokes each time you need to perform these tasks, you can create a macro to do it for you. A **macro** is a list of computer instructions that can be activated with one (or more) preset keystrokes. The Macro feature in Word records all the mouse actions or keystrokes you would use to accomplish a task and then stores them in a separate file that can be invoked with a few simple keystrokes, much like the memory dialing feature on many telephones. Anything you can do with a mouse or on the keyboard, and more, can be saved in a macro.

There are two steps to using basic macros: creating the macro (defining and saving it) and then running the macro (invoking it for use). The following exercise creates a macro that will type a company heading and date.

CREATING A MACRO

When designing a macro, you may want to first perform the task step by step in Word, listing each mouse/keyboard action in proper sequence on paper. Creating the actual macro is then simply a matter of reperforming the mouse/keyboard actions back into the program.

You should also give some thought to the name you select for a macro. This is important: a macro's name should remind you of its function. You can create macro names that are invoked through the Macro Menu command. You can also assign macros to shortcut keys, menus, or toolbars. For example, a macro that prints out selected pages of a document might be named "Pages" or "Printer." Its shortcut keys might be Alt + P (the mnemonic "P" reminds you of "page" or "print").

Macros are invoked by first invoking the Macro command and then typing the full name of the macro (as you will see). You can create an unlimited supply of these macros. They are easier to remember, because their longer names can better indicate their use, although they take a few more keystrokes to invoke. Macros that are assigned to shortcut keys are easy to use but hard to remember because their names do not provide much of a clue to their use.

CREATING A MACRO.   This exercise creates a macro that types the heading shown in Figure WP3-24.

STEPS

1 **Open a new document if needed**

FIGURE WP3-24 ■ THE MACRO WILL PRODUCE THIS HEADING

The XYZ Company
New York, New York 10001

January 22, 1996

2 Click *Tools* and then *Macro* for the *Macro* dialog box

The *Macro* dialog box will appear as in Figure WP3-25a.

3 Type **HEADING** to name the macro

Tip: Do not use spaces, commas, or periods in a macro name.

FIGURE WP3-25 ■ CREATING A NEW MACRO

(a) The *Macro* dialog box.
(b) The *Record Macro* dialog box.

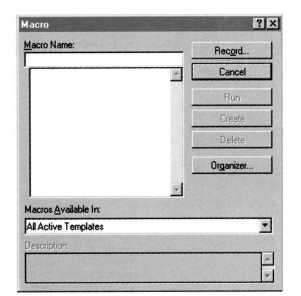

(a)

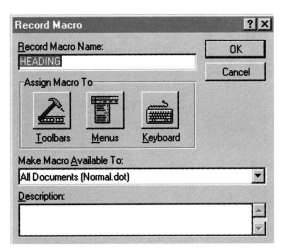

(b)

4 Click the *Record* button

A *Record Macro* dialog box appears, as shown in Figure WP3-25b.

5 Click the *OK* button (or press ↵ to continue)

A Macro Recorder toolbar (as in Figure WP3-26a) now appears on your screen, indicating that the program will record any mouse actions or keystrokes you now enter. The mouse pointer also displays a tape icon (as in Figure WP3-26b) indicating that macro recording is on. Note that the time it takes you to enter each command does not affect the recorded macro; only the mouse actions or keystrokes are entered. You may want to refer to Figure WP3-24 and your screen as you create the heading.

Now perform the mouse commands, as follows:

6 Click the *Center* toolbar button
[**Ctrl** + **E**]

7 Type   **The XYZ Company**   and press ↵

8 Type New York, New York 10001 and press ↵

9 Click the *Align Left* toolbar button
[**Ctrl** + **L**]

10 Press ↵ to create a blank line

Here's an interesting use of an insert function that will automatically place the system date into the document in an appropriate form. Although not required by the macro, it is another notable feature of Word and further demonstrates the flexibility of macros.

11 Click *Insert* and then *Date and Time*

12 Press   **Pg Up**   to move to the top of the list

> Note: It is important to press the Pg Up key as part of the macro, even if you are currently located at the top of the list. This way, the highlight will always be placed correctly for the next action, no matter when you use the macro in the future.

13 Press ↓ three times to move to the desired date format

FIGURE WP3-26 ■ RECORDING THE MACRO

(a) The Macro Recorder toolbar.
(b) The *Tape* icon indicates that the macro is being recorded.

(a)   (b)

14 Press ↵ to select it

The current date should now appear on your screen.

15 Press ↵ twice to leave a blank line after the date

This completes the mouse actions and keystrokes for now. To end the macro recording,

16 Click the *Stop* button on the macro recorder toolbar   [Alt + T , M , O]

17 Close the document *without* saving it.

The HEADING macro is saved as part of Word's "Normal" template. It is now available for use with any document that uses this template.

CREATING A SHORTCUT MACRO.   For comparison, create a shortcut macro that types a closing, as in Figure WP3-27.

STEPS

1 Open a new document

2 Click *Tools* and then *Macro*

Note that the HEADING macro appears in the macro list. You are now going to record a second macro named CLOSING as follows:

3 Type **CLOSING**

4 Click *Record*

The *Record Macro* dialog box appears. You can now assign the macro to a toolbar, menu, or shortcut keyboard action. This exercise will assign a shortcut key:

Keyboard

5 Click *Keyboard* in the *Assign Macro To* box

FIGURE WP3-27 ■ THE CLOSING MACRO WILL PRODUCE THIS TEXT

Sincerely yours,

Martin Parker

WP

A *Customize* dialog box appears as shown in Figure WP3-28. You can now indicate the shortcut keys that will be used. For example, you will use the "C" key as a mnemonic for "CLOSING."

6 **Press** **Alt** **+** **C** **to assign these keys to the macro**

The dialog box indicates that this key combination is currently unassigned. If it were already assigned to some other purpose, you could simply choose another combination, such as Alt + E (for "End") or even Alt + Ctrl + C.

7 **Click _Assign_**

The Shortcut keys move to the Current Keys list.

8 **Click the _Close_ button**

The macro recorder appears as before. Drag the recorder out of the way (click and drag its title bar). You can now type the macro:

9 **Press** ↵ **twice to skip two lines**

10 **Type** **Sincerely yours,**

11 **Press** ↵ **three times to skip two more lines**

FIGURE WP3-28 ■ **THE _CUSTOMIZE_ DIALOG BOX**

After selecting *Keyboard,* the *Customize* dialog box lets you assign shortcut keys that will invoke the macro.

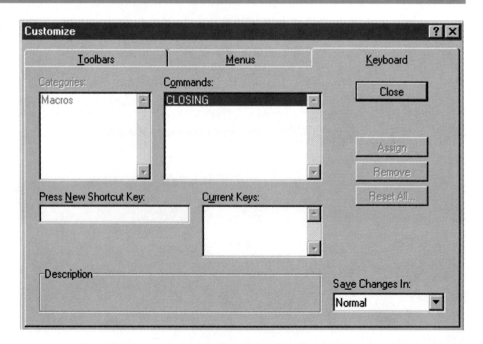

▢12 **Type your name and press ↵**

▢13 **Click the *Stop* button to end**   **[Alt + T , M , O]**

This new macro is now saved both with a name and shortcut key and is available for use.

▢14 **Close the document (again, there is no need to save as a document)**

INVOKING A MACRO

The method by which you invoke a macro depends on how it was saved. The following exercises demonstrate invoking macros by name and by shortcut keys.

INVOKING A MACRO BY NAME.   Macros can be invoked, when needed, through the *Macro* dialog box, as follows:

▢1 **Close any open document and then open a new document**

▢2 **Click *Tools* and then *Macro***

The Macro dialog box appears.

▢3 **Type   HEADING   in the *Macro Name* text box**

> **Tip: You could also select a macro by clicking its name in the list or pressing the Tab key and then using the arrow keys to highlight its name.**

▢4 **Click the *Run* button (or press ↵)**

The heading is quickly typed by the macro and appears on your screen. If the macro was recorded correctly, the date should match the system date, and the insertion point should be correctly positioned to allow you to begin typing a letter.

▢5 **Press ↵ to insert a blank line for now**

INVOKING A MACRO BY SHORTCUT KEY.   If you assigned a shortcut key to a macro, you need not invoke it by name. Instead, simply tap the appropriate keys that you assigned. For example, to invoke the CLOSING shortcut keys,

▢1 **Press Alt + C**

WP

The CLOSING macro will skip two additional lines on the screen and type the words "Sincerely yours" and your name.

There is no hard-and-fast rule for naming macros. In general, assign shortcut keys for often-used tasks, saving the multiletter names for less utilized macros.

2 **Close the document without saving**

EDITING A MACRO

Macros can be replaced, deleted, or edited to change or expand their function. To replace a macro with a new one, simply create a new macro with the same name, press Y to replace, and then type the new macro. To erase a macro, highlight its filename in the *Open* dialog box and delete it.

The following exercise demonstrates a simple edit routine to add a line to your heading macro, as in Figure WP3-29.

STEPS

1 **Open a new document**

2 **Click *Tools* and then *Macro***

3 **Type** **HEADING** **in the *Name list* box or click it in the list**

4 **Click the *Edit* button**

Your document window lists your macro, as in Figure WP3-30a. In addition, a Macro toolbar appears at the top. You can add additional lines, delete, or edit as you would any other text. For example,

5 **Press ↓ twice to move the insertion point before *Insert "The XYZ Company"***

6 **Select the two macro command lines as in Figure WP3-30b by clicking and dragging the mouse pointer over them** [**F8** , →]

 7 **Click *Edit* and then *Copy* to copy the selection** [**Ctrl** + **C**]

FIGURE WP3-29 ■ THE AMENDED MACRO

The amended HEADING macro will display this three-line heading.

The XYZ Company
1234 Fifth Avenue
New York, New York 10001

April 6, 1996

FIGURE WP3-30 ■ EDITING A MACRO

(a) Opening a macro file through the *Edit Macro* dialog box (Tools, Macro, Edit) allows you to edit it directly.
(b) Selecting macro commands to be copied for the insertion of new text.
(c) The completed macro.

```
HEADING
Sub MAIN
CenterPara
Insert "The XYZ Company"
InsertPara
Insert "New York, New York 10001"
InsertPara
LeftPara
InsertPara
InsertDateTime .DateTimePic = "MMMM d, yyyy", .InsertAsField = 0
InsertPara
InsertPara
End Sub
```

(a)

```
Sub MAIN
CenterPara
Insert "The XYZ Company"
InsertPara
Insert "New York, New York 10001"
InsertPara
```

(b)

```
Sub MAIN
CenterPara
Insert "The XYZ Company"
InsertPara
Insert "1234 Fifth Avenue"
InsertPara
Insert "New York, New York 10001"
InsertPara
```

(c)

WP

8 **Click the beginning of the line** [F8]

9 **Click *Edit* and then *Paste*** [↵ , Ctrl + V]

10 **Press → seven times to move the insertion point after "Insert"**

11 **Shut off the Insert mode (press Insert)**

12 **Type   "1234 Fifth Avenue"   (use Figure WP3-30c as a guide)**

13 **Click *File* and then *Close*** [Alt + Shift , F]

14 **Click *Yes* to keep the changes** [↵]

The macro has been modified and saved.

15 **Invoke the heading macro to verify its result**

Tip: It is also possible to assign a macro to a toolbar or menu. See the appendix.

☑ CHECKPOINT

✓ Create a macro named SELF that prints your name and address on three centered lines.
✓ Create a macro named WPCHECK5 (and assign it to the shortcut ALT + W) that will underline the next word already typed on the screen (*Hint:* use the Select mode, then search for a space, then underline.)
✓ Use the SELF macro to print your name
✓ Position the insertion point before your first name and use WPCHECK5 shortcut to underline it.
✓ Print the results.

MODULE 5: FOOTNOTES AND ENDNOTES

Footnotes and **endnotes** are text added to your document to provide references, explanations, or comments. They may be referenced in the text by a footnote or endnote number. Footnotes are usually placed at the bottom of the page on which they are referenced, whereas endnotes are usually listed at the end of a document. Because the procedures for using footnotes and endnotes are virtually identical, only footnotes will be presented here. Both footnotes and endnotes can be accessed through the *Insert* menu.

CREATING A FOOTNOTE

When you create a footnote, Word numbers and formats it for you. It is a difficult typing task to properly place footnotes on a page. Word eliminates this problem by automatically adjusting each page so that the footnote will fit correctly. Creating a footnote is a relatively simple matter: position the insertion point in the text where the footnote marker will appear, invoke the Footnote command, and type the footnote. The following exercise lets you experience this firsthand.

STEPS

1 **Close any open document and open EXWP3-2**

You must first position the insertion point where the footnote number is desired. (The footnote format used in the exercise is one of many styles; you may prefer to use some other format in the future.)

2 **Move the insertion point to Page 2, after the quotation on the second line of the first paragraph, as in Figure WP3-31a**

3 **Click *Insert* and then *Footnote***

A dialog box appears as shown in Figure WP3-31b. From here, you can select footnotes or endnotes, as well as various options. For now,

4 **Click the *OK* button (or press ↵)**

FIGURE WP3-31 ■ CREATING FOOTNOTES

(a) The insertion point is in the text where the footnote reference is desired.
(b) The *Footnote and Endnote* dialog box.
(c) The footnote is typed in the footnote area.

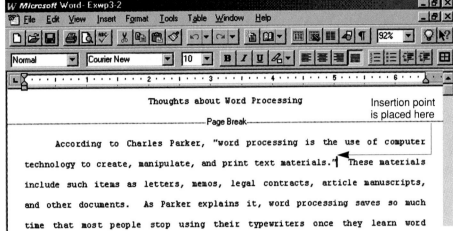

(a)

(b)

(c)

The insertion point moves to the footnote entry area at the bottom of the page. In addition, a footnote number appears to its left and the Footnote bar appears below the document.

Tip: You can press the shortcut keys Alt + Ctrl + F instead of Steps 3–4.

5   Type the footnote as shown in Figure WP3-31c

Do not press the Enter key when you reach the right margin, but type as you normally would. You are free to use Backspace, Delete, and Insert as needed to correct errors.

WP

6 After you finish typing, press ↵

7 Click the *Close* button of the Footnote bar   [**Alt** + **Shift** + **C**]

Your document will now display a "1" positioned after the quotation mark. Create one more footnote as follows:

8 Position the insertion point after the word "office" in the second paragraph, as shown in Figure WP3-32a

9 Click *Insert*, *Footnote*, and then the *OK* button

10 Type the second footnote as shown in Figure WP3-32b

11 After you finish typing, press ↵

12 Click the *Close* button   [**Alt** + **Shift** + **C**]

The footnotes are now completed.

FIGURE WP3-32 ■ PLACING A SECOND FOOTNOTE

(a) Place the insertion point at the new position.
(b) The second footnote has been typed.

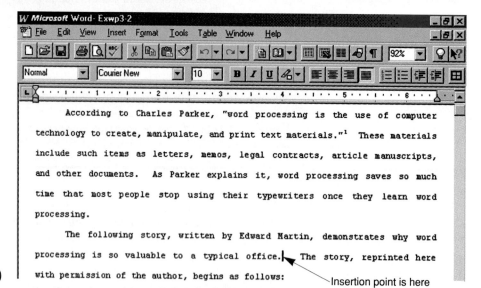

Tip: Use Word's Page Layout view to display the footnotes as they would appear on a printed page.

13 Save the document as EXWP3-4a

Figure WP3-33 displays the entire page as it will appear when printed. Word automatically creates the subscripted references and the horizontal line separating the footnotes from the text. As you will see shortly, these can be changed to suit other footnote styles.

If you were to add a third footnote on this page, an appropriate number of document text lines would be moved to the next page automatically to ensure that the new footnote would end at the bottom margin. Similarly, removing a footnote would cause text lines from the next page to move up to this page.

You may create new footnotes at any time, and in any position in your document. All subsequent footnotes will be renumbered automatically to reflect the new addition.

FIGURE WP3-33 ■ PRINTED FOOTNOTES

When printed, footnote references appear as superscripts, with the full citation properly positioned at the bottom of the page (partial text shown).

According to Charles Parker, "word processing is the use of computer technology to create, manipulate, and print text materials."[1] These materials include such items as letters, memos, legal contracts, article manuscripts, and other documents. As Parker explains it, word processing saves so much time that most people stop using their typewriters once they learn word processing.

The following story, written by Edward Martin, demonstrates why word processing is so valuable to a typical office.[2] The story, reprinted here with permission of the author, begins as follows:

Andrea sat nervously in front of the microcomputer screen. She stretched her fingers over the keybaord while Elissa Roberts, manager of Freddy Johnson's Travel Agency, looked on. Andrea had skipped lunch to finish this work, stopping only when the stiffness in her neck and fingers forced her to take a break. This was her first big assignment since completing the word processing course at Oakridge University. She could have used more practice with the word processor--especially on this keyboard, which differed from the one she used at school. Her fingers kept pressing the wrong key for SHIFT, forcing her to backspace and retype more often than usual. If only she were better acquainted with the layout, she'd be fine. But there was no time for that now. Andrea knew that time was short, and excuses wouldn't help. The job simply had to be completed.

Andrea had arrived at work earlier that morning to learn that an important meeting had been moved up, well ahead of schedule. With only hours left before the meeting, Andrea had been asked to put her word processing training to the test--a typewriter

---

[1] Parker, Charles S., <u>Understanding Computers and Information Processing: Today and Tomorrow (Third Edition)</u>. Chicago: The Dryden Press, 1990: 372.

[2] Adapted from Martin, Edward G. and Burstein, Jerome S., <u>Computer Systems Fundamentals</u>. Chicago: The Dryden Press, 1990: 149, 182.

WP

THE *NOTE OPTIONS* DIALOG BOX

Word's default footnote style is acceptable for most applications, but it can be changed to suit your specific needs through a *Note Options* dialog box. Examine the screen as follows:

> **1** Click *Insert* and then *Footnote*

> **2** Click *Options* for the *Note Options* dialog box

A *Note Options* dialog box should appear as in Figure WP3-34. It can be used to change the numbering method, numbering style, spacing, or position of notes. For example, the *Restart Each Page* check box resets the footnote counter on each page; the number format drop-down list lets you select other numbering schemes. You may want to experiment with this dialog box in the future. but for now do not make any alterations.

> **3** Click the *Cancel* button to exit the dialog box   [Esc]

> **4** Click the *Cancel* button again to exit the *Footnote and Endnote* dialog box   [Esc]

EDITING A FOOTNOTE

Like other text, footnotes (and endnotes) can be edited to correct a reference or modify a comment. The following exercise examines the editing process.

> **1** Switch to Page Layout view if you're not already there (select *View*, *Page Layout*)

FIGURE WP3-34 ■ **THE *NOTE OPTIONS* DIALOG BOX**

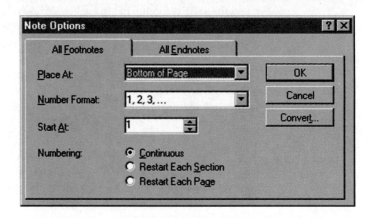

2 Move to the bottom of page 2

Your screen should resemble Figure WP3-35a. At this point, you can modify the footnote, using the arrow keys, Backspace, Delete, or Insert as needed. Try this quick change:

3 Delete the words "Adapted from" (include the space)

Your screen should resemble Figure WP3-35b.

4 Save again as EXWP3-4a

> **Tip:** You can also edit a footnote by first double-clicking the desired footnote number in the text by mouse instead of Steps 1 and 2 above. Then, close the footnote "pane" when you're done editing.

DELETING A FOOTNOTE

Footnotes can also be removed from the text easily. This exercise deletes the first footnote.

STEPS

1 Open EXWP3-4a if it is not on your screen

WP

FIGURE WP3-35 ■ **EDITING A FOOTNOTE**

(a) Positioning the insertion point in Page Layout view.
(b) The edited footnote.

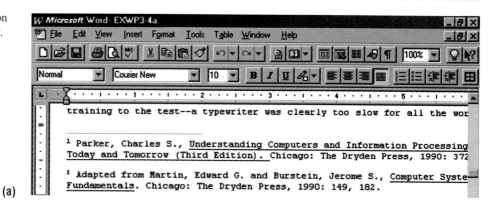

(a)

(b)

2 **Move the insertion point before the "1" of the first footnote on Page 2**

The insertion point is placed correctly when it falls between the quotation mark and the footnote number, as shown in Figure WP3-36a.

3 **Select the footnote number (drag the mouse over it or press** **Shift** **+** **→** **)**

As shown in Figure WP3-36b the footnote is highlighted and "Footnote Refe" shows in the Formatting toolbar's style box.

4 **Press** **Delete**

The "1" disappears from the screen and the second footnote is automatically renumbered. Footnote deletions (like insertions) affect the footnote numbers that follow. If you are using sequential footnote numbers *throughout* your document (the default setting), then all footnotes after the deleted one will be renumbered. If you have opted to start footnotes anew on each page, then only this page will be amended.

> **Tip:** Footnotes affect text layout throughout the document. You should use Page Layout view mode when you create, edit, or delete footnotes to ensure that the final printed layout will be acceptable. In addition, if you accidentally delete a footnote, use the Edit Undo command to restore it.

5 **Close the document** *without* **saving it**

☑ **CHECKPOINT**

✓ In a new document window copy any paragraph from this book.
✓ Add a footnote at the end noting the page where you found it. Save it as WPCHECK6.

FIGURE WP3-36 ■ **DELETING A FOOTNOTE**

(a) Position the insertion point to the left of the footnote to be deleted.

(a)

      According to Charles Parker, "word processing is the use of computer technology to create, manipulate, and print text materials."¹ These materials and other documents. As Parker explains it, word processing saves so much

(b) Select the footnote by dragging the mouse or pressing Shift + →.

(b)

      According to Charles Parker, "word processing is the use of computer technology to create, manipulate, and print text materials."▮ These materials and other documents. As Parker explains it, word processing saves so much

✓ Insert a footnote at the end of the first sentence. Type the citation as "New foot-note, p. ___," filling in the appropriate page number.
✓ Save again as WPCHECK6 and print.
✓ Delete the second footnote.

MODULE 6: ORGANIZING DATA WITH OUTLINES AND SORTS

Word offers two features to help organize your text. Word's **Outline feature** helps you create properly numbered outlines of up to nine levels of numbering—each level determined by its tab position. Word's **Sort feature** allows you to arrange text in alphabetical or numerical order. The following exercise creates and modifies the outline shown in Figure WP3-37.

PREPARING AN OUTLINE

The first step in preparing an outline is to invoke the Outline feature as follows:

STEPS

1 **Launch Word or close any open document**

WP

FIGURE WP3-37 ■ THE OUTLINE TO BE CREATED WITH WORD'S OUTLINE FEATURE

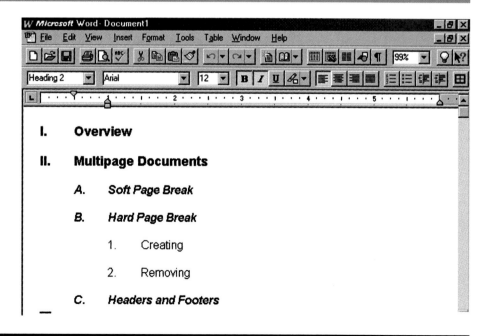

To activate the *Outline* menu,

2 Click *View* and then *Outline* to switch to the Outline view (or click the *Outline* button on the status bar)

Your screen should resemble Figure WP3-38a.

3 Click *Format* and then *Heading Numbering*

A *Heading Numbering* dialog box appears as in Figure WP3-38b.

4 Accept the first format by clicking the *OK* button (or pressing ↵)

Your screen should appear as Figure 3-39a. Note that an Outline toolbar now appears. In addition, an outline icon and the first number of the outline item (I.) appears on the screen.

5 Type Overview and press ↵

As shown in Figure WP3-39b, the next number sequence ("II.") appears.

FIGURE WP3-38 ■ **USING WORD'S OUTLINE FEATURE**

(a) The Outline view has been invoked.
(b) The *Heading Numbering* dialog box lets you select a numbering style.

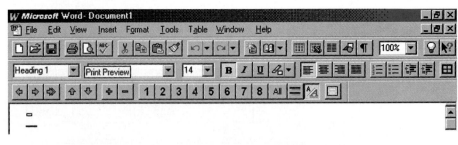

(a)

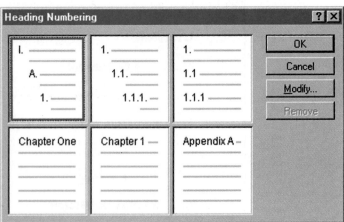

(b)

FIGURE WP3-39 ■ CREATING AN OUTLINE

(a) The first number has been set by the program.
(b) The next outline number appears when you press the Enter key.
(c) The Tab key will change the level of the outline number.

(a)

(b)

(c)

6 Type **Multipage Documents** and press ↵

As expected, a "III." appears on the next line.

CHANGING TO A LOWER LEVEL.   There is no third line at this level, so you must now change to the next level.

STEPS

1 Press **Tab** to move to a lower level

As in Figure WP3-39c, the "III." has changed to an "A." in the second level. Continue to type as you did before.

> **Tip:** You can also press the "demote" button on the toolbar to change to a lower level.

2 Type **Soft Page Break** and press ↵

Notice that the outline stays within the same level. A "B." now appears on the screen.

3 Type **Hard Page Break** and press ↵

Now move to the next lower level with the same process as before.

4 Press **Tab**

The "C." changes to a " 1." as it becomes the third level.

5 Type **Creating** and press ↵

The outline now stays within the third level as a "2." and appears on the screen.

6 Type **Removing** and press ↵

A "3." appears and awaits your entry.

> **Note: A minus sign at the left of a line indicates a heading that has no subtext (additional levels of text). A plus sign shows a heading with subtext.**

RETURNING TO A HIGHER LEVEL. To return to a higher outline level at this point, you simply use Shift + Tab as follows.

STEPS

1 Press **Shift** + **Tab**

The "3." changes to a "C."—the next entry in the higher level of the outline.

> **Tip: Pressing the "promote" toolbar button will also return the outline to a higher level.**

2 Type **Headers and Footers**

Now turn off the outline feature as follows:

3 Click *View* and then *Normal*

Your completed outline should resemble Figure WP3-37.

4 Save this document as OUTLINE1

EDITING THE OUTLINE

Like any other text, outlines can be easily modified. Adding or deleting lines automatically adjusts the sequence of outline numbers that follow. Inserting or removing tabs alters the outline level of that particular line. You can change the style and numbering scheme of the entire outline as well.

ADDING LINES. Inserting new lines into the outline renumbers all subsequent lines.

STEPS

1. **Open OUTLINE1 if it is not on your screen**

2. **Turn on the Outline view**

3. **Position the insertion point *after* the "w" in "Overview"**

4. **Press ↵**

As shown in Figure WP3-40, a new number is added in sequence at the proper level, and all subsequent numbers on that level have been renumbered.

5. **Type   Preparing**

DELETING LINES.   Deleting existing lines in an outline will renumber all subsequent lines.

STEPS

1. **Position the insertion point to the end of "II. Preparing" if it is not already there**

2. **Press   Backspace   to delete this entire line and then press   Delete   to remove its numeral (II.)**

The subsequent numbers have been readjusted in sequence.

WP

FIGURE WP3-40 ■ CHANGING THE OUTLINE

Adding a line inserts a new number into the outline.

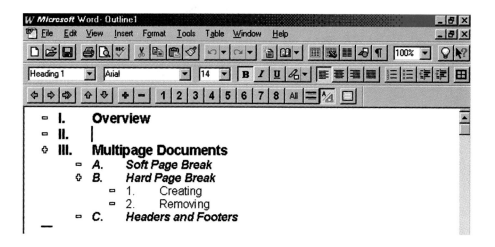

REARRANGING OUTLINE "FAMILIES."   An outline *family* is the selection of all subsequent lines contained within a given outline level. You can move or copy these selections as easily as other text selections. Unlike normal moving, however, the Outline feature will renumber all subsequent levels to reflect the change.

STEPS

   1   Open OUTLINE1 if it is not on your screen and switch to Outline view, if needed

2   Point to the *Plus* icon to the left of "II." until a pointer with arrows at each end appears (as in Figure WP3-41a)

3   Click the *Plus* icon to select the family (as in Figure WP3-41b)

   4   Click the *Move Up Arrow* button on the Outline toolbar to move the family up one level

5   Click anywhere to turn off the select mode

The selection has moved, and all appropriate numbers have been changed to reflect their new position as shown in Figure WP3-41c.

6   Save this document as OUTLINE2

FIGURE WP3-41   ■   REARRANGING OUTLINE "FAMILIES"

(a) Position the mouse pointer to the extreme left.
(b) Click the icon to select the family.
(c) Click the *Move Up* button to reposition the text.

I.   Overview
II.   **Multipage Documents**
    A.   *Soft Page Break*
    B.   *Hard Page Break*
       1.   Creating
       2.   Removing
    C.   *Headers and Footers*
(a)

I.   Overview
II.   **Multipage Documents**
    A.   *Soft Page Break*
    B.   *Hard Page Break*
       1.   Creating
       2.   Removing
    C.   *Headers and Footers*
(b)

I.   **Multipage Documents**
    A.   *Soft Page Break*
    B.   *Hard Page Break*
       1.   Creating
       2.   Removing
    C.   *Headers and Footers*
(c)   **II.**   **Overview**

MODIFYING THE OUTLINE FORMAT

If the default outline style is not appropriate, you can choose six other outline formats or invent your own. To prepare for these exercises,

STEPS

1. Launch Word or close any open document

2. Open the OUTLINE1 document

 3. Switch to Outline view

PARAGRAPH NUMBERING.   Like new page numbers, any outline number can be given any desired value, as follows:

STEPS

1. Move insertion point to first line of the outline

2. Click *Format* and then *Heading Numbering*

3. Click the *Modify* button

A *Modify Heading Numbering* dialog box appears as shown in Figure WP3-42a.

4. Click the *Start At* entry box

5. Delete the entry, type **3** , and click the *OK* button

As shown in Figure WP3-42b, the outline has been renumbered starting with your choice—III.

OUTLINE FORMAT.   At the beginning of the outline section, you used the default outline style. You can also change the style of an existing outline. Note that the insertion point can be anywhere *within* the outline when changing outline style.

STEPS

1. Place the insertion point anywhere within the outline

2. Click *Format* and then *Heading Numbering*

3. In the dialog box, click the style box at the center of the top line

4. Click the *OK* button

FIGURE WP3-42 ■ **RENUMBERING OUTLINES**

(a) The *Modify Heading Numbering* dialog box.
(b) The starting number has been changed.

Modify Heading Numbering   [?] [X]

Number Format

Text Before:	Bullet or Number:	Text After:
[ ]	[I, II, III, ... ▼]	[.] [Font...]

Start At: Include from Previous Level:
[I ▲▼]   [Nothing ▼]

Level 1
I.
_____
_____

Number Position

Alignment of List Text: [Left ▼]

Distance from Indent to Text: [0.5" ▲▼]

Distance from Number to Text: [0" ▲▼]

☑ Hanging Indent

[ ] Restart Numbering at Each New Section

Preview
```
I. ————————
   A. ————————
      1. ————————
         a) ————————
            (1) ————————
               (a) ————————
                  (i) ————————
                     (a) ————————
                        (i) ————
```

[OK]
[Cancel]

(a)

```
✧ III.   Multipage Documents
    ▫ A.    Soft Page Break
    ✧ B.    Hard Page Break
        ▫ 1.    Creating
        ▫ 2.    Removing
    ▫ C.    Headers and Footers
▫ IV.   Overview
```

(b)

CANCELING CHANGES.   To cancel a change, use the same dialog box. To cancel the paragraph number settings or other outline settings, try this:

STEPS

[1] Click *Format* and then *Heading Numbering*

[2] Click the *Remove* button

[3] Switch to Normal View (*View, Normal*)

The removal of these enhancements will return the outline to standard outline form.

[4] Close the document without saving

SORTING

Word's sort feature allows you to arrange text in alphabetical or numerical order. You can sort lists, lines of text, paragraphs, or merge records. You can also invoke sort when the insertion point is positioned in a table to sort the table rows just as easily (tables are discussed in "Module 7: Graphics and Tables"). This brief exercise will examine basic sort techniques. Once you have mastered them, feel free to experiment with all the variations.

> **Tip:** It is a good idea to save the original document *before* sorting and to save the sorted results as a new document (with a new filename). This way, not only can you open the document if your sort does not perform as expected, but you will always have the text in its original order if you need to use it again.

PREPARING FOR THE SORT. For this exercise, you will need to create the document shown in Figure WP3-43 as follows:

STEPS

1 Launch Word or close any open document

2 Switch to Normal view if needed

Now, do Steps 3 through 5 to set the tabs at 2 inches and 4 inches from the left margin.

3 Change the tab button on the left side of the ruler bar to "L" if needed [**Alt** + **F** , **T**]

4 Click the 2" mark on the ruler bar [**2** , **Alt** + **S**]

FIGURE WP3-43 ■ THE SORT DATA

Data are placed in columns, one tab apart.

Customer	City	State
Edwards	New York	NY
Smith	Washington	DC
Parker	Santa Fe	NM
Bonacci	Fort Worth	TX
Martin	Rochester	NY
Charles	Albuquerque	NM
Williams	Boston	MA
Hayes	Fort Worth	TX
Perkins	Chicago	IL

WP

5 Click the 4″ mark on the ruler bar [**4** , **Alt** + **S** , ↵]

Tabs are now set at the 2 inch and 4 inch marks as shown at the top of Figure WP3-43.

6 Type the data as shown in Figure WP3-43, pressing **Tab** to advance to the next column
and ↵ at the end of each line

7 Save this document as SORT1

SORTING WITH ONE KEY. Basic sorting involves two simple decisions: you
must decide what portion of the document will be sorted and what key (or keys) will be
used. A *key* is a piece of data (such as name or zip code) that provides the basis for the
sort. *Any* key can be used. If the key you select uniquely identifies each item (that is,
there are no duplicate key values) then you only need one key to completely sort your
list. Social security number and driver's license number are examples of unique keys,
but last name would work as well if all the last names on your list were different (as in
this example). To sort,

STEPS

1 Indicate the selection of text to be sorted as in Figure WP3-44a

(Reminder: Move to the "E" in "Edwards," invoke the select mode, and then move
below the last line of the list.)

> **Tip: The selection to be sorted should include only data, not titles, headings, or
> summary lines. Otherwise, these lines would be sorted along with the data and appear
> somewhere in the resulting list.**

2 Click *Ta̲ble* and then *Sort Text* for the *Sort Text* dialog box

A *Sort Text* dialog box resembling Figure WP3-44b will appear. This dialog box allows
you to control such factors as keys, record selection (what records will be included), sort
order (whether the sort will be ascending or descending), and type of sort. You should always review this dialog box to make sure that the settings are correct for the sort you desire. If they are not what you want, change them appropriately.

At present, the default settings are fine: the leftmost column (Paragraphs) will be
used as the key, and each line in the data selection will be sorted in ascending order (A
to Z).

3 Click the *OK* button to perform the sort [↵]

4 Click anywhere to deselect the text

The sort appears on your screen in Figure WP3-44c.

FIGURE WP3-44 ■ SORTING WITH ONE KEY

(a) Text selection to be sorted.
(b) *Sort Text* dialog box.
(c) Sorted text.

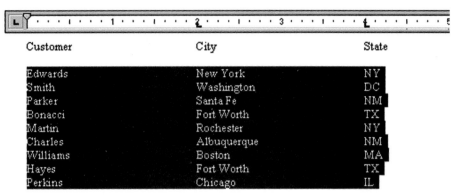

(a)

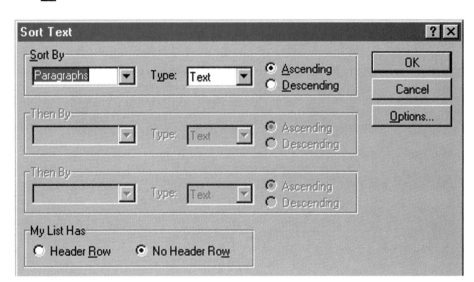

(b)

Customer	City	State
Bonacci	Fort Worth	TX
Charles	Albuquerque	NM
Edwards	New York	NY
Hayes	Fort Worth	TX
Martin	Rochester	NY
Parker	Santa Fe	NM
Perkins	Chicago	IL
Smith	Washington	DC
Williams	Boston	MA

(c)

Tip: To undo the sort, select *Edit* and then *Undo Sort* (or press Ctrl + Z).

> **5**   Save this document as SORT2

> **Tip:** Although it is not evident in this result, Word sorts special characters (such as @ or *) first, followed by numbers, uppercase letters, and then lowercase letters. Thus, "apple" would come after "Cat" and after "*zoo."

SORTING WITH TWO KEYS.   Many times, the key you select does not uniquely identify each item (that is, there are duplicate key values), and you may want to add a second key to differentiate among the duplicates. This exercise, for example, will sort the list of data using "State" as the first (primary) key and "City" as a secondary key.

STEPS

1   Indicate the selection of text to be sorted as in Figure WP3-45a.

2   Click *Table* and then *Sort Text*

You can now identify the first key ("State"), which can be found in the third column of data. Word uses the tab column to identify the key (the left margin counting as the first column). Using Figure WP3-45b as a guide, do the following:

3   Click the *Sort By* drop-down arrow

4   Click *Field 3* to select it   [↓ ,   **Tab**]

5   Click the *Then By* drop-down arrow

6   Click *Field 2* to select it   [↓ ,   **Tab**]

7   Click the *OK* button to perform the sort   [↵]

8   Click anywhere in the document to cancel the select mode   [→]

The resultant sort, in state and then city order, appears as shown in Figure WP3-45c.

9   Save this document as SORT3

10 Close the document

In the future, you may want to experiment with sort order, numerical sorts, and selecting records. Simply invoke the *Sort Text* dialog box from the *Table* menu and follow the command structure.

☑ **CHECKPOINT**

✓   Prepare an outline of this module (you may use the outline at the chapter's beginning as a reference).

FIGURE WP3-45 ■ SORTING WITH TWO KEYS

(a) Text selection to be sorted.
(b) *Sort Text* dialog box with two keys.
(c) Sorted text.

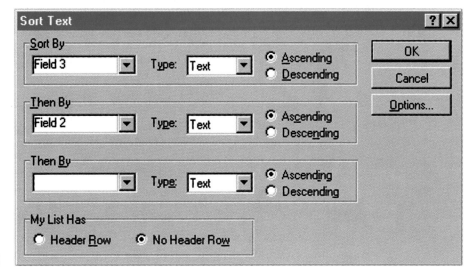

Customer	City	State
Bonacci	Fort Worth	TX
Charles	Albuquerque	NM
Edwards	New York	NY
Hayes	Fort Worth	TX
Martin	Rochester	NY
Parker	Santa Fe	NM
Perkins	Chicago	IL
Smith	Washington	DC
Williams	Boston	MA

(a)

Sort Text

Sort By
Field 3   Type: Text   ● Ascending   ○ Descending

Then By
Field 2   Type: Text   ● Ascending   ○ Descending

Then By
   Type: Text   ● Ascending   ○ Descending

My List Has
○ Header Row   ● No Header Row

OK   Cancel   Options...

(b)

Customer	City	State
Smith	Washington	DC
Perkins	Chicago	IL
Williams	Boston	MA
Charles	Albuquerque	NM
Parker	Santa Fe	NM
Edwards	New York	NY
Martin	Rochester	NY
Bonacci	Fort Worth	TX
Hayes	Fort Worth	TX

(c)

✓ Save as WPCHECK7.
✓ Change the outline style to Appendix form.
✓ Move the last section ("Sorting . . . ") to the beginning of the outline.
✓ Save as WPCHECK7 and print.

WP

MODULE 7: GRAPHICS AND TABLES

Word's **graphics feature** lets you combine lines or images with text. This capability is useful when you are producing such documents as newsletters and reports, where graphic images, diagrams, company logos, or even pictures are needed.

Simple graphics—lines and boxes—can be drawn directly on the screen. More complicated graphic images can be created with Word's Drawing program or other graphics programs, saved on disk, and brought into the document.

BORDERS AND HORIZONTAL LINES

Word's Borders feature allows you to create horizontal or vertical lines around selected text or objects. These simple graphic lines can add emphasis or make a page more pleasing to the eye. The following exercise creates a horizontal graphic line as part of a letterhead as shown in Figure WP3-46.

STEPS

1 Launch Word or start a new document

2 Type the centered heading shown in Figure WP3-46

3 Press ↵ twice, then press ↑ once to move up one line

4 Click the *Borders* button on the Formatting toolbar

A Borders toolbar appears above the ruler bar as shown in Figure WP3-47a.

5 Click the *Bottom Border* button.

Tip: To cancel a setting, click the button again.

6 Click the *Borders* button on the Formatting toolbar to remove the Borders toolbar.

FIGURE WP3-46 ■ CREATING A HORIZONTAL LINE

The Border command can be used to create a horizontal line.

Your Name
1234 Randall Avenue
Los Angeles, CA 90211
(213) 555-9876

FIGURE WP3-47 ■ USING THE BORDERS FEATURE

(a) The Borders toolbar.
(b) The *Paragraph Borders and Shading* dialog box.

(a)

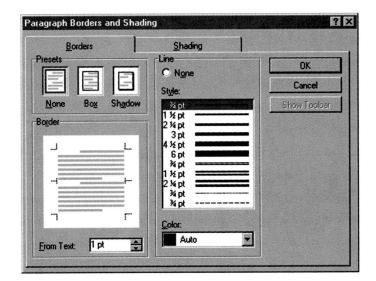

(b)

The image on your screen should resemble Figure WP3-46.

> **7** **Save this document as LETTERHD**

> **8** **Close the document window**

You can select any text and then choose which lines you will place around it using the same approach as you used for horizontal lines.

CREATING TABLES IN WORD

An extension of simple lines or boxes in Word's powerful Table feature, which can quickly create and edit boxes to present data in columns. The following exercise illustrates the basics of this process by creating the table shown in Figure WP3-48.

THE BASIC TABLE FORM.   To create the basic table form, do the following:

FIGURE WP3-48 ■ A WORD TABLE

This table will be created with Word's Table feature.

PHONE LIST		
Last	**First**	**Phone**
Your Last Name	Your First Name	999-555-1234
Martin	Edward	718-555-1234
Parker	Charles	505-555-9876
Kee	Charles	201-555-5678

STEPS

1 Launch Word or close any open document

2 Open a new document

 3 Click the *Insert Table* button on the Standard toolbar

A table box appears as shown in Figure WP3-49a.

FIGURE WP3-49 ■ SPECIFYING THE TABLE SIZE

(a) The *Table Insert* button accesses the table box.
(b) The 5 × 3 table has been set.
(c) The *Insert Table* dialog box can also specify a table size.

(a)

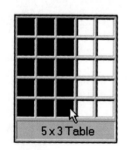

(b)

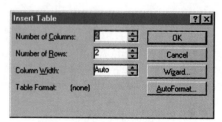

(c)

4 Point to the upper-left corner of the box, as shown in Figure WP3-49a

5 Click and drag the mouse pointer three cells right and five cells down so that the box reads "5 x 3" as shown in Figure WP3-49b

6 Release the mouse button to accept

Tip: If you make a mistake, click the *Undo* button or select *Edit, Undo* to cancel.

The basic form (set to 3 columns and 5 rows) appears on your screen as in Figure WP3-50a. If gridlines do not appear, try selecting *Table* and then *Gridlines* to display them.

ENTERING TABLE DATA.   Tables are composed of *cells* formed by the intersection of columns and rows. You can use the arrow keys or the Tab key to move to each cell. Text can be entered into each cell individually as follows:

STEPS

1 Press ↓ to move to the first cell in the second row (Ln 2)

2 Type Last and press Tab

3 In the second cell, type First and press Tab

4 In the third cell, type Phone and press Tab

Your screen should resemble Figure WP3-50b.

5 Complete the rest of the table by filling in the rows for Martin, Parker, and Kee in the three remaining rows of your table (as in Figure WP3-50c)

Tip: If you press the Enter key by mistake, the cell will expand one row. Press the Backspace key to remove the hard return, and then press the Tab key correctly.

6 Save this document as TABLE

TABLE ENHANCEMENTS.   A table can be enhanced while the form is being created or after it has been filled with text. As long as your insertion point is within the table, you can access these enhancements by invoking the Table command as follows:

STEPS

1 Move the insertion point to the upper-left cell (on Ln 1)

FIGURE WP3-50 ■ **CREATING THE BASIC TABLE**

(a) The 5-row by 3-column table has been created.
(b) Each cell is entered individually.
(c) The data have been entered.

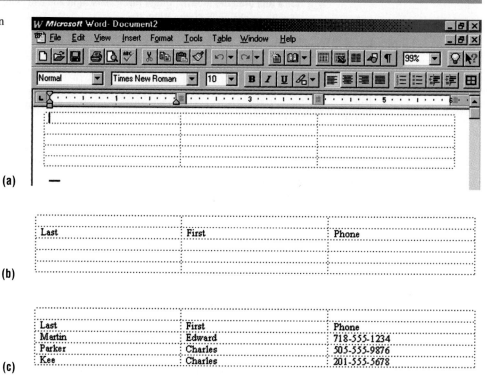

(a)

(b)

Last	First	Phone
Martin	Edward	718-555-1234
Parker	Charles	505-555-9876
Kee	Charles	201-555-5678

(c)

Next, select all cells in the row as follows:

2 Click the mouse and then drag it across the top three cells to select them (as in Figure WP3-51a), then release the mouse   [**Shift** + **End** three times]

FIGURE WP3-51 ■ **ENHANCING THE TABLE**

(a) The top row of cells has been selected.
(b) All three cells have been merged to create one cell.

(a)

Last	First	Phone
Martin	Edward	718-555-1234
Parker	Charles	505-555-9876
Kee	Charles	201-555-5678

(b)

Last	First	Phone
Martin	Edward	718-555-1234
Parker	Charles	505-555-9876
Kee	Charles	201-555-5678

3 Click *T<u>a</u>ble* and then *<u>M</u>erge Cells*

4 Click anywhere to end the select mode   [↓]

The Row 1 cells have joined to form one long cell as in Figure WP3-51b. You can merge as many cells as you want to form larger boxes, in rows and in columns.

5 Move to the leftmost cell in the second row ("Last")

6 Select *all cells* in this row as before

Remember, to select, drag the mouse over the cells or press Shift + End three times.

7 Click *F<u>o</u>rmat, <u>F</u>ont* and then *<u>B</u>old* for bold   [**Ctrl** + **B**]

8 Click anywhere to end the select mode   [↓]

Now, to insert a row for new data:

9 Move to the first cell in the third row (Ln 3—"Martin")

10 Click *T<u>a</u>ble* and then *<u>I</u>nsert Rows*

11 Click anywhere to end the select mode   [→]

Now, try adding shading to a row of cells:

12 Move to the first cell in the second row (Ln 2—"Last")

13 Select the entire row (drag the mouse or press   **Shift**   +   **End**   three times)

14 Click *F<u>o</u>rmat* and then *<u>B</u>orders and Shading*

15 If needed, click the *Shading* tab to open that dialog box as shown in Figure WP3-52
                                                                          [**Alt** + **S**]

16 Click the *20%* shade   [**Alt** + **D** , ↓]

17 Click the *OK* button   [↵]

One more enhancement—adding solid grid lines to the table. At present, the dashed lines appear only on the screen. You can add solid lines that will appear in the printed version as follows:

18 Move the insertion point to the upper-left cell in the table.

19 Click *T<u>a</u>ble* and then *Select T<u>a</u>ble* to highlight the entire table

20 Click *F<u>o</u>rmat* and then *<u>B</u>orders and Shading*

FIGURE WP3-52 ■ THE *TABLE BORDERS AND SHADING* DIALOG BOX

---

21 If needed, click the *Borders* tab to access its dialog box   [**Alt** + **B**]

22 Click *Grid* in the *Presets* box

23 Click the *OK* button   [↵]

24 Click anywhere to clear the select mode   [↓]

COMPLETING THE TABLE.   With these enhancements set, you can now fill the empty cells with text.

STEPS

1 Move to the first row of the table

2 Click the *Center* toolbar button   [**Ctrl** + **E**]

3 Type   **PHONE LIST**

4   **In the first cell of row 3 (below "Last"), type your LAST name**

5   **Move to the next cell and type your FIRST name**

6   **Move to the next cell and type your PHONE number**

7   **Resave this document as TABLE**

Your screen should resemble Figure WP3-48. When printed, your table will be stylized like the table shown in the figure. Make sure your printer is ready and then print the table if you want.

When no longer needed, tables can be deleted by selecting Table, Select Table and then Delete Rows. You can select a table and press the Delete key to remove the text, but retain the table form.

ADDING GRAPHICS BOXES

Word's Graphics features also contain commands that allow you to create separate graphics boxes into which you can insert images, graphs, diagrams, charts, or even other documents. Of course, these other items must be available on disk. These boxes are like little windows on the screen. Document text automatically wraps around the window, as shown in Figure WP3-53. The following exercise demonstrates the creation and editing of a graphics box.

STEPS

1   **Close any open document**

2   **Open the EXWP3-6 text document**

> **Note: If you do not have EXWP3-6 on your disk, change the initial document font to Times New Roman 12 pt, type in the paragraph text shown in Figure WP3-54, and save it as EXWP3-6.** *Remember:* **Do not press the Enter key until you reach the end of the paragraph.**

FIGURE WP3-53 ■ COMBINING PICTURES WITH TEXT

This is an example of incorporating a graphics picture into a Word document. The picture can be positioned anywhere in the document, and its size can be adjusted to fit appropriately into the text. The graphic picture in this example contains a diagram of a 3-1/2" disk that was saved in a bit-mapped graphics file with the name DISK. This particular file was saved as a monochrome (one-color) graphic to save space on your practice disk, but any bit-mapped image (color or monochrome) can be combined with your text.

WP

FIGURE WP3-54 ■ **THE EXWP3-6 TEXT**

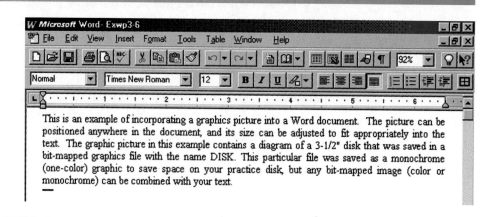

INSERTING A PICTURE. You can now incorporate the graphic material into your document by inserting the picture as follows:

STEPS

1 Position the insertion point at the beginning of the document

2 Select *Insert* and then *Picture*   [**Alt** + **I** , **P**]

An *Insert Picture* dialog box appears. This box works in a similar fashion to the *Open* and *Save As* dialog boxes. You can type a filename or select it from the list, as follows:

3 If needed, change the "Look In" drive to A: (or B:) as shown in Figure WP3-55a

4 Select the DISK.BMP file by highlighting it

> **Tip:** You can tell Word to preview any selected picture by clicking the *Preview Picture* check box or pressing Alt + P.

5 Click the *OK* button (or press ↵) to insert the picture into the document at the current insertion point position

The image of the disk now occupies the upper left portion of your screen. For now, the text has been pushed below it and to the right, as shown in Figure WP3-55b. But, don't be concerned, for this will change shortly.

6 Save this document as GRAPHIC1

FIGURE WP3-55 ■ INSERTING A PICTURE INTO A DOCUMENT

(a) The *Insert Picture* dialog box.
(b) The picture appears at the upper left of the screen.

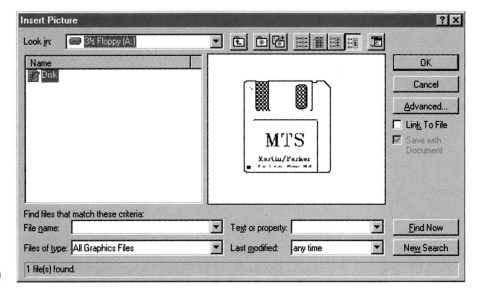

(a)

(b)

> ‎This is an example of incorporating a graphics picture into a Word document. The picture can be positioned anywhere in the document, and its size can be adjusted to fit appropriately into the text. The graphic picture in this example contains a diagram of a 3-1/2" disk that was saved in a bit-mapped graphics file with the name DISK. This particular file was saved as a monochrome (one-color) graphic to save space on your practice disk, but any bit-mapped image (color or monochrome) can be combined with your text.

EDITING A PICTURE.   Most picture parameters can be adjusted. You can add captions, adjust the box size, shift its position on the page, or change the type of border that surrounds it. You can even adjust the graphic itself. First, to select a picture,

STEPS

1 **Point to the image**

2 **Click the mouse**

Note that the command places selection handles (small square boxes) on the border of the box to indicate that it is selected as in Figure WP3-56a. To unselect the box, simply click outside it.

Note only mouse actions are presented for some of the changes. If you do not have a mouse, simply review the section.

FIGURE WP3-56 ■ SELECTING A PICTURE

(a) Clicking an image selects it for use.
(b) Right-clicking an image also accesses its *Shortcut* menu.

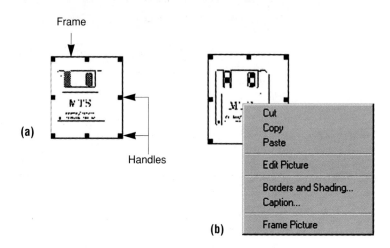

3 Now, click outside the picture box to deselect it for now.

WRAPPING TEXT AROUND A PICTURE FRAME. Currently, the picture frame that you added to the document has pushed the text below it so that there is a large, blank area to the right of the image. You can alleviate this by wrapping the text around the edges of the frame.

> Note: To wrap text, Word requires at least one inch between the frame edge and a margin (or another frame). Because the frame is currently at the left margin, the text will wrap to its right side only.

To wrap the text around the frame,

STEPS

1 If needed, close any open document and then open GRAPHIC1

 2 Switch to the Page Layout view (click the appropriate status bar button or press Alt + V , P)

3 Point to the image and *right-click* the mouse (that is, press the mouse's *right* button)

As shown in Figure WP3-56b, right-clicking the mouse not only selects the graphic (indicated by the rectangular frame and handles that appear around it) but also invokes a *Shortcut* menu.

4 Click the *Frame Picture* menu item (or ↓ to it and press ↵)

A shaded frame is added to the rectangular box, and text is now wrapped to the right of the image, as shown in Figure WP3-57a.

> **Tip:** If the text did not wrap, the Wrap-around feature may not be set. Try selecting *Format, Frame, Around*, and *OK*.

FIGURE WP3-57 ■ WRAPPING TEXT AROUND A PICTURE FRAME

(a) The text wraps to the right of a frame positioned at the left margin.
(b) Text wraps on both sides of a centered frame.

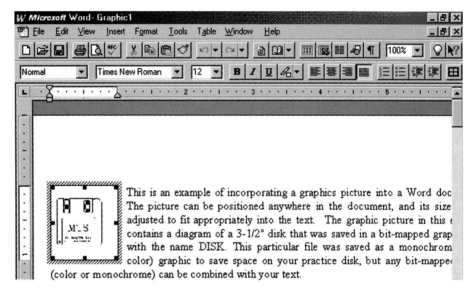

(a)

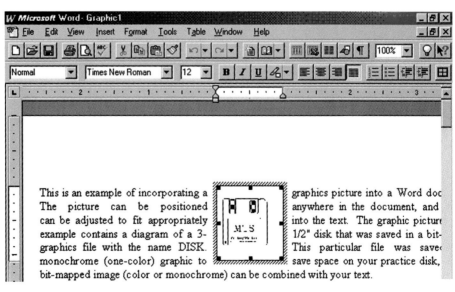

(b)

WP

5 Click anywhere outside the frame to deselect it

6 Save the document again as GRAPHIC1

POSITIONING THE FIGURE. The box containing the picture can be repositioned both horizontally (across the page) and vertically (in relation to the paragraph). To change the horizontal position of the box to the right margin,

STEPS

1 Open GRAPHIC1 and invoke the Page Layout view, if needed

2 Click the image to select the frame

3 Point anywhere within the frame, then drag the rectangular box to the right side of the screen

4 Release the mouse

The text automatically rewraps around the image.

5 Try repositioning the image in different locations—center, top, bottom (see Figure WP3-57b)

6 Close the document window *without* saving it

> **Tip:** You can "drag and drop" a selected figure to any position by a mouse. Simply drag the figure to the new position and then release ("drop") the mouse button.

SIZING THE FIGURE. The default size of the box can be adjusted as follows:

STEPS

1 Open GRAPHIC1

2 If needed, switch to Page Layout view

3 Click the disk image once to select it

4 Point to the lower-right graphic handle as shown in Figure WP3-58

The pointer changes to a double-pointed arrow.

5 Click and hold the mouse button

FIGURE WP3-58 ■ RESIZING A PICTURE FRAME

Clicking the corner handle
activates the scaling message
on the status bar.

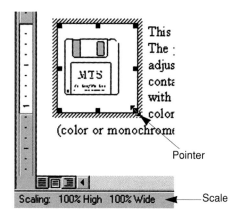

Note that the current height and width scaling percentages appear in the status bar, as in Figure WP3-58.

6 **Drag the pointer up and left, until the status bar scaling displays "75%." You may have to move the mouse slowly back and forth as you reach this exact scaling.**

7 **Release the mouse**

The image has decreased in size appropriately.

> **Tip: Use a corner handle when you want to maintain an image's proportions (height:width ratio). Using an edge handle—top, bottom, left or right—allows you to change the height or width separately.**

8 **Deselect the graphic figure (remember, simply click outside of the figure)**

9 **Save this document as GRAPHIC2**

EDITING THE IMAGE ITSELF. Word also allows you to "play" with the image to adjust its size, position, and orientation within the box. This exercise is a quick demonstration of some of the edit features.

> **Tip: If you make a mistake, select the graphic and then select *Format, Picture, Reset, OK.***

Cropping a picture means trimming its size. When you crop a picture, you can adjust its position, or change it's relative size within the frame. To crop a picture:

1   **Click the picture to select it**

You can now select a handle depending on which edge you wish to move. For example,

2   **Point to the center handle on the right frame edge, as shown in Figure WP3-59a**

3   **Press and hold   Shift**

The pointer changes to a crop mark, as shown in Figure WP3-59b.

4   **Press and hold the left mouse button**

The status bar displays the current crop setting of *0″ Right.*

5   **While continuing to press both the Shift key and the mouse button, drag the right frame edge to the left until the status bar displays a .15″ crop, as shown in Figure WP3-59c**

6   **Release the mouse and Shift key (in either order)**

You have just trimmed .15″ from the right side of the image.

7   **Using the same technique as in Steps 2–6, crop the top frame by .12″ and the bottom frame by .15″**

8   **When you are done, click outside the picture frame to deselect it**

FIGURE WP3-59   ■   CROPPING A PICTURE FRAME

(a) The pointer is positioned at a handle.
(b) Pressing the Shift key changes the pointer to a crop marker.
(c) As you move the marker, the crop measurement appears on the status bar.

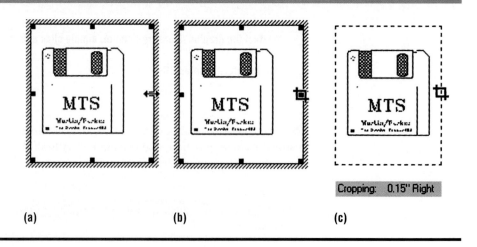

Cropping: 0.15" Right

(a)   (b)   (c)

You can now enlarge the new image as follows:

9 **Click the frame and then drag the lower-right handle until the status bar shows a 200% scaling**

10 **Release the mouse and then deselect the frame**

11 **Save the document again as GRAPHIC2**

Placing a border around an image can further highlight a graphic image. Try the following:

STEPS

1 **Click the picture to select it**

 2 **Click the *Borders* toolbar button**

A Borders toolbar appears, as shown in Figure WP3-60a.

3 **Click the *Outside Border* button on the Borders toolbar**

4 **Click outside the frame to deselect it**

WP

FIGURE WP3-60 ■ ADDING PICTURE ENHANCEMENTS

(a) The Border toolbar.
(b) The completed picture with added shading.

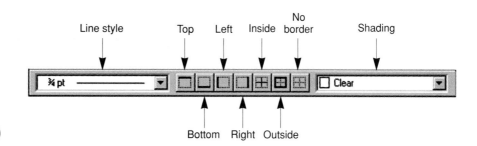

(a)

(b)

This is an example of incorporating a graphics picture into a Word document. The picture can be positioned anywhere in the document, and its size can be adjusted to fit appropriately into the text. The graphic picture in this example contains a diagram of a 3-1/2" disk that was saved in a bit-mapped graphics file with the name DISK. This particular file was saved as a monochrome (one-color) graphic to save space on your practice disk, but any bit-mapped image (color or monochrome) can be combined with your text.

Note that a single line has been added around the frame. One more sample change:

5 Click the picture again to select it

6 Click the drop-down arrow on the Borders toolbar's *Shading* entry box

7 Click *10%* (or ↓ to it and press ↵)

When printed, your document will resemble Figure WP3-60b.

8 Click the *Borders* button on the Standard toolbar to turn off this feature

9 Click outside the picture frame to deselect it

10 Save the document again as GRAPHIC2

ADDING CAPTIONS TO A PICTURE. A caption can be used to identify a figure or image. You can add a caption to a picture as follows:

1 Click the picture to select it

2 Click *Insert,* and then *Caption*

A *Caption* dialog box appears. This box allows you to change the label settings and numbering schemes, but for now,

3 Type `:` `Spacebar` (a colon and a space) and then DISK.BMP

4 Click the *OK* button

5 Unselect the picture

The caption will appear beneath the picture's image.

6 Save the document again as GRAPHIC2

7 Print the document

8 Exit Word

☑ CHECKPOINT

✓ Create your own letterhead with your name, address, and telephone number.
✓ Next create a horizontal line below it. Save as WPCHECK8.

✓ Create a two-column table that lists each course you are taking this semester with the instructor's name to the right of each course.
✓ Retrieve the DISK graphic and center it on the page.
✓ Add a figure caption that contains your name. Do *not* save.

MODULE 8: SHARING INFORMATION AMONG PROGRAMS

At times you may want to move information from Word to another software package, such as a spreadsheet, database, or even another word processing program. Conversely, you may want to move information prepared in another program into Word. Fortunately, there is a way to translate information into other software formats. In fact, if you are using Word with other Microsoft Office programs, such as Excel or Access, the procedure is almost automatic.

The exercises in this module use two files that were contained on the student data disk included with this book: EMPLOY.WP and EMPLOY.XLS (a spreadsheet). Figures

FIGURE WP3-61 ■ **SAMPLE FILES TO SHARE**

(a) The EMPLOY.WP document.
(b) The EMPLOY.XLS spreadsheet.

```
Employee List

                 Home          Annual     Date
Sales Staff      Phone         Salary     Hired
----------------------------------------------------
Burstein, J.     408-555-1010  $23,450    06-Jul-78
Laudon, J.       914-555-9876   33,600    07-Oct-81
Martin, E.       718-555-1234   31,750    01-Nov-79
Parker, C.       505-555-5678   37,500    25-Apr-82
Williams, D.     312-555-0202   38,000    17-Feb-75
----------------------------------------------------
(a)  Total                      $164,300
```

	A	B	C	D
1	Employee List			
2		Home	Annual	Date
3	Sales Staff	Phone	Salary	Hired
4	Burstein, J.	408-555-1010	$23,450	06-Jul-78
5	Laudon, J.	914-555-9876	33,600	07-Oct-81
6	Martin, E.	718-555-1234	31,750	01-Nov-79
7	Parker, C.	505-555-5678	37,500	25-Apr-82
8	Williams, D.	312-555-0202	38,000	17-Feb-75
9	Total		$164,300	
10				

(b)

WP3-61a and WP3-61b present the contents of these files. Both should have been copied to your data disk when you began this chapter and are now available for use. (If they are not, review the "Preparing for This Chapter" section at the beginning of this chapter.)

EXPORTING AND IMPORTING

Export and *Import* commands facilitate data transfer by converting data into formats that can be read by other software packages. **Exporting** *saves* data in another format; **importing** *retrieves* data that has been saved in another format.

DIRECT CONVERSION.   The easiest way to share data is to translate them into a form that another program can readily understand. Some slight adjustments may have to be made, but these are usually minimal. Typically, direct conversions are offered for the most popular software packages. You'll try some direct conversions soon.

ASCII—THE COMMON DENOMINATOR.   When direct conversion is not available, *ASCII* conversion may still allow data transfer. **ASCII** (pronounced "ask-key") stands for American Standard Code for Information Interchange. It is one of a few standard formats adopted by the computer industry for representing typed characters. ASCII eliminates the symbols unique to each software package, providing a common style for sharing data. Word refers to ASCII files as "plain-text" or "MS-DOS Text" format.

EXPORTING FILES FROM WORD

Word files may be exported (saved) into another format when using the *Save As* dialog box to save. The dialog box offers a Save File as Type list with format options. To prepare for exporting exercises,

STEPS

1   Launch Word or close any open document

2   Open the EMPLOY.WP file on Drive A (type its name or switch the file type to "All Files" to select it)

CREATING AN ASCII FILE.   In Word, an ASCII file is often equivalent to an MS-DOS Text with Line Breaks file. To save a copy of the EMPLOY.WP document in ASCII format,

STEPS

1   Click *File* and then *Save As* for its dialog box

2   Type   EMWP.TXT   in the *Filename* text box

3   Click the "▼" button at the right of the *Save File as Type* box for its drop-down list

[**Alt** **+** **T**]

4 Use the scroll bar to scroll up to *MS-DOS Text with Line Breaks* and then click it   [↑]

5 Click the *OK* button to save in that format   [⏎]

> **Tip:** The .TXT extension is optional, but it is useful to indicate that the file is saved in text (ASCII) format.

> **Note:** Word can save documents in 22 standard formats. Scroll through the *Save File as type* drop-down list to see the options.

EXPORTING TO A SPREADSHEET.   Any ASCII file can be read by a spreadsheet program. However, two minor procedural adjustments are needed: (1) Prior to exporting, set the document's left margin to zero so that the text will be placed correctly in the spreadsheet, and (2) use a .PRN extension. ASCII files are called "print files" in spreadsheet programs and identified with the .PRN extension. If a .PRN extension is not used, the document may not be recognized when you try to open it in a spreadsheet.

EXPORTING TO A DATABASE PROGRAM.   ASCII files can also be read by database programs. Data can be in column form as in the EMPLOY.WP file (Figure WP3-61a) where each field is a fixed distance from the left margin. Data can also contain fields of variable lengths, as long as they are enclosed in quotes and separated by commas.

Again, the procedure is identical to creating other ASCII files, except that you must first adjust settings and remove characters that the database may not understand, and then save the file with an appropriate extension.

Data in column form must contain only the lines that represent records, and all numeric data must be free of commas and dollar signs.

STEPS

1 Open EMPLOY.WP

As shown in Figure WP3-62, you must first remove all lines that do not contain record data as follows:

2 Delete the *first* four lines

3 Delete the *last* two lines

You must now remove dollar signs and commas from numeric data, making sure that you do not change the relative position of the value. To do this, use the overtype mode or search and replace to change each dollar sign to a space.

WP

FIGURE WP3-62 ■ **PREPARING DATA IN OTHER FORMATS**

(a) Fixed Columns—Systems Data Format (SDF).
(b) Variable-length format—Delimited.

(a)
```
Burstein, J.     408-555-1010     23450   07/06/78
Laudon, J.       914-555-9876     33600   10/07/81
Martin, E.       718-555-1234     31750   11/01/79
Parker, C.       505-555-5678     37500   04/25/82
Williams, D.     312-555-0202     38000   02/17/75
```

(b)
```
"Burstein, J.","408-555-1010",23450,07/06/78
"Laudon, J.","914-555-9876",33600,10/07/81
"Martin, E.","718-555-1234",31750,11/01/79
"Parker, C.","505-555-5678",37500,04/25/82
"Williams, D.","312-555-0202",38000,02/17/75
```

Tip: To remove commas, insert a space to the left of the number and then delete its comma. This way, all numbers will maintain their decimal position from the left margin.

4 Remove the $ symbol and commas from the numeric data

5 Change the date format to MM/DD/YY.

Your screen should resemble Figure WP3-62a. You can now save the adjusted file in ASCII format.

6 Click *File* and then *Save As*

7 Type **EMWP.SDF** in the *File name* text box

8 Change the format to *MS-DOS Text with Line Breaks*

9 Click the *OK* button to save in that format   [↵]

The .SDF extension identifies this file format as "System Data Format"—a format that is readable by most database programs.

Data can also be prepared in Word in a variable-length format as in Figure WP3-62b. Character fields are enclosed in quotes, and fields are separated by commas (one record on each line). This is a standard mail merge format used in some word processing programs and is also readable by most database programs.

10 Close the document

11 Open EMWP.SDF

12 Edit the document to make it look like Figure WP3-62b removing spaces and inserting commas or quotes where appropriate

13 Save the document as an MS-DOS Text File with Line Breaks named EMWP.DEL

14 Close the document

In this case, the .DEL extension identifies this file as a standard "delimited" file. ("Delimited" means "separated with commas.")

IMPORTING FILES INTO WORD

ASCII text files (or files saved in many other word processing formats) can be read directly with Word's Open command. Once opened, they can be modified and saved with normal commands. Here are a few examples:

1 Close any open document

2 Open the EMWP.TXT file

The ASCII file is now converted into Word and appears on your screen. The columns may not align if you are using a proportional font such as Times New Roman. Try this:

3 Select the entire document as a block

4 Select a monospaced font such as Courier.

5 Shut off the selection mode

The entire text now aligns neatly.

6 Close the document *without* saving

IMPORTING FROM A SPREADSHEET.   There are a few ways to import spreadsheet data into Word. Print files created by a spreadsheet can be opened as any other ASCII file. There is no need to repeat the process here.

Word can also retrieve a worksheet directly into a table format—a technique that is highly recommended; it can also place a spreadsheet graph directly into a graphics box. Here are a few examples:

1 Launch Word or close any open document

2 Open EMPLOY.XLS (type EMPLOY.XLS in Filename entry line)

> Tip: The .XLS extension indicates a worksheet created in Excel format. With the proper convert programs, Word will also import other spreadsheet formats, such as Quattro or Lotus 1-2-3.

An *Open Worksheet* dialog box appears as in Figure WP-63. At this point, you can import the entire worksheet or define a range to be imported. To import the worksheet as a table with a defined range of A1..D9:

3 Press **Tab** to move to Name or Cell Range

4 Type **A1:D9**

5 Click the *OK* button   [↵]

Your screen should now display the worksheet. You could now adjust the columns and data as needed.

6 Close the document without saving

> Tip: Like other files, the text is placed at the current insertion point, allowing you to add spreadsheet data to existing documents already on the screen.

IMPORTING A SPREADSHEET GRAPHIC.   You can also import graph files (with .PIC or other standard extensions) directly into Word graphic boxes. To accomplish this in the future, use the same procedure as outlined in "Module 7: Adding Graphics and Tables" presented earlier in this chapter, being sure to use the proper extension as part of the filename.

FIGURE WP3-63 ■ IMPORTING A WORKSHEET

The *Open Worksheet* dialog box.

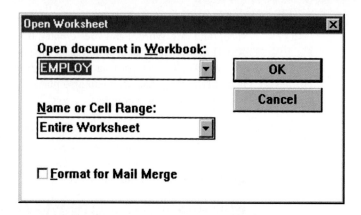

IMPORTING FILES FROM A DATABASE. ASCII files created by a database program (whether saved delimited or in system data format) can also be read directly with normal Open File commands. The following exercises demonstrate opening some database files into Word.

STEPS

■1 **Close any open document**

■2 **Open EMWP.SDF**

The document appears on your screen resembling Figure WP3-62a (your fonts may differ).

■3 **Close the document without saving**

A delimited file can also be opened directly into Word and then modified, or it can be translated directly into a secondary merge file (as you will see shortly). The first method is accomplished in the normal manner:

■4 **Open EMWP.DEL**

The file appears on your screen (resembling Figure WP3-62b). These data are not that useful in this form, but can be adjusted easily. For example, you might find and replace to remove the quotation marks and replace the delimiting commas with tabs. Do this as follows:

■5 **Click *Edit* and then *Replace* for the *Replace* dialog box**   [**Ctrl** + **H**]

■6 **Press " to search for quotes**

■7 **Click *Replace All* to replace the quotes with nothing**

■8 **Click the *OK* button**

In effect, this command removes the quotes from the file.

■9 **Click the Word window (anywhere)**   [**Alt** + **F6**]

■10 **Move to the beginning of the document**   [**Ctrl** + **Home**]

All quotes have been removed. You can now replace the delimiting commas with tabs. This is not as easy as it first appears, for you do not want *all* commas removed—the comma after the last name should remain. Of course, you could delete the commas individually or use replace with confirm, but this would be tedious in a long file. Here's a trick—in this document, only the comma after the last name is followed by a space (all other commas *are not*); therefore, you can replace the last name commas with a different character, then replace all the other commas with tabs, and finally replace the original commas where they belong. It may seem like a long process, but these three Replace commands save time and effort in a long document. Try it:

11 Activate the *Replace* dialog box

12 Delete the quote mark in the *Find What* text box

13 Press `,` `Spacebar` in the *Find What* text box to search for a comma and space

> Note: Including the space *as part of the search condition* eliminates all the other commas from this Replace command.

14 Press `Tab` to move the insertion point to the *Replace With* text box

15 Press `*` `Spacebar` to replace with an asterisk and space

16 Click the *Replace All* button

17 Click the *OK* button

18 Activate the Word Window (click anywhere)   [→]

The commas after last name have been replaced with asterisks; only the delimiting commas remain. Now replace all these commas with tabs:

19 Move to the beginning of the document

20 Activate the *Replace* dialog box

Remember, to activate, either click Edit, Replace, or press Ctrl + H.

21 Delete the comma *and* space

22 Press `,` `Tab` to move the insertion point to Replace With

> Note: To find or replace with a code, you must use the *Special* drop-down list.

23 Delete the asterisk

24 Click *Special*

25 Click the *Tab Character*   [T]

Your screen should now resemble Figure WP3-64a.

26 Click the *Replace All* button to replace all "," with Tab

27 Click the *OK* button   [↵]

FIGURE WP3-64 ■ CONVERTING A DELIMITED FILE

(a) The *Replace* dialog box will replace all commas with tabs.
(b) The completed file with tabs added.

(a)

(b)

Burstein, J.	408-555-1010	23450	07/06/78
Laudon, J.	914-555-9876	33600	10/07/81
Martin, E.	718-555-1234	31750	11/01/79
Parker, C.	505-555-5678	37500	04/25/82
Williams, D.	312-555-0202	38000	02/17/75

Now, replace the original commas in their proper position.

28 **Move to the top of the document**

29 **Replace all asterisks (*) with commas (,)**

30 **When done, click *OK* or press ↵ and close the *Replace* dialog box**

Your screen should resemble Figure WP3-64b (except for Font style).

Tip: If you are going to use delimited files often, you may want to save all these keystrokes in a macro for future use.

You could now add dollar signs and commas to the salary column and then use the document normally in Word.

31 **Save this file as EMWP, as a Word document**

32 **Close the document**

TRANSLATING DELIMITED FILES INTO DATA SOURCES.   Delimited files can also be converted for use as Word data source files. These files can then be merged into *main* documents as you have seen in Module 3. The following exercise demonstrates the technique. To prepare the file, you must first add a header row as follows:

STEPS

1   Open the EMWP.DEL document (remember to switch the file type to All Files before selecting the filename)

2   Move to the top of the document, and make sure that insert mode is on

3   Type   "NAME", "PHONE", "SALARY", "DATE"   and press ↵ as shown in Figure WP3-65a

4   Delete any extra blank lines that may appear beneath the last data line

5   Save the file as EMWP2.DEL using the MS-DOS Text with Line Breaks file format

6   Close the document window

You are now ready to try the conversion.

7   Open a new document

> **Note:** In actual use, you would open a main document in Step 7 to be merged with the data.

8   Click *Tools* and then *Mail Merge* to access the Mail Merge

The *Mail Merge Helper* dialog box will appear. You can now create the main document as you normally would (as follows):

9   Click the *Create* button

10   Click *Form Letters*

FIGURE WP3-65 ■ ADDING A HEADER ROW TO A DELIMITED FILE

```
"NAME","PHONE","SALARY","DATE"
"Burstein, J.","408-555-1010",23450,07/06/78
"Laudon, J.","914-555-9876",33600,10/07/81
"Martin, E.","718-555-1234",31750,11/01/79
"Parker, C.","505-555-5678",37500,04/25/82
"Williams, D.","312-555-0202",38000,02/17/75
```

11 Click *Active Window*

12 Click *Get Data*

13 Click *Open Data Source*

14 Type   **A:EMWP2.DEL**   and press ↵

> **Note: You could also change the drive to A, and the file type to All Files (*.*) and then select the filename EMWP2.DEL from the list.**

A *Header Record Delimiters* dialog box appears as shown in Figure WP3-66b.

15 Click the drop-down arrow on the *Field Delimiter* box   [**Alt** + **F**]

16 Click the comma symbol (beneath [Tab])   [↓]

17 Click the *OK* button   [↵]

Because you used a blank main document, the fields will not match the data source. A dialog box will warn you of this. To continue for now,

18 Click the *Cancel* button

You can now examine the data in the file.

19 Click *Edit* and choose a file

FIGURE WP3-66 ■   THE DATA SOURCE APPEARS IN A DATA FORM

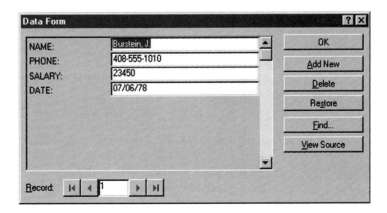

WP

A Data form appears as shown in Figure WP3-66. Note that the data has been correctly arranged under each field name.

20   **Click the *OK* button**   [↵]

The data source can now be merged with a main document. To end for now,

21   **Close all windows without saving (respond with "No" twice)**

LINKING DATA FROM OTHER OFFICE APPLICATIONS

Typically, Word is used in conjunction with other Microsoft Office applications, such as Excel or Access. Office is known as a **suite** program—a set of separate applications that work together as one large program. Some suite applications provide additional menus or toolbar buttons that let you easily transfer data to the other applications.

You have already learned some basic methods for sharing data among applications through ASCII files and file conversions. However, if you have other Office applications and a mouse, you can also use two additional techniques that allow you to combine data from different applications, namely, *linking* and *embedding*.

> **Tip:** Linking and embedding techniques will also work, for the most part, between any Windows programs.

LINKING AND EMBEDDING.   An **object** is a form of information. Linking or embedding describes the two options available to you for transferring an object (or selection) from one application to another.

Embedding copies a selection from one program to another without changing the original. It is identical to copying except that it involves two programs. You might, for example, embed data from an Excel worksheet into a Word document.

Linking, on the other hand, establishes an ongoing connection between the program that provides the object (known as the *source*) and the one that receives it (the *container*). Change the source object and the container is automatically updated. For example, if an Excel selection is linked with Word, changes in the Excel worksheet will also appear in the Word document.

Because you must have access to other Office programs to accomplish these tasks, a brief description of the process will be presented. You may want to try these techniques with the EMPLOY.XLS file and any Word document, after you've learned how to use Excel.

LINKING A SELECTION.   The following paragraphs describe how to link a block of data from the Excel workbook file "EMPLOY" to a Word document (named "WORD1"). The Word file does not exist, but is used only for illustrative purposes. You can use a new document or any existing Word file. The procedure assumes you have experience with Excel. If not, do not perform these steps now, but use them as a guide in the future.

STEPS

1. Start your computer, enter Windows, and launch Word

   Note: You must start with the source document to create a link.

2. Launch Excel through the Start button and open the EMPLOY workbook

3. Identify the selection to be linked, such as the block A4:D8

 4. Click *Edit, Copy*

The selected block of cells is copied to the Windows Clipboard and is available for linking.

5. Click the *Microsoft Word* button on the taskbar to switch to Word

6. Open the destination document—WORD1

7. Position the insertion point where you want the object to appear

8. Click *Edit, Paste Special*

9. In the dialog box, click *Paste Link* and then *OK*

The data block from the EMPLOY workbook appears in the WORD1 document as a table and is dynamically linked to the original workbook. For example,

10. Click the *Microsoft Excel* button on the taskbar to switch back to Excel

11. Change some data within the selected block; for example, change Cell A8 to *Kee, C.* and Cell C6 to *40,000*

12. Switch back to Word (using the taskbar) to see that the data have been changed as well

13. Switch to Excel and exit without saving

If you were to make changes to the EMPLOY workbook in the future and Word were not currently active, the changes would appear the next time you opened the WORD1 document for use.

EMBEDDING A SELECTION.   Embedding a selection simply copies it into the other application, without creating a link between the two files.

STEPS

1. Identify the selection as you did in linking by following Steps 1–7 above

WP

2   In Word, click *Edit, Paste*

The data are copied, but will now remain static. Changes you make in EMPLOY.XLS will not affect the WORD1 document.

3   Close the WORD1 document and Word without saving

4   Switch to Excel and exit without saving the workbook

☑   **CHECKPOINT**

✓   Using Word and the correct file extensions: Export the EMPLOY.WP document into a file named EMWP.W52 in WordPerfect 5.2 format.
✓   Close the document.
✓   Import the EMWP.W52 document into a new document window.
✓   Place two blank lines at the end of the text. After these lines, import the range A5:D9 of the EMPLOY.XLS workbook as a table.
✓   Save the file as EMCHECK. Close the document.

SUMMARY

■   Document pages can be divided by soft page breaks, which are inserted automatically by Word, or hard page breaks, which are created by the user. Soft page breaks change their location as the document is modified; hard page breaks remain fixed unless removed by the user.
■   Headers and footers are lines of descriptive text that can appear on every printed page of a multipage document. Headers are placed at the top of the document page; footers at the bottom. Headers and footers can be created, edited, or deleted.
■   Word's Page Number feature allows numbers to be placed at the top or bottom of each printed page, positioned at the left, center, or right. Each page will be consecutively numbered unless changed by the user.
■   The Go To command allows the user to reposition the insertion point on any page of a multipage document.
■   Word allows the user to work with up to nine documents at one time. Each document is placed in its own window. The user can then use the *Window* menu or press Ctrl + F6 to switch between them to read text or copy text from one to the other. Document windows may also be arranged with one above the other.
■   Merge is the process by which information from two sources is combined to produce a third document. Merge usually combines a main document (which contains text and instructions for merging) with a data source (which contains the specific data to be merged). Both files may be created through the Mail Merge Helper and then combined with Merge commands.
■   A macro is a list of computer instructions that can be activated with one (or more) preset keystrokes. Macros must first be defined and saved before you can invoke them for use. Macro names can be up to eight characters in length. A macro assigned to a Shortcut key can be invoked quickly by simply pressing the shortcut. Macros with longer names must be invoked through the *Macro* dialog box.

- Footnotes and endnotes are text added to your document to provide source references, more detailed explanations, or comments. Footnotes are usually placed at the bottom of the page where they are referenced. Endnotes are usually listed at the end of the document. These notes can be inserted, edited, deleted, and renumbered as needed.
- Word's Outline feature eases the task of creating and editing outlines using a number of standard formats.
- Word's Graphics feature allows lines and images to be combined with text in the same document. Borders and lines can be quickly created using the Borders toolbar. Tables allow text to be professionally displayed in columns and rows. Separate graphics boxes can also be created into which graphic images can be inserted. These boxes are like little windows on the screen around which document text will automatically wrap. Graphics boxes can be repositioned and resized as needed.
- ASCII file format is a standard for data transfer. It excludes all special symbols, providing a common data style.
- Files can be exported from (saved in another format) or imported into (retrieved from a compatible format) Word.
- Data in fixed-length columns can be saved in ASCII files for use with spreadsheets or database programs. Data in variable-length fields can be saved in a delimited format. Delimited files separate with commas and surround character data with quotation marks.
- Word's normal commands will convert most files into Word format.
- Linking and embedding allow information from one program to be added to another.

WP

KEY TERMS

Shown in parentheses are the page numbers on which key terms are boldfaced.

Arrange All (WP158)	Footnote (WP180)	Main document (WP162)
ASCII (WP218)	Go To (WP153)	Merge (WP162)
Cropping (WP214)	Graphics feature (WP200)	Object (WP228)
Data source (WP162)	Hard page break (WP142)	Outline feature (WP187)
Embedding (WP228)	Header (WP144)	Soft page break (WP141)
Endnote (WP180)	Importing (WP218)	Sort feature (WP187)
Exporting (WP218)	Linking (WP228)	Suite (WP228)
Footer (WP144)	Macro (WP172)	

QUIZ

TRUE/FALSE

____ 1. The location of a soft page return within the text will change if text is inserted or deleted before it.

____ 2. Headers do not usually appear on a document's first page.

____ 3. Page numbers and headers are displayed in Outline view for easy editing.

____ 4. The Go To command is used to switch to another document file.

___ 5. Word can display up to nine documents on one screen at the same time.

___ 6. In a merge operation, the data to be merged is kept in a main document.

___ 7. Merged documents can be previewed by mouse or keyboard.

___ 8. Anything that can be typed on a keyboard can be saved in a macro.

___ 9. Footnotes and their reference numbers appear within work screen text when in Page Layout view.

___ 10. The Word Graphics feature does not allow the user to insert pictures on the screen.

MULTIPLE CHOICE

___ 11. A _____ is displayed as an untitled single dotted line on the work screen.
   a. soft page break
   b. hard page break
   c. merged document
   d. table cell

___ 12. Which of these is *not* an option for page number placement?
   a. Top right of each page
   b. Bottom left of each page
   c. Right center of page
   d. Bottom center of page

___ 13. The most important reason for using multidocuments at one time is for
   a. referencing footnotes
   b. comparing files
   c. numbering pages
   d. copying text

___ 14. How does Word indicate the active document when more than one document is displayed at the same time?
   a. The title bar of the Word window is highlighted.
   b. The title bar of the active document window is highlighted.
   c. A pop-up screen lists the active document's number.
   d. A box is drawn around the active document area.

___ 15. Which of these is *not* a requirement for data source files?
   a. All records must contain the same number of fields.
   b. All fields must be listed in the *Field Names in Header Row* box.
   c. A field name *cannot* include spaces.
   d. Each record must be separated by a soft page break.

___ 16. Which one of these macros can be invoked by pressing just the Ctrl + Shift keys and the letter H?
   a. Ctrl + Shift + H
   b. H
   c. Shift + H
   d. MACRO-H

___ 17. Which Word feature cannot be removed with the Delete key?
   a. Headers
   b. Footnotes
   c. Hard page breaks
   d. Soft page breaks

___ 18. Which command allows the user to create a horizontal line?
   a. Hard Return
   b. Borders

c. Create line
d. Single line

___ 19. Which of these features allows Word to display graphic images contained in figure boxes?

a. Macro
b. Multidocument windows
c. Show/hide feature
d. WYSIWYG

___ 20. The Borders toolbar includes commands for all but which one of these functions?

a. Shading
b. Outside border
c. Top border
d. Insert graphic

MATCHING

Select the lettered item from Figure WP3-A that best matches each phrase below:

___ 21. This item can be used to preview merged documents.
___ 22. This feature allows you to switch to Page Layout view.
___ 23. This is the document window in which keyboard commands will currently operate.

WP

FIGURE WP3-A ■ MATCHING EXERCISE

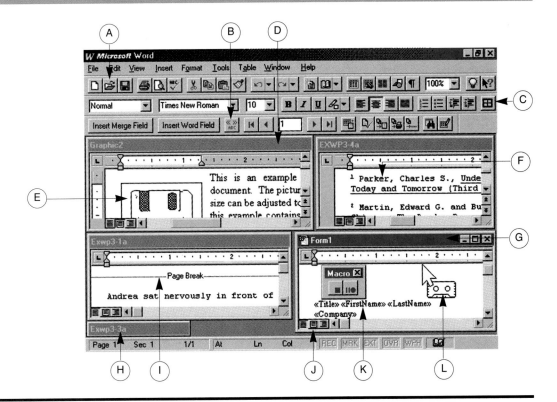

___ 24. This page divider is created directly by the user and it remains fixed at a specific text location unless the user removes it.

___ 25. This is an example of a minimized document.

___ 26. This spot marks the position where data will be inserted.

___ 27. This item can be used to draw a border around a picture or text.

___ 28. This text, usually appearing at the bottom of each page and identified by number, is added to a document to provide source references, more detailed explanations, or comments.

___ 29. This item indicates that a macro is being recorded.

___ 30. This results from using Word's graphics feature

ANSWERS

True/False: 1. T; 2. T; 3. F; 4. F; 5. T; 6. F; 7. F; 8. T; 9. T; 10. F
Multiple Choice: 11. a; 12. c; 13. d; 14. b; 15. d; 16. a; 17. d; 18. b; 19. d; 20. d
Matching: 21. b; 22. j; 23. g; 24. i; 25. h; 26. k; 27. c; 28. f; 29. l; 30. e

EXERCISES

I. OPERATIONS

Provide the Word mouse or keyboard actions required to do each of the following operations. For each operation, assume a system with a hard disk and a diskette in Drive A. A ten-page document called LETTER1 has been opened onto the work screen. Further assume that the default drive has been set to Drive A, and that the following files are contained on the data disk: LETTER1, LETTER2, ROSTER, and COMPUTE.PCX. There are also two macros: one named ZAP and the other named SPELL (which is also saved as the shortcut ALT + S).

1. Create a hard page break after the first paragraph.

2. Create a header that states "Reference Letter 1."

3. Number all pages beginning with Page 2, positioning the number at the bottom center of each page.

4. Renumber Page 2 to show a page number of "1."

5. Open LETTER2 and arrange the document windows.

6. Copy the first paragraph of LETTER2 to the end of LETTER1.

7. Close LETTER2 and open a new document window.

8. Merge the data contained in the ROSTER file with the LETTER2 data source.

9. Invoke the SPELL macro and then the ZAP macro.

10. Create a macro named BYE that will save the current document back onto disk and then close the document.

11. Delete the third footnote in the LETTER1 file.

12. Draw a horizontal line.

13. Display the image contained in the COMPUTE.PCX file.

II. COMMANDS

Describe clearly what command is initiated or what is accomplished in Word by the actions described below. Assume that each exercise part is independent of any previous parts.

1. Pressing the Ctrl + Enter keys

2. Clicking the document icon of a document window

3. Pressing the Alt + V, H keys

4. Pressing the Ctrl + G, 4, Enter keys

5. Dragging a margin marker to a new location on the ruler bar

6. Pressing the Ctrl + F6 keys

7. Pressing the Alt + T, R, Alt + D keys

8. Pressing the Alt + V, O keys

9. Pressing the Ctrl + L keys

10. Pressing the Alt + T, M, Alt + O keys

11. Double-clicking a graphic object

12. Pressing the Alt + I, N keys

13. Pressing the Alt + A, T keys

14. Pressing the Alt + A, I keys

III. APPLICATIONS

Perform the following operations using your computer system. You will need a hard drive or network with Word on it. You will also need your data disk to store the results of this exercise and to open the DISK graphic. In a few words, tell how you accomplished each operation and describe its result. Save the document after each operation is completed so that you can continue this exercise later. *Note:* An application may contain skills selected from more than one module. If you did not perform the tutorials for that module, skip the corresponding exercises within the application.

APPLICATION 1: GENERAL PRACTICE: REPLICATING AN ARTICLE

1. To prepare for this exercise, select an article that contains at least 600 words from a recent magazine or newspaper. Bring a copy of it or the original article to your computer's location. Boot your computer and start Word.

2. Type the headline of the article centered on the first page of your document. Skip two lines. Center your name, class, and date on three separate lines beneath the heading.

3. Create a hard page break on the line after the date, and set line spacing to double-spaced text at the beginning of Page 2. Save your document with the name ARTICLE.

4. Using a font style and margin settings that approximate the article, type the article heading once again at the top of Page 2, centered and underlined at the top of the page. Skip a line. Type the article's text exactly as it appears. End paragraphs where they end in the article and indent as needed. Copy as much of the article as you need to fill two full pages—approximately 600 words.

5. Create a header that displays your full name to start on the page after the title page and continue on all other pages.

6. Add page numbering at the bottom center of the page starting after the title page. Renumber this page to be counted as Page 1.

7. Place a footnote at the end of the heading on the first full page of typing. In the footnote reference, indicate the author (if known) and the source, date, and page numbers of the article you selected.

8. Edit the header you created earlier to display your class designation in parentheses after your name.

9. Copy the first paragraph of the document into a new document. Skip a line and type your name after the copied paragraph. Save this new document as ARTICLE1. Close the document and return to ARTICLE.

10. Move to the title page of the ARTICLE document. Place one horizontal line under the date.

11. Move to the second paragraph of the typed article. Import the DISK.PCX graphic (or use any other graphic you may have) and position it two lines below the top of this paragraph, on the right side of the page.

12. Add a caption to the graphic that reads "Figure 1. A Sample." Set the width and height of the graphic to 200% of its original size. Save the ARTICLE document with these changes.

13. Print out copies of ARTICLE and ARTICLE1. Attach a copy of the original article to your work.

14. Create an outline of at least two levels that summarizes the key points made in the article. Save this outline as ARTICLE2.

15. Open ARTICLE2 and change the outline to another numbering style of your choice. Then, move one family section of text to the end of the outline. Save this outline as ARTICLE3.

APPLICATION 2: GENERAL PRACTICE: REVIEWING CLASS NOTES

1. To prepare for this exercise, select a set of recent class notes from a class of your choice. Bring a copy of it, or the original notes, to your computer's location. Boot your computer and start Word.

2. Type the course title and designation centered on the first page of your document. Beneath this line, type a line that identifies the instructor and the date the notes were

taken. Skip three lines. In the lower-left corner of the page, type your name and the current date.

3. Create a hard page break on the line after the date.

4. Set line spacing to double-spaced text at the beginning of Page 2. Save your document with the name NOTES.

5. Using an appropriate font style and size to be easily readable, type the class notes in a format that matches the original as closely as possible. Outline and indent as needed. The notes should occupy more than one page.

6. Create a header that identifies the class and date on which the notes were taken. The header should skip the title page and continue on all other pages.

7. Add page numbering at the top right of the notes pages starting after the title page. The first page of notes should be numbered as Page 1.

8. Place a footnote at the end of the notes on the last page of typing. In the footnote reference, indicate the course and date of the notes you have typed.

9. Add a second footnote somewhere within the notes to further explain the entry or make some comment about what you have typed. Allow this footnote to be renumbered as the first footnote. Print the document.

10. Delete the footnote that you created in Exercise #9.

11. Copy the entire set of notes into a new document. Change the font style and size to a smaller setting. Change the line spacing back to single-spaced. Save this new document as NOTES1. Close the document and return to NOTES.

12. Move to the first page of the notes. Add a centered title that identifies the class and date of the notes and then place one horizontal line under the date.

13. Print out copies of NOTES and NOTES1. Attach a copy of the original class notes to your work.

14. Create an outline of at least two levels that summarizes the key points made in the notes. Save this outline as NOTES2.

15. Open NOTES2 and change the outline to another numbering style of your choice. Print this outline but do not save it.

APPLICATION 3: SORTING A VIDEO LIST WITH MULTIPLE DOCUMENTS AND MACROS

1. Boot your computer; start Windows and launch the Word program

2. Open the WORK1-4B video list you created in Chapter 1 or type it now. *Note:* If you plan to type the list, first complete Exercise #3 below to set your tabs properly. Then, type the list as shown, pressing the Tab key between each entry and the Enter key at the end of each line. You can then skip Exercise #4.

   You can also create the list by following the instructions in Chapter 1, Application 4—Steps 1–8.

3. At the start of the document, set new tab markers at .5″, 1.5″, and 4.5″, so that the first column starts at the left margin, with each succeeding column starting at the next tab marker.

STAR TREK NEXT GENERATION VIDEO COLLECTION

TAPE	COUNTER	EPISODE	STAR DATE
A	0000	Encounter at Farpoint	41153.7
A	1200	Where No One Has Gone Before	41263.1
A	2350	11001001	41365.9
A	3100	The Neutral Zone	41986.0
A	4000	Tin Man	43779.3
A	4850	Darmok	45047.2
B	0000	A Matter of Time	45349.1
B	1150	Violations	45429.3
B	2325	Power Play	45571.2
B	3005	Ethics	45587.3
B	3990	Cause and Effect	45652.1
B	4765	I, Borg	45845.2
C	0000	The Inner Light	45944.1
C	1250	Realm of Fear	46041.1
C	3125	A Fistful of Datas	46271.5
C	2465	Ship in a Bottle	46424.1
C	4100	Face of the Enemy	46519.1
C	4870	Lessons	46693.1
D	0000	The Chase	46731.5
D	1175	Parallels	47391.2
D	2290	Inheritance	47410.2
D	3010	Thine Own Self	47611.2
D	4025	Masks	47615.2
D	4755	Journey's End	47751.2

4. Delete or add tabs as needed within each row of text so that its columns align neatly as shown in the figure.

5. Save the adjusted list as VIDEO1.

6. Identify the list of records to be sorted (omitting the top title line), and then sort the list by EPISODE (Field 3). Save the list as VIDEO2 and then print the results.

7. Sort the list by two fields, TAPE and COUNTER. That is, sort by TAPE and, where the TAPE is the same, sort further by COUNTER. Print the results.

8. Clear all document windows. Open VIDEO1 into one window, and VIDEO2 into a second document window. Sort the list in VIDEO2 by STARDATE.

9. Arrange the two documents so that they appear on the screen at the same time. Examine both lists and describe how the two lists compare. Write a brief explanation of what you observed. Close all documents.

10. Open the VIDEO1 document. Using the same technique as in Exercise #6, create a macro named EPISORT that will select the text block and then sort it by EPISODE. Invoke the macro.

11. Create a second macro named DATASORT, assign it to the Shortcut keys Alt + D, that will select the entire text block no matter how many additional lines you might add, and then sort it by STARDATE. *Hint:* After positioning the insertion point beneath the title row, use the F8 sequence to select the remainder of the document.

12. Add two more lines of text to your list, creating dates and names as desired.

13. Invoke the macro you created in Exercise #11 by name and then by Shortcut keys. Print the result, then exit the document *without* saving it.

14. Exit Word and Windows.

APPLICATION 4: CREATING AND SORTING A PHONE TABLE

1. Boot your computer; start Windows and launch the Word program.

2. Type your name, class, and date at the upper left of a new document. Skip two lines.

3. Create a table with three columns and ten rows. Label the top cells in the table "Last," "First," and "Phone," respectively.

4. In the remaining rows, type information for nine friends (or just make up the data). Save the document as PHONE1.

5. Change the font to another proportional font of your choice. Boldface the labels in the title row of the table.

6. Insert an additional row and data for a tenth friend.

7. Sort the table by last name (*Note:* When sorting, each column of the table corresponds to a tabbed field.) Save the table as PHONE2.

8. Sort the table by phone number and then save it as an ASCII text file.

9. Print copies of PHONE1 and PHONE2.

10. Close all documents and exit Word.

APPLICATION 5: PRODUCING MERGED LETTERS OF INQUIRY

1. Boot your computer; start Windows and launch the Word program.

2. In a new document window, use the Mail Merge Helper to identify the main document as the active window with the name INQFORM1.

3. Create a Data Source with the following fields: Title, FirstName, LastName, Position, Company, Address1, Address2, Area. Save the form as INQDATA1.

4. Return to the INQFORM1 letter. Type the text and insert field markers as shown so that your letter resembles the sample at the top of page 240. Don't worry if the lines of text do not wrap exactly as shown in the sample.

5. Save this form letter as **INQFORM1.**

6. Place the two records at the bottom of page 240 into the INQDATA1 data source.

7. Now, add two more records using data of your choice.

8. Merge the INQFORM1 main document with the INQDATA1 data source.

9. Print the letters that result from this merge.

Your name
Your address
Your city, state zip

Today's date

<<Title>> <<FirstName>> <<LastName>>
<<Position>>
<<Company>>
<<Address1>>
<<Address2>>

Dear <<Title>> <<LastName>>:

I am a senior at Pilemore College and plan to graduate in June with a degree in **Sand Castle Sculpting.** I will be continuing my education in the <<Area>>, and am interested in seeking part-time employment to help finance my education toward a Masters degree in Fine Arts. At the conclusion of my studies, I plan to pursue a full-time career in this field.

I would appreciate any information concerning part-time jobs with <<Company>>, as well as any application forms or other pertinent information. I will be in the <<Area>> during the next three months and would be happy to meet with you to discuss any opportunities.

Thank you for your time and attention. I look forward to hearing from you at your earliest convenience.

Sincerely,

Your name

Title:	Ms.		*Title:*	Mr.
FirstName:	Dinah		*FirstName:*	Gene
LastName:	Soar		*LastName:*	Poole
Position:	Director of Antiquities		*Position:*	Artistic Director
Company:	Museum of Sand Wonders		*Company:*	The Sedimentary Foundation
Address1:	1234 Tar Pit Way		*Address1:*	1000BC Metamorphic Lane
Address2:	Las Yackos, AR 54321		*Address2:*	Sands Point, NY 12345
Area:	Southwest		*Area:*	Northeast

10. Close all documents without saving.

APPLICATION 6: PRODUCING MERGED LETTERS OF RESPONSE

1. Boot your computer; start Windows and launch the Word program.

2. In a new document window, use the Mail Merge Helper to identify the Main Document as the active window with the name INQFORM2.

3. Create a Data Source with the following fields: Title, FirstName, LastName, Address1, Address2, Date. Save the form as INQDATA2.

4. Return to the INQFORM2 form letter. Type the text and insert field markers as shown so that your letter resembles the sample on the next page. Don't worry if the lines of text do not wrap exactly as shown in the sample.

5. Save this form letter as INQFORM2.

6. Place the two records on page 242 into the INQDATA2 data source.

7. Now, add one more record using your name and other data of your choice.

8. Merge the INQFORM2 main document with the INQDATA2 data source.

9. Print the letters that result from this merge.

10. Close all documents without saving.

WP

MASTERY CASES

The following mastery cases allow you to demonstrate how much you have learned about this software. Each case describes a fictitious problem or need that can be solved using the skills you have learned in this chapter. Although minimum acceptable outcomes are specified, you are expected and encouraged to design your response (files, data, lists) in ways that display your personal mastery of the software. Feel free to show off your skills. Use real data from your own experience in your solution, although you may also fabricate data if needed.

These mastery cases allow you to display your ability to perform some or all of the following:

- Create and use headers and page numbers.
- Merge documents.
- Create tables.
- Sort data.
- Import graphics.

CASE 1: PREPARING A COURSE HISTORY TABLE

In anticipation of applying for graduate schools or jobs, you want to present your college course history in an effective and pleasing manner. Using tables and fonts, headers and page numbering, prepare a table that lists, sorted by title, all the courses you will have completed in your degree displaying their titles, designations, and grades.

The Sedimentary Foundation
1000BC Metamorphic Lane
Sands Point, NY 12345

Mr. Gene Poole
Artistic Director

Today's date

<<Title>> <<FirstName>> <<LastName>>
<<Address1>>
<<Address2>>

Dear <<Title>> <<LastName>>:

Please be advised that we have received your letter of <<Date>> concerning possible employment at The Sedimentary Foundation. As you know, our organization is well known throughout the world. Each year, we receive as many inquiries for employment as there are grains of sand on a beach. Unfortunately, we have only two artist's openings available--truly an "unsettling" situation.

I am enclosing with this letter our employee brochure and an application form. Please complete the form and return it to me with photographs of some of your best work. If, after reviewing the material, we require additional information or an interview, we will contact you.

Thank you for your interest in the Foundation and best wishes for your future success.

Sincerely,

Title:	Mr.		*Title:*	Ms.
FirstName:	Philip		*FirstName:*	Wanda
LastName:	DeLake		*LastName:*	Jobb
Address1:	2000 Pebble Drive		*Address1:*	4321 Liftoff Blvd.
Address2:	Boulder, CO 11223		*Address2:*	Cape Canaveral, FL 13579
Date:	November 1, 199X		*Date:*	October 7, 199X

CASE 2: CREATING YOUR OWN LETTERHEAD

Using fonts and a layout of your choice, create letterhead stationery for yourself that includes your name and address followed by a horizontal line beneath. Place an appropriate graphic in the letterhead, correctly sized and positioned as needed. (Use the DISK.BMP file if you have none.) *Extra:* Create a macro that will copy this letterhead into a new document.

CASE 3: CREATING A MERGED MEMORANDUM

You have decided to send the memo you created in Mastery Case 3 of Chapter 1 to a number of people. Using the memo as a main document, create an appropriate field list and data source, and add data for five people. Modify the memo to accept data for the fields you have chosen. Enhance the main document with font changes or imported graphics as desired. Print the memos.

WP

WORD 7.0 FOR WINDOWS 95
FEATURE AND OPERATION REFERENCE

Note: Word keys include both keystrokes that are common to most Windows applications and those that are unique to Word.

COMMON WINDOWS KEYS

Common Windows keys include basic menu and dialog box operations, file management, window manipulation, and editing commands.

ALT

Pressed alone, the Alt key activates the section highlight on the active window's menu bar. The highlight may then be removed to a menu bar item using the arrow keys. If used in combination with other keys, the Alt key is held down when striking another key. The other key is usually a function key (F1 through F12), the underlined letter of a menu item, button, or other option that has an underlined letter.

- **Alt** + **F4** exits Word (or any Windows application) or any dialog box.
- **Alt** + **Backspace** or **Ctrl** + **Z** undoes the last action.
- **Alt** + **Spacebar** opens Word's window's (or any application window's) control-menu.
- **Alt** + **–** (**Minus**) opens the control-menu of a document window.
- **Alt** + **Tab** switches to the last application used when operating multiple applications. Pressing and holding the Alt key while tapping the Tab key scrolls through running applications.
- **Alt** + **Esc** switches to the next running application when operating multiple applications. An application can be running as a window or a toolbar button.
- **Alt** + **Enter** switches a non-Windows application that was started in Windows between running in full screen and a window.
- **Alt** + **Print Screen** copies an image of the active application window (or dialog box) to the Clipboard for future pasting.

ARROW KEYS

- Move the insertion point one character at a time in the direction of the arrow when editing data within a text box or drop-down box.

■ Move the selection highlight in the direction of the arrow, to each item on a menu or list (in a list box or drop-down box).

The arrow keys can also be used in conjunction with other keys to perform such tasks as resizing a window, moving a selection (data, chart, table, or object), or moving a drawing or editing tool.

BACKSPACE

Erases single characters to the left of the insertion point.

CAPS LOCK

Keeps the Shift key active so that all characters are typed in uppercase.

CTRL

The Control key is used with another key to invoke a command.

■ **Ctrl** + **Alt** + **Delete** exits the current application if it stops responding to the system.

■ **Ctrl** + **B** turns on/off the bold feature.

■ **Ctrl** + **C** or **Ctrl** + **Insert** copies a selection (data, chart, table, or object) to the Windows Clipboard for future pasting.

■ **Ctrl** + **Esc** opens the *Task List* dialog box.

■ **Ctrl** + **F4** closes the active document window.

■ **Ctrl** + **F6** or **Ctrl** + **Tab** moves the highlight to another document window or icon.

■ **Ctrl** + **I** turns on/off the Italics feature.

■ **Ctrl** + **N** turns off the Bold, Italics, or Underline feature.

■ **Ctrl** + **O** opens a file.

■ **Ctrl** + **P** prints the current document or range (selection).

■ **Ctrl** + **S** saves the current document to a file.

■ **Ctrl** + **U** turns on/off the underline feature.

■ **Ctrl** + **V** or **Shift** + **Insert** pastes the contents of the Windows Clipboard to a desired location.

■ **Ctrl** + **X** or **Shift** + **Delete** cuts (moves) a section to the Windows Clipboard for future pasting.

■ **Ctrl** + **Z** or **Alt** + **Backspace** undoes the last action.

DELETE

The Delete key erases the following:

■ Single characters to the right of the insertion point when editing data in a cell, text box, or drop-down box.

■ A selection.

END

- Moves the insertion point to the end of a line when editing data.
- Moves the selection highlight to the last item in a menu, list box, or drop-down box.

ENTER

- Enters typed data into a cell or inserts a hard return.
- Invokes a command from a menu selection or dialog box.

ESC

- Cancels a menu or dialog box before a command is invoked.
- Returns a cell to its previous content before completing a new entry.

HOME

- Moves the insertion point to the beginning of a line of data in a cell, text box, or drop-down box.
- Moves the selection highlight to the beginning of a list in a menu, list box, or drop-down box.

NUMLOCK

Activates the numeric keypad that is on the right side of most keyboards. NumLock works as a toggle key; pressing it once activates the keypad, while pressing it again de-activates the keypad.

PG UP AND PG DN (PAGE UP AND PAGE DOWN)

Moves screen one page up or one page down.

PRINT SCREEN (PRTSC)

Captures an image of a screen to the Clipboard.

SHIFT

Works like the Shift key on a typewriter; when it is held down and a letter or number is pressed, an uppercase letter or symbol assigned to the number key is produced. Other commands invoked when pressing the Shift key and another key include the following:

- **Shift** + → expands the selection highlight to the right.
- **Shift** + ← expands the selection highlight to the left.
- **Shift** + **Delete** or **Ctrl** + **X** cuts (moves) a selection to the Windows Clipboard for future pasting.
- **Shift** + **Insert** or **Ctrl** + **V** pastes the content of the Windows Clipboard to a desired location.
- **Shift** + **Tab** moves the dotted selection rectangle to the previous option in a dialog box.

TAB

Moves the dotted selection rectangle to the next option in a dialog box.

WORD KEYS

Special keys used by Word in addition to those used in Windows are described below. For the specific location of these keys, check your particular keyboard.

ENTER ↵

Serves two principal functions: (1) enters a hard return into a document and (2) completes a Word command, after typing in text or keystroke sequences.

ESC (ESCAPE) Esc

Commonly used to backtrack from Word menus to the document screen.

HOME Home

Used with arrow keys to move the insertion point in various ways.

INS (INSERT) Insert

Used to toggle between the insert mode and the overtype mode. When in the insert mode (the default mode), characters being typed in are inserted at the insertion point, and any text to the right of the insertion point moves farther right. When in the overtype mode, characters being typed in replace characters already on the screen.

TAB Tab

Used to reach a preset Tab stop.

WORD MOUSE OPERATIONS

A mouse is an input device that allows you to control a mouse pointer (graphical image) on your screen. As you move your mouse, the mouse pointer moves in a similar fashion. See Figure WP1-2 in Chapter 1 for mouse pointer forms and common mouse action terms.

Your mouse can be used to select Windows and Word features. Some Word special features accessible by mouse are summarized below. Refer to Figure WP1-3 in Chapter 1 for the location of some of these features. (Detailed applications of these features are incorporated within the "Summary of Common Word Operations" section of this appendix.)

CLOSING A DOCUMENT WINDOW

Double-clicking a document window's *Document* icon is a quick way to close that window.

DRAG AND DROP

Word's "Drag and Drop" feature offers a quick way to cut and paste a selection of text or a graphics box within the same document. This is done by "dragging" the selected text or graphics box to its new location and then "dropping" it (releasing your mouse). (Remember, you must first select your text or graphics box before "dragging and dropping.")

EXITING WORD BY MOUSE

Double-clicking Word's program icon is a quick way to close the program.

MOVING THE INSERTION POINT BY MOUSE

Pointing to a new location within a document and clicking your mouse is a quick way to move the insertion point.

RESIZING BUTTONS

Clicking a resizing button is a quick way to change the size of a window. These mouse actions can be used to resize the Word window and document window(s).

When at maximum size, a document window's resizing button is located near the right end of the menu bar. At other times, a document window's resizing buttons appear in the upper right corner of its window.

	Resizing Button	Resizing Effect When Clicked
▬	Minimize	Reduces the window to a toolbar button
▣	Restore	Restores the window to its previous size
▢	Maximize	Enlarges the window to full screen

RULER BAR

Using Word's ruler bar is a quick way to access certain *Layout* menu features by mouse. To activate or deactivate the ruler, select *View* and then *Ruler*. A horizontal ruler bar appears.

To use the ruler bar to edit left or right margins, tab positions, table column widths, and column widths, simply drag and drop their respective markers.

SCROLL BARS

Clicking the arrow button at either end of a scroll bar is a quick way to scroll through your document or list box. Dragging the square button (or "elevator") along the scroll bar is another quick way to scroll. After scrolling, move your mouse pointer to the new location and click it. This will move the insertion point or highlight to that location.

SELECTING TEXT BY MOUSE

Text selection is a process of highlighting (marking) text for application of other Word features. Such features include assigning special formats; deleting, moving, or copying text, and saving a selection of text.

Text selection techniques by mouse include the following:

To Select a	Use This Mouse Action
Block of text	Drag mouse over text
Word	Double-click the word
Graphic	Click the graphic
Sentence	Hold Ctrl and click the sentence
Paragraph	Triple-click anywhere in the paragraph
Line	Point to line from left margin and click
Several lines	Point to first line from left margin and drag down
Vertical block of text	Hold Alt and then drag down

SHORTCUT MENUS

Shortcut menus provide quick access to a variety of features. To select a *Shortcut* menu feature by mouse, simply click it (left mouse button). Pointing to and clicking the right mouse button in the following locations on the Word window will open a *Shortcut* menu:

- Columns
- Dialog boxes
- Endnotes
- Fields
- Footnotes
- Frames
- Graphics
- OLE objects
- Ruler bar
- Scroll bars
- Selected text and left margin
- Status bar
- Tables
- Text
- WordArt window

THE TOOLBARS

The toolbars, as in Figure WPA-1, provide quick access by mouse to frequently used Word features. There are seven standard toolbars that appear at various times in Word: Standard, Formatting, Borders, Drawing, Database, Forms, and a general Microsoft toolbar. By default, the Standard and Formatting toolbars appear below the menu bar when you start Word.

The reference letter next to each button in the chart below refers to the position of the button on the toolbars in Figure WPA-1.

FIGURE WPA-1 ■   MOUSE POINTER SYMBOLS AND MOUSE ACTIONS

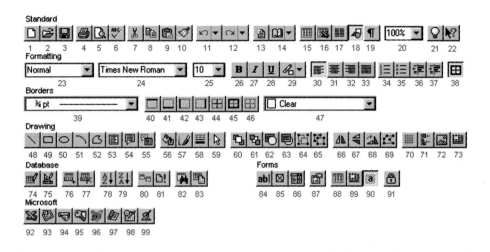

Toolbar	#	Button Name	Function
Standard	1	New	Creates a new document with NORMAL template
	2	Open	Opens an existing document or template
	3	Save	Saves the active document or template
	4	Print	Prints the active document
	5	Print Preview	Shows full pages as they will be printed
	6	Spelling	Checks spelling in the active document
	7	Cut	Cuts the selection and places it in the Clipboard
	8	Copy	Copies the selection and places it in the Clipboard
	9	Paste	Inserts the Clipboard contents at the insertion point
	10	Format Painter	Copies the selection's format to another location
	11	Undo	Reverses the last action
	12	Redo	Redoes the last action that was undone
	13	Auto Format	Automatically formats a document
	14	Insert Address	Inserts an address from the Address Book
	15	Insert Table	Inserts a table
	16	Insert Excel	Inserts an Excel Worksheet object
	17	Columns	Changes the column format of the selected sections
	18	Drawing	Shows/hides the Drawing toolbar
	19	Show/Hide	Shows/hides nonprinting characters
	20	Zoom Control	Adjusts the scale of the editing view
	21	Tip Wizard	Invokes/Closes Tip Wizard
	22	Help	Accesses the Help feature

(continued)

(continued from previous page)

Toolbar	#	Button Name	Function
Formatting	23	Style	Applies or records a style
	24	Font	Changes the font of the selected text
	25	Font Size	Changes the font size of the selected text
	26	Bold	Bold toggle (on/off)
	27	Italic	Italic toggle (on/off)
	28	Underline	Underline toggle (on/off)
	29	Highlight	Selects/deselects highlighter pen
	30	Align Left	Aligns the paragraph at the left indent
	31	Center	Centers the paragraph between indents
	32	Align Right	Aligns the paragraph at the right indent
	33	Justify	Aligns the paragraph at both indents
	34	Numbering	Creates a numbered list
	35	Bullets	Creates a bulleted list
	36	Decrease Indent	Decreases indent or promotes one level
	37	Increase Indent	Increases indent or demotes one level
	38	Borders	Shows/hides the border toolbar
Borders	39	Line Style	Changes border line styles
	40	Top Border	Changes the top border of the selection
	41	Bottom Border	Changes the bottom border of the selection
	42	Left Border	Changes the left border of the selection
	43	Right Border	Changes the right border of the selection
	44	Inside Border	Changes the inside border of the selection
	45	Outside Border	Changes the outside border of the selection
	46	No Border	Removes the border from the selection
	47	Shading	Changes the shading pattern of the selection
Drawing	48	Line	Inserts a line drawing object
	49	Rectangle	Inserts a rectangle drawing object
	50	Ellipse	Inserts an ellipse drawing object
	51	Arc	Inserts an arc drawing object
	52	Freeform	Inserts a freeform drawing object
Drawing	53	Text Box	Inserts a textbox drawing object
	54	Callout	Inserts a callout drawing object
	55	Format Callout	Formats selected callouts or sets callout defaults
	56	Fill Color	Changes the fill color
	57	Line Color	Changes the line color
	58	Line Style	Changes the line style
	59	Select Drawing Object	Selects drawing object
	60	Bring to Front	Brings selected drawing object to the front
	61	Send to Back	Sends selected drawing object to the back
	62	Bring in Front of Text	Brings selected drawing forward one layer

(continued)

(continued from previous page)

Toolbar	#	Button Name	Function
	63	Send Behind Text	Sends selected drawing object back one layer
	64	Group	Groups the selected (selected with Shift)
	65	Ungroup	Ungroups the selected group of objects
	66	Flip Horizontal	Flips selection left to right
	67	Flip Vertical	Flips selection top to bottom
	68	Rotate Right	Rotates selection 90 degrees to the right
	69	Reshape	Shows resizing handles on freeform shape
	70	Snap to Grid	Sets up an aligning grid for objects
	71	Align Drawing Objects	Aligns selected drawing objects
	72	Create Picture	Opens a window to create a picture object
	73	Insert Frame	Inserts an empty frame or encloses the selection
Database	74	Data Form	Edits a list or table in a form
	75	Manage Fields	Adds or deletes a field from a database
	76	Add New Record	Adds a record to a database
	77	Delete Record	Removes a record from a database
	78	Sort Ascending	Sorts records in ascending order
	79	Sort Descending	Sorts records in descending order
	80	Insert Database	Inserts data from an external source
	81	Update Fields	Updates and displays selected fields
	82	Find Record	Finds a record in a mail merge data source
	83	Mail Merge Main Doc	Accesses a mail merge main document
Forms	84	Text Form Field	Inserts a text form field
	85	Check Box Form Field	Inserts a check box form field
	86	Drop-Down Form Field	Inserts a drop-down form field
	87	Form Field Options	Accesses form field options
	88	Insert Table	Inserts a table
	89	Insert Frame	Inserts a frame
	90	Form Field Shading	Changes shading options
	91	Protect Form	Turns protection on/off for the active document
Microsoft	92	Excel	Starts or switches to Excel
	93	PowerPoint	Starts or switches to PowerPoint
	94	Mail	Starts or switches to Mail
	95	Access	Starts or switches to Access
	96	FoxPro	Starts or switches to FoxPro
	97	Project	Starts or switches to Project
	98	Schedule+	Starts or switches to Schedule+
	99	Publisher	Starts or switches to Publisher

DISPLAYING AND HIDING A TOOLBAR.   To display or hide a toolbar:

1 Click *View*, and then *Toolbars*

2 Click the check box to select or clear the desired toolbar

3 Click *OK*

MOVING THE TOOLBAR.   The toolbar can be moved (and reshaped) from its current location to a new location anywhere within the Word window.

1 Click within the toolbar and hold the mouse button

2 Drag the toolbar to your desired new location and drop it there

CREATING A CUSTOMIZED TOOLBAR.   You can create your own custom toolbar by doing the following:

1 Select *Tools, Customize*

2 Select the Toolbars tab in the *Customize* dialog box

3 Select the desired toolbar in the *Categories* box

4 Select the desired buttons

5 Click the *Close* button to exit the dialog box

EDITING A TOOLBAR.   You may add, move, or delete buttons from any toolbar.

TO ADD A BUTTON TO A TOOLBAR

1 Display the toolbar in the window

2 Select *Tools, Customize, Toolbar*

3 Select the desired category

4 Drag the desired button to the toolbar

5 Click the *Close* button

TO MOVE A BUTTON

1 Display the toolbar

2 Select _Tools_, _Customize_, _Toolbar_

3 Point to the button that you desire to move

4 Drag the button to its new location and drop it there

5 Click the _Close_ button

TO DELETE A BUTTON

1 Repeat Steps 1–3 in "To Move a Button"

2 Point to the button that you desire to delete

3 Drag the button off of the toolbar

4 Click the _Close_ button

INSERTION POINT MOVEMENT

The Insertion Point Moves	When You Press
One character right	$[\rightarrow]$
One character left	$[\leftarrow]$
One line up	$[\uparrow]$
One line down	$[\downarrow]$
One word right	[Ctrl] +$[\rightarrow]$
One word left	[Ctrl] +$[\leftarrow]$
To the beginning of the current line	[Home]
To the end of the current line	[End]
To the beginning of current paragraph	[Ctrl] + $[\uparrow]$
To the beginning of previous paragraph	[Ctrl] + $[\uparrow][\uparrow]$
To the beginning of the next paragraph	[Ctrl] + $[\downarrow]$
To the top of the document	[Ctrl] + [Home]
To the bottom of the document	[Ctrl] + [End]
One screen back (up)	[Pg Up]
One screen forward (down)	[Pg Dn]
Bottom of screen	[Ctrl] + [Pg Dn]
Top of screen	[Ctrl] + [Pg Up]
One page back (up)	[Alt] + [Ctrl] + [Pg Up]
One page forward (down)	[Alt] + [Ctrl] + [Pg Dn]

SUMMARY OF COMMON WORD OPERATIONS

Following is a brief, step-by-step summary showing how to perform several common Word tasks.

ALIGNING TEXT

Word automatically defaults to ragged-right edge (left alignment). To change to full justification:

1 Click *Layout, Justification*, and then *Full*   [**Ctrl** + **J**]

Note: Besides *Left* (Ctrl + L) and *Justify* (Ctrl + J), other options that can be chosen in Step 1 are *Right* (Ctrl + R) and *Center* (Ctrl + E) or *All*

USING THE TOOLBAR TO CHANGE ALIGNMENT.   To change the alignment using the toolbar:

1 Point to an alignment button on the Formatting toolbar

2 Click the button

ARRANGING DOCUMENT WINDOWS

When you are working with more than one document window, Word allows you to arrange them one on top of the other. To do so,

1 Click *Window*

2 Click *Arrange All*

AUTOCORRECT AND AUTOTEXT

The AutoCorrect feature allows you to correct and insert items as you type. It also lets you retrieve and insert an item by typing a few keystrokes or clicking the *AutoText* button.

With the AutoCorrect feature, Word automatically replaces common misspellings and words that are complicated to spell. For example, if you always type "wrod" instead of "word," you can create an AutoText entry named "wrod." Whenever you type *wrod* followed by a space or punctuation mark, Word replaces it with "word."

You can create AutoText entries (previously known as glossary entries) for text and graphics you use less frequently or don't want Word to insert automatically. For example, you can store a standard business letter greeting. The AutoText feature works like the AutoCorrect feature, but you decide when you want to make the re-placements.

BOLDING TEXT

Bolding enables you to output text with thicker strokes than normal text.
  Before typing the text, do the following:

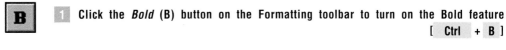

1 Click the *Bold* (B) button on the Formatting toolbar to turn on the Bold feature
[**Ctrl** + **B**]

2 Type the text to be bolded

3 Click the *Bold* (B) button again to turn off the Bold feature   [**Ctrl** + **B**]

After typing in the text,

1 Select the text to be bolded

2 Click the *Bold* button on the Formatting toolbar

3 Click outside of the selected text area to turn off the select mode

CANCELING A COMMAND

Canceling a command enables you to abort a partially completed menu or prompt, back out of Word's menu system, and return to your document.

1 Press Esc for Cancel

2 If you are not fully back to the document, continue pressing Esc until you return there

CENTERING TEXT

The centering command enables text to be centered on a line, either before or after you type in the text.
  Before typing in the text,

1 Click the *Center* button on the Formatting toolbar   [**Ctrl** + **E**]

2 Type the text to be centered

3 Press ↵

After typing in the text,

1 Move the insertion point to the beginning of the text to be centered

2 Click the *Center* button on the Formatting toolbar   [**Ctrl** + **E**]

CHANGING THE DEFAULT DRIVE ("LOOK IN" DRIVE)

The default drive usually must be changed when you enter Word so files are saved to and opened from a data diskette.

1 Click *File* and then *Open* for the *Open* dialog box (or click the *Open File* button on the power bar)

2 Click the *Look in* drop-down box

3 Click the desired drive or folder

4 Press ↵

5 Press **Esc** to return to your document

CLOSING A DOCUMENT

Closing a document allows you to start fresh, on a new document. It is the same as closing a document window.

1 Click *File* and then *Close*   [**Ctrl** + **F4**]

If you have not saved your document or have changed your document without resaving it, a dialog box will appear asking you if you wish to save.

2 Click *Yes* or *No* or *Cancel,* depending on whether you want to save your current document   [**Y** , **N** , or **Esc**]

Double-clicking the document window's document icon will also close the document.

COPYING TEXT

Copying allows a duplicate version of a selection of text to be placed in another section of a document.

1 Select the text to be copied

2 Click *Edit* and then *Copy* (or click the *Copy* button on the toolbar)   [**Ctrl** + **C**]

3 Move the insertion point to the location where you wish to copy the text

4 Click *Edit* and then *Paste* (or click the *Paste* button on the toolbar)   [**Ctrl** + **V**]

USING SHORTCUT KEYS TO COPY TEXT AND GRAPHICS.   Use the following Shortcut keys to copy text and graphics.

To	Press
Copy text or graphics	[Ctrl] + [C]
Copy formats	[Ctrl] + [Shift] + [C]
Move text or graphics	[F2]
Paste text or graphics	[Ctrl] + [V]
Paste formats	[Ctrl] + [Shift] + [V]

DELETING TEXT AND CODES

Deleting physically removes text from a document.

DELETING A CHARACTER OR A WORD AT A TIME.   Complete the following instructions:

To Delete	Press
The current character	[Delete]
The character to the left	[← Backspace]
The word before the insertion point	[Ctrl] + [← Backspace]
The word after the insertion point	[Ctrl] + [Delete]
Selected text	[Ctrl] + [X]

DELETING A SELECTION OF TEXT

1 **Select the text to be deleted**

2 **Press Delete**

DRAG AND DROP FEATURE

Word's Drag and Drop feature is a quick way to cut and paste a selection of text or a graphics box within the same document.

TO DRAG AND DROP TEXT

1 **Select text to be dragged and dropped**

2 **Move your mouse pointer anywhere on the selected text**

3   "Drag" the selection to your desired new location

4   Release your mouse to "drop" the selection in its new location

5   Double-click *EXT* on the status bar or press **F8** to turn off the select mode

TO DRAG AND DROP A GRAPHIC

1   Click the graphics box to select it

2   "Drag" the graphics box to your desired new location

3   Release your mouse to "drop" the selection in its new location

4   Double-click *EXT* on the status bar or press **F8** to turn off the select mode

EQUATION EDITOR

Equation Editor lets you add fractions, exponents, integrals, and other mathematical elements to a document. Equation Editor applies most of the formatting for you and adjusts spacing between elements.

TO CREATE AN EQUATION WITH EQUATION EDITOR

1   Position the insertion point

2   Select *Insert, Object*

3   Select the *Create New tab*

4   Under Object Type, select *Microsoft Equation 2.0,* and then *OK*

(Word displays the Equation Editor toolbar and menu.)

5   Create an equation by typing text and by choosing symbols, operators, and templates from the Equation Editor toolbar and menu

6   When you finish, click in the Word document window to return to Word. To edit the equation, double-click it

EXITING WORD

Three ways to exit Word are as follows:

EXITING BY *PROGRAM* ICON OR SHORTCUT KEYS

1   Double-click Word's *Program* icon box to close it   [**Alt** + **F4**]

EXITING BY CONTROL-MENU

1 Click Word's *Program* icon box for its control menu   [**Alt** + **F4**]

2 Click *Close* to close the Word window   [**C**]

EXITING BY MENU BAR

1 Click *File* and then *Exit* to close Word

FINDING TEXT

Finding text requires you to identify the string of characters you want to search. There are separate Find and Replace commands (see "Replacing Text").

1 Place the insertion point where you want to begin the search

2 Click *Edit* and *Find* for the *Find* dialog box

3 Type the search string

4 Select any desired option

5 Click the *Find Next* button to move to the first occurrence of this text

6 Perform Step 5 to move to the remaining occurrences of this text

SEARCH CRITERIA WILDCARDS.   You can use wildcards in the *Find What* box in the *Find or Replace* dialog box to conduct various searches (see Figure WPA-2).

FONTS

Different fonts can be used to print text in a special way. Depending on the printer you have, you may or may not be able to take full advantage of the features in Word's Font command. Font changes affect text that you type from the insertion point forward or selected text.

TO CHANGE THE FONT FROM THE INSERTION POINT FORWARD OR FOR SELECTED TEXT

1 Move the insertion point to the location that you desire the new font to begin or select text

2 Click *Format* and then *Font* for its dialog box   [**F9**]

3 Click the desired font name   [→]

FIGURE WPA-2 ■ SEARCH CRITERIA WILDCARDS

To Find	Use This Wildcard	Examples
A single character	?	c?t finds "cat" and "cut"
A string of characters	*	m*d finds "mad" and "muzzled"
One of the listed characters	[ ]	p[iu]n finds "pin" and "pun"
A single character in the range	[-]	[l-n]ight finds "light," "might," and "night."Ranges must be in ascending order
Any single character except those listed inside the brackets	[!]	p[!a]st finds "pest" and "post," but not "past"
"t" occurrences of the previous character or expression	{t}	be{2}t finds "beet" but not "bet"
One or more occurrences of the previous character or expression	@	so@n finds "son" and "soon"
The beginning of a word	<	<(host) finds "host" and "hostile," but not "ghost"
The end of a word	>	(ang)> finds "hang" and "sang," but not "anger" or "wrangler"

---

4 **Click the desired font size**

5 **Click the desired appearance option(s)**   [↵]

6 **Click the *OK* button**

Note: To remove formatting, press Ctrl + Spacebar.

TO CHANGE THE INITIAL FONT OF A DOCUMENT

1 **Click *Format* and then *Font* for the *Font* dialog box**   [F9]

2 **Click the desired font from the *Font Name* list box**   [Alt + T]

3 **Click the *Font Size* text box and type in the desired size (or click the desired size from the *Font Size* list box)**

4 **Select the *Default* button**

5   Confirm by selecting "Yes"

6   If you want to save the new format permanently, select "Yes"

FOOTNOTES

Word enables you to create, edit, and delete footnotes.

TO CREATE A FOOTNOTE

1   Position the insertion point at the place in your document where you would like the footnote to appear

2   Click *Insert, Footnote, Footnote, Autonumber, OK*   [**Alt** + **Ctrl** + **F**]

The footnote number will automatically appear on your screen. Next,

3   Type the text of the footnote

When you are finished,

4   Click the *Close* button   [**Alt** + **Shift** + **C**]

TO EDIT A FOOTNOTE

1   Switch to Page View

2   Move to the footnote

3   Edit the note as you would edit ordinary text

4   Switch view if needed

TO DELETE A FOOTNOTE

1   Select the reference footnote number within the document

2   Press **Backspace** or **Delete**

Note: If you wish endnotes rather than footnotes, follow the instructions above, but choose the *Endnote* option instead of the *Footnote* option after you click *Insert*.

FORMATTING CHARACTERS WITH SHORTCUT KEYS

Use the following shortcut keys to apply character-formatting styles.

CHANGING FONT OR FONT SIZE

To	Press
Change the font	[Ctrl] + [Shift] + [F]
Change the font size	[Ctrl] + [Shift] + [P]
Increase the font size to the next size	[Ctrl] + [Shift] + [>]
Decrease the font size to the previous size	[Ctrl] + [Shift] + [<]
Increase the font size by 1 point	[Ctrl] + []]
Decrease the font size by 1 point	[Ctrl] + [[]

CHANGING TEXT FORMATTING

To	Press
Change the case of letters	[Shift] + [F3]
Create all capital letters	[Ctrl] + [Shift] + [A]
Make text bold	[Ctrl] + [B]
Underline text	[Ctrl] + [U]
Italicize text	[Ctrl] + [I]
Create small capital letters	[Ctrl] + [Shift] + [K]
Apply subscripts	[Ctrl] + [=]
Apply superscripts	[Ctrl] + [Shift] + [=]
Remove formatting set by Shortcut keys or menus	[Ctrl] + [Shift] + [Z]

GRAMMAR CHECK

Word's grammar check identifies sentences with potential errors in grammar or style. Word offers three "stylistic rule" groups: formal, business, and casual.

1 **Click _Tools_ and then _Grammar_**

2 **Select options in answer to each problem found**

3 **Select _OK_ when done**

> Note: To change the "rule" used, select Tools, Options, Grammar tab. Then select the new rule and *OK*.

GRAPHICS BOXES

The Graphics feature in Word enables you to draw boxes around text or figures for emphasis.

TO CREATE A GRAPHICS BOX

1 Click *Insert*, *Picture*

2 Select *Insert*, *Frame*

TO EDIT A GRAPHICS BOX

1 Click the desired Graphics box to be edited to select it

2 Click *Graphics* and then *Edit*

3 Adjust any of the parameters that define the graphic

HEADERS AND FOOTERS

Headers and footers contain brief information that identifies a page. You can create headers and/or footers for odd pages, even pages, or all pages.

1 Move the insertion point to the desired page

2 Click *View* and then *Header and Footer* for its toolbar

3 Switch to Footer if desired

4 Type the header or footer

5 Click the *Close* button on the toolbar to close it   [**Alt** + **Shift** + **C**]

> Note: To learn how to place page numbers in headers and footers, see the note accompanying the section on "Numbering Pages."

HELP FEATURE

The Help feature lets you learn more about a particular feature in Word without having to turn to the printed reference manual.

REQUESTING HELP FROM A DOCUMENT SCREEN.   If you are in the middle of typing a document and need help,

1 Click *Help*   [**F1**]

The HELP window now appears.

2 Follow the instructions on the screen telling you what to do next

THE HELP SEARCH FEATURE.   The Help Search feature allows you to get help on a desired topic. To access this feature,

1 Click *Help* and then *Search*

2 Type in the desired topic or select it from the list by clicking it

3 Click the *Show Topic* dialog box

4 Click the desired topic from the list box

5 Click the *Go To* button

TO GET INFORMATION ABOUT INDIVIDUAL MENU COMMANDS

1 On the *Standard toolbar*, click the *Help* button. The mouse pointer changes to a question mark

2 Click the desired menu and then click the command for which you want information. Word displays the Help window

INDENTING PARAGRAPHS

Indenting is appropriate both for a numbered (or bulleted) list of sentences or paragraphs and for sentences or paragraphs that are not numbered.

1 If preparing a number or bullet list, click the appropriate button; otherwise, go directly to Step 2

2 Click the *Increase Indent* toolbar button   [**Ctrl** + **M**]

3 Type the text, letting the right margin wrap

4 End the indent

INDEX PREPARATION

Indexes can be prepared in two ways: (1) by marking words or phases in the document or (2) by creating a list of words that you want indexed and storing the list in a file (called a *concordance file*). You can identify words for an index by using either one of the two ways or by combining them. Once you've identified the words and phrases for the index, a separate procedure is required to create the index itself. The first technique is shown here:

MARKING WORDS OR PHRASES IN A DOCUMENT

1 Move the insertion point anywhere on the word you want indexed or, if it is a phrase, select the text involved

2 Press **Alt** + **Shift** + **X** The selected text appears in the *Main Entry* box.

3 Edit the text if needed

4 Type a subentry if desired

5 Select the *Mark* or *Mark All* button

Repeat Steps 1 through 5 for every word or phrase you want to mark.

6 Click the *Close* button

PREPARING A CONCORDANCE FILE

1 Begin with a fresh document screen

2 Select *Table*, *Insert Table*, *OK*

3 In the first column, type the first index entry exactly as you want it in the index and press **Tab**

4 In the second column, type the entry as it will appear in the index and press **Tab** (*Note:* The entries in both columns can be identical.)

5 Repeat Steps 3 and 4 for each index entry

6 Save the document

Note: While entries in the concordance file do not need to be in alphabetical order, index creation will be faster if you sort the list (see "Sorting Items in a List"). Word automatically assumes that each entry in the concordance file is a heading; if it is to be a subheading, you must mark it in this file by using the steps described earlier under "Marking Words or Phrases in a Document."

CREATING THE INDEX.   After you have marked entries for indexing, you can create the index itself.

1 Assuming the index is to be at the end of the document, move the insertion point there

2 Select *Insert* and then *Index and Tables*

3 Select the *Index* tab

4 Select a desired format

5 Select the *OK* button

When you print the document, the index will be included. If you later need to update the index, and page-number references have changed, you will need to recreate the index.

INSERTING A FILE INTO THE CURRENT DOCUMENT   Inserting a file into your current document allows you to make one document part of another.

1 Place the insertion point where you want the inserted file to begin

2 Click *Insert* and then *File* for the *File* dialog box

3 Type the name of the file or select it from the *File Name* list box

4 Click the *OK* button for insertion of file into current document (or click the *Cancel* button to cancel)

INSERTING TEXT

Inserting allows text to be added at the insertion point, pushing existing text over to the right. To insert text:

1 Make sure the insert mode is active

Note: The insert mode is the default mode; if the overtype indicator ("OVR") appears in the status bar on your screen, you are not in the insert mode and must press the Insert key to get there.

2 Move the insertion point to the place where you want to insert text

3 Type the text to be inserted

Note: The text of your document will be reformatted automatically.

USING SHORTCUT KEYS TO INSERT TEXT AND GRAPHICS.   Use the following Shortcut keys to insert text and graphics:

To insert	Press
A field	[Ctrl] + [F9]
An AutoText entry	*AutoText entry name* + [Alt] + [Ctrl] + [V]
A line break	[Shift] + [Enter]
A page break	[Ctrl] + [Enter]
A column break	[Ctrl] + [Shift] + [Enter]
An optional hyphen	[Ctrl] + [Hyphen]
A nonbreaking hyphen	[Ctrl] + [Shift] + [Hyphen]
A nonbreaking space	[Ctrl] + [Shift] + [Spacebar]
A double opening quotation mark	[Ctrl] + [`] followed by [Shift] + ["] (*Note:* shares a key with ~)
A double closing quotation mark	[Ctrl] + ['] followed by [Shift] + ["]

LINE NUMBERS

Adding line numbers lets you refer to specific lines in a document, as in a script or legal contract. You can add line numbers to *sections* of a document or to the entire document. Word adds numbers to every line except tables, footnotes, endnotes, headers, and footers.

TO ADD LINE NUMBERS

1. Position the insertion point in the section in which you want the lines numbered. If you have not divided your document into sections, line numbers are added to the entire document

2. Select *File, Page Setup*

3. Select the *Layout* tab

4. Choose the *Line Numbers* button

5. Select the *Add Line Numbering* check box

You can set these options:

- To start with a number other than 1, type or select a line number in the *Start At* box.
- Select Auto or specify a distance between the line number and the text by typing or selecting a measurement in the *From Text* box.
- To increment numbers by other than one, type or select the increment in the *Count By* box. For example, if you want Word to print every second line number, type 2.

6. When you finish setting options, click *OK* twice

> Note: Word prints line numbers in the margin. If the margins are too narrow, the line number will not be printed.

LINE SPACING

The line spacing option allows text to be single-spaced, double-spaced, and so on.
    Move to the line in your text preceding the place at which you want to begin the new spacing.

1 Click *Format*, *Paragraph*, and then the *Indents and Spacing* tab

2 Select the desired line spacing   [**Ctrl** + **1** , **5** , or **2**]

3 Click the *OK* button

MACROS

A macro is a set of keystrokes that are automatically invoked when summoned. While Word allows macro names, you can also assign macros to Shortcut keys, menus, or toolbars for easy execution.

TO CREATE A MACRO

1 Double-click the "REC" indicator on the status bar for the *Record Macro* dialog box
            [**Alt** + **T** , **M** , **O**]

2 In the *Record Macro* dialog box, type a name

3 To assign a macro to a toolbar, menu, or shortcut key, choose the appropriate button

4 Select the *OK* button or press ↵

5 Enter the keystrokes that you want the macro to represent

6 Repeat Step 1 to stop recording the macro and save it

TO RUN A MACRO

1 Select *Tools, Macro*

2 Select the macro from the list

3 Select *Run*

If you assigned the macro to a toolbar, menu, or Shortcut key, press as appropriate.

MARGIN ADJUSTMENT

Word allows you to adjust the top, bottom, left, and/or right margins of your document.

1 Move the insertion point to the section in which you desire the change to begin

2 Click *File* and then *Page Setup* and the *Margins* tab

3 Type in the new margin setting(s) over the current margin settings (or click the triangle buttons on the right of the text boxes)

4 Click the *OK* button to return to the document

USING THE RULER BAR TO MAKE MARGIN ADJUSTMENTS.   Left and right margin adjustments can be quickly made by mouse using the ruler.

1 Click the *View* and then *Ruler* if needed

2 Drag the Left or Right Margin marker to the desired position and then release the mouse

Note: Hold the Alt key while dragging the mouse to display ruler measurements.

MERGING FILES

Merging files enables you to create customized form letters. Assuming you have followed the procedures described in the text to create a main document (form) and data source file (the customized information to place in the letter), follow the steps below to merge the two into a third document.

1 Open the main document into the active window

2 Click the *View Merged Data* button on the Mail Merge toolbar.

Word displays the data from the first record in the data source merged into the main document.

3 Click the arrows in the toolbar (or type a number) to see other record's data

4 You can use the toolbar to print, save all the merged data in a new document, or select other options

MOVING TEXT

Moving text is an action that physically removes (cuts) a selection of text from one place in a document and puts (pastes) it in another.

1   Select the text to be moved

2   Click *Edit* and then *Cut*   [**Ctrl**   +   **X**   ]

3   Move the insertion point to the new location in the document

4   Click *Edit* and then *Paste*   [**Ctrl**   +   **V**   ]

MOVING TEXT USING THE DRAG AND DROP FEATURE.   To drag and drop text using a mouse,

1   Select the text to be cut and pasted

2   Move your pointer anywhere on the selected text until the pointer appears as an arrow

3   "Drag" the selection to your desired new location

4   Release your mouse to "drop" the selection in its new location

5   Click anywhere outside the selection to turn off the select mode

MULTICOLUMN TEXT

Word enables you to create multicolumn text, similar to that which you see in a newspaper. To define columns before you type in the text or convert a noncolumn file to multicolumn,

1   Click *Format, Columns* for the *Columns* dialog box

2   Type the desired number of columns (or click a preset option)

3   Click *OK* to create newspaper type columns (the default)

4   Type text going into the first column

5   Press   **Ctrl**   +   ↵   to move to the next column

> Note: Use the *Columns* dialog box to change the margins or distance between the multiple columns.

USING THE TOOLBAR TO CREATE COLUMNS.   To quickly create columns using the toolbar:

1   Click the *Columns* button on the Standard toolbar

2 Drag to the desired column size (up to 6) and then release the mouse

EDITING COLUMNS.   The ruler bar or *Columns* dialog box can be used to edit the setup of the columns.

1 Click *View* and then *Ruler* to turn it on

2 Drag and drop the column markers at the desired new location(s)

NEW DOCUMENT

To create a new document:

1 Select *File*, *New*   [**Ctrl** + **N**]

2 Select a template

3 Click *OK*   [↵]

(Also see *Templates.*)

NUMBERING PAGES

The Word default is no page numbers. To number pages of a Word document:

1 Place the insertion point at the beginning of the page where the page numbers will start

2 Click *Insert, Page Numbers* for the *Page Numbers* dialog box

3 Select the desired position

4 Select the desired alignment

5 If desired, select "Show number on first page"

6 Select the *OK* button

> **Note:** You can also print page numbers within a header or a footer by placing the insertion point where you want the number to print in the header or footer and clicking the *Page Numbers* button on the Header and Footer toolbar.

OPENING DOCUMENTS

Opening a file is the act of fetching a document from disk and loading it into memory. To open a file,

1 Click *File* and then *Open* for the *Open* dialog box   [**Ctrl** + **O**]

2 Either type the filename to be opened into the *File name* text box or select it from the *Files* list box

3 Click the *OK* button

USING THE TOOLBAR TO OPEN A DOCUMENT.   To use the toolbar to open a document, replace Step 1 with the following:

1 Click the *Open File* button on the toolbar for the *Open File* dialog box

ORPHANS AND WIDOWS

For eliminating orphans and widows, see "Page Breaks."

PAGE BREAKS

Word has features that enable you to force page breaks when you want them, to keep certain selections of text (such as tables or paragraphs) from being split between two pages, and to eliminate orphans and widows in a document.

HARD PAGE BREAKS.   To produce a hard break,

1 Place the insertion point where a new page will begin

2 Click *Insert* and then *Break*   [**Ctrl** + **↵**]

3 Click the *OK* button

CONDITIONAL PAGE BREAKS.   To keep lines of a paragraph from being split by a soft page break,

1 Place the insertion point in the paragraph that is to remain intact

2 Click *Format, Paragraph*

3 Select the *Text Flow* tab

4 Under Pagination, select the *Keep Lines Together* check box

5 Click the *OK* button

ELIMINATING ORPHANS AND WIDOWS.   Orphans and widows are aesthetically undesirable line breaks. The first line of a paragraph is called an orphan when it is separated from the rest of the paragraph by a page or column break. The last line of a paragraph is called a widow when it is separated from the rest of the paragraph by being forced onto a new page or column.

By default, Word does not allow widows or orphans to occur. To check—or change—the setting,

1 Select *Format, Paragraph*

2 Select the *Text Flow* tab

3 Under *Pagination,* select the *Widow/Orphan Control* check box ("X" to eliminate or "clear" to allow)

4 Select *OK*

PRINTING DOCUMENTS

Word allows several printing options, including printing an entire document, a single page, or a range of pages.

PRINTING THE ENTIRE DOCUMENT

1 Click *File* and then *Print* for the Print dialog box (or click the *Print* button on the toolbar)

2 Click the *OK* button

PRINTING A SINGLE PAGE

1 Position the insertion point anywhere on the page you want to print

2 Click *File* and then *Print* (or click the *Print* button on the toolbar)

3 Click *Current Page*

4 Click the *OK* button

PRINTING A RANGE OF PAGES

1 Click *File* and then *Print* (or click the Print button on the toolbar)

2 Click *Pages*

3 Type the numbers corresponding to the range of pages to be printed

Examples:

11, 17 (means pages 11 and 17 only)
11–17 (means pages 11 through 17)
10, 12–14 (means pages 10, 12, 13, and 14)
11– (means from page 11 on)
–11 (means up to page 11)

4 **Click the *OK* button to print**

STOPPING OR CANCELING A PRINT JOB. To stop or cancel a job that is printing, simply press ESC, double-click the *Print* toolbar button, or select *File, Print, Stop Print.*

REPLACING TEXT

Replacement requires you to identify both the text string you want to search for in the document as well as the text string with which you want to replace it.

1 **Place the insertion point where you want to begin the search**

2 **Click *Edit* and then *Replace* for the *Replace* dialog box**   [**Ctrl** + **H**]

3 **Type a search string in the *Find What* text box**

4 **Press** **Tab** **to move the insertion point with the *Replace With* text box**

5 **Type the replacement text**

> **Note: Select the *Special* button to use special text and formatting characters.**

6 **Click either *Replace All* for replacement without confirmation or *Replace* for replacement with confirmation**

7 **If you selected *Replace,* confirm replacement by selecting *Replace* and repeat (note that if you do not wish to replace an item, select *Find Next* to continue)**

8 **Click the *Cancel* button to end**

RESTORING DELETED TEXT

Word allows you to see and restore your most recent deletions.

1 **Click *Edit* and then *Undo***   [**Ctrl** + **Z**]

2 **To undo multiple actions, click the undo down arrow**

RULER BAR

Word's ruler bar feature allows quick access to certain Layout features with the mouse.

1   Click _View_ and then _Ruler_ to display it

2   Drag and drop markers to change left or right margins, tab positions, table column widths, and column widths

Note that a dotted vertical line will appear in the document window as a guide when you drag a marker. The ruler attaches to a document window when activated and detaches when the window is closed. To deactivate the ruler without closing the document window,

1   Click _View_ and then _Ruler_ to hide it again if desired

Operations of tab markers and ruler buttons are described under their related functions within this appendix.

SAVING DOCUMENTS

Saving a document places onto disk a copy of the active document in main memory.

1   Click _File_ and then _Save As_ for the _Save As_ dialog box

2   Type a document name or accept the document name in the _File name_ text box (if previously saved)

3   Click the _OK_ button

4   If needed, click the _Yes_ button to replace

> **Note:** The _Save_ command of the _File_ menu will resave a file without confirmation. This command can also be invoked by clicking the _Save_ button on the Standard toolbar.

SAVING AND OPENING SELECTIONS OF TEXT

Use this feature to save frequently used blocks of text.

TO SAVE

1   Select the text to be saved

2   Click _File_ and then _Save As_

3   Give the selection a name

4   Click the _OK_ button

TO OPEN. See procedures described under "Opening Documents."

SCROLL BARS

Scroll bars allow quick scanning of a document or list box. Word opens with vertical (right wall of document window) and horizontal (above status bar) scroll bars. A vertical scroll bar also appears on the right side of a list box when its contents exceed its view space. Text must occupy the document window before you can operate its scroll bar(s).

TO SCROLL USING THE ARROW BUTTON

1 Click the arrow button at either end of the scroll bar until you have reached your desired location or item

Note that the insertion point or highlight does not move its position as you scan with scroll bars. To move the insertion point or highlight,

2 Move the mouse pointer to the position where you want the insertion point or highlight

3 Click your mouse to insert the insertion point or highlight

TO SCROLL USING THE SQUARE BUTTON. The square ("elevator") button on a scroll bar allows you to scroll up or down (left or right for a horizontal scroll bar) in your document or list box.

1 Drag the square button on the scroll bar until you have reached your desired position

2 Move the mouse pointer to the position where you want the insertion point or highlight to appear

3 Click your mouse to insert the insertion point or highlight

SELECTING TEXT

Use this procedure to assign special formats; to delete, move, or copy text; and to save selections of text, such as frequently used paragraphs.

SELECTING TEXT BY MOUSE

1 Use one of the mouse techniques on page 279 to select

2 Perform editing or formatting procedures

3 Click anywhere outside the highlighted area to turn off the select mode, if necessary

Selection	Mouse Action
Block of text	Drag mouse over text
Word	Double-click the word
Sentence	Hold the Ctrl key and click anywhere in the sentence
Paragraph	Triple-click anywhere in the paragraph
Line	Point to line from left margin and click
Several lines	Point to first line from left margin and drag down

SELECTING TEXT BY KEYBOARD

1 **Move the insertion point to the beginning of the text to be selected**

2 **Press and hold Shift and then use the arrow keys to select the desired text**

Note that the selected text is highlighted on the screen.

3 **Perform editing or formatting procedures**

4 **Press an arrow key to turn off the select mode, if necessary**

SORTING ITEMS IN A LIST

To sort a list of items alphabetically,

1 **Select the list of items to be sorted**

2 **Click *Table* and then *Sort Text***

3 **Click the *OK* button**

SPELLING

The spelling checker is used to flag and subsequently correct potentially misspelled words and double words.

1 **Click *Tools* and the *Spelling* for the *Spelling* dialog box**   **[F7]**

You can also click the Spelling button on the Standard toolbar.

STARTING A NEW DOCUMENT

You can start a new document from an existing template, or you can use a wizard. If you create a document using a wizard, Word bases the document on the Normal document template. The styles used in the document reflect the formatting that you select.

TO START A NEW DOCUMENT

1 Select *File* and then *New*

2 Under *New,* select the *Document* option button

3 In the *Template* box,

■ To create from an existing template, tab to and select the template you want to use, and then choose the *OK* button.
■ To create by using a wizard, select the wizard you want to use, and then choose the *OK* button.
■ If you select a wizard, Word displays dialog boxes that lead you through the layout steps. Select the options you want. Choose the *Finish* button to close the dialog box.

Word gives the new document a temporary name until you save it with a unique filename.

SWITCHING AMONG MULTIPLE DOCUMENTS

Word's switching feature enables you to store multiple documents separately in memory and toggle among them.

1 Open the first document

2 Open the second document

3 Click *Window* and then the *Document Name* to switch back to the desired document

[**Ctrl** + **F6**]

Use Step 3 whenever you want to toggle between documents.

SYMBOLS

In addition to the keys shown on the keyboard, many fonts also include bullets, symbols, and other special marks.

TO INSERT SYMBOLS BY COMMAND

1 Position the insertion point

2 Select *Insert, Symbol*

3 In the *Font* box, type or select the font that contains the symbol you want to insert

4 Double-click the desired symbol character. To see an enlarged version of the symbol in the dialog box, click the symbol character, or use the arrow keys to move to the symbol

5 When you finish inserting symbols, select the *Close* button.

TO INSERT SYMBOLS BY TYPING THE CHARACTER CODE

1 Position the insertion point

2 Make sure the Num Lock key is on

3 From the *Formatting* toolbar, choose the font that contains the symbol you want to insert

4 Hold down [Alt], and then, using the numeric keypad, type 0 (zero) followed by the appropriate code

TAB STOP SETTINGS

Word, like most word processors, has default tab stop settings. However, you can change any of these by following the procedure described next.

1 Select the paragraph(s) in which you want to change the tab stops

2 Click *View* and then *Ruler* to turn on the ruler if needed

3 Click the left tab alignment button if needed to change tab type

4 Point under the desired location of the ruler bar and click to place tab stop

5 Repeat Step 3 to set additional tabs

6 Click *OK* to end

TABLES

Word's Table feature can be used to create attractive tables to put in documents as well as to create invoices.

TO CREATE A TABLE FORM

1 Place the insertion point where you desire to create a table

2 Click *Table* and then *Insert Table*

3 Type the number of columns and press Tab

4 Type the number of rows

5 Click the *OK* button to accept the form

USING THE TOOLBAR TO CREATE A TABLE. Word's Standard toolbar offers a quick way to create a table.

1 **Place insertion point where table is desired**

2 **Click the *Insert Table* button**

A table grid appears beneath the toolbar.

3 **Drag your mouse over the grid to create columns and rows**

4 **Release your mouse when you have selected the desired table**

Note that a message box appears below the grid showing the number of rows and columns that you are creating as you drag your mouse on the grid.

TO FILL TABLE WITH TEXT OR EDIT TABLE

1 **Place the insertion point in the table**

2 **Type or edit text in the current cell**

3 **Press `Tab` to move to the next cell or `Shift` + `Tab` to move to the previous cell**

TEMPLATES

Word offers a set of basic templates that can be selected when creating a new document. Templates control layout and fonts, and contain prompts for various data that you will type. The available templates are as follows:

Template	Description
Blank Document	Word's DEFAULT template (G)
Fax Wizard	Creates customized Fax cover sheet (L)
Fax	Contemporary/Elegant/Professional Fax cover sheets (L)
Letter Wizard	Selects from prewritten letter forms (L)
Letter	Contemporary/Elegant/Professional letters (L)
Memo Wizard	Creates customized memos (M)
Memo	Contemporary/Elegant/Professional memos (M)
Report	Contemporary/Elegant/Professional report forms (R)

(G) General   (L) Letters & Faxes   (M) Memos   (R) Reports

You can choose a template when starting a new document. Then, fill in the appropriate data as shown in the template. Save the document normally.

THESAURUS

The thesaurus is used to find synonyms and antonyms for words.

1 **Place the insertion point on the word you want to look up**

2 **Click _Tools_ and then _Thesaurus_ for the Thesaurus window**   [**Shift** + **F7**]

If the word is found, you will see a list of synonyms and antonyms in the thesaurus's list box.

To choose one of the words from the list box,

3 **Use the vertical scroll bar, if necessary, to locate your selection**   [**Tab**]

4 **Click your selection**

5 **Click the _Replace_ button to replace**

TOOLBARS

To select a toolbar item,

1 **Point to the button**

2 **Click the button**

For detailed operations of the toolbar, see the toolbar section of this appendix.

UNDERLINING TEXT

Underlining enables you to output text that is underlined.
Before typing in the text,

1 **Click the _Underline (U)_ button on the toolbar to turn on the underline feature**
[**Ctrl** + **U**]

2 **Type the text to be Underlined**

3 **Click the _Underline (U)_ button on the toolbar again to turn off the Underline feature**
[**Ctrl** + **U**]

After typing the text,

1 **Select the text to be underlined**

2 **Click the _Underline (U)_ button on the toolbar**   [**Ctrl** + **U**]

UNDO

The Undo feature reverses the last change you made. Also, see "Restoring Deleted Text."

 1 Click *Edit* and then *Undo* (or click the *Undo* button on the toolbar)   [**Ctrl** + **Z**]

VIEW MODES

Word offers five view modes:

- *Normal view* (default) is a simplified WYSIWYG view of the document, which omits page settings. This screen is useful for text entry, editing, and formatting.
- *Page Layout* view is a full-featured WYSIWYG mode that presents the document exactly as it will appear when printed.
- *Outline view* "collapses" the document so that only its major headings are displayed.
- *Master Document view* allows you to manage a large document by creating separate subdocuments and then combining them.
- *Full Screen view* maximizes the space available for your document by removing all toolbars, rulers, and menus. You must then use Shortcut keys until you exit by pressing Alt + V, U.

TO SELECT A VIEW BY MENU

1 Click *View*

2 Click the desired view mode

To select a view by toolbar, click the desired view on the toolbar directly above the status bar.

WORDART

WordArt allows you to add designs and shapes to your text.

TO CREATE A TEXT EFFECT WITH WORDART

1 Position the insertion point where you want to add the effect

2 Select *Insert* and then *Object*

3 Select the *Create New* tab

4 In the *Object Type* box, select *MSWordArt 2* and then the *OK* button

Word displays the WordArt toolbar, text entry box, and menu.

5 In the *Enter Your Text Here* box, type the text you want to format

6 Select the text effect options you want. If you type new text, choose the *Update Display* button to view the changes

7 When you finish, click in the Word document window

ZOOMING

The Zoom command (View menu) can be used to magnify or reduce the view of a page. To invoke the Zoom command,

1 Move the insertion point to the desired page to be zoomed

2 Click *View* and then *Zoom*

3 Type the desired zoom percent

4 Click the *OK* button

To quickly access zoom, click the *Zoom* box on the toolbar.

QUICK REFERENCE TO FEATURES

Feature	Menu Selections	Shortcut Keystrokes
Alignment		
Menu	Format, Paragraph, Alignment	
Left-align	Format, Paragraph, Alignment, Left	[Ctrl] + [L]
Right-align	Format, Paragraph, Alignment, Right	[Ctrl] + [R]
Center	Format, Paragraph, Alignment, Center	[Ctrl] + [E]
Justify	Format, Paragraph, Alignment, Justify	[Ctrl] + [J]
Arrange windows	Window, Arrange All	[Alt] + [W] [A]
Autotext	Edit, Autotext	
Bold text	Format, Font, Bold	[Ctrl] + [B]
Bookmark	Edit, Bookmark	
Cancel command	[Esc]	[Esc]
Center Text	Format, Paragraph, Alignment, Center	[Ctrl] + [E]
Clear		[Delete]
Close document	File, Close	[Ctrl] + [F4]
Copy text	Edit, Copy	[Ctrl] + [C]
Cut text	Edit, Cut	[Ctrl] + [X]
Date	Insert, Date and Time	[Alt] + [I] [T]

(continued)

Feature	Menu Selections	Shortcut Keystrokes
Delete		
Current character	[Delete]	[Delete]
Character to left	[← Backspace]	[← Backspace]
Current word	[Ctrl] + [← Backspace]	[Ctrl] + [← Backspace]
Previous word		[Ctrl] + [Delete]
Selection of text		Select Text, [Delete]
Exiting Word	File, Exit	[Alt] + [F4]
Find file	File, Find File	
Find text	Edit, Find	[Ctrl] + [F]
Font dialog box	Format, Font	
Footers	View, Header and Footer	[Alt] + [V] [H]
Footnotes	Insert, Footnote	
Goto	Edit, Goto	[Ctrl] + [G]
Grammar check	Tools, Grammar	[Alt] + [T] [G]
Headers	View, Header and Footer	[Alt] + [V] [H]
Help feature	Help	[F1]
Index	Insert, Index and Tables	
Insert a file into the current document	Insert, File	[Alt] + [I] [I]
Insert (toggle) key	[Insert]	[Insert]
Italic font	Format, Font, Italic	[Ctrl] + [I]
Link objects	Edit, Links	
Macro		
Record	Tools, Macro, Record	
Run	Tools, Macro, Run	[Alt] + [F] [U] [Alt]+ [M]
Margins	File, Page Setup, Margins	[Alt] + [F] [U] [Alt] + [M]
Merge	Tools, Merge	[Shift] + [F9]
Move selected text	Edit, Cut	[Ctrl] + [X]
New file	File, New	[Ctrl] + [N]
Open file dialog box		
Open document	File, Open	[Ctrl] + [O]
Select a file	File, Open, Tab [↓]	[Ctrl] + [O] [Tab] [↓]
Change directories	File, Open, Directories	[Ctrl] + [O] [Alt] + [D]
Change default drive	File, Open, Drives	[Ctrl] + [O] [Alt] + [V]
Change type	File, Open, Type	[Ctrl] + [O] [Alt] + [T]
Outline feature	Tools, Outline	[Alt] + [T] [O]
Page break	Insert, Break	[Ctrl] + [↵]
Page Number dialog box	Insert, Page Numbers	[Alt] + [L] [P] [N]
Page setup	File, Page Setup	
Paste text	Edit, Paste	[Ctrl] + [V]
Paste special	Edit, Paste Special	
Picture	Insert, Picture	

(continued)

Feature	Menu Selections	Shortcut Keystrokes
Print	File, Print	[Ctrl] + [P]
Print preview	File, Print Preview	
Replace	Edit, Replace	
Restore deleted text	Edit, Undelete	
Retrieve file	Insert, File	
Ruler bar	View, Ruler	[Alt] + [Shift] + [F3]
Save	File, Save	[Ctrl] + [S]
Save As		
Selection of text	Select text, File, Save As	[Alt] + [F] [A]
Full document without closing or exiting	File, Save As	[Alt] + [F] [A]
Full document with closing	File, Close	
Full document with exit	File, Exit	[Alt] + [X]
Full document into another format	File, Save As, Type	[Alt] + [F] [A] [Alt] + [T]
Password protect	File, Save As, Options, Save Protection Password	
Select entire document	Edit, Select All	
Shortcut menus	Right-click mouse	[Shift] + [F10]
Show/hide	Tools, Options, All, OK	
Small caps font		[Ctrl] + [Shift] + [K]
Sort feature	Tools, Sort	[Alt] + [T] [R]
Spacing	Format, Paragraph, Line Spacing	[Ctrl] + [1] [5] [2]
Special character	Insert, Symbol	[Alt] + [0] + code
Spelling tool	Tools, Spelling	[F7]
Summary info	File, Summary Info	[Ctrl] + [F6]
Switch Documents	Window, #	[Ctrl] + [F6]
Table of contents	Insert, Index and Tables	
Tab set	Format, Tabs	[Alt] + [O] [T]
Thesaurus	Tools, Thesaurus	[Shift] + [F7]
Toolbars	View, Toolbars	
Underline		[Ctrl] + [U]
Undo	Edit, Undo	[Ctrl] + [Z]
Upper/lowercase conversion	Format, Change Case	
View modes	View, then select view	
Zoom	View, Zoom	[Alt] + [V] [Z]

WORD'S MENU SYSTEM

Word's menu bar provides a menu system that allows you to access its features by mouse or keyboard. Figure WPA-3 provides an overview of each menu bar item's submenu.

FIGURE WPA-3 ■ WORD'S MENU SYSTEM

File   Edit   View   Insert   Format   Tools   Table   Window   Help

File

New...	Ctrl+N
Open...	Ctrl+O
Close	
Save	Ctrl+S
Save As...	
Save All	
Properties	
Templates...	
Page Setup...	
Print Preview	
Print...	Ctrl+P
1	
Exit	

Edit

Undo Typing	Ctrl+Z
Repeat Typing	Ctrl+Y
Cut	Ctrl+X
Copy	Ctrl+C
Paste	Ctrl+V
Paste Special...	
Clear	Del
Select All	Ctrl+A
Find...	Ctrl+F
Replace...	Ctrl+H
Go To...	Ctrl+G
AutoText...	
Bookmark...	
Links...	
Object	

View

- • Normal
- Outline
- Page Layout
- Master Document
- Full Screen
- Toolbars...
- ✔ Ruler
- Header and Footer
- Footnotes
- Annotations
- Zoom...

Insert

- Break...
- Page Numbers...
- Annotation
- Date and Time...
- Field...
- Symbol...
- Form Field...
- Footnote...
- Caption...
- Cross-reference...
- Index and Tables..
- File...
- Frame
- Picture...
- Object...
- Database...

Format

- Font...
- Paragraph...
- Tabs...
- Borders and Shading...
- Columns...
- Change Case...
- Drop Cap...
- Bullets and Numbering..
- Heading Numbering...
- AutoFormat...
- Style Gallery...
- Style...
- Frame...
- Picture...
- Drawing Object...

Tools

Spelling...	F7
Grammar...	
Thesaurus...	Shift+F7
Hyphenation...	
Language...	
Word Count...	
AutoCorrect...	
Mail Merge...	
Envelopes and Labels...	
Protect Document...	
Revisions...	
Macro...	
Customize...	
Options...	

Table

Insert Table...	
Delete Cells...	
Merge Cells	
Split Cells...	
Select Row	
Select Column	
Select Table	Alt+Num 5
Table AutoFormat...	
Cell Height and Width...	
Headings	
Convert Text To Table..	
Sort Text...	
Formula...	
Split Table	
✔ Gridlines	

Window

- New Window
- Arrange All
- Split
- ✔ 1 Document1

Help

- Microsoft Word Help Topics
- Answer Wizard
- The Microsoft Network...
- WordPerfect Help...
- About Microsoft Word

GLOSSARY

Alignment.   The arrangement of text horizontally on a page in relation to the left or right margins. (WP96)

Arrange All.   A Word command that allows you to view all open document windows on the screen simultaneously, one above the other. (WP158)

ASCII.   Abbreviation for the American Standard Code for Information Interchange, a standard format adopted by the computer industry for representing typed characters. (WP218)

At message.   A status bar message that displays the vertical position of the insertion point within the current page. (WP15)

Backspace key.   A key that removes the character to the immediate left of the cursor. (WP43)

Bold.   A text enhancement in which printed text appears darker. (WP47)

Center.   To align text so that it is equally spaced from the right and left margins. (WP44)

Clicking.   To press and release the left mouse button quickly after pointing to an object (button, menu bar, text, icon, etc.). (WP4)

Column message.   A status bar message that displays the current horizontal character position of the insertion point from the left margin. (WP15)

Cropping.   The process of trimming away parts of a graphic you do not want to display. (WP214)

Data source.   A document used in a merge process that contains specific data to be merged into another document. (WP162)

Delete key.   A key that removes the character at the insertion point. (WP41)

Dialog box.   A window that requests or gives information for a specific task. (WP2)

Double-clicking.   Rapidly pressing and releasing the left mouse button twice after pointing to an object (button, menu bar, text, icon, etc.). (WP5)

Embedding.   Copying objects from one application to another without changing the original. (WP228)

Endnote.   Text added to the end of a document to provide source references, more detailed explanations, or comments. (WP180)

Exporting.   The saving of data into another program's format. (WP218)

Find.   A word processing feature that locates each occurrence of a specified text string in the current document. (WP106)

Footer.   Text containing descriptive information that appears at the bottom of each page in a multipage document. (WP144)

Footnote.   Text added to a document, usually appearing at the bottom of each page and identified by number, to provide source references, more detailed explanations, or comments. (WP180)

Go To.   A word processing command that relocates the insertion point on any named page of a multipage document. (WP153)

Grammar check.   An auxiliary program that checks the grammar in the current document. (WP121)

Graphics feature.   A Word feature that allows you to combine lines and images with text in the same document. (WP200)

Hard page break.   A page divider created by the user that remains fixed at a specific text location unless removed by the user. (WP142)

Hard return.   A line break inserted into the text by the user (Enter). (WP33)

Header.   Text containing descriptive information that appears at the top of each page in a multipage document. (WP144)

Help prompt.   A Word feature that uses the title bar to display messages describing a button or other area of the window as you point to it while pressing and hold the right mouse button. Help prompts also appear when selecting (highlighting) a menu item. (WP16)

Icon.   A small graphical picture representing an application or document window. (WP2)

Importing.   The retrieval of data that was saved in another program's format. (WP218)

Indent.   A word processing feature that indents an entire paragraph without changing margins elsewhere in the document. (WP98)

Insert mode.   The default Word setting in which existing text is pushed forward as new text is typed. (WP37)

Insertion point.   A blinking vertical line that shows where the next keystroke typed in a document or dialog box will appear. (WP13)

Justified text.   Alignment of text so that it falls exactly at a margin. (WP96)

Layout. The arrangement of text and white space on a page. (WP90)

Line message. A status bar message, expressed in text lines, that indicates the insertion point's vertical position on the page. (WP15)

Linking. Inserting into Word a copy of text or graphic material created in another program, while maintaining a connection between the two programs so that changes in the original source file automatically update the linked copy. (WP228)

Macro. A list of computer instructions or keystrokes that can be activated with one or more preset keystrokes. (WP172)

Main document. A document used in a merge process that contains text and instructions for the merge. (WP162)

Menu bar. An item located below an application window's title bar. This offers menu items that open to submenus that can access the application's features. (WP8)

Merge. A process by which information from two sources is combined to form a third document. (WP162)

Mouse pointer. A graphical image on the screen that is controlled by an input device called a mouse. (WP4)

Normal view. Word's default view mode. It provides a WYSIWYG ("What-You-See-Is-What-You-Get") screen that displays a simplified view of your document. (WP30)

Object. A table, chart, graphic, equation, or other information that is often created in one application and then displayed in another. (WP228)

OLE (Object Linking and Embedding). A Windows feature that allows an object created in one program (the "source file") to be shared with another program.

Outline feature. A word processing feature that creates properly numbered outlines of up to eight levels of numbering. (WP187)

Overtype mode. A Word setting, invoked by the Insert key, in which existing text is replaced by new text that is typed. (WP40)

Page layout view. A full-featured WYSIWYG view mode that presents the document exactly as it will appear when printed. (WP30)

Page message. A status bar message, expressed as a number, that indicates the document page on which the insertion point is currently positioned. (WP14)

Program icon. An icon located at the upper left corner of a program window. Clicking it opens a control-menu that contains commands to resize or close the window. (WP11)

Pull-down menu. A menu that opens as a result of selecting a menu bar item (either clicking the item or pressing the Alt key + Underlined letter of the menu bar item). It provides a list of commands related to the respective menu bar item. (WP8)

Relative tab. A tab setting measured in relation to the left margin setting. (WP100)

Replace. A word processing feature that locates each occurrence of a specified text string in the current document and replaces it with another. (WP107)

Resizing button. Generally at the upper right corner of a window when available. Allows for quick window resizing by mouse by clicking it. Resizing buttons include the Maximize button, Minimize button, and Restore button. (WP9)

Ruler bar. An optional indicator appearing at the top of the document window that displays current margins and tab settings. (WP10)

Scroll bars. Used to scroll (move) through a document containing text (and graphics) with a mouse. (WP14)

Section message. A status bar message that indicates the current document section. (WP15)

Select. A feature that allows highlighting of a segment of contiguous text. (WP80)

Selection enhancement. A process by which a formatting change is made to a selection of text that is already on the screen. (WP86)

Shortcut keys. Keystrokes that may include the use of function keys (F1–F12), which provide quick keyboard access to certain commands. (WP6)

Shortcut menu. A pop-up menu, activated with the right mouse button, that provides quick access to specific Word features. (WP10)

Soft page break. A page divider automatically created or relocated by a word processor when text reaches the end of a page. (WP141)

Soft return. A line break inserted into the text automatically by Word's word-wrap feature so that text will not go beyond the right margin setting. (WP34)

Sort feature. A Word feature that allows you to arrange text in alphabetical or numerical order. (WP187)

Spelling check. A word processing feature that identifies potentially misspelled words in the current document. (WP116)

Status bar. An indicator line, located near the bottom of the Word window, that displays information about the document, the current insertion point, and text enhancement settings. (WP10)

Tab. A formatting feature that allows text to be placed in specific positions on a line. (WP100)

Text string. A collection of contiguous characters or words. (WP105)

Thesaurus. A word processing feature that suggests synonyms for selected words. (WP119)

Title bar. An item located at the top center of a window or dialog box. This indicates the name of the window or dialog box. (WP7)

Toolbar. A Word feature that can provide quick access to frequently used features by mouse. (WP8)

Underline. A text enhancement, invoked by the Ctrl + U keys, in which text is underscored for emphasis. (WP46)

Undo. A Word command that allows you to reverse (cancel) changes you have made in a document. (WP44)

Word processing. The use of computer technology to create, manipulate, save, and print text materials. (WP2)

Wordwrap. A word processing feature in which text that does not fit at the right margin is automatically moved to the next line by the insertion of a soft return. (WP34)

Workspace. The interior area of a window. (WP10)

Zoom. A Word command that allows you to enlarge or reduce the image of your document on the screen (between 10% and 200%). (WP36)

INDEX

MICROSOFT EXCEL 7.0 FOR WINDOWS 95

EDWARD G. MARTIN
CHARLES S. PARKER
CHARLES E. KEE

This manual contains numerous features that help you master the material quickly and reinforce your learning:

- *A Table of Contents.* A list of the manual's contents appears on the first page of the manual. Each chapter starts with an *outline,* a list of learning *objectives,* and an *overview* that summarizes the skills you will learn.

- *Bold Key Terms.* Important terms appear in bold type as they are introduced. They are also conveniently listed at the end of each chapter, with page references for further review.

- *Color as a Learning Tool.* In this manual, color has been used to help you work through each chapter. Each step is numbered in green for easy identification. Within each step, text or commands that you should type appear in orange. Single keys to be pressed are shown in yellow boxes. For example,

  1 Type **WIN** and press ↵

- *Step-by-Step Mouse Approach.* This manual stresses the mouse approach. Each action is numbered consecutively in green to make it easy to locate and follow. Where appropriate, a mouse shortcut (toolbar icon) is shown in the left margin; a keyboard shortcut may be shown in brackets at the right, as follows:

  1 Click *Edit, Cut*   [**Ctrl** + **X**]

As your skills increase, the "click this item" approach slowly gives way to a less-detailed list of goals and operations so that you do not mindlessly follow steps, but truly master software skills.

- *Screen Figures.* Full-color annotated screens provide overviews of operations that let you monitor your work as you progress through the tutorial.

- *Tips.* Each chapter contains numerous short tips in bold type at strategic points to provide hints, warnings, or insights. Read these carefully.

- *Checkpoints.* At the end of each major section is a list of checkpoints, highlighted in red, which you can use to test your mastery of the material. Do not proceed further unless you can perform the checkpoint tasks.

- *Summary and Quiz.* At the end of each chapter is a bulleted summary of the chapter's content and a 30-question quiz with true/false, multiple-choice, and matching questions.

- *Exercises.* Each chapter ends with two sets of written exercises (Operations and Commands) and six guided hands-on computer applications that measure and reinforce mastery of the chapter's concepts and skills. Each pair of applications present problems relating to school, personal, and business use.

- *Mastery Cases.* The final page of each chapter presents three unguided cases that allow you to demonstrate your personal mastery of the chapter material.

- *A Note about the Manual's Organization.* The topics in this manual are arranged in order of increasing difficulty. Chapters 1 and 2 present beginning and intermediate techniques and should be completed in sequence, for each skill builds upon the previous one. However, Chapter 3 includes several *independent* modules that present advanced skills. These modules may be followed in any order, or omitted, as time and interest allow.

- *End-of-Manual Material.* The manual also provides a comprehensive reference *appendix* that summarizes commands and provides alphabetical listings of critical operations, a *glossary* that defines all key terms (with page references), and an *index* to all important topics.

WHAT'S NEW IN MICROSOFT EXCEL 7.0 FOR WINDOWS 95

1. *Answer Wizard:* A special feature that searches for help based on a question that you ask.

2. *Easier Number Formatting:* Number formatting is done by examples instead of format codes.

3. *AutoCalculate:* Excel automatically sums, averages, or counts a range (marked area) of numbers and displays its result in the status bar (bottom of screen).

4. *AutoCorrect:* Text typed can be corrected automatically for proper capitalization and spelling.

5. *Easier Document Management:* Document management commands are available through either the *Open* or *Save As* dialog box. These commands include renaming, copying, cutting and pasting, printing, deleting, creating an icon (called a shortcut), and changing file properties.

6. *Improved Drag-and-Drop Features:* A range of cells can be quickly moved or copied between different worksheets and workbooks using drag-and-drop techniques.

MICROSOFT EXCEL 7.0
FOR WINDOWS 95

1

SPREADSHEET BASICS:
CREATING A WORKSHEET

SS

OBJECTIVES

After completing this chapter, you will be able to

1   Explain the general capabilities of a spreadsheet program.
2   Describe the procedures to launch and exit Microsoft Excel.
3   Explain the various components of the Microsoft Excel and workbook windows.
4   Explain the differences between a constant value and formula.

5   Enter data into a workbook, perform basic edits on the data, and save the workbook on a disk.
6   Insert and delete columns and rows.
7   Close a workbook, create a new workbook, open a file, and prepare a printed copy.

OVERVIEW

Chapter 1 introduces the concept of electronic spreadsheets by presenting the basic techniques for using Microsoft Excel, a well-known Windows-based spreadsheet package. First, you will learn how to start Windows 95 and then launch Microsoft Excel, how to interpret the screen, and how to enter and save data. Once you have mastered these basics, you will examine constant values and formulas. Printing and editing techniques are introduced next. Although this chapter is based on Microsoft Excel Version 7.0 for Windows 95, many of the techniques discussed will work with earlier releases as well.

ELECTRONIC SPREADSHEETS

A computerized **spreadsheet** is the electronic equivalent of the multicolumned paper used by accountants. A spreadsheet, or **worksheet,** is used to display data in columnar (column and row) form. Spreadsheet programs are used to create balance sheets, payroll reports, income statements, and other financial documents. They allow users to enter, edit, and manipulate data in the form of words, numbers, and formulas. More important, spreadsheet programs include a recalculation feature, which automatically recalculates formulas when interdependent values are changed. This feature allows you to evaluate "What if?" questions by modifying values and seeing their mathematical consequences quickly and easily.

All modern spreadsheet programs are based on the original VisiCalc program created in the 1970s and thus are remarkably similar in features and layout. Today, Microsoft Excel is a widely used spreadsheet program. Microsoft Excel combines spreadsheet features with graphics and file management.

The instructions in this module pertain to Microsoft Excel Version 7.0 for Windows 95. Microsoft Excel is a Windows 95 program based on a *graphical user interface*, or *GUI* (pronounced "gooey"), which uses symbols and menus instead of typewritten commands to help you communicate with the computer. It is similar to using a red traffic light to indicate "stop." Many GUI symbols and operations have become standard throughout the industry. This makes communicating with the computer more universal.

The GUI environment in which Microsoft Excel operates is called *Windows 95*. In this environment, you work with rectangular boxes called *windows* and symbols (pictures) called *icons.*

Microsoft Excel is also a *what-you-see-is-what-you-get,* or *WYSIWYG* (pronounced "wizzy-wig"), electronic spreadsheet. This means that you work in a screen that resembles your final printed page. For example, if you create a column (bar) chart in your spreadsheet, the display on your screen looks like the chart that will appear on the final printed page.

You can invoke Microsoft Excel's capabilities by mouse or keyboard. This book uses mouse actions as the primary approach to invoke features. Where appropriate, shortcut keystrokes are shown at the right margin. Many *shortcut keys* are common to most Windows programs. For example, pressing the Alt and F4 keys together will exit most Windows programs.

It is highly recommended that you use a mouse when operating Microsoft Excel for Windows. This approach is easier visually and is sometimes quicker than using a keyboard. In addition, this text often refers to Microsoft Excel as simply "Excel" and Windows 95 as "Windows."

GETTING STARTED

Before you begin, be certain you have all the necessary tools: a hard disk or network that contains Windows 95 and Microsoft Excel for Windows 95 and a formatted disk on which you will store the documents you create. This text assumes that you will be using Microsoft Excel on a hard-disk drive, although directions for networks are included.

STARTING WINDOWS 95

Before launching any Windows program, you must first start Windows. As mentioned earlier, in the Windows environment, you work in rectangular boxes called *windows.* A window that contains a program is called a *program window,* and a window that contains a document is called a *document window.* A window may also request or provide information to perform a task, in which case the window is called a *dialog box.*

USING A HARD-DISK DRIVE. This text assumes that the Windows and Excel programs are on your hard disk, which is identified as Drive C. To start Windows, follow these steps:

STEPS

1 **Turn on your computer to boot (start) the operating system**

Windows should start automatically. A "Starting Windows 95" message may appear. If your system boots to a menu, go to Step 3 in the next section, "Using a Network." If a C:\> prompt appears on your screen,

2 **Type WIN and press ↵ (This key may also be labeled "Enter" or "Return")**

Note: Throughout this manual, text or commands that you should type will be shown in a box, as in WIN .

You should now be at the Windows 95 screen as in Figure SS1-1. (The actual contents of your screen may differ.)

3 **If a *Welcome to Windows 95* dialog box appears, click the *Close* button**   **[Esc]**

4 **Insert your data disk into Drive A**

USING A NETWORK. Excel may be available to you through a local area network (LAN). If so, Excel is kept on another computer's hard-disk drive that is shared by many users. To use Excel, you must access the program from your own microcomputer. So many network configurations are in use today that it is difficult to predict which one you

FIGURE SS1-1 ■ THE WINDOWS 95 SCREEN

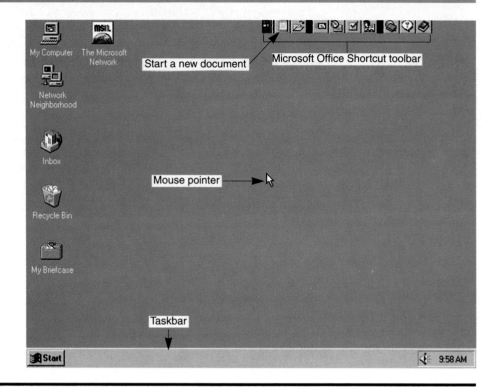

will use. Check with your instructor for exact directions. In general, however, to start Excel you will follow these steps:

STEPS

1 Boot the network operating system (perhaps with your own disk)

2 Type any command needed to get the network menu

3 Insert a data diskette into Drive A

4 Select (or type) the appropriate command shown on your screen to access Windows.

THE WINDOWS 95 SCREEN.   Your screen should now resemble Figure SS1-1. (Note: The contents of your screen may differ depending on how it was programmed.) The Windows 95 screen has two primary parts: the taskbar and the desktop. The *taskbar* is the bar at the bottom of the screen with a *Start* button on its left side and a message area with the system's time on its right. The *desktop* is the large area above the taskbar. Occupying the upper left side of the desktop are several icons, starting with the *My Computer* icon.

Another object that should currently appear on your screen is a small graphical image resembling an arrow. This is called the *mouse pointer* or *pointer.* You control its movements by using a *pointing device.* Pointing devices are input devices (hardware) that help you to communicate with a computer. The most common pointing device is a *mouse.* Other pointing devices may include a trackball, pointing stick, track pad, or electronic pen. These pointing devices are more commonly used with portable computers.

MOUSE AND KEYBOARD OPERATIONS

Skip this section if you are already familiar with using a mouse and keyboard.

In Excel, as with most programs in Windows, the primary input device for accessing *commands* is a mouse or other pointing device. As such, most command steps presented in this manual refer to mouse operations. Keyboard commands, where available as *shortcut keys,* are presented in brackets [ ] to the right of a mouse command. Also, when a command can be invoked by using a button or other graphic feature, its icon is presented in the left margin of a command. For example (do not invoke command!),

---

STEPS

     1 Click the *Start* button on the taskbar for the *Start* menu   **[Ctrl + Esc]**

Shortcut keys provide quick keyboard access to specific commands. They may involve pressing a function key alone or in conjunction with the Ctrl, Alt, or Shift keys. *Function keys* are labeled F1–F12, and they may be located at the extreme left of your keyboard or across the top in one horizontal row. The Ctrl, Alt, or Shift keys may also be used in conjunction with other keys.

POINTING.   Often, the mouse pointer resembles a small arrow on your screen. You control its movements by using a pointing device. In Excel, the mouse pointer may appear in forms displayed in Figure SS1-2a. A mouse or other pointing device generally has at least two buttons (left and right). You can perform several actions using a mouse. The most basic is *pointing.* This involves moving your mouse on a flat surface, and thus the mouse pointer on your screen to a desired item or area. If you are using a pointing device other than a mouse, refer to its manual for operating instructions.

In the following exercises, you will practice pointing and other basic mouse techniques. Figure SS1-2b summarizes these mouse actions. (You can also use the numeric keypad to invoke mouse actions, as is outlined in Figure SS1-2c and discussed later in the section titled "MouseKeys.")

To *point* (move) your mouse pointer,

STEPS

     1 Slowly move your mouse on a flat surface or mouse pad (a small rubber pad) and notice the direction in which the mouse moves on your screen

FIGURE SS1-2 ■ **MOUSE SYMBOLS AND MOUSE ACTIONS**

(a) Common Excel mouse symbols.
(b) Common mouse actions.

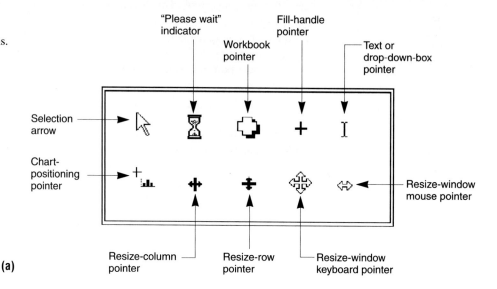

(a)

Mouse Actions	Explanations
Point	Move the mouse, and thus the mouse pointer, to the desired item.
Click	Press and quickly release the left mouse button.
Right-click	Press and release the right mouse button.
Double-click	Rapidly press and release the left mouse button twice.
Drag	Press and hold the left mouse button, move the pointer to the desired location, and release the button to select.

(b)

(continued)

Note: If you run out of space, simply lift your mouse, place it in the original position, and start again.

2 Point to the *My Computer* icon at the top left corner of your desktop

3 Slowly point to the *Start* button at the left side of the taskbar and wait

The caption "Click here to begin" should briefly appear. Many buttons in the Windows 95 environment offer brief descriptions when you point to them.

CLICKING. The second most common mouse action is *clicking*. This involves pointing to an item and then rapidly pressing and releasing your left mouse button.

FIGURE SS1-2 ■ *(continued)*

(c) In order to use the numeric keypad for mouse actions, the *MouseKeys* feature and Num Lock must be on. When on, a *Mouse* icon appears in the message area of the taskbar. Double-clicking this icon opens the *Accessibility Options Properties* dialog box for adjusting or turning off the *MouseKeys* feature.

Mouse Icon Appearance	Operation	Numeric KeyPad Keys
	Horizontally, vertically (1)	←, →, ↑, ↓
	Diagonally (1)	Home, End, Pg Up, Pg Dn
	Click	5
	Double-click	+
	Switch to right-click (2)	−, 5 or +
	Switch to both click (2)	*, 5 or +
	Switch back to normal (left) click	/
	Drag Turn on mouse button hold down	Ins (Do not hold)
	Drag Mouse (1)	←, →, ↑, ↓, Home, End, Pg Up, Pg Dn
	Turn off mouse button hold down	Del (Do not hold)

(1) Pressing and holding the Ctrl key with these keys speeds up the pointer movement. Pressing and holding Shift with these keys slows down the pointer movement.

(c) (2) When on, pressing the 5 key invokes their action.

SS

STEPS

1 **Click the *Start* button (point to the *Start* button and then rapidly press and release your left mouse button)**   [Ctrl + Esc]

The *Start* menu should appear. This is the main menu in Windows. You will use it shortly to launch (start) Excel. For now, you will use it to further practice mouse operations. Note also that each option is listed with a corresponding icon to its left and that each option has an underlined letter. For example, the <u>H</u>elp option has an icon of a book with a question mark and the letter "H" is underlined. You can use the underlined letter to access the option by keyboard.

As you proceed with the next exercise, watch the mouse pointer as you move it within a menu. It moves with a selection highlight to each item you point to. In addition, pointing to menu items with a ▶ to its far right opens a submenu. Try this:

2 **Slowly point to *Settings* for its submenu**   [S]

Although you can select a submenu item by pointing to and then clicking it, you will practice this later. Now, to close the *Start* menu without selecting anything,

3 Click an open space on the desktop to close the menu without selecting   [**Esc**]

Note: A menu item without a ▶ to its far right starts a feature or opens a window.

For now, keep the *Start* menu opened as you proceed to the next step. Here you will practice invoking a direct command from the *Start* menu,

4 Click the *Start* button   [**Ctrl** + **Esc**]

5 Point to *Help*

As you move your mouse pointer, notice again that the selection highlight moves with it to *Help*.

6 Click *Help* to open the *Help* dialog box (Remember, to click, rapidly press   [**H**]
and release your left mouse button.)

The *Help* dialog box now appears on your screen. Remember, a *dialog box* is a window that either provides or requests information. For example, the *Help* dialog box can provide information on a desired topic. Dialog box operations are discussed in detail later.
To close the dialog box,

7 Click the *Cancel* button at the bottom right of the box   [**Esc**]

RIGHT-CLICKING.   Pointing to an item and clicking your *right mouse button*, or *right-clicking* generally results in opening its *Shortcut menu*. A *Shortcut* menu contains common commands you can invoke on the related item. For example,

STEPS

1 Right-click a blank area of the desktop for its *Shortcut* menu

The desktop's *Shortcut* menu now appears. To select a menu item, you can either click (left mouse button) it or press its underlined letter. Menu items that appear in a lighter color are not currently available. For now, to close the *Shortcut* menu without selecting a command,

2 Click (left mouse button) anywhere outside the *Shortcut* menu   [**Esc**]

You can also close a *Shortcut* menu by opening another item or another *Shortcut* menu. Try opening these *Shortcut* menus:

3 Right-click an open area of the taskbar for its *Shortcut* menu

4   Right-click the *Start* button for its *Shortcut* menu

5   Right-click the *My Computer* icon for its *Shortcut* menu

6   Click (left mouse button) anywhere outside the Shortcut menu to close it   [**Esc**   ]
without selecting a command

Different *Shortcut* menus are available for many items in the Windows environment and Excel. In some cases, different *Shortcut* menus are available for each part of an item. For example, in Steps 3 and 4 you received two different *Shortcut* menus from right-clicking two different areas of the taskbar. Excel offers a multitude of *Shortcut* menus to help you access commands faster. Excel *Shortcut* menus are demonstrated later.

DOUBLE-CLICKING.   Another commonly used mouse action is *double-clicking*. This involves first pointing to an item and then rapidly pressing and releasing your left mouse button twice. Double-clicking an icon on your screen resizes it to a window. Double-clicking also has a variety of other uses that are discussed as needed.

Before beginning the next exercise, notice that the *My Computer* icon is a different color than the other icons on the desktop. This indicates that it is the *active* (or *current*) icon. Keyboard commands will generally affect this icon. For example (do not invoke), if you press the Enter key, the icon would open to a window. To open the *My Computer* icon to a window by mouse requires double-clicking it. Try this:

STEPS

1   Double-click the *My Computer* icon (Rapidly press and release your left mouse button twice.)

The *My Computer* icon now resizes to a window. If it did not, repeat Step 1. (The contents of your window may differ.) To close it,

⊠   **2**   Click the *Close* button (the button with an "X" in it) at the top right   [**Alt**   +   **F4**   ]
of the window

The "X" button is referred to as the *Close* button. It is available on most windows and is a shortcut to closing a window. It closes any window and thus the program, document, or other feature encased in it.

Many Windows programs also support a feature called *drag and drop*. This feature allows you to use a mouse to move a selection (marked items, either text or graphics) from one place to another. This feature is illustrated in later chapters.

MOUSEKEYS.   Although you can invoke many commands by using shortcut keys, Windows offers a feature called **MouseKeys**. This feature allows you to use the numeric keypad to invoke the common mouse actions. These actions include clicking, right-clicking, double-clicking, and dragging and dropping. If you do not intend to use MouseKeys to invoke mouse actions or if the feature is not available, skip this section. Check with your instructor before activating this feature.

To use MouseKeys, you will need to turn on the *Use MouseKeys* feature. This feature is part of the Accessibility Properties, which can be accessed through the Control Panel. (Note: The Accessibility feature must be installed on your system.)

SS

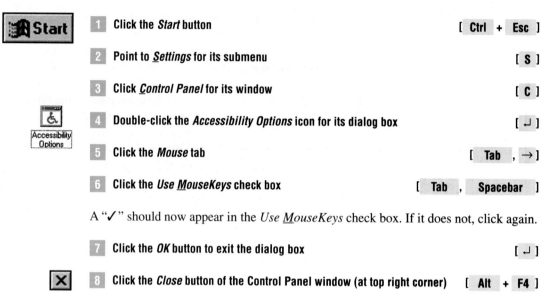

1	Click the *Start* button	[**Ctrl** + **Esc**]
2	Point to *Settings* for its submenu	[**S**]
3	Click *Control Panel* for its window	[**C**]
4	Double-click the *Accessibility Options* icon for its dialog box	[**⏎**]
5	Click the *Mouse* tab	[**Tab** , **→**]
6	Click the *Use MouseKeys* check box	[**Tab** , **Spacebar**]

A "✓" should now appear in the *Use MouseKeys* check box. If it does not, click again.

7	Click the *OK* button to exit the dialog box	[**⏎**]
8	Click the *Close* button of the Control Panel window (at top right corner)	[**Alt** + **F4**]

When the MouseKeys feature is on, a mouse icon appears in the message area of the taskbar. You can use the numeric keypad (NumLock=on) to invoke mouse actions by following the instructions in Figure SS1-2c. Also when this feature is on, the numeric keypad cannot be used for number entry.

Keystrokes required to operate the Microsoft Excel menu system are discussed under the section titled "Operating Menus."

LAUNCHING MICROSOFT EXCEL

The procedure to launch Excel is the same as that used to launch any Windows program. In Windows, *launching* is a process of starting a program. (Note: Excel is usually part of the Microsoft Office, a group of programs that you can use to perform a variety of tasks.)

1	Click the *Start* button	[**Ctrl** + **Esc**]

To open the *Programs* submenu,

2	Point to *Programs* on the *Start* menu	[**P**]

Note that the letter "P" is underlined. This indicates that you can press "P" instead of Step 2 if you want to select it by keyboard.

The *Programs* submenu now appears to the right of the *Start* menu. If Excel appears on the *Programs* submenu, go to Step 4. If Excel is located in a group other than Microsoft Office, use the proper group in place of Microsoft Office in Step 3. If *Microsoft Office* appears on the *Programs* submenu,

3	Point to *Microsoft Office* for its submenu

4 **Click** *Microsoft Excel* **to launch it**

A Microsoft Excel copyright screen may appear briefly but it is quickly replaced by the Microsoft Excel window as in Figure SS1-3. Now, if needed,

5 **Click the** *Maximize* **button to enlarge the window to its**   [**Alt** + **Spacebar** , **X**]
maximum size

> **Tip:** If your system has Microsoft Office, you can also launch Excel from within the Microsoft Office shortcut toolbar. When activated, this toolbar appears at the top right of your screen as in Figure SS1-1. To launch Excel, click the *Start a New Document* button on the toolbar (second button from the left). Click the *Blank Workbook* icon and then click the *OK* button.

> **Note:** The keyboard commands presented in this manual are based on the assumption that Excel was installed using its default settings. Check with your instructor to determine if the Lotus 1-2-3 transition features have been activated. If so, follow your instructions or select only the *Microsoft Excel Menus* option in the *Transition* tab of the *Options* dialog box (*Tools* menu).

FIGURE SS1-3 ■ **THE MICROSOFT EXCEL WINDOW**

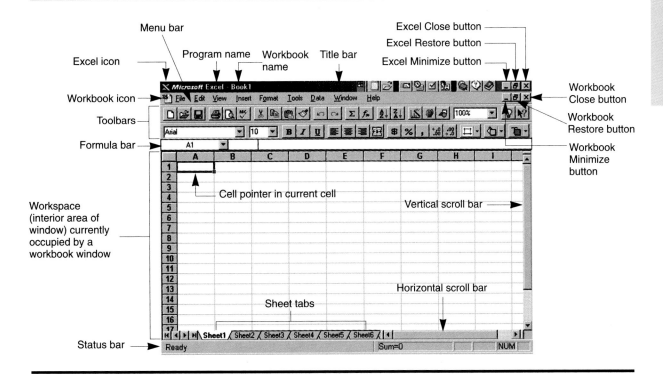

☑ CHECKPOINT

- ✓ Describe how to start Windows.
- ✓ What is the desktop and taskbar?
- ✓ What is a mouse and mouse pointer?
- ✓ What are shortcut keys?
- ✓ Describe how to launch Excel.

UNDERSTANDING MICROSOFT EXCEL

The Microsoft Excel window, as shown in Figure SS1-3, is the main program window that appears each time you launch the program. Occupying its workspace (interior window space) is a new workbook that looks like a big grid. In Excel, a **workbook** is a document file whose contents are viewed through a *workbook window*. (Workbook windows are document windows.) They are similar to binders with accounting paper (paper with columns and rows). Each page in a workbook is called a **sheet.** Sheets (there are 16 in the default workbook) may contain worksheets, charts, or other information. The content of a sheet can be very large; the portion of the sheet that appears in your workbook window represents only a small portion of the entire sheet.

There is only one Microsoft Excel window. However, depending on your computer's memory, multiple workbooks may be opened in its workspace, each encased in its own workbook window.

THE MICROSOFT EXCEL WINDOW

Like all program windows, the Microsoft Excel window (Figure SS1-3) has standard Windows and unique Excel features. Locate each feature on your screen as you read about its operation.

TITLE BAR.   The *title bar* is generally at the top of a window. It is a standard Windows feature that identifies the window—in this case, Microsoft Excel. It also has a program icon at its left end, two resizing buttons (currently, the *Minimize* and *Restore* buttons) and a *Close* (X) button at its right end.

A program icon is a graphical symbol that represents the program. Double-clicking it closes the window and single-clicking it opens the window's control-menu. Right-clicking the title section of the title bar also opens the window's control-menu. Control-menu operations are further discussed under "Using a Control-Menu."

A window can also be resized quickly by either double-clicking the title bar or clicking a resizing button with your mouse. Try this:

STEPS

1 Point anywhere within the Microsoft Excel title bar (except for the program icon or resizing buttons)

2 Double-click it (rapidly click your left mouse button twice)

The Excel window now appears as a smaller window. Note also that the *Restore* button (a button with two overlapping rectangle boxes) in the right end of the title bar has been replaced by a *Maximize* button (a button with a rectangular box).

3 **To return the window to a full screen (maximized),**   [**Alt** + **Spacebar** , **X**]
   point to and click the *Maximize* button

> **Tip:** Instead of clicking the *Maximize* button in Step 3, you can also double-click the title bar again to resize the window to full screen.

> **Tip:** Right-clicking the title bar also opens the window's control-menu.

MENU BAR.   Excel's *menu bar* is located directly below its title bar. A *menu bar*, which is present only in program windows, provides mouse or keyboard access to an application's commands through pull-down menus. A **pull-down menu** provides a list of commands related to the menu bar item. For example, the menu bar item *File*, opens to a pull-down menu with file management commands. Menu bar operations are discussed under the "Operating Menus" section.

TOOLBARS.   Just below the menu bar are two Excel toolbars: the Standard toolbar and the Format toolbar. Each **toolbar** contains *command buttons* and *drop-down boxes* that you can use to access Excel features by mouse. **Command buttons** are mouse shortcuts to a program's features. For example, clicking the *Print* button starts the printing process. A **drop-down box** first appears as a rectangular box with a ▼ button at its right. Clicking the ▼ button opens a drop-down list. For example, clicking the ▼ button of the *Font* drop-down box (displaying "Arial") of the Formatting toolbar opens a drop-down list of available fonts. See the "Toolbars" subsection under the "Operating Command Buttons" section of this chapter for a further discussion of the toolbar operations.

FORMULA BAR.   Beneath the toolbars is Excel's formula bar. The **formula bar** provides information about data entered into a worksheet. See "The Formula Bar" subsection of this discussion for a detailed examination of its operation.

WORKSPACE AND WORKBOOK WINDOW.   Located between the formula bar and the status bar is the workspace. This is the large interior space of the window that is currently occupied by a workbook window. See the next section "The Workbook Window: Columns, Rows, and Cells" for further discussion on workbooks.

STATUS BAR.   At the bottom of the window is Excel's status bar. The **status bar** displays messages regarding the operation in progress or a selected command on its left side and toggle switch (on/off switch) indicators on its right side. Currently, your status bar's left side displays "Ready," indicating that Excel is ready for your next operation. Your status bar may also display "CAPS" (Caps Lock), "NUM" (Number Lock), and "SCRL" (Scroll Lock) on its right side when these toggle switches are set in the on position. Pressing a toggle key, for example, the Caps Lock key, turns the feature on or off.

Excel also has an **AutoCalculate** feature that will quickly sum a range (marked set) of numbers. Its results are displayed in the AutoCalculate message area on the status bar. This area currently shows "SUM=0." AutoCalulate operations are discussed later.

THE WORKBOOK WINDOW: COLUMNS, ROWS, AND CELLS

Look at the workbook window on your screen and in Figure SS1-3. It currently displays an electronic spreadsheet called a *worksheet*. Worksheets are divided into vertical *columns* and horizontal *rows*. The letters along the top border (A through I) designate columns, and the numbers in the left border (1 through 17) designate rows. Columns are lettered A through Z, then AA through AZ, BA through BZ, and so on. Rows are numbered consecutively starting with 1. The intersection of a column and a row forms a box called a **cell.** Each cell is identified by its column and row coordinates (**cell addresses**). For example, Cell A1 is formed by the intersection of Column A and Row 1 (the column letter is always listed first, followed by the row number).

New workbook windows always display the first 9 columns and 18 rows, but this changes as you adjust column widths or move the cell pointer. The worksheet itself can contain as many as 16,384 rows and 256 columns, depending on available computer memory.

THE CURRENT CELL.   The **current cell** is the one that will receive the next data you enter or be affected by the next command. The screen identifies the current cell in two ways. First, the cell is visually indicated in the worksheet area with a **cell pointer** (or *pointer*) a rectangular box with dark borders that outlines one cell. Second, the cell address is listed in the left side of the formulas bar (fifth row from top). These two indicators in Figure SS1-3 show that the current cell is A1.

MOVING AROUND THE WORKSHEET.   You can move the cell pointer from cell to cell by using the mouse or the keyboard. With the mouse, simply point to a desired cell and click. With the keyboard, press the Up, Down, Left, or Right arrow key. Try this to move the cell pointer to Cell 5:

STEPS

---

1 **Click** *Cell E5*   [→ to Cell E1, ↓ to Cell E5]

Notice how the cell pointer's position and the cell address change.

SCROLLING BY KEYBOARD.   If you move the pointer past the right-most screen column (or below the bottom row), the worksheet in the workbook window will **scroll,** or reposition itself automatically, to display the current cell. Because the commands to move the cell pointer beyond the current display area by mouse and keyboard are quite different, they are addressed separately. Try this keyboard exercise first:

1 Move to Cell I5

As shown in Figure SS1-4a, Column A is still on the screen.

2 Press → once

As shown in Figure SS1-4b, Column J now appears, and Column A has disappeared. But remember that the screen is merely a window to a larger spreadsheet. Columns or rows may not be shown in the worksheet window's workspace, but they are still part of the spreadsheet.

3 Move back to Cell A5   [← as needed, or Home]

Column A reappears. Figure SS1-5 lists the keys that relocate your pointer. You can move one cell at a time with an arrow key, or you can move one screen at a time with the Pg Up and Pg Dn keys. To examine the effect of these keys on the screen,

4 Press a few of the keys listed in Figure SS1-5

Now, to move the cell pointer quickly to Cell A1, the *home cell,*

5 Press Ctrl + Home

FIGURE SS1-4 ■ SCROLLING BY KEYBOARD

(a) The pointer is placed at the edge of the screen.
(b) As the pointer is moved to the right by pressing the Right arrow key, Column J appears on the screen as Column A disappears.

(a)

(b)

SS

FIGURE SS1-5 ■ POINTER MOVEMENT KEYS

↑	Moves the pointer up one cell.
↓	Moves the pointer down one cell.
→	Moves the pointer right one cell.
←	Moves the pointer left one cell.
Pg Up	Moves the pointer up one screen.
Pg Dn	Moves the pointer down one screen.
Alt + **Pg Dn**	Moves the pointer right one screen.
Alt + **Pg Up**	Moves the pointer left one screen.
Home	Moves the pointer to the left end of a row.
End	Holding this key and pressing an arrow key moves the pointer to the edge of the worksheet that is in the direction of the arrow.
Scroll Lock	When pressed, the worksheet moves and the pointer remains stationary as an arrow key is pressed.
F5	Opens the *Go To* dialog box to go to a cell. For example, pressing the F5 key, typing the cell address A6, and then pressing the enter key will cause the pointer to go to Cell A6.
Ctrl + **End**	Moves the pointer to the last cell in the lower right corner of a worksheet.
Ctrl + **Home**	Moves the pionter to Cell A1.
Ctrl + ←	Moves the pointer left to the intersection of a blank and a nonblank cell.
Ctrl + →	Moves the pointer right to the intersection of a blank and a nonblank cell.
Ctrl + ↑	Moves the pointer up to the intersection of a blank and a nonblank cell.
Ctrl + ↓	Moves the pointer down to the intersection of a blank and a nonblank cell.

SCROLLING BY MOUSE.   Moving the cell pointer by mouse to a cell beyond the current display requires the use of a **scroll bar,** a common Windows tool that allows you to view the contents of a window that is not in the current viewing area. As shown in Figure SS1-3, a workbook window has both a horizontal and a vertical scroll bar.

You can access scroll bars only by mouse. They do not move the cell pointer, only the display area. Once a desired cell is in view, you may use the mouse to move the cell pointer by pointing to the desired cell and then clicking it.

Scroll bars have arrow buttons at each end. Clicking a scroll bar's arrow button will scroll (move) the spreadsheet one row or column in the direction of that arrow. Scroll bars also contain a scroll box. By dragging the scroll box along the scroll bar you can quickly scroll through the spreadsheet. Try this exercise:

1 **Point to the** ↓ **button of the vertical scroll bar (near the lower right side of window) and click it twice**

As shown in Figure SS1-6a, Row 17 fully appears as Row 1 disappears. The cell pointer also disappears, because it is still in Cell A1. Now, try moving the cell pointer to Cell A17.

2 **Click** *Cell A17*

The cell pointer now appears in Cell A17 as shown in Figure SS1-6b.

3 **Press** **Ctrl** + **Home** **to move to Cell A1**

COMMON WINDOWS FEATURES. Like all document windows, workbook windows have a workbook (document) icon, title bar, resizing buttons, and a *Close* button. The location of these features depends on the size of the window. For instance, whenever the workbook window on your screen is *maximized* (enlarged to its maximum size), it shares its title bar with the Microsoft Excel window's title bar. As shown in Figure SS1-3, the title bar's caption, "Book1," next to the words "Microsoft Excel" is the current workbook's name. "Book1" also indicates that you have not assigned a specific name to the workbook.

FIGURE SS1-6 ■ **SCROLLING BY MOUSE**

(a) Clicking the down arrow button of the vertical scroll bar displays Row 17
(b) Clicking Cell A17 moves the pointer there.

(a)

(b)

SS

As in Figure SS1-3, a maximized workbook's icon occupies the left end of the menu bar and its resizing buttons and *Close* buttons occupy the right end. Try the following steps to resize the workbook window to a smaller window in the Microsoft Excel window's workspace.

STEPS

  1 Click the *Restore* button (near the right end of the menu bar)   [**Ctrl** + **F5**]

> **Tip:** You can also use the workbook window's control-menu to resize it. Click its workbook icon and then *Restore* or press Alt + – for its control-menu, and then press R to restore.

As shown in Figure SS1-7, the workbook window should now be a smaller window with its own title bar. Its control-menu box appears at the top left and two resizing buttons are at the top right.

UNIQUE EXCEL FEATURES.   A workbook window, as shown in Figure SS1-7, has several unique Excel features, including sheet tabs, tab-scroll buttons, and tab, horizontal, and vertical split bars. *Sheet tabs* are used to identify sheets in a workbook and enable you to switch back and forth between them. Remember, a sheet is like a page in a book and may contain a worksheet, chart, or other information. Although additional sheets can be added, 16 sheets are available in a new workbook. *Tab-scroll* buttons can

FIGURE SS1-7 ■ THE WORKBOOK WINDOW

A less-than maximized workbook window has its own title bar. It appears similar to Excel's title bar.

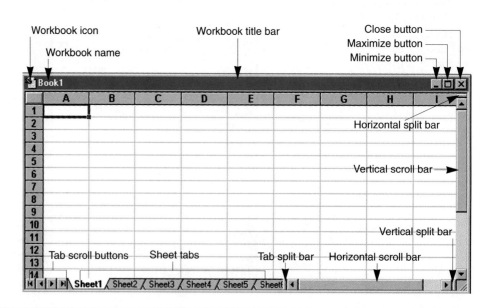

be used to scroll through multiple sheets by clicking them with your mouse. Dragging a *split bar* with your mouse will split the workbook window into separate panes (parts). This allows you to view different areas of multiple sheets (tab split bar) or a single sheet (horizontal or vertical split bar) at the same time. Multiple sheet operations and workbook window splitting techniques are discussed later.

To enlarge your workbook window back to its maximum size,

STEPS

    1   **Click to the *Maximize* button (near the right end of title bar)**   [**Ctrl** + **F10**]

THE FORMULA BAR

The *formula bar,* shown in Figure SS1-8a, is located below the Format toolbar. It provides information about the current cell address (location) and its content. The formula bar has three parts: name box (left side), entry area (right side), and command button(s).

THE NAME BOX.   The **name box,** located on left side of the formula bar, provides information about the current cell address. Your name box should show "A1," which indicates that the cell pointer is in Cell A1. You can also use the name box to move the cell pointer to different areas of the current workbook. Simply click the box, type in the desired cell address, and then press ↵ .

FIGURE SS1-8 ■ THE FORMULA BAR

(a) The formula bar is located below the Format toolbar.
(b) As data is entered into a cell, it appears in both the cell and the entry area of the formula bar. Three command buttons also appear to the left of the entry area when entering data.

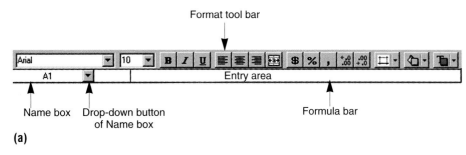

(a)

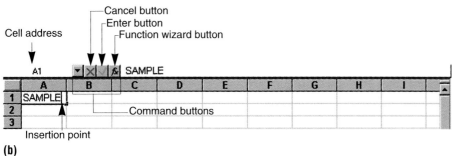

(b)

ENTRY AREA. The **entry area,** located on the right side of the formula bar, displays the content of the current cell. You can also use it to enter or edit data in the current cell.

COMMAND BUTTONS. Currently, the formula bar displays only the drop-down button of the name box. Clicking this button will open a drop-down list of the workbook's named areas. Naming areas of a workbook are discussed later.

When data is entered into a cell, the formula bar becomes active and three other command buttons appear. Try this:

STEPS

1 Move the cell pointer to Cell A1

2 Type **SAMPLE** (do not press enter)

Note: As you type "SAMPLE," it appears in both the entry area and the current cell. In addition, a vertical blinking line, called the *insertion point,* also moves to the right in the current cell as you type. The insertion point indicates where the next character you enter will appear.

Your formula bar and Cell A1 content should appear as Figure SS1-8b. Note also that the *Cancel* (X), *Enter* (✓), and *Function Wizard (fx)* buttons appear to the left of "SAMPLE" on the formula bar. At this point you can edit the entry or accept it into Cell A1 by either clicking the *Enter Box* button or pressing the Enter key. You can use the *Function Wizard* button to place a function (built-in formula) in the current cell. Functions are discussed later. For now, do the following to cancel the entry:

3 Click the *Cancel* (X) button on the formula bar   [Esc]

Note: The formula bar also becomes active when editing cell contents.

THE HELP FEATURE

Microsoft Excel's on-line Help feature includes standard Windows Help features such as the *Contents* tab for general program help, and the *Index* and *Find* tabs for specific help. It also has an Answer wizard, which provides help when you enter a question. To open the Help Topics window,

STEPS

1 Click *Help* (on the menu bar) and then *Microsoft Excel Help Topics*   [F1]

At this point you can use any of the tabs by clicking it and then following its instructions.

A context-sensitive help feature can be accessed from most dialog boxes. To invoke it in the *Help Topics* dialog box,

 2 Click the *? (Help)* button near the right end of the *Help Topics* dialog box

Your mouse pointer now changes to a Help pointer (see left margin). You can now click the item you desire help on in the dialog box. Try this:

3 Click the list box (the area within the tab that has a white background)

A Help caption should now appear. To exit the dialog box,

 4 Click the *Close* button at the right side of the dialog box's title bar   [**Alt** + **F4**]

You may continue working through the module or close Excel and then shut down Windows by doing as follows:

 5 Click Excel's *Close* button (right side of title bar)   [**Alt** + **F4**]

 6 Click the *Start* button   [**Ctrl** + **Esc**]

7 Click *Sh̲ut Down* and then the *Y̲es* button

Other exiting techniques will be demonstrated later.

☑ CHECKPOINT

✓ Start Windows, launch Excel, and then move to Cell J10. In what two ways can you tell that J10 is the current cell?
✓ Describe the key components of the Excel window.
✓ Describe the key components of a workbook window.
✓ Describe how to access Excel's on-line Help feature.
✓ Close Excel and then shut down Windows.

OPERATING MENUS

Like all Windows programs, Excel has a menu system that you can use to access its many features. The Excel menu system contains standard Windows menu features, such as a menu bar (main menu) with pull-down menus and a control-menu with window manipulating features. Excel also offers *Shortcut* menus, which provide quick access to specific features.

STEPS

1 Start Windows and then launch Excel, if needed

□   **2** If needed, click Excel's *Maximize* button to enlarge   [**Alt** + **Spacebar** , **X**]
     the window to its maximum size

USING A MENU BAR

Excel's menu bar gives you access to most of the program's features through pull-down menus. Each provides a list of commands related to its menu bar item. When you select a menu bar item, a pull-down menu is opened. This module will refer to a pull-down menu simply as a menu.

> **Note: Click = point to and click.**

OPENING AND CLOSING A MENU.   To open a menu by mouse, simply click its menu bar item. With the keyboard, you must press the Alt key and the underlined letter of the menu bar item. Try this to open the *File* menu:

STEPS

1 Click *File*   [**Alt** + **F**]

At this point you can get a brief description of a menu item or select one. These techniques will be demonstrated shortly. For now, to close a menu without selecting a menu item,

2 Click any open space outside the menu   [**Alt** once or **Esc** twice]

IDENTIFYING A MENU ITEM'S FUNCTION.   Moving the selection highlight to a menu item displays its function in the status bar. Pointing moves the selection highlight by mouse. With the keyboard you must use the arrow keys. Try this:

STEPS

1 Click *File* for the file menu again   [**Alt** + **F**]

The top of your file menu should appear as Figure SS1-9.

2 Point to *Save* (do not click)   [↓ , ↓ , ↓]

Now the message "Saves document" appears on the status bar.

3 Press **Alt** to close the *File* menu without selecting a command

SELECTING A MENU ITEM.   Once a menu is open, simply click the desired menu item or press its underlined letter to select it. Try this to select *Exit* from the *File* menu to exit Excel:

FIGURE SS1-9 ■ A SAMPLE OF A PULL-DOWN MENU

Clicking a menu bar item
opens its pull-down menu.
This figure only displays the
top portion of the *File* menu.

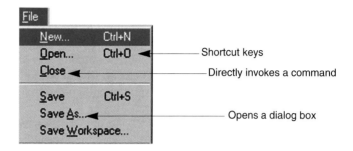

STEPS

1 Click *File* for the *File* menu   [**Alt** + **F**]

2 Click *Exit*   [**X**]

You should now have exited Excel. To launch Excel again,

STEPS

1 Click the *Start* button   [**Ctrl** + **Esc**]

2 Point to *Programs* for its submenu   [**P**]

3 If needed, point to *Microsoft Office* for its submenu   [↓ **as needed**]

4 Click *Microsoft Excel*   [↵]

**Tip: Another way to open a menu and select a menu item by keyboard is to press the
Alt key first to turn on the highlight. (The Alt key is a toggle [on/off] switch that activates or deactivates the highlight bar.) Once turned on, the highlight can be moved to
a menu bar item by pressing an arrow key and then the Enter key to open the menu.
Next, press the Down arrow key to move the highlight to the desired menu item and
press the Enter key to select the item.**

MENU INDICATORS

Excel uses standard Windows menu indicators or conventions in its menu system. These
conventions apply to all types of menus—pull-down menus, control-menus, and *Shortcut* menus. The *File* menu will be used as an example to help you understand these menu
conventions.

STEPS

1   Click *File*   **[Alt + F]**

The top portion of the *File* menu should appear again as shown in Figure SS1-9.

     Menu items with *neither* a triangle pointer (▶) at their extreme right (not shown in Figure SS1-9) nor an ellipsis (...), such as *Close* directly invoke a command. If shortcut keys can be used to invoke a menu item directly, they are displayed at the extreme right of the item. For example, the shortcut keys Ctrl + O are displayed to the right of *Open*.

     Figure SS1-10a summarizes menu bar mouse and keyboard actions required to open pull-down menus and select menu items. A list of standard windows menu indicators is displayed in Figure SS1-10b. To exit the *File* menu:

2   Click any open space in the window   **[Alt]**

USING A CONTROL-MENU

Like all windows, the Excel and workbook windows (and icons, when minimized) have a *control-menu* that contains options to manipulate and close a window. Any dialog box also has a control-menu. Figure SS1-11 displays examples of control-menus.

     To open the control-menu of any window, simply right-click its title bar. By keyboard, press the Alt + Spacebar keys to open a program window or dialog box's control-menu. Pressing the Alt + Minus keys will open a workbook window's control-menu. Try this:

FIGURE SS1-10 ■ **MENU BAR SELECTIONS**

(a) Mouse and keyboard actions to select menu bar and menu items.
(b) Menu conventions.

(a)

Selecting a	Mouse Actions	Keyboard Actions
Menu bar item letter	Point to and click the item	Press the Alt key and the item's underlined letter
Menu item	Point to and click the item	Press the item's underlined letter

(b)

Menu items with	Explanation
Ellipsis (...)	Opens to a dialog box or another window
▶ at far right	Opens to a submenu
No notation	Invokes a command or other feature
Keys at far right	Shortcut key(s) to invoke the menu item using the keyboard
✓ to left of item	A toggle (on/off) feature that has been activated
Dimmed (or not visible) characters	A menu item not currently available

FIGURE SS1-11 ■ CONTROL-MENUS

(a) Excel's control-menu can be used to resize, move, or close its window.
(b) A workbook's control-menu can be used to resize, move, or close its window.
(c) A dialog box's control-menu can be used to move or close its window.

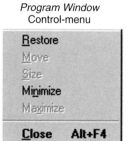

Program Window
Control-menu

Restore	
Move	
Size	
Minimize	
Maximize	
Close	**Alt+F4**

(a)

Workbook Window
Control-menu

Restore	Ctrl+F5
Move	Ctrl+F7
Size	Ctrl+F8
Minimize	Ctrl+F9
Maximize	Ctrl+F10
Close	**Ctrl+W**

(b)

Dialog box
Control-menu

| Move | |
| **Close** | **Alt+F4** |

(c)

STEPS

1   Right-click (click the right mouse button) an empty area of the title bar for Excel's control-menu   [**Alt** + **Spacebar**]

Tip: You can also open a program window's control-menu by clicking the *Program* icon at the left side of the title bar. Clicking a *Workbook* icon will open a workbook window's control-menu.

At this point you can select a control-menu item by clicking it or pressing its underlined letter. For now,

2   Click anywhere outside the control-menu to close it without selecting   [**Esc**]

Note: Control-menus use the same menu indicators as the menu bar. Their operations are demonstrated throughout this module.

USING A *SHORTCUT* MENU

Shortcut menus provide quick access to specific Excel features. You open a ***Shortcut*** **menu** by pointing to certain areas of the Excel window and workbook and right-clicking (clicking the right mouse button). Try this:

STEPS

1   Right-click an open space in the center of the workbook window

SS

A *Shortcut* menu should appear similar to Figure SS1-12. At this point you can select a *Shortcut* menu item by clicking it. For now,

2   **Click (left button) outside of the *Shortcut* menu to close it**   **[Esc]**

☑ CHECKPOINT

✓   Describe the procedures to open and close a pull-down menu by mouse and keyboard.
✓   What do menu items followed by a triangle (▶) at their extreme right or an ellipsis (…) represent?
✓   Describe the actions required to open and select from a *Shortcut* menu.
✓   Describe the actions to open a control-menu (Excel's and a workbook's).
✓   Describe how to close a window using its control-menu box.

OPERATING COMMAND BUTTONS

Many Excel features can be quickly accessed by mouse using command buttons. (Remember, command buttons can be used to invoke certain commands directly.) For example, as demonstrated earlier, double-clicking Excel's *Program* icon (left side of title bar) closes the window.

Standard Windows command buttons include the *Program* and *Workbook* (document) icons, resizing buttons, and the *Close* button. Unique Excel command buttons are mainly available through toolbars. They are a series of pictures or symbols that appear below the menu bar. Clicking a toolbar button will access the feature it represents. Excel also has a variety of other command buttons, for example, the *Enter* button, which appears on the formula bar when entering data into a cell.

FIGURE SS1-12 ■ *SHORTCUT* MENU

Right-clicking certain areas of the Excel window will open a *Shortcut* menu. This *Shortcut* menu appears when right-clicking a cell in the worksheet.

You will now learn more about the resizing buttons and toolbar buttons.

> **Note: Many buttons are only accessible by mouse. In this module, command buttons are displayed in the left margin of their related commands, where available.**

RESIZING BUTTONS

There are three types of resizing buttons: *Minimize, Restore,* and *Maximize.* Resizing buttons generally appear at the right end of a window's title bar. A maximized workbook window's resizing buttons, however, appears at the right end of the menu bar. Each one is described briefly below. (Do not invoke command.)

- Clicking a *Minimize* button reduces the window to an icon (also called a minimized window).

- Clicking a *Restore* button reduces a maximized window to a smaller window. A maximized window is one that is enlarged to its largest size. The *Restore* button appears only when a window is maximized.

- Clicking a *Maximize* button resizes the window to a full screen (also called a *maximized* window). The *Maximize* button appears only when a window is less than its largest size.

Resizing buttons are used as needed within this manual.

TOOLBARS

Excel opens with a Standard toolbar and a Format toolbar below its menu bar as in Figure SS1-13a. *Toolbars* provide mouse shortcuts to Excel's features through command

FIGURE SS1-13 ■ STANDARD AND FORMAT TOOLBARS

(a) Excel launches with the Standard and Format toolbars below its menu bar.
(b) Clicking the ▼ button of a drop down box opens its list.

Menu bar
Standard tool bar
Format tool bar

(a)

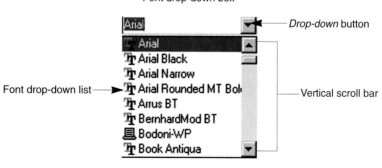

Font drop-down box

Font drop-down list

Drop-down button

Vertical scroll bar

(b)

buttons and drop-down boxes. The *Standard toolbar* can be used for accessing file management, editing, data manipulation, charting, and a variety of other commonly used commands. The *Format toolbar* can be used to access worksheet formatting commands.

Excel also comes with a variety of other specialized toolbars that automatically appear when you invoke a command that relates to their operation. For example, the Chart toolbar appears when you create a chart. These toolbars can also be turned on or off manually through the menu bar or a *Shortcut* menu. All toolbars can be edited. In addition, Excel allows you to create your own custom toolbar. Specialized toolbar operations will be discussed as needed. See the appendix to create a custom toolbar.

IDENTIFYING A TOOLBAR BUTTON'S FUNCTION.   Pointing to a toolbar button will display its function in a caption box below it and in the left side of the status bar. Try this:

STEPS

1 Point to the *Print* button on the Standard toolbar (do not click)

A caption box with the word "Print" appears below the button and the message "Prints active document" appears in the status bar.

2 Point to another toolbar button and view its function

USING TOOLBAR BUTTONS.   Clicking a toolbar button normally invokes a command or opens a dialog box. Some toolbars contain drop-down boxes that appear as a box with a drop-down list button at its right. For example, the *Font* (type style) drop-down box at the left end of the Format toolbar opens to a drop-down list of available fonts (typefaces) similar to Figure SS1-13b. Try this:

STEPS

1 Point to the ▼ button of the *Font* drop-down box

2 Click it

A *Font* drop-down list similar to Figure SS1-13b now appears. (Note: Your font list may differ depending on the available fonts in your system.) To select from a drop-down list, simply click the desired item. For now, close the drop-down list without selecting a new font.

3 Click an open space outside of the drop-down list   [**Esc**]

☑ **CHECKPOINT**

✓ What is a command button?
✓ Identify and describe the three different types of *Resizing* buttons.

✓   Where are toolbars located?

✓   What are toolbar buttons? How can you get a description of a toolbar button's functions?

✓   How do you open a drop-down box's list?

A QUICK START: THE BASICS

The following exercises demonstrate how to create, save, and open a spreadsheet. Use these techniques to save your work and return to it later. For clarity, keys are displayed in uppercase letters, but you need not type them this way: Excel recognizes *a5* as easily as *A5*.

SETTING THE DEFAULT DRIVE

Each time you begin Excel, you should confirm (and set if needed) the drive (for example, Drive A) that Excel uses to hold your data disk. This is essential to ensure that your work will be saved on your data disk. You can use either the *Save As* or *Open File* dialog box to verify and change (if needed) the default drive. The procedures are the same for both dialog boxes. Try this to use the *Save As* dialog box to check the default drive and change it to Drive A (if needed):

STEPS

1   **If needed, insert your data disk into Drive A**

 2   **Click *File*, *Save As* for its dialog box**   [**F12**]

A *Save As* dialog box similar to Figure SS1-14a should appear. (Note: The content of your dialog box may differ depending on how Excel was programmed.)

The *Save As* dialog box has a variety of common Windows features as described in Figure SS1-14b. These features operate the same way in most dialog boxes. To select a feature by mouse, click the desired item; to select by keyboard, press the Alt key and the underlined letter of the option.

Now, examine the drop-down box for your drives. If Drive A appears, then just read Steps 2 and 3 and then do Step 4. If another drive appears, do the following to set it to Drive A.

 3   **Click the ▼ button of the *Save in* drop-down box**

(If using the *Open* dialog box, click the ▼ button of the *Look in* drop-down box.)

4   **Click *3½ Floppy (A:)***

At this point, you can either use the dialog box to save a file or exit the dialog box. To exit the dialog box with the new drive setting:

FIGURE SS1-14 ■ **THE *SAVE AS* DIALOG BOX**

(a) The *Save As* dialog box.
(b) Parts of the *Save As* dialog box.

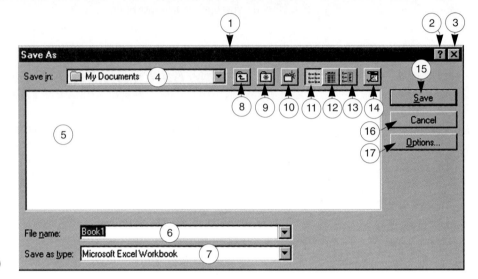

(a)

	Item	Descripiton
1	Title bar	Identifies the dialog box. Right-click for control-menu. Drag to move dialog box.
2	"?" *(Help)* button	Click to change to Help pointer, and then click item for help on its operation.
3	"X" *(Close)* button	Click to close the dialog box.
4	*Save-in* box	A drop-down box that is used to set the default drive and directory.
5	*Files list* box	A list box that displays the files in the default directory.
6	*File name* box	A text box that is used to enter a file's name for saving.
7	*Save As Type* box	A drop-down box that can be used to save a document in a specific file type.
8	*Up One Level* button	Click to display file structure up one level in the *Files* list box.
9	*Look in Favorites* button	Displays *Favorite* folders in *Files* list box.
10	*Create New Folder* button	Click to create a new folder.
11	*List* button	Click to list the content of the default directory in the *Files* list box without details. This is the default display.
12	*Details* button	Click to display file details in the *Files* list box.
13	*Properties* button	Click to open the *Properties* dialog box of a selected item.
14	*Commands and Settings* button	Click for menu with sorting , network, and properties options.
15	*Save* button	Click to save a document to disk.
16	*Cancel* button	Click to cancel the dialog box.
17	Options button	Click for a dialog box with options to create a backup upon saving, add a password, and make file read-only.

(b)

[X] **5** Click the *Cancel* or *Close* button   [**Esc**]

Drive A will remain as the default drive until Excel is exited or the default is changed.

ENTERING DATA

The first step in the creation of a spreadsheet is to enter data in the desired cells. In this brief exercise, you will simply type your name and a number.

STEPS

1 Press **Ctrl** + **Home** to move to Cell A1 and type your first name

Your name appears in the entry and in the cell. If you typed incorrectly, you can use the Backspace key to erase the entry and then retype it.

2 Move to Cell A3

Note that as you moved the cell pointer, the previous entry stays in Cell A1.

3 Type **75** and press ↵

As you have seen here, an entry can be placed into a spreadsheet cell either by pressing the Enter key or by moving the cell pointer.

SAVING A WORKBOOK

A workbook can be saved using the Save or Save As command (from the *File* menu). Both commands open the *Save As* dialog box if invoked on an unsaved workbook. (Remember, a document file in Excel is called a *workbook*.) Invoking the **Save** command on a previously saved workbook will quickly resave it under its original name. Invoking the **Save As** command on a previously saved workbook will alert you if a file with the same name exists on the disk. This command also allows you to save the file under a different name, thereby keeping the original workbook under its old name. This is useful when saving an updated workbook. Both commands are demonstrated here:

STEPS

  1 Click *File* and then *Save*   [**Ctrl** + **S**]

The *Save As* dialog box should appear since this is the first time you are saving this workbook. As seen earlier, you can use this dialog box to set the default drive. You can also use it to save a workbook in the Microsoft Excel workbook format (the default) or another program's format, change the default directory, assign a password to the workbook, and to perform a variety of other save options. Note also the that selection highlight is in the *File name* list box on the name Book1. As you type a new filename, Book1 will disappear.

SS

2 Type **SAMPLE**

3 Click the *Save* button   [↵]

The mouse pointer briefly appears as an hourglass (indicating "please wait"). The message "Saving Sample" briefly appears in the message area of your status bar as your workbook is being saved to disk. Your workbook has been saved on the disk in the default drive with the name "SAMPLE.XLS." Excel automatically adds a ".XLS" filename extension to identify your file as an Excel workbook, (Depending on your system's display settings, the XLS may appear in the title bar or *Save As* dialog box.) The filename "SAMPLE" also appears in the title bar after it is saved.

> **Tip: The ".XLS" filename extension also associates the file with Excel. Associated document files in the Window's environment allow you to open the file with its program at the same time through My Computer, Explorer, or a *Shortcut* icon. Refer to your Windows on-line help for detailed instructions on associated file operations.**

Once you have saved a workbook, you can use either the Save As or Save command to resave it. Remember, the Save command resaves a file without confirmation. First try the Save As command to resave the workbook SAMPLE.

4 Click *File* and then *Save As* for its dialog box   [**F12**]

When the dialog box appears, it displays the current name of the workbook, in this case, "SAMPLE" in the *File Name* text box.

5 Click the *Save* button to accept the current name   [↵]

Since a "SAMPLE" file already exists on your disk, Excel offers you a dialog box with the choices *Yes* or *No*.

6 Click the *Yes* button to replace the old

The *Yes* button replaces the previous file on the disk with the new one. The *No* button returns you to the spreadsheet *without* saving.

Now, try the Save command to resave the file without confirmation.

  7 Click *File* and then *Save*   [**Ctrl** + **S**]

Your file is now resaved under its previous name.

CLOSING A WORKBOOK

Closing a workbook removes it (and its window) from Excel's workspace. Although you can open many workbooks in Excel's workspace, each additional workbook uses more system memory. Many opened workbooks may therefore affect the operating efficiency of your system. Unless otherwise needed, you should close any workbook not in use. Multiple workbook operations are discussed later.

A workbook can be closed by using the Close command in the *File* menu or control-menu. It can also be closed by clicking its *Close* button, double-clicking its window's icon, or pressing Ctrl + F4 or Ctrl + W. These closing techniques are presented throughout this text. Now, to close the active workbook by menu bar (remember, the active workbook is the one currently in use),

STEPS

1   Click *File* for its menu

2   Click *Close* to close the workbook

> **Tip:** If changes were made or the workbook was never saved, a dialog box will appear with the options *Yes*, *No*, and *Cancel*. Click *Yes* to save or resave the workbook and then close it.

Your Excel workspace should now be blank and the menu bar only displaying *File* and *Help* options.

CREATING A NEW WORKBOOK

At this point you can create a new workbook, open a saved workbook, or exit Excel. The latter two options are discussed in the sections to follow. The **New** command (from the *File* menu) opens a new blank workbook in Excel's workspace.

STEPS

1   Click *File* and then *New* for its dialog box   [**Ctrl** + **N**]

2   Click *OK* for a new workbook   [↵]

A new workbook with the title "BOOK2" appears in its own window in Excel's workspace. Excel automatically labels new workbooks in sequence as you create them (for example, BOOK1, BOOK2, and so on). As seen earlier, you can change this workbook name upon saving the workbook. For now, use the workbook window's *Close* button to close it.

> **Caution:** In the next command, be sure to use the workbook's icon that is currently located to the left of the *File* option on the menu bar. *Do not* use Excel's icon that is at the left end of its title bar.

3   Click the workbook's *Close* button at the right side of menu bar   [**Ctrl** + **F4**]

Excel's workspace is now empty again.

> **Tip:** You can also close a workbook by double-clicking its icon (on the left side of the menu bar), pressing the Ctrl +W, or using its control-menu. To use the control-menu, click the workbook icon (or press Alt+-), and then click *Close*.

OPENING A WORKBOOK

The **Open** command (from the *File* menu) retrieves a saved workbook into a workbook window. Excel offers several ways to open a saved workbook. Two common ways include opening it by typing the name of the workbook or selecting it from a list.

TYPING A WORKBOOK'S NAME. If you know a workbook's name, the most direct way to open the worksheet is to type its name in the *File Name* text box of the *Open File* dialog box. Try this:

STEPS

1 Click *File* and then *Open* for its dialog box   [**Ctrl** + **O**]

An *Open File* dialog box should appear as shown in Figure SS1-15. Notice that its components are similar to those of the *Save As* dialog box.

2 Type **SAMPLE**

FIGURE SS1-15 ■ THE *OPEN FILE* DIALOG BOX

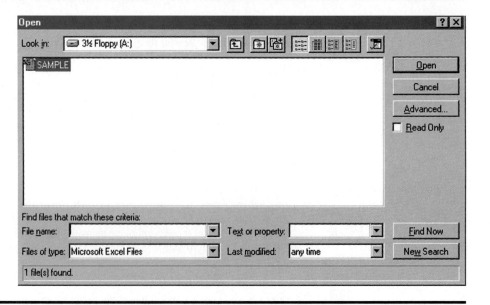

> **Note:** If you have just restarted Excel, make sure you set the default drive to A before opening (use the *Look in* drop-down box).

3 Click the *Open* button to open the file   [↵]

SELECTING A WORKBOOK FROM A LIST.   If you do not remember the name of a worksheet or its exact spelling, you can open a file by selecting from the *Files* list box of the *Open File* dialog box. As with the *Save As* dialog box, the *Open* dialog box's *Files* list box is located below the toolbar. Try this:

STEPS

1 First, close the current workbook by double-clicking its icon   [**Ctrl** + **W**]
    (located at the left end of the menu bar)

 2 Click *File* and then *Open*   [**Ctrl** + **O**]

3 Click SAMPLE from the *Files* list box

4 Click the *Open* button   [↵]

> **Tip:** You can avoid Steps 3 and 4 by double-clicking SAMPLE in the *Files* list box.

SELECTING A WORKBOOK FROM THE FILE MENU.   The last four workbooks used can also be opened directly from the *File* menu. Try this,

STEPS

 1 Close the current workbook using the *File* menu (*File, Close*)   [**Ctrl** + **F4**]

2 Click *File* for its menu

Note that the last workbook(s) used appear listed above the Exit command on the *File* menu.

3 Click *1 Sample* to open it

EXITING EXCEL AND SHUTTING DOWN WINDOWS

There are several ways to exit Excel or any Windows program. You can click Excel's *Close* button; click *File, Exit;* double-click its *Program* icon, press the Alt + F4 *shortcut* keys, or use the Close command of the Excel control-menu.

SS

Since all Windows programs can be closed using the same techniques, the next exercise will close the Excel window using its *Close* button. This is one of the quickest and most common ways to exit it. Windows will then be shut down using the *Start* menu. You may want to practice the other exiting techniques on your own.

STEPS

 1 Click Excel's *Close* button at the right end of the title bar   [**Alt** + **F4**]

 2 Click the *Start* button   [**Ctrl** + **Esc**]

3 Click *Shut Down* for its dialog box

At this point you can select one of the options of the *Shut Down Windows* dialog box, cancel the shut down by clicking <u>*N*</u>*o,* or do the following to complete the shut down process.

4 Click the <u>*Yes*</u> button to shut down Windows

5 Wait for the message "It's now safe to turn off your computer." to appear.

6 Turn off your system

Use these basic methods for saving and exiting as you work through the remainder of this chapter. You may stop at any point, remembering to save your work so that you can open it later.

☑ CHECKPOINT

  ✓ Describe the difference between the Save As and Save commands.
  ✓ Describe how to close a workbook.
  ✓ Type your name in Cell B5 and then close the workbook window without saving.
  ✓ Describe how to open a new workbook.
  ✓ Exit the Excel program and then shut down Windows.

CREATING A WORKSHEET

We will now examine some of the intricacies of creating and using spreadsheets. First prepare your program:

STEPS

1 Start Windows and then launch Excel

 2 Maximize the Excel window if needed

(Remember, click the *Maximize* button or press Alt + Spacebar and then X.)

CONSTANT VALUES AND FORMULAS

The data you enter into a cell are classified as either *constant values* or *formulas.* Constant values are data directly entered into a cell, whereas, formulas are preceded by an equal (=) sign. Examples of constant values and formulas are in Figure SS1-16.

CONSTANT VALUES.   A **constant value** may be text or a numeric value. Text—such as a report title or street address—can consist of any combination of alphabetic (A–Z), numeric (0–9), or special characters (?, *, and so forth.). A **numeric value**—such as 2 or 3.5—is simply a number without any alphabetic text. It can also include dates, times, currency, percentages, fractions, or scientific notation. Numeric values can be used in mathematical operations (as in formulas, which are discussed next) whereas, text cannot. A constant value will not change unless you edit it. Editing techniques are discussed later.

Numeric values generally start with a numeral, a decimal point, or a minus symbol (as in –2.3). Excel also reads numerals in brackets [ ] as negative numbers.

In most cases, Excel recognizes data the way you entered it. An example of this is a social security number or an address. At times you may want to restrict a numeric value from being available for use in a mathematical operation—for example, an account number that contains only numeric values. In such cases, type an apostrophe (') before entering the number to instruct Excel to recognize it as text.

FORMULAS.   A **formula,** such as =A1*2, performs a mathematical operation on data in other cells. Formulas may include a sequence of constant values, cell addresses, operators (*/+−^), or functions. A **function,** such as =SUM(A1:A5), is a predetermined formula built into the spreadsheet. After you enter a formula into a cell, the entry appears in the *entry area of the formula bar,* but the numeric value resulting from the calculation appears in the *cell.* The value can in turn be used in other calculations. Also, the program will recalculate the value as values in related cells are altered. All formulas must start with an equal sign (=).

SS

FIGURE SS1-16 ■ **EXAMPLES OF CONSTANT VALUES AND FORMULAS**

Example	Description	Entered on the Keyboard As
Revenue	Text constant value	Revenue
.15	Numeric constant value	.15
$2,000,000	Numeric constant value	$2000000
.6*A5/100-B2	Formula	=.6*A5/100-B2
SUM(A1:A4)	Formula-function	=SUM(A1:A4)
C3-D2	Formula	=C3-D2
3rd Quarter	Text constant value	3rd Quarter

DISTINGUISHING CONSTANT VALUES FROM FORMULAS.   If you don't start with an equal sign when entering data, it will be recognized as a constant value. For example,

1 Move to Cell A1

2 Type   718-555-1234   and press ↵

As shown in Figure SS1-17a, the entry *718-555-1234* appears as you entered it. In this case, the data has been entered as a text constant value and may be interpreted as a telephone number. Now, try this to enter the data as a formula:

3 Move to Cell A3

4 Press =

5 Type   718-555-1234   and press ↵

> **Tip:** Remember, instead of pressing the Enter key in Steps 2 and 5, you can click the Enter (✓) button on the formula bar to accept the entry.

As in Figure SS1-17b, your entry yields a mathematical result of –1071.

Similarly, formulas that begin with a cell reference (such as A1*5) will be mistaken for text constant value, since they begin with a letter. Try this:

6 Move to Cell C1

FIGURE SS1-17 ■ **CONFUSING CONSTANT VALUES AND FORMULAS**

(a) Data entered without an equal sign (=) are recognized as constant values.
(b) Data entered with an equal sign (=) are recognized as formulas. The result of a formula's calculation is displayed in the cell.
(c) A mathematical operation that is entered without an equal sign (=) is mistaken for a constant value.

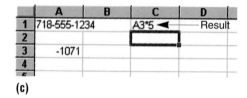

(a)   (b)

(c)

7 Type **A3*5** and press ↵

As shown in Figure SS1-17c, the cell displays the data as it was typed, not its mathematical result. Such formulas should be typed with an initial equal symbol (=) to indicate that they are formulas.

8 Move to Cell C1, type **=A3*5** and press ↵

The result of the formula (in this case, –5355) now appears in Cell C1. Now to close the workbook without saving.

9 Click the workbook window's *Close* button (right end of the menu bar)   [**Ctrl** + **F4**]

10 Click the *No* button

ENTERING CONSTANT VALUES AND FORMULAS

You are now ready to start a new workbook and enter data for the sales worksheet shown in Figure SS1-18. To do this, move to each cell using the arrow keys (or mouse), type the constant value or formula indicated, and then press the Enter key (or an arrow key).

STEPS

1 If needed, launch Excel or close any open workbook

2 If needed, click *File, New, OK* for a new workbook

SS

FIGURE SS1-18 ■ THE SALES WORKSHEET MODEL

Leave Cells D4 through D8 empty for now.

	A	B	C	D	E	F
1	Your Name				M/D/YY	
2						
3	Agent	Region A	Region B	Totals		
4	Michaels	500	200			
5	Martin	200	450			
6	Parker	300	325			
7	Williams	50	125			
8	Totals					
9						
10						
11						

3   Move the cell pointer to Cell A1

ENTERING TEXT CONSTANT VALUES.   You will first practice entering text (in this case, column headings) into the spreadsheet.

1   Type your name and press ↵

Your name is recognized as text because it begins with an equal sign (=). If your name exceeds the width of the cell, its letters will extend right and cover Cell B1 (this is fine for now).

2   Move to Cell E1

3   Type today's date (Use M/D/YY format)

4   Press ↵

> **Tip:**   To retype or correct a cell entry, simply type over the original entry, which will be replaced when you press the Enter key. To erase an entry, move to the cell and click *Edit* and then *Clear*. With the keyboard, move to the cell and press the Delete key.

Using Figure SS1-18 as a guide,

5   Enter the titles in Cells A3, B3, C3, and D3

6   Enter the names (or words) in Cells A4 through A8

Notice that Excel automatically left-aligns the text.
    To save the workbook on your data disk as SHEET1,

7   Click *File, Save* for the *Save As* dialog box   [**Ctrl**   **+**   **S**   ]

8   Type   SHEET1   in the File name text box

> **Note:**   Skip Step 9 if your default drive is already A.

9   If needed, set the default drive to A by clicking the ▼ button of the *Save in* drop-down box, and then click *3½ Floppy (A:)*.

10   **Click the _Save_ button**   [↵]

You should save a spreadsheet often as you develop it. The few seconds it takes may prove valuable later if your work is lost or incorrectly modified.

ENTERING CONSTANT VALUES/NUMERIC VALUES.   When you have finished entering the text, you are ready to enter the numeric values. Although data can be entered in any order, it is good practice to create row and column titles (text) before entering specific values.

1   **Move to Cell B4**

You can type numbers using the numeric keys on the top row of the regular keyboard or the keys on the numeric keypad after pressing the Num Lock key.

> **Tip:** If your keyboard does not have separate arrow keys, remember to press the Num Lock key again before you attempt to use the numeric keypad to move the pointer.

2   **Type   500   and press ↓**

Remember that pressing the arrow key also enters data. Notice, too, that the entry was recognized as a value because it starts with a number. It will be right-aligned in the cell.

3   **Enter the remaining values in Cells B5 through B7**

4   **Enter the values in Cells C4 through C7**

Your spreadsheet should resemble Figure SS1-18. Notice that there are no entries in Cells B8 or C8. These will come later.

5   **Save again as   SHEET1   (_File_, _Save_ or Ctrl + S)**

> **Tip:** You can also enter data into a cell by clicking the Enter (✓) button on the formula bar after typing it into a cell.

ENTERING FORMULAS BY USING MATHEMATICAL OPERATORS.   You can now enter formulas using cell references (locations) and mathematical operators that will automatically compute totals and enter the results into the worksheet. A **mathematical operator** is a character used in a formula that tells the program to perform a certain calculation. Only the plus (+) operator is used in this section. Other mathematical operators are discussed under the "Mathematical Operators" section.

1 Move to Cell D4

Cell locations that are part of formulas can be typed or pointed to. In this example, you will type the first formula, but point to the second.

2 Type `=B4+C4` and press ↵

Remember that the initial equal symbol is needed to indicate that this entry is a formula. The formula will compute the total (700) for Cells B4 and C4, which contain all of Michaels' sales figures. Now, enter the next Column D formula—for Cell D5—using the pointing method:

3 Move to Cell D5 and press `=` (equal)

4 Press ← twice to move to Cell B5

Note that a light-color-dashed cell pointer appears and moves to Cell B5 as you press the ← key. In addition, Excel types the B5 cell address for you in the formula bar and Cell D5.

5 Press `+`

6 Move to Cell C5

This address is also placed on the formula bar and Cell D5.

7 Press ↵ to accept the formula =B5+C5

8 Move back to Cell D5 for a moment

Note that =B5+C5 appears in the formula bar while 650, the result of the formula, appears in Cell D5 as in Figure SS1-19a.

Although this example shows typed formulas for clarity, you may use either method to enter formulas: either type the entire formula or type the math operators but *point* to the cells. Now, complete the Column D entries:

9 In Cell D6, type `=B6+C6`

10 In Cell D7, type `=B7+C7` and press ↵

Your workbook should resemble Figure SS1-19b. If it does not, return to the cell that is incorrect, retype, and enter the correction.

FIGURE SS1-19 ■ USING FORMULAS

(a) Moving the cell pointer to a cell that contains a formula will display its formula in the formula bar. Note that only the result of the formula appears in the cell.

(b) The sales worksheet with total formulas added is shown in Column D.

(c) Adding the SUM function in Row 8 completes the worksheet.

(a)

	A	B	C	D	E	F	
	D5	▼	=B5+C5 ◀— Formula				
	A	B	C	D	E	F	
1	Your Name				M/D/YY		
2							
3	Agent	Region A	Region B	Totals			
4	Michaels	500	200	700			
5	Martin	200	450	650 ◀—			
6	Parker	300	325				

Result of formula

(b)

	A	B	C	D	E	F	G
1	Your Name				M/D/YY		
2							
3	Agent	Region A	Region B	Totals			
4							
5	Michaels	500	200	700			
6	Martin	200	450	650			
7	Parker	300	325	625			
8	Williams	50	125	175			
9	Totals						
10							

(c)

	A	B	C	D	E	F
1	Your Name				M/D/YY	
2						
3	Agent	Region A	Region B	Totals		
4	Michaels	500	200	700		
5	Martin	200	450	650		
6	Parker	300	325	625		
7	Williams	50	125	175		
8	Totals	1050	1100	2150		
9						
10						

11 Save the SHEET1 workbook again   [Ctrl + S]

ENTERING FORMULAS—FUNCTIONS. Although you could enter formulas using cell references and mathematical operators to compute the totals in Row 8, an easier method uses one of Excel's many built-in functions. For example, the formula =B4+B5+B6+B7 typed into Cell B8 would correctly compute the total of the sales figures in Row B, but it is cumbersome to use. Imagine having to total 100 cells—the typing would take forever. Instead, you can invoke a built-in SUM function as follows:

STEPS

1 Move to Cell B8

2 Type =SUM(B4:B7) and press ↵

The SUM function instructs the program to compute the total for all the cell values listed in the range specified within the parentheses (more on range shortly). That is, the program will add all the cells between B4 and B7, which includes B4, B5, B6, and B7. If you wanted to add all cells from Z1 to Z1000, you would type the range as (Z1:Z1000). As you can see, this is much easier than typing every cell address.

Enter the remaining functions as follows:

3 In Cell C8, type =SUM(C4:C7)

4 In Cell D8, type   =SUM(D4:D7)   and press ↵

Your screen should resemble Figure SS1-19c. If it does not, return to the cell that is incorrect, retype, and enter the correction.

5 Save the SHEET1 workbook again and then close it

Note that Cell D8 contains the grand total, which can be computed many ways. The function SUM(D4:D7) summed the totals for each agent, but you could have also summed the totals for each region with =B8+C8, or you could have totaled all the individual sales figures with SUM(B4:C7). See the appendix for a comprehensive list of functions.

> **Tip:** There are many ways to compute a result. Although you should be consistent and rational, as long as your math is correct it doesn't matter what formula or function you use.

THE RECALCULATION FEATURE

A powerful spreadsheet feature is **automatic recalculation,** which recalculates formulas whenever values in related cells are changed. This feature allows you to update or modify values and see their mathematical consequences immediately.

STEPS

1 Launch Excel or close any open workbook

 2 Click *File, Open*   [Ctrl + O]

3 Type   SHEET1   in the *File name* text box

4 If needed, click the / button of the *Look in* drop down box and then *3½ Floppy (A:)* to set the default drive to A

5 Click the *Open* button   [↵]

6 Move to Cell B4

7 Type   600   and press ↵

This action changes Michaels' Region A sales from 500 to 600. As shown in Figure SS1-20, not only did the value in Cell B4 change, but also, because of automatic recalculation, values changed in Cells B8, D4, and D8. Compare the results with the original spreadsheet in Figure SS1-19c. Every cell whose value depended on the value in Cell B4 has changed.

FIGURE SS1-20 ■ THE RECALCULATION FEATURE

A change in Cell B4 causes related cells (D4, B8 and D8) to change as well.

	A	B	C	D	E	F	
1	Your Name				M/D/YY		
2							
3	Agent	Region A	Region B	Totals			
4	Michaels	600	200	800			
5	Martin	200	450	650			
6	Parker	300	325	625	These cells change automatically to show new results		
7	Williams	50	125	175			
8	Totals	1150	1100	2250			
9							
10							
11							

ANSWERING "WHAT IF?" QUESTIONS.   The recalculation feature greatly expands the utility of electronic spreadsheets. Certainly, interrelating cells with formulas simplifies worksheet use, but it also allows easy modification and enhanced decision making. Most businesspeople go through an extensive series of "What if?" scenarios when making key decisions. For example, what if Region A totals are 10 percent lower? Or what if Williams increases Region A sales to 500?

The ultimate effect of a change often depends on dozens of interdependent figures. Consider all the values that must be recalculated to answer a simply stated financial question like, "What if some of my income is deferred into the next fiscal year?" How does this one action affect personal income-tax deductions, adjustments, and, ultimately, tax liability? On the company's side, how are its payments for social security, withholding, pensions, and bonuses affected?

To examine how making changes affect column and row totals,

STEPS

1 Change a few values in Cells B4 through C7

2 Close the workbook without saving when you are finished

Remember, to close a workbook without saving, click its *Close* button (right side of menu bar) and then click the *No* button. With the keyboard, press the Ctrl + F4 keys and then the N key.

A FURTHER WORD ON FORMULAS AND CONSTANT VALUES.   In the last exercise, you modified cells with numeric constant values, but not those with formulas. Remember that a workbook shows a formula's *result,* not the formula itself. Although a formula result of 200 and a numeric constant value of 200 may look identical in a cell, they are not interchangeable. Formulas are "flexible" in that they can be recalculated; constant numeric values are not. If you replace a formula with a value, even though the number appears to be the same, the result can no longer be recalculated. Therefore, if you erase a formula by mistake, do not simply type its current result back into the cell. Instead, retype the *formula* to ensure that future recalculations will be mathematically correct.

MATHEMATICAL OPERATORS

As discussed earlier, a *mathematical operator* is a character used in a formula that tells the program to perform a certain calculation. A number of operators are available for you to use:

^ (caret)	exponentiation
* (asterisk)	multiplication
/ (slash)	division
+ (plus)	addition
– (minus)	subtraction

As in normal mathematics, when these operators are used in combination, the *hierarchy of operations,* or order of precedence of the operators, is as follows: (1) exponentiation is performed first; (2) multiplication and division are performed next, in order reading from left to right; and (3) addition and subtraction are last, also performed in order from left to right.

When parentheses surround parts of a formula, however, the operation inside the parentheses takes precedence. More than one pair of parentheses are evaluated from innermost to outermost, and from left to right.

> **Tip:** The sentence "Please excuse my dear Aunt Sally" (for Parentheses, Exponentiation, Multiplication, Division, Addition, Subtraction) is a helpful mnemonic device for remembering the hierarchy of operations.

To see how the hierarchy works, consider the following formula:

$$=A1/A2-A3*A4^2$$

This results in the following sequence of computations:

1 The value in Cell A4 is raised to the second power

2 The value in Cell A1 is divided by the value in Cell A2

3 The value in Cell A3 is multiplied by the result of Step 1

4 Step 3's result is subtracted from the result of Step 2

If A1 = 6, A2 = 4, A3 = 2, and A4 = 3, the result would be + 6/4 – 2*3^2, or –16.5.
    Now consider the same formula with added parentheses:

$$=A1/(A2-A3)*A4^2$$

This formula produces a different sequence:

1 Cell A3's value is subtracted from the value in Cell A2

2 The value in Cell A4 is raised to the second power

3 The value in Cell A1 is divided by the result of Step 1

4 The result of Step 3 is multiplied by the result of Step 2

This formula, using the same cell values as before, yields a result of 27.

Figure SS1-21 provides further practice with evaluating the hierarchy of operations by listing a few illustrative formulas and their results.

☑ CHECKPOINT

✓ On a new workbook, type in the number 1234 as a text constant value in Cell A1. Which character did you type before the number?
✓ What key must be entered to identify an entry as a formula?
✓ In Cell A3, enter a formula that will add 5 to a value in Cell A2.
✓ What is the result of the formula $6 + (3*2)^2-(12/2)*7$?
✓ Describe the mathematical operators that can be used in an Excel formula.

THE RANGE CONCEPT

Although data can be manipulated cell by cell, much of a spreadsheet's power comes from its ability to affect a large group of cells at one time. Many of Excel's commands (formatting, copying, moving, printing, erasing, inserting, sorting, and charting, to name a few) rely on your ability to describe a *range* of spreadsheet cells. As shown in Figure SS1-22, a **range** is a rectangular grouping of one or more cells. Because of its shape, a range can easily be identified by indicating its diagonal corners. That is, to identify a range, specify the cell in its upper left corner, followed by a colon (for separation

SS

FIGURE SS1-21 ■ SOME HIERARCHY EXAMPLES

If A1 = 3, A2 = 4, A3 = 5, A4 = 6:

Mathematical Operation	Answer
=A1/A2 + A3*A4	30.75
=A1/(A2 + A3)*A4	2.0
=(A1/A2 + A3)*A4	34.5
=(A1^2 + A3)/(A2 + A4)	1.4
=A4 − A1/A2*A3	2.25
=(A4 − A1)/(A2*A3)	0.15

FIGURE SS1-22 ■ EXAMPLES OF TYPICAL RANGES

	A	B	C	D	E	F	G	H	I	
1										
2										
3		25		640	318	32	←—D3:F3			
4		710								
5		715	←— B3:B10							
6		920								
7		920			512	512	512			
8		215			512	512	512			
9		110			512	512	512			
10		25			512	512	512			
11	Multiple ranges				512	512	512			
12					512	512	512			
13					512	512	512			
14			800		512	512	512			
15					512	512	512			
16					512	512	512	←— E7:G16		
17										
18			C14:C14							

purposes), and then the cell in its lower right corner. Thus, the range E8:G19 indicates all 36 cells in the Cell E8 through Cell G19 (Columns E, F, and G; Rows 8 and 19). Ranges can contain a single cell or many cells grouped in one or more rows or columns.

Excel also allows the selection of several (multiple) ranges that may be separate, touching, or overlapping. This process is discussed in the appendix. The following exercise explores the fundamentals of specifying a single range.

STEPS

1 Launch Excel or close any open workbook

 2 If needed, open a new workbook (Click *File*, *New*, *OK* or press   Ctrl + N , ↵)

3 Enter the data into eight cells as shown in Figure SS1-23a

Assume you want to create two sums in Cells B7 and C7, which will total their respective columns. You can specify a range by typing its endpoints or pointing to them.

TYPING A RANGE FOR A FUNCTION

The most direct way to identify a range is to type it, as you did in the section on functions. Try one more here:

STEPS

1 Move to Cell B7

FIGURE SS1-23 ■ IDENTIFYING RANGES

(a) Data for cells B2 through C5.

(b) Pointing to the first cell in a range places its cell address in the formula bar and cell.

(c) Pressing and holding the Shift key while moving the pointer selects the range with a light dashed outline and types the cell address in the formula bar and cell.

(d) The completed range has been entered.

	A	B	C	D
1				
2		10	7	
3		7	6	
4		81	78	
5		2	1	
6				
7				
8				

(a)

C2   =SUM(C2

	A	B	C	D
1				
2		10	7	
3		7	6	
4		81	78	
5		2	1	
6				
7			100 =SUM(C2	
8				

(b)

C2   =SUM(C2:C5

	A	B	C	D
1				
2		10	7	
3		7	6	
4		81	78	
5		2	1	
6				
7			100 =SUM(C2:C5	
8				

(c)

	A	B	C	D
1				
2		10	7	
3		7	6	
4		81	78	
5		2	1	
6				
7		100	92	
8				

(d)

2 Type   **=SUM(B2:B5)**

3 Press ↵

The cells included within the parentheses of the SUM function identify a range whose upper left corner is Cell B2 and whose lower right corner is Cell B5. The function then computes the sum of this cell range.

POINTING TO A RANGE FOR A FUNCTION

You may prefer to point to cells to specify a range. Not only does this save typing, but the screen will also visually display the range as you define it. Try this:

STEPS

1 **Move to Cell C7**

2 **Type =SUM(** (but do *not* press the Enter key)

(Be sure to type an opening parenthesis after SUM.)

Tip: Clicking the Function wizard (*fx*) button opens a dialog box with a list of functions.

Of course, you could type the range (C2:C5) as before, but try pointing instead, as follows:

3 Click *Cell C2*   [↑ to C2]

Notice how the program simultaneously types the cell address (C2) in the entry area of the formula bar and in Cell C7 as shown in Figure SS1-23b. A "Point" message also appears in the status bar.

4 Press and hold Shift while clicking *Cell C5*   [**Shift** + ↓ to Cell C5]

Cell C5's address appears on the formula bar and in the current cell as shown in Figure SS1-23c. Notice, too, that a light-dashed outline appears around the cell range C2 through C5—a helpful visual indication of the selected range. To complete the function,

5 Press ↵

Note that Excel automatically places a ")" at the end of the function. Your screen should now resemble Figure SS1-23d.

6 Save as SAMPLE2 by clicking *File, Save As*

(Remember to change the default drive to A if needed.) For clarity, this module gives instructions that specify ranges by typing them, but you may point or type ranges as you prefer. Keep in mind, though, that you cannot mix techniques within one range specification. If you type the first cell in a range, you must type the second. If you point to the first, point to the second.

SELECTING A RANGE FOR TOOLBAR OR MENU COMMANDS

You can also set a range for use with many toolbar or menu commands using a mouse or the keyboard. Do the following to prepare for the next exercises:

STEPS

1 Move to Cell C7

2 Click *Edit, point to Clear* **and then click** *All* **to erase the sum**   [**Delete**]

3 Move to Cell C2

A few common techniques to set a range prior to clicking a toolbar button are discussed next.

SELECTING A RANGE USING THE SHIFT KEY.   To select the range C2:C7 using the Shift key as part of the command,

1 Press and hold Shift while clicking *Cell C7*   [Shift + ↓ five times]

Before invoking the Auto Sum command, note that Excel's AutoCalculate feature displays the sum of the items in the range in the status bar (SUM=92). The *AutoCalculate* feature can therefore serve as an on-line calculator. It allows you to sum items without entering a formula in a cell.

At this point, you can invoke a command to affect the range by using the menu bar or toolbar. Try this:

Σ   **2** Point to and click the *Auto Sum* button

The sum will appear at the bottom cell of the range, which must be left empty. Now, to remove the range,

3 Click *Cell C7* (or any cell)   [↓ to Cell C7]

SELECTING A RANGE BY DRAGGING.   To set a range by dragging your mouse over the desired range,

1 In Cell C7, click *Edit, Clear, All,* and then Cell C2

2 Point to *Cell C2* and then press and hold the left mouse button

3 While holding the mouse button, point to *Cell C7*

4 Release the button

The range *C2:C7* is highlighted. Steps 2 and 3 is called dragging and Step 4, dropping. Now that your range has been selected, you can invoke a variety of commands by using toolbar or menu commands. Try this:

   5 Point to and click the Auto Sum button

6 Remove the selection highlight (click any other cell)

7 Close the workbook without saving

> **Tip:** These range selection techniques can be used whenever a range is selected before invoking a command.

SS

SELECTING MULTIPLE RANGES.   Many commands can also be invoked on multiple ranges. To select a multiple range, select the first range using any of the previous techniques. Press and hold the Ctrl key while selecting each additional range.

 CHECKPOINT

✓   Create the worksheet in Figure SS1-23 and then, using the pointing method, create a sum in Cell B7 that totals all cells from B2 to B5.
✓   Using the typing method, create a sum in Cell C7 that totals all cells from C2 to C5.
✓   Using either typing or pointing, create a sum in D7 that totals all cells from B2 to C5. Save as SAMPLE2.
✓   How do you delete a cell entry?
✓   Describe the procedures to use the Auto Sum toolbar button.

PRINTING A WORKSHEET

Most spreadsheets are ultimately printed on paper. To prepare for this exercise,

STEPS

1   Launch Excel or close any open workbook

2   Open SHEET1

You are now ready to print the spreadsheet. In this exercise, you will print the entire worksheet, from Cell A1 to Cell E10. Excel allows you to print to your screen (using the Print Preview feature) or to a printer. You may also print a selected range of a worksheet, multiple worksheets, specific pages of a worksheet, the entire workbook, or multiple copies. The exercises in this section illustrate print previewing, printing the current worksheet, and then printing a selected range of a worksheet.

PRINTING TO THE SCREEN

Excel's Print Preview feature allows you to view a worksheet or a selected range of a worksheet as it will appear on paper. Try this:

STEPS

1   Click *File* and then *Print Preview* for its window

The top of your Print Preview window should appear similar to Figure SS1-24a. To enlarge the view of the worksheet,

2   Click the *Zoom* toolbar button   [↵]

Your screen should resemble Figure SS1-24b. The Print Preview toolbar can also be used to invoke a variety of other commands. Now, to return to the workbook,

FIGURE SS1-24 ■ THE PRINT PREVIEW WINDOW

(a) The print preview
window.
(b) Zooming the view of a
worksheet.

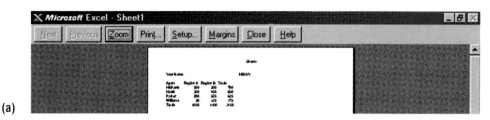

(a)

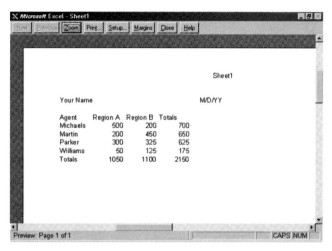

(b)

---

3 Click the *Close* toolbar button   [Esc]

> **Tip:** To zoom in on a particular area of the worksheet while in the Print Preview window, point to and then click the area.

PRINTING TO A PRINTER

To print the current worksheet to your printer,

STEPS

1 Turn on your printer

2 Click *File* and then *Print* for its dialog box   [Ctrl + P]

The *Print* dialog box should appear as in Figure SS1-25a. Note that its default setting is to print the current worksheet (selected sheet[s]). Other print options include printing a specific range of a worksheet (selection), the entire workbook, specified pages, and

FIGURE SS1-25 ■ PRINTING THE CURRENT WORKSHEET

(a) The *Print* dialog box.
(b) The printed worksheet.

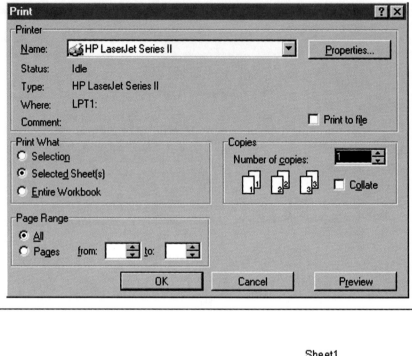

(a)

(b)

multiple copies. You can also access the Print Preview feature and make page setup changes using this dialog box. To print the entire worksheet,

3 **Click the *OK* button**   [↵]

The contents of your printed worksheet should appear as in Figure SS1-25b. Note that the column and row identifiers do not appear on the printed spreadsheet, only in the contents of the worksheet cells themselves. Excel also prints the tab's name in the top center of the worksheet and the page number at the bottom. In this case, "Sheet1" and "Page 1." Later you will learn how to change this.

PRINTING A SELECTED RANGE

At times, you may want to print only a portion of a worksheet. To do so, you must first tell Excel your desired range. For example, to print only Columns A and B of SHEET1, follow these steps:

STEPS

1 Select the range A1:B8

2 Click *File* and then *Print* for its dialog box   [**Ctrl** + **P**]

3 Click the *Selection* option in the Print What group

To print the selected range,

4 Click the *OK* button   [↵]

Your printed copy should resemble Figure SS1-26. As before, column and row identifiers are not printed.

5 Close the workbook without saving

> **Tip:** You can also use the Print Area feature to print a selected range. To do so, click *File*, point to *Print Area*, click *Set Print Area*, select the desired print range, click *File*, *Print*, *OK*.

SS

FIGURE SS1-26 ■ PRINTING A SELECTED RANGE

Sheet1

Your Name

Agent	Region A
Michaels	500
Martin	200
Parker	300
Williams	50
Totals	1050

CHECKPOINT

✓ What does the Print Preview command do?
✓ What does the Zoom command do in the Print Preview window?
✓ Print out the cells in Column B only.
✓ Print out the cells in Columns B and C on a new page.
✓ Print both of these ranges on the *same page*.

EDITING A WORKSHEET

At some point, you may want to change cell data. Perhaps you want to correct a mistake or change a constant value or formula. To prepare for this exercise,

STEPS

1 **Launch Excel or close any open workbook**

2 **Open SHEET1**

It should resemble Figure SS1-19c.

REPLACING CELL CONTENTS

There are three basic ways to change the contents of a cell: (1) move to the cell and retype its contents, (2) use the Edit mode to insert or delete characters, or (3) erase a cell's contents through the *Command* menu. The following exercises briefly present each technique.

RETYPING. The most direct way to replace cell contents is to move to the cell and retype its data. For example,

STEPS

1 **In Cell A4, type** **Smith**

2 **In Cell C5, type** **575** **and press** **↵**

The previous contents (Michaels and 450) have been replaced with the new entries. This technique works well when completely different data must be entered, but you must retype the entire entry even when minor changes are needed.

EDITING. A better method for minor adjustments is to use the Edit mode. This is particularly useful when you have created long formulas and do not want to reenter them. Any cell data can be edited with the following procedure:

STEPS

■ 1   **Move to Cell B7**

■ 2   **Double-click *Cell B7* to invoke the Edit mode**   [F2]

Note that "Edit" appears on the left side of the status bar. You can now use the arrow keys to move the insertion point and then type additional characters (or delete them) as needed.

■ 3   **If needed press the arrow keys to move the insertion point before the 5 in 50.**

Your Cell B7 should resemble Figure SS1-27.

■ 4   **Type 1**

The new character is inserted at the insertion-point location. Notice that the number now reads *150.*

■ 5   **Press ↵ to accept the change**

Here's another example:

■ 6   **Move back to Cell B7**

■ 7   **Double-click Cell B7**   [F2]

Again, the cell contents appear on the entry line.

■ 8   **Move the insertion point before the *1* in *150***

■ 9   **Press Delete**

The 150 has been changed back to 50.

■ 10   **Press ↵ to accept the change**

FIGURE SS1-27 ■ EDITING A CELL

Double-clicking a cell or pressing F2 invokes the Edit mode and activates the insertion point.

6	Parker	300
7	Williams	→50
8	Totals	1050

Insertion point

SS

After double-clicking the cell or pressing F2, you may use the Home key to move quickly to the beginning of a long cell entry, or press the End key to move to the end. Try this on your own. You may also want to experiment with the Insert key (which turns on the typeover feature) and the Backspace key.

ERASING CELLS.   At times, you will simply want to erase cell contents. The *Edit* menu offers a Clear command for this purpose.

STEPS

1 **Move to Cell E1**

2 **Click _Edit_, point to _Clear_, and then click _All_**   [**Delete**   ]

The date is gone.

> **Tip:** When you use the *Edit* menu to invoke the Clear command, a *Clear* submenu offers four options: *All* deletes everything in the cell, *Formats* deletes only style formats, *Contents* deletes the constant value or formula in the cell, and *Notes* deletes any note attached to the cell. *Format* relates to text and graphic enhancement.

You can also erase a range of cells by specifying the range *before* pressing the Enter key as follows:

3 **Move to Cell D3**

4 **Press and hold   Shift   while clicking _Cell D8_**

5 **Click _Edit_, point to _Clear_ and then click _All_**   [**Delete**   ]

6 **Click _Cell D3_ (or any cell) to remove the range selection highlight**

All data in Cells D3:D8 have been deleted.

UNDOING AN ACTION.   The **Undo** command (in the *Edit* menu) can be used to undo your last action. Try this:

STEPS

1 **Click _Edit_ and then _Undo Clear_**   [**Ctrl**   +   **Z**   ]

The last set of erased cells returns to the screen.

2 Remove the range selection

3 Close the workbook without saving

INSERTING AND DELETING ROWS OR COLUMNS

Rows or columns can be added to or removed from your worksheet using the Rows or Columns command (in the *Insert* menu). The following exercise inserts rows before and after the list of names in SHEET1, inserts a column between the region sales data, and then deletes it.

INSERTING A ROW.   The basic technique for inserting a row is to position the pointer where you want the new row to appear and then invoke the Rows command (in the *Insert* menu). Try this:

STEPS

1 Open SHEET1

2 Move to Cell A4 (any cell in Row 4 will do)

Your screen should resemble Figure SS1-28a.

3 Click *Insert* and then *Rows*

A new row appears in Row 4, as shown in Figure SS1-28b. All rows below the new one have been moved down one row and all formulas have been adjusted.

4 Move to Cell B9 and examine its contents in the formula bar

FIGURE SS1-28 ■ INSERTING A ROW

(a) The Cell pointer is positioned in Row 4, where the new row will be inserted. (b) When the new row is inserted, all rows below it shift down one row.

	A	B	C	D	E	F
1	Your Name				M/D/YY	
2						
3	Agent	Region A	Region B	Totals		
4	Michaels	500	200	700		
5	Martin	200	450	650		
6	Parker	300	325	625		
7	Williams	50	125	175		
8	Totals	1050	1100	2150		
9						
10						
11						

(a)

	A	B	C	D	E	F
1	Your Name				M/D/YY	
2						
3	Agent	Region A	Region B	Totals		
4						
5	Michaels	500	200	700		
6	Martin	200	450	650		
7	Parker	300	325	625		
8	Williams	50	125	175		
9	Totals	1050	1100	2150		
10						
11						

(b)

Note that the formula has been adjusted to reflect the added row. The formula range now reads B5:B8 instead of B4:B7. The program automatically adjusts all formulas affected by adding rows (or columns).

A note of caution: Rows added *outside* a function's stated range will *not* be included in the adjusted function range. For a new row to be included, it must be added *within* the endpoints—upper left to lower right cell of the function's range. For example, you just added a row *above* the old Row 4, outside the range B4:B7. If you were to type data into this row, it would not be included in the column total (unless, of course, you edited the range yourself to include it). However, if you had added the row within the range endpoints—that is, between Row 4 and Row 7—the program would automatically extend the range to include it. Keep this in mind when adding rows or columns. Now, add one more row as follows:

5 **Stay in Cell B9 (any cell in Row 9 will do)**

6 **Click _Insert_ and then _Rows_**

7 **Save this spreadsheet as SHEET2 (click _File_, _Save As_)**

To insert more than one row, you must first select the desired range to be inserted.

8 **Move to Cell A2**

9 **Press and hold   Shift   while clicking _Cell A4_ to select a range of three rows**

Three rows are now selected on the screen to be added. Note that the first cell of a selected range contains the cell pointer (the anchor cell). All subsequent cells of the range are highlighted.

10 **Press and hold   Shift   while clicking _Cell A3_**

Now only two rows are selected (including Cell A2). You can adjust the number of rows to be added before invoking the insertion feature.

11 **Click _Insert_ and then _Rows_ to insert the two rows**

Two rows have now been added to your worksheet.

INSERTING A COLUMN.   You can insert a column (in this case, between Columns B and C) by following the same procedure, but choose *Columns* instead of *Rows* from the *Insert* menu.

---

1 **Move to Cell C6 (any cell in Column C will do)**

2 **Click _Insert_ and then _Columns_ to insert a column**

A new column has been inserted at Column C, and all columns that follow have been moved to the right.

3   **Move to Cell E7 and examine this cell's contents**

The formula now reads =B7+D7, reflecting that Column C is now Column D.

4   **Save this spreadsheet as SHEET3**

> **Tip: Formulas do not include the inserted row or column in their calculations but simply adjust their current cell references to their new locations. Only ranges can expand automatically to reflect inserted rows or columns.**

DELETING A ROW OR COLUMN.   You can delete rows and columns with a similar technique—move to the row or column to be deleted, and use the *Delete* dialog box of the *Edit* menu.

STEPS

1   **Open SHEET3 (if needed)**

2   **Move to Cell C7 (any cell in Column C will do)**

3   **Press *Edit* and then *Delete* for the *Delete* dialog box**

4   **Click *Entire Column* and then the *OK* button**

The column is gone. All columns to its right are shifted left, and all formulas are readjusted to reflect the change.

    More than one row or column can be deleted by selecting its range, as before.

5   **Move to Cell C2 (any cell in Row 2 is fine)**

6   **Press and hold   Shift   while clicking *Cell C3* to highlight two rows of cells**

7   **Click *Edit* and then *Delete* for the *Delete* dialog box**

8   **Click the *Entire Row* and then the *OK* button**

Column D and Row 10 should now display the totals. If they do not, use the Undo command or open SHEET3, and repeat the Delete procedure. To exit Excel without saving the worksheet and then shut down Windows,

 9   **Click Excel's *Close* button and then the *No* button**

10 Click the *Start* button

11 Click *Shut Down*

12 Click the *Yes* button

[**Ctrl** + **Esc**]

☑ CHECKPOINT

✓ Open SHEET1. With typeover, change *Williams* in Cell A7 to *West* and *200* in C4 to *375*. Use the Edit mode to remove the "s" in *Totals* in Cells D1 and A8.

✓ Insert a row at Row 6. Fill in the four new cells with Burstein, *100, 150,* and the formula *=B6+C6*. Print the worksheet.

✓ Insert a column at Column A, save as SHEET3a, and exit Excel and shut down Windows.

✓ Describe how to delete a row.

✓ Describe how to delete a column.

SUMMARY

■ A spreadsheet, or worksheet, displays data in columnar form. It is composed of cells formed by vertical columns and horizontal rows.

■ The Excel window has a title bar, menu bar, toolbars, formula bar, workspace, and status bar.

■ The workbook window occupies Excel window's workspace and displays only a portion of the entire spreadsheet, identifying columns with letters and rows with numbers. Each cell is identified by a cell address, which displays the cell's column and row coordinates.

■ The current cell will receive data or be affected by the next command. The current cell is indicated by a cell pointer that resembles a dark-bordered rectangle in the workbook window and a cell address in the name box of the formula bar.

■ When the cell pointer is moved off the workbook window's display area by keyboard, the worksheet will scroll—or reposition itself—to display the current cell. Scrolling by mouse requires using the vertical or horizontal scroll bars of the workbook window.

■ Excel features can be accessed by mouse or keyboard through its menu bar. Each menu bar item opens to a pull-down menu. Selecting by mouse involves clicking the menu bar item and then the menu item. With the keyboard, pressing the Alt key and the underlined letter of the menu bar item opens its menu. Pressing the underlined letter of the menu item selects the item.

■ Toolbars contain a series of command buttons and drop-down boxes that provide quick access to the program's features by mouse. Shortcut keys are also available for many commands to provide fast keyboard access to Excel features.

■ The status bar, the bottom row of the Excel window, displays the mode indicator (which shows what the program is doing), a description of a selected command, the Autocalculate message, the caps lock, the number lock, and the scroll lock indicators.

■ Constant values are data directly entered into a cell. Data may include text or numeric values. Text includes any combination of alphabetic (A–Z), numeric (0–9), or special characters (?, *, and so forth). Numeric values are numbers without any alphabetic text that can be used in mathematical operations. A constant value will not change unless you edit it.

■ Formulas must start with an equal sign (=). They perform mathematical operations on data in other cells. They may include a sequence of constant values, cell addresses, operators (*/=−^), and functions.

■ A function is a predetermined formula built into the spreadsheet.

■ Formulas follow the hierarchy of operations: parentheses, exponentiation (^), multiplication (*) or division (/), and addition (+) or subtraction (−).

■ The recalculation feature automatically recalculates formulas when values in related cells are changed. This feature allows "What if?" questions to be investigated.

■ A range is a rectangular grouping of cells. It is identified by specifying diagonal corners—its upper-left cell and lower-right cell (or lower-left and upper-right cells)—separated by a period. Ranges can be designated by typing, pointing, or dragging.

■ The chapter presented the following commands (Remember, to select from a pull-down menu by mouse, click the menu bar item for its pull-down menu, and then click the menu item. By keyboard, press the Alt + underlined letter of the menu bar item for its pull-down menu, and then press the underlined letter of the menu item.)

Command	Menu Bar	Shortcut Key(s)
Save a workbook	*File, Save*	Ctrl+S
Save a workbook with a different filename	*File, Save As*	F12
Open a workbook	*File, Open*	Ctrl+O
Create a new workbook	*File, New*	Ctrl+N
Print a workbook/worksheet	*File, Print*	Ctrl+P
Close a workbook	*File, Close*	Ctrl+F4 or Ctrl+W
Exit Excel	*File, Exit*	Alt+F4
Undo an action	*Edit, Undo*	Ctrl+Z
Help	*Help, Microsoft Excel Help Topics*	F1
Edit a cell	Double-click the cell	F2
Clear a cell	*Edit, Clear, All*	Delete
Insert a row or column	*Insert, Row or Column*	
Delete a row or column	*Edit, Delete, Entire Row* or *Entire Column, OK*	

KEY TERMS

Shown in parentheses are the page numbers on which key terms are boldfaced.

AutoCalculate (SS14)
Automatic recalculation (SS44)
Cell (SS14)

Cell address (SS14)
Cell pointer (SS14)
Closing (SS32)
Command buttons (SS13)

Constant value (SS37)
Current cell (SS14)
Drop-down box (SS13)
Entry area (SS20)

Formula (SS37) Numeric value (SS37) Sheet (SS12)
Formula bar (SS13) Open (SS34) *Shortcut* menu (SS25)
Function (SS37) Pull-down menu (SS13) Spreadsheet (SS2)
Mathematical operator Range (SS47) Status bar (SS13)
  (SS42) Save (SS31) Toolbar (SS13)
MouseKeys (SS9) Save As (SS31) Undo (SS58)
Name box (SS19) Scroll (SS14) Workbook (SS12)
New (SS33) Scroll bar (SS16) Worksheet (SS2)

QUIZ

TRUE/FALSE

____ 1. A workbook may contain only a worksheet.
____ 2. Columns are identified by letters.
____ 3. The current cell is visually identified by the cell pointer.
____ 4. Pressing the Home key moves the cell pointer to the center of the worksheet.
____ 5. The current cell address is normally displayed in the formula bar.
____ 6. The menu bar pull-down menu can be opened by pressing the Ctrl key and the underlined letter of the item.
____ 7. To close Excel or a workbook window, click its *Close* (X) button.
____ 8. Formulas must start with an apostrophe to be recognized by the program.
____ 9. Excel functions must begin with an = symbol.
____ 10. Excel treats the typed entry E1 + E2 as a constant value.

MULTIPLE CHOICE

____ 11. Which of these is *not* part of the Excel window?
       a. Menu bar
       b. Taskbar
       c. Workspace
       d. Status bar
____ 12. Which of the following displays the column and row coordinates of a cell?
       a. Formula bar
       b. Cell pointer
       c. Status bar
       d. Window
____ 13. ____ refers to automatically repositioning the worksheet area window to show the current cell.
       a. Windowing
       b. Addressing
       c. Pointing
       d. Scrolling
____ 14. Which of these is *never* displayed in the formula bar?
       a. Entry area
       b. Cell address

    c. Date and time

    d. Command button(s)

___ 15. Which of these displays a one-word message that shows what the spreadsheet is currently doing?

    a. Status bar

    b. Toolbar

    c. Menu bar

    d. Cell pointer

___ 16. Which key(s) can be used to open a pull-down menu?

    a. The Alt key

    b. The Alt key and the underlined letter of a menu bar item

    c. The Esc key

    d. The underlined letter of a menu bar item

___ 17. Which one of these cell entries is *not* a formula?

    a. =35+C7

    b. =A5*B6

    c. =SUM(B7:B23)

    d. 52

___ 18. A phone number entry typed as 718-555-1212 will be treated as which of the following by Excel?

    a. A function

    b. A formula

    c. A constant value number

    d. A constant value text

___ 19. The range "rectangle" is normally specified from

    a. Upper left to lower right

    b. Upper left to upper right

    c. Upper right to lower right

    d. Lower left to lower right

___ 20. How would =SUM(B2:B5) change after a column is inserted with the cell pointer in Cell B3?

    a. =SUM(B3:B6)

    b. =SUM(C2:C5)

    c. =SUM(B2:B6)

    d. =SUM(C2:C6)

MATCHING

Select the lettered item from the figure on page SS66 that best matches each phrase below:

___ 21. A series of command buttons that can be used to access Excel features quickly.

___ 22. Displays a window's name.

___ 23. The Excel cell pointer.

___ 24. A standard Windows feature that opens to pull-down menus containing commands related to the program.

___ 25. The function command in Cell D8.

___ 26. The area of the Excel window called the formula bar.

___ 27. The AutoCalculate feature.

___ 28. The name box.

FIGURE SS1-A ■ **MATCHING FIGURE**

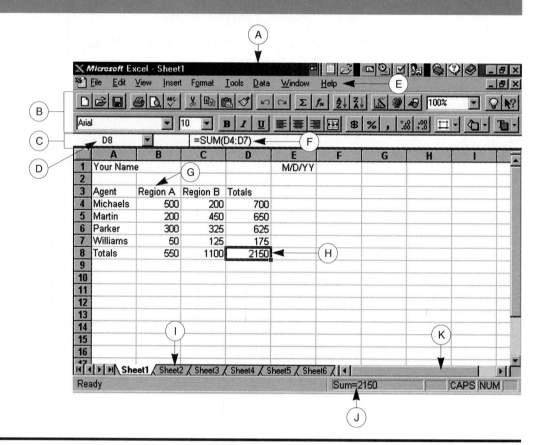

___ 29. The area of the window that indicates what the spreadsheet is currently doing.
___ 30. A constant value.

ANSWERS

True/False: 1. F; 2. T; 3. T; 4. F; 5. T; 6. F; 7. T; 8. F; 9. T; 10. T
Multiple Choice: 11. b; 12. a; 13. d; 14. c; 15. a; 16. b; 17. d; 18. d; 19. a; 20. b
Matching: 21. b; 22. a; 23. h; 24. e; 25. f; 26. c; 27. j; 28. d; 29. l; 30. g

EXERCISES

I. OPERATIONS

Provide the Excel mouse approach and keyboard approach actions (as appropriate) required to do each of the following operations. For each operation, assume a hard-disk system with a data diskette in Drive A. Further assume that the data diskette contains files named JULY and OCTOBER.

1. Start Windows and then launch Excel.

2. Set the default drive to A as you open OCTOBER.

3. Erase the contents of Cell E7.

4. Insert a row at Row 9.

5. Delete Column C.

6. Display a total of Cells B5 through B22 in Cell B24.

7. Print the worksheet so that it includes all cells up to Row 5 and Column F.

8. Save the workbook with its same name—OCTOBER.

9. Save the workbook with a new name—NOVEMBER.

10. Close the workbook.

11. Exit the program and then shut down Windows.

II. COMMANDS

Describe fully, using as few words as possible, what command is initiated or what is accomplished in Excel by the actions described below. Assume that each exercise part is independent of any previous parts.

1. Pressing the Ctrl + Home keys

2. Clicking the *Close* button of any window

3. Right-clicking a cell in a worksheet

4. Typing =C5*C6 and then pressing →

5. Pressing the Alt + F4 keys

6. Pressing the F1 key

7. Double-clicking the Excel title bar

8. Pressing the Ctrl + P keys

9. Pressing the Ctrl + F4 keys

10. Pressing the Ctrl + Esc keys

11. Pressing the Ctrl + Z keys

12. Pressing the Ctrl + S keys

13. Typing '165

III. APPLICATIONS

Perform the following operations, briefly tell how you accomplished each operation, and describe its results. Note: Of the six applications, each pair relates to school, home, and business, respectively.

APPLICATION 1: CLUB BUDGET

Save the workbook as CLUB1 after each operation is completed so that you can continue this exercise later. (Remember to set the default drive to A before saving the workbook.)

1. Start Windows and then launch Excel

2. Create the following spreadsheet. Enter your name in Cell A1 and the current date in Cell A2 as shown. Complete the rest of your spreadsheet to match the example.

	A	B	C	D	E	F
1	Your Name					
2	Date					
3						
4	ART CLUB BUDGET					
5						
6			JAN	FEB	MAR	TOTAL
7						
8	Meeting Expenses		50	60	70	
9	Art Supplies		75	50	80	
10	Guest Speakers		50	100	50	
11	Field Trips		150	125	100	
12	Art Exhibitions		300	350	400	
13						
14	Total Funds Needed					
15						
16						

3. Enter a formula in Cell F8 that will total the three months meeting expenses.

4. Enter similar formulas in Cells F9 through F12 to accomplish the same result on each respective row.

5. Enter a SUM function in Cell F14 to total all the expenses that appear in Column F.

6. Save this workbook as CLUB1. (Be sure to set the default drive to A if you haven't already done so.)

7. Type   **1st QUARTER**   in Cell D1. Print the spreadsheet.

8. Change the amount in Cell C9 to 65 and Cell E11 to 140.

9. Insert a Row 11 (between *Guest Speakers* and *Field Trips*). Type **Awards** in Cell A11, **75** in Cell C11, **100** in Cell D11, and **125** in Cell E11.
   Type a formula in Cell F11 to compute the total as before.

10. Type   **REVISED**   in Cell D2. Print the entire spreadsheet.

11. Delete Row 10 to remove *Guest Speakers*.

12. Print part of the spreadsheet that includes all cells from Cells A6 through Cell C12.

13. Place a SUM function in Cell C14 through Cell E14 to total each month's expenses.

14. Save the workbook as CLUB1, print the entire worksheet, exit the program and then shut down Windows.

APPLICATION 2: GPA

Save the workbook in this exercise as GPA1 after each operation is completed so that you can continue this exercise later. (Remember to set the default drive to A before you save the workbook.)

1. Start Windows and then launch Excel.

2. Create the following spreadsheet. Enter your name in Cell A1 and the current date in Cell A2 as shown. Complete the rest of your spreadsheet to match the example.

	A	B	C	D	E	F
1	Your Name					
2	Date					
3						
4	GRADES					
5						
6	COURSE	TERM	GRADE	CREDITS	POINTS	TOT.PTS.
7						
8	MUS101	9203	A	2	4	
9	ART102	9203	B	3	3	
10	BUS101	9203	A	3	4	
11	BUS105	9201	B	3	3	
12	HIS104	9301	B	3	3	
13						
14						

3. Enter a formula in Cell F8 that will multiply the credits in Cell D8 by the points in Cell E8.

4. Enter similar formulas in Cells F9 through F12 to accomplish the same result on each respective row.

5. Enter a SUM function in Cell F14 to total the five courses that appear in Column F.

6. Save this worksheet as GPA1. (Remember to set the default drive to A, if you haven't already done so.)

7. Type **SPRING 19XX** in Cell F1. Print the entire spreadsheet.

8. Change the grade in Cell C9 to A and the points in Cell E9 to 4.

9. Insert a row at Row 11 (between BUS101 and BUS105). Type **ENG103** in Cell A11, **9203** in Cell B11, **B** in Cell C11, **4** in Cell D11, and **3** in Cell E11. Type a formula in Cell F11 to compute the value as before.

10. Type   **UPDATED**   in Cell F2. Print the entire spreadsheet.

11. Delete Row 12 to remove BUS105.

12. Print the part of the spreadsheet that includes all cells from Cell A6 through Cell F12.

13. Place a SUM function in Cell D14 that totals the credits column.

14. Save the workbook as GPA1, print the entire worksheet, exit the program, and then shut down Windows.

APPLICATION 3: CHECKBOOK

Save the workbook as CHECK1 after each operation is completed so that you can continue this exercise later. (Remember to set the default drive to A before saving the workbook.)

1. Start Windows and then launch Excel.

2. Create the following spreadsheet. Enter your name in Cell A1 and the current date in Cell A2 as shown. Complete the rest of your spreadsheet to match the example.

	A	B	C	D	E	F	G	H
1	Your Name							
2	Date							
3								
4	CHECKING ACCOUNT							
5								
6	DATE	CHECK#	PAYEE		PMT	DEPOSIT	BALANCE	
7								
8	1-Jan		Deposit pay check			1200		
9	4-Jan	106	R. Landlord		600			
10	10-Jan	107	Telephone Co.		65			
11	15-Jan		Deposit pay check			1200		
12	28-Jan	109	Electric Co.		80			
13								
14								

3. Enter a formula in Cell G8 that substracts Cell E8 (PMT) from Cell F8 (Deposit) the starting balance.

4. Enter a formula in Cell G9 that starts with Cell G8, adds Cell F9, and then subtracts Cell E9 to calculate the balance.

5. Enter similar formulas in Cells G10 through G12 to accomplish the same result.

6. Save this workbook as CHECK1. (Remember to set the default drive to A if you haven't already done so.)

7. Type   **JAN 19XX**   in Cell E1. Print the spreadsheet.

8. Change the amount in Cell E9 to 700 and Cell F11 to 1400.

9. Insert a Row 11 (between *10-Jan* and *15-Jan*). Type   **12-Jan**   in Cell A11,   **108**   in Cell B11,   **Water Co.**   in Cell C11, and   **45**   in Cell E11. Type a formula in Cell G11 to compute the balance as before.

10. Type   **CORRECTED**   in Cell E2. Print the entire spreadsheet.

11. Delete Row 12 to remove *28-Jan.* and then adjust the formula in Cell G12

12. Print part of the spreadsheet that includes all cells from Cells A9 through Cell E12.

13. Place a SUM function in Cell E14 and Cell F14 to total the payments and deposits column.

14. Save the workbook as CHECK1, print the entire worksheet, exit the program, and then shut down Windows.

APPLICATION 4: INVESTMENTS

Save the workbook as INVEST1 after each operation is completed so that you can continue this exercise later. (Remember to set the default drive to A before saving the workbook.)

1. Start Windows and then launch Excel.

2. Create the following spreadsheet. Enter your name in Cell A1 and the current date in Cell A2 as shown. Complete the rest of your spreadsheet to match the example.

	A	B	C	D	E	F
1	Your Name					
2	Date					
3						
4	INVESTMENTS					
5						
6	TYPE		DATE	PRICE	QUANTITY	TOTAL
7						
8	CDs		2/5/XX	1000	7	
9	TEDDY CORP.		3/15/XX	10.75	200	
10	SAVINGS BONDS		4/20/XX	50	5	
11	BLASTER CORP.		7/2/XX	5.25	300	
12	ACE MUSIC CORP.		10/20/XX	20.5	100	
13						
14						

3. Enter a formula in Cell F8 that will multiply the price in Cell D8 by the quantity in Cell E8.

4. Enter similar formulas in Cells F9 through F12 to accomplish the same result on each respective row.

5. Enter a SUM function in Cell F14 to total the five investments that appear in Column F.

6. Save this workbook as INVEST1. (Remember to set the default drive to A if you haven't already done so.)

7. Type **YEAR ENDED 12/31/XX** in Cell E1. Print the spreadsheet.

8. Change the amount in Cell E10 to 100 and Cell D12 to 10.25.

9. Insert a row at Row 5 and then type **PURCH** in Cell D6.

10. Insert a column at Column D (between *DATE* and *PRICE*). Type **SELLING** in Cell D6, **PRICE** in Cell D7, **1030** in Cell D9, **12** in Cell D10, **100** in Cell D11, **6** in Cell D12, and **15.75** in Cell D13.

11. Insert a column at Column G (between *QUANTITY* and *TOTAL*). Type **TOTAL** in Cells G6 and H6, **SALES** in Cell G7, **PURCH** in Cell H7, **PROFIT/** and in Cell I6, and **(LOSS)** in Cell I7.

12. Enter formulas in Cells G9 through G13 that will multiply the selling price in Column D by the quantity in Column F.

13. Enter formulas in Cells I9 through I13 that will subtract the TOTAL PURCHASES (Column H) from TOTAL SALES (Column G).

14. Place a SUM function in Cell G15 and Cell I15 to total overall sales, purchases, and profit/(losses).

15. Save the workbook as INVEST1, print the entire worksheet, exit the program, and shut down Windows.

APPLICATION 5: INVENTORY

Save the workbook as STOCK1 after each operation is completed so that you can continue this exercise later. (Remember to set the default drive to A the first time you save the worksheet.)

1. Start Windows and then launch Excel.

2. Create the following spreadsheet. Enter your name in Cell A1 and the current date in Cell A2 as shown. Complete the rest of your spreadsheet to match the example.

	A	B	C	D	E
1	Your Name				
2	Date				
3					
4	INVENTORY				
5					
6	ITEM	COST	QUANTITY	VALUE	
7					
8	Disk	0.75	115		
9	Paper	5.25	21		
10	Ribbon	3.15	7		
11	Labels	10.65	11		
12					
13	TOTAL				
14					
15					

3. Enter a formula in Cell D8 that will multiply the disk cost in Cell B8 by the quantity in Cell C8.

4. Enter similar formulas in Cells D9 through D11 to accomplish the same result on each respective row.

5. Enter a SUM function in Cell D13 to total the four values that appear in Column D.

6. Save this worksheet as STOCK1. (Remember to set the default drive to A if you haven't already done so.)

7. Type **EX1-7** in Cell D1. Print the entire spreadsheet.

8. Change the cost in Cell B8 to 1.25 and the quantity in Cell C10 to 9.

9. Insert a row at Row 9 (between *Disk* and *Paper*). Type **Disk Box** in Cell A9, **3.25** in Cell B9, and **1** in Cell C9. Type a formula in Cell D9 to compute the value as before.

10. Type **EX-109** in Cell D1. Print the entire spreadsheet. Save as STOCK1.

11. Delete Row 7. Do *not* save again.

12. Erase Cell D1 and type [EX-12] in Cell C1. Print the part of the spreadsheet that includes all cells from Cell A1 to C11. Do *not* save again.

13. Exit the program without saving and then shut down Windows.

APPLICATION 6: TICKETS

Save the workbook in this exercise as TICKET1 after each operation is completed so that you can continue this exercise later. (Remember to set the default drive to A the first time you save the worksheet.)

1. Start Windows and then launch Excel.

2. Create the following spreadsheet (on page 74). Enter your name in Cell A1 and the current date in Cell A2 as shown. Complete the rest of your spreadsheet to match the example.

3. Enter a formula in Cell E8 that will multiply the ticket price in Cell B8 by the amount sold in Cell D8.

4. Enter similar formulas in Cells E9 through E11 to accomplish the same result on each respective row.

5. Enter a SUM function in Cell E13 to total the four receipts that appear in Column E.

6. Save this workbook as TICKET1. (Remember to set the default drive to A, if you haven't done so already.)

7. Type **MATINEE** in Cell E1. Print the entire spreadsheet.

8. Change the price in Cell B8 to 65 and the quantity in Cell C10 to 175.

9. Insert a row at Row 9 (between *Orchestra* and *Lodge*). Type **Box Seat** in Cell A9, **65** in Cell B9, **20** in Cell C9, and **15** in Cell D9. Type a formula in Cell E9 to compute the value as before.

10. Type **EVENING** in Cell E1. Print the entire spreadsheet.

11. Delete Row 7 and insert a column at Column E.

	A	B	C	D	E	
1	Your Name					
2	Date					
3						
4	TICKETS					
5						
6	SEAT	PRICE	QUANTITY	SOLD	VALUE	
7						
8	Orchestra	60	500	245		
9	Lodge	50	300	123		
10	Mezzanine	30	200	87		
11	Balcony	15	250	168		
12						
13						

12. Type **EMPTY** in Cell E6. Create a formula in Cell E7 that subtracts the contents of Cell D7 from Cell C7. Enter similar formulas in Cells E8 through E11. Print the part of the spreadsheet that includes all cells from Cell A1 to Cell F11.

13. Place a SUM function in Cell E13 that totals the column.

14. Save the workbook as TICKET1, print the entire worksheet, exit the program, and then shut down Windows.

MASTERY CASES

The following mastery cases allow you to demonstrate how much you have learned about this software. Each case describes a fictitious problem or need that can be solved using the skills you have learned in this chapter. Although minimum acceptable outcomes are specified, you are expected and encouraged to design your response (files, data, lists) in ways that display your personal mastery of the software. Feel free to show off your skills. Use real data from your own experience in your solution, although you may also fabricate data if needed.

These mastery cases allow you to display your ability to:

- Launch Excel.
- Enter data into a worksheet.
- Save the worksheet on disk.
- Use ranges and formulas.
- Print the worksheet.
- Edit the worksheet.

CASE 1: TRACKING YOUR EXAM GRADES

You would like to keep track of all your exam grades by course. Prepare a spreadsheet listing each course that you have taken. Next, list all exam grades that you earned across from each course. Make up courses and exam grades if needed. Be sure to head each column, for example, COURSE, EXAM 1, and so on. Create a column titled AVERAGE to the right of the last exam grade and calculate the average exam grade for each course. Save and print the worksheet.

CASE 2: CREATING A HOLIDAY SHOPPING BUDGET

You would like to keep track of your holiday shopping. Prepare a spreadsheet with columns for the Person, Gift, Budget (amount you want to spend), Actual, and Difference. Enter a list of persons that you desire to buy a gift for and the type of gift. Make up a budget price for each gift and enter it into the Budget column. Now, make up an actual price (different from the budget price) for each gift and place it in the Actual column. Calculate the difference between actual and budget in the Difference column and then the overall total of each column. Save and print the budget.

CASE 3: CREATING A SALES REPORT

You have your own computer business and have completed your first year of operation. Create a simple sales report listing several of your products and displaying the units sold and their prices. Be sure to identify your company name, report title (Sales Report) and year-end date. Include columns for the Product, Units Sold, Unit Price, and Total. Calculate the sales dollars for each product in the Total column. Also calculate overall totals for the Units Sold and Total columns. Save and print your sales report.

2

ENHANCING SPREADSHEETS: RANGE AND DEFAULT CHANGES, FORMATS, AND FUNCTIONS

SS

OBJECTIVES

After completing this chapter, you will be able to

1 Explain how to align and format data.
2 Describe the procedures to copy and move cell contents.
3 Explain the effects of worksheet default changes.
4 Describe and differentiate among the three ways to change column widths: resetting the default, individually, and by column-range.
5 Enhance a worksheet with different fonts, colors, and lines.

6 Differentiate between relative and absolute references.
7 Examine functions and describe how to select them using the Function wizard.
8 Describe techniques for handling large spreadsheets.
9 Demonstrate advanced printing techniques such as compressing page data and displaying column and row titles, column and row indicators, and grid lines.

OVERVIEW

Building on the skills developed in Chapter 1, in Chapter 2 you will examine commands that enhance your ability to create or modify spreadsheets efficiently, and commands that enhance the appearance of the spreadsheet itself. First, range and default changes that alter the appearance of spreadsheet cells are presented.

You will then learn how to adjust data alignment, format numeric values and formula results, and adjust column widths to better present your data. This chapter then explores the use of different type faces (called *fonts*), colors, and lines to enhance the look of your worksheet. Next, methods to overcome cell-reference problems are discussed, followed by a closer look at using functions. Finally, techniques are presented for managing large spreadsheets, both on the screen and on the printer.

USING RANGES IN COMMANDS

Unlike *default changes* that can affect the entire worksheet (as you will soon see), commands that use ranges change only specified cells. Some of the more useful commands control data alignment, numeric value and formula result formatting, copying, and moving. To prepare for these exercises, first create the spreadsheet in Figure SS2-1 as follows:

STEPS

1 **Start with a new blank workbook on your screen**

FIGURE SS2-1 ■ THE INITIAL WORKSHEET

Note that column headings in Columns B through D do not line up neatly over their column values.

	A	B	C	D	E
1	Chapter Exercises				
2	Your Name				
3	Date				
4					
5	Employee	Hours	Pay	Gross	
6	Burstein	40	5.65		
7	Laudon	35	4		
8	Martin	38	5.75		
9	Parker	25	6.75		
10	Williams	32	3.5		
11					
12					

Note: Exercises in this chapter require your computer to be on and Excel to be active.

2 Enter the data shown in Figure SS2-1

Note that *Chapter Exercises* is typed completely in Cell A1, *Employee* in Cell A5, *Hours* in Cell B5, and so on.

3 Save the workbook as SS2-1a (remember to set the default drive to A when saving)

ALIGNING DATA

A quick look at the worksheet reveals a frequent irritant—some column headings may not line up neatly over their respective numeric values. In Figure SS2-1, for example, it is difficult to determine whether "Pay" refers to Column B or C. This results because of the column's **alignment**—the position of data in a cell. Text is left-aligned in cells by default (whereas numeric values and formula results are always positioned on the right). The alignment of data in a cell can be changed using the *Format Cells* dialog box or *Format* toolbar buttons. This process involves first selecting the range to be changed and then invoking the desired command.

ALIGNING DATA WITHIN A CELL.   The following exercise changes the data alignment in Cells B5 through D5:

STEPS

1 Move to Cell B5—the left corner of the desired range

2 Press and hold Shift while clicking *Cell D5* to select the range B5:D5   [Shift + →]

3 Click *Format, Cells,* and then the *Alignment* tab for the   [Ctrl + 1 , A]
   Alignment section of the *Format Cells* dialog box

You can use the *Format Cells* dialog box, shown in Figure SS2-2, to make alignment changes on a range of data, multiple ranges, or a table (discussed later). Although only text-alignment changes are demonstrated here, the procedures for other alignment changes are the same.

4 Click *Right* to select right horizontal alignment

5 Click the *OK* button   [↵]

6 Move to Cell D6

The text is now right-aligned, as shown in Figure SS2-3.

SS

FIGURE SS2–2 ■ THE *FORMAT CELLS* DIALOG BOX

The *Format Cells* dialog box can be used to change the format of a range of data, multiple ranges, or a table.

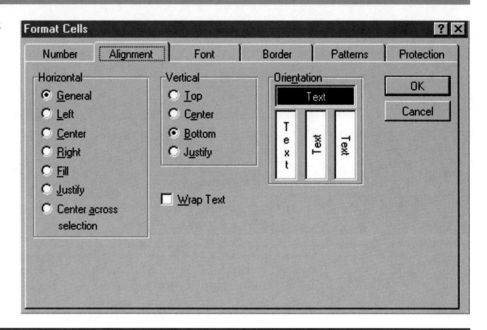

 Tip: Instead of following Steps 3 and 4, you can simply click the *Right-align* toolbar button. Other alignment toolbar buttons include a *Left-align, Center-align,* and *Center-across columns* button.

Now complete the worksheet by adding formulas for *Gross* as follows:

7 In Cell D6, type `=B6*C6`

FIGURE SS2-3 ■ ALIGNING DATA

The data in Row 5 have been right-aligned over their respective values.

	A	B	C	D	E
1	Chapter Exercises				
2	Your Name				
3	Date				
4					
5	Employee	Hours	Pay	Gross	
6	Burstein	40	5.65		
7	Laudon	35	4		
8	Martin	38	5.75		
9	Parker	25	6.75		

8 In Cell D7, type `=B7*C7`

9 Complete similar entries for Cells D8, D9, and D10

Your worksheet should now resemble Figure SS2-4. If it does not, repeat Steps 7 though 9.

10 Save this worksheet again as SS2-1A   [**Ctrl** + **S**]

Try changing Column A data to the right, center, and then left. You can readjust data alignments of any range at any time. However, text that exceeds the width of a column (as in Cell A1 in this example) will always appear left-aligned. Numeric values and formula results that exceed a column's width may appear in scientific notation (for example, 1.12E+15).

If your worksheet does not resemble Figure SS2-4 when you are finished,

11 Close the current workbook without saving and then open the SS2-1A workbook again before continuing.

> **Tip:** The *alignment* dialog box can also be used to change the alignment of a range of values.

CENTER-ALIGNING DATA ACROSS COLUMNS.   When creating a title that applies to more than one column, the center-across columns option of the *Format Cells* dialog box is very helpful. Try this to center-align the title WEEKLY PAYROLL across Cells A through D.

SS

FIGURE SS2-4 ■ USING FORMULAS

Formulas that calculate the gross pay have been added in Column D.

	A	B	C	D	E
1	Chapter Exercises				
2	Your Name				
3	Date				
4					
5	Employee	Hours	Pay	Gross	
6	Burstein	40	5.65	226	
7	Laudon	35	4	140	
8	Martin	38	5.75	218.5	
9	Parker	25	6.75	168.75	
10	Williams	32	3.5	112	
11					
12					

The default format makes it difficult to compare numbers.

1 Move to Cell A5

2 Insert a Row (*Insert*, *Rows*)

3 Type   WEEKLY PAYROLL   and press ↵

4 Move back to Cell A5 and select the Range A5:D5

 5 Click *Format*, *Cells*, the *Alignment* tab,   [**Ctrl** + **1** , **A** , **Alt** + **A** , **↵**]
Center across selection, *OK* to center the title

6 Move to Cell A1

Your worksheet should appear as Figure SS2-5.

 7 Resave the workbook as SS2-1a and then close it

ADJUSTING NUMBER FORMAT

As you have learned, numeric data may contain only numerals, decimal points, or math expressions. By default, these data appear in cells without commas, dollar signs, or trailing zeros after the decimal point. This is true whether data are entered as numeric constants (as in Columns B and C in Figure SS2-5), or are the result of a formula (as in Column D). Although this may be satisfactory for some spreadsheets, it is usually desirable to adjust a number's **format**—the way a number is displayed in a cell—from its

FIGURE SS2-5 ■ CENTER-ALIGNING DATA ACROSS COLUMNS

The title "WEEKLY PAYROLL" has been centered across cells A5 through D5.

	A	B	C	D	E
1	Chapter Exercises				
2	Your Name				
3	Date				
4					
5		WEEKLY PAYROLL			
6	Employee	Hours	Pay	Gross	
7	Burstein	40	5.65	226	
8	Laudon	35	4	140	
9	Martin	38	5.75	218.5	
10	Parker	25	6.75	168.75	
11	Williams	32	3.5	112	
12					
13					

default state to a more useful style. Changing a format can add commas or dollar signs to a range of numeric data. It can also standardize the number of decimal places shown in each cell or even hide a cell's contents. Excel comes with a variety of build-in number formats (codes). You can accept the default format (general), select from a build-it format, or create your own custom format. Figure SS2-6 displays a sample of Excel number formats. Refer to this figure as you make the following format changes. The next exercises examine the most popular of these options, but you can invoke them all using similar techniques.

GENERAL NUMBER FORMAT.   The *general format* is the default format for all new worksheets. As in Figure SS2-5, the general format displays a number as an integer (as in Cell B7—40), decimal fraction (as in Cell C7—5.65), or scientific notation (not displayed—1.4E+7).

When entering data into a general formatted cell, Excel automatically selects the correct format for that data, as in Figure SS2-7. For example, try the following:

FIGURE SS2-6 ■ NUMBER FORMATS

Category	Display Options
1. General	Default number format that automatically formats a number based on the symbol entered with it
2. Number	General number format used to set decimal place and negative number display, and to insert a 1,000 comma separator
3. Currency	General monetary value format used to set decimal place and negative number display, to insert dollar signs and 1,000 comma separator
4. Accounting	Specialized monetary value format used to align dollar signs, 1,000 comma separator, and decimals uniformly in a column
5. Date	Date number format used to set date or date and time displays
6. Time	Time number format used to set time or date and time displays
7. Percentage	Percentage number format used to insert a percentage sign to the left of a number with a set decimal place
8. Fraction	Fraction number format used to set fraction display
9. Scientific	Scientific number format used to set numbers in scientific display with a set decimal place
10. Text	Text number format used to display numbers as text
11. special	Special number format used for zip codes, phone numbers, and social security numbers
12. Custom	Custom number format used to create user defined number format

FIGURE SS2–7 ■ **THE GENERAL NUMBER FORMAT**

Data entered into a cell with a certain symbol(s) of cells with the general number format (the default) will be automatically formatted.

	A	B	C	D	E	F	G
1	FORMAT						
2	SELECTED						
3							
4	CURRENCY			$1,000	◄————	Type $1000	
5	NUMBER WITH COMMA STYLE			1,000	◄————	Type 1,000	
6	PERCENTAGE			10%	◄————	Type 10%	
7	DATE			1/1/96	◄————	Type 1/1/96	
8							
9							
10							

STEPS

1 Close any open workbook (*File*, *Close* or Ctrl + F4)

2 Open a new workbook (*File*, *New* or Ctrl + N , ↵)

3 Type the titles in Cells A1 and A2 from Figure SS2-7

4 Move to Cell A4 and type CURRENCY

5 In Cell D4, type $1000 (be sure to place a "$" before typing 1000 and do not place a ","
after the 1—Excel will automatically do this), and press ↵

6 In Cell A5, type NUMBER WITH COMMA STYLE

7 In Cell D5, type 1,000 (be sure to place a comma after the 1) and press ↵

8 In Cell A6, type PERCENTAGE and press ↵

9 In Cell D6, type 10%

10 In Cell A7, type DATE

11 In Cell D7, type 1/1/96 and press ↵

Your worksheet should resemble Figure SS2-7. Note that Excel automatically selected the correct number format for each entry. Also note that the alignment may differ slightly from one number format to another as in Cells D4 and D5.

12 Save this workbook as FORMATS and then close it

ACCOUNTING NUMBER FORMAT.   The accounting number format is a very useful format for presenting financial information. It includes several built-in number formats, all of which use the 1,000-comma separator, insert a dollar sign against the left margin of a cell, place negative numbers in brackets, and set zero values as hyphens (-). This format also decimal-aligns numbers.

> **Tip: When making format changes, it is highly advisable to use toolbar buttons where available. For example, the $ toolbar button formats data in the accounting style that uses the dollar sign and two decimal places, as in $1,000.00 (note that the dollar sign is left-aligned, whereas the number is right-aligned. The , (comma) toolbar button formats data in the accounting style that omits the dollar sign and uses two decimal places, as in 1,000.00. Both toolbar buttons decimal-align numbers in a column.**

Although the quicker method to make format changes is to use a toolbar button, the *Number* tab of the *Format Cells* dialog box is used next. This displays all number format options available. Try this:

STEPS

1 Close any open workbook

2 Open the SS2-1a workbook

3 Move to Cell C7

4 Press and hold   Shift   while clicking *Cell C11* to select the range C7:D11

5 Click *Format, Cells*, the *Number* tab, and the   [Ctrl + 1 , N , Alt + C , A]
   Accounting category (in the *Category* list box)

Your Number tab content (Format Cells dialog box) should appear as Figure SS2-8. Note that the Sample indicator at the bottom left of the dialog box displays $5.65. This is the number format that will appear in the selected range after you perform the next step. Also note that the you can use this this tab to change the default decimal setting of 2 and use dollar sign setting.

> **Tip: The active cell must contain data for the Sample indicator of the *Number* tab (*Format Cells* dialog box) to display a sample.**

For now,

6 Click *OK* button   [↵]

$ > **Tip: Quickly invoke the accounting-dollar sign, two-decimal format by clicking the $ toolbar button in place of Steps 5 and 6.**

FIGURE SS2-8 ■ **THE ACCOUNTING NUMBER FORMAT**

Excel automatically selects the correct format for data entered into a cell that is initially in General format (Excel's default setting).

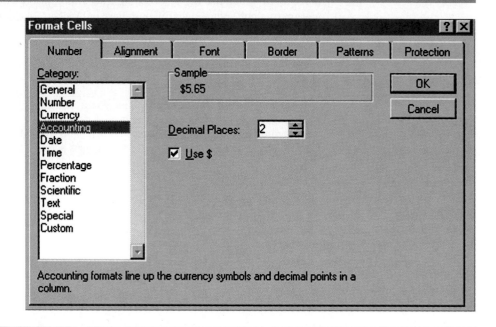

---

7 **Move to Cell A1**

Your worksheet should now resemble Figure SS2-9a. Note that all data in the range C7:D11 has been formatted to the dollar sign, two-decimal accounting formula. Now to format the data in the range C8:D11 in the comma, two-decimal accounting format (no dollar sign),

8 **Select the range _C8:D11_**

9 **Click _Format, Cells_, the _Number_ tab, the _Accounting_ category (in the Category list box), click _Use $_, OK**   [**Ctrl** + **1** , **N** , **Alt** + **C** , **A** , **Alt** + **U** , **↵**]

10 **Move to Cell A1**

As in Figure SS2-9b, the data in Cells C8 through D11 have now been changed to the no dollar sign, two-decimal format (note that this format inserts 1,000 comma separators and also aligns decimals.)

11 **Save the workbook as SS2-1b**

Cells may also be formatted before entering data. To do so, select the desired range and invoke the format command. Try this:

12 **Move to Cell D13**

13 **Format Cell D13 for the dollar sign, two-decimal accounting format**

FIGURE SS2-9 ■ CHANGING NUMBER FORMATS

(a) All numbers in the range C7:D11 have been formatted to dollar sign, two decimal-accounting style.

	A	B	C	D	E
1	Chapter Exercises				
2	Your Name				
3	Date				
4					
5		WEEKLY PAYROLL			
6	Employee	Hours	Pay	Gross	
7	Burstein	40	$ 5.65	$ 226.00	
8	Laudon	35	$ 4.00	$ 140.00	
9	Martin	38	$ 5.75	$ 218.50	
10	Parker	25	$ 6.75	$ 168.75	
11	Williams	32	$ 3.50	$ 112.00	
12					

(a)

(b) All numbers in the range C8:D11 have been reformatted to no dollar sign, two decimal-accounting style.

	A	B	C	D	E
1	Chapter Exercises				
2	Your Name				
3	Date				
4					
5		WEEKLY PAYROLL			
6	Employee	Hours	Pay	Gross	
7	Burstein	40	$ 5.65	$ 226.00	
8	Laudon	35	4.00	140.00	
9	Martin	38	5.75	218.50	
10	Parker	25	6.75	168.75	
11	Williams	32	3.50	112.00	
12					

(b)

(c) Cell D13 has been formatted to dollar sign, two decimal-accounting style, after which a SUM function has been entered to total the range D7:D11.

	A	B	C	D	E
1	Chapter Exercises				
2	Your Name				
3	Date				
4					
5		WEEKLY PAYROLL			
6	Employee	Hours	Pay	Gross	
7	Burstein	40	$ 5.65	$ 226.00	
8	Laudon	35	4.00	140.00	
9	Martin	38	5.75	218.50	
10	Parker	25	6.75	168.75	
11	Williams	32	3.50	112.00	
12					
13	TOTAL			$ 865.25	
14					
15					
16					

(c)

SS

14 In Cell D13, enter   =SUM (D7:D11)

15 In Cell A13, type TOTAL and then press ↵

Your worksheet should now resemble Figure SS2-9c. If it does not, repeat Steps 13 through 16.

16 Save the workbook as SS2-1C and then close it

CHANGING DECIMAL PLACES.   Clicking the *Increase Decimal* or *Decrease Decimal* toolbar button with your mouse is a quick way to change the decimal places. Try this:

STEPS

1 Create a new workbook (*File, New* or Ctrl + N)

2 Type **.7** into Cells C3 through C7

3 Type **.7** into Cells E3 through E7

4 Place a SUM function in Cells C9 and E9 to total the columns

Your worksheet should appear as SS2-10a. Note that Excel automatically formats the cells for the required decimal places. Although you can use the *Number* tab of the *Format Cells* dialog box to set the decimal place, an easier way is to use toolbar buttons. Try this:

5 Select the range C3:C7

 6 Click the *Increase Decimal* button once

Two decimal places now appear in the selected range.

 7 Click the *Increase Decimal* button five more times

The cells in the selected range now display ######## indicating that the cell values contain more characters than the cell's width. At this point, you can change the column width (discussed later) or reduce the number of decimal places. Now, to reduce the decimal place back to one

 8 Click the *Decrease Decimal* button six times (or as needed)

Your worksheet should resemble Figure SS2-10a again.

DISPLAY VERSUS CONTENTS. Formatting alters the display, or *appearance* of a cell, but does not change the actual cell contents. This can lead to some peculiar results. For example, format the numbers in Cells E3 through E9 to no decimal places:

FIGURE SS2-10 ■ DISPLAY VERSUS CONTENTS

Formatting cells with too few decimal places may display incorrect results because the display is changed, not the number itself.

B	C	D	E	F	G
	0.7		0.7		
	0.7		0.7		
	0.7		0.7		
	0.7		0.7		
	0.7		0.7		
	3.5		3.5		

B	C	D	E	F	G
	0.7		1		
	0.7		1		
	0.7		1		
	0.7		1		
	0.7		1		
	3.5		4		

(a)   (b)

1 Select the range E3:E9

2 Click the *Decrease Decimal* button

3 Move to Cell E10

The worksheet now appears as Figure SS2-10b. Note that the numbers and total in Column C correctly show that .7 added five times totals 3.5. Now, look at Column E where these cells have been reformatted as whole numbers (using the *Decrease Decimal* button). This column now shows 1+1+1+1+1=4! This occurs because each cell has been formatted to display a whole number, but the values in the cells remain as .7 and 3.5. Keep in mind that values may appear rounded to conform to formatting settings but are used unchanged in other spreadsheet formulas.

4 Close the workbook without saving

OTHER FORMAT CHANGES.   The *Number* tab (*Format Cells* dialog box) offers a variety of number formats as previously listed in Figure SS2-6. The steps to select a different number format code from the *Number* tab are the same as those described in the previous sections. To create custom number format codes, see your on-line help.

COPYING CELLS

Although data can be *typed* into individual cells, it is much more efficient to *copy* data from one cell to another as needed. Any data can be copied. Constant values copy exactly; formulas including functions (unless the program is told otherwise) will have their cell references automatically adjusted to reflect their new location. For example, the formula =B7*C7 in Cell D7 (see Figure SS2-9c) multiplies hours (in B7) by pay (in C7). The formula =B8*C8 in Cell D8 does exactly the same thing for the corresponding cells in *its* row. Every formula in Column D is identical except its cell references, which must be relative to the row the formula is on. You created these formulas by typing each one—a lot of wasted effort. You can save time and reduce typing errors by *copying* one cell into others. **Copying** replicates the contents of a cell in other cells, automatically adjusting relative references to reflect the new cell address. It also copies any formatting or alignment that you have previously set.

The following exercises demonstrate the importance of the Copy command. To prepare for this exercise,

1 Open the SS2-1C workbook (if needed)

2 Select the cell range D8:D11 (the source range)

3 Press Delete to erase cells D8:D11

4   **Move to Cell D8**

Your worksheet should resemble Figure SS2-11. If it does not, repeat these steps before continuing.

The copy procedure has four parts: (1) selecting the **source range** to be copied, (2) invoking the Copy command (from the *Edit* menu), (3) selecting the **destination range** to which the selection will be copied, and (4) pressing the Enter key or invoking the Paste command (*Edit* menu).

> **Tip:** When you copy a cell's content, you copy all of that cell's format and alignment settings.

COPYING ONE CELL.   Assume that you have just finished entering the formula in Cell D7 and want to copy it into the rest of a column (or row) of cells. For example, the following exercise shows how to copy Cell D7 to several cells in Column D (D8:D11).

STEPS

1   **Move to Cell D7 (the cell you want to copy)**

   2   **Click *Edit, Copy***   [**Ctrl** + **C**]

The Excel status bar now displays the message "Select destination and press ENTER or choose Paste," as shown in Figure SS2-12a. Like all Windows applications, the Copy command first copies the selection to the Windows Clipboard, a holding application. This process allows for the possibility of copying and moving data among multiple applications. Multiple application copying and moving techniques are discussed in the appendix.

FIGURE SS2-11 ■ **PREPARING TO COPY**

Cells D8 through D11 have been erased to show the results of the copy procedure.

	A	B	C	D	E
1	Chapter Exercises				
2	Your Name				
3	Date				
4					
5		WEEKLY PAYROLL			
6	Employee	Hours	Pay	Gross	
7	Burstein	40	$ 5.65	$ 226.00	
8	Laudon	35	4.00		
9	Martin	38	5.75		
10	Parker	25	6.75		
11	Williams	32	3.50		
12					
13	TOTAL			$ 226.00	
14					
15					
16					

FIGURE SS2-12 ■ COPYING AND PASTING

(a) The message "Select destination and press Enter or choose Paste" appears in the title bar when the copy command is invoked.
(b) Once a desired range has been copied to the Clipboard, the destination range is selected.
(c) This is the completed copy.

| ◄ ◄ ► ►| Sheet1 ⟋ Sheet2 ⟋ Sheet3 ⟋ Sheet4 ⟋ Sheet5 ⟋ |
| Select destination and press ENTER or choose Paste |

(a)

	A	B	C	D	E	F
1	Chapter Exercises					
2	Your Name					
3	Date					
4						
5		WEEKLY PAYROLL				
6	Employee	Hours	Pay	Gross		
7	Burstein	40	$ 5.65	$ 226.00		
8	Laudon	35	4.00			
9	Martin	38	5.75			
10	Parker	25	6.75			
11	Williams	32	3.50			
12						
13	TOTAL			$ 226.00		
14						

(b)

	A	B	C	D	E	F
1	Chapter Exercises					
2	Your Name					
3	Date					
4						
5		WEEKLY PAYROLL				
6	Employee	Hours	Pay	Gross		
7	Burstein	40	$ 5.65	$ 226.00		
8	Laudon	35	4.00	$ 140.00		
9	Martin	38	5.75	$ 218.50		
10	Parker	25	6.75	$ 168.75		
11	Williams	32	3.50	$ 112.00		
12						
13	TOTAL			$ 865.25		
14						

(c)

> **Tip:** If the desired range to be copied is greater than one cell, select the range before invoking the copy command in Step 2.

The destination is the desired location in which the selection will be duplicated. This location can be a cell or a range of cells. To select the destination range D8:D11,

3 ▸ Move to Cell D8

4 ▸ Press and hold Shift while clicking Cell D11   [Shift + ↓ to Cell D11]

The destination range D8:D11 should now be highlighted as in Figure SS2-12b.
    To **paste** (transfer the copied selection from the Clipboard) to the destination range:

5 ▸ Click _Edit_, _Paste_   [Ctrl + V]

6 ▸ Move to Cell D8

If you had wanted to copy the formula into one cell only (such as D8), you would have skipped Step 4 altogether. It was needed only to specify a destination range greater than one cell.
    Your screen should resemble Figure SS2-12c. If it does not, repeat Steps 1 through 6. Examine the contents of the newly created cells. Note that the formula-cell addresses have been copied _relative_ to each row and that the formatting matches the copied cell.
    To match your original worksheet in Figure SS2-9c, change the no dollar sign, two-decimal accounting format [,] in these cells as follows:

7 ▸ Select the range D8:D11

SS

8 Click the , Toolbar button

9 Move to Cell A1

10 Close the workbook without saving

A few words of caution: If the Copy and Paste commands do not work as expected, you can retrieve the saved worksheet. You can also use the Undo feature immediately after copying to negate the Copy command.

COPYING A RANGE OF CELLS. You can copy a range of cells almost as easily as copying one cell. For example, suppose you wanted to copy all the data and formulas in Rows 7 through 10 starting at Row 12. This exercise demonstrates the technique.

STEPS

1 Open the SS2-1C workbook

2 Select the range A7:D11

Note that the range is highlighted as shown in Figure SS2-13a.

3 Click *Edit, Copy* to copy the range to the Clipboard   [**Ctrl** + **C**]

The title bar now displays the message "Select destination and press ENTER or choose Paste." When copying a range of cells, you need to specify only the *upper-left cell* where you want the copy to begin. The program knows exactly where to put the rest.

FIGURE SS2-13 ■ COPYING A RANGE OF CELLS

(a) Selecting the copy range.
(b) The range has been copied starting at Row 12.

(a)

	A	B	C	D	E
1	Chapter Exercises				
2	Your Name				
3	Date				
4					
5		WEEKLY PAYROLL			
6	Employee	Hours	Pay	Gross	
7	Burstein	40	$ 5.65	$ 226.00	
8	Laudon	35	4.00	140.00	
9	Martin	38	5.75	218.50	
10	Parker	25	6.75	168.75	
11	Williams	32	3.50	112.00	
12					
13	TOTAL			$ 865.25	
14					
15					

(b)

	A	B	C	D	E
1	Chapter Exercises				
2	Your Name				
3	Date				
4					
5		WEEKLY PAYROLL			
6	Employee	Hours	Pay	Gross	
7	Burstein	40	$ 5.65	$ 226.00	
8	Laudon	35	4.00	140.00	
9	Martin	38	5.75	218.50	
10	Parker	25	6.75	168.75	
11	Williams	32	3.50	112.00	
12	Burstein	40	$ 5.65	$ 226.00	
13	Laudon	35	4.00	140.00	
14	Martin	38	5.75	218.50	
15	Parker	25	6.75	168.75	
16	Williams	32	3.50	112.00	

4   Move to Cell A12

5   Click *Edit, Paste*   [**Ctrl** + **V**]

6   Move to Cell A12

The copying is completed, and the spreadsheet should now resemble Figure SS2-13b. If it does not, repeat Steps 1 through 6. Examine your worksheet carefully. Note that constant values were copied exactly, whereas formulas were copied relative to their locations. In addition, all alignments and formatting were duplicated in the copied cells.

     Practice copying one cell to another, one cell to a range of cells, and ranges of cells, and ranges of cells to other ranges. Use cells in both rows and columns until you are satisfied with the effect of each procedure.

7   Close the workbook without saving

MOVING CELLS

Cell contents can be moved from one location to another using the Cut and Paste commands. The Cut and Paste commands (*Edit* menu) relocate the contents of a cell (or range of cells) *without* changing the cell references. For example, the formula =A1*A2 stays constant no matter where it is moved. In addition, unlike the Copy command, the **Cut** command *erases* (moves) the contents of the Source range and places it in the Windows Clipboard for future pasting.

     A warning about moving: a formula (function) does not change when its cell is moved, but *other* formulas that refer to the cell do! They adjust to reflect the new location of the moved cell. This is useful, unless the moved cell is a range endpoint. For example, if Cell A1 is moved to Cell B10, the formula =SUM(A1:A5) will now read =SUM(B10:A5)—yielding incorrect results. Use care when moving cells—save workbooks before moving cells or be prepared to invoke the Undo command.

     The following exercises demonstrate the Cut and Paste commands. First, move the date in Cell A3 to D1:

STEPS

1   Open the SS2-1C workbook

2   Move to Cell A3

3   Click *Edit, Cut* to move the selection to the Clipboard   [**Ctrl** + **X**]

In the Windows environment, moving involves a *cut-and-paste* process. The Cut command moves the selection from its current position to the Clipboard, and the Paste command copies the selection from the Clipboard to the desired new location. Now to move the selection to Cell D1,

4   Move to Cell D1

5 Click *Edit, Paste*   [**Ctrl** + **V**]

Now, try moving the column headings from Rows 5 and 6 to Cell A4.

6 Move to Cell A5

7 Select the range A5:D6

8 Click *Edit, Cut*   [**Ctrl** + **X**]

9 Move to Cell A4

10 Click *Edit, Paste*   [**Ctrl** + **V**]

11 Move to Cell A1

Your spreadsheet should now resemble Figure SS2-14. If it does not, repeat Steps 1 through 10.

12 Save this workbook as SS2-1D and then close it

TRANSPOSING CELLS

Copying replicates cells in other spreadsheet locations by maintaining their row or column orientation. That is, a *row* of cells must be copied to another *row;* a *column* of cells to another *column*. However, what if you need to shift a column of cells to form a row, or vice versa? Of course, you could move a row of data cell by cell to form a column, but this is tedious and will not work for formulas or functions. To remedy this situation, Excel offers a Paste Special option called the Transpose command that allows

---

FIGURE SS2-14 ■ CUTTING AND PASTING

The Cut and Paste commands
(*Edit* menu) can reposition
one or more cells without
retyping or erasing.

	A	B	C	D	E
1	Chapter Exercises			Date	
2	Your Name				
3					
4		WEEKLY PAYROLL			
5	Employee	Hours	Pay	Gross	
6					
7	Burstein	40	$ 5.65	$ 226.00	
8	Laudon	35	4.00	140.00	
9	Martin	38	5.75	218.50	
10	Parker	25	6.75	168.75	
11	Williams	32	3.50	112.00	
12					
13	TOTAL			$ 865.25	
14					
15					

you to copy cells while switching columns and rows in the process. **Transpose** copies cell contents while exchanging the orientation of columns and rows automatically.

For example, this exercise converts the column of cells in Figure SS2-15a to a row orientation (as shown in Figure SS2-15b).

STEPS

1   **Create a new workbook**

2   **Enter text in Cells B2 through B6 as in Figure SS2-15a**

3   **Select the range B2:B6**

4   **Click _Edit_, _Copy_**   [**Ctrl** + **C**]

5   **Click Cell D2**

6   **Click _Edit_, _Paste Special_ for its dialog box**

7   **Click the _Transpose_ check box, then click _OK_**

8   **Move to Cell D2**

Your worksheet should resemble Figure SS2-15b.

Once a range has been transposed, you can delete or erase unneeded cells.

9   **Move to Cell B2**

FIGURE SS2-15 ■ TRANSPOSING CELLS

(a) The original column of cells.

(b) Transposing has moved Column B to Row 2.

	A	B	C	D	E	F	G	H	I
1									
2		Hours							
3		40							
4		35							
5		38							
6		25							
7									
8									

(a)

	A	B	C	D	E	F	G	H	I
1									
2		Hours		Hours	40	35	38	25	
3		40							
4		35							
5		38							
6		25							
7									
8									

(b)

SS

10 Select the range B2:B6

11 Press **Delete**

12 Move to Cell A1

Experiment with this command on your own—create another row or column of cells (or both) and transpose them.

13 Close the workbook without saving

USING RANGE NAMES

A **range name** can be used in a formula, function, or command, used in place of actual cell addresses. For example, if the name PAY is assigned to the range C6:C10, then PAY can be used in any operation that refers to these cells—=SUM(PAY) totals the range.

Using range names is simpler than specifying cell addresses. Range names take less time to select and are easier to remember. The following exercises illustrate the creation, use, modification, and deletion of range names.

CREATING NAMES. Any valid range can be given a name. For this exercise, you will create two ranges—NAMES for the range A4:A10 and TIME for the range B6:B10. In general, range names should begin with alphabetic characters, not with any symbols that Excel might misinterpret as formulas or cell addresses.

STEPS

1 Open the SS2-1D workbook

2 Move to Cell A5

3 Select the range A5:A11

4 Click *Insert*, *Name*, *Define* for its dialog box

5 Type **NAMES** and click *OK*

For the second range name,

6 Select the range B7:B11

7 Click *Insert*, *Name*, *Define* for its dialog box

8 Type **TIME** and click *OK*

9 Move to Cell A1 and resave the SS2-1d worksheet

> **Tip:** When you save the worksheet, range names are saved with it. If you do not save the worksheet, the range names will not be there when the worksheet is opened. Range names can also be created using the *Name* box (left side of the formula bar). To do so, select the desired range, click the *Name* box, type the name, and press Enter.

REVIEWING OR MODIFYING NAMES.   You have created two range names. You can easily review (or modify) them by following this procedure:

STEPS

1   Click *Edit, Go To* for its dialog box   [**Ctrl** + **G**]

The *Go To* dialog box appears as in Figure SS2-16a. Note that all current range names are displayed in the *Go To* list box.

2   Double-click *TIME* in the Go To list box (or click TIME, *OK*)

The range is selected. Its cell addresses are displayed in the *Name* box (formula bar) and on the worksheet screen as shown in Figure SS2-16b. At this point, you could simply look at the range address or modify it by typing a new one. When you have finished examining the screen,

3   Move to Cell A1

> **Tip:** You can also select a name from the *Name* drop-down list by clicking the ↓ button of the *Name* box (formula bar) and then clicking the desired name.

SS

FIGURE SS2-16 ■ NAME RANGES

(a) The *Go To* dialog box displays current names defined in the worksheet. (b) The selected range is identified in the formula bar and highlighted on the screen.

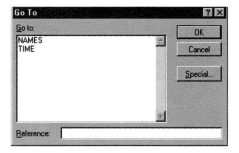

(a)   (b)

USING NAMES. Once range names are created, they can replace their corresponding cell addresses in any Excel procedure. These exercises illustrate how range names can be used in Print and Print Preview commands, and in a function.

STEPS

1   Click *Edit, Go To*   [Ctrl + G]

2   Double-click *NAMES*

3   Click *File, Print*   [Ctrl + P]

4   Click *Selection*

5   Click *Preview*, the *Zoom* toolbar button to print the NAMES range to the screen

The print range A5:A11 defined under the range name NAMES now appears in the Print Preview screen as in Figure SS2-17. To print this range instead of print previewing it, turn on your printer and replace Step 5 with clicking the *OK* button (or pressing the Enter key).

6   Press Esc to return to the Excel window

For an example of range name use in a function,

7   Move to Cell B13

8   Type =SUM(TIME) and press ↵

FIGURE SS2-17 ■ PRINT PREVIEWING AND PRINTING BY RANGE NAME

The Print Preview window has been set to display only the selected range.

Sheet1

Employee

Burstein
Laudon
Martin
Parker
Williams

9　**Move to Cell B13**

As shown in Figure SS2-18a, the =SUM function has correctly totaled the indicated range.

DELETING NAMES.　When there is no longer any need for a range name, it can be deleted without harming the range itself or any formulas that refer to it.

STEPS

1　**Click _Insert_, _Name_, _Define_ for its dialog box**

2　**Click TIME**

3　**Click _Delete_, OK**

The range name TIME has been deleted. As shown in Figure SS2-18b, all cells remain undisturbed except for Cell B13. Since TIME no longer exists, the message "#NAME?" appears in Cell B13.

4　**Move to Cell B13 and press　Delete**

5　**Close the workbook without saving**

☑ CHECKPOINT

✓　Open the SS2-1D workbook. Format the cells.
✓　Right-align all employee names and center-align hours in the Pay column to accounting using the currency, two-decimal format.

FIGURE SS2-18　■　USING RANGE NAMES

(a) Range names can also be used in formulas.
(b) Deleting a name that is used in a formula invokes the message "#NAME?" in the cell that it is used.

(a)　(b)

✓ Copy the formula in D7 to E7; then copy E7 into all cells from E8 to E11. Transpose the names in Cells A7:A11 to Row 16.
✓ Name the cell range A5:A11 PEOPLE.
✓ Use the range name PEOPLE to move this range to Column F, starting in F5. Save as PAYROLL.

RESETTING WORKSHEET DEFAULTS

Excel has many default settings. Some default settings affect the view of the window, others affect the behavior of the program (for example, the default number format) or the worksheet. This section focuses on worksheet default settings and will refer to them simply as *default changes*.

Whereas range changes adjust only a part of the spreadsheet, default changes are designed to affect the spreadsheet as a whole. **Default changes** change default settings that determine spreadsheet appearance. In general, default changes affect all the cells in a worksheet *except* those cells whose appearance (format, alignment, or column width) is set individually or by a range change. Although default changes can be used at any time, they are typically performed before data are entered into individual cells, so that the general appearance of all worksheet cells can be established. The following exercises demonstrate how default changes can affect the worksheet. First, prepare a demonstration worksheet as follows:

STEPS

1 Close any open workbook and then open a new workbook

2 In Cell A1, type LEFT

3 In Cell A2, type RIGHT

4 In Cell A3, type 1234.5

5 In Cell A4, type 5678.9

6 Press ↵

7 Change Cell A2's alignment to right horizontal

8 Format Cell A4 to the comma, one-decimal accounting format

9 Move to Cell A1

Your spreadsheet should match Figure SS2-19. If it does not, fix the appropriate cells before continuing.

10 Save this workbook as SS2-2A

FIGURE SS2-19 ■ **DEMONSTRATION WORKSHEET FOR DEFAULT CHANGES**

	A	B	
1	LEFT		
2	RIGHT		
3	1234.5		
4	5,678.9		
5			
6			

Notice that Cell A1 (which was typed without alignment or format changes) has been automatically assigned the current default setting of *left-align*. Cell A3 (which has no range format adjustment) uses the current default format of general. You are now ready to explore changing default settings.

> **Note: Before invoking a default change, the cell pointer must be in a cell whose default changes have not been changed.**

FORMAT

Default formats are identical to the range formats you have already learned, but default formats will affect all the cells in the spreadsheet that use the default setting.

STEPS

1 Open the SS2-2A workbook and move to Cell A1 if needed

2 Click *Format, Style* for its dialog box

The *Style* dialog box should appear as shown in Figure SS2-20. This dialog box displays the current style default settings and can be used to change these settings. Note the number style is currently set to general format.

3 Click *Modify, Number* tab

4 Click *Number* in the *Category* list box

5 Click the ▼ button of the Decimal Places box to reduce it to 0

6 Click *OK, OK*

Examine the worksheet on your screen and in Figure SS2-21. Notice that Cell A3 now uses the new default format, but Cell A4 does not. This is because default changes do not

FIGURE SS2-20 ■ THE *STYLE* DIALOG BOX

This dialog box allows you to change the default style settings of the worksheet.

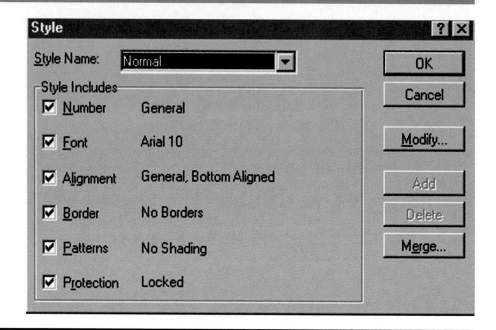

affect cells that have been formatted by range changes. This is true whether the range change was invoked before or after a default change.

Range changes always override worksheet default changes. Only cells with no specific format will reflect the new style default settings. If you want a formatted cell to use the default setting, you must remove its format. This can be done by using the *Clear, Formats* command from the *Edit* menu. The following exercise examines this further.

7 Type **2468.1** in Cell B3 and press ↵

Notice that the cell, which displays 2,468, automatically uses the default format setting.

FIGURE SS2-21 ■ RANGE VERSUS WORKSHEET DEFAULT CHANGES

	A	B	
1	LEFT		
2	RIGHT		
3	1,235		
4	5,678.9 ◄————		Formatted cell remains unchanged
5			
6			

8   **Move to Cell B3 again**

9   **Click *Format, Cells, Number* tab, Number, ▲ button of the *Decimal* places to set it to 2 (use 1000 separator (,), 2 decimal), *OK***

Note that now the cell displays 2468.10—the range format just added *overrides* the global default setting. To remove the cell's range format,

10   **Click *Edit, Clear, Formats* to delete range formats**

Note that the cell's display returns to the worksheet default setting.

11   **Save this workbook as SS2-2B**

ALIGNMENT

As you have seen, data alignment within a cell can be changed at any time by a range change.

The default changes do *not* affect data aligned by a range change already on the worksheet. It simply changes how new data will be aligned. As always, you can still change the alignment with a range change. This exercise changes the default alignment from general (automatic) to center-align.

STEPS

1   **Open the SS2-2B workbook if needed**

2   **Move to Cell A1**

3   **Click *Format, Style, Modify, Alignment* tab**

4   **Click *Center* for center horizontal alignment and then click *OK, OK***

Examine the worksheet on your screen and in Figure SS2-22a. Notice that only the data in Cells A1, A3, and B3, whose alignment was not changed by a range command, is centered.

5   **In Cell B1, type** TEST1

6   **In Cell B2, type** TEST2 **and press** ↵

7   **Move to Cell B2 and left-align the data**

In examining your changes and Figure SS2-22b, note that the data in Cell B1, TEST1, was automatically assigned the default alignment—center. TEST2 in Cell B2 remained left-aligned because it was aligned by a range change. Any data entered into a new cell or one that was not formatted with a range change will appear center-aligned.

8   **Save this workbook again as SS2-2B**

FIGURE SS2-22 ■ **ENTERING NEW DATA**

(a) This illustrates changing the Default alignment to center-horizontal align.
(b) New data entries are aligned with the default setting unless the cell was formatted with a range command.

(a)

(b)

COLUMN WIDTH

The worksheet default changes for column width allow you to change the width of all columns in the spreadsheet *except* those whose widths have been set individually or as a range (you will learn these commands shortly). The following exercise adjusts the default column width.

STEPS

1 **Open the SS2-2B workbook if needed**

2 **Move to Cell A1**

3 **Click *Format*, *Column*, *Standard Width* for its dialog box**

Note that the default column width displayed in the *Standard Width* dialog box is 8.43.

4 **Type 12 in the *Standard Column Width* text box**

5 **Click *OK* to set the default column width to 12**

Examine the worksheet on your screen and in Figure SS2-23a. Notice that all columns are now 12 characters wide. Because they are wider, fewer columns (only A through G) can be displayed on the worksheet screen. Try one more change:

6 **Click *Format*, *Column*, *Standard Width***

7 **Type 4 in the *Standard Column Width* text box and click *OK***

As shown in Figure SS2-23b, the columns are now four characters wide, allowing many more columns to be displayed at one time. A number of other notable changes are caused by the column-width adjustment. First, regardless of alignment, text that exceeds the new cell width (such as in Cells B1 and B2) are displayed at the left edge of the cell. In addition, the right side of some labels may be hidden by cell entries to their right (as in

FIGURE SS2-23 ■ CHANGING THE DEFAULT COLUMN WIDTH

(a) Column widths have been changed to 12 characters using the *Standard Width* dialog box.
(b) Setting the column widths too narrow can overlap labels and obscure values.

	A	B	C	D	E	F	G
1	LEFT	TEST1					
2	RIGHT	TEST2					
3	1,235	2,468					
4	5,678.9						
5							
6							

(a)

	A	B	C	D	E	F	G	H	I	J	K	L	M	N	O	P	Q	R
1	LEFT	EST1																
2	IGHT	TEST2																
3	####	####																
4	###																	
5																		
6																		

(b)

Cell A2). Finally, values may appear as number symbols (####) filling a specific cell. Number symbols (#) such as the ones in Cells A3 and A4 indicate that the value in the cell cannot be displayed in its entirety. The value is still in the cell but it cannot be seen. There are two ways to remedy the situation—either change the cell's format to one that occupies less space or make the column wider.

8 **Change the default width back to 8.43**

9 **Close the workbook without saving**

☑ **CHECKPOINT**

✓ What is the difference between a range change and a default change?
✓ Open the SS2-1D worksheet. Change to the comma, zero-decimal default number format.
✓ Which cells changed? Why?
✓ Change the default alignment to center.
✓ Change the default column width to 15. Save as DEFAULT.

ADJUSTING COLUMN WIDTH

Although default column widths can be reset, you may also want to change the width of one or more individual columns. You can widen columns to accommodate longer text or value formats, or shorten columns to fit more columns on a page. The following exercises demonstrate the use of *Column* cascading menus from the (*Format* menu), which

SS

allow you to change column width, reset column default settings, and even hide columns from view.

CHANGING INDIVIDUAL COLUMN WIDTH

Column widths can be adjusted by using the *Column Width* dialog box or by dragging and dropping the border to the right of the column letter. Assume you want to change the widths of Columns B and D. The following exercises demonstrate both techniques.

THE *COLUMN WIDTH* DIALOG BOX.   You can set a single column width or a range of column widths by using the *Column Width* dialog box. Try the following:

STEPS

1 Open the SS2-1D workbook

2 Move to Cell B6 (any cell in Column B is fine)

Your worksheet should resemble Figure SS2-24a.

3 Click *Format*, *Column*, *Width* for its dialog box

FIGURE SS2-24 ■ CHANGING INDIVIDUAL COLUMN WIDTH

(a) The initial worksheet columns are set to a default of 8.43 characters.
(b) This illustrates the *Column Width* dialog box.

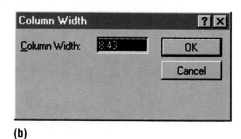

(a)

(b)

(c)

The current width (8.43) appears in the *Column Width* text box of the *Column Width* dialog box as shown in Figure SS2-24b. Assume you want to change the width of this column to 6.

4   Type **6** in the *Column Width* text box to set the width to six characters

5   Click *OK* to set new column width

As shown in Figure SS2-24c, the width of Column B has changed.

DRAGGING AND DROPPING A COLUMN WIDTH.   A column's width can also be changed by dragging and dropping the border to the right of a column letter. As you try the next exercise, examine the cell address area (left side) of the formula bar for character-width messages. (If you do not have a mouse, use the *Column Width* dialog box to change Column D's width to 12 characters.)

STEPS

1   Slowly move your mouse pointer to the border to the right of the Column letter D until it changes to a resizing column-width pointer as in Figure SS2-25a

2   Press and hold the left mouse button while moving the mouse and border (drag) to the left until the message "Width:7:00" appears in the name box (formula bar) area as in Figure SS2-25b

FIGURE SS2-25 ■ DRAGGING AND DROPPING A COLUMN WIDTH

(a) Slowly moving your mouse pointer to the border to the right of a column letter changes it to a resizing column-width pointer.
(b) As you drag the resizing column-width pointer, the column's new character width appears in the name box (formula bar). A horizontal line indicating where the new column border will appear is displayed below the pointer until the mouse is released.
(c) Column D has been resized to 12 characters.

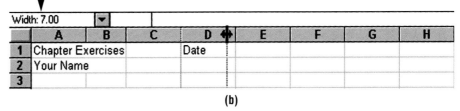

3 Release the mouse

Column D is now narrowed by about one character. Using the same technique, change Column D's width to six characters:

4 Again, move your mouse pointer to the border to the right of the Column letter D

5 Drag the border to the left until "Width:6.0" appears in the selection indicator area

6 Release the mouse

Note that the column is now too narrow to show certain numeric data. Instead, number signs (####) fill the cell. Now use the same technique to increase the column width to 12 characters:

7 Point to the border to the right of the Column letter *D*

8 Drag the border to the right until "Width:12.0" appears in the cell address area

9 Release the mouse

As shown in Figure SS2-25c, Column D is now 12 characters wide.

RESETTING TO THE DEFAULT WIDTH. Once column widths have been set individually, they do not respond to default changes. However, you can cancel the individual width and return the column to the default setting with a similar command sequence.

STEPS

1 Move to Cell D6 (any cell in Column D is fine)

2 Click *Format, Column, Standard Width* for its dialog box

3 Click the *OK* button

Column D returns to the default width.

4 Reset Column B's width to the default

5 Close the workbook without saving

CHANGING WIDTH IN A COLUMN RANGE

The *Column Width* dialog box can also be used to change the width of a range of columns. For this exercise, assume that you want to change Columns B, C, and D to 15 characters.

STEPS

1 Open the SS2-1D worksheet

2 Move to Cell B6 (or any cell in Column B)

3 Select the range B6:D6

4 Click *Format, Column, Width* for its dialog box

5 Type **15** in the *Column Width* text box

6 Click *OK*

7 Move to Cell B6

8 Close the workbook without saving

All three column widths have been changed to 15. You may also reset columns to the default by selecting *Standard Width* instead of *Width* in Step 4.

HIDING AND UNHIDING COLUMNS

At times, you may want to hide a column from view without harming its data or formulas (which continue to work correctly). This is especially useful when you want to eliminate specific columns from a printed copy of a spreadsheet.

HIDING COLUMNS.   Assume that you want to hide Columns B and C from the SS2-1D worksheet as shown in Figure SS2-26.

STEPS

1 Open the SS2-1D workbook

2 Move to Cell B6 (or any cell in Column B)

3 Select the range B6:C6

4 Click *Format, Column, Hide* to hide Columns B and C

The columns are hidden. Notice (as in Figure SS2-26) that the border highlight displays Column A followed by Column D—a clear indication that some columns are missing. Note, too, that the Gross values still reflect the data from the hidden columns. You could now continue to use, save, or print the worksheet.

There may be some text overlap problems, as in Row 1. These can be left alone or fixed as needed. For example, remove the date in Cell D1 as follows:

FIGURESS2-26 ■ **HIDING COLUMNS**

Columns B and C are hidden in this worksheet.

	A	D	E	F	
1	Chapter E Date				
2	Your Name				
3					
4	WEEKLY PAYROLL				
5	Employee	Gross			
6					
7	Burstein	$ 226.00			
8	Laudon	140.00			
9	Martin	218.50			
10	Parker	168.75			
11	Williams	112.00			
12					
13	TOTAL	$ 865.25			
14					
15					

5 In Cell D1, press **Delete**

UNHIDING COLUMNS. The procedure to "show," or redisplay, hidden columns is almost identical to the Hide command sequence:

STEPS

1 Move to Cell A1 (or any cell in Column A)

2 Select the range A1:D1

3 Click *Format*, *Column*, *Unhide*

4 Move to Cell A1

The hidden columns are redisplayed.

5 Close the workbook without saving

☑ CHECKPOINT

✓ Open the SS2-1D worksheet. Use the *Column Width* dialog box to change Column A's width to four.
✓ Change Column B's width to six by the drag and drop technique.
✓ Reset the width in Columns A and B to the default setting.
✓ Hide Column C, print the worksheet, and then redisplay the column.
✓ Change the default width to 15. Do *not* save this spreadsheet.

ENHANCING A WORKSHEET WITH FONTS, COLORS, AND LINES

Excel contains commands that enhance the appearance of your worksheet. As shown in Figure SS2-27, you can change the type styles or size of data for more professional-looking print; add lines and borders for better clarity; and emphasize data with color, highlighting, or shading. The following exercises introduce you to these enhancement features by modifying the WEEKLY PAYROLL worksheet in workbook SS2-1D to create the final worksheet as in Figure SS2-27.

Do the following to prepare for the exercises in this section.

STEPS

1   **Open the SS2-1D workbook**

2   **Move to Cell A1**

3   **Delete Rows 1, 2, and 3 (Select the range A1:A3, _Edit, Delete, Entire Row, OK_)**

4   **Move to Cell A3 and delete Row 3**

5   **Move to Cell A8 and delete Row 8**

6   **Move to Cell A1**

Your worksheet should appear as Figure SS2-28. If not, close the workbook without saving and then repeat Steps 1 through 6.

7   **Save this workbook as SS2-1E**

Font commands used in the following exercise can be invoked on a single cell, a range of cells, or before entering data.

FIGURE SS2-27 ■ **A WORKSHEET WITH FONT, COLOR, LINE, AND OTHER ENHANCEMENTS**

	A	B	C	D	E
1	WEEKLY PAYROLL				
2	Employee	Hours	Pay	Gross	
3	Burstein	40	$ 5.65	$ 226.00	
4	Laudon	35	4.00	140.00	
5	Martin	38	5.75	218.50	
6	Parker	25	6.75	168.75	
7	Williams	32	3.50	112.00	
8	TOTAL			$ 865.25	
9					
10					

FIGURE SS2-28 ■ **THE ADJUSTED WORKSHEET**

Extra rows have been deleted in preparation for the worksheet enhancements in this section.

	A	B	C	D	
1		WEEKLY PAYROLL			
2	Employee	Hours	Pay	Gross	
3	Burstein	40	$ 5.65	$ 226.00	
4	Laudon	35	4.00	140.00	
5	Martin	38	5.75	218.50	
6	Parker	25	6.75	168.75	
7	Williams	32	3.50	112.00	
8	TOTAL			$ 865.25	
9					

CHANGING A FONT

A **font** is a typeface. Excel and Windows offer a number of basic font faces, sizes, and styles (bold, italic) from which to choose. Your system may also have other fonts available.

Assume that you want to emphasize the title "WEEKLY PAYROLL" by selecting a different font face, font size, and font style as in Figure SS2-27. As you will soon see, these changes can be done through the Format toolbar or the *Font* tab of the *Format Cells* dialog box.

CHANGING A FONT FACE. The default *font face* used by Excel is Arial. This is the typeface that currently appears on your screen. To change it to another font face:

STEPS

1 Move to Cell A1, if needed

The text "WEEKLY PAYROLL," which is aligned to fit across Columns A through D, should appear in the entry area of your formula bar.

 2 Click the ▼ button of the *Font* drop-down box (Format toolbar) for its list

 3 Click the ▼ button of the Font list scroll bar until Times New Roman is visible, similar to Figure SS2-29

4 Click *Times New Roman* to select it

The title, "WEEKLY PAYROLL," should now appear in the font face Times New Roman as in Figure SS2-30a.

Tip: The *Font* tab of the *Format Cells* dialog box can also be used to make font changes. To access it, click *Format, Cells, Font* tab, select the font, *OK.*

FIGURE SS2-29 ■ CHANGING A FONT FACE

Clicking the ▼ button of the *Font* drop-down box (Format toolbar) opens its list.

CHANGING FONT SIZE.   A font's size is measured in points. A *point* is a typesetting unit of measure equivalent to 1/72 of an inch. As displayed in the *Font Size* drop-down box of the Format toolbar, Excel's default point size is 10 points. To change the point size:

STEPS

1 Click the ▼ button of the *Font Size* drop-down box (Format toolbar)

2 Click *16* in the *Font Size* list

The title, "WEEKLY PAYROLL," should now resemble Figure SS2-30b.

FIGURE SS2-30 ■ CHANGING A FONT

(a) The font face has been changed to Times New Roman.
(b) Changing a font's size to 16 points enlarges its typeface.
(c) The Bold feature darkens a font's type face for emphasis.

(a)

(b)

(c)

SS

CHANGING FONT STYLE. Font styles available with many fonts include regular (the default), *italic*, **bold,** and ***bold italic.*** You can change the font style using the *Font* tab (in the *Format Cells* dialog box); however, using the toolbar or shortcut keys is more efficient. Try this:

STEPS

B

1 Click the *Bold* button (Format toolbar) to boldface the title   [**Ctrl** **+** **B**]

I

2 Click the *Italic* button (Format toolbar)   [**Ctrl** **+** **I**]

The title, "WEEKLY PAYROLL," should now appear in Bold Italic. Now, to remove the italic style:

I

3 Click the *Italic* button again   [**Ctrl** **+** **I**]

The title, "WEEKLY PAYROLL," should now resemble Figure SS2-30c. Font-style commands are toggle (on/off) commands and, as mentioned earlier, can also be invoked before entering data.

4 Resave this workbook as SS2-1E

CHANGING COLOR

Both the background and font colors can be changed. Although the following exercise changes Cells A2 through D2's cell-background color to black and the characters to white, as in Figure SS2-31a, you can use any color available on Excel's color palette.

CHANGING BACKGROUND COLOR. The background color is the color of the interior space of a cell. To change the background color:

STEPS

1 Select the range A2:D2

FIGURE SS2-31 ■ **CHANGING BACKGROUND AND CHARACTER COLORS**

(a) The character color of the data in Cells A2 through D2 are changed to white.
(b) The background color of Cells A2 through D2 are changed to black.

(a)

(b)

2 Click the ▼ button of the *Color* button (Format toolbar) for the cell color palette

3 Click the *Black* palette box

4 Move to Cell A2

The background color of Cells A2:D2 are now black as in Figure SS2-31b. Since the character color is also black, they blend into the background and are not currently distinguishable. This will be corrected in the following section when you change the color of the characters to white.

CHANGING CHARACTER COLOR.   The default color of text is black; however, this can easily be changed as follows:

STEPS

1 Select the range A2:D2

2 Click the ▼ button of the *Font Color* button (Format toolbar) for the Font color palette

3 Click the *White* palette box

4 Move to Cell A1

The text in Cells A2 through D2 should appear as Figure SS2-31a.

5 Resave the workbook as SS2-1E

ADDING LINES

Excel's Border commands allow you to draw lines around each cell or outlines around ranges of cells for emphasis. Only lines, double-lines, color changes, and outlines are discussed here.

CREATING LINES.   To create lines (including double-lines) as in Figure SS2-32a,

STEPS

1 Open the SS2-1E workbook if needed

2 Select the range A7:D7

3 Click the ▼ button of the *Borders* button (Format toolbar) for a palette of borders

4 Click the *Single line* border box (see left margin)

FIGURE SS2-32 ■ ADDING LINES

(a) Border lines (single and double) have been added to the bottom of Cells A7 through D7, and A8 through D8.
(b) Vertical lines have been added to the worksheet.
(c) A double-line outline has been drawn around the outer borders of the worksheet.

	A	B	C	D	E
1	WEEKLY PAYROLL				
2	Employee	Hours	Pay	Gross	
3	Burstein	40	$ 5.65	$ 226.00	
4	Laudon	35	4.00	140.00	
5	Martin	38	5.75	218.50	
6	Parker	25	6.75	168.75	
7	Williams	32	3.50	112.00	
8	TOTAL			$ 865.25	
9					
10					

(a)

	A	B	C	D	E
1	WEEKLY PAYROLL				
2	Employee	Hours	Pay	Gross	
3	Burstein	40	$ 5.65	$ 226.00	
4	Laudon	35	4.00	140.00	
5	Martin	38	5.75	218.50	
6	Parker	25	6.75	168.75	
7	Williams	32	3.50	112.00	
8	TOTAL			$ 865.25	
9					
10					

(b)

	A	B	C	D	E
1	WEEKLY PAYROLL				
2	Employee	Hours	Pay	Gross	
3	Burstein	40	$ 5.65	$ 226.00	
4	Laudon	35	4.00	140.00	
5	Martin	38	5.75	218.50	
6	Parker	25	6.75	168.75	
7	Williams	32	3.50	112.00	
8	TOTAL			$ 865.25	
9					
10					

(c)

⑤ Move to Cell A8 and then select the range A8:D8

⑥ Click the ▼ button of the Borders toolbar button for a palette of borders again

⑦ Click the *Double-line* border box

⑧ Move to Cell A1

Tip: In place of Steps 4 through 7, you can click the top single line, bottom double-line border box of the Border palette.

Your worksheet should appear as Figure SS2-32a, Now, to add vertical lines,

9 Select the range A3:C7

10 Click the ▼ button of the *Borders* toolbar button for a palette of borders

11 Click *Right Vertical* Border box ↵

12 Move to Cell B2

13 Save the workbook as SS2-1F

CHANGING LINE COLOR.   Now, to add white vertical lines to Cells B2 and C2:

STEPS

1 Select the range A2:C2

2 Click *Format, Cells, Border* tab   [Ctrl + 1 , B]

3 Click *Right* in the Border group

4 Click the ▼ button of the *Color* drop-down box for the color palette

5 Click the *White* box in the color palette

6 Click *OK*

7 Move to Cell A1

8 Resave the workbook as SS2-1F

Your worksheet should now appear as Figure SS2-32b.

CREATING AN OUTLINE.   The outline feature places a line or lines around a selected range. To create a double-line border around the worksheet:

STEPS

1 Select the range A1:D8

2 Open the *Format Cells* dialog box and select the *Border* tab   [Ctrl + 1 , B]

3 Click *Outline* in the Border group

4 Click the *Double-line box* in the Style group

SS

5   Click *OK*

6   Move to Cell A1

Your worksheet should appear as Figure SS2-32c.

7   Save this workbook as SS2-1G and then close it

PROVIDING ADDITIONAL EMPHASIS

If you have a mouse, you can use the Drawing toolbar to add a variety of additional features such as drop shadows, captions, arrows, and other objects.

   To add a drop shadow, as in Figure SS2-27, to your SS2-1G workbook:

STEPS

1   Open the SS2-1G workbook

2   Select the range A1:D8

3   Click the *Drawing* button (Standard toolbar) for the Drawing toolbar

4   Click the *Drop Shadow* button on the Drawing toolbar

At this point, you can use the Drawing toolbar to create other objects in your worksheet. Feel free to experiment with this toolbar on your own. For now, to close the toolbar:

5   Click the *Drawing* button (Standard toolbar) to remove the Drawing toolbar

Note that drop-shadow borders have *handles* (small square boxes). This means that the drop-shadow border is selected. In Excel, a drop-shadow border is considered an object (drawing). Objects in the Windows environment, like data, must be selected before they can be edited. See the appendix for further information on creating and editing objects in Excel. For now,

6   Click Cell A1 (or any other cell) to deselect the drop shadow

Your worksheet should appear as in Figure SS2-27.

7   Save the workbook as SS2-1H and then close it

☑   CHECKPOINT

   ✓   What is a font?
   ✓   Open the SS2-1D workbook and change the font face and size of the data in Rows 4 and 5.
   ✓   Change the background and character colors in the range A7:A11.

✓   Delete any blank rows of the worksheet and place border lines around the data.
✓   Add a drop-shadow to the worksheet. Save the workbook as ENHANCE and then close it.

CELL REFERENCES

If you *type* every formula in your spreadsheet (a tedious task), you need never worry about different types of cell references. However, it is more likely that you will use the Copy and Paste commands extensively to *copy* formulas into cells rather than type all of them.

To prepare for these exercises (and practice some of the skills you have learned in this chapter), create the worksheet shown in Figure SS2-33, as follows:

STEPS

1 Close any open workbook and then open a new one

2 Make the following default changes:

■   Number format: Comma, two decimals (*Format, Style, Modify, Number* tab, *Number, Use 1000 Separator [,], OK, OK*)
■   Column width: 12 (*Format, Column, Standard Width*)

3 Use the *Column Width* dialog box (*Format, Column, Width*) to set Column A's width to 25

4 Type the cell entries shown in Figure SS2-33

5 Right-align the contents of Cells B2:D3

FIGURE SS2-33 ■ THE INITIAL SS2-3A WORKSHEET BEFORE FORMULAS ARE ADDED

	A	B	C	D	E
1	Bookstore Discounts				
2		Book	0.10	Sale	
3	Title	Price	Discount	Price	
4					
5	The Rough-Faced Girl	16.95			
6	Will's Mammoth	14.95			
7	Foolish Rabbit's Mistake	12.00			
8	Ghost Stories of Japan	8.50			
9	The Hungry Tigress	16.00			
10					
11					

Your screen should resemble Figure SS2-33. If it does not, repeat Steps 1 through 5.

6   **Save this workbook as SS2-3A**

RELATIVE AND ABSOLUTE REFERENCES

The standard copy procedure, which you have seen, uses cell references that are relative. A **relative reference** is a cell address that, when copied, is automatically adjusted to reflect its new position in the worksheet. However, you may not want the copied cell address to change at all.

Examine the discount worksheet in Figure SS2-34a. If you enter the formula =B5*C2 in Cell C5, the correct discount will be calculated for the first book. However, if this formula was copied down the column, the relative references in it would be changed automatically to =B6*C3, =B7*C4, and so on. This would be incorrect, for although the book price reference in Column B should change relative to each row, the discount percentage reference (C2) *must remain constant*. This problem calls for an

FIGURE SS2-34 ■ ABSOLUTE AND RELATIVE REFERENCES

(a) An absolute reference has been typed.
(b) The formula is placed in Cell C5.

C5			=B5*$C$2		
	A	**B**	**C**	**D**	**E**
1	Bookstore Discounts				
2		Book	0.10	Sale	
3	Title	Price	Discount	Price	
4					
5	The Rough-Faced Girl	16.95	=B5*$C$2		
6	Will's Mammoth	14.95			
7	Foolish Rabbit's Mistake	12.00			
8	Ghost Stories of Japan	8.50			
9	The Hungry Tigress	16.00			
10					
11					

(a)

	A	**B**	**C**	**D**	**E**
1	Bookstore Discounts				
2		Book	0.10	Sale	
3	Title	Price	Discount	Price	
4					
5	The Rough-Faced Girl	16.95	1.70		
6	Will's Mammoth	14.95			
7	Foolish Rabbit's Mistake	12.00			
8	Ghost Stories of Japan	8.50			
9	The Hungry Tigress	16.00			
10					
11					

(b)

(continued)

absolute reference—a cell address reference that always refers to the same cell re-gardless of where it is copied. Absolute references are easily created:

1 Open the SS2-3A workbook if needed

2 Move to Cell C5

3 Type =B5 (do not press the Enter key yet)

You need do nothing else to this reference, because you want it to remain relative.

4 Type *C2 (do not press the Enter key yet)

To make C2 an absolute reference,

5 Press F4 (Absolute)

Notice that dollar symbols have been placed before the column letter and row number in the cell address ($C$2), as in Figure SS2-34a. The dollar symbols indicate that the row and column references are "locked" in the identified worksheet—they are absolute ref-erences that will not be changed if this formula is copied. (The F4 function key places these symbols for you, but you may type them yourself instead, as long as you place them correctly.)

6 Press ↵ to complete the entry

The formula in Cell C5 (and its result of 1.70) should resemble the contents shown in Figure SS2-34b. If it does not, retype it now. When the formula is correctly entered, it can be copied into the remaining cells.

7 Copy Cell C5 into the range C6:C9

Examine the formulas in Cells C5:C9, as shown in Figure SS2-34c. Notice that the rel-ative reference (B5) has been changed in each row, whereas the absolute reference ($C$2) remains unchanged in each formula.

Complete the spreadsheet now by entering a formula with relative references (ones that will change when copied) to calculate the sale price:

8 In Cell D5, enter =B5-C5 and then press ↵

9 Copy this formula into cells D6:D9

10 Move to Cell A1

Your worksheet should resemble Figure SS2-34d.

11 Save this workbook as SS2-3B

FIGURE SS2-34 ▪ *(continued)*

(c) The relative reference in Cell C5 has been changed in each row, whereas the absolute reference remains constant.

(d) The completed worksheet has both relative and absolute references.

(c)

	A	B	C	D	E
1	Bookstore Discounts				
2		Book	0.10	Sale	
3	Title	Price	Discount	Price	
4					
5	The Rough-Faced Girl	16.95	1.70		
6	Will's Mammoth	14.95	1.50		
7	Foolish Rabbit's Mistake	12.00	1.20		
8	Ghost Stories of Japan	8.50	0.85		
9	The Hungry Tigress	16.00	1.60		
10					
11					

(d)

	A	B	C	D	E
1	Bookstore Discounts				
2		Book	0.10	Sale	
3	Title	Price	Discount	Price	
4					
5	The Rough-Faced Girl	16.95	1.70	15.26	
6	Will's Mammoth	14.95	1.50	13.46	
7	Foolish Rabbit's Mistake	12.00	1.20	10.80	
8	Ghost Stories of Japan	8.50	0.85	7.65	
9	The Hungry Tigress	16.00	1.60	14.40	
10					
11					
12					

MIXED REFERENCES

Other circumstances may require the use of a **mixed reference**—a cell-address reference that is part absolute and part relative. Mixed references use one dollar sign to lock in either a row or column coordinate, but they leave the other coordinate relative. For example,

STEPS

1 Close any open workbook and then open a new workbook

2 In Cell B1, type `=$A1` and press [↵]

3 Now copy Cell B1 to the range C1:C10

4 Move to Cell C1

Examine the cell contents of any cell in Column C. Notice that the Column A reference remains, but the row changes relative to its new location. In the mixed reference =$A1, the dollar sign before the *A* has made the column absolute—it remains constant when copied—whereas Row 1 is free to change. Similarly, in a mixed reference such as =A$1, Column A is relative, whereas Row 1 is absolute.

5 Close the workbook without saving

> **Tip:** Pressing the F4 key while the cell pointer is on a cell address changes the reference from relative to absolute and then to mixed references. The cycle is =A1 →
> =$A$1 → =A$4 → =$A4 → =A1.

FIXING CIRCULAR REFERENCES

A **circular reference** is an error condition that occurs in a spreadsheet when a cell formula refers to itself either directly or indirectly. This is usually caused by a mistyped or misplaced formula. Figure SS2-35 displays two examples of circular references. In Figure SS2-35a, Cell B2's formula includes a direct reference to itself—clearly a problem. Figure SS2-35b, on the other hand, displays an *indirect* circular

FIGURE SS2-35 ■ CIRCULAR REFERENCES

(a) A *direct* circular reference is placed in the same cell.
(b) An *indirect* circular reference can involve many cells.

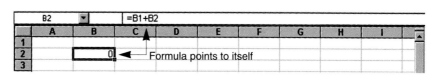

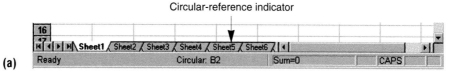

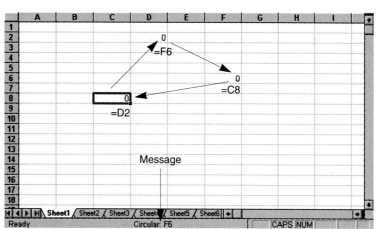

reference—Cell D2's formula refers to a cell, which refers to another cell, which in turn refers back to Cell D2. Create the circular reference in Figure SS2-35a to see the effect:

STEPS

1 **Close any open workbook and open a new one**

2 **In Cell B2, type** `=B1+B2` **and press ↵**

When a circular reference occurs, a dialog box indicating "Cannot resolve circular references," as in Figure SS2-36a, appears.

3 **Click *OK***

"Circular: B2" now appears in the status bar, as in Figure SS2-36b. This circular reference indicator will remain the same until changed.

4 **In Cell B2, press** **Delete**

5 **Close the workbook without saving**

☑ **CHECKPOINT**

✓ Describe the difference between a relative and absolute reference. Which key invokes the absolute reference?
✓ Define the components and effect of a mixed reference.
✓ What is a circular reference and where does Excel identify that one exists in a worksheet?
✓ Open SS2-3A Delete Column D. Create a border line beneath the column headings. Change the discount rate to 15 percent.

FIGURE SS2-36 ■ **CIRCULAR REFERENCE MESSAGES**

(a) If you enter a circular reference, this dialog box appears to warn you.
(b) If a circular reference has been entered into a worksheet, the status bar displays its cell position.

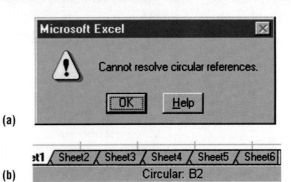

(a)

(b)

✓ Create a mixed reference in Cell D5 to calculate the final book price by subtracting the discounted price from the book price. Save the workbook as SS2-4A.

FUNCTIONS

Excel offers more than 100 built-in formulas, called *functions,* that perform a variety of useful calculations. You can use functions for arithmetic, statistical, financial, string, or date and time calculations. Functions are also available for creating conditional formulas or performing table lookups (see Chapter 3). An extensive list of Excel's functions is included in the appendix.

FUNCTION STRUCTURE

Although Excel functions perform different tasks, each shares a common structure, as shown in Figure SS2-37. All functions must begin with an "=" symbol and a function name that identifies the desired calculations. In addition, many functions include *arguments* (enclosed in parentheses) that indicate the data or range of cells that should be used in the calculation.

A FUNCTION SAMPLER

Figure SS2-38 lists a few illustrative examples of functions. Each has been applied to the data in Figure SS2-39 to calculate an answer (in Column C of the worksheet). If you want to see the effect of each yourself,

---

STEPS

1 Close any open workbook and then open a new one

2 Enter the data in Cells A1 through A5 of Figure SS2-39

FIGURE SS2-37 ■ ANATOMY OF A FUNCTION

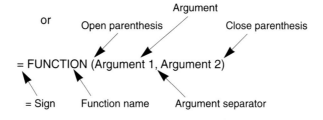

= FUNCTION

or

= FUNCTION (Argument 1, Argument 2)

FIGURE SS2-38 ■   SOME SAMPLE FUNCTIONS

This is an illustrative sample *of a few of* the many functions. s = a string or a cell address that contains a string. v = a value or a cell address that contains a value. n = a number.

Function	Explanation
SUM(range)	Calculates the sum of the range
AVERAGE(range)	Calculates the average of nonempty cells
MAX(range)	Lists the highest value in the range
MIN(range)	Lists the lowest value in the range
COUNT(range)	Lists the number of nonempty cells
STDEVP(range)	Calculates the standard deviation
ROUND(v,n)	Rounds *v* to *n* decimal places
SQRT(v)	Calculates the square root of *v*
ABS(v)	Calculates the absolute value of *v*
INT(v)	Calculates the integer value of *v*
RAND( )	Calculates a random number from 0 to 1
LEFT(s,n)	Returns the first *n* characters of *s*
RIGHT(s,n)	Returns the last *n* characters of *s*
LEN(s)	Counts the characters in *s*
LOWER(s)	Converts *s* to lowercase
PROPER(s)	Changes the first letter in *s* to uppercase and the rest to lowercase
REPT(s,n)	Duplicates *s* *n* times
PMT(p,i,n)	Calculates a periodic payment amount needed to pay off a loan of *rate* interest for the period, *nper* payments, *pu* principal, or present value
NOW	Calculates a value that corresponds to the current date and time
DATE(y,m.d)	Calculates a date number for a set of year, month, and day values

3   Enter the data in Cells A7 and A12 of Figure SS2-39

4   Type each function shown in Figure SS2-39 in the corresponding cell in Column C

(That is, start in C1 and type   **=SUM(A1:A7)** . Then type each succeeding function in the cell below the previous one.) Examine the result of each function, based on the spreadsheet's data, before entering the next function.

The results in Column C should match the spreadsheet (except for Cell C11, which generates a random number, and C19, which depends on the current date). Check your entries and retype them if your results differ.

5   Save this workbook as SS2-4 and then close it

FIGURE SS2-39 ■ A WORKSHEET SAMPLER OF FUNCTIONS

Note: Your results in Column C should match, except for Cell C11, which generates a random number and C19, which depends on the current date.

	A	B	C	D	E	F	G	H	I
1	11		78.6		◄	=SUM(A1:A7)			
2	1		13.1		◄	=AVERAGE(A1:A7)			
3	49		49		◄	=MAX(A1:A7)			
4	0		-3		◄	=MIN(A1:A7)			
5	-3		6		◄	=COUNT(A1:A7)			
6			17.91973		◄	=STDEVP(A1:A7)			
7	20.6		21		◄	=ROUND(A7,0)			
8			7		◄	=SQRT(A3)			
9			3		◄	=ABS(A5)			
10			20		◄	=INT(A7)			
11			0.996198		◄	=RAND()			
12	SAMPLE		SAM		◄	=LEFT(A12,3)			
13			LE		◄	=RIGHT(A12,2)			
14			6		◄	=LEN(A12)			
15			sample		◄	=LOWER(A12)			
16			Sample		◄	=PROPER(A12)			
17			SAMPLESAMPLE		◄	=REPT(A12,2)			
18			($49.02)		◄	=PMT(A2,A1,A3)			
19			16740		◄	=INT((NOW())-DATE(A3,A2,A1))			
20									

USING THE FUNCTION WIZARD

Excel's **Function wizard** is a feature that can help you quickly identify a function's operation and its required arguments. It also simplifies using functions by providing a two-step function-entry guide. This process, as illustrated next, involves first selecting a desired function from a list and then filling in its arguments.

STEPS

1 Open workbook SS2-4 if needed

2 Move to Cell C20

3 Click *Insert, Function* for the function   [**Shift** + **F3**]

Note that the Function wizard's title bar displays "Function Wizard - Step 1 of 2."

4 Click *All* in the *Function Category* list box to select it

5 Use the vertical scroll bar of the *Function Name* list box to scroll to PMT and then click it.

Your *Function wizard's* dialog box should resemble Figure SS2-40a. (Note that the position of PMT in your *Function Name* list box may differ.) Just below the function category, the selected function is displayed with its required arguments and a brief description of its operation.

FIGURE SS2-40 ■ THE FUNCTION WIZARD

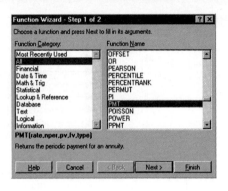

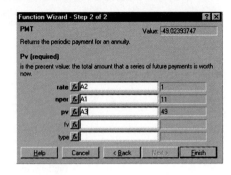

(a)   (b)

6 Click the *Next* button for the *Function wizard - Step 2 of 2* dialog box

7 Type **A2** in the *rate* text box and then press **Tab**

8 Type **A1** in the *nper* (number of periods) text box and then press **Tab**

9 Type **A3** in the pv (present value)

Your *Function wizard - Step 2 of 2* dialog box should resemble Figure SS2-40b. To the right of each cell reference that you entered is the current data it contains. Note also that the *Value* box (upper-right corner) displays the result of the function ($49.02393747).

10 Click the *Finish* button

The result of the PMT function, ($49.02) in Cell C20, should be the same as in Cell C18.

> **Tip: The Function wizard can also be used to place a function within a formula using cell references and mathematical operators and within another function. For example, the formula in Cell C19 "=INT((NOW())−DATE(A3,A2,A1))"**

11 Close the workbook without saving

☑ CHECKPOINT

✓ What is a function and the different ways that it can be entered?
✓ Can functions be inserted within a function? Give an example.
✓ Open SS2-4a. Type in function formulas to calculate the total and average book prices in Rows 11 and 12.

✓ Use the Function wizard to insert function formulas to calculate the maximum and minimum book prices in Rows 13 and 14.

✓ Use a data function to place the system date in the cell next to your name. Resave the workbook as SS2-4a.

MANAGING LARGE SPREADSHEETS

As spreadsheets grow large, they become more difficult to manage on the screen. Row or column data may disappear off the screen as the cell pointer is moved, making it harder to enter data in the proper cells. Results generated by "What if?" scenarios may be located far from data-entry cells, and thus not easily read as changes are made. Excel offers two command windows—*Titles* and *Split*—that alleviate the problems associated with large spreadsheets. Note that these features affect only the screen; they do not alter how worksheets print.

FREEZING

The **Freeze Panes** command (*Window* menu) freezes columns, rows, or both along the top and left of the worksheet. Once frozen, these cells remain in constant view no matter where the cell pointer moves in the worksheet.

FREEZING PANES.   The following exercise demonstrates the procedure for freezing panes on the screen:

STEPS

1 Open the SS2-1H workbook

Position the cell pointer one row *below* the rows you want to freeze and one column to the *right* of the columns to freeze. In this example, you will freeze Rows 1 through 2 and Column A.

2 Move to Cell B3, as shown in Figure SS2-41a

The columns to the left of this cell, and the rows above it, can now be frozen.

3 Click *Window*, *Freeze Panes* to freeze both rows and columns

4 Move the cell pointer to Cell J3

Note how Column A remains on the screen, as in Figure SS2-41b. To return to the first cell past the frozen panes (Cell B3),

5 Move to Cell B3

6 Move to Cell B18

FIGURE SS2-41 ■ **FREEZING PANES**

(a) The cell pointer is positioned below the row and to the right of the column to be frozen.
(b) Frozen columns remain on the screen as it scrolls right.
(c) Frozen rows remain on the screen as it scrolls down.

(a)

	A	B	C	D	E	F	G	H	I
1	**WEEKLY PAYROLL**								
2	Employee	Hours	Pay	Gross					
3	Burstein	40	$ 5.65	$ 226.00					
4	Laudon	35	4.00	140.00					
5	Martin	38	5.75	218.50					
6	Parker	25	6.75	168.75					
7	Williams	32	3.50	112.00					
8	TOTAL			$ 865.25					
9									
10									

(b)

	A	C	D	E	F	G	H	I	J
1	**WEPAYROLL**								
2	Employee	Pay	Gross						
3	Burstein	$ 5.65	$ 226.00						
4	Laudon	4.00	140.00						
5	Martin	5.75	218.50						
6	Parker	6.75	168.75						
7	Williams	3.50	112.00						
8	TOTAL		$ 865.25						
9									
10									
11									

(c)

	A	B	C	D	E	F	G	H	I
1	**WEEKLY PAYROLL**								
2	Employee	Hours	Pay	Gross					
6	Parker	25	6.75	168.75					
7	Williams	32	3.50	112.00					
8	TOTAL			$ 865.25					
9									
10									

Note how Rows 1 and 2 remain on the screen, as in Figure SS2-41c.

You can freeze panes anywhere. You should consider doing so especially on large spreadsheets where the benefit of titles becomes significant.

> **Tip:** To freeze just the rows, click the row number of the row below the row you want to freeze and then click _Window, Freeze Pane_. To freeze only the columns, click the column letter of the column to the right of the columns you want frozen, and then click _Window, Freeze Pane_.

UNFREEZING PANES.   You need not be in any particular cell to unfreeze titles. Simply,

STEPS

1 Click _Window_

2 Click _Unfreeze Panes_

SPLITTING

The **Split** command splits the worksheet window into separate **panes,** either horizontally, vertically, or both. This allows you to see two or four different parts of the spreadsheet at the same time. These panes are two (or four) copies of the same spreadsheet.

SPLITTING PANES.   The following exercise creates a vertical window (but could just as easily create a horizontal one).

STEPS

1 Open the SS2-1H worksheet (if needed)

When creating a pane, you must first position the cell pointer in the row that will be the top edge of the new pane (if horizontal) or the column that will be its left edge (if vertical). You will use Column D:

2 Move to Cell D1, as shown in Figure SS2-42a

3 Click _Window_ for the _Window_ menu

4 Click _Split_

Note how two panes appear side by side as in Figure SS2-42b.

SS

FIGURE SS2-42 ■ SPLITTING

(a) The cell pointer is placed where the window will be split.
(b) The cell pointer is in the right pane but can be switched to the left by clicking any cell in the left pane or by pressing the F6 key.

	A	B	C	D	E
1	WEEKLY PAYROLL				
2	Employee	Hours	Pay	Gross	
3	Burstein	40	$ 5.65	$ 226.00	
4	Laudon	35	4.00	140.00	
5	Martin	38	5.75	218.50	
6	Parker	25	6.75	168.75	
7	Williams	32	3.50	112.00	
8	TOTAL			$ 865.25	
9					
10					

(a)

	A	B	C	D	E
1	WEEKLY PAYROLL				
2	Employee	Hours	Pay	Gross	
3	Burstein	40	$ 5.65	$ 226.00	
4	Laudon	35	4.00	140.00	
5	Martin	38	5.75	218.50	
6	Parker	25	6.75	168.75	
7	Williams	32	3.50	112.00	
8	TOTAL			$ 865.25	
9					
10				◄— Split bar	

(b)

SWITCHING PANES.   You can now move the cell pointer in the right pane as needed. If you wish to adjust the left pane, you must switch the cell pointer to it.

STEPS

1   Click *Cell C1* (or any cell) in the left pane   [**F6**]

You can now move in the pane. To switch back to the right pane,

2   Click *Cell D1* (or any cell) in the right   [**F6**]

REMOVING THE SPLIT.   When you no longer need two (or more) panes on the screen, you can clear them as follows:

STEPS

1   Click *Window,* for the *Window* menu

2   Click *Remove Split*

You may practice the split procedure by creating a horizontal pane by moving the cell pointer to Column A and the respective row and then invoking the Split command (*Window* menu). You can also create a vertical and horizontal split by placing the cell pointer in any desired cell except for Row 1 or Column A and then invoking the Split command.

3   Close the workbook without saving

☑   CHECKPOINT
- ✓   What is the difference between freezing and splitting?
- ✓   Open workbook SS2-3B. Freeze titles in Column A.
- ✓   Set a vertical pane in Column C. Switch to the spreadsheet on the right.
- ✓   Split the worksheet at Column C. Move to the other side of the split bar and then unsplit the worksheet.
- ✓   Unfreeze the column and then close any open worksheet.

PRINTING TECHNIQUES

Large spreadsheets may also require the use of additional print features to enhance the appearance of the spreadsheet on paper. Such features include creating page breaks and using print options.

PAGE BREAKS

Excel automatically creates a new page when printed data fill a page (as determined by top and bottom margins). However, you can control page breaks yourself by adding a row in your spreadsheet with special print-control characters. The following exercise, which creates a page break after Row 8, shows you how to do this.

STEPS

1 **Open the SS2-1G workbook**

The cell pointer should be first placed in the *leftmost* column of the range you are printing, in the row where you want the new page to start.

2 **Move to Cell A6**

3 **Click *Insert, Page Break***

As shown in Figure SS2-43, Excel inserts a row of dimmed dashed lines representing a forced page break. When this worksheet is printed, a new page will begin at Row 9.
    To remove a page break:

4 **Move to Cell A6 (if needed)**

5 **Click *Insert, Remove Page Break***

PAGE SETUP OPTIONS

A number of *Page Setup* options are available through the *Page Setup* dialog box. This dialog box can be accessed through the *File* menu, the *Print* dialog box, or the *Print Preview* dialog box. As displayed in Figure SS2-44, the *Page Setup* dialog box includes the following options:

SS

FIGURE SS2-43 ■ PAGE BREAKS

Page breaks can be inserted as needed.

Page-break indicator

FIGURE SS2-44 ■ **THE** *PAGE SETUP* **DIALOG BOX**

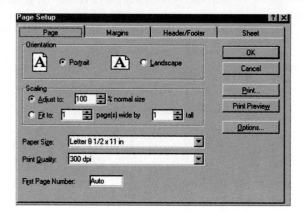

- *Page tab:* Changes orientation and scales data so you can fit more (or less) on each page
- *Margin tab:* Adjusts margins
- *Header/Footer tab:* Places a header at the top or a footer at the bottom of each page
- *Sheet tab:* Prints column and row titles on each page and offers other printing options

SCALING PAGE DATA. When you are working with a large worksheet, the *Scaling group* options of the *Page* tab (*Page Setup* dialog box) allow you to compress the data size. Data, columns, or rows can be compressed to a single page or custom compressed. Try this:

STEPS

1 Click *File*, *Page Setup* for its dialog box

The *Page Setup* dialog box, as shown in Figure SS2-44, should appear on your screen.

You can select either the *Adjust to* (the default) or *Fit to* option button in the scaling group to control the compression of your worksheet data. The *Adjust to* option is preset to 100% and allows you to control the size of the printed data. To change it, you can either click the up or down triangle buttons to the right of the *Adjust to* text box or type in a desired size. Try this:

2 Click the ▼ button of the *Adjust to* text box until the size is reduced to 75%

3 Click *Print Preview*

4 Click the *Zoom* toolbar button

Your worksheet now appears scaled to 75% of its original size. You can print the worksheet instead of print previewing it by replacing Steps 3 and 4 with clicking the *Print* button (or pressing 1). Now, reset the scaling to 100%.

5 Click the *Setup* toolbar button for its dialog box

6 Click the ▼ button of the *Adjust to* text box to increase to 100%

The *Fit* to option is helpful when you want to compress a large worksheet's width and/or length to that of a page or a desired number of pages. Like the *Adjust to* option, you can change the *Fit to* option either by clicking the up or down triangle buttons to the right of its text boxes or by typing in a desired size. For now,

7 Click *OK* to return to the Print Preview window

8 Click *Close* to return to your worksheet

REPEATING COLUMN OR ROW TITLES. *Print titles* are the printed versions of frozen panes; that is, for print titles, you can select columns, rows, or both to be repeated on every page of a printed spreadsheet. This option is useful for multipage worksheets where top or side labels would normally appear only on the first page. To select print titles,

STEPS

1 Open the SS2-1G worksheet (if needed)

2 Click *File*, *Page Setup* for its dialog box

3 Click the *Sheet* tab

The Print Titles group of the Sheet tab allows you to specify the range of rows to repeat at the top of a page and/or columns to repeat at the left of a page. To specify the top two rows as a print title:

4 Click the *Rows to Repeat at Top* text box

5 Type `1:2` to repeat Rows 1 through 2

6 Click *Print Preview*

If this worksheet contained multiple pages, Rows 1 and 2 would appear on the top of each printed page. To print column titles on each page of a multiple-page worksheet, you would select the *Columns to Repeat at Left* text box of the *Sheet* tab and type in the first column letter of the range, a colon, and then the last column letter. For example, if you desired to print the column titles of Columns A through C on each page of a multiple-page worksheet, type A:C in the *Columns to Repeat at Left* text box.

7 Close the Print Preview window

8 Close the worksheet without saving

OTHER PRINT OPTIONS. The *Print group* box of the *Page Setup* dialog box (Figure SS2-45a) contains five print-display check boxes: Gridlines, Notes (prints any cell notes defined in the worksheet), Draft Quality (prints without grid lines and less graphics), Black and White (prints worksheet in pure black and white), and Row and Column Headings (includes row numbers and column letters). Try this:

FIGURE SS2-45 ■ OTHER PRINT OPTIONS

(a) The Print group options of the *Sheet* tab can be used to control certain displays of a worksheet.
(b) Activating the *Gridline* and *Row and Column Headings* check boxes will result in this worksheet when printed.

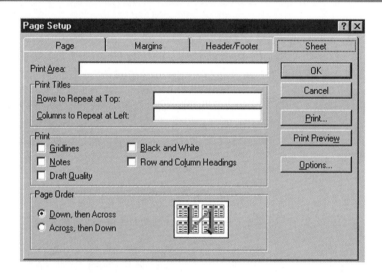

(a)

(b)

STEPS

1   **Open the SS2-1F workbook**

2   **Click _File, Page Setup_**

3   **Click the _Sheet_ tab**

4   **Click _Gridlines_ to insert an "X" from the check box**

5   **Click _Row and Column Headings_**

6   **Click _Print Preview_**

7   **Click _Zoom_ (if needed)**

Your worksheet should appear as Figure SS2-45b. Note that only the border lines that you created appear in the worksheet. In addition, the row numbers and column letters also appear.

8   **Close the Print Preview window and close the worksheet without saving**

9   **Exit Excel and then shut down Windows (if desired)**

A FINAL NOTE ABOUT PRINT OPTIONS.   Excel comes with a variety of Print options that can be controlled through the _Page Setup_ dialog box (_File_ menu). Print options are saved with your spreadsheet; they need not be reentered each time you want to print. In addition, as mentioned earlier, some printers may not support all Excel print options. In these cases, the worksheet image that appears in the Print Preview window may differ from your printed page. For example, some printers may not print reverse color (white text on a black background), italics, underlining, and graphics as they appear in the Print Preview window. In addition, you may have to restart your printer to cancel previous settings.

☑ **CHECKPOINT**

✓   Open the SS2-3B workbook. Place a page break between _Will's Mammoth_ and _Foolish Rabbit's Mistake._

✓   Print Preview the worksheet and then remove the page break.

✓   Using the _Page Setup_ dialog box, create title rows that include Rows 1 through 3.

✓   Activate the Row and Column headings and deactivate grid lines options.

✓   Print the worksheet and save it as SS2-5.

SUMMARY

Specific mouse actions or keystrokes for the following commands can be reviewed in the chapter or in the appendix.

- Commands that use ranges affect only specified cells, not the entire spreadsheet. Range data alignment changes previously typed data in their cells. Range format changes adjust number displays, but not the number itself. Popular formats include general (the default), which automatically selects the correct format, and accounting, which contains built-in format codes that will display numbers with dollar signs; comma, two-decimal places; and in brackets (negative numbers).

- The Copy and Paste commands replicate the contents of a cell (or cell range) into other cells. Other commands related to Copy and Paste include the Transpose command (which exchanges rows and columns) and the Cut and Paste command (which erases the original cells).

- Range names can be used in place of specific cell addresses in all commands and formulas.

- Default changes affect the entire worksheet by changing configuration or default settings. Default format and column-width changes affect all cells that have not been set with range changes. Default alignment changes set a new default for data entry; they do not affect existing range alignment changes.

- The default column width for the entire worksheet can be changed. Column width can also be changed individually or by column range (for adjacent columns). In addition, columns can be hidden completely.

- Font (character type style) changes include font face, size, style (bold or italic), and color. All can be changed using either toolbar buttons or the *Font* tab of the *Format Cells* dialog box. Cell background color can also be changed by using toolbar buttons or the *Pattern* tab of the *Format Cells* dialog box.

- Border lines can be added to cell walls by using the *Border* button (Format toolbar) or the *Border* tab of the *Format Cells* dialog box.

- Drop-shadow backgrounds and other graphic images can be added to a worksheet using the Drawing toolbar and a mouse.

- Cell references can be relative, absolute, or mixed. Relative references (such as =A1) are automatically adjusted to reflect their new location, absolute references (such as =$A$1) remain constant, and mixed references (such as =A$1) have only one coordinate absolute.

- Circular references occur when a formula refers to itself directly or indirectly. They are indicated by the "Circular" (cell reference) message in the status bar.

- Functions perform useful calculations for arithmetic, statistical, financial, string, logical, and date and time applications. All functions begin with an "=" symbol and may include arguments to indicate data or ranges.

- Screen techniques to manage large spreadsheets include the use of freezing and splitting panes that allow you to view different parts of the spreadsheet on one screen. Print techniques include scaling (compressing) page data and displaying column or row titles, column or row indicators, and removing grid lines.

KEY TERMS

Shown in parentheses are the page numbers on which key terms are boldfaced.

Mixed reference (SS122)   Range name (SS96)   Split (SS131)
Panes (SS131)   Relative reference (SS120)   Transpose (SS95)
Paste (SS91)   Source range (SS90)

QUIZ

TRUE/FALSE

____ 1. Only the alignment of text in a cell can be changed.
____ 2. The general format automatically selects the correct number format for data entered.
____ 3. The Cut and Paste commands move cell content to a new location.
____ 4. Transposing cells changes them from text to formulas.
____ 5. Any range can be replaced with a range name.
____ 6. Default alignment changes affect all existing data in a spreadsheet.
____ 7. Data entered into a new cell is automatically assigned the default settings.
____ 8. A font is a type style.
____ 9. Borders are lines that can be placed horizontally.
____ 10. Worksheets can be split horizontally or vertically.

MULTIPLE CHOICE

____ 11. Which of the following refers to the way a number is displayed in a cell?
   a. Range
   b. Format
   c. Freeze
   d. Value
____ 12. Which of the following numbers has been formatted as currency with two decimals?
   a. 1234.56
   b. $1234.2
   c. $1,234
   d. $1,234.00
____ 13. Which item must be specified first when copying cells?
   a. Range name
   b. Worksheet name
   c. Range destination
   d. Source range
____ 14. Which command (or commands) transfers cell contents to a new location and then erases the original cell?
   a. Cut and Paste
   b. Copy and Paste
   c. Transpose
   d. Format
____ 15. Which of the following changes is *not* an example of a worksheet enhancement change?
   a. Transpose adjustments
   b. Font changes

    c. Border line changes

    d. Drop-shadow borders

___ 16. When is it most effective to issue default changes?

    a. After text is returned

    b. After all formatting has been completed

    c. Before data are entered into cells

    d. Before printing or saving a worksheet

___ 17. What is the default number format?

    a. General

    b. Accounting

    c. Currency

    d. Worksheet

___ 18. What do the number signs (####) that fill a cell indicate?

    a. The cell is too narrow to show a number.

    b. The cell is too narrow to show the data.

    c. The cell has a border line in it.

    d. The data in the cell must be retyped.

___ 19. Which of these commands cannot be used to change column width?

    a. Dragging the right border next to the column letter

    b. Clicking *Format, Column Width*

    c. Pressing Alt + O, C, W

    d. Clicking *Column Width,* and then *Worksheet*

___ 20. How would you describe the reference (or references) contained in the formula =$A$1*B3?

    a. A mixed reference

    b. An absolute reference followed by a relative reference

    c. A relative reference followed by an absolute reference

    d. A currency format followed by a fixed format

MATCHING

Select the lettered item from the following figure that best matches each phrase:

___ 21. Toolbar buttons that change the alignment of data in a cell.

___ 22. The result of a font change.

___ 23. Contains a formula that is formatted—accounting, dollar sign, two decimals.

___ 24. Created by invoking the split command.

___ 25. Toolbar buttons that can be used to change the background color of a cell or characters.

___ 26. Can be created by using the *Border* tab of the *Format Cells* dialog box.

___ 27. Contains commands to change the format of cells, row and column settings, and style settings.

___ 28. Contains commands to split or freeze panes.

___ 29. Can be used to change the format of number displays by mouse.

___ 30. Can be used to invoke certain font-style changes quickly.

ANSWERS

True/False: 1. F; 2. T; 3. T; 4. F; 5. T; 6. F; 7. T; 8. T; 9. T; 10. T

Multiple Choice: 11. b; 12. d; 13. d; 14. a; 15. a; 16. c; 17. a; 18. a; 19. d; 20. b

Matching: 21. e; 22. j; 23. i; 24. k; 25. h; 26. l; 27. a; 28. b; 29. f; 30. d

FIGURE SS2-A ■ MATCHING FIGURE

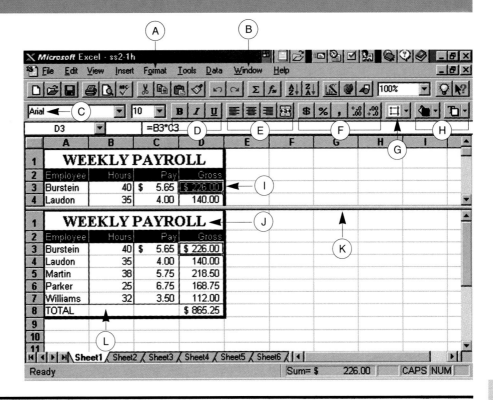

EXERCISES

I. OPERATIONS

Provide the actions (as appropriate) required to do each of the following operations.

1. Right-align cells B5:F8.

2. Change the format of cells C1:C6 to accounting, no dollar sign, two decimals.

3. Display accounting, dollar sign, two decimals in cells D5:D20.

4. Copy Cell B6 to Cell B7.

5. Copy Cell C7 to Cells C8:C15.

6. Copy Cells A1:A8 to Cells B1:B8.

7. Create a range name called JANUARY for range F5:F25.

8. Change the column width to 20 by the drag and drop technique.

9. Change the column width of Columns E and F to 10.

10. Reset the width of Column F to the default setting.

11. Add a border line to Cells A5:H5.

12. Create an absolute reference to Cell T6.

13. Freeze vertical titles in Columns A and B.

14. Create an unsynchronized horizontal pane at Row 5.

II. COMMANDS

Describe fully, using as few words as possible in each case, what command is initiated or what is accomplished in Excel by the actions described below. Assume that each exercise part is independent of any previous parts.

1. Pressing the Shift + F3 keys

2. Clicking the ▼ button of the font drop-down box

3. Dragging the right border next to a column letter

4. Pressing the F5 key

5. Clicking the toolbar button containing a picture of two documents

6. Pressing the Ctrl + N keys

7. Pressing F6 after invoking the split command

8. Pressing the Ctrl + 1 keys

9. Clicking the toolbar button that looks like a clipboard with paper

10. Pressing the ' (apostrophe) key, 10, and then the Enter key

III. APPLICATIONS

Perform the following operations and briefly describe how you accomplished each operation and what its results were.

APPLICATION 1: CLUB BUDGET
Save the workbook as CLUB2 after each operation is completed so that you can continue this exercise later. (Remember to set the default drive to A before saving the workbook.)

1. Open the CLUB1 workbook (created in Chapter 1).

2. Right-align the data in Cells C6 through F6.

3. Format the range C8:F8 and C14:F14 with the accounting, dollar sign, two-decimal format.

4. Format the range C9:F12 with the accounting, no dollar sign, two-decimal format.

5. Delete the empty Row 7 and then Row 12.

6. Place a single-lined border in the range C11:F11 and then place a double-lined border in the range C12:F12.

7. Change the standard (default) column width to 12 and then the column width of Column F to 15.

8. Insert three columns to the left of Column F (see Chapter 1).

9. Copy the range C7:E12 to the range F7:H12.

10. Type **APR** in Cell F7, **MAY** in Cell G7, and **JUN** in Cell H7.

11. Delete the range I7:I11, place a SUM function to total the range C7:H7, and then copy the formula to the range I8:I11.

12. Format the range I8:I11 in the accounting, no dollar sign, two-decimal format.

13. Change the numbers in Cells F7 to 80, G9 to 75, H11 to 325.

14. Change the font of Cell A4 to 14 point Times New Roman and then boldface that cell's content and the range C6:I6.

15. Save the workbook as CLUB2, print the entire worksheet without grid lines, and then exit the program.

APPLICATION 2: ADDITIONAL GPA

Save the workbook in this exercise as GPA2 after each operation is completed so that you can continue this exercise later.

1. Open the GPA1 workbook (created in Chapter 1).

2. Center all the data in Cells B6 through C12. Right-align the data in Cells D6 through F6.

3. Format Cells D8 through F14 to number format, no decimals (0).

4. Insert a row below Row 10 (see Chapter 1).

5. Copy Cells A10 through F10 into the new Row 11. Type **ART205** in Cell A11, **9301** in Cell B11, **A** in Cell C11, **2** in Cell D11, and **4** in Cell E11.

6. Move the word *Grades* in Cell A4 to Cell C3.

7. Create the name CREDITS for the range D8 to D13. In Cell D15, enter an =SUM function that totals the range named CREDITS.

8. Change the default column width to 8, and the default alignment to right-aligned.

9. Change the column width of Columns A and B to 7.

10. Reset Column B's width to the default setting.

11. Hide Column B, print the spreadsheet, then unhide the column.

12. Type **PART OF** in Cell G5 and **TOTAL** in Cell G6. Create a formula in Cell G8 to divide F8 (relative reference) by F15 (absolute reference). Copy this formula into Cells G9 through G13. Format Column G to percent, two decimal (0.00%).

13. Add a double-lined outline border around the range A4:G15.

14. Place a formula in Cell F4 to calculate the current GPA as (Total Points)/(Total Credits). Format this cell to number format, two decimals (0.00). Place the title "GPA" in Cell E4.

15. Print the spreadsheet and then save it again as GPA2.

APPLICATION 3: CHECKBOOK

Save the workbook as CHECK2 after each operation is completed so that you can continue this exercise later. (Remember to set the default drive to A before saving the workbook.)

1. Open the CHECK1 workbook (created in Chapter 1).

2. Format the range E8:G12 with the accounting, no dollar sign, two-decimal format.

3. Change the column width of Column C to 20, and delete Row 7 and Column D.

4. Add single-lined borders to the right walls of the range A6:D11, and then add double-lined borders to the right walls of the range E6:E11.

5. Change the font and font size of the text in Cell A4 to 16 point Times New Roman and boldface the text; then center-align it across the range A4:F4.

6. Change the character color to white in the range A6:F6 and then change the background color of the same range to black.

7. Change the color of the single-lined borders on the right walls of Cells A6:D6 and the double-lined border on the right wall of Cell E6 to white.

8. Place a double-lined outline border around the range A4:F11 and then delete Row 5.

9. Right-align the data in cells A6, B6, D6, E6, and F6.

10. Insert a row between the rows beginning with 12-Jan and 28-Jan. Type **14-JAN** in Cell A11, **Transfer from savings** in Cell C11, and **2000** in Cell E11.

11. Copy the formula in Cell F10 to Cells F11 and F12. (Use the Paste Special command of the *Edit* menu to paste "only" the formula.)

12. Italicize "Deposit pay check" in Cells C7.

13. Save the workbook as CHECK2, print the entire worksheet with the grid option off, and then exit the program.

APPLICATION 4: INVESTMENTS

Save the workbook as INVEST2 after each operation is completed so that you can continue this exercise later. (Remember to set the default drive to A before saving the workbook.)

1. Open the INVEST1 workbook (created in Chapter 1).

2. Change the font in Cell A4 to 18 point Times New Roman, boldface, and then center-align the text across the range A4:I4.

3. Delete Row 8.

4. Change the default (standard column width) to 12, change the column width of Column A to 20, delete Column B, and change the width of Column B and E to nine.

5. Right-align the data in the range C6:H7 and B7:B12.

6. Format the ranges C8:D12, F8:H8, and F14:H14 to accounting, dollar sign, two decimals.

7. Format the range E8:E12 to accounting, no dollar sign, no decimals and the range F9:H12 to accounting, no dollar sign, two decimals.

8. Type **RETURN ON** in Cell I6 and **INVEST** in Cell I7. Create a formula in Cell I8 to divide H8 (relative reference) by G8 (absolute reference). Copy this formula into Cells I9 through I12.

9. Right-align the range I6 and I7, and then format I8:I12 to percentage, two decimals (0.00%).

10. Place a single-lined border at the bottom of Cells A7 through I7 and A12 through I12 and a double-lined border at the bottom of the Cells F14 through G14.

11. Hide Columns B through E, print the spreadsheet with grid lines, and then unhide the columns.

12. Insert a column in D. Type the word **DATE** in Cells B6 and D6, **SOLD** in B7 and **PURCH** in D7, **7/10/YY** in D8, **9/15/YY** in D9, **10/25/YY** in D10, **12/20/YY** in D11, and then **5/3/YY** in D12.

13. Right-align the range B8:B12 and D8:D12 and then change Column D's width to nine.

14. Save the workbook as INVEST2. Print the entire worksheet without grid lines, in landscape orientation, scaled to print on one page. Exit the program.

APPLICATION 5: ADDITIONAL INVENTORY

Save the worksheet as STOCK2 after each operation is completed so that you can continue this exercise later.

1. Open the "STOCK1" workbook (created in Chapter 1).

2. Right-align the data in Cells B6 through D6.

3. Format cells B8 and D8 to accounting, dollar sign, two decimals. Format the rest of the cells in Columns B and D to accounting, no dollar sign, two decimals. Format Cell D14 to accounting, dollar sign, two decimals.

4. Move the word *Inventory* in Cell A4 to Cell C4.

5. Create the name COUNT for the range C8:C12. In Cell C14, enter an =SUM function that totals the range named COUNT.

6. Change the default column width to 12 and the default alignment to right-aligned.

7. Change the column width of Columns A and B to 15.

8. Reset Column B's width to the default setting.

9. Hide Columns B and C, print the spreadsheet, and then unhide the two columns.

10. Type **PART OF** in Cell E5, and **TOTAL** in Cell E6. Create a formula in Cell E8 to divide D8 (relative reference) by D14 (absolute reference). Copy this formula into Cells E9 through E12. Format Column E to percent, one decimal.

11. Insert a row below Row 9 (see Chapter 1).

12. Copy cells A9 through E9 into the new Row 10. Type **Templates** (left-justified) in Column A, **.7** in Cell B10, and **100** in Cell C10.

13. Add border lines where appropriate.

14. Print the spreadsheet and then save it again as STOCK2.

SS

APPLICATION 6: ADDITIONAL TICKETS

Save the workbook in this exercise as TICKET2 after each operation is completed so that you can continue this exercise later.

1. Open the TICKET1 workbook (created in Chapter 1).

2. Right-align the data in Cells B6 through F6.

3. Format Cells B7 and F7 to accounting, dollar sign, no decimals. Format the rest of the cells in Columns B and F to accounting, no dollar sign, no decimals. Format Cell F14 to accounting, dollar sign, no decimals.

4. Insert a row below Row 10 (see Chapter 1).

5. Copy Cells A10 through F10 into the new Row 11. Type **Rear Mezz** in Cell A11, **20** in Cell B11, **100** in Cell C11, and **0** in Cell D11.

6. Center align *Tickets* in Cell A4 across the range A4:F4.

7. Create the name SEATS for the range C8 to C13. In Cell C15, enter a SUM function that totals the range named SEATS. Copy the formula to Cell D15 so that the SUM function totals Column D. Format Columns C, D, and E to accounting, no dollar sign, no decimals.

8. Change the default column width to 10 and the default alignment to right-aligned.

9. Change the column width of Columns A and B to 12.

10. Reset Column B's width to the default setting.

11. Hide Columns B and C, print the spreadsheet, and then unhide the two columns.

12. Type **PART OF** in Cell G5, and **TOTAL** in Cell G6. Create a formula in Cell G7 to divide F7 (relative reference) by F14 (absolute reference). Copy this formula into Cells G8 through G12. Format Column G to percent, two decimals (0.00%).

13. Add border lines where appropriate.

14. Print the spreadsheet and then save it again as TICKET2.

MASTERY CASES

The following mastery cases allow you to demonstrate how much you have learned about this software. Each case describes a fictitious problem or need that can be solved using the skills you have learned in this chapter. Although minimum acceptable outcomes are specified, you are expected and encouraged to design your response (files, data, lists) in ways that display your personal mastery of the software. Feel free to show off your skills. Use real data from your own experience in your solution, although you may also fabricate data if needed.

These mastery cases allow you to display your ability to

■   Use ranges in commands.
■   Reset worksheet defaults.
■   Adjust column width.

- Enhance a worksheet with fonts, colors, and lines.
- Use absolute cell references.
- Use Print options.

CASE 1. MODIFYING YOUR EXAM GRADES

Open the exam grades workbook that you created for Mastery Case 1 of Chapter 1. Right-align appropriate titles. Change the font and font size of the title characters. Select an appropriate format for the grades. Adjust column widths to the minimal width necessary for each column. Add border lines to further enhance the spreadsheet. Save and print the worksheet *without* grid lines.

CASE 2. MODIFYING YOUR HOLIDAY SHOPPING BUDGET

Open the holiday-shopping workbook that you created for Mastery Case 2 of Chapter 1. Change the font and font size of the titles. Format the first row of numbers and the totals in the accounting, dollar sign, two-decimal style. Format all other numbers in the accounting, no dollar sign, two-decimal style. Add a Percent Difference column, and place formulas to yield the difference in a percentage for each gift, and then format appropriately. Add border lines to further enhance the worksheet. Save and print *without* grid lines.

CASE 3. MODIFY YOUR SALES REPORT

Open the sales report workbook that you created for Mastery Case 3 of Chapter 1. Add two columns to calculate the tax and adjusted total. Place your state sales tax rate in a cell above the TAX title; use the actual rate or invent your own. Insert cell formulas in the Tax column that will multiply the total by that tax rate (use an absolute reference). Create appropriate formulas to calculate the adjusted total to reflect the sales tax. Adjust format, column width, and fonts to best present your data. Save and print your report.

SS

3

ADVANCED SPREADSHEETS: CHARTS, DATA MANAGEMENT, MACROS, MULTIPLE WORKBOOKS, MULTIPLE SHEETS, AND SHARING DATA

OUTLINE

SS

OBJECTIVES

After completing this chapter, you will be able to do any of the following (based on your selection of modules):

1. Create column (bar) charts, line charts, and pie charts from columnar data.
2. Distinguish among the purposes and procedures for using conditional functions such as IF, VLOOKUP, and HLOOKUP.
3. Use database techniques to create number sequences and data distributions, as well as to sort, query, and copy data within the spreadsheet to a query table.
4. Understand, create, and invoke macros.
5. Use data from other spreadsheets by linking, copying, and combining cells from other spreadsheet files or sheets.
6. Explain and demonstrate data-protection techniques.
7. Explain and demonstrate linking, embedding, and import and export techniques.

OVERVIEW

Chapter 3 presents an advanced set of spreadsheet techniques, including charts, conditional functions, databases, spreadsheet links, macros, and spreadsheet security. Each procedure is presented as a separate module that can be studied independently of the others. Study the modules that are most useful to you.

Using files available on disk and others created by the reader, the chapter presents a series of eight learning modules. Module 1 examines creating charts from spreadsheet data. Conditional functions are presented next in Module 2, including an IF function and table lookup functions. Module 3 introduces the reader to database techniques, including fill sequences, sorts, data distributions, queries, and query tables. Each submodule of this section can be studied separately as desired. This is followed by Module 4, which presents methods for automating procedures with macros. Modules 5 and 6 examine techniques for linking workbooks and sheets. Module 7 looks at protection techniques for improving data security. The chapter concludes with sharing data among programs (Module 8).

PREPARING FOR THIS CHAPTER

This text comes with a data diskette that contains files for you to use with this chapter. These files reduce the amount of initial data entry you must do in each module. If you do not have this disk (or you want to practice entering data), you can create the files as you need them.

The files from the Dryden data diskette must first be copied onto your data disk so they will be available for use. Check with your instructor or lab technician to see if the files are available, or do the following steps to use the My Computer program.

STEPS

1 **Start Windows**

First, you must copy the files from the Dryden File disk's Excel folder to your hard disk as follows:

2 **Double-click the *My Computer* icon for its window similar to Figure SS3-1**

(The contents of your window may differ.)

3 **Insert the Dryden File disk in Drive A**

4 **In the *My Computer* window, double-click the *3½ Floppy (A:)* icon**

5 **In the *3½ Floppy (A:)* window, click the *Excel* folder**

6 **Select *Edit, Copy***   [**Ctrl** + **C**]

You have now told Windows to copy the the contents of Drive A's Excel folder. You can now specify into which drive it should be copied.

Double-clicking the *My Computer* icon will laumch it. (Your window may differ.)

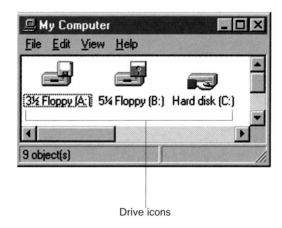

Drive icons

---

7 On the taskbar, click the *My Computer* button to reopen its window

8 In the My Computer window, double-click the *Drive C* icon to open its window

9 In the Drive C window's menu bar, click *Edit, Paste*   [**Ctrl** + **V**]

The files are now copied into a new Excel folder on Drive C, which appears within the Drive C window. You can now transfer the files onto your own data disk.

10 Remove the Dryden disk and place your disk in Drive A.

11 In the Drive C window, double-click the *Excel folder* icon to open its window

12 In the Excel folder's menu bar, click *Edit, Select All*   [**Ctrl** + **A**]

13 In the same menu, click *Edit, Copy*   [**Ctrl** + **C**]

14 On the taskbar, click the *3½ Floppy (A:)* button to reopen its window

15 Press **F5** to "refresh" the contents of the window and return to its root directory

16 In the *3½ Floppy (A:)* window menu, click *Edit, Paste*   [**Ctrl** + **V**]

The files have been copied onto your disk's root directory and are now available for use. You no longer need the Excel folder in Drive C and can remove it or leave it alone as follows:

17 If you want to remove the Excel folder from Drive C, perform the following steps:

   a.   On the taskbar, click the *Drive C* icon to reopen its window

     b.   Click the *Excel* folder icon to select it

     c.   Press Delete

     d.   Click *Yes* to send the Excel folder and its contents to the Recycle Bin

    18   Click the *Close* button of each window to close it   [Alt + F4 as needed]

    19   Click anywhere in the desktop to deselect the *My Computer* icon

MODULE 1: CHARTS

Most people understand information faster when it is presented as a **chart**—a pictorial representation of data. The chart features in Excel allow you to develop charts quickly from worksheet data, such as the one shown in Figure SS3-2b. The following exercises demonstrate how to construct, save, and print charts. To prepare for these exercises, open or create the spreadsheet shown in Figure SS3-2a as follows:

STEPS

    1   Launch Excel, switch to Drive A, and then open the GADGETS workbook from your data disk

    2   If you do not have this workbook (or if you prefer to create one yourself), type it now, matching the data shown in Figure SS3-2a, and save it as GADGETS

The following exercise creates column (bar) chart shown in Figure SS3-2b. A **column (bar) chart** displays numeric data as a set of evenly spaced bars whose relative heights indicate values in the range being charted.

     To create a simple column chart, follow five basic steps: (1) select the range of data to be charted, (2) invoke the Chart command (*Insert* menu), (3) point to the first cell in the left corner of the chart's desired location (destination), (4) click, and (5) follow the five steps in Excel's ChartWizard.

CREATING A CHART

The following chart-creating technique uses Excel's *ChartWizard.* This feature uses five ChartWizard dialog boxes to walk you through the chart-creating process. This technique requires a mouse, although some keyboard commands have been supplied.

     To create a column chart (Excel's default chart),

STEPS

    1   Move to Cell A3

FIGURE SS3-2 ■ TRANSFORMING WORKSHEET DATA INTO A CHART DISPLAY

(a) GADGETS worksheet.
(b) Completed column (bar) chart of GADGETS data.

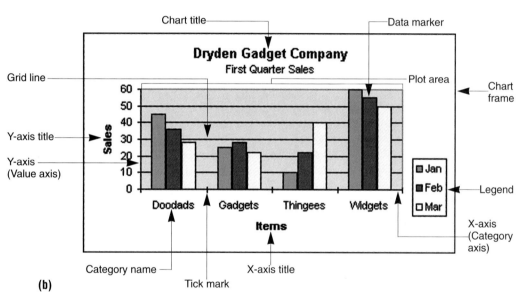

(a)

(b)

2 **Select the range A3:D7 as in Figure SS3-3a**

Be sure not to include the Total column (Column E) in the data range.

3 **Click _Insert,_ and then point to _Chart_ for the _Chart_ submenu**

A *Chart* submenu should appear as in Figure SS3-3b. At this point, you can either insert the chart on the current sheet or on a new sheet. Placing a chart on a new sheet inserts it on a sheet separate from the current worksheet. For now, to insert a chart within the current sheet,

4 **Click _On This Sheet_**

FIGURE SS3-3 ■ PREPARING TO CREATE A CHART

(a) Selecting the chart.
(b) The chart submenu.

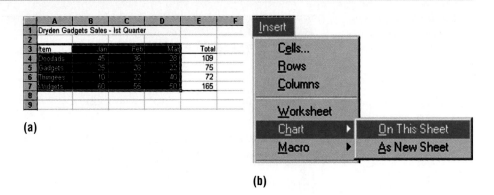

(a)

(b)

Your mouse pointer will now change to a charting pointer (see left margin). The next step is done exclusively by mouse.

> **Tip:** Clicking *As New Sheet* in place of Step 4 will place the chart on a separate sheet within the workbook. See "Module 5: Using Multiple Sheets" for using more than one sheet in a workbook.

5 Point to the upper-left corner of *Cell A9* and click

The *ChartWizard Step 1 of 5* dialog box appears as in Figure SS3-4a. At this point, compare your selected range of data to be charted to the Range text box. It should read "=$A$3:$D$7." (Note that the ranges are inserted as absolute references.) If not, click cancel and repeat Steps 1 through 5.

6 Click the *Next >* button for the *Step 2* dialog box   [↵]

The *ChartWizard Step 2 of 5* dialog box now appears as in Figure SS3-4b. You can now select a chart type by clicking its button (or by pressing the Alt and underlined letter of the chart type). To accept the default (Column chart),

7 Click the *Next >* button for the *Step 3* dialog box

This dialog box, as in Figure SS3-4c, allows you to select a format (for the chart type previously selected) by clicking the desired format button (or by pressing the desired format number). Again, to accept the default setting,

8 Click the *Next >* button for the *Step 4* dialog box

Note the Sample Chart display in this dialog box as in Figure SS3-4d. This is a picture of how the chart will look in the worksheet. This dialog box can also be used to switch the orientation of the data series between rows and columns. The *Columns* option button should be selected as in the figure. If not, do Step 9, otherwise go to Step 10.

(a) The *ChartWizard chart data range* dialog box.
(b) The *ChartWizard chart type* dialog box.
(c) The *ChartWizard chart format* dialog box.
(d) The *ChartWizard data series* dialog box.

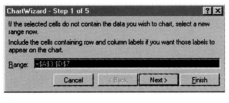
(a)

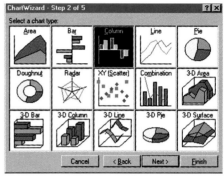
(b)

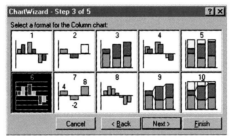
(c)

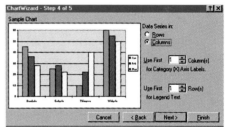
(d)

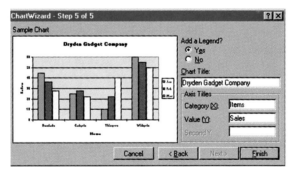
(e)

9 If needed, click the *Columns* option button

10 Click the *Next >* button for the *Step 5* dialog box   [↵]

This dialog box is used to add a legend and titles. The legend is automatically created, as in this case, when the data is included in the data range in Step 2 above. To add chart and axis titles,

11 Click the *Chart Title* text box

12 Type ▓Dryden Gadget Company▓ in the *Chart Title* text box

13 Press ▓Tab▓ to move to the *Category (X)* text box

14 Type ▓Items▓ in the *Category (X)* text box and press ▓Tab▓

15 Type ▓Sales▓ in the *Category (Y)* text box

Your *ChartWizard Step 5 of 5* dialog box appears as in Figure SS3-4e. If not, repeat Steps 11 through 15. Now, to complete the chart,

16 Click the *Finish* button   [↵]

Your worksheet should resemble Figure SS3-5a. Note that the column titles are currently not readable. This will be adjusted soon when the chart is resized.

The small square boxes on the frame of the Chart are called **selection handles,** and they indicate that its outer frame is selected. Later, these handles will be used to resize the chart by mouse. A Chart toolbar also appears on your screen and can also be used to edit the chart.

17 Move to Cell A1 by clicking it (this will also remove the handles from the chart and the chart toolbar)

18 Save this workbook as GADGETS1 and then close it

CHARTING SPECIFIC RANGES.   To chart specific ranges you must select them as multiple ranges. The first range is selected by using normal selection techniques, you must press and hold the Ctrl key when selecting the beginning of each additional range. For example, to chart only the Total Sales of the GADGETS worksheet,

STEPS

1 Open the GADGETS worksheet

2 Select the range A3:A7

To select the additional range E3:E7,

3 Press and hold ▓Ctrl▓ while clicking Cell E3 (the first cell in the next range)

4 Press and hold ▓Shift▓ while clicking Cell E7 to select the range E3:E7

Both ranges should now be selected. If not, repeat Steps 2 through 4.

5 Click *Insert,* point to *Chart,* and then click *On This Sheet*

6 Point to the left corner of Cell B9 and click for the ChartWizard

7 Click the *Next* > button of dialog boxes Step 1 through Step 4

8 In the *Step 5* dialog box, click the *Chart Title* text box to place the insertion point there

9 Type Dryden Gadget Sales and then press   Tab

10 In the *Category (X)* text box, type Items and then press   Tab

11 In the *Value (Y)* text box, type Total Sales

12 Click the *Finish* button

A chart with the Total Sales data appears.

13 Save this worksheet as MULTIPLE and then close it

Later you can use techniques from the sections that follow to resize the chart and change the titles and legend.

MANIPULATING A CHART

A chart is considered an object (picture) in the Windows environment. As such, it can be resized, moved, and copied. Resizing a chart involves enlarging or reducing its size. Moving a chart relocates it from its current position (*source*) to a new location (*destination*). Copying involves duplicating the chart in a new location.

Before a chart can be resized, moved or copied, its frame must be selected. To select the chart's frame, click anywhere on the chart. At this point, a chart can be resized by dragging one of its selection handles. Move it by dragging the entire chart to a new location, or copy it by holding the Ctrl key while dragging it to a new location.

> **Tip:** The Cut or Copy and Paste or Paste Special commands can also be used to move or copy a selected chart.

RESIZING THE CHART FRAME.   To resize a chart,

STEPS

1 Open the GADGETS1 workbook

2 Click anywhere on the chart to select it

3 If the Chart toolbar does not appear, right-click anywhere on the toolbars for its *Shortcut* menu, and then click *Chart* for its toolbar

Selection handles and the Chart toolbar should appear as in Figure SS3-5a.

 4 Click the ▼ button of the vertical scroll bar five times to position the viewing area of the worksheet as in Figure SS3-5b

FIGURE SS3-5 ■ **RESIZING A CHART**

(a) Clicking the chart selects it and turns on the Chart toolbar for editing.
(b) A scrollbar can be used to adjust the viewing area of the worksheet.
(c) Dragging a selection handle will resize the chart.
(d) Dragging the selected chart will move it.

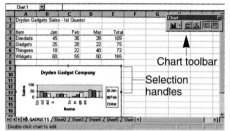

(a)

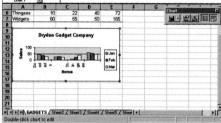

(b)

(c)

(d)

---

5 Slowly point to the bottom-right selection handle of the chart until the pointer changes to a double arrow

6 Drag the selection handle (and the outline of the chart border) to the bottom-right corner of Cell F21

7 Release the mouse

Your chart should now resemble Figure SS3-5c. Note that the column titles are now readable.

8 Resave the workbook as GADGETS1

MOVING A CHART. Dragging a selected chart will move it. Try this:

STEPS

1 If needed, click the chart to place selection handles on the frame

2 Point anywhere within the chart

3 Drag the chart to move it one column to the right as in Figure SS3-5d

4 Resave the workbook as GADGETS1

> **Tip:** You can also use the Cut and Paste commands (*Edit* menu) to move a chart after its frame is selected.

COPYING A CHART.   To copy a chart,

STEPS

1 If needed, click the chart to select its frame

2 Point anywhere within the chart

3 Press and hold   Ctrl   while dragging to the right of the current chart (or any desired empty area in the worksheet)

> **Note:** A plus (+) sign appears to the right of the mouse pointer when you are dragging. This indicates that you are copying.

4 Release your mouse

You should now have two of the same charts next to each other.

5 Close the workbook without saving

> **Tip:** You can also use the Copy and Paste commands (*Edit* menu) to copy a chart after its frame is selected.

EDITING CHART PARTS

Clicking a chart once, as seen earlier, selects its frame. This allows you to resize, move, or copy it by mouse. Once a chart's frame is selected, double-clicking a chart will turn on the chart edit mode, which allows you to edit its contents.

ADDING A SUBTITLE.   Try this to add a subtitle to the chart:

STEPS

1 Open the GADGETS1 workbook and then if needed, click the chart once to select it

Your status bar should display the message "Double-click chart to edit."

2   **Double-click the chart**

The frame of the chart should appear as in Figure SS3-6a. At this point, you can edit any part of the chart by first clicking it. The *Insert* and *Format* menus also change to reflect Chart editing commands.

3   **Click the title "Dryden Gadget Company" to select it**

4   **Point to the end of the title after "y" and click to place the insertion point there**

An insertion point should appear at the end of the title as in Figure SS3-6b. The message "Title" also appears in the Name box of the formula bar.

5   **Press ↵ to move the insertion point to the next line**

6   **Click the ▼ button of the *Font size* drop-down box (Formatting toolbar), click the ▼ button of the vertical scroll bar to view 8, and then click it**

7   **Click the *Bold* (B) toolbar button (to turn it off)**   [**Ctrl** + **B**]

8   **Type** **First Quarter Sales**

You can edit other parts of the chart or turn off the edit mode. To turn off the chart edit mode,

9   **Double-click Cell F7 (or any cell outside the chart)**

Your chart should resemble Figure SS3-2b. Examine your screen and the figure to learn each part's name.

10   **Resave the workbook as GADGETS1**

FIGURE SS3-6 ■ **EDITING A CHART**

(a) Double-clicking a selected chart puts it in edit mode.
(b) Clicking on the title places an insertion point there for editing text.

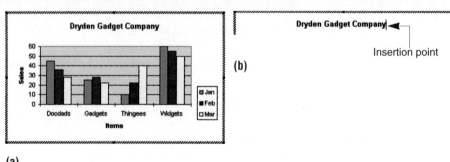

(a)

Tip: Double-clicking some chart parts when in the chart edit mode will open a dialog box. These boxes can be used to edit the chart part's attributes.

GRID LINES.   Grid lines can improve the readability of charts. Excel automatically places horizontal (*y*-axis) grid lines in major intervals on a column chart, as in Figure SS3-2b. You can modify the chart to have the grid lines appear at minor intervals to provide greater reference readability or you can remove the grid lines. You can also add vertical (*x*-axis) grid lines with major or minor intervals. These changes can be made through the *Grid lines* dialog box, which is accessed through the *Insert* menu. Try this to remove the grid lines:

STEPS

1   Click the chart to select it

2   Double-click the chart for the chart edit mode

3   Click *Insert, Grid lines*

4   In the Value (y) Axis group, click *Major Grid lines* to unselect it, and then click *OK*

The gridlines should now disappear from your chart. Now, use the *Grid lines* dialog box to reinsert the grid lines.

5   Repeat Steps 3 and 4 to reinsert the grid lines

6   Double-click the outside of the chart to deselect it

7   Close the workbook without saving

CHART TYPES

Excel offers 15 types of charts that may be selected as you create a chart or after you're done (see the "Creating a Chart" section). Each chart type also has many variations, called *subtypes*. Do the following to prepare for the exercises in this section:

STEPS

1   Open the GADGETS1 workbook

2   Click the ▼ button of the vertical scroll bar to reposition the viewing area of the chart and workbook as in Figure SS3-7a

3   Click the chart

FIGURE SS3-7 ■ **PREPARING TO CHANGE CHART TYPES**

(a) Repositioning the viewing area at the workbook.
(b) Selecting and resizing the chart.

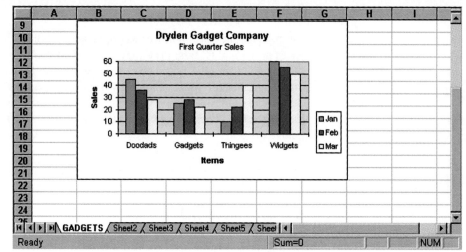

(a)

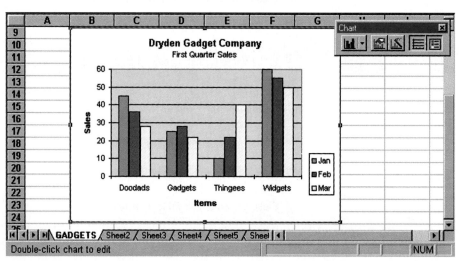

(b)

4 Slowly point to the bottom-center selection handle of the chart until the pointer changes to a double arrow

5 Drag the selection handle (and the outline of the chart border) three cells down and then release

Your chart should appear as in Figure SS3-7b.

CHANGING THE CHART TYPE. To change the chart type of an existing chart you must first select a chart, turn on the edit mode, and then select *Format, Chart Type* for its dialog box.

To change to a line chart,

1 **Double-click it to turn on the chart edit mode**

2 **Click *Format, Chart Type* for its dialog box**

3 **Click the *Line Chart* button**

4 **Click *OK***

Your line chart should appear as Figure SS3-8a. A **line chart** displays numeric data as a set of points along a line. It is useful for showing trends over time. Now, using the same technique as above, change the chart to a pie chart. At this point, you can also double-click any cell outside the chart to unselect it. For now, keep the chart in edit mode and try the following other chart type changes:

FIGURE SS3-8 ■ CHANGING CHART TYPE

(a) Line chart.
(b) Pie chart.
(c) 3-D Bar chart.
(d) Stacked column (subtype) chart.

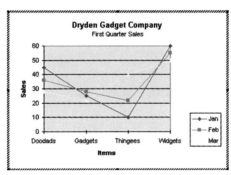

(a)

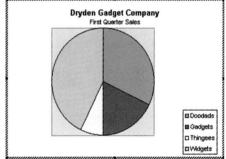

(b)

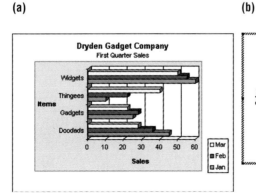

(c)

(d)

SS

5 Use the *Chart Type* dialog box to select a pie chart (*Format, Chart Type*)

A pie chart similar to Figure SS3-8b should now appear. A **pie chart** displays data as parts of a whole circle, where each data "slice" corresponds to a percentage of the total.

Excel also offers 3-D charts. These charts are also accessible through the *Chart Type* dialog box. Try this:

6 If needed, select the chart and invoke the chart edit mode

7 Click *Format, Chart Type* for its dialog box

8 Click the *3-D* option button

9 Click the *3-D Bar* chart button

10 Click *OK*

Now, realign the x-axis title—Sales—to horizontal.

11 Click the x-axis title—Sales—to select it

12 Click *Format, Selected Axis Title* for its dialog box

13 If needed, click the *Alignment* tab

14 Click the horizontal *Text* orientation button

15 Click *OK*

16 Click the *Legend* to select it (Mar, Feb, Jan)

17 Drag the Legend up to align with the bottom of the chart's plot area, as in Figure SS3-8c

18 Double-click Cell A9 or any cell outside the chart to deselect it and turn off the chart edit mode

Your chart should resemble Figure SS3-8c. A *3-D bar chart* is a bar chart with horizontal orientation.

19 Save this workbook as GADGETS2 and close it

CHANGING THE CHART SUBTYPE.   Each chart type has a variety of subtype displays. Subtype displays are selected through the Option feature of the *Chart Type* dialog box. Try this:

1 Close any open workbook

2 Open the GADGETS1 workbook

3 Click and then double-click the chart to switch to chart edit mode

4 Click *Format, Chart Type* for its dialog box

5 Click the *Options* button for the *Format Column Group* dialog box

6 If needed, click the *Subtype* tab

7 Click the *Stacked Column* chart button (center button)

8 Click *OK*   [↵]

9 Double-click any cell outside the chart to turn off the chart edit mode.

Your chart should resemble Figure SS3-8d. A *stacked column* chart places each set of data in bars on top of the previous set in one column to display the total.

10 Close the workbook without saving

"EXPLODING" DATA

As shown in Figure SS3-8a, a pie chart displays data as parts of a circle. In an *exploded* pie chart, one or more data slices are separated from the whole for emphasis (shown in Figure SS3-9b). You will now learn how to "explode" a pie chart and then resize it for better viewing.

EXPLODING A PIE CHART.   The quickest way to create an exploded pie chart is to drag the desired slices away from the pie. Try this:

STEPS

1 Open the GADGETS1 workbook

2 Select the chart frame and then activate the chart edit mode

3 Use the *Chart Type* dialog box to select a pie chart (*Format, Chart Type, Pie, OK*)

Your pie chart should again resemble Figure SS3-8b. Now, add titles and percentage labels for each of the pie's slices using the Autoformat dialog box.

4 Click *Format, Autoformat* for its dialog box

5 Click the number 7 format button

6 Click *OK*   [↵]

Your chart should now display percentage and label information as in Figure SS3-9a. Now to explode its slices,

7 **Point to the *Widgets* slice of the pie chart**

8 **Drag it away from the pie chart until it resembles Figure SS3-9b**

9 **Double-click any cell outside the chart to deselect and turn off the chart edit mode**

Your pie chart should now resemble Figure SS3-9b. Note that the slices are reduced in size. This will be adjusted next.

RESIZING CHART COMPONENTS.   Like resizing a chart's frame, resizing its components involves first selecting the item and then dragging one of the selection handles. The next exercise enlarges the *plot area* (the area containing the graph) for better viewing, as in Figure SS3-9d.

STEPS

1 **Click and then double-click the chart to turn on the chart edit mode**

FIGURE SS3-9 ■ **EXPLODING A PIE CHART**

(a) Format information has been added to the chart.
(b) Dragging a pie's slice explodes the pie chart.
(c) The plot frame of a chart is selected.
(d) Dragging a plot-frame selection handle resizes the chart.

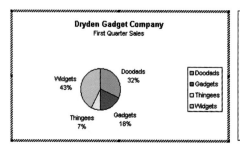

(a)

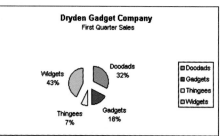

(b)

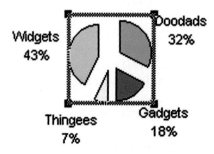

(c)

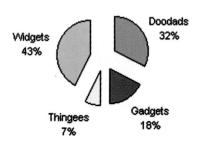

(d)

2 **Point to the center of the plot area and click to select it**

A square selection box with selection handles at each corner should appear as in Figure SS3-9c.

3 **Slowly point to the top-left selection handle until the pointer turns into a double arrow**

4 **Drag the *selection handle* away from the center to enlarge the plot area as in Figure SS3-9d**

5 **Double-click any cell outside the chart to turn off the chart edit mode**

Your chart should resemble Figure SS3-9d.

6 **Save the workbook as GADGETS3 and then close it**

PRINTING A CHART

A chart may be printed with its related worksheet data or alone.

PRINTING A WORKSHEET WITH A CHART.   To print a chart in its related worksheet,

STEPS

1 **Open the GADGET1 workbook and turn on your printer**

 2 **Click *File*, *Print*, OK**

PRINTING A SPECIFIC CHART.   To print a specific chart in a worksheet,

STEPS

1 **Click and then double-click the chart to select it and turn on the edit mode**

 2 **Click *File*, *Print*, OK**

3 **Close the workbook without saving and exit Excel**

☑ CHECKPOINT

✓ On a new workbook, list five names in Column A and five math test scores in Column B. Create a column chart displaying these data.

✓ On the worksheet, add reading scores in Column C. Add these new data to the chart and show the data in line-chart form. Adjust or add titles accordingly.

✓   Adjust the data to display only the reading scores in a pie chart with the first score exploded.

✓   Change the format of the exploded pie chart to include percentages and other label information.

✓   Resize the exploded pie chart and print it.

MODULE 2: CONDITIONAL FUNCTIONS

Conditional functions include logical and other special functions such as IF and lookup tables. These functions add limited decision-making capabilities to your worksheet by automatically selecting alternate results based on a condition that you have specified.

THE IF FUNCTION

The **IF function** is a logical spreadsheet function of the form IF(test,t,f). It takes one of two actions (*t* or *f*) depending on the truth of the stated condition (test). If the *test is true,* IF performs action *t;* if the *test* is false, it performs action f. For example, the function IF(A1 = A2,1,0) placed in Cell A3 will return a 1 in A3 if A1 equals A2, or a 0 if it does not.

A condition is typically expressed as a *logical formula* (a formula that uses one of the logical operators shown in Figure SS3-10a) or a range that contains a logical formula. However, the condition can be *any* formula, cell reference, string, or number. Any condition that equals zero is considered to be *false.* The actions to be taken (*t* or *f*) can be constant values or formulas.

Examine the IF examples in Figure SS3-10b. See if you can determine why each IF statement acted the way it did. Note that IF functions can also be nested one inside the other to create tests for multiple conditions (see Examples 9 and 10 in Figure SS3-10b). You may want to type each condition in a cell in Column C and compare your results with those in the figure.

USING IF FUNCTIONS.   An IF function is useful when there are two possible courses of action. Figure SS3-11 displays a few practical applications of this concept.

1   **Close any open workbook**

2   **Open the PAYROLL workbook from your data disk**

3   **Examine each formula as it is discussed in the text**

(If you do not have this workbook, examine the functions shown at the bottom of Figure SS3-11.)

Column B uses an IF function to mark employees whose sales do not exceed quota. For example, Cell B5 remains blank because *sales* (C5) exceeds *quota* (D5). However, Cell B6 shows a minus sign because C6 does not exceed D6.

FIGURE SS3-10 ■ THE IF FUNCTION

(a) Logical operators.
(b) IF examples.

Symbol	Explanation	Example
<	Less than	A1<A2
>	Greater than	A1>A2
=	Equal to	A1=A2
>=	Greater than or equal to	A1>=A2
<=	Less than or equal to	A1<=A2
<>	Not equal to	A1<>A2
NOT	Logical NOT test	NOT(A1,A2)
AND	Logical AND test	AND(A1>A2,A2>A3)
OR	Logical OR test	OR(A1>A2,A2<A3)

(a)

Using the following spreadsheet, the IF function shown at the left will return the result displayed on the right:

	A	B	C
1	7	5	
2	5	Hello	
3			

IF Statement	Result
1. =IF(A1>A2,1,0)	1
2. =IF(A1=A2, "yes", "no")	no
3. =IF(A1<>B2,A1*5,A2*3)	35
4. =IF(B1, "Text OK, A2)	Test OK
5. =IF(AND(A1=7,B1>10), "OK", "—")	—
6. =IF(OR(A1=7,B1>B10), "OK", "A3")	OK
7. =IF(B2="Hello",A1,A2)	7
8. =IF(A1>5,SUM(A1:A2),0)	12
9. =IF(A3>A1,"YES",IF(B2="Hello",1,2))	1
10. =IF(A1>A2,IF(B1>A1,"YES","NO"),0)	NO

(b)

Note: Examples 9 and 10 are nested IF statements.

Gross pay is divided into two columns: Column G shows the *regular* portion of gross up to the first 40 hours; Column H shows the additional *overtime* pay (or 0 if hours do not exceed 40).

FIGURE SS3-11 ■ AN IF APPLICATION TO PAYROLL

	A	B	C	D	E	F	G	H	I	J	K
1	Dryden Weekly Payroll and Commission Report									11-01-XX	
2											
3							SALARY			Adj.	
4	Employee	Q?	Sales	Quota	Hrs	Pay	Gross	OT	Comm	Gross	
5	Burstein		$ 1,100	$ 900	43	$5.65	$ 226.00	$ 25.43	$ 65.00	$ 316.43	
6	Laudon	-	1,000	1,200	35	4.00	140.00	-	50.00	190.00	
7	Martin	-	850	900	45	5.75	230.00	43.13	42.50	315.63	
8	Parker		1,275	1,000	25	6.75	168.75	-	77.50	246.25	
9	Williams		1,450	1,300	51	3.50	140.00	57.75	80.00	277.75	
10	Totals		$ 5,675	$5,300			$ 904.75	$126.30	$ 315.00	$ 1,346.05	
11											
12	Notes:		Cell	Formula or Function							
13			B5	=IF(C5>D5," ","-")							
14			G5	=IF(E5>40,F5*40,F5*E5)							
15			H5	=IF(E5>40,(E5-40)*F5*1.5,0)							
16			I5	=C5*0.05+(C5>D5)*(C5-D5)*0.05							
17											

USING CONDITIONS WITHOUT IFS. Note that Column I provides alternatives without actually using an IF function. It calculates commission as 5 percent of sales and then automatically adds a 5 percent bonus for those sales that exceed the quota. The C5>D5 in Cell I5's formula does the trick. It is a *condition.* Like IF, it evaluates to 1 if the condition is true (sales exceed quota), or to 0 if it is false. Since the bonus is multiplied by this value, the bonus automatically is 0 if C5 does not exceed D5.

Using a condition alone is a shortcut to the IF function. It takes a lot more thought, but it can save space in the worksheet file.

> **Tip: If you need more than two alternatives, explore the use of Excel's CHOOSE function as listed in the appendix.**

TABLE LOOKUPS: VLOOKUP AND HLOOKUP

Lookup tables are logical spreadsheet functions of the form VLOOKUP (lookup_value, table_array, col_index_num,...) or HLOOKUP (lookup_value, table_array, row_index_num...) both use a two-dimensional table to return values that fall within set intervals; VLOOKUP uses a vertical table, whereas HLOOKUP uses a horizontal one.

This exercise examines a VLOOKUP table that returns the amount of tax for a given income and category.

STEPS

1 **Launch Excel or close any open workbook**

2 **Open the TAX workbook from your data disk**

3 **If you do not have the TAX workbook (or if you want the practice), type it now, matching the data shown in Figure SS3-12a, and save it as TAX**

To create a lookup, you should first name the lookup table range. Although you could type cell addresses, a range name makes the function more understandable.

FIGURE SS3-12 ■ LOOKUP TABLES

(a) This is the TAX workbook.
(b) The VLOOKUP function returns one of the cell values from the tax table.

	A	B	C	D	E	F
1	TAX TABLE EXAMPLE					
2						
3	Income:					
4	Category:					
5	Your TAX is:					
6						
7		Category				
8	Income	1	2	3	4	
9	$ 25,000	$ 7,250	$ 6,525	$ 5,870	$ 5,278	
10	25,500	7,413	6,671	5,999	5,376	
11	26,000	7,575	6,793	6,118	5,500	
12	26,500	7,685	6,901	6,217	5,599	
13						
14						

(a)

	A	B	C	D	E	F
1	TAX TABLE EXAMPLE					
2						
3	Income:		$ 25,625			
4	Category:		2			
5	Your TAX is:		$ 6,671			
6						
7		Category				
8	Income	1	2	3	4	
9	$ 25,000	$ 7,250	$ 6,525	$ 5,870	$ 5,278	
10	25,500	7,413	6,671	5,999	5,376	
11	26,000	7,575	6,793	6,118	5,500	
12	26,500	7,685	6,901	6,217	5,599	
13						
14						

(b)

SS

4 Select the range A9:E12

5 Click *Insert, Name, Define* for its dialog box

6 Type `Tax` and click *OK*

The entries in the first column of the table will be used for comparison; the remaining columns contain the values that will be returned.

7 In Cell C5, type   `=VLOOKUP(C3,TAX,C4+1)`

The "+1" in the VLOOKUP function instructs Excel to look one cell to the right of the indicated column number. For instance, typing the number 2 in Cell C4 instructs Excel to look in Column C of the range.

8 Press ↵

This lookup function compares the value in Cell C3 with each cell in the first column of the tax table. For this to work properly, values in the first column must be in ascending sequential order. When Excel finds a cell in the first column that is closest to the value in C3 *without exceeding it,* Excel moves across that row to the column specified by the value in Cell C4. (Currently, "#N/A" messages may appear in cells until you complete the remaining cells.)

9 In Cell C3, enter an income of `25625`

10 In Cell C4, enter an offset of `2` and then press ↓

Your screen should now resemble Figure SS3-12b. The VLOOKUP function locates the row that contains a value close to, but not exceeding, 25625. It then uses the offset value to locate the proper column and return the appropriate cell.

11 Save this workbook as TAX1 and then close it

Change the income and offset values in Cells C3 and C4, and examine the value returned in C5. Incomes that exceed the highest value in the table will use the last row of the table. Incomes that are less than the first value in the table will return an error message.

☑ CHECKPOINT

✓ On a new workbook, type 10 numbers between zero and 100 in Column A.
✓ Create an IF function in Column B that will multiply each cell in Column A by two if the value exceeds 50, and otherwise return a zero in the Column B cell.
✓ Using the worksheet you just created, create a VLOOKUP table that will return a letter grade in Column C for each number in Column A as follows: "F" for 0-59, "D" for 60-69, "C" for 70-79, "B" for 80-89, and "A" for 90 and above.
✓ Create an HLOOKUP table that does the same task just outlined.
✓ What is the purpose of adding a "+1" to a lookup argument?

MODULE 3: DATA MANAGEMENT

Although Excel is used primarily as a spreadsheet, any related data placed in rows and columns can also be treated as an Excel *database table*—an organized collection of data. As shown in Figure SS3-13, each worksheet row forms a *record,* and each column contains one *field*—a category of data common to each record. The entries in any field (column) must be consistent—either all values (including formulas) or all text, but not some of each.

The top row of the database must contain *field names* that identify all the fields in the database. This row must be followed immediately by the first record—blank rows or separator lines cannot be used. More than one database can appear within the same worksheet as space permits.

The following exercises examine various database commands. In preparation for these exercises,

STEPS

1 Close any open worksheet and then open the GRADES workbook

2 If you do not have the GRADES workbook (or want the practice), type it now, matching the data shown in Figure SS3-13, and then save it as GRADES

Note: If you create the worksheet yourself, *type* the letters in Column F even though they are generated by a VLOOKUP table in this example. You do not need the lookup table to use the database.

SS

FIGURE SS3-13 ■ THE SPREADSHEET AS A DATABASE

	A	B	C	D	E	F	G	H	I	J
1	STUDENT GRADES				Field names					
2								Grade		
3		STUDENT	TEST 1	TEST 2	AVERAGE	GRADE		Lookup		
4		Jerry	56	87	72	C		0	F	
5		Elissa	92	96	94	A		60	D	
6		Andrea	98	90	94	A		70	C	
7		Edward	56	80	68	D		80	B	
8		Charles	84	90	87	B		90	A	
9		Rita	85	93	89	B				
10		Lesley	72	85	79	C	Record			
11										
12	Database									
13		Field								
14										

MODULE 3A: GENERATING A SEQUENCE OF NUMBERS

A useful data feature are Excel's Fill commands, which generate number sequences in a given range. For example, assume you want to give each student in the database a student number, starting with 101 and increasing by one for each student on the list. You could type these numbers yourself, but it is easier to let Excel do it by either using the *Fill* submenu or the fill handle.

STEPS

1   Open the GRADES workbook if needed

2   Move to Cell A4

THE FILL SUBMENU.   To use the *Fill* submenu to generate a sequence of numbers beginning with 101 in Cell A4 and ending with107 in Cell A10,

STEPS

1   Type 101 and press ↵

2   Select the fill range A4:A10

3   Click *Edit,* point to *Fill* for its submenu

The *Fill* submenu contains commands to fill a range. The first five commands fill a range in the direction of the command. The Series command fills a range with a series of numbers or dates and the Justify command rearranges text to fill a range of cells.

4   Click *Series* for its dialog box

The *Series* dialog box should appear as Figure SS3-14a. At this point, you can change the default step value, stop value, type, or series in row or column. The *step value* is the value added to each number to generate the next number in the sequence. A *type* is the frequency with which a sequence number will appear.
   At this point you can change the different series options. For now, to accept this range and other default settings,

5   Click the *OK* button

6   Press ↑ to deselect and move to Cell A3

The range is instantly filled with the proper values as if you had typed them (as shown in Figure SS3-14b).

7   Save this workbook as GRADES1 and then close it

FIGURE SS3-14 ■ DATA FILL

(a) The Fill parameters have been set in the *Fill* dialog box.
(b) This is the complete fill.

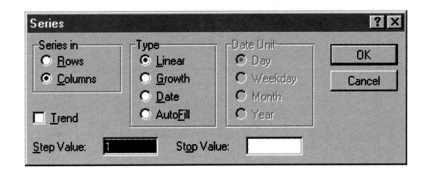

(a)

(b)

	A	B	C	D	E	F	G	H	I	J
1	STUDENT GRADES									
2								Grade		
3		STUDENT	TEST 1	TEST 2	AVERAGE	GRADE		Lookup		
4	101	Jerry	56	87	72	C		0	F	
5	102	Elissa	92	96	94	A		60	D	
6	103	Andrea	98	90	94	A		70	C	
7	104	Edward	56	80	68	D		80	B	
8	105	Charles	84	90	87	B		90	A	
9	106	Rita	85	93	89	B				
10	107	Lesley	72	85	79	C				
11										
12										

THE FILL HANDLE.   The small square box at the bottom-right corner of Excel's cell pointer is called the **fill handle.** It is a feature that can be used to quickly fill a range with a sequence of numbers or other data by mouse. If only one number is placed in a cell of the fill range, the fill handle will copy that number to the empty cells in that range. Try this:

STEPS

1　Open the workbook GRADES

2　Move to Cell A4

3　Type **101** and press ↵

4　Move back to Cell A4

5　Slowly point to the fill handle of the cell pointer until the mouse pointer turns into a (+) (see left margin)

6　Drag the fill handle to Cell A10 and then release your mouse

Note that 101 has been copied to the range A5:A10. Now, do the following to generate a sequence of numbers using the fill handle.

7 Press Delete to remove the contents of the range A4:A10

8 In Cell A4, type 101 and press ↵

9 In Cell A5, type 102 and press ↵

10 Select Cells A4 and A5

 11 Drag the fill handle to Cell A10 and then release your mouse

12 Press ↑ to move to Cell A3

Your worksheet should resemble Figure SS3-14b again.

13 Close the worksheet without saving

MODULE 3B: SORTING DATA

Data that are listed vertically in any range can also be *sorted,* or arranged in order. Data are normally sorted in ascending order (from lowest value to highest), but they can also be sorted in descending, or reverse, order (highest to lowest). The following exercise sorts the test data in alphabetical order by student name.

> **Note:** Before you sort, it is usually good practice to save your worksheet. This way, if the sort does not work as expected, you can always open the worksheet and try again. The Undo feature will also return the worksheet to its "presort" state.

IDENTIFYING THE DATA RANGE. The first step in the sort process is to identify the data range to be sorted.

STEPS

1 Open the GRADES workbook

2 Move to Cell B4

3 Select the range B4:F10

Notice (as shown in Figure SS3-15a) that the data range includes *all* columns of the records (rows) to be sorted, not just the student name column. Columns and rows that are left out of the data range *will not be sorted.* The top row of field names is purposely not included in the data range, or it too would be sorted.

FIGURE SS3-15 ■ SORTING DATA

(a) The data range includes all fields and records but not field names.
(b) This is the *Sort* dialog box.
(c) The entire data range has been sorted alphabetically.

(a)

	A	B	C	D	E	F	G	H	I	J
1	STUDENT GRADES									
2								Grade		
3		STUDENT	TEST 1	TEST 2	AVERAGE	GRADE		Lookup		
4		Jerry	56	87	72	C		0	F	
5		Elissa	92	96	94	A		60	D	
6		Andrea	98	90	94	A		70	C	
7		Edward	56	80	68	D		80	B	
8		Charles	84	90	87	B		90	A	
9		Rita	85	93	89	B				
10		Lesley	72	85	79	C				
11										
12										

(b)

Sort   **? X**

Sort By
STUDENT ▼   ⊙ Ascending   ○ Descending

Then By
▼   ⊙ Ascending   ○ Descending

Then By
▼   ⊙ Ascending   ○ Descending

My List Has
⊙ Header Row   ○ No Header Row

OK   Cancel   Options...

(c)

	A	B	C	D	E	F	G	H	I	J
1	STUDENT GRADES									
2								Grade		
3		STUDENT	TEST 1	TEST 2	AVERAGE	GRADE		Lookup		
4		Andrea	98	90	94	A		0	F	
5		Charles	84	90	87	B		60	D	
6		Edward	56	80	68	D		70	C	
7		Elissa	92	96	94	A		80	B	
8		Jerry	56	87	72	C		90	A	
9		Lesley	72	85	79	C				
10		Rita	85	93	89	B				
11										
12										

SS

SETTING KEYS.   The second step is to select key fields, or *keys,* to be used for the sort. As you will soon see, key fields are selected using drop-down boxes in the *Sort* dialog box (*Data* menu).

STEPS

1   **Click** *Data, Sort* **for its dialog box**

The *Sort* dialog box should now appear as in Figure SS3-15b. You can select up to three sort key fields using this dialog box. The key field selected in the *Sort By* drop-down box will sort before the key field selected in the *Then By* drop-down box, and so on. You can also select the order of each key field's sort (ascending or descending).

Excel automatically selects STUDENT as the *Sort By* key field and the default sort order—ascending. Although you can select another key or a different sort order, none is needed in this exercise.

PERFORMING THE SORT.   The last step is to activate the sort.

STEPS

1   **Click the** *OK* **button**

2   **Press** ↑ **to deselect, move to Cell B3**

3   **Save this workbook as GRADES3**

Examine your screen and Figure SS3-15c. Notice that records within the data range have been sorted into alphabetical order according to the key field—STUDENT. All tests and averages have been moved as well, since they were part of the data range. The title, field names, and grade lookup table were unaffected.

SORTING WITH TWO KEYS.   This exercise demonstrates sorting with two keys: *average* as the *Sort By* key and *student* as the *Then By* key.

STEPS

1   **Select the range B4:F10**

2   **Click** *Data, Sort* **for its dialog box**

3   **Click the** ▼ **button of the** *Sort By* **drop-down box**

4   **Click AVERAGE from the drop-down list**

5   **Click the** *Descending* **option button of the Sort By group**

6   Click the ▼ button of the *Then By* drop-down box

7   Click STUDENT from the drop-down list

Your *Sort* dialog box selections should resemble Figure SS3-16a. If not, redo Steps 3 through 7.

8   Click *OK*   [↵]

9   Press ↑ to deselect and move to Cell B3

FIGURE SS3-16 ■ THE COMPLETED SORT

(a) This is the *Sort* dialog box with two key field selections.
(b) These data have been sorted by Average Grade and Student name.

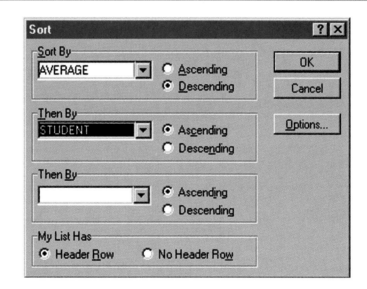

(a)

	A	B	C	D	E	F	G	H	I	J
1	STUDENT GRADES									
2								Grade		
3		STUDENT	TEST 1	TEST 2	AVERAGE	GRADE		Lookup		
4		Andrea	98	90	94	A		0	F	
5		Elissa	92	96	94	A		60	D	
6		Rita	85	93	89	B		70	C	
7		Charles	84	90	87	B		80	B	
8		Lesley	72	85	79	C		90	A	
9		Jerry	56	87	72	C				
10		Edward	56	80	68	D				
11										
12										

(b)

The completed sort appears in Figure SS3-16b. Note that the rows are ordered first according to the average test grade in decreasing order (AVERAGE, descending order). Where primary fields are identical—as for Andrea and Elissa—the rows are further ordered in normal alphabetical order by name (STUDENT, ascending order).

10 **Close the workbook without saving**

> **Tip:** You can also sort a range by using the ascending or descending toolbar buttons.

MODULE 3C: CREATING A DATA DISTRIBUTION

Excel can also prepare a data distribution of values in a range. A **data distribution** (or *frequency distribution*) is a count of spreadsheet values (within a *values range*) that fall within specified numeric intervals (listed in a *bin range*). The following exercise creates a data distribution that determines how many test grades are less than or equal to 60, greater than 60 but less than 70, and so on, up to a grade of 100.

The first step is to select two unused adjacent columns where the distribution will appear. Use Columns H and I starting at Row 12, as shown in Figure SS3-17a. Column H will hold the upper limit of each interval or *bin;* the distribution will appear in Column I.

CREATING THE BINS.   Increasing values can now be entered into the appropriate bins to create a specific interval for counting. The program interprets the contents of each bin you create as "less than or equal to this number." Thus, the first value of 60 will collect any value that is less than or equal to 60.

STEPS

1 **Open the GRADES1 workbook**

Now place some identifying labels as follows:

2 **In Cell H10, type   Distribution**

3 **In Cell H11, type   Up to**

These two titles are simply reminders for future reference; they are not needed for the actual calculations.

4 **In Cells H12 through H16, enter the numbers as shown in Figure SS3-17a**

Your screen should resemble Figure SS3-17a, with 60, 70, 80, 90, and 100 appearing in Cells H12 through H16. If it does not, retype these cells now.

INVOKING THE DISTRIBUTION.   Once the bins have been created, you can invoke the command to calculate the distribution.

FIGURE SS3-17 ■ CREATING A DATA DISTRIBUTION

(a) Creating the bins.
(b) The completed
distribution of test grades.

(a)

	A	B	C	D	E	F	G	H	I	J
1	STUDENT GRADES									
2								Grade		
3		STUDENT	TEST 1	TEST 2	AVERAGE	GRADE		Lookup		
4	101	Jerry	56	87	72	C		0	F	
5	102	Elissa	92	96	94	A		60	D	
6	103	Andrea	98	90	94	A		70	C	
7	104	Edward	56	80	68	D		80	B	
8	105	Charles	84	90	87	B		90	A	
9	106	Rita	85	93	89	B				
10	107	Lesley	72	85	79	C		Distribution		
11								Up to		
12								60		
13								70		
14								80		
15								90		
16								100		
17										
18										

(b)

	A	B	C	D	E	F	G	H	I	J
1	STUDENT GRADES									
2								Grade		
3		STUDENT	TEST 1	TEST 2	AVERAGE	GRADE		Lookup		
4	101	Jerry	56	87	72	C		0	F	
5	102	Elissa	92	96	94	A		60	D	
6	103	Andrea	98	90	94	A		70	C	
7	104	Edward	56	80	68	D		80	B	
8	105	Charles	84	90	87	B		90	A	
9	106	Rita	85	93	89	B				
10	107	Lesley	72	85	79	C		Distribution		
11								Up to		
12								60	2	
13								70	0	
14								80	2	
15								90	6	
16								100	4	
17									0	
18										

STEPS

1 **Select the frequency-distribution-results range I12:I17 (the "I" in "I12" and "I17" stands for Column I—do not use "112" or "117")**

Note that this range includes one cell more (Cell I17) than the corresponding bin numbers.

2 **Type** **=FREQUENCY(C4:D10,H12:H16)** **but *do not* press Enter**

The range C4:D10 is the *data-array range;* it includes all the data in the TEST 1 and TEST 2 columns. The H12:H16 is the *bin-array range* and includes the distribution criteria. To produce the distribution shown in Figure SS3-17b,

3 **Press** **Ctrl** + **Shift** + **↵**

Step 3 copies the frequency function to each cell in the distribution-results range as an absolute formula, which is encased in brackets ({ }).

4 **Press** ↑ **to deselect and move to Cell I11**

Your worksheet should resemble Figure SS3-17b.

The results can be interpreted as follows: two tests were 60 or less; no tests were between 61 and 70; two tests were between 71 and 80; six tests were between 81 and 90; and finally, four tests were greater than 90 but less than or equal to 100. The final zero beneath the distribution shows that no tests were above the last bin limit. The sum of the counts shown in the distribution is 14—the number of tests in the values range.

5 **Save this workbook as GRADES2 and then close it**

Since the distribution range contains frequency functions, changing a test score in the data-array range automatically updates the distribution results. You can calculate as many distributions as you want by changing the number of bin rows, their upper limits, or the data-array range to be counted once the FREQUENCY functions have been placed in the distributions results range.

MODULE 3D: INFORMATION RETRIEVAL—DATA QUERIES

A **database query** is a question asked of a database. Database query commands let you locate (and edit) records in a database table that meet certain criteria. Although database queries are more useful in large spreadsheets, the principles of creating and using queries can be learned more easily on a smaller scale.

To query an Excel database table, use the Filter commands that are accessed through the *Data* menu. **Filter** commands find and extract records in a database that match a specific criteria. **Criteria** are conditions that are used to find matching records in a database.

FILTERING DATA.   Excel's AutoFilter command can be used to filter records based on criteria specified through drop-down list boxes. The results of the filtering process are displayed in place of the source database table. The table is not lost, but rather hidden, and may be redisplayed using the Show All command (*Filter* menu). Try this to filter the database to display information based on the criteria STUDENT=Jerry.

STEPS

1 **Open the GRADES workbook**

2 **Move to Cell B3, the first cell in the Field Names row**

3 **Save the workbook as GRADES4**

4 **Click *Data*, point to *Filter*, and then click *AutoFilter* to turn on the AutoFilter feature and filter mode**

Drop-down list buttons (▼) should appear at the right end of each field name cell as in Figure SS3-18a.

5 **Click the ▼ button in Cell B3 for the STUDENT drop-down list**

6 **Click *Jerry* from the drop-down list**

Excel filtered the record meeting the criteria "STUDENT=Jerry" as in Figure SS3-18b.

By using the custom option of the filter drop-down list, you can filter students who match other search conditions. Try this:

7 **Click *Data, Filter, Show All* to redisplay the entire database**

8 **Click the ▼ button of the TEST1 drop-down box (in Cell C3) for the TEST1 drop-down list**

9 **Click *(Custom...)* for the *Custom AutoFilter* dialog box**

10 **Type 80**

11 **Click the ▼ button of the operator drop-down box and click <**

Your dialog box should appear as Figure SS3-19a.

12 **Click *OK***

FIGURE SS3-18 ■ FILTERING RECORDS

(a) The AutoFilter command places drop-down list buttons at the right end of each field name's cell.
(b) Setting a filtering criterion with a drop-down list will display only the result of the filter.

(a)

	A	B	C	D	E	F	G	H	I	J
1	STUDENT GRADES									
2								Grade		
3		STUDEN ▼	TEST ▼	TEST ▼	AVERAG ▼	GRAD ▼		Lookup		
4		Jerry	56	87	72	C		0 F		
5		Elissa	92	96	94	A		60 D		
6		Andrea	98	90	94	A		70 C		
7		Edward	56	80	68	D		80 B		
8		Charles	84	90	87	B		90 A		
9		Rita	85	93	89	B				
10		Lesley	72	85	79	C				
11										
12										

(b)

	A	B	C	D	E	F	G	H	I	J
1	STUDENT GRADES									
2								Grade		
3		STUDEN ▼	TEST ▼	TEST ▼	AVERAG ▼	GRAD ▼		Lookup		
4		Jerry	56	87	72	C		0 F		
11										
12										

FIGURE SS3-19 ■ CUSTOM DATA FILTERING

(a) This is the *Custom AutoFilter* dialog box.
(b) This screen shows filtered data.

(a)

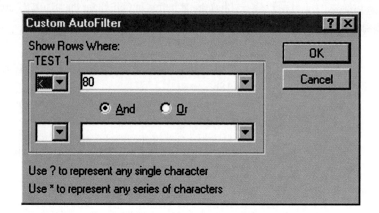

(b)

	A	B	C	D	E	F	G	H	I	J
1	STUDENT GRADES									
2								Grade		
3		STUDEN ▾	TEST ▾	TEST ▾	AVERAG ▾	GRAD ▾		Lookup		
4		Jerry	56	87	72	C		0	F	
7		Edward	56	80	68	D		80	B	
10		Lesley	72	85	79	C				
11										
12										

Your worksheet should resemble Figure SS3-19b. If not, repeat Steps 6 through 11. Note that only the records that meet the criterion "Test1<80" are displayed.

13 Close the workbook without saving

Tip: You can use the *Form* dialog box (*Data*, *Form*) to find, change, or delete records in a database.

USING MULTIPLE CRITERIA.   More than one search criterion can be used at a time. These criteria can be identified using logical connectors, such as AND or OR. Logical connectors are available through the *Custom AutoFilter* dialog boxes.

Multiple criteria can be set in a single field or in multiple fields using similar techniques. Try this multiple-criteria entry to find records whose average (single field) exceeds 59 *and* is also less than 70.

Note: An AND connector requires that all criteria be met for a record to be selected.

1 Open the GRADES4 workbook

2 Click _Data_ point to _Filter,_ and then click _AutoFilter_

3 Click the ▼ button of Cell E3 for the AVERAGE drop-down list

4 Click _(Custom...)_ for the _Custom AutoFilter_ dialog box

5 Type 59

6 Click the ▼ button of the first _Operator_ drop-down box (it currently displays an "=" sign)

7 Click >

8 Click the ▼ button of the second _Operator_ drop-down box

9 Click <

10 Click the second value drop-down box to place the insertion point

11 Type 70

Your dialog box should appear as in Figure SS3-20a.

12 Click _OK_   [↵]

The result of your multiple criteria search appears as in Figure SS3-20b.

13 Close the workbook without saving

ADVANCED FILTERING. As mentioned earlier, multiple criteria that pertain to different fields can also be set with an AND or an OR connector. You can use the _AutoFilter_ drop-down list boxes to set criteria for more than one field, thereby creating an AND connector. OR connectors containing different fields require the use of the _Advance Filter_ dialog box. The next exercise explores an OR connector entry using Excel's Advanced Filter feature.

1 Open the GRADES4 workbook

2 Move to Cell A2 and insert four new rows below it

3 In Cell B3, type TEST 2 (with a space between TEST and 2)

4 In Cell B4, type >=C8+10

FIGURE SS3-20 ■ MULTIPLE CRITERIA SEARCHES

(a) Entering multiple-criteria information.
(b) The results of the multiple-criteria search.

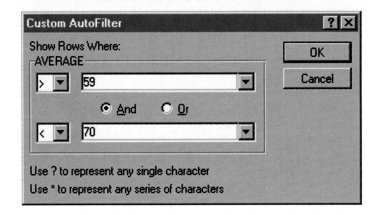

(a)

(b)

	A	B	C	D	E	F	G	H	I	J
1	STUDENT GRADES									
2								Grade		
3		STUDEN ▾	TEST ▾	TEST ▾	AVERAC ▾	GRAD ▾		Lookup		
7		Edward	56	80	68	D		80	B	
11										
12										

---

5 In Cell C3, type **AVERAGE**

6 In Cell C5, type **<90**

Placing criteria in different rows, as in Steps 4 and 5 above, invokes an OR connector. The above entries should agree with the corresponding cells at the top of Figure SS3-21a.

7 Move to Cell B7 (or any cell in the database table)

8 Click *Data*, point to *Filter*, and then click *Advanced Filter*

9 Click the *Criteria Range* text box

10 Type **B3:C5**

Your dialog box should resemble Figure SS3-21b. Note that Excel places the list range as long as the cell pointer is positioned in one of the cells in the database.

11 Click *OK*   [ ]

FIGURE SS3-21 ■ USING MULTIPLE CRITERIA

(a) This screen shows the result of filtering.
(b) The *Advanced Filter* dialog box can be used to filter data based on multiple criteria specified on a worksheet.

	A	B	C	D	E	F	G	H	I	J
1	STUDENT GRADES									
2										
3		TEST 2	AVERAGE							
4		>=C8+10		— Criteria						
5			<90							
6								Grade		
7		STUDENT	TEST 1	TEST 2	AVERAGE	GRADE		Lookup		
8		Jerry	56	87	72	C		0	F	
11		Edward	56	80	68	D		80	B	
12		Charles	84	90	87	B		90	A	
13		Rita	85	93	89	B				
14		Lesley	72	85	79	C				
15										
16										

(a)

(b)

Advanced Filter   ? ✕

Action
○ Filter the List, in-place
○ Copy to Another Location

OK
Cancel

List Range: $B$7:$F$14
Criteria Range: B3:C5
Copy to:

☐ Unique Records Only

The results of your multiple criteria search should agree with those at the bottom of Figure SS3-21a.

12 **Resave the workbook as GRADES4**

CREATING A QUERY TABLE.   A filter list can also be copied to another location as a separate query table. This is done by selecting the *Copy to Another Location* option button of the *Advanced Filter* dialog box.

STEPS

1 **Open the GRADES4 workbook, if needed**

SS

2   Delete the content of range B3:C5 and move to Cell B3

3   Click *Data,* point to *Filter,* and then click *Show All* to clear all previous filter settings

4   In Cell B3, type   TEST 1

5   In Cell B4, type   =85

6   Move to Cell B7

7   Click *Data,* point to *Filter,* and then click *Advanced Filter*

8   Click the *Copy to Another Location* option button

9   Press   Alt   +   C   to highlight the content of the *Criteria Range* text box and press   Delete   to remove prior settings

10   Type   B3:B4   and press   Tab

11   Type   B16:F18   in the *Copy to* text box

Your dialog box should resemble Figure SS3-22a.

12   Click *OK*   [↵]

Your worksheet should now resemble Figure SS3-22b. Filter commands can also be applied to the copied filter list.

13   Save this workbook as GRADES5

Now try creating another query table to contain the record of students who received A's as final grades.

STEPS

1   Open the GRADES5 workbook, if needed

2   In Cell D3, type   GRADE

3   In Cell D4, type   A

4   Move to Cell B7

5   Click *Data,* point to *Filter,* and then click *Advanced Filter*

6   Click the *Copy to Another Location* option button

(a) The *Copy to another location* option can be used to create a query table.
(b) This is a query table containing the results of the filtering process.

Advanced Filter

Action
- ○ Filter the List, in-place
- ● Copy to Another Location

OK

Cancel

List Range: `$B$7:$F$14`

Criteria Range: `B3:B4`

Copy to: `B16:F18`

☐ Unique Records Only

(a)

	A	B	C	D	E	F	G	H	I	J
1	STUDENT GRADES									
2										
3		TEST 1		—Criteria						
4		85								
5										
6								Grade		
7		STUDENT	TEST 1	TEST 2	AVERAGE	GRADE		Lookup		
8		Jerry	56	87	72	C		0	F	
9		Elissa	92	96	94	A		60	D	
10		Andrea	98	90	94	A		70	C	
11		Edward	56	80	68	D		80	B	
12		Charles	84	90	87	B		90	A	
13		Rita	85	93	89	B				
14		Lesley	72	85	79	C				
15										
16		STUDENT	TEST 1	TEST 2	AVERAGE	GRADE		—Query table		
17		Rita	85	93	89	B				
18										

Database table —

(b)

---

7 Press **Alt** + **C** to highlight the content of the *Criteria Range* text box and press **Delete** to remove prior settings

8 Type **D3:D4** and press **Tab**

9 Type **B19:F21** in the *Copy to* text box as in Figure SS3-23a

10 Click *OK*

11 Click the ▼ of the vertical scroll bar until the new query table is visible as in Figure SS3-23b

12 Save this workbook as GRADES6 and then close it

FIGURE SS3-23 ■ CREATING AN ADDITIONAL QUERY TABLE

(a) Select the *Copy to another location* option, and then enter the *Criteria Range* and *Copy to* range in the dialog box.
(b) The result of the second query table.

(a)

(b)

	A	B	C	D	E	F	G	H	I	J
6								Grade		
7		STUDENT	TEST 1	TEST 2	AVERAGE	GRADE		Lookup		
8		Jerry	56	87	72	C		0	F	
9		Elissa	92	96	94	A		60	D	
10		Andrea	98	90	94	A		70	C	
11		Edward	56	80	68	D		80	B	
12		Charles	84	90	87	B		90	A	
13		Rita	85	93	89	B				
14		Lesley	72	85	79	C				
15										
16		STUDENT	TEST 1	TEST 2	AVERAGE	GRADE				
17		Rita	85	93	89	B				
18										
19		STUDENT	TEST 1	TEST 2	AVERAGE	GRADE		Second		
20		Elissa	92	96	94	A		query table		
21		Andrea	98	90	94	A				

Now, only two records that match these criteria—*Elissa* and *Andrea*—are copied into the query table as shown in Figure SS3-23b.

MODULE 3E: USING DATA FUNCTIONS

Data functions, as listed in Figure SS3-24, combine the qualities of statistical functions with lookup and database concepts to include only selected records in a specific calculation. Data functions follow the form DFUNCTION (*input, offset, criteria*). In this format, the criteria range tells the program which records in the input range to include in the calculation of the column listed in the *offset*. The following exercise demonstrates its use.

FIGURE SS3-24 ■ DATABASE FUNCTIONS

DAVERAGE	Averages the values in a database field based on certain criteria
DCOUNTA	Counts the nonblank cells in a database field based on certain criteria
DMIN	Finds the smallest value in a database field based on certain criteria.
DSTDEVP	Calculates the population standard deviation of the values in a database field based on certain criteria.
DSUM	Totals the field values in a database field based on certain criteria.
DVARP	Calculates the population variance of the values in a database field based on certain criteria.

STEPS

1 **Open the CHECKS workbook**

Your screen should resemble Figure SS3-25, which depicts a simple checkbook management system. (While you are in this spreadsheet, you may want to examine the use of

FIGURE SS3-25 ■ THE CHECKS WORKSHEET

	A	B	C	D	E	F	G
1	CHECKBOOK						
2							
3	NUMBER	DATE	TRANSACTION	AMOUNT	BALANCE		
4		07-Oct	Deposit	$ 1,000.00	$ 1,000.00		
5	101	07-Oct	Rent	415.00	585.00		
6	102	12-Oct	Utilities	66.75	518.25		
7	103	14-Oct	Phone	54.50	463.75		
8	104	21-Oct	Ed's Applicances	350.32	113.43		
9	105	30-Oct	Charlie's Record Shop	67.07	46.36		
10		01-Nov	Deposit	625.00	671.36		
11	106	03-Nov	Dryden Books	124.15	547.21		
12	107	03-Nov	Rent	415.00	132.21		
13	108	04-Nov	Phone	42.65	89.56		
14	109	08-Nov	Utilities	75.46	14.10		
15							
16			TRANSACTION				
17				Total:			

Column B's DATE function or Column E's IF function.) Note that titles have already been entered and formats selected to help structure your results.

2 Click ▼ on the vertical scroll bar until rows 17, 18, and 19 are visible

3 Move to Cell E17

At this point, you can either use Excel's Function wizard to help you enter functions arguments or simply type them. The Steps 3 through 10 use the Function wizard to enter the first function 5DSUM(A3:E14,4,C16:C17). All other functions in this exercise are presented as type-in data.

4 Click *Insert, Function* for the Function wizard   [**Shift** + **F3**]

5 Click *Database* in the *Function Category* list box

6 Click DSUM in the *Function Name* list box

7 Click the *Next>* button   [↵]

8 Type **A3:E14** in the database text box and press **Tab**

9 Type **4** in the field text box and press **Tab**

10 Type **C16:C17** in the criteria text box

Your *Function wizard* dialog box should resemble Figure SS3-26a.

11 Click the *Finish* button   [↵]

This formula translates as "within the stated input range (A3:E14), total the fourth off-set column (AMOUNT) for those records that match the criteria in cells C16:C17."

Since the criteria range is empty, all records are included—the function simply calculates the total of Column D.

12 Format Cells E17 and E18 to the accounting-dollar sign, two-decimal format

13 In Cell C17, type **Deposit** and press ↵

As shown in Figure SS3-26b, the total now reflects only those records whose transaction matches the label "Deposit."

14 In Cell E18, type **=DAVERAGE(A3:E14,4,C16:C17)** and press ↵

15 In Cell E19, type **=DCOUNTA(A3:E14,4,C16:C17)** and press ↵

These formulas average and count the deposits, respectively, as shown in Figure SS3-26c. When entering database functions, you can use named ranges for the input and criteria, or you can specify a cell address that contains a value for the offset.

FIGURE SS3-26 ■ ENTERING DATABASE FUNCTIONS

(a) The Function Wizard can be used to help enter a database function.
(b) The DSUM in cell C17 adds all records whose transactions show "Deposit."
(c) The DAVERAGE and DCOUNTA functions have been added.
(d) Changing the criterion to "Rent" automatically changes the results of all database functions.

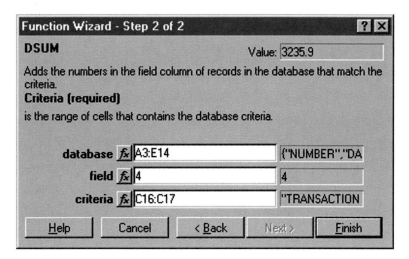

(a)

(b)

(c)

(d)

16 Save this workbook as CHECKS1

17 In Cell C17, type Rent and press ↵

As shown in Figure SS3-26d, all the database functions now reflect results for the new criterion, *Rent*. By redefining the criteria range, you can also specify multiple criteria as you did for data queries.

18 Close the workbook without saving

☑ CHECKPOINT

✓ Open the GRADES workbook. Sort the data in Columns B through F by TEST 2 scores from highest to lowest.
✓ Resort by STUDENT and TEST 1 score in normal order.
✓ Generate a sequence of numbers in Column J that starts with 50, counts by fives, and ends at 95.
✓ Using the GRADES workbook, create a database that finds all records whose Test 1 *or* Test 2 score exceeds 89.
✓ Extract the STUDENT and AVERAGE fields for these records into a range starting in Row 20.

MODULE 4: MACROS

A **macro** is a set of mouse actions, keystrokes, or command instructions for automating a task. Macros save time that you might normally spend performing repetitive tasks. The more mouse actions or keystrokes involved in a procedure, the more time is saved, and the more likely it is that you will want to automate it with a macro.

CREATING A MACRO

Macros can be created by following a simple procedure: planning, recording, assigning, and saving. The following exercise creates a simple macro that automatically changes a column width to 12.

PLANNING A MACRO.   The first step in creating a macro is to identify all the steps required. An easy way to plan a macro is to perform the task while recording each action (mouse and keystroke) on paper. For example,

STEPS

1 Open the GRADES workbook

2 Delete Columns F, G, H, and I (select the range *F1:I1*, click *Edit, Delete, Entire Column*, and then *OK*)

3 Delete Column A

These actions remove columns that are not needed in this exercise and provide some demonstration space. Get a piece of paper and a pen or pencil before continuing.

4 Write each action on paper as you change Column A's width to 12

When you have finished, these actions should appear on your paper:

Click *Format, point to Column, click Width*, type **12**, click *OK* (By keyboard, **Alt** + **O**, **C**, **W**, **1**, **2**, ↵)

5 **Save this workbook as MACRO1**

You can now create a macro in four steps: assigning the macro a name and description in the *Record New Macro* dialog box, turning on the macro recorder, recording the actual macro mouse/keyboard actions in a *module sheet,* and turning off the macro recorder.

> **Tip: Macro commands can also be created from scratch and entered directly into a workbook, menu, or shortcut keys. This technique requires knowledge of Visual Basic, a programming language. Refer to your on-line help for information on Visual Basic.**

RECORDING A MACRO.   After a macro has been planned, you are ready to record the macro's mouse/keystroke actions.

STEPS

1 **Click *Tools*, point to *Record Macro*, click *Record New Macro* for its dialog box**

2 **Type   COLUMN_WIDTH_12   in the *Macro Name* text box and press   Tab**

Note that you can use up to 256 characters for a macro name; however, it cannot have any blank spaces separating words.

3 **Type   CHANGE THE COLUMN WIDTH TO 12   in the *Description* text box**

Your *Record New Macro* dialog box should appear as in Figure SS3-27.

4 **Click *OK* to turn on the macro recorder**

FIGURE SS3-27 ■ RECORDING A NEW MACRO

This dialog box is used to name, describe, and turn on the Macro recorder.

Excel uses *Visual Basic,* a programming language, for macro commands. When the macro recorder is turned on, Excel adds a new sheet called the **module sheet** to store your actions in Visual Basic code. Although not currently visible, this sheet is added behind Sheet 16 in the workbook. Methods to access the module sheet are discussed later.

5   Click *Format*, point to *Column*, click *Width*   [**Alt** + **O** , **C** , **W**]

6   Type **12**

7   Click *OK*   [↵]

8   Click the *Stop Macro* toolbar button to turn off the macro recorder [**Alt** + **T** , **R** , **S**]

> **Tip:** You can also click *Tools*, point to *Record Macro*, and then click *Stop Recording* in place of Step 8.

9   Resave this workbook as MACRO1

RUNNING A MACRO

Once macros have been created, they are available for use. You can run them using the *Macro* dialog box, a shortcut key, the *Tools* menu, or a macro button. The latter three options first require the macro to be assigned to them and are discussed in the next section. Try this to run the macro using the *Macro* dialog box,

STEPS

1   Open the MACRO1 workbook, if needed

2   Move to Column B (any row)

3   Click *Tools*, *Macro* for its dialog box

4   Click COLUMN_WIDTH_12

The top portion of your *Macro* dialog box should resemble Figure SS3-28a. Note that this dialog box lists all macros created and saved with a workbook. It also displays a description of the macro as entered when created.

5   Click *Run* to run the macro   [↵]

Column B's width has now been changed to 12 as in Figure SS3-28b.

FIGURE SS3-28 ■ RUNNING A MACRO

(a) The *Macro* dialog box
(*Tools* menu) can be used to
run a macro using its name.
(b) These are the results of
running the macro in Column
B to increase its width to 12.

(a)

(b)

ASSIGNING A MACRO

As mentioned earlier, a macro can also be run from shortcut keys, the *Tools* menu or a
button. To do so you must first assign the macro commands to one of these items.

ASSIGNING TO SHORTCUT KEYS.   A macro can be assigned to shortcut keys
either during its recording or after by using the *Macro Options* dialog box. This dialog
box can be invoked from the *Record New Macro* dialog box when recording a macro,
or from the *Macro* dialog box after a macro has been recorded. These macros will be
referred to as *one-letter macros*. They generally involve the use of the **Ctrl** or **Ctrl**
+ **Shift** keys and one letter. The **Ctrl** or **Ctrl** + **Shift** keys are automatically selected by Excel when assigning a macro to shortcut keys to prevent conflict with previously
programmed Excel or user-defined shortcut keys.
   To assign the macro COLUMN_WIDTH_12 to the shortcut keys **Ctrl** + **Shift**
+ **W** :

STEPS

1 Click *Tools*, *Macro* for its dialog box

2 Click COLUMN_WIDTH_12

3 Click the *Options* button for the *Macro Options* dialog box

4 Click the *Shortcut Key* check box

5 Click the text box next to "Ctrl+"   [**Alt** + **T**]

6 Type **W** and note that "Ctrl+Shift" appears before it

7 Click *OK, Close*   [↵ ,   **Alt** + **F4**]

Now, try running the macro using its shortcut keys.

8 Move to Column D (any row)

9 Press **Ctrl** + **Shift** + **W**

Column D's width should now be 12.

10 Save the workbook as MACRO2 and then close it

Tip: When assigning a macro to shortcut keys, try to use a letter that is easy for you to remember and relates to the macro's function.

ASSIGNING TO THE *TOOLS* MENU.   The procedures to assign a macro to the *Tools* menu is similar to assigning it to a shortcut key. Again, a macro can be assigned to the menu either during its recording or after by using the *Macro Options* dialog box. Try this:

STEPS

1 Open the MACRO1 workbook

2 Click *Tools, Macro* for its dialog box

3 Click *COLUMN_WIDTH_12*

4 Click the *Options* button for the *Macro Options* dialog box

5 Click the *Menu Item on Tools Menu* check box

6 Click the *Menu Item on Tools Menu* text box

7 Type   **Column WD12**

8 Click *OK, Close*

9 Save the workbook as MACRO3

To run the macro using the *Tools* menu,

10 Move to Column D

11 **Click** *Tools*

12 **Click** *Column WD12*

ASSIGNING TO A BUTTON.   To assign a macro to a button on the current worksheet,

STEPS

1 **Click the** *View, Toolbars, Drawing* **check box, then click** *OK*

The Drawing toolbar should now appear in your Excel window. This toolbar can be used to create a button or other objects (pictures or symbols) in your worksheet.

2 **If needed, drag the Drawing toolbar's title bar to move it away from Cell F3**

3 **Click the** *Create* **button on the Drawing toolbar (bottom left button)**

Note that the mouse pointer changes to a "+."

4 **Point to the top-left corner of Cell F3 (or any desired location for the position of the macro button)**

5 **Drag the mouse pointer down to the bottom-left corner of Cell F4 and then across its right cell wall to create a button filling the Cells F3 and F4**

A button briefly appears and then the *Assign macro* dialog box appears.

6 **Click** *COLUMN_WIDTH_12* **and then** *OK*

7 **Point before the "B" in Button 1 and then drag across to select it as in Figure SS3-29a**

8 **Press** Delete **to remove it**

9 **Type** COL W12 **for the button's name**

Your macro button should appear as Figure SS3-29b.

At this point, you can move to any cell not occupied by the button to turn off the button edit mode. Now use the macro button to change Column C's width to 12:

10 **Click to Cell C1 or any cell in Column C**

11 **Click the COL W12 macro button to change the column width to 12**

12 **Click the** *Close* **button of the Drawing toolbar or click** *View, Toolbars, Drawing, OK*

To edit a macro button, right-click it.

FIGURE SS3-29 ■ CREATING A MACRO BUTTON

(a) Dragging over a macro button's name selects it for editing.
(b) Once selected, simply type in a desired macro-button name.

E	F	G
	Button 1	

E	F	G
	COL W12	

(a)   (b)

> **Tip:** You can also remove a toolbar by using the toolbar *Shortcut* menu. Simply point to any toolbar, click the right mouse button, and then click the desired toolbar to turn it off/on. Clicking a toolbar's control-menu box will also close it.

13 Resave the workbook as MACRO3

ADDING ANOTHER MACRO

More than one macro can be created and saved within the same workbook. Now that you have learned how to create and invoke a simple macro, try applying these techniques to a more complicated macro. In the next exercise, you will create a print macro named PRINT_COL_AB on the MACRO3 workbook and assign it to the shortcut keys Ctrl + Shift + Print. This macro will print only Columns A and B.

STEPS

1 Open the MACRO3 workbook, if needed, and turn on your printer

2 Click *Tools*, point to *Record Macro*, *Record New Macro* for its dialog box

3 Type PRINT_COL_AB in the *Macro Name* text box and press Tab

4 Type PRINT ONLY COLUMNS A AND B in the *Description* text box

5 Click the *Options* button

6 Click the *Shortcut Key* check box and then press Tab

7 Type **P** (Use capital)

8 Click *OK* to turn on the macro recorder

9 Click *Edit*, *Go To*   [Ctrl + G]

10 Type **C1** and click *OK*

11 Select the range C1:D1

12 Click *Format*, point to *Column*, and then click *Hide*

13 Click *File*, *Print*, OK   [Ctrl + P , ↵]

The worksheet should print with only the STUDENT and TEST 1 columns. Now we'll
return the worksheet display back to its original view.

14 Click *Format*, point to *Column*, and then click *Unhide*

15 Click the *Stop Macro* toolbar button to turn off the macro recorder

16 Move to Cell A1

17 Press Ctrl + Shift + P to invoke the macro

18 Save the workbook as MACRO4 and then close it

EDITING A MACRO

Editing a macro requires knowledge of Visual Basic. As such, it is generally easier to
delete a macro with a limited amount of statements and then rerecord it. Steps to delete
a macro follow. (Do not perform these steps unless you want to delete a macro.)

STEPS

1 Click *Tools*, *Macro* for the *Macro* dialog box

2 Click the macro to be deleted

3 Click the *Delete* button

For further information on editing a macro, see the appendix and Excel's on-line
Help.

☑ CHECKPOINT

✓ On a new worksheet, create a macro (with documentation) named ROW2 that will
    insert two rows at the current pointer position. Invoke it.

SS

✓ Create a macro named PAPER that will print the range A1:C15 to the printer. Invoke it.
✓ Create a macro button for each of the two macros.
✓ Assign the ROW2 macro to a shortcut key. Invoke it.
✓ Assign the PAPER module to the *Tools* menu.Invoke it.

MODULE 5: USING MULTIPLE WORKBOOKS

You need not restrict your use of Excel to one workbook file at a time. Excel allows you to copy or move parts of a workbook or combine other workbooks with the current one. You can also create links between cells of *different* workbooks that will update values as if they were all part of one large spreadsheet.

In Excel, a workbook window is used to display a portion of a single workbook. Depending on your system's memory, you can create or open more than one workbook window in Excel's workspace at the same time. This makes manipulating data between multiple workbooks easier.

A new workbook initially has 16 sheets in its workspace. However, up to 255 sheets can be created and stored in a single workbook. Working with a workbook is similar to working with a book that contains 16 or more pages. An individual sheet is similar to a page in the book.

The exercises in this section first explore creating and manipulating multiple workbooks on your screen and then manipulating their contents. As you work in this and the next module, remember that each workbook window contains only one workbook that may contain 16 or more sheets. Multiple sheets are discussed in "Module 6: Using Multiple Sheets."

SWITCHING BETWEEN WINDOWS

Since workbook windows are document windows (a window within an application window), standard Windows commands can be applied to manipulate them and their contents.

STEPS

1 **Close any open workbooks**

2 **Open the BOOKS, the SALES, and then the TAPES workbooks**

> **Tip:** You can select more than one workbook to be opened from the *Open file* dialog box by holding the Ctrl key while clicking each additional workbook.

As each additional file is opened, it is placed in its own window on top of the previously opened file. You can switch to another opened workbook window using the *Window* menu or shortcut keys.

3 Click *Window* and then 2 SALES to switch to it

4 Press   Ctrl   +   F6   to use shortcut keys to switch back to the TAPES workbook

5 Press   Ctrl   +   F6   again or use the *Window* menu to switch to the BOOKS workbook

6 Close all worksheet windows without saving.

ARRANGING WINDOWS

In the previous exercise, you viewed multiple workbook windows on separate screens. It is possible to display several files on one screen at the same time. The Arrange command (*Window* menu) opens to a dialog box that allows you to arrange your workbook windows in a tile, horizontal, vertical, or cascade format. A sample of each window arrangement is shown in Figure SS3-30.

STEPS

1 Open the BOOKS, SALES, and TAPES workbooks

2 Click *Window*, *Arrange* for its dialog box

3 If an "x" appears in the *Windows of Active Workbook* check box, click it to remove it

4 Click *Tiled*, *OK* to tile windows as in Figure SS3-30a

5 Click *Window*, *Arrange*

6 Click *Horizontal*, *OK* to display the windows as in Figure SS3-30b

7 Click *Window*, *Arrange*

8 Click *Vertical*, *OK* to display the windows as in Figure SS3-30c

9 Click *Window*, *Arrange*

10 Click *Cascade*, *OK* to display the windows as in Figure SS3-30d

11 Close all workbooks without saving

Your Excel workspace should now be blank.

> **Tip: To make a window active, simply click its title bar. To move a window by mouse, drag its title bar.**

SS

FIGURE SS3-30 ■ ARRANGING WORKBOOK WINDOWS

Standard display formats of
workbook windows.
(a) Tiled.
(b) Horizontal.

(a)

(b)

(continued)

RESIZING WINDOWS

Any workbook window can be resized within Excel's workspace. Resizing is helpful
when using multiple windows to display the desired content of each window. Standard
Windows resizing commands include Restore (resize to a previous size or to a smaller
window), *Minimize* (shrink to an icon), and *Maximize* (enlarge to maximum size). A window may also be resized to a custom size. When resizing with the keyboard, you must
use the window's control-menu.

> **Tip:** The following resizing techniques can also be used to resize an application win-
> dow (for example, the Excel window).

FIGURE SS3-30 ■ *(continued)*

(c) Vertical.
(d) Cascaded.

(c)

(d)

STANDARD WINDOW RESIZING. Try the following to resize the BOOKS workbook window:

1 **Open the BOOKS workbook**

If the BOOKS workbook is less than full size, *not* occupying Excel's entire workspace, perform Step 2. Otherwise, go to Step 3.

2 **If needed, click the Books window *Maximize* button (located at the top right corner of window)** [**Ctrl** + **F10**]

SS

3 Click the workbook window's *Restore* button (located near the
right end of the menu bar)

[**Ctrl** + **F5**]

The Books window should appear as a smaller window as in Figure SS3-31a. (The
size of your window may differ.) Note that it now has its own title bar and two resizing buttons.

4 Click the workbook window's *Minimize* button

[**Ctrl** + **F9**]

The BOOKS file should now appear as an icon at the bottom left of Excel's workspace
as in Figure SS3-31b. To return the worksheet to its maximum size,

5 Click the *Maximize* button of the Books icon

[**Ctrl** + **F10**]

FIGURE SS3-31 ■ **RESIZING A WORKSHEET WINDOW**

(a) The Restore command
reduces the size of a
maximized window.
(b) The Minimize command
reduces a workbook window
to this icon.
(c) Dragging a corner or wall
of a window resizes it.

Maximize button
Minimize button

Books

	A	B	C	D	E	F	G
1	Book Sales						
2		Book	Units	Total			
3	Book Title	Price	Sold	Sales			
4	The Rough-Faced Girl	$ 16.95	25	$ 423.75			
5	Will's Mammoth	14.95	76	1,136.20			
6	Foolish Rabbit's Mistake	12.00	15	180.00			
7	The Hungry Tigress	16.00	67	1,072.00			

BOOKS / Sheet2 / Sheet3 / Sheet4 / Sheet5 / Sheet6

(a)

Restore button   Maximize
button

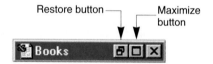

Books

(b)

Books

	A	B	C	D	E	F	G
1	Book Sales						
2		Book	Units	Total			
3	Book Title	Price	Sold	Sales			
4	The Rough-Faced Girl	$ 16.95	25	$ 423.75			
5	Will's Mammoth	14.95	76	1,136.20			
6	Foolish Rabbit's Mistake	12.00	15	180.00			
7	The Hungry Tigress	16.00	67	1,072.00			
8	Totals		183	$ 2,811.95			
9							
10							
11							

BOOKS / Sheet2 / Sheet3 / Sheet4 / Sheet5 / Sheet6

(c)

Tip: Double-clicking a workbook icon or a window's title bar will also resize it.

CUSTOM WINDOW RESIZING.   Windows may be resized to a desired size. Try the following to custom-resize the BOOKS window as shown in Figure SS3-31c:

STEPS

1   Open the BOOKS file, if needed

 2   Click the workbook window's *Restore* button to reduce the   [Ctrl + F5]
window's size (near right side of menu bar)

3   Point slowly to anywhere on the bottom wall of the window until the   [Ctrl + F8]
mouse pointer changes to a pointer with two arrows on each side

4   Drag the bottom wall's outline down until Row 11 appears   [↓]

5   Drop (release mouse button) the bottom wall's outline to complete the resizing   [↵]

The Books window should resemble Figure SS3-31c.

6   Maximize the window

7   Exit Excel without saving

Tip: To resize the entire window, slowly point to either bottom corner of the window until the pointer changes to a diagonal pointer with two arrows at each end. Then drag the corner in or out.

MANIPULATING DATA BETWEEN WORKBOOKS

Now that you have learned how to manipulate workbook windows on your screen, you are ready to perform data transfers between files. These transfers include copying, moving, combining, and linking data from one workbook to another.

COPYING DATA.   The commands to copy data from one workbook to another are similar to those for copying cell data from one range to another. The main difference is that the destination of the copied data is in another workbook. Try this to copy the Name and then the Grade columns of the GRADES file onto two new worksheet files:

STEPS

1   Launch Excel and open the GRADES workbook

2 Move to Cell B3

3 Select the range B3:B10

 4 Click *Edit, Copy* to copy the selected range to the Clipboard   [**Ctrl** + **C**]

 5 Click *File, New, OK* for a new workbook window (file)   [**Ctrl** + **N** , **↵**]

 6 Click *Edit, Paste*   [**Ctrl** + **V**]

7 Move to Cell B1

> **Tip:** To move data from one file to another, replace Step 4 with *Edit* and *Cut* (or the Ctrl + X keys).

8 Save this workbook as NAMES

Your Names window should resemble Figure SS3-32a. Note that the Grades window is currently hidden behind the NAMES workbook. To switch back to the Grades window, copy the Grades column, and then paste it to a new workbook,

9 Click *Window, 2 GRADES*   [**Ctrl** + **F6**]

10 Move to Cell F3

11 Select the range F3:F10

12 Click *Edit, Copy*   [**Ctrl** + **C**]

FIGURE SS3-32 ■ COPYING DATA BETWEEN WORKBOOKS

(a) The Copy and Paste commands (*Edit* menu) were used to copy this text to a new workbook.
(b) The *Values* option of the *Paste Special* dialog box was used to copy the formulas from the GRADES workbook to Column B of the new workbook.

	A	B	C
1	STUDENT		
2	Jerry		
3	Elissa		
4	Andrea		
5	Edward		
6	Charles		
7	Rita		
8	Lesley		
9			
10			

(a)

	A	B	C
1	STUDENT	GRADE	
2	Jerry	C	
3	Elissa	A	
4	Andrea	A	
5	Edward	D	
6	Charles	B	
7	Rita	B	
8	Lesley	C	
9			
10			

(b)

13 Click *Window, 1 NAMES*   [**Ctrl** + **F6**]

Since the grades in the range F4:F10 were originally entered as formulas, they can be transferred to the new worksheet as formulas or values. To copy them as values,

14 Click *Edit, Paste Special* for its dialog box

15 Click *Values, OK*

16 Move to Cell A1

17 Save this workbook again as NAMES

The NAMES file should resemble Figure SS3-32b.

18 Close any open workbook

> **Tip: Tiling the source and destination worksheet windows before copying may make the copy process easier visually.**

LINKING FILES.   Excel also allows you to link values *between* workbooks; that is, cells in other workbooks (called *server cells*) can be connected to cells in the current workbooks (called *client cells*). As shown in Figure SS3-33, when server cells are linked to client cells, changes in the server file are automatically reflected in the client file when it is opened—a useful technique when consolidating data from a number of workbooks.

The process of linking cells is similar to copying; however, instead of selecting the Paste command, you select **Paste Link.** This command automatically places a *linking formula* that refers to the server cell (source) in the client cell. (Note: These formulas can also be typed in.) The following exercise creates links between two server files (BOOKS and TAPES) shown in Figure SS3-33 and then the consolidated client file (SALES).

SS

STEPS

1 Open the BOOKS workbook and maximize it if needed

2 Move to Cell C8

3 Select the range C8:D8

4 Click *Edit, Copy* to copy the range C8:D8 to the Clipboard   [**Ctrl** + **C**]

5 Open the SALES workbook

6 Change Column C's width to 12

7 Move to Cell B4

FIGURE SS3-33 ■ **LINKING FILES**

Changes in the server *cells* are automatically reflected in the client cells.

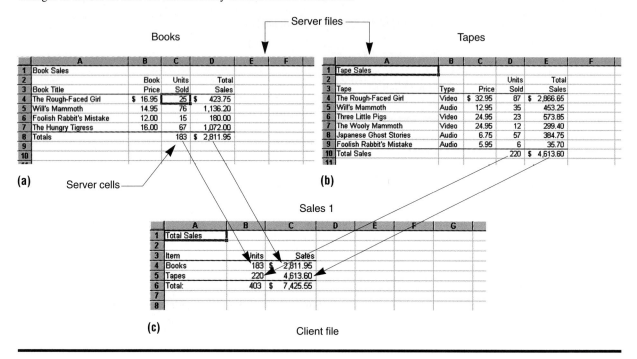

Server files

Books

Tapes

(a)

Server cells

(b)

Sales 1

(c)   Client file

---

8   Click *Edit*, Paste *Special*, Paste *Link*

This links Cells C8 and D8 in the BOOKS file to Cells B4 and C4 in the SALES file by pasting linking formulas ({=[WORKBOOK NAME.XLS]SHEETNAME!ABSOLUTE RANGE}). As shown in Figure SS3-34a, the total for units and sales from the BOOKS file immediately appears.

9   Open the TAPES workbook

10   Move to Cell D10

11   Select the range D10:E10

12   Click *Edit*, *Copy*   [**Ctrl** + **C**]

13   Click *Window* and then *2 SALES* to switch to it   [**Ctrl** + **F6**]

14   Move to Cell B5

15   Click *Edit*, Paste *Special*, Paste *Link*

16   Format Column C to resemble Figure SS3-34b (accounting-dollar sign, two decimals in Cell C4 and accounting-no dollar sign, two decimals in Cell C5)

FIGURE SS3-34 ■ CREATING LINKS

(a) The link to the BOOKS file has been establised in Cell B4 of the SALES file.
(b) This is the completed file with all links.

(a)

B4	▼	{=[BOOKS.XLS]BOOKS!$C$8:$D$8}		
	A	**B**	**C**	**D**	**E**
1	Total Sales				
2					
3	Item	Units	Sales		
4	Books	183	2811.95		
5	Tapes				
6	Total:	183	$ 2,811.95		
7					
8					

(b)

C5	▼	{=[TAPES.XLS]TAPES!$D$10:$E$10}		
	A	**B**	**C**	**D**	**E**
1	Total Sales				
2					
3	Item	Units	Sales		
4	Books	183	$ 2,811.95		
5	Tapes	220	4,613.60		
6	Total:	403	$ 7,425.55		
7					
8					

As shown in Figure SS3-34b, these link formulas have brought data from the two server workbooks into the consolidation, where they are totaled and formatted.

17 **Move to Cell A1**

18 **Save this workbook as SALES1**

To see the link effect, make the following change to the BOOKS worksheet:

19 **Switch to the Books window**

Remember, use the *Window* menu or press the Ctrl and F6 keys.

20 **In Cell C4, type 86 and press ↵**

Your worksheet should resemble Figure SS3-35a.

21 **Resave the workbook as BOOKS1**

SS

FIGURE SS3-35 ■ LINKED WORKBOOK FILES

(a) Changes are made in the
server worksheet.
(b) These changes are
automatically transferred to
the client worksheet.

(a)

	A	B	C	D	E
1	Book Sales				
2		Book	Units	Total	
3	Book Title	Price	Sold	Sales	
4	The Rough-Faced Girl	$ 16.95	86	$ 1,457.70	
5	Will's Mammoth	14.95	76	1,136.20	
6	Foolish Rabbit's Mistake	12.00	15	180.00	
7	The Hungry Tigress	16.00	67	1,072.00	
8	Totals		244	$ 3,845.90	
9					
10					

(b)

	A	B	C	D	E
1	Total Sales				
2					
3	Item	Units	Sales		
4	Books	244	$ 3,845.90		
5	Tapes	220	4,613.60		
6	Total:	464	$ 8,459.50		
7					
8					

22 **Switch to the Sales1 window**

Your worksheet should resemble Figure SS3-35b, the linked cells in Row 4 reflect the
changes in the Books window.

23 **Close all the workbooks without saving**

> **Tip: When working with more than one worksheet window, you may use the Tile or
> Cascade command to view the files more easily.**

Objects (pictures) may also be linked among workbooks. In addition, Excel files may be
linked to other application files. See the "Sharing Information with Other Programs"
module for these operations.

☑ CHECKPOINT

✓ Open any three workbooks and apply each Arrange command (*Window* menu).
✓ Open the TAPES workbook and resize it to an icon and back to a window.

✓ Use the GRADES workbook. Copy Column C to a workbook named TEST1.
✓ In the GRADES workbook, insert a column between TEST 2 and AVERAGE. Combine the TEST1 workbook into this column. Do not save.
✓ Change the link formulas in the SALES1 workbook window to retrieve the appropriate numbers for WILL'S MAMMOTH only, not the totals from the server files. Do not save.

MODULE 6: USING MULTIPLE SHEETS

Until now, you have been working with only one sheet in a workbook. A *sheet,* as discussed earlier, may contain a worksheet, chart, or other information. Sheets are similar to pages in a book. Each new workbook opens with 16 sheets. Excel allows you to create up to 239 more sheets (or 255 sheets in total) in a workbook.

Using multiple sheets in a single workbook lets you keep a set of related worksheets together. For example, a budget workbook may use 13 sheets: a summary sheet and one sheet for each month.

To prepare for the exercises in this section,

STEPS

1 **Close any open workbook**

2 **Open the SHEET2 workbook (created in Chapter 1)**

USING SHEET TABS

Sheet tabs appear at the bottom of a workbook window, as in Figure SS3-36a. Sheet tabs can be used to switch to another sheet. They are used to identify a sheet and can be renamed.

Although a workbook opens with 16 sheets, only six sheet tabs (you can identify them on Sheets 1 through 6) are currently visible in the sheet-tab view area. (The number of sheets may differ.) To view other sheet tabs in a workbook, use the *tab-scrolling*

SS

FIGURE SS3-36 ■ SHEET TABS

(a) Sheet tabs are located at the bottom of the workbook.
(b) Clicking a sheet tab makes that sheet active.

(a)

(b)

buttons (left of the tab-viewing area). You can also enlarge the tab-viewing area by dragging the *tab-split* bar.

SWITCHING BETWEEN SHEETS.   Clicking a sheet tab will switch to that sheet and make it active. Try this,

STEPS

1   Click the *Sheet 3* tab   [**Ctrl** + **Pg Dn** twice]

Sheet 3 will appear on top as in Figure SS3-36b. Now to move back to Sheet 1.

2   Click the *Sheet 1* tab   [**Ctrl** + **Pg Up** twice]

NAMING SHEET TABS.   Each sheet can be assigned a name with up to 31 characters on its tab. To assign a name to a tab,

STEPS

1   Double-click *Sheet1*'s tab for the *Rename Sheet* dialog box

2   Type   **Total Regions**   and click *OK*

3   Double-click *Sheet2's* tab

4   Type   **Region A**   and click *OK*

5   Double-click *Sheet3's* tab

6   Type   **Region B**   and press ↵

7   Switch to the Total Regions Sheet (click its sheet tab) and move to Cell A1

8   Save this workbook as REGIONS1

Your sheet tabs should now resemble those in Figure SS3-37.

SHEET TAB SCROLLING.   Tab-scrolling buttons are used to view tabs not currently visible in the sheet-tab viewing area. These buttons are accessible only by mouse.

FIGURE SS3-37 ■ **RENAMING SHEET TABS**

Sheet tabs from Sheets 1 through 3 have been renamed using the *Rename Sheet* dialog box.

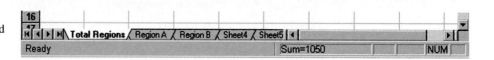

As indicated in Figure SS3-38a, there are four tab-scrolling buttons: First Tab, Previous Tab, Next Tab, and Last Tab. Try this to quickly view the last sheet tabs.

 1 Click the *Last Tab* scroll button

Your tab-viewing area now displays Sheets 12 through 16, as in Figure SS3-38b. Note that the active sheet has not changed. To change the active sheet, click the desired sheet tab. For example,

2 Click *Sheet 15's* tab to make it active

3 Now, click the *Previous Tab* button one tab to the left

Your tab-viewing area should resemble Figure SS3-38c. To return to the Total Regions sheet (Sheet 1),

4 Click the *First Tab* scroll button

5 Click *Total Regions* tab

Tip: The sheet-tab viewing area can also be enlarged by dragging the tab split bar to the right or reduced by dragging the bar to the left.

FIGURE SS3-38 ■ SHEET-TAB SCROLLING

(a) Tab-scrolling buttons can be used to view different sheet tabs in the sheet-tab viewing area.
(b) Clicking the *Last Tab* scroll button moves the view to the last tabs in the workbook.
(c) Clicking the *Previous Tab* scroll button moves the view one tab to the left.

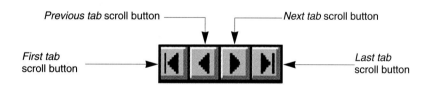

(a)

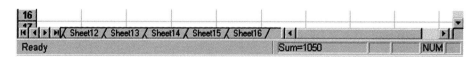

(b)

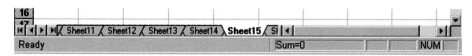

(c)

MANIPULATING DATA BETWEEN SHEETS

You can copy, move, or link data from one sheet to another just as from one worksheet file to another. In the following exercise, you will create the Region A and Region B sheets from the data in the Total Regions sheet and then link them.

COPYING DATA. To copy data from one sheet to another, you use the same commands as for copying data from one file to another. The only difference is the copied data's destination—another worksheet.

1	Open the REGIONS1 workbook if needed	
2	In the Total Regions sheet, move to Cell A3	
3	Select the range A3:B10	

 | 4 | Click *Edit, Copy* | [**Ctrl** + **C**]

5	Click the *Region A* sheet tab	[**Ctrl** + **Pg Dn**]

 | 6 | Click *Edit, Paste* | [**Ctrl** + **V**]

7	Move to Cell A1 in the Region A sheet	

Your Region A sheet should resemble Figure SS3-39a. Now copy ranges A3:A10 and C3:C10 to the Region B sheet.

> **Tip:** To move data from one sheet to another, replace Step 4 with *Edit* and then *Cut* (or the Ctrl and X keys).

8	Click the *Total Regions* sheet tab	[**Ctrl** + **Pg Up**]
9	Select the range A3:A10	

 | 10 | Click *Edit, Copy* | [**Ctrl** + **C**]

11	Click the *Region B* sheet tab	[**Ctrl** + **Pg Dn** twice]

 | 12 | Click *Edit, Paste* | [**Ctrl** + **V**]

13	Click the *Total Regions* sheet tab	[**Ctrl** + **Pg Up** twice]

 | 14 | Select the range C3:C10 | |

15	Click *Edit, Copy*	[**Ctrl** + **C**]

FIGURE SS3-39 ■ COPYING DATA BETWEEN SHEETS

(a) Range A3:B10 has been copied from the Total Regions Sheet to the A1:B8 range of the Region A sheet. (b) Ranges A3:B10 and C3:C10 have been copied from the Total Regions Sheet to the A1:B8 and B1:B8 ranges of the Region B sheet.

	A	B	C
1	Agent	Region A	
2			
3	Michaels	500	
4	Martin	200	
5	Parker	300	
6	Williams	50	
7			
8	Totals	1050	
9			
10			
11			
12			
13			
14			
15			
16			

Total Regions \ **Region A** /
Ready

(a)

	A	B	C	D
1	Agent	Region B		
2				
3	Michaels	200		
4	Martin	450		
5	Parker	325		
6	Williams	125		
7				
8	Totals	1100		
9				
10				
11				
12				
13				
14				
15				
16				

Total Regions / Region A \ **Region B** /
Ready

(b)

16 **Click the *Region B* sheet tab**   [**Ctrl** + **Pg Dn** twice]

17 **Move to Cell B1**

18 **Click *Edit, Paste***   [**Ctrl** + **V**]

19 **Move to Cell B1**

20 **Resave this workbook as REGIONS1**

The Agent and Region B data columns have now been copied to the Region B sheet as shown in Figure SS3-39b.

> **Tip: To copy formulas as values, use the Paste Special command instead of the Paste command in Step 17.**

LINKING SHEETS.   The procedures to link values between sheet cells are similar to those for copying worksheet cells, except you use the Paste Link command instead of the Paste command. Remember, the Paste Link command connects cells in other sheets (called *server cells*) to the current sheet. Changes in the server sheet will automatically be reflected in the client sheet.

SS

The next exercise uses the Region A and Region B sheets as servers and the Total Regions sheet as the client.

STEPS

1 **Move to the Total Regions sheet**

2 **Delete data in the range B5:C8**

3 **Move to Cell B5**

The cells in range B5:C8 should now be empty, as shown in Figure SS3-40a. Also note that the totals show "0," because they are formulas that use the data in the range B5:C8.

FIGURE SS3-40　■　LINKING SHEETS

(a) The data in the range B5:C8 have been removed for the linking exercise.
(b) The range B3:B6 has been paste-linked from the Region A sheet to the B5:B8 range of the Total Regions sheet.
(c) The completed client sheet.
(d) Changes in the server sheet (Region B) is automatically reflected in the client sheet (Total Regions).

(a)

	A	B	C	D	E
1	Your Name				M/D/YY
2					
3	Agent	Region A	Region B	Totals	
4					
5	Michaels			0	
6	Martin			0	
7	Parker			0	
8	Williams			0	
9					
10	Totals	0	0	0	
11					
12					
13					
14					
15					
16					

Total Regions / Region A / Region B / Sheet4 / S

Ready

(b)

B5 ▼ {=Region A!$B$3:$B$6}

	A	B	C	D	E
1	Your Name				M/D/YY
2					
3	Agent	Region A	Region B	Totals	
4					
5	Michaels	500		500	
6	Martin	200		200	
7	Parker	300		300	
8	Williams	50		50	
9					
10	Totals	1050	0	1050	
11					
12					
13					
14					
15					
16					

Total Regions / Region A / Region B / Sheet4 / S

Select destination and press ENTER or choose Paste

(c)

	A	B	C	D	E
1	Your Name				M/D/YY
2					
3	Agent	Region A	Region B	Totals	
4					
5	Michaels	500	200	700	
6	Martin	200	450	650	
7	Parker	300	325	625	
8	Williams	50	125	175	
9					
10	Totals	1050	1100	2150	
11					

(d)

	A	B	C	D	E
1	Your Name				M/D/YY
2					
3	Agent	Region A	Region B	Totals	
4					
5	Michaels	500	400	900	
6	Martin	200	450	650	
7	Parker	300	325	625	
8	Williams	50	125	175	
9					
10	Totals	1050	1300	2350	
11					

4   Move to the Region A sheet   [**Ctrl** + **Pg Dn**]

5   Move to Cell B3

6   Select the range B3:B6

 7   Click *Edit, Copy*   [**Ctrl** + **C**]

8   Click the *Total Regions* sheet tab   [**Ctrl** + **Home**]

9   Move to Cell B5

10 Click *Edit, Paste Special, Paste Link*

Your Total Regions sheet should resemble Figure SS3-40b. Note that the totals automatically update. Note also that the formula in Cell B5 (formula bar) has the sheet reference 'Region A'! to indicate its linked source.

11 Using the same techniques, copy and paste link range B3:B6 of the Region B sheet to range C5:C8 of the Total Regions sheet,

12 Move to Cell A1

Your final linked Total Regions sheet should resemble Figure SS3-40c.

13 Save this workbook as REGIONS2

To see the linked effect, make the following changes to the Region B sheet,

14 Switch to the Region B sheet   [**Ctrl** + **Pg Dn** twice]

15 In Cell B3, type **400** and press ↵

16 Switch to the Total Regions sheet   [**Ctrl** + **Pg Up** twice]

Your Total Regions sheet has been automatically updated as in Figure SS3-40d.

17 Save this workbook as REGIONS3 and then close it

☑ CHECKPOINT

✓   Open the GADGETS workbook, and then save it as BUDGET1.
✓   Name Sheet1 "1st Quarter," Sheet2 "January," Sheet3 "February," and Sheet4 "March."
✓   Copy the item name and corresponding monthly sales data from the 1st Quarter sheet into each respective month's sheet. Save the workbook as BUDGET2.

SS

✓ Delete the data in the range B4:D7 in the 1st Quarter sheet. Use the Paste-Link command to insert linking formulas to place and link data from the January, February, and March sheets into the 1st Quarter sheet. Save the workbook as BUDGET3.

✓ Change some of the data in the February sheet and switch to the 1st Quarter sheet to see the changes.

MODULE 7: PROTECTING THE SPREADSHEET

Computers follow your *instructions,* not your *intentions.* All too often, formulas or functions are mistakenly erased, replaced, or copied over. Lookup tables, macros, and databases (usually placed off-screen) are accidentally deleted or destroyed. Although the Undo feature allows you to cancel immediate mistakes, it is not useful for mistakes that go unnoticed—especially when other people use your spreadsheet. One way to prevent many of these mishaps is to "protect" cells.

Cells can be protected with a two-step process: (1) cells in which changes may occur must be marked unprotected (unlocked), and then (2) the protection feature must be turned on.

SETTING THE UNPROTECTED RANGE

Before you turn on the protection feature, you must specify which should remain unprotected (unlocked). Unprotected cells allow changes after the protection feature is on. To designate the C4:D10 range of the GRADES worksheet to be unprotected,

STEPS

1 Open the GRADES workbook

2 Move to Cell C4

3 Select the range C4:D10

4 Click *Format, Cells, Protection* tab   [**Ctrl** + **1** , **P** , →]

5 Click the *Locked* check box to remove the "X"

The *Locked* check box should be empty as in Figure SS3-41.

6 Click the *OK* button   [↵]

7 Move to Cell B6

8 Save this workbook as PROTECT1

The unprotected cell range has now been set.

FIGURE SS3-41 ■ THE PROTECTION TAB

This tab is used to specify an unlocked range before invoking the protection feature.

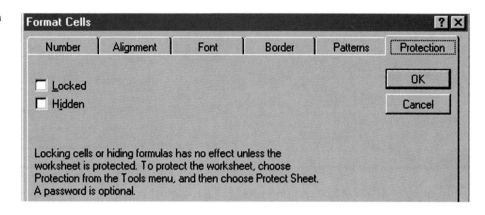

ACTIVATING THE PROTECTION FEATURE

Excel's **protection feature** can be activated on a sheet or workbook. When on, only cells that were specified as unprotected prior to its activation will be available for change. Try this:

STEPS

1 Open the PROTECT1 workbook, if needed

2 Click *Tools,* point to *Protection,* and then click *Protect Sheet* for its dialog box

Your *Protect* sheet dialog box should resemble Figure SS3-42.

At this point, you may assign an optional password by typing it into the *Password* text box. You may also restrict the protection to just the Contents, Objects, or Scenarios of the sheet or workbook by removing the "X" from the respective check boxes. For now, to close the dialog box without a password and turn on the protection feature,

3 Click the *OK* button   [↵]

All cells except for the ones designated earlier as unprotected are protected.

4 Move to Cell B6—the ANDREA entry

5 Try typing Meryl

A dialog box with the message "Locked cells cannot be changed." appears. A locked cell is a protected cell.

6 Click the *OK* button to remove the dialog box   [↵]

FIGURE SS3-42 ■ THE PROTECTION FEATURE

This dialog box can be used to turn on the protection feature, assign a password, and restrict the protection.

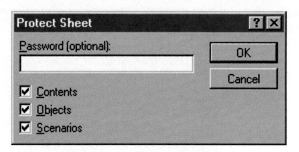

7 Move to Cell D8

8 Type **100** and then press ↵

Note that AVERAGE and GRADE cells still automatically update. The protection feature protects the formulas in these cells from being altered. It does not affect their operations.

9 Save this workbook as PROTECT2 and then close it

> **Tip:** To make a change in a protected cell, you must first turn off the protection feature by selecting _Tools, Protection, Unprotect sheet_ or _Unprotect Workbook._ Make the desired change and then turn on the protection feature again.

A final word about protection: The _Protection_ tab (_Format Cells_ dialog box) simply allows you to identify those cells that are exempt from protection. The _Protect_ sheet or _Protect workbook_ dialog box (_Tools_ menu) allows you to protect the entire file except for those cells identified as unprotected with the _Protection_ tab. Both commands are needed to invoke protection. Adding a password when invoking the protection feature may strengthen the protection form.

☑ CHECKPOINT

✓ What does the protection feature do?
✓ How do you unprotect a range of cells?
✓ Open the GRADES workbook and unprotect the range of cells in C4:D10.
✓ Turn the Protection feature on and change a few grades in the unprotected range.
✓ Change "Rita" in Column A to "Karen" (you will have to disable the protection feature first, then enable it).

MODULE 8: SHARING INFORMATION WITH OTHER PROGRAMS

Earlier you learned how to copy, move, and link information both between sheets within a workbook and between different workbooks. Here you will explore several techniques to share information between Excel workbooks and documents of other programs. These techniques include linking, embedding, importing, and exporting.

LINKING AND EMBEDDING

Typically, Excel is used in conjunction with other Microsoft Office programs, such as Word, Access, or PowerPoint. Office is known as a suite program—a set of separate programs that work together as one large program. Some suite programs provide additional menus or toolbar buttons that let you easily transfer information to other programs.

If you have other Microsoft Office programs and a mouse, you can use *linking and embedding* techniques to combine information from different programs.

> **Tip:** Linking and embedding techniques will also work, for the most part, between any Windows programs that support it.

In linking and embedding, an **object** is a set of information. The document with the original information is called the **source file.** The document receiving the information is called the **container file** or **compound document.**

The term **OLE** (short for object linking and embedding) refers to transferring information from one program to another as an object. When you OLE an object, it retains its source file's display format in the container file. For example, if you OLE a range of an Excel worksheet into a Word document, it will appear there in an Excel worksheet format. This will be demonstrated shortly.

Objects may also be linked or embedded into a container file in formats that may differ from their source. These formats as described in Figure SS3-43, may include text, a picture, or bitmap. Only OLE (objects linked or embedded as objects) operations are demonstrated here. You may want to try the other format options on your own.

Linking establishes an ongoing connection between the source file that provides the object and the container file that receives it. The object remains stored in the source file. The copy of the object in the container file is automatically updated whenever the source file's object is changed. For example, if an Excel object is linked with Word, changes in the Excel worksheet appear in the Word document.

Embedding inserts an object from the source file into a container file. The object then becomes part of the container file. Any changes in the source file do not appear in the embedded object.

You can, of course, change information in the embedded object. An embedded object is edited using its source program without changing the source file. You might, for example, embed information from a Word document into an Excel worksheet and then change only the information in the container file.

FIGURE SS3-43 ■ **FORMAT OPTIONS**

Objects can be linked or embedded in any of the following formats if available in *Paste Special* dialog box of the container program.

Format Option	Information's Format in the Container File	Edit Procedures
Object	Source file's format.	Double-click the object in the container file and then edit it. If linked, this action will switch to the source file. If embedded, this action will display the embedded information in the source program within the container file.
Text	Container file's text format, including font style, table, or other text formats.	If linked, switch to the source file and then edit; otherwise edit directly in container file.
Unformatted Text	Text format without any formatting	If linked, switch to the source file and edit; otherwise edit directly in container file.
Picture	Container program's graphic image format. It is faster to work and requires less disk space than a Bitmap file. It also prints better than a Bitmap file when using a high-quality printer.	If linked, switch to the source file and then edit; otherwise, double-click for the container program's graphics editor.
Bitmap	Graphic image composed of a series of dots.	If linked, switch to the source file; otherwise, double-click for the container program's graphics editor.

This text assumes that you have access to other Microsoft Office programs to accomplish the next exercises.

LINKING AN OBJECT.   The following exercise links a range of the Excel GADGETS worksheet to a Word document. Although the procedure assumes you have experience with Word, you can perform the steps as outlined.

STEPS

1   Start your computer and Windows

2   Launch Excel and open the GADGETS workbook

3   Select the range A3:D7 as in Figure SS3-44

4   Click *Edit, Copy* to copy the selection to the Clipboard   [**Ctrl** + **C**]

FIGURE SS3-44 ■ SELECTING THE INFORMATION TO BE LINKED OR EMBEDDED

	A	B	C	D	E	F
1	Dryden Gadgets Sales - Ist Quarter					
2						
3	Item	Jan	Feb	Mar	Total	
4	Doodads	45	36	28	109	
5	Gadgets	25	28	22	75	
6	Thingees	10	22	40	72	
7	Widgets	60	55	50	165	
8						
9						
10						

Note: You must start with the source file to create a link.

Remember, the Copy command copies a selection to the Clipboard, a program that temporarily holds the selection for future pasting or paste linking into another location. Now you will use the Paste Link command to paste and link your object into a new Word document.

5 Launch Word (it should be part of the *Microsoft Office* submenu)

6 Type   The following object is linked to the GADGETS workbook.

7 Press ↵ twice to skip two lines.

8 Click *Edit, Paste Special* for its dialog box

This dialog box lets you either paste (the default) or paste link. You also have several format options, which are described in Figure SS3-43. To paste link as an Excel Object,

9 Click *Microsoft Excel Worksheet Object* in the *As* list box

10 Click the *Paste Link* option, then click *OK*

The range A3:D7 from the GADGETS worksheet appears in the Word document as in Figure SS3-45. It is also dynamically linked to the original Excel worksheet. For example,

11 Double-click the linked object in Word

FIGURE SS3-44 ■ **THE OBJECT IN THE CONTAINER FILE**

The following object is linked to the GADGETS workbook.

Item	Jan	Feb	Mar
Doodads	45	36	28
Gadgets	25	28	22
Thingees	10	22	40
Widgets	60	55	50

The object is now displayed in its source file and program. This allows you to edit the object in Excel.

12 **Move to Cell C4**

13 **Type 50 and press ↵**

The data have now been automatically changed in both the source and container files. This is because linked information is stored with the source file. To see this change in the container file,

14 **Click Microsoft Word's taskbar button to switch to it**

Examine the document and note that it reflects the source file changes.

15 **Close Microsoft Word without saving**

16 **Close Excel without saving**

If you had saved the Word document and later made changes to the GADGETS worksheet while the Word document was not opened, the changes would appear the next time you opened it. Of course, this will only happen if both source and container files and programs are available in the same system.

EMBEDDING AN OBJECT. Embedding an object simply inserts it into the container file with the ability to edit the object using the source program. Upon saving the edited container file, you are given the option to change the source file.

STEPS

1 **Identify the object as you did in linking by following Steps 1–5 above**

2 Type   The following object was embedded from the GADGETS workbook.

3 Press ↵ twice to skip two lines.

4 Click *Edit, Paste Special* for its dialog box

5 Click *Microsoft Excel Worksheet Object* in the *As* list box

6 Click the *Paste* option, and then click *OK*

The information is now embedded as an object and is part of the container file. Changes in the source file are not typically reflected in the container file.

Embedded objects are edited using their source program but not source file. Changes made here are only reflected in the container document. However, upon re-saving the container file, you will be given the option to update the source file. Try this:

7 Double-click the embedded object

Note that the object appears within Excel in the object's frame. At this point you can edit the object using Excel. For now,

8 Click outside the object to return to the Word document

☒ **9** Close Word without saving

☒ **10** Close Excel without saving

> **Tip:** To link or embed an entire document (file), use the Object command of the *Insert* menu. This command can also be used to embed a new object into a container file. For example, you can create a worksheet in Word using Excel. Once the new object is embedded, you can also link it. See your on-line instructions for details.

EXPORTING AND IMPORTING

Export and import commands facilitate data transfer by converting data into formats that can be read by other software packages. **Exporting** *saves* data in another format; **importing** *opens* data that have been saved in another format.

DIRECT CONVERSION.   The easiest way to share data is to translate them into a form that another program can readily understand. For example, a spreadsheet can be converted directly into a database file or vice versa. Some slight adjustments may have to be made, but those are usually minimal. Typically, direct conversions are offered for the most popular software packages.

ASCII—A COMMON DENOMINATOR. When direct conversion is not available, *ASCII* conversion may still allow data transfer. **ASCII** (pronounced "ask-key") stands for the American Standard Code for Information Interchange. It is one of a few standard formats adopted by the computer industry for representing typed characters. ASCII eliminates the symbols unique to each software package, providing a common style for sharing data.

EXPORTING DATA FROM EXCEL

The following exercises export data from the BOOKS workbook into forms that can be read by a variety of word-processing and database applications.

STEPS

1 Launch Excel and change the default drive to A

2 Open the BOOKS workbook

Your screen should resemble Figure SS3-46.

EXPORTING AN ASCII FILE TO A WORD PROCESSOR. To save a worksheet as an ASCII file, *Text(OS/2 or MS-DOS)* must be selected in the *Save File as Type* drop-down box of the *Save As* dialog box. The extension ".TXT" is automatically added to the filename when you save in this file type (format). Spreadsheet data that are saved in ASCII format can be read directly by many word processing programs. This exercise creates an ASCII file called BOOKS.TXT. Note that the ".TXT" may not be visible in your dialog box. This depends on your system settings. However, by changing the display of the dialog box to "Detail," you will be able to see the file's type.

FIGURE SS3-46 ■ THE BOOKS WORKSHEET

	A	B	C	D	E
1	Book Sales				
2		Book	Units	Total	
3	Book Title	Price	Sold	Sales	
4	The Rough-Faced Girl	$ 16.95	25	$ 423.75	
5	Will's Mammoth	14.95	76	1,136.20	
6	Foolish Rabbit's Mistake	12.00	15	180.00	
7	The Hungry Tigress	16.00	67	1,072.00	
8	Totals		183	$ 2,811.95	
9					
10					

STEPS

1 Click *File*, *Save As* for its dialog box   [F12]

2 Type **BOOKS1** in the *File name* text box

 3 Click the ▼ button of the *Save as Type* drop-down box

4 Click *use the scroll bar* to scroll to *Text(OS/2 or MS-DOS)* and click it

5 Click the *Save* button and then *OK*

The BOOKS.TXT file has now been saved on your disk as an ASCII file. It can be read by WordPerfect or other word processing programs

6 Click *File*, *Save As* again   [F12]

 7 Click the *Details* toolbar button

Note that "Text Document" appears under the *Type* button indicating that the books file is a text or ASCII file. Keep the details display on for the rest of the exercises in this section.

8 Click *Cancel* and then close the workbook without saving

GENERAL EXPORTING TO A DATABASE.   Excel files can be exported to a variety of database file types using the *Save File as Type* drop-down box (*Save As* dialog box). In many cases, the data in the worksheet must first be placed into columnar form as discussed in the next section. Those database file types that are not available through the *Save File as Type* drop-down box, may require the file to be saved in ASCII format (Text).

DATA IN COLUMNAR FORM.   Before worksheets can be copied into ASCII files for database use, all numeric data must be free of dollar signs and commas.

STEPS

1 Open the BOOKS workbook

2 Change Column B to the number, two-decimal format (select the range B4:B7, then select *Format*, *Cells*, *Number* tab, *Number*, *OK*)

3 Change Column D to the number, two-decimal format (use the range D4:D7)

ASCII files intended for database use can contain only records. Titles, summary rows, and underlining must be omitted (or deleted) for the save range before the worksheet is saved in ASCII format. In this case, we'll save only Rows 4 through 7.

4 Delete Rows 1, 2, and 3

5   **Delete Row 5**

6   **Remove the border line at the bottom of Cells A4:D4 (*Format*, *Cells*, *Border* tab, *Bottom*, *OK*)**

7   **Move to Cell A1**

Your worksheet should resemble Figure SS3-47.

8   **Click *File*, *Save As***   **[F12]**

9   **Type**   `BOOKS2`

10   **Click the ▼ button of the *Save as Type* drop-down box**

11   **Use the scroll bar to locate *Text (OS/2 or MS-DOS)* and then click it**

12   **Click the *Save* button, *OK* to save as an ASCII file**

This file includes only the four rows that contain data as in Figure SS3-47 (the titles, border lines, and summary rows are omitted from the file). This ASCII file is now available to be read into an existing database file.

13   **Close the workbook without saving**

DIRECT DATABASE EXPORTING.   An Excel file can also be directly exported into a variety of database file types that are available through the *Save File as Type* drop-down box. When preparing a spreadsheet for a direct database conversion, you can leave in one row of titles. Type this:

STEPS

1   **Open the BOOKS workbook**

2   **Change the cells in Columns B and D to the number, two-decimal format**

FIGURE SS3-47 ■ **EXPORTING TO AN ASCII FILE**

The title and total rows have been deleted to prepare the worksheet to be saved as an ASCII file.

	A	B	C	D	E
1	The Rough-Faced Girl	16.95	25	423.75	
2	Will's Mammoth	14.95	76	1136.20	
3	Foolish Rabbit's Mistake	12.00	15	180.00	
4	The Hungry Tigress	16.00	67	1072.00	
5					
6					
7					

3 Delete Rows 1, 2, and then 6

4 Remove the border line at the bottom of Cells A1:D1, A5:D5 (*Format, Cells, Border* tab, *Bottom, OK*)

5 Move to Cell A1

Your worksheet should resemble Figure SS3-48. Note that a row of column titles is included in the worksheet.

6 Click *File, Save As*   [F12]

7 Type **BOOKS3**

8 Click the ▼ button of the *Save File as Type* drop-down box

9 Use the scroll bar to locate *DBF 4 (dBASEIV)* and then click it

10 Click the *Save* button, *OK* to save as a dBASEIV file

Any database format available in the *Save File as Type* drop-down box can be selected in Step 9, if desired.

11 Close the workbook without saving

IMPORTING DATA INTO EXCEL

The following exercises show you how to import data from database and ASCII files into Excel.

IMPORTING AN ASCII FILE.   ASCII text files can be read by Excel using an Open command. However, they remain as rows of text—they do not contain mathematical formulas or separate cell entries.

FIGURE SS3-48 ■ DIRECT DATABASE CONVERSION

Direct database exporting in Excel allows you to retain a one-line title row.

	A	B	C	D	E
1	Book Title	Price	Sold	Sales	
2	The Rough-Faced Girl	16.95	25	423.75	
3	Will's Mammoth	14.95	76	1136.20	
4	Foolish Rabbit's Mistake	12.00	15	180.00	
5	The Hungry Tigress	16.00	67	1072.00	
6					
7					
8					

The worksheets that result may require formatting, changing the column width, or separating the data into distinct columns. The following exercise imports the BOOKS text file and then alters it into a more usable form. To prepare for this exercise,

STEPS

1 Launch Excel if needed

2 Click *File, Open* for its dialog box (and switch to the A drive, if needed)   [**Ctrl** + **O**]

3 If needed, click the *Details* toolbar button

Note that the BOOKS text file does not appear in the *File Name* list box; only Microsoft Excel files appear. To display other file type in the list box you must use the *Files of Type* drop-down box.

4 Click the ▼ button of the *Files of Type* drop-down box and then *Text Files* (The *File Name* list box now displays all text documents.)

5 Click *BOOKS1* in the *File Name* list box and then the *Open* button

The *Text Import Wizard Step 1 of 3* dialog box appears as in Figure SS3-49a to assist you in importing your ASCII (text) file.

6 Click *Next>* to accept the default original type of data and move to the *Step 2 of 3* dialog box as in Figure SS3-49b

7 Click *Next>* to accept the default delimiter settings and move to the *Step 3 of 3* dialog box as in Figure SS3-49c

8 Click *Finish* to accept the default conversion column and data format

9 Change Column A's width to 25 and Column D's width to 12

10 Add bottom border lines to Rows 3 and 7

11 Format Cells B5:B7 and D5:D7 with accounting-no dollar sign, two decimals

12 Format Cells B4, D4 and D8 with accounting-dollar sign, two decimals

13 Move to Cell A1

14 Save the workbook as BOOKS4 (be sure the *Save as Type* drop-down box indicates *Microsoft Excel Workbook* before saving)

Your worksheet should resemble Figure SS3-50.

15 Close the workbook and exit Excel

FIGURE SS3-49 ■ THE TEXT IMPORT WIZARD

This wizard is used for importing text documents into Excel.
(a) Step 1 allows you to select the file type for importing.
(b) Step 2 lets you specify the delimiters.

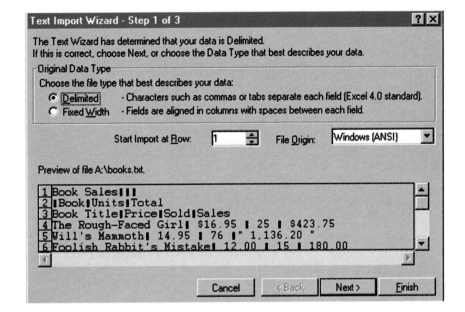

(a)

(b)

(continued)

IMPORTING A DATABASE "TEXT" FILE. A "TEXT" document produced by a database program can be opened as any ASCII file. You may be able to use the worksheet as is, or you may have to use the Text Import wizard to separate individual data

FIGURE SS3-49 ■ *(continued)*

(c) Step 3 allows you to select the Column Data format.

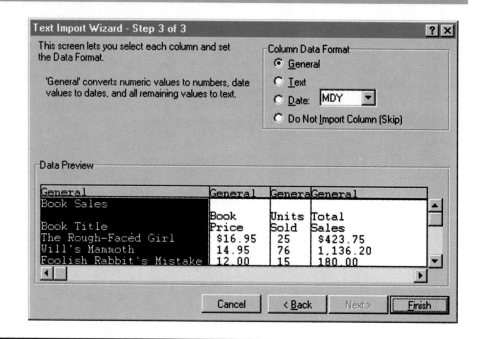

columns or adjust formats and widths. You can try this technique with the BOOKS3 text file in the next Checkpoint exercise.

 CHECKPOINT

✓ What is object linking and embedding?
✓ How do you activate a linked object for editing?

FIGURE SS3-50 ■ **THE IMPORTED DATABASE FILE**

	A	B	C	D	E
1	Book Sales				
2		Book	Units	Total	
3	Book Title	Price	Sold	Sales	
4	The Rough-Faced Girl	$ 16.95	25	$ 423.75	
5	Will's Mammoth	14.95	76	1,136.20	
6	Foolish Rabbit's Mistake	12.00	15	180.00	
7	The Hungry Tigress	16.00	67	1,072.00	
8	Totals		183	$ 2,811.95	
9					

✓ Describe the difference between exporting and importing a file.

✓ Using Excel and the correct file extensions, export the GRADES workbook to an ASCII file named GRADES2 for use by a database program.

✓ Import the BOOKS2 file using the Text Import wizard and save as a workbook named BOOKS5. Print the worksheet.

SUMMARY

Specific mouse actions and keystrokes for the following commands can be reviewed in the chapter or in the appendix.

- Charts present information in picture form. Creating a chart includes selecting the chart data, invoking the Chart command (from the *Insert* menu), and selecting the chart's location.

- Chart enhancements include options such as titles, grids, and legends that can be customized.

- Conditional functions add decision-making capabilities to worksheets. The IF function takes one of two actions based on the condition's truth. The CHOOSE function returns a value in a list based on a calculated value. Table lookups—VLOOKUP and HLOOKUP—use a two-dimensional table to return values that correspond to specified intervals.

- Spreadsheet data can be treated as a database; rows are records and columns are fields. The top row of a database must identify field names.

- The Fill command generates an evenly spaced sequence of numbers.

- The FREQUENCY function creates a frequency distribution of numbers displaying how many values in a value range fall within specified numeric intervals listed in a bin range.

- The Sort command (*Data* menu) arranges any data range in ascending order (lowest to highest) or descending order (highest to lowest) based on a primary key and two optional keys.

- Data queries are questions asked of a database. The Filter command can be used to extract records from a database, based on specified criteria. The *Form* dialog box can be used to change or delete records in a database.

- Criteria are cell entries used as tests to select records. Multiple criteria can be placed in one cell or separate cells. Complexed criteria placed in one row are connected by an AND operator, whereas complexed criteria in two or more rows are connected by an OR operator.

- Data functions, like DSUM, DAVG, and DMAX, combine statistical functions with input and criteria ranges to limit calculations to selected records in the database.

- A macro is a set of mouse actions, keystrokes, or command instructions for automating a task. Macros must be planned and named. Once named, a macro can be assigned to a shortcut key, the *Tools* menu, or a macro button for invoking.

- Macros can be entered by using the Record command to record keystrokes or mouse actions, or by typing macro commands directly. The latter method requires knowledge of Visual Basic.

- Ranges can be copied into other workbooks or sheets or other application files.

- *Client* cells in the current worksheet or sheet can be linked to *server* cells in other workbooks or sheets with a linking formula (use the Paste Link command of the

SS

Paste Special dialog box in the *Edit* menu). When server cells are changed, client cells are automatically updated.

■ The protection feature prevents all cells from being edited or deleted except those cells unprotected by the *Protection* tab of the *Format Cells* dialog box (*Format* menu) before turning on the protection feature.

■ The term OLE, or object linking and embedding, refers to transferring information from one program to another as an object. An object is a set of information. The source file is the document with the original information and the container file or compound document is the document receiving the information.

■ Import and Export commands facilitate data transfer among programs.

■ ASCII is one of a few standard formats adopted by the computer industry for representing typed characters.

■ The *Text Import Wizard* dialog box separates data from an imported ASCII file into distinct columns.

KEY TERMS

Shown in parentheses are the page numbers on which key terms are boldfaced.

ASCII (SS228)	Embedding (SS223)	Macro (SS194)
Chart (SS152)	Exporting (SS227)	Module sheet (SS196)
Column chart (SS152)	Fill handle (SS175)	Object (SS223)
Container file (or com-	Filter (SS182)	OLE(SS223)
pound document)	IF function (SS168)	Paste link (SS209)
(SS223)	Importing (SS227)	Pie chart (SS164)
Criteria (SS182)	Line chart (SS163)	Protection feature (SS221)
Data distribution (SS180)	Linking (SS223)	Selection handles (SS156)
Database query (SS182)	Lookup tables (SS170)	Source file (SS223)

QUIZ

TRUE/FALSE

____ 1. A chart may be inserted on a current sheet or on a new sheet.

____ 2. A line chart is useful for showing trends over time.

____ 3. An IF statement selects one of two possible actions.

____ 4. Values that exceed the highest VLOOKUP table value return an error message.

____ 5. A data distribution is also known as a frequency distribution.

____ 6. An alphabetical list that runs from Z to A is sorted in descending order.

____ 7. The Filter command and the *Form* dialog box can be used to query data.

____ 8. Criteria may include field names and records to be searched.

____ 9. Complexed criteria placed on adjacent rows (below each other) are linked by an OR logical connection.

____ 10. Macros can record all keystrokes except function keys.

MULTIPLE CHOICE

____ 11. The chart command can be invoked from which menu?
  a. *Chart* menu
  b. *Insert* menu
  c. *Format* menu
  d. *Tools* menu

____ 12. Which chart option improves data estimation when reading a chart?
  a. Grid
  b. Title
  c. Color
  d. Legend

____ 13. What result is returned by =IF(A1=5,"A","B") if Cell A1 = 0?
  a. A
  b. B
  c. 5
  d. 0

____ 14. To what does a column in a spreadsheet database correspond?
  a. A record
  b. A cell
  c. A table
  d. A field

____ 15. Which command creates a sequence of numbers separated at equal intervals?
  a. Frequency
  b. Fill
  c. Sort
  d. Key

____ 16. Which rows should be included in a data-sort process?
  a. Field names and record row
  b. Field names only
  c. Record names only
  d. Primary key column only

____ 17. Which command displays, in sequence, records that match specified criteria?
  a. Filter
  b. Form
  c. Sort
  d. Fill

____ 18. Which of these ranges does *not* include field names?
  a. Criteria range
  b. Sort range
  c. Query table
  d. Database table

____ 19. Which Paste Special command creates a special connection between a source and destination copy?
  a. Cut link
  b. Copy link
  c. Paste
  d. Paste-link

____ 20. Which sheet-linking formula follows proper format?
  a. **A2**File
  b. +{{B3}}File
  c. {='Region B'!$B$3:$B$6}
  d. +[D7]in File

SS

MATCHING

Select the lettered item from the figure below that best matches each phrase.

_____ 21. Can be used to invoke a macro.

_____ 22. Can be dragged to fill a range of cells with a sequence of data or copies of the same data.

_____ 23. This is used to identify and switch to different sheets in a workbook.

_____ 24. A pictorial representation of data.

_____ 25. The protection feature can be turned on or off using this menu.

_____ 26. This item can be used to scroll to the last sheet tab in the viewing area.

_____ 27. This menu can be used to invoke the Filter commands.

_____ 28. A workbook reduced to its minimum size.

_____ 29. Can be created by the Paste-Link command.

_____ 30. Opens to a drop-down list for filtering a database.

ANSWERS

True/False: 1. T; 2. T; 3. T; 4. F; 5. T; 6. T; 7. T; 8. F; 9. T; 10. F

Multiple Choice: 11. b; 12. a; 13. b; 14. d; 15. b; 16. c; 17. a; 18. b; 19. d; 20. c

Matching: 21. i; 22. l; 23. k; 24. f; 25. b; 26, j; 27. c; 28. h; 29. e; 30. g

---

FIGURE SS3-A ■ **MATCHING FIGURE**

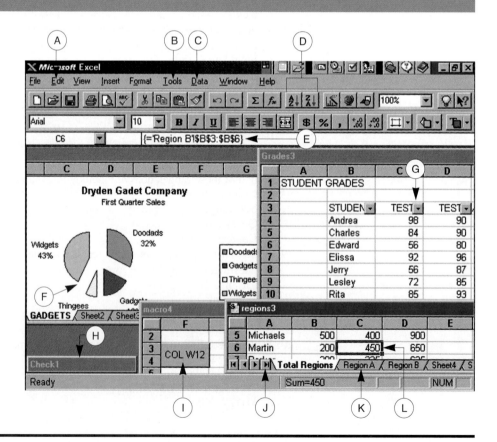

EXERCISES

I. OPERATIONS

Provide the Excel actions required to do each of the following operations.

1. Create a column chart.

2. Change the column chart to a pie-chart display.

3. Create an IF function that returns YES if A1>0, or NO if it does not.

4. Create an IF function that returns C1*5 if B1 = 2, or zero if it does not.

5. Fill a column with even numbers from 10 to 40 starting at Cell B6.

6. Create a data distribution of test grades in the range called EXAMS showing how many grades fall between each 10-point interval from zero to 100.

7. Sort cells D5:D20 in ascending order.

8. Use a criteria range to locate records whose name (in Column A) starts with an S and whose age (in Column B) exceeds 18. Assume the records start in Row 8.

9. Create a query table for the name and age of the records found in the previous exercise.

10. Create an average of grades (listed in Column D) for those cells in the input range B1:D20 whose grade (listed in Column C) is 12.

11. Create a macro to set the default format to fixed, two decimals.

12. Copy the formulas in B5:C12 to a file called NEW.

13. In Cell L4, link Cell A25 in the APRIL file.

14. Protect the entire worksheet except for cells C4:C10.

II. COMMANDS

Describe fully, using as few words as possible, what command is initiated, or what is accomplished, in Excel by the following actions. Assume that Excel has already been invoked, and that each exercise is independent of any previous exercises. If the series of actions is not complete, indicate what action should be taken to finalize the command.

1. Double-clicking a chart's title

2. Typing `=IF(A1<>1, "Error","OK")`

3. Typing `=IF(B1 = "Smith",5 1 A1,A1)`

4. Typing `=VLOOKUP(C5,$MONEY,3)`

5. Clicking *Window, Arrange, Tile, OK*

6. Pressing the `Ctrl` + `F6` keys

7. Clicking *Tools, Protection, Protect Sheet*

8. Clicking *Window, Arrange, Cascade, OK*

9. Typing `=DAVG(A1:A10,2,D5:D6)`

10. Typing `{='Region A' !$B$3:$B$6}`

III. APPLICATIONS

Perform the following operations, briefly explain how you accomplished each operation, and describe its results.

APPLICATION 1: ADVANCE CLUB BUDGET

Save the workbook in this exercise as indicated so that you can continue this exercise later if desired.

1. Open the CLUB2 workbook (created in the Chapter 2).

2. Create a column chart showing the expense dollars by month. Add appropriate titles and resize the chart to adequately display its contents. Save the workbook as EXPENSE1. If a graphics printer is available, print the worksheet with the chart.

3. Create a pie chart that is formatted to display percentages for each slice. Save the workbook as EXPENSE2. Print only the pie chart, if a graphics printer is available.

4. Create a three-dimensional bar chart showing expenditures for each type of expense for individual months. Save the workbook as EXPENSE3. Print only the three-dimensional bar chart, if a graphics printer is available, and close the workbook.

5. Open the CLUB2 workbook. Sort the data in Cells A7 through H11 using Column A as the primary key (use ascending order). Save this workbook as CLUB3 and print it.

6. Select the range A6:I11 as the database table. Filter the database for only those records whose TOTAL data exceed $500. Print and save this workbook.

7. Change the criteria in the previous exercise to filter records whose JUN data is less than 100 and whose TOTAL data exceed $500. Print and save.

8. Create a macro button in Column M that will print only the columns that display TOTAL. (Hint: Your macro can hide the columns that you do not wish to print.) Print and save this workbook.

9. Unhide the columns that were hidden by the macro. Protect Cells B12:I12 and I7:I11.

10. In Cell H13, create a DAVERAGE function to calculate the average funds needed for a month. Save and print the workbook.

11. Exit the program.

APPLICATION 2: ADVANCED GPA

Save the workbook in this exercise as GPA3 after each operation is completed (unless otherwise indicated) so that you can continue this exercise later.

1. Open the GPA2 workbook (created in Chapter 2).

2. Create a column chart showing the total points earned for each course taken. Add appropriate titles. (Hint: Select the ranges A8:A13 and F8:F13 as multiple ranges

before invoking the Chart command.) Save the worksheet as GPA_B. Print the image if a graphics printer is available.

3. Create a pie chart showing the total points of each course. Save the workbook as GPA_P. Print the image if a graphics printer is available. Compare the percentages shown in the chart with the values in Column G.

4. Change the default width to 10. In Column H, add an IF function that will mark with two asterisks any course whose point value is four. Label and format as needed. Change the width of Column H to 2. Print the worksheet and save it.

5. Create this lookup table named CONVERT, starting in Cell J2 (the titles start in J2, the table begins in J3):

Grade	Points
F	0
D	1
C	2
B	3
A	4

Replace the current entry in Cell E7 with a VLOOKUP function that compares the grade with that in this chart and returns the points automatically. Copy the function correctly into the remaining cells in the column. Print the worksheet and save it.

6. Sort the data in Cells A8:H13 using *only* COURSE as the primary key (in ascending order). Print the spreadsheet. Now sort by TERM as the primary key and COURSE as the secondary key (both in ascending order). Print and save the workbook.

7. Delete Row 7 (the empty row) and create a data table for the range A6:F12. Use the Advanced Filter command to create a query table in Cells A35:F39 that includes only those records from the data table whose GRADE is B. Print and save.

8. Change the criteria in the previous exercise to select records only if their TERM is 9301 *and* their GRADE is A. Create a query table of these records. Print and save.

9. In Cell J24, create a DSUM function to calculate the total credits only for courses in business. (Hint: You may use a LEFT function.) Create a function below it to count the number of courses in this category. (Use Cells M22 and M23 for the criterion.) Title cells as needed.

10. Create a macro that will print only the columns that display courses and grades when invoked with **Ctrl** and **T** keys. (Hint: You may want to use a column hide and unhide routine.) Invoke the macro and then print the entire worksheet. Save the workbook.

11. Create a macro button that will print Columns A through F of the worksheet. Invoke the macro. Save the workbook.

12. Copy the COURSE and TERM columns to a new workbook called GPA3A. Open a new workbook. Copy GPA3A into this blank workbook starting in Cell A1. Print, but do not save.

13. Open the GPA3A workbook from the previous exercise (or create it if needed). Delete the rows that contain courses in ART or MUSIC. For the remaining rows, use the Paste link command to link formulas in Column C that will open the grades from the GPA3 worksheet. Save as GPA3B and print.

14. Open GPA3. Protect all cells from change except the rows with data entry (from Column A to Column E). Save the workbook.

15. Exit the program.

APPLICATION 3: ADVANCED CHECKBOOK

Save this workbook as CHECK3 after each operation is completed (unless otherwise indicated) so that you can continue this exercise later.

1. Open the CHECK2 workbook (created in Chapter 2).

2. Create a line chart showing the BALANCE during the time period from 01-Jan through 15-Jan. (Hint: Select the ranges A7:A12 and F7:F12 as multiple ranges before invoking the Chart command.) Add appropriate titles and resize the chart to adequately display its contents. Save the workbook as LCHECK. If a graphics printer is available, print the workbook with the chart. Close the workbook.

3. Open the CHECK2 workbook again. In Row 15, create a DMIN function to find the lowest balance. Title the cells as needed.

4. Copy the DATE and BALANCE columns to Sheet 2. Rename Sheet 1, CHECKS, and Sheet 2 BALANCES. Save and print the entire workbook with all sheets.

5. Select the range A6:F12 as the database table. Filter only the deposits. Save and print the workbook.

6. Display the entire database table. Filter only the check payments. Save and print this workbook.

7. Display the entire database table. Create a macro that automatically adds the formula in the Balance column to the next cell below when invoked.

8. Assign the macro to the *Tools* menu.

9. Add the following data and invoke the BALANCE macro in the BALANCE column as needed.

DATE	CHECK#	PAYEE	PMT	DEP
20-Jan	109	M-Charge	340.00	
31-Jan		Deposit pay check		1,400.00

10. Reformat the worksheet as needed. Save and then print the workbook.

11. Protect Rows 4 and 6 and all data in the BALANCE column. Save the workbook and close it.

12. Open the CHECK2 workbook again. Format the worksheet as an ASCII file, save it as CHECKS.TXT, and then close it.

13. Use the Text Import wizard to convert the CHECKS.TXT file into an Excel workbook.

14. Exit the program.

APPLICATION 4: ADVANCED INVESTMENTS

Save the workbook as INVEST3 after each operation is completed (unless otherwise indicated) so that you can continue this exercise later.

1. Open the INVEST2 workbook (created in Chapter 2).

2. Create a line chart for TOTAL SALES and TOTAL PURCH for each stock. (Hint: Select the ranges A8:A12, G8:G12 and H8:H12 as multiple ranges before invoking the Chart command. Add appropriate titles and resize the chart to adequately display its contents. Print the chart if a graphics printer is available.

3. Change the default (standard) width to 11. In Column K, add an IF function to mark with an asterisk (*) any return on investment less than 5.00%. Change the width of Column K to 2. Save the workbook and then print it without the chart created in the previous step.

4. Sort the data in Cells A8:J12 by TYPE in ascending order. Print and save.

5. Sort the data in Cells A8:J12 by TYPE in ascending order and also by PROFIT/(LOSS) in descending order.

6. Select the range A7:J12 as the database table. Filter the database for those investments whose profit is greater than $500.

7. Copy the TYPE, DATE SOLD, SELLING PRICE, QUANTITY, and TOTAL SALES columns to SHEET 2.

8. Copy the TYPE, DATE PURCH, PURCH, PRICE, QUANTITY, and TOTAL PURCH columns to SHEET 3.

9. Rename Sheet 1's tab to TOTAL; Sheet 2's tab to SALES; and Sheet 3's tab to PURCHASES.

10. In the TOTAL sheet, delete the data in the range A8:H12. Create linking formulas in the cells of the deleted range to link to the appropriate information from the SALES and PURCHASES sheets. (Hint: Use the Paste-Link command of the *Special Paste* dialog box.) Save the workbook.

11. Protect all of the data in the TOTAL sheet and the columns containing formulas in the SALES and PURCHASES sheets.

12. Change some of the data in the SALES and PURCHASES sheets and examine the results in the TOTAL sheet. Save the workbook.

13. Print the entire workbook (all sheets).

14. Exit the program.

APPLICATION 5: ADVANCED TAPES

1. Open the TAPES workbook. (If you do not have TAPES, enter the worksheet shown in the figure).

2. Create a column chart showing units sold for each title. (Hint: Select the ranges A4:A9 and D4:D9 as multiple ranges before invoking the Chart command.) Add appropriate titles. Save the workbook as CATALOG1 and then print the worksheet.

3. In Column F, add an IF function that will mark with a plus sign any title whose sales exceed $500. Format as needed. Print the worksheet and save it as CATALOG.

	A	B	C	D	E	
1	Tape Sales					
2				Units	Total	
3	Tape	Type	Price	Sold	Sales	
4	The Rough-Faced Girl	Video	$ 32.95	87	$ 2,866.65	
5	Will's Mammoth	Audio	12.95	35	453.25	
6	Three Little Pigs	Video	24.95	23	573.85	
7	The Wooly Mammoth	Video	24.95	12	299.40	
8	Japanese Ghost Stories	Audio	6.75	57	384.75	
9	Foolish Rabbit's Mistake	Audio	5.95	6	35.70	
10	Total Sales			220	$ 4,613.60	
11						

4. Create this lookup table named SHIPPING starting in Cell H4:

Price	Shipping
$ 0.00	$0.50
10.00	1.25
20.00	2.00
30.00	2.75

Title Column G "Shipping." Create a VLOOKUP function in Column G that compares the price with that in this chart and returns the shipping cost *multiplied by the units sold.* Format Column G as needed. Print the worksheet and save it.

5. Sort the data in Cells A4:G9 using *only* TYPE as the primary key and TAPE as the secondary key (use ascending order for both). Print the spreadsheet and save it.

6. Create a data table for the range A3:E9. Use the Advanced Filter command to create a query table in Cells A18:E22 that includes only those records from the data table whose prices exceed $15. Print and save.

7. Change the criteria to select records only if their TYPE is "Video" *and* they sold more than 20 units. Create a query table of these records. Print and save.

8. In Row 25, create a DSUM function to calculate the sum of SALES only for videos. Create a function below it to count the number of audio tapes. Title cells as needed.

9. Create a macro that will print only the tape TITLES when invoked with the Ctrl and T keys. Invoke the macro and print the entire worksheet. Save the worksheet.

10. Create a macro button that will print Columns A through E of the worksheet. Invoke the macro. Save the worksheet.

11. Copy the tape TITLE and TYPE to a new worksheet file called CATALOG2. Open a new worksheet. Combine CATALOG2 into this blank worksheet file starting in Cell A1. Print, but do not save.

12. Open the CATALOG2 worksheet from the previous exercise (or create one). Change Column A's width to 30. Delete the rows that contain audio tapes. For the three remaining rows, create linking formulas using the Paste Link command (*Paste Special* dialog box) in Column C that will open the units sold from the CATALOG worksheet. Save as CATALOG2 and print.

13. Open CATALOG. Protect all cells from change except the six rows with data entry (from Column A to Column D).

14. Save the workbook and exit the program.

APPLICATION 6: ADVANCED TICKETS

Save the workbook in this exercise as TICKET3 after each operation is completed (unless otherwise indicated) so that you can continue this exercise later if desired.

1. Open the TICKET2 worksheet (created in Chapter 2).

2. Create a column chart showing the quantity of each seat type. (Hint: Select the ranges A7:A12 and C7:C12 as multiple ranges before invoking the Chart command.) Add appropriate titles and resize the chart to adequately display its contents. Save the workbook as TICK_B1. Add a second series of data for tickets sold and save it as TICK_B2. If a graphics printer is available, print the worksheet with the chart.

3. Remove the second set of data. Now, create a pie chart showing the *value* of each seat type. Save the workbook as TICK_P. Print the chart only if a graphics printer is available. Compare the percentages shown in the chart with the values in Column G.

4. Change the default width to 8. In Column H, add an IF function that will mark with an asterisk (*) any seat type whose value exceeds $5,000. Format as needed. Change the width of Column H to 2. Print the worksheet and save it as TICKET3.

5. Create this lookup table named HANDLING, starting in Cell J2 (the titles start in J2, the table begins in J3):

Price	Shipping
$10.00	$1.50
30.00	2.00
50.00	2.25

Format to match the sample. Title Column I "Handling." Create a VLOOKUP function in Column I that compares the ticket price with those in this chart and returns the handling cost *multiplied by the number of tickets sold.* Extend the existing border lines to cover the added columns. Format the column to match Column F. Print the worksheet and save it.

6. Sort the data in Cells A7:I12 using *only* SEAT as primary key (in ascending order). Print the spreadsheet. Now sort by PRICE as primary key and SEAT as secondary key (both in descending order). Print and save the spreadsheet.

7. Create a data table for the range A6:F12. Use the Advanced Filter command to create a query table in Cells H19:M23 that includes only those records from the data table whose SOLD data exceed 100. Print and save.

8. Change the criteria in the previous exercise to select records only if their EMPTY data are less than 100 seats *and* their VALUE data exceed $2,000. Create a query table of these records. Print and save.

9. In Cell B33, create a DSUM function to calculate the sum of tickets sold only for seats that cost $50 or more. Create a function below it to total the number of avail-

able seats in this category. (Use Cells G22 and G23 for the criterion.) Title cells as needed.

10. Create a macro in Column M that will print only the columns that display seat types and number of empty seats when invoked with Ctrl and T keys. (Hint: You may want to use a column hide and unhide routine.) Invoke the macro and then print the entire worksheet. Save the workbook.

11. Create a macro button that will print Columns A through F of the worksheet. Invoke the macro. Save the workbook.

12. Copy the SEAT and PRICE columns to a new worksheet file called TICKET3A. Open a new workbook. Copy TICKET3A into this blank workbook, starting in Cell A1. Print, but do not save.

13. Open the TICKET3A workbook from the previous exercise (or create it if needed). Delete the rows that contain seats that sell for $50 or more. For the remaining rows, use the Paste-Link command to insert linking formulas in Column C that will open the seats sold from the TICKET worksheet. Save as TICKET3B and print.

14. Open TICKET. Protect all cells from change except the rows with data entry (from Column A to Column F). Save the workbook.

15. Exit the program.

APPLICATION 7: LINKING AND EMBEDDING

1. Launch Excel and open the TAPES workbook. (If you do not have TAPES, enter the worksheet shown in the figure of Application 5: Advanced Tapes).

2. Select and then Copy the range A3:C9 to the Clipboard.

3. Launch Word.

4. Type   **The following is our latest tape price list:**

5. Skip two lines.

6. Paste-link the copied range from the Clipboard (use the default format) to your Word document.

7. Save the Word document as PRICELIST and then print it.

8. Switch to Excel and make the following changes:

Cell	Change
C4	27.95
B7	Audio
B8	Video
C9	10.95

9. Save the revised workbook as REVISEDTAPES.

10. Switch to Word to see that the linked data are automatically updated.

11. Save the revised Word document as REVISEDPRICELIST and then print it.

12. Close Word and Excel, and then shut down Windows.

MASTERY CASES

The following mastery cases allow you to demonstrate how much you have learned about this software. Each case describes a fictitious problem or need that can be solved using the skills you have learned in this chapter. Although minimum acceptable outcomes are specified, you are expected and encouraged to design your response (files, data, lists) in ways that display your personal mastery of the software. Feel free to show off your skills. Use real data from your own experience in your solution, although you may also fabricate data if needed.

These mastery cases allow you to display your ability to

- Create charts.
- Use conditional functions.
- Create macros.
- Use multiple workbooks.
- Use multiple sheets.
- Protect cells in a workbook.
- Share data among programs.

CASE 1. ANALYZING YOUR EXAM GRADES

Open the exam grades workbook that you created for Mastery Case 1 of Chapter 2. Create a column chart showing your AVERAGE in each course. Print the workbook with the chart. Create a distribution of your final grades (AVERAGE column) assuming an A is 100-90, a B is 89-80, a C is 79-70, and so on. Copy the COURSE and AVERAGE columns to Sheet 2 of the workbook. Link the AVERAGE column between the sheets. Add data for two new classes to the workbook. Save and print the entire workbook (all sheets). Add other enhancements to make the workbook more attractive. Save the workbook and print Sheet 1.

CASE 2. ANALYZING YOUR HOLIDAY SHOPPING

Open the holiday-shopping workbook that you created for Mastery Case 2 of Chapter 2. Create a pie chart to show the actual amount that you spent for each person on your list. Print the worksheet with the chart. Sort your data in ascending order by ACTUAL amount spent on each person. Save and print the workbook. Create a query table that displays only those records in which the actual amount spent is more than the budget amount. Add other enhancements to make the workbook more attractive. Save and print your budget.

CASE 3. ANALYZING YOUR SALES REPORT

Open the sales report workbook that you created for Mastery Case 3 of Chapter 2. Create a pie chart to show the relative amount that each product has contributed to total sales. Print the worksheet with the chart. Create and execute a macro that will print only the PRODUCT and UNITS SOLD columns. Protect the PRODUCT and UNIT PRICE columns. Add other enhancements to make the workbook more attractive. Save and print your sales report.

Appendix: FEATURE AND OPERATION REFERENCE EXCEL MOUSE OPERATIONS

A mouse is an input device that allows you to control a mouse pointer (graphical image) on your screen. As you move your mouse on a flat surface, the mouse pointer moves on the screen in a similar fashion. See Figure SS1-2A in Chapter 1 for mouse-pointer forms and common mouse actions.

A summary of some Excel features that are accessible by mouse follows. Refer to Figure SS1-3 in Chapter 1 for the location of some of these features. Detailed applications of these features are incorporated within other sections of this appendix.

 ### CANCEL BUTTON

Clicking the *Cancel* button (X) (in the formula bar) cancels the data being entered. The *Cancel* button appears on the formula bar only when data are being entered into a cell.

 ### CLOSE BUTTON

Clicking the *Close* button (X) of any window closes it. The *Close* button of the Excel (program) window, a restored workbook (document) window, and a dialog box is located at the right end of each of their title bars. A window's close button is at the right end of the menu bar.

DRAGGING AND DROPPING

Excel's Drag and Drop feature offers a quick way to move a selection of cells or an object within the same worksheet. To drag a selection, point to it, and then press and hold the left mouse button while moving (dragging) the pointer and the selection to its new location. Pressing and holding the Ctrl key while dragging and dropping will generally copy a selection.

 ### ENTER BUTTON

Clicking the *Enter* button (formula bar) will place data into the cell. The *Enter* button appears on the formula bar only when data are being entered into a cell.

 ### FUNCTION *WIZARD* BUTTON

Clicking the function *Wizard* button (formula bar) opens a Function wizard.

MENU BAR

Clicking a menu bar item opens its pull-down menu. Clicking a pull-down menu item selects that item.

MOVING THE CELL POINTER

Pointing to a desired location in a worksheet and clicking it moves the cell pointer there.

PROGRAM OR *WORKBOOK* ICON

Double-clicking a *Program* or *Workbook* icon quickly closes a window. Clicking a *Program* or *Workbook* icon once opens the window's control menu.

   Program or *workbook* icon is normally located at the left side of its window's title bar. A maximized workbook window's *Workbook* icon, however, is located at the left end of the menu bar.

RESIZING BUTTONS

Clicking a resizing button is a quick way to change the size of a window. Standard resizing buttons include the following:

Resizing Button	Resizing Effect When Clicked
Minimize	Reduces the window to an icon
Restore	Restores the window to its previous size
Maximize	Enlarges the window to its maximum size

Two resizing buttons generally occupy the upper-right corner of a window. A maximized workbook window's resizing buttons are located at the right end of the menu bar.

SCROLLING

Clicking the arrow buttons at either end of a scroll bar or dragging the scroll box along a scroll bar allows you to see areas of a worksheet or list not currently in the viewing area without moving the cell pointer or highlight. To move the pointer or highlight to a position or item in the current display area, simply point to it and click.

SELECTING A COLUMN

Clicking the letter of a column selects the entire column.

SELECTING A CHART

Clicking a chart's frame selects it. Double-clicking a selected chart puts it in the chart edit mode. Once in edit mode, simply click the chart's part to select it. Note that a selected chart has selection handles on its frame.

SELECTING A RANGE

A range is a selection of cells that resembles a highlighted rectangular area. Dragging the mouse pointer over desired cells selects them. A range of cells can also be selected by clicking the first cell of the desired range and then pressing and holding the Shift key while clicking the last cell of the range.

SELECTING A ROW

Clicking a row number selects the entire row.

SELECTING AN OBJECT

Clicking an object selects it by placing selection handles on its frame.

SELECTING MULTIPLE RANGES

To select multiple ranges, select the first range and then press and hold the Ctrl key while selecting each additional range.

SELECTING THE ENTIRE WORKSHEET

Clicking the top-left corner of worksheet where rows and column indicators intersect selects the entire worksheet.

SHEET TABS

Clicking a workbook's sheet tab allows you to switch to that sheet.

SHORTCUT MENUS

Right-clicking certain areas of Excel's window opens a *Shortcut* menu. *Shortcut* menus provide quick access to a variety of features. To select a *Shortcut* menu item by mouse, simply click it.

SPLITTING A WORKSHEET

To split a worksheet, drag the horizontal or vertical splitter bar to the desired split position in the worksheet and then release (drop) the splitter bar.

STATUS BAR

The status bar has a variety of indicators (messages) and selectors. To see a description of a toolbar button in the status bar, point to the button. To see a description of a menu item, open the menu and use the arrow keys to move the highlight to it.

SWITCHING AMONG MULTIPLE WINDOWS

Clicking anywhere on a workbook window will make it the active window when multiple windows are in use.

TAB-SCROLLING BUTTONS

Clicking a *Tab-scrolling* button will move tabs into the sheet-tab-viewing area. *Tab* buttons include (left to right) the *First Tab, Previous Tab, Next Tab,* and *Last Tab.*

TITLE BAR

Double-clicking a window's title bar resizes the window.

KEYBOARD OPERATIONS

Many Excel operations can be performed by keyboard. They include common Windows keys and those that are unique to Excel. Common Windows keys concern basic menu and dialog-box operations, file management, window manipulation, and editing commands. They also include keys that provide quick access to commands called *shortcut keys.* Many of these keys generally follow the structure for standard Windows shortcut keys. For example, pressing Alt + F4 exits any program or dialog box. Keys used to perform mouse actions such as clicking, right-clicking, double-clicking, and dragging and dropping are called *MouseKeys.* Windows Accessibility Options must be installed on your system to use MouseKeys.

Other keyboard options available with the Accessibility Options include Sticky Keys, FilterKeys, and ToggleKeys. *StickyKeys* allows you to use the Alt, Ctrl, or Shift keys by pressing each key at a time. *FilterKeys* is an option that instructs Windows to ignore repeated keystrokes. *ToggleKeys* provides a sound when the Num Lock, Caps Lock, or Scroll Lock is pressed.

COMMON WINDOWS KEYS

Common Windows keys concern basic menu and dialog-box operations, file management, window manipulation, and editing commands. They also include a variety of shortcut keys.

ALT   Pressed alone, the Alt key activates the selection highlight on Excel's (or any active program window's) menu bar. The highlight may then be moved to a menu bar item using the arrow keys. If used in combination with other keys, the Alt key is held down when striking another key. The other key is usually a function key (F1 through F12), the underlined letter of a menu item, button, or other option that has an underlined letter.

- Alt + F4 exits Excel (or any Windows program) or any dialog box.
- Alt + Spacebar opens the Excel window's (or any program window's) control menu.
- Alt + – (minus) opens the control-menu of a workbook (or document) window.

- Alt + Tab switches to the last program used when operating multiple programs.
- Alt + Esc switches to the next running program when operating multiple applications. A program can be running as a window or taskbar button.
- Alt + Print Screen copies an image of the active program window (or dialog box) to the Clipboard for future pasting.

ARROW KEYS

- Move the cell pointer one cell at a time in the direction of the arrow.
- Move the insertion point one character at a time in the direction of the arrow when editing data within a cell, text box, or drop-down box.
- Move the selection highlight in the direction of the arrow to each item on a menu or list (in a list box or drop-down box).

The arrow keys can also be used in conjunction with other keys to perform such tasks as resizing a window, moving a selection (data, chart, table, or object), or moving a drawing or editing tool.

BACKSPACE
Erases single characters to the left of the insertion point.

CAPS LOCK
Keeps the Shift key active so that all characters are typed in uppercase.

CTRL
The Control key is used with another key to invoke a command.

- Ctrl + Alt + Delete exits the current program if it stops responding to the system.
- Ctrl + B turns the bold feature on and off.
- Ctrl + C copies a selection (data, chart, table, or object) to the Windows Clipboard for future pasting.
- Ctrl + Esc opens the *Start* menu.
- Ctrl + F4 closes the active workbook (document) window.
- Ctrl + G invokes the Goto command.
- Ctrl + F6 moves the highlight to another workbook (document) window or icon.
- Ctrl + H starts Find/Replace feature.
- Ctrl + I turns the italic feature on and off.
- Ctrl + N creates a new workbook.
- Ctrl + O opens a file.
- Ctrl + P prints the current worksheet (document) or range (selection).
- Ctrl + S saves the current workbook (document) to a file.
- Ctrl + U turns the underline feature on and off.
- Ctrl + V pastes the contents of the Windows Clipboard to a desired location.
- Ctrl + X cuts (moves) a selection to the Windows Clipboard for future pasting.
- Ctrl + Y repeats close.
- Ctrl + Z undoes the last action.

■ Ctrl + 1 opens the *Format Cells* dialog box.

DELETE
The *Delete* key erases the following:

■ Single characters to the right of the insertion point when editing data in a cell, text box, or drop-down box.
■ A selection (individual cell, range, or object).

END
■ Moves the insertion point to the end of a line when editing data in a cell, text box, or drop-down box.
■ Moves the selection highlight to the last item in a menu, list box, or drop-down box.

ENTER
■ Enters typed data into a cell (spreadsheet programs only).
■ Invokes a command from a menu selection or dialog box.

ESC
■ Cancels a menu or dialog box before a command is invoked.
■ Returns a cell to its previous content before completing a new entry.

F1
Opens the Help window of any Windows program.

FUNCTION KEYS
Numbered F1 through F12, the function keys are used alone, or in combination with the Alt, Ctrl, and Shift keys, to invoke Excel or another program's commands.

HOME
■ Moves the insertion point to the beginning of a line of data in a cell, text box, or drop-down box.
■ Moves the selection highlight to the beginning of a list in a menu, list box, or drop-down box.

INSERT
In certain situations, allows the insertion of characters at the insertion point when editing data in a cell, text box, or drop-down box.

NUM LOCK
Activates the numeric keypad that is on the right side of most keyboards. Num Lock works as a toggle key; pressing it once activates the keypad, while pressing it again deactivates the keypad.
It also activates the numeric keypad for use as MouseKeys when the feature is on.

PG UP AND PG DN (PAGE UP AND PAGE DOWN)
Moves one screen page up or one down.

PRINT SCREEN (PRT SC)
Captures an image of a screen to the Clipboard.

SHIFT

Works like the Shift key on a typewriter; when it is held down and a letter or number is pressed, an uppercase letter or symbol assigned to the number key is produced. Other commands invoked when pressing the Shift key and another key include the following:

- Shift + → expands the selection highlight to the right.
- Shift + ← expands the selection highlight to the left.
- Shift + Tab moves the dotted selection rectangle to the previous option in a dialog box.

TAB

Moves the dotted selection rectangle to next option in a dialog box.

UNIQUE EXCEL KEYS

Unique Excel keys allow users to invoke commands that relate only to Excel features. The keys listed here assume that the transition check boxes in the *Transition* tab of the *Options* dialog box are empty. To check, select *Tools, Options, Transition* tab.

FUNCTION KEYS.   Excel commands invoked by pressing a function key alone or with another key(s) are listed below.

- F1 (Help)

  Invokes the Excel Help feature.

- Shift + F1

  Invokes context-sensitive Help.

- F2 (Edit)

  Puts Excel in edit mode, which displays the contents of the current cell in the Entry area of the formula bar for editing.

- Shift + F2

  Invokes the Note command (*Insert* menu).

- Ctrl + F2

  Opens the Info window.

- F3

  Pastes a name into a formula.

- Shift + F3

  Invokes the Function wizard.

- Ctrl + F3

  Invokes the Define command (Insert menu, Name submenu).

- Ctrl + Shift + F3

  Invokes the Create command (*Insert* menu, *Name* submenu).

- F4

  Changes a cell or range from relative to absolute or vice versa, or repeats last action.

- Ctrl + F4

  Closes the active workbook window.

- Alt + F4

  Exits Microsoft Excel.

- F5 (Goto)

  Moves cell pointer to a specified location.

- Ctrl + F5

  Restores workbook window size.

- F6 (Pane)

  Moves cell pointer between panes on a single sheet.

- Shift + F6

  Moves to previous pane.

- Ctrl + F6

  Moves to next workbook window.

- Ctrl + Shift + F6

  Moves to previous workbook window.

- F7

  Invokes the spell-checker program.

- Shift + F7

  Invokes the Move command (workbook window control-menu).

- F8

  Toggles the extend mode on and off.

- Shift + F8

  Toggles the add mode on and off.

- Ctrl + F8

  Invokes the Size command (workbook window control-menu).

- F9 (Calculate) or Ctrl + =

  Recalculates all workbook sheets.

- Shift + F9

  Calculates only the active sheet.

- Ctrl + F9

  Minimizes the workbook window.

- F10 or Alt (Menu)

  Activates the selection highlight on the menu bar.

- Shift + F10

  Opens the *Shortcut* menu.

- Ctrl + F10

  Maximizes the workbook window.

- F11

  Inserts new chart sheet.

- Shift + F11

  Inserts new sheet.

- Ctrl + F11

  Inserts new Microsoft Excel macro sheet.

- F12

  Invokes Save As command (*File* menu).

- Shift + F12

  Invokes the Save command (*File* menu).

- Ctrl + F12

  Invokes the Print command (*File* menu).

OTHER EXCEL KEYS   These Excel keys do not involve the use of function keys.

- =

  Starts a formula.

- Alt + =

  Places the AutoSum formula in the current cell address.

- Alt + Page Up

  Moves left one screen.

- Alt + Page Down

  Moves right one screen.

- Alt + ⏎

  Inserts a carriage return.

- Ctrl + ; (semicolon)

  Enters the system date.

- Ctrl + ' (apostrophe)

  Copies the formula from the cell above the current cell into the cell or formula bar.

- Ctrl + ' (single left quotation mark)

  Switches between displaying values or formulas in cells.

- Ctrl + 0 (zero)

  Hides selected columns.

- Ctrl + 6

  Switches between hiding objects, displaying objects, and displaying placeholders for objects.

- Ctrl + 7

  Displays or hides the Standard toolbar.

- Ctrl + 8

  Shows or hides the outline symbols.

- Ctrl + 9

  Hides selected rows.

- Ctrl + A
    - Selects the entire worksheet.
    - Displays Step 2 of the Function wizard, after a valid function name is entered in a formula.

- Ctrl + Alt + Tab

  Inserts a tab.

- Ctrl + D

  Fills a selection down.

- Ctrl + Delete

  Deletes data to the end of the line.

- Ctrl + End

  Moves the cell pointer to the last cell in your worksheet (lower-right corner).

- Ctrl + Home

  Moves the cell pointer to the beginning of the worksheet.

- Ctrl + – (minus sign)

  Deletes the selection.

- Ctrl + Page Up

  Moves the cell pointer to the previous sheet in the workbook.

- Ctrl + Page Down

  Moves the cell pointer to the next sheet in the workbook.

- Ctrl + R

  Fills a selection to the right.

- Ctrl + Shift + : (colon)

  Enters the system time.

- Ctrl + Shift + "

  Copies the value from the cell above the current cell into the cell or formula bar.

- Ctrl + Shift + (

  Unhides selected columns.

- Ctrl + Shift + A

  Inserts the argument names and parentheses for the function after a valid function name is entered in the formula.

- Ctrl + Shift + End

  Expands a selection to the last cell in a worksheet (lower-right corner).

- Ctrl + Shift + Home

  Expands a selection to the beginning of the worksheet.

- Ctrl + Shift + + (plus)

  Inserts blank cells at the cell pointer.

- Ctrl + Shift + Spacebar

  Selects all objects on a sheet after the first one is selected.

- Ctrl + Shift + ↵

  Enters the formula as a range formula.

- Ctrl + Spacebar

  Selects the entire column.

- Ctrl + ← or Ctrl + →

  Moves the cell pointer up or down to the edge of the current data region.

- Ctrl + ↑ or Ctrl + ↓

  Moves the cell pointer up or down to the edge of the current data region.

- Ctrl + ⏎

  Fills a range of cells with the current entry.

- End, arrow key

  Moves the cell pointer by one block of data within a row or column.

- End

  Turns on/off the end mode.

- End, Shift + ⏎ *

  Expands a selection to the last cell in the current row.

- End, ⏎ *

  Moves the cell pointer to the last cell in the current row.

- End, Shift + arrow key

  Expands a selection to the end of the data block in the direction of the arrow.

- End, Shift + Home

  Expands a selection to the last cell of a worksheet (lower-right corner).

- End, Home

  Moves the cell pointer to the last cell of a worksheet (lower-right corner).

- Enter (⏎)

  Completes the cell entry.

- Esc

  Cancels an entry in a cell, formula bar, or menu.

- Home

  - Moves the cell pointer to the beginning of the row.
  - Moves the insertion point to the start of the line.

- Page Up

  Moves the cell pointer one screen up.

- Page Down

  Moves the cell pointer one screen down.

- Scroll Lock

  Turns the scroll lock on or off.

- Shift + arrow key

  Expands a selection by one cell.

- Shift + Backspace

  Reduces the selection to the active cell.

- Shift + Home

  Expands a selection to the beginning of the row.

- Shift + Page Up

  Expands a selection one screen up.

- Shift + Page Down

  Expands a selection one screen down.

- Shift + Spacebar

  Selects the entire row.

- Shift + Tab
  Enters a cell entry and moves to the previous cell in the row or range.
- Tab
  - Moves the cell pointer among unlocked cells in a protected worksheet.
  - Enters a cell entry and moves to the next cell in the row or range.

MOUSEKEYS

MouseKeys is a feature of the Accessibility Options that you can access through the Control Panel. It allows you to use the numeric keypad to invoke mouse actions such as clicking, right-clicking, double-clicking and dragging and dropping. To use any Accessibility Option, the program must first be installed on your system. This can be checked through Windows Add/Remove Programs feature.

CHECKING FOR THE ACCESSIBILITY OPTIONS FEATURE.   If the *Accessibility Options* icon appears in the Control Panel, then it has been installed on your system and ready for use. To check,

1 **Click the** *Start* **button**   [**Ctrl** + **Esc**]

2 **Point to** *Settings*

3 **Click** *Control Panel*

4 **Examine the Control Panel window for the** *Accessibility Options* **icon**

If the *Accessibility Options* icon does not appear and you have the Windows 95 CD-ROM (you must also have a CD-ROM drive) or setup disks, go to the "Installing Accessibility Options" section for installation procedures. If you want to turn on the *MouseKey* option, see the "Turning On/Off MouseKeys" section. To exit the Control Panel,

 5 **Click the Control Panel's** *Close* **button**

INSTALLING ACCESSIBILITY OPTIONS.   The Accessibility Options can be installed using the *Add/Remove Programs* dialog box.

1 **Click the** *Start* **button**   [**Ctrl** + **Esc**]

2 **Point to** *Settings*

3 **Click** *Control Panel*

4 **Double-click the** *Add/Remove Programs* **icon**

5 **Click the** *Windows Setup* **tab**

6 Click the *Accessibility Options* check box

7 Click the *Apply* button

8 Insert the Windows 95 CD-ROM or appropriate disk as requested on the screen

9 Click the *OK* button

TURNING ON/OFF MOUSEKEYS.   The MouseKeys feature can be turned on or off using the *Mouse* tab of the *Accessibility Properties* dialog box. When the MouseKeys feature is on, you can use the numeric keypad to invoke mouse actions. To turn the MouseKeys feature on or off,

 1 Click the *Start* button   [Ctrl + Esc]

2 Point to *Settings* for its submenu

3 Click *Control Panel* for its window

 4 Double-click the *Accessibility Options* icon for its dialog box

5 Click the *Mouse* tab

6 Click the *Use MouseKeys* check box

7 Click the *OK* button to exit the dialog box

 8 Click the *Close* button of the Control Panel window

   When the MouseKeys feature is on, a mouse icon appears in the message area of the taskbar. Double-clicking this icon will also open the *Accessibility Properties* dialog box.

USING MOUSEKEYS.   When the MouseKeys feature is on, the mouse pointer movement can be controlled by using the numeric keypad. See Figure SS1-2c for their operations.

DIALOG BOX OPERATIONS

A dialog box is a window that requests or gives information. It operates similar to a program window; however, it cannot be resized. A dialog box has a title bar that displays its name with a *Close* button, *Help* (?) button, and a control-menu (right-click the title bar to open it). It may also have tabs, which are different parts of a dialog box.

USING DIALOG BOX OPTIONS

To access Windows on-line help in using dialog box options,

1 **Click the *Start* button**   [**Ctrl** + **Esc**]

2 **Click *Help***

3 **Click the *Index* tab**

4 **Type   DIALOG BOXES, USING   or click it in the list box**

5 **Click the *Display* button**

6 **Click *The Basics* in the *Topics Found* dialog box**

7 **Click the *Display* button**

8 **Click the *Using dialog boxes* button**

Your Windows Help window should appear as in Figure SSA-1. Dialog boxes may have one or more these components. To learn how to operate them, simply click the desired component on the screen. When you are done,

9 **Click the *Close* button of the window**

FIGURE SSA-1   ■   DIALOG BOX OPTIONS

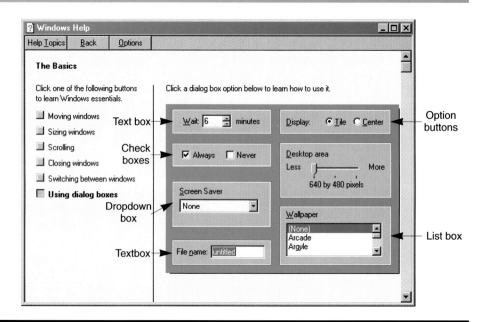

PARTS OF A DIALOG BOX

Most dialog parts are identified in Figure SSA-1. These and other dialog box components are described next.

CHECK BOX.   A square box identified by its title to the right. A "✔" or "X" indicates that the option has been selected. More than one check box can be selected at a time.

COMMAND BUTTON.   A Command button directly invokes the item it represents when clicked.

DROP-DOWN BOX.   A drop-down box initially appears as a single line box with a ▼ button on its right. Clicking the ▼ button opens a drop-down list. Some drop-down boxes allow text entry for selecting.

GROUP BOX.   A group box is an area of a dialog box containing related option buttons or check boxes.

INFORMATION BOX.   An information box generally displays information about a current dialog box selection.

LIST BOX.   A box that lists available options in alphabetical order.

OPTION BUTTON.   A small circle with its title to the right. A • (dot) indicates that the option is selected. Only one option can be selected in a group.

TAB.   Identifies a section of a dialog box. Clicking a tab displays that section's format.

TEXT BOX.   A text box allows text entry to communicate with the computer.

SUMMARY OF EXCEL FEATURES

Following is a chart that summarizes some of Excel's most popular features. When invoking menu commands by mouse, simply click the item(s) (or point to the item if it opens a submenu). With the keyboard, press the Alt key and the underlined letter of the menu bar item. Otherwise perform the actions as indicated.

FEATURE	COMMANDS	*SHORTCUT* KEYS
Aligning data		
Range	Select the range, *Format, Cells, Alignment* tab, select the desired option(s) (or alignment toolbar buttons, *OK*)	Ctrl + 1, A, Alt + underlined letter of desired option(s), ↵ *(continued)*

FEATURE	COMMANDS	SHORTCUT KEYS
Aligning data		
Default	*Format, Style, Modify, Alignment* tab, select the desired option(s), *OK, OK*	
Center across columns	Select the range, *Center Across Columns* toolbar button.	
Bold	*Bold* toolbar button	Ctrl + B
Border lines	*Format, Cells, Borders* tab, select desired options, *OK*	Ctrl + 1, B, select desired options, ↵
Canceling		
Pull-down menu (menu bar)	Click outside of menu	Alt once or Esc twice
Back one menu level	Click other menu item	Esc
Undo last command	*Edit, Undo*	Ctrl + Z
Change directories		
Default	*Tools, Options, General* tab, type the identity of the new directory (e.g., A:\), *OK*	
Current session	*File, Open or Save As,* ▼ button of the *Look in* or *Save in* box, select desired drive/directory *Close* button	Ctrl + O or Alt + F, A, Alt + I, select drive/ directory, Alt + F4
Charts		
Create on current sheet	Select the range to be charted, *Insert, Chart, On This* Sheet, move *chart pointer* to desired position of top left corner of chart, click for standard size chart or drag to create a custom size chart	
Create on a new sheet	Select the range to be charted, *Insert, Chart, As a New Sheet*	
Change chart type	Click, double-click chart for edit mode, *Format, Chart Type,* select the desired chart type, *OK*	
Chart options: headings, legends or data labels, turn grid lines on or off, or change the chart's name	Click, double-click chart for edit mode, *Insert or Format*	
Clear (erase)	*Select the desired range and*	
All	*Edit, Clear, All*	
Cell styles	*Edit, Clear, Format*	
Cell contents (w/o styles)	*Edit, Clear, Contents*	
Cell notes	*Edit, Clear, Notes*	

(continued)

FEATURE	COMMANDS	*SHORTCUT* KEYS
Column width		
Range	Select the range, *Format, Column, Width,* type in desired width, *OK* (or drag the border between column letter)	
Default	Select the range, *Format, Column, Standard Width,* type in desired width, *OK*	
AutoFit selection	Select the range, *Format, Column, AutoFit Selection*	
Copy a selection		
Copy to Clipboard	*Edit, Copy*	Ctrl + C
Paste to new location	*Edit, Paste*	Ctrl + V
Delete		
Rows	*Edit, Delete Entire Row*	
Columns	*Edit, Delete Entire Column*	
Sheets	*Edit, Delete Sheet*	
Edit cell data	Double-click cell	F2
Embedding a selection (object)	Select source range, *Edit, Copy,* move to destination, *Edit, Paste Special, Paste, OK*	
Enter data into a cell	Click desired cell, type data, click confirm (✓) button to accept or cancel (x) button to cancel	Arrow keys to desired cell, type data, press ↵ to accept or press Esc to cancel
Exit Excel		
By menu bar	*File, Exit*	
By title bar	*Close* button	Alt + F4
By *Excel* program icon	Double-click the *Excel* program icon	
By control-menu	Right-click title bar, *Close*	Alt + Spacebar
Fonts		
Range	Select the range, *Format, Cells, Font* tab, select desired option(s), *OK*	Select the range, Ctrl + 1, F, Alt + underlined letter of each desired option, ↵
Default	*Format, Style, Modify, Font* tab, select the desired option(s), *OK, OK*	
Format	*Format, Style, Modify,* desired tab, select the desired option(s), *OK, OK*	
Freezing panes		
Row titles	Move one row below the row to be frozen, *Window, Freeze Pane*	
		(continued)

FEATURE	COMMANDS	*SHORTCUT* KEYS
Freezing panes		
Column titles	Move one column to the right of column to be frozen, *Window, Freeze Pane*	
Both	Move one row below and one column to the right of the row and columns to be frozen, *Window, Freeze Pane*	
Unfreeze	*Window, UnFreeze*	
Function wizard	*Insert, Function*	Shift + F3
Italic	*Italic* toolbar button	Ctrl + I
Help		
Excel	*Help, Microsoft Excel Help Topics*	F1
Dialog box	? button on right end of title bar	F1
Hide/Unhide		
Hide columns	Select the range, *Format, Column, Hide*	
Unhide columns	Select the range, *Format, Column, Unhide*	
Hide sheets	Select the Sheets, *Format, Sheet, Hide*	
Unhide sheets	Select the Sheets, *Format, Sheet, Unhide*	
Insert		
Rows	*Insert, Rows*	
Columns	*Insert, Columns*	
Worksheet	*Insert, Worksheet*	
Launch Excel	In Windows, *Start* button, *Program, Microsoft Excel (or Microsoft Office, Microsoft Excel)*	
Link a selection (object) between sheets or workbooks or with other programs	Select source range, *Edit, Copy,* move to destination , *Edit, Paste Special, Paste Link, OK*	
Move a selection		
Move to Clipboard	*Edit, Cut*	Ctrl + X
Paste to new location	*Edit, Paste*	Ctrl + V
Open file(s)	*File, Open,* type filename or select it from the list, *Open* button	Ctrl + O, type filename, ↵
Page break	*Insert, Page Break*	
Password	*File, Save As,* type filename, *Options,* type password, *OK,* type password again, *OK, Save*	F12, type filename, Alt + O, type password, ↵, type password again, ↵, ↵ *(continued)*

FEATURE	COMMANDS	SHORTCUT KEYS
Print		
Preview	*File, Preview*	
To paper	*File, Print,* select *Print what options, Page Range options,* and *Copies Options, OK*	Ctrl + P, select *Print what options, Page Range options,* and *Copies Options,* ↵
Print options		
Orientation, scaling, paper size, quality, and page numbering	*File, Page Setup, Page* tab, select desired options, *OK*	
Set page margin	*File, Page Setup, Margins* tab, select desired options, *OK*	
Header/footer	*File, Page Setup, Header/Footer* tab, select desired options, *OK*	
Print area, print titles (rows and columns), grid lines, notes, draft quality, black and white, row and column headings, and page order	*File, Page Setup, Sheet,* select desired options, *OK*	
Protection (lock)		
Protect sheet or workbook	*Tools, Protection, Protect Sheet,* or *Protect Workbook,* if desired type password, *OK*	
Unprotect sheet or Workbook	*Tools, Protection, Unprotect Sheet,* or *Unprotect Workbook*	
Unprotect ranges within a protected sheet or workbook	Before turning on protection, select the unprotected (unlocked), *Format, Cells, Protection* tab, *Locked, OK*	
Range		
Select a single range	Drag over desired cells or click the first cell, press and hold Shift while clicking the last cell	Shift + arrow key
Select multiple ranges	Select the first range, press and hold Ctrl while selecting each additional range	
Select all	*Edit, Select All*	Ctrl + A
Select a column	Click its column letter	
Select a row	Click its row number	
Unselect	Click the range, or any cell outside the range	Any arrow key
Repeat	Type character, ↵, move back to cell, *Format, Cells, Alignment tab, Fill, OK*	

(continued)

FEATURE	COMMANDS	*SHORTCUT* KEYS
Save		
Workbook	*File, Save* or *Save As*	Ctrl + S or F12
Workspace	*File, Save Workspace*	
Spell check	*Tools, Spelling*	F7
Select		
Cells	See "Range"	
Chart or graphic object	Click the item	
Sheets		
Insert new	*Insert, Worksheet*	
Delete	*Edit, Delete Sheet*	
Switch to	Click *Sheet* tab or use *Tab Scroll* buttons	Ctrl + Pg Up or Ctrl + Pg Dn
Shortcut menu	Right-click the item	
Split view		
On	*Window, Split*	
Off	*Window, UnSplit*	
Switch between split panes	Click desired pane	F6
Transposing data	Select the range to be transposed, *Edit, Copy,* move to first cell to display transposed cells, *Edit, Paste Special, Transpose, OK*	
Underline	*Underline* toolbar button	Ctrl + U
Undo	*Edit, Undo*	Ctrl + Z

DATABASE COMMANDS

Excel provides a variety of database features that can be invoked on spreadsheet data. Worksheet data must first be organized into rows and columns called a database table. Each worksheet row should form a record—a collection of related fields—and each column should contain one field—a category of data common to each record. The database table is the source in a database query operation. A query is a question asked of a database. The following is a summary of some of the more popular Excel database features.

DISTRIBUTING DATA

To set up a frequency distribution that tallies the number of data values in a range that fall into each of several contiguous intervals (if data are already in a range, skip Step 1),

1 Place the data values to be tallied into a range

2 Set up a bin range (column), leaving the column to the right of the bin range empty

3 Select the frequency distribution results range (be sure to include one cell more than the corresponding bin numbers)

4 Type   =FREQUENCY (data array range, bin array range   (but *DO NOT* press   Enter   )

5 Press   Ctrl   +   Shift   + ↵ to copy the frequency function to each cell in the distribution results range as an absolute formula, which is encased in brackets ({ })

6 Press an arrow key to deselect

FILTERING RECORDS

Before you can filter records that meet a specified condition, you need to organize your data into a database table. (See Figure SS3-13 in Chapter 3).

To filter records from a database table,

1 Select the database table

2 Click *Data, Filter, AutoFilter*

3 Use ▼ button of each field's title to set filter criteria

To unfilter records,

4 Click *Data, Filter, Show All*

MICROSOFT ACCESS

Excel's *Data* menu (menu bar) offers three commands to share worksheet data directly with Microsoft Access, a database program. (Access, like Excel, is also part of the Microsoft Office suite.)

To convert a worksheet database table to an Access table,

1 Select the database table

2 Click *Data, Convert to Access*

3 Follow the Excel Import wizard

To create an Access form from a worksheet database table,

1 Select the database table

2 Click *Data, Access Form*

To create or refresh an Access report from a worksheet database table,

1 Select the database table

2 Click *Data, Access Report*

QUERY TABLES

A query table can be created by extracting records from a database table. To create a complex criteria range,

1 In an area outside of the database table, type desired criteria labels (in the same row as each other) that identically correspond to those column labels (titles) that you want to analyze from the database table. For example, to analyze the database column labeled TEST 1, you must use that same label as a criteria label in the criteria range.

2 Use one of the following guidelines to enter comparison criteria in the criteria range:

   - To find records that meet all criteria in a row, type the criteria in the same row in cells next to each other.
   - To find records that meet more than one criterion for the same column, use the same column label in a new column.
   - To find records that meet all criteria in the first row *or* the second row, type the criteria in different rows.

3 Select the database table range

4 Click *Data, Filter, Advanced Filter* for its dialog box

5 Click *Copy to Another Location* option button

6 Click the *Criteria Range* text box

7 Type in the *Criteria* range

8 Press `Tab` and type in the *Copy* to range

9 Click *OK*   [↵]

To just filter the database table instead of creating a new table, skip Steps 5 and 8 above.

SORTING DATA

Excel sorts data according to the "numbers first" collating sequence. This sequence is described by the following ordering:

1. **Blank cells**

2. **Data starting with numbers (in numerical order)**

3. **Data starting with letters (in alphabetical order)**

4. **Data starting with other characters**

5. **Numbers**

    To sort a range,

    1 **Select the range of data to be sorted**

    2 **Click *Data, Sort* for its dialog box**

    3 **Use the *Sort By* drop-down box to set the first sorting key**

    4 **Select the sorting order by either clicking the *Ascending* or *Descending* option button**

    5 **If desired, use the *Then By* and *Then By* drop-down boxes to set second and third sorting keys**

    6 **If Step 5 is performed, select the desired sorting order for each key (ascending or descending)**

    7 **Click *OK* to sort**

TABLE LOOKUPS

To look up an entry in a specified column (vertical lookup) or row (horizontal lookup) in a table that corresponds to a value in a specific cell,

1 **Move the cell pointer to the cell that will contain the result of the lookup**

2 **Click *Insert, Function* for the *Function Wizard* dialog box**   [**Shift** + **F3**]

3 **Click *Lookup & Reference* in the *Function Category* list box**

4 **Use the scroll bar of the *Function Name* list box to locate *VLOOKUP* or *HLOOKUP*, depending on whether you wish to do a vertical or horizontal lookup, and click it**

5 **Click *Next>* to move to Step 2 of the dialog box**   [↵]

6 **Enter the cell address of the data on which the search is to be based in the *lookup_value* text box and press Tab**

7 **Enter the range corresponding to the table to be searched in the *table_array* text box and press Tab**

8 Type the offset, which is the number of columns (or rows) between the lookup column (or row) and the first table column (or row) in the *col_index_num* (or *row_index_num*) text box and press ↵

FUNCTIONS

Microsoft Excel offers more than 200 functions. To view a complete alphabetical on-line list and description of functions,

1 Click *Insert, Function* for the *Function Wizard* dialog box   [**Shift** + **F3**]

2 Click *All* in the *Function Category* list box

3 Locate the desired function in the *Function Name* list box (use the scroll bar if necessary)

4 Click the desired function in the *Function Name* list box

Note that a description of the currently selected function appears below the *Function Category* list box.

To use a selected function,

5 Click *Next>* for Step 2   [↵]

6 Enter the arguments of the function

Note: To move from one text box to another, use **Tab** .

7 Click *Finish*   [↵]

To exit the Function wizard prior to completing an entry,

8 Click *Cancel*   [**Esc**]

Following is a list of the primary functions. If you need more advanced functions, use the Function wizard to help you locate and use them. (Remember to type an [=] sign before entering a function.)

- **ABS(x)**
  Calculates the absolute (positive) value of the value *x*.
- **ACOS(x)**
  Calculates the arc cosine of the angle x, where x is expressed in radians.
- **ADDRESS (row_num, column_num, abs_num, a1, sheet_text)**
  Returns a cell reference as text to a single cell in a worksheet.
- **AND (logical1, logical2,...)**

Returns TRUE if all its arguments are true.

■ **AREAS (range)**

Returns the number of areas in a range.

■ **ASIN(x)**

Calculates the arc sine of the angle x, where x is expressed in radians.

■ **ATAN(x)**

Calculates the arc tangent of the angle x, where x is expressed in radians.

■ **ATAN2(x,y)**

Calculates the radian angle whose tangent is y/x, where y and x are any values.

■ **AVERAGE (range)**

Averages values in a range.

■ **CEILING (x, significance)**

Calculates a number rounded to the nearest integer or the nearest multiple of significance.

■ **CELL(attribute,range)**

Returns information about a specified attribute for the first cell in a range. Some of the attributes for which information is provided are formatting, location, or contents.

■ **CHAR(x)**

Returns the character that corresponds to x (where x is between 1 and 255).

■ **CHOOSE(index_num, value1, value2...)**

Uses the offset (index_num) value to return the contents of one of the cells in the argument list. For instance, an offset of zero would return the contents of the first cell in the list.

■ **CLEAN(text)**

Removes nonprintable characters from text.

■ **CODE(text)**

Displays the number code that corresponds to the first character in a text string.

■ **COLUMN (cell_reference)**

Counts the column number of a cell reference.

■ **COLUMNS(range)**

Counts the number of columns in a range.

■ **COS(x)**

Calculates the cosine of the angle x, where x is expressed in radians.

■ **COUNT (value1,value2,...)**

Counts the numbers that are in the list of arguments.

■ **COUNTA(value1,value2,...)**

Counts the number of nonblank cells in a range.

■ **COUNTBLANK (range)**

Counts the number of blank cells in a range.

■ **DATE(yy,mm,dd)**

Calculates the date number for a given year/month/day combination.

- **DATEVALUE(date string)**

Converts a date string (such as "5–Jan-95") into an equivalent date number.

- **DAVERAGE(database_range,field_offset,criteria_range)**

Averages the values in a field of the database range that meet the criteria specified in the criteria range.

- **DAY(date_number)**

Calculates a serial number that corresponds to the day in the date number.

- **DCOUNT (database_range,field, criteria_range)**

Counts the number of cells containing numbers from a specified database and criteria.

- **DCOUNTA(database_range,field_offset,criteria_range)**

Counts the number of nonblank cells in a field of the input range that meet the criteria specified in the criteria range.

- **DDB(initial cost,salvage value,useful life,period,factor)**

Calculates the double-declining balance depreciation of an asset for one period, based on the asset's initial cost, salvage value, and useful life.

- **DMAX(database_range,field_offset,criteria_range)**

Finds the largest value in a field of the database range that meets the criteria specified in the criteria range.

- **DMIN(database_range,field_offset,criteria_range)**

Finds the smallest value in a field of the database range that meets the criteria specified in the criteria range.

- **DOLLAR(x, decimal)**

Converts a number to text, using the currency format.

- **DSTDEVP(database_range,field_offset,criteria_range)**

Finds the population standard deviation of the values of a field in the database range that meets the criteria range.

- **DSUM(database_range,field_offset,criteria_range)**

Finds the sum of the values of a field in the database range that meets the criteria specified in the criteria range.

- **DVAR(database_range,field_offset,criteria_range)**

Finds the population variance of the values of a field in the database range that meets the criteria specified in the criteria range.

- **EVEN(x)**

Rounds a number up to the nearest even integer.

- **EXACT(text_string1,text_string2)**

Check to see that two text-string values are equivalent.

- **EXP(x)**

Calculates the number e raised to the power x.

- **FALSE( )**

Returns the value FALSE.

- **FIND(find_textstring,within_targettextstring,start number)**

Locates the starting position of the find text string within the target text string. The start number is the first character of the search.

- **FREQUENCY (data_array, bin_array)**

  Returns a frequency distribution as a vertical display.

- **FV(rate, nperiod, payment, PV, type)**

  Calculates the future value of a series of equal payments made over a number of periods at a specified periodic interest rate.

- **HLOOKUP(lookup_value,table_array,row_index_num...)**

  Uses the lookup value x to look across the first row in the range (array) to find the value closest to but not larger than x; then it goes down that column the number of offset rows specified and selects the contents of the cell there.

- **HOUR(time_number)**

  Calculates the integer that corresponds to the hour in a time number.

- **IF(condition,result_if_true,result_if_false)**

  Returns one result if a condition is true, another if a condition is false.

- **INDEX(...)**

  Finds the value in the cell located at the specific row offset and column offset of the first cell in the range.

- **INT(x)**

  Truncates the value x to a whole number.

- **IRR(values, guess)**

  Calculates the internal rate of return of cash flows in a range. The estimate represents your initial guess of this rate.

- **ISERR(x)**

  A TRUE is returned if the value is any error value except #N/A.

- **ISNA(x)**

  Checks if an #N/A condition is present. If it is, a TRUE is returned.

- **ISNUMBER(x)**

  Tests whether a cell reference contains a number. Returns TRUE if it is a number.

- **LEFT(text_string,n)**

  Returns the first n characters of the text string.

- **LEN(text_string)**

  Counts the number of characters in a string.

- **LN(x)**

  Calculates the natural (base e) logarithm of the value x.

- **LOG(x)**

  Calculates the common (base 10) logarithm of the value x.

- **LOWER(text_string)**

  Converts all characters in a text string to lowercase characters.

- **MAX(number1,number2,...)**

  Finds the highest value in a range.

■ **MID(text_string,start_number,n)**

Extracts *n* contiguous characters from a text string, beginning at the start number. The start number corresponds to the first letter of the string.

■ **MIN(number1,number2,...)**

Finds the lowest value in a range.

■ **MINUTE(time_number)**

Calculates the integer that corresponds to the minute in a time number.

■ **MOD(number,divisor)**

Returns the remainder (modulus) that is produced when a number is divided by a divisor.

■ **MONTH(serial_number)**

Calculates the serial number that corresponds to a month.

■ **N(range)**

Returns the value in the first cell of a range if the cell contains a text number.

■ **NA( )**

Returns the error value #N/A.

■ **NOW( )**

Returns a number that corresponds to the current time according to your computer's clock.

■ **NPV(rate,value1,value2,...)**

Calculates the net present value of the cash flows in a range, at a specified periodic interest rate.

■ **PI**

Returns the value of [1] (3.14159. . .).

■ **PMT(rate,nper,pu,fv,type)**

Calculates the payment made in each of a specified number of periods that, at a specified periodic interest rate, is equivalent to a present value (such as a loan).

■ **PROPER(text_string)**

Converts the first letter in each word of a text string to uppercase and converts the other letters to lowercase.

■ **PV(rate,nper,pmt,fv,type)**

Calculates the present value of a series of equal payments, at a specified periodic interest rate, over a specified number of periods.

■ **RAND( )**

Generates a random value between 0 and 1.

■ **RATE(nper,pmt,pv,fv,type,guess)**

Calculates the periodic interest rate necessary for a present value to accrue to a future value, within a specified number of periods.

■ **REPLACE(old_text_string,start_num,num_chars,new_text_string)**

Replaces characters in the old text string with characters from the new string. The start number and length determine where replacement starts in the original text string and how many characters are to be replaced. The start number corresponds to the first letter in the original text string.

- **RIGHT(text_string,n)**

  Returns the last *n* characters of the text string.

- **ROUND(x,num_digits)**

  Rounds a value *x* to a specified number of decimal places.

- **ROWS(range)**

  Counts the number of rows in a range.

- **SECOND(time_number)**

  Calculates the serial number that corresponds to the second in a time number.

- **SIN(x)**

  Calculates the sine of the angle *x,* where *x* is expressed in radians.

- **SLN(initial_cost,salvage_value,useful_life)**

  Calculates the straight-line depreciation of an asset for each period, based on the asset's initial cost, salvage value, and useful life.

- **SQRT(x)**

  Calculates the square root of the value *x.*

- **STDEVP(range)**

  Calculates the population standard deviation of values in a range.

- **SUM(range)**

  Sums the values in a range.

- **SYD(initial_cost,salvage_value,useful_life,period)**

  Calculates the sum-of-the-year's-digits depreciation of an asset for one period, based on the asset's initial cost, salvage value, and useful life.

- **T(value)**

  Converts its argument to text.

- **TAN(x)**

  Calculates the tangent of the angle *x,* where *x* is expressed in radians.

- **TIME(hr,min,sec)**

  Calculates the time number for an hour/minute/second combination.

- **TIMEVALUE(time_string)**

  Converts a time string (such as "14:30:58") into an equivalent time number.

- **TRIM(text_string)**

  Removes leading, consecutive, and trailing blanks from a text string.

- **TRUE( )**

  Returns the value TRUE.

- **UPPER(string)**

  Converts all characters in a string to uppercase characters.

- **VALUE(text_string)**

  Converts a string that looks like a number into a value. For example, the text string 55.3 becomes the value 55.3.

- **VAR(range)**

  Calculates the population variance of values in a range.

- **VLOOKUP(lookup_value,table_array,col_index_num,...)**

  Uses the lookup value *x* to look down the first column in the range (array) to find the value closest to but not larger than *x;* then it goes across that row the number of offset columns specified and selects the contents of the cell there.

- **YEAR(date_number)**

  Calculates the year from a date number.

MICROSOFT EXCEL'S MENU SYSTEM

Microsoft Excel's menu bar provides a menu system that allows you to access its features by mouse or keyboard. Figure SSA-2 provides an overview of each menu bar

FIGURE SSA-2 ■ EXCEL'S MENU SYSTEM

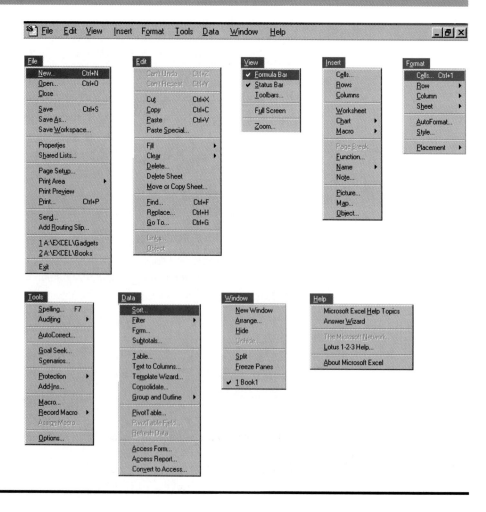

item's pull-down menu. To see a description of a pull-down menu item in the status bar, first open the related pull-down menu by clicking its menu bar item or pressing the Alt key and the underlined letter of the item. Next, point (but do not click) or use the arrow keys to move the selection highlight to the desired menu item without pressing the Enter key.

MACRO COMMANDS

Macros are short programs consisting of mouse actions, keystrokes, and special functions called *macro commands.* Excel uses Visual Basic, a programming language, for its macros. You can create macros by using the macro recorder (*Tools, Record Macro, Record New Macro*) or you can write them directly into a Visual Basic module. A *module* is a sheet that Excel uses to store macro command statements. When on, the macro recorder automatically types the correct Visual Basic macro statement as you perform an action by mouse or keyboard on a module sheet.

MACROS—CREATING AND ASSIGNING

Macros are stored mouse and keystroke sequences that you can invoke by holding down the Ctrl or Ctrl + Shift keys while pressing another (letter) key that, in effect, is the name of the macro. Macros can also be assigned to and invoked from the *Tools* menu or a macro button.

As mentioned earlier, macros can be created by using Excel's Macro Recording feature or written from scratch.

To create a macro using Excel's Recording feature,

1 Click *Tools, Record Macro, Record* for the *Record New Macro* dialog box

2 Type a desired MACRO NAME in the *Macro Name* text box and press

Note that you can use up to 256 characters for a macro name; however, it cannot have any blank spaces separating words.

3 Type a *description* of the macro in the *Description* text box

4 Click *OK* to turn on the macro recorder   [↵]

Excel uses **Visual Basic,** a programming language, for macro commands. When the macro recorder is turned on, Excel adds a new sheet called the *module sheet* to store your actions in Visual Basic code. Although not currently visible, this sheet is added behind Sheet 16 in the workbook.

5 Perform desired mouse/keyboard actions

6 Click the *Stop Macro* toolbar button or click *Tools,* point to *Record Macro,* and then click *Stop Recording* to turn off the macro recorder

MACROS—ASSIGNING

A macro can be run using the *Macro* dialog box (*Tools* menu), shortcut keys, the *Tools* menu, or a button. To run a macro using the latter three methods requires first assigning the macro commands to one of these items.

ASSIGNING TO *SHORTCUT* KEYS.   A macro can be assigned to shortcut keys either during its recording or afterward by using the *Macro Options* dialog box. You can invoke this dialog box from the *Record New Macro* dialog box when recording a macro or from the *Macro* dialog box after a macro has been recorded. These macros will be referred to as *one-letter macros*. They generally involve the use of the Ctrl or Ctrl + Shift keys. Excel automatically selects when assigning a macro to shortcut keys. This is to prevent conflict with previously programmed Excel or user-defined short-cut keys.

1 Click *Tools, Macro* for its dialog box

2 Click MACRO NAME to be assigned

3 Click the *Options* button for the *Macro Options* dialog box

4 Click the *Shortcut Key* check box

5 Click the text box next to *Ctrl+*

6 Type the *desired one-letter* character for the macro

7 Click *OK, Close*

ASSIGNING TO THE *TOOLS* MENU.   The procedures to assign a macro to the *Tools* menu is similar to assigning it to a shortcut key. Again, you can assign a macro to the menu either during its recording or after by using the *Macro Options* dialog box.

1 Click *Tools, Macro* for its dialog box

2 Click MACRO NAME to be assigned

3 Click the *Options* button for the *Macro Options* dialog box

4 Click the *Menu Item on Tools Menu* check box

5 Click the *Menu Item on Tools Menu* text box

6 Type a menu NAME for the macro

7 Click *OK, Close*

ASSIGNING TO A BUTTON.   To assign a macro to a button on the current worksheet, try the following exercise:

1 Click *View, Toolbars*

2 Click the *Drawing* check box, *OK*

The Drawing toolbar should now appear in your Excel window. This toolbar can be used to create a button or other objects (pictures or symbols) in your worksheet.

3 Click the *Create Button* toolbar button

Note that the mouse pointer changes to a "+."

4 Point to the top-left corner of any desired location for the position of the macro button

Note that the mouse pointer changes to a "+."

5 Drag the mouse pointer down to create and size the button and then release

A button briefly appears and then the *Assign macro* dialog box appears.

6 Click MACRO NAME to be assigned and then *OK*

7 Point before the "B" in *Button* on the button and then drag across to select it

8 Press **Delete** to remove it

9 Type a desired BUTTON NAME

At this point, you can move to any cell not occupied by the button to turn off the button edit mode.

10 Move to a different cell to exit the button edit mode

MACROS—RUNNING

Once macros have been created, they are available for use. They can be run using the *Macro* dialog box, a shortcut key, the *Tools* menu or macro button. The latter three options first require the macro to be assigned to them.

To run a macro using the *Macro* dialog box,

1 Click *Tools, Macro* for its dialog box

2 Click the desired macro   [**Tab, arrow keys to select desired macro**]

The *Macro* dialog box lists all macros created and saved with a workbook. It also displays a description of the macro as entered when created.

3 Click *Run* to run the macro   [↵]

To invoke a one-letter macro,

1 Hold down **Ctrl** (or **Ctrl** + **Shift**) and then press the letter that corresponds to the name of the macro

To run the macro using the *Tools* menu,

1 Click *Tools*

2 Click the desired **MACRO NAME**

To invoke a macro from a button,

1 Click the desired button

WRITING A MACRO

Writing a macro from scratch involves the use of Visual Basic codes. Although these codes are complicated, Excel provides an on-line help with example codes for many common commands. These codes can be copied from the Help window into a module sheet. To insert a module sheet (or switch to an existing one) and then copy a Visual Basic macro code, do the following: (Note: The procedures below can also be used for editing a macro.)

1 Click *Insert, Macro, Module* for a new module sheet or click an existing module sheet tab.

2 Click *Help, Content, Programming with Visual Basic*

3 Click *Search* for its dialog box

4 Use the scroll bar to locate the desired code, click it, *Show Topics*

5 Click the desired topic in *Select a Topic,* choose the *Go To* list box, and click *Go To*

6 Click *Example* for the Visual Basic Reference Example window

7 Click the *Copy* button for the *Copy* dialog box

8 Select the code and other information to copy

9 Click the *Copy* button to copy to the Clipboard   [**Ctrl** + **C**]

At this point, you can switch to the module sheet and paste the codes and then switch back to the on-line help and copy another code or exit help. To switch to the module sheet and paste without closing help,

10 Click the module sheet and move the insertion point to the desired paste location

11 Click *Edit, Paste*   [**Ctrl** + **V**]

12 Press Alt + Tab to switch to Help windows not needed and close them (for example, the windows that relate to the last code copied)

13 Switch to the Search window.

14 Repeat Steps 4 through 13 as desired

15 Close the Help windows

16 Resave the workbook with the new macro commands

17 Run the macro to see it operate

THE STEP FEATURE

Macros work so quickly that it is often difficult to locate errors when a macro does not work as expected. The Step feature helps locate errors by allowing a macro to be run one instruction at a time. This feature can be used in conjunction with the steps in the "Writing a Macro" section to edit a macro.

1 Click *View, Toolbars, Visual Basic, OK* for its toolbar

2 Click *Tools, Macro*

3 Click the macro to be edited

4 Click the *Step* button to turn on the step mode

When using the keyboard only, the Visual Basic toolbar will not appear on your screen. The macro's current command sequence appears in a rectangular box. Although you can invoke the Step Into and Step Over commands from the *Run* menu, it is much easier to use toolbar buttons or shortcut keys. The Step Into command invokes the next macro command statement. The Step Over command skips the next command statement.

5 Click the *Step Into* toolbar button   [F8]

Each time you invoke the Step Into command, the program performs the next macro command in the sequence. You can then examine the effect of each command and locate the error. See your Excel manual for further information regarding Visual Basic codes. Keep repeating Step 5 to continue the process, and then make editing changes or do the following to end it.

6 Click *Run, End*

7 If needed, turn off the Visual Basic toolbar (click its *Close* button)

8 Resave the workbook

> **Note:** To go to and edit a macro's module sheet quickly, select *Edit* in the *Macro* dialog box. Note that the *Run* menu bar item also appears when you display a module sheet.

TOOLBARS

Toolbar buttons provide quick access to Excel's commands by mouse. Toolbar buttons are grouped in sets and appear below the edit line of the Excel window.

To receive a description of a toolbar's function in the status bar,

1 **Point to the desired toolbar button**

To invoke a command using a toolbar button,

1 **Point to the desired toolbar button**

2 **Click the toolbar button**

To turn on/off toolbar button sets,

1 **Click *View, Toolbars***

2 **Click the desired toolbar's check box**

3 **Click *OK***

To change the toolbar button's size,

1 **Click *View, Toolbars* for its dialog box**

2 **Click the *Large Buttons* check box**

3 **Click *OK***

To customize a toolbar,

1 **Click *View, Toolbars, Customize* for its dialog box**

2 **Follow the directions of the dialog box to make your desired changes**

3 **Click *Close***

4 **Click *OK***

FIGURE SSA-3 ■ EXCEL TOOLBARS

Standard Toolbar

1 2 3 4 5 6 7 8 9 10 11 12 13 14 15 16 17 18 19 20 21* 22

Format Toolbar

23 24 25 26 27 28 29 30 31 32 33 34 35 36 37 38 39

40 41 42 43 44 45 46 47

53 54 55 56 57 58 59 60 61 62 63 64

48 49 50 51 52

65 66 67 68 69 70 71 72 73

Tip Wizard Toolbar

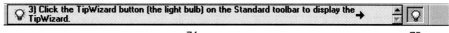

74 75

76 77

94 95 96 97 98 99 100 101

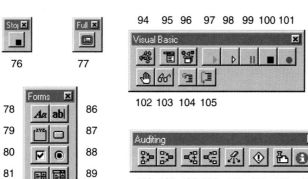

78 86
79 87
80 88
81 89
82 90
83 91
84 92
85 93

102 103 104 105

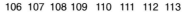

106 107 108 109 110 111 112 113

114 115 116 117 118 119

120 121 122 123 124 125 126

As in Figure SS1-3, Excel opens with Standard and Format toolbars below its menu bar. Some toolbars automatically appear when you invoke a related command. For example, the Chart toolbar appears when you invoke the Chart command or place an existing chart in edit mode.

Excel comes with 13 preset toolbars, which are displayed in Figure SSA-3. These toolbars can be turned on or off using the toolbars command of the *View* menu. You can also turn a toolbar on or off using its *Shortcut* menu.

A toolbar can be moved by dragging its background or title bar. It can also be resized when not attached to the Excel window. Toolbars in this state are called *floating* toolbars and they have their own title bars and control boxes. To resize a floating toolbar, drag one of its walls or corners.

Existing toolbars can also be customized and new toolbars can be created. Use Excel's on-line help to guide you through these operations.

The toolbar button numbers in the following chart correspond to Figure SSA-3.

Toolbar Button #	Description
	Standard Toolbar
1	Opens a new workbook
2	Opens a saved workbook
3	Saves the current workbook
4	Prints the current sheet, selection, or entire workbook
5	Print Previews the current sheet
6	Starts the Spell Checker
7	Cuts a selection to the Windows Clipboard
8	Copies a selection to the Windows Clipboard
9	Pastes a selection from the Windows Clipboard
10	Starts the Format Painter
11	Undoes the last action
12	Repeats the last action
13	Sums values in a range or above the cell pointer
14	Starts the Function wizard
15	Sorts a range in ascending order
16	Sorts a range in descending order
17	Starts the Chart wizard
18	Starts the Mapping feature
19	Turns the Drawing toolbar on or off
20	Zooms the Workbook view
21	Turns the Tip wizard toolbar on or off
22	Offers context-sensitive help
	Format Toolbar
23	Changes the font
24	Changes the font size
25	Turns the boldface feature on and off
26	Turns the italicize feature on and off

Toolbar Button #	Description
27	Turns the underline feature on and off
28	Left-aligns data in a cell
29	Center-aligns data in a cell
30	Right-aligns data in a cell
31	Center-aligns data across columns
32	Formats numbers (and formula results) in the accounting $-style format
33	Formats numbers (and formula results) in the percentage-style format
34	Formats numbers (and formula results) in the accounting no $-style format
35	Increases decimal place by one
36	Decreases decimal place by one
37	Places border(s) in cell or a range
38	Changes cell background color
39	Changes font color
	Query and Pivot Toolbar
40	Starts the Pivot Table wizard
41	Edits the Pivot Table field
42	Ungroups
43	Groups
44	Hides detail
45	Shows detail
46	Shows pages
47	Refreshes data
	Chart Toolbar
48	Changes chart type
49	Sets to default chart type
50	Offers Chart wizard
51	Turns horizontal grid lines on or off
52	Edits legends
	Drawing Toolbar
53	Draws a line
54	Draws a rectangular shape
55	Draws an ellipse
56	Draws an arc
57	Draws a free-form object
58	Creates a text box
59	Draws an arrow
60	Draws free hand
61	Draws a filled rectangle
62	Draws a filled ellipse
63	Draws a filled arc
64	Draws a filled free-form object
65	Creates a button
66	Selects an object

Toolbar Button #	Description
67	Moves selected object to the front
68	Moves selected object to the back
69	Groups objects
70	Ungroups objects
71	Reshapes objects
72	Creates a drop shadow
73	Creates a pattern
	Tip Wizard Toolbar
74	Offers *Tip Wizard* box
75	Changes tip
	Stop Toolbar
76	Stops macro recording
	Full Toolbar
77	Switches to or from the full-screen display
	Form Toolbar
78	Creates a label
79	Creates a group box
80	Creates a check box
81	Creates a list box
82	Edits a combination list
83	Creates a scroll bar
84	Controls properties
85	Switches toggle grid on or off
86	Edits box
87	Creates a button
88	Creates an option button
89	Creates a drop-down control
90	Edits a combination drop-down control
91	Creates a spinner control
92	Moves to object macro or creates a new one
93	Runs the current dialog
	Visual Basic
94	Inserts a new Visual Basic module sheet
95	Edits menus
96	Shows procedures, objects, methods, and properties
97	Runs a macro
98	Steps through a Macro command
99	Resumes a macro after the Pause command is invoked
100	Stops macro recording or the execution of a running macro
101	Starts the macro recorder
102	Turns the breakpoint on or off at the insertion point
103	Shows the value of a mathematical expression
104	Executes the next macro statement stepping into procedure

Toolbar Button #	Description
105	Executes the next macro statement stepping over procedure
	Auditing
106	Traces and displays cells that the current cell refers to (precedents)
107	Removes one level of tracer precedent arrows
108	Displays formulas that use the current cell (dependents)
109	Removes one level of tracer dependent arrows
110	Removes all tracer arrows
111	Traces and displays cells causing error in the selected cell
112	Creates and attaches a note to the current cell
113	Displays the info window
	Work Group
114	Searches for user-specified files
115	Attaches a routing slip to the current workbook
116	Sends electronic mail
117	Revises a read-only file to include the last update
118	Toggles a workbook from read-only to read-write status
119	Adds, displays, or edits scenarios
	Microsoft Toolbar
120	Starts Microsoft Word
121	Starts Microsoft PowerPoint
122	Starts Microsoft Access
123	Starts Microsoft Fox Pro
124	Starts Microsoft Project
125	Starts Microsoft Schedule+
126	Starts Microsoft Mail

GLOSSARY

Absolute reference. A cell address reference that always refers to the same cell regardless of where it is copied (SS121).

Alignment. The position of data in a cell—either left, right, or centered (SS79).

ASCII (American Standard Code for Information Interchange). One of a few standard formats for transferring data among software programs (SS228).

AutoCalculate. An Excel feature that automatically sums numbers in a range displaying the result in the status bar (SS14).

Automatic recalculation. A spreadsheet program feature that automatically recalculates formulas when values in related cells are changed (SS44).

Cell. The intersection of a column and a row in a spreadsheet (SS14).

Cell address. The column and row coordinates of a cell (SS14).

Cell pointer. A rectangular box the size of one cell used in the worksheet to point to cells, thereby making them active (SS14).

Chart. A pictorial representation of data (SS152).

Circular reference. A condition that occurs in a spreadsheet when a cell formula refers to itself either directly or indirectly (SS123).

Closing. This command (*File* menu) removes a workbook (and its window) from Excel's workspace (SS32).

Column. A vertical group of contiguous single cells extending down the entire length of a spreadsheet.

Column (Bar) chart. A chart that displays numeric data as a set of evenly spaced bars whose relative heights indicate values in the range being graphed (SS152).

Command buttons. A series of pictures or symbols that represents a command. They are mouse shortcuts to access a command. Clicking or double-clicking a command button invokes the command it represents. Many of Excel's command buttons are located on toolbars and are called toolbar buttons (SS13).

Constant values. Data directly entered into a cell. They may be text or numeric values (SS37).

Container file (compound document). The file in a linking or embedding operation that receives a copy of an object or other selection from a source file (SS223).

Copying. Replicating the contents of a cell in another cell, while adjusting relative references to reflect the new position of the cell in the spreadsheet (SS89).

Criteria. Cell entries placed in a criteria range that are used as tests by Excel to find matching records in a database (SS182).

Current cell. The spreadsheet cell that will receive the next data entered or be affected by the next command (SS14).

Cut. This command erases the contents of the source range and places it in the Windows Clipboard for future pasting (SS93).

Database query. A question asked of a database table (SS182).

Data distribution. A frequency distribution, or count, of spreadsheet values that fall within specified numeric intervals (SS180).

Default changes. Settings that Excel uses for the entire worksheet—Excel screens or files (SS100).

Destination range. The new location of a selection (data, chart, table, or object) in a copy or move operation, or the location of a new chart, table, object, or query that results from data in a source range (SS90).

Drop-down box. It first appears as a one-line rectangular box with a ↓ button at its right side. Clicking that button opens the box to a drop-down list. Some drop-down boxes allow you to enter text into them (SS13).

Embedding. This is used to copy objects from one application to another without changing the original (SS223).

Entry area. Located on the right side of the formula bar, the entry area displays the content of the current cell. It can also be used to enter or edit data in the current cell (SS20).

Exporting. The process of saving a file in a format other than the software's default format so that it can be read by other programs (SS227).

Fill handle. A small square box at the bottom right corner of Excel's cell pointer, it can be used to quickly fill a range with a sequence of numbers or other data by mouse (SS175).

Filter. A set of commands that can be used to find and extract records in a database to match a specific criteria (SS182).

Font. A typeface style (SS112).

Format. The way in which Excel displays a number in a cell (SS82).

Formula. A value entry or function in a spreadsheet that directs the program to perform a mathematical operation on numeric constants or values in other cells (SS37).

Formula bar. Located below Excel's toolbars, the formula bar displays information about data entered into a worksheet (SS13).

Freeze panes. Rows or columns that are locked in place at the top or left of the spreadsheet (SS129).

Function. A predetermined formula built into the spreadsheet package (SS37).

IF function. A logical spreadsheet function of the form IF (c,a,b) that returns one of two options (a or b) to the spreadsheet cell based on the truth of the stated condition (c) (SS168).

Importing. The process of retrieving a file that was saved in a format other than the default format for the current program (SS227).

Line chart. A chart that displays numerical data as a set of points along a line (SS163).

Linking. This is an ongoing connection between the program that provides the object (known as the *source*) and the one that receives it (the *destination*). The destination is automatically updated (SS223).

Lookup tables. A logical spreadsheet function of the form VLOOKUP (X, range, column-offset) or HLOOKUP (X, range, row-offset), which uses a two-dimensional table to return values that fall within set intervals (SS170).

Macro. A set of mouse actions, keystrokes, or command instructions for automating an Excel task (SS194).

Mathematical operator. A character used in a formula that tells the program to perform a certain calculation (SS42).

Mixed reference. A cell address reference that is part absolute and part relative (SS122).

Module sheet. A sheet used to record and edit macro commands (SS196).

Name box. Located on the left side of the formula bar, the name box displays information about the current cell address (SS19).

New. This command opens a new blank workbook in Excel's workspace (SS33).

Numeric value. A value entry in a spreadsheet consisting of only numbers, which may be preceded by a negative symbol or include a decimal point (SS37).

Object. A set of data (SS223).

OLE (Object Linking and Embedding). Describes the two options (see *Linking* and *Embedding*) used to transfer data from one application to another (SS223).

Open. A command that can be used to open a file (SS34).

Panes. A split in the worksheet screen, either horizontally or vertically, that allows you to view two parts of a worksheet at the same time (SS131).

Paste. An *Edit* menu command that places the contents of the Windows Clipboard into a desired location (SS91).

Paste link. An Edit menu Paste Special command that pastes a selection (data, chart, table, or object) from the Windows Clipboard into another worksheet or application's document with a link (SS209).

Pie chart. A chart that displays data as parts of a whole circle, where each data "slice" corresponds to a percentage of the total (SS164).

Protection feature. A feature that can be activated on a sheet or workbook. When on, only cells that were specified as unprotected prior to its activation will be available for change (SS221).

Pull-down menus. Menus accessed from the menu bar that contain commands to activate Excel's features (SS13).

Range. A rectangular grouping of one or more cells in a spreadsheet (SS47).

Range name. A name used to identify a range on a worksheet (SS96).

Relative reference. A cell address reference that, when copied, is automatically adjusted to reflect its new position in the worksheet (SS120).

Save. This command will resave a workbook under its original name (SS31).

Save As. A command that is used to save a new file or resave an existing file with confirmation (SS31).

Scroll. A process by which a program automatically repositions the data on the screen to display the current work area (SS14).

Scroll bars. Many appear on the right or bottom of any window or list box whose size does not permit its entire contents to be visible. They provide mouse access to scrolling (moving) through a window or list box's contents (SS16).

Selection handles. Selection markers that appear on the borders of a chart (or its components), table, or object when selected. Drag to resize the item (SS156).

Sheet. A page in a workbook (SS12).

***Shortcut* menus.** Menus that are available by pointing to certain areas of the Excel screen and right-clicking (SS25).

Source file. The file in a linking or embedding operation that contains the original object or selection (SS223).

Source range. The selected data to be edited, copied, moved, or used to create a chart, table, or object or in a query operation (SS90).

Split. A command (*View* menu) that splits a single worksheet into two panes (screens) either horizontally or vertically to allow you to view both parts at the same time (SS131).

Spreadsheet. The electronic equivalent of multicolumned paper used to display data in columnar (column and row) form (also known as a worksheet) (SS2).

Status bar.   Located at the bottom of the Excel window, the status bar displays information about the mode of operation and toggle switches (SS13).

Toolbar.   A series of command buttons and drop-down boxes, usually located below Excel's menu bar, that provides mouse shortcuts to Excel's features (SS13).

Transpose.   A command that copies cell contents while changing the positions of columns and rows (SS95).

Undo.   A command that cancels the most recent operation (SS58).

Workbook.   A document file in Excel whose contents are viewed through a workbook window. It may contain a worksheet, chart, or other information (SS12).

Worksheet.   The electronic equivalent of multicolumned paper used to display data in columnar (column and row) form (also called a spreadsheet) (SS2).

INDEX

MICROSOFT POWERPOINT 7.0 FOR WINDOWS 95

EDWARD G. MARTIN
CHARLES S. PARKER

This manual contains numerous features that help you master the material quickly and reinforce your learning:

- *A Table of Contents.* A list of the manual's contents appears on the first page of the manual. Each chapter starts with an *outline,* a list of learning *objectives,* and an *overview* that summarizes the skills you will learn.

- *Bold Key Terms.* Important terms appear in bold type as they are introduced. They are also conveniently listed at the end of each chapter, with page references for further review.

- *Color as a Learning Tool.* In this manual, color has been used to help you work through each chapter. Each step is numbered in green for easy identification. Within each step, text or commands that you should type appear in orange. Single keys to be pressed are shown in yellow boxes. For example,

    1 Type WIN and press ↵

- *Step-by-Step Mouse Approach.* This manual stresses the mouse approach. Each action is numbered consecutively in green to make it easy to locate and follow. Where appropriate, a mouse shortcut (toolbar icon) is shown in the left margin; a keyboard shortcut may be shown in brackets at the right, as follows:

    1 Click *Edit, Cut*   **[Ctrl + X]**

As your skills increase, the "click this item" approach slowly gives way to a less-detailed list of goals and operations so that you do not mindlessly follow steps, but truly master software skills.

- *Screen Figures.* Full-color annotated screens provide overviews of operations that let you monitor your work as you progress through the tutorial.

- *Tips.* Each chapter contains numerous short tips in bold type at strategic points to provide hints, warnings, or insights. Read these carefully.

- *Checkpoints.* At the end of each major section is a list of checkpoints, highlighted in red, which you can use to test your mastery of the material. Do not proceed further unless you can perform the checkpoint tasks.

- *Summary and Quiz.* At the end of each chapter is a bulleted summary of the chapter's content and a 30-question quiz with true/false, multiple-choice, and matching questions.

- *Exercises.* Each chapter ends with two sets of written exercises (Operations and Commands) and six guided hands-on computer applications that measure and reinforce mastery of the chapter's concepts and skills. Each pair of applications present problems relating to school, personal, and business use.

- *Mastery Cases.* The final page of each chapter presents three unguided cases that allow you to demonstrate your personal mastery of the chapter material.

- *A Note about the Manual's Organization.* The topics in this manual are arranged in order of increasing difficulty. Chapters 1 presents beginning and intermediate techniques and should be completed in sequence, for each skill builds upon the previous one. However, Chapter 2 includes several *independent* modules that present advanced skills. These modules may be followed in any order or omitted, as time and interest allow.

- *End-of-Manual Material.* The manual also provides a comprehensive reference *appendix* that summarizes commands and provides alphabetical listings of critical operations, a *glossary* that defines all key terms (with page references), and an *index* to all important topics.

WHAT'S NEW IN MICROSOFT POWERPOINT 7.0 FOR WINDOWS 95

1. *AutoClip Art:* Scans your presentation for appropriate clips or images.

2. *Enhanced AutoContent Wizard:* Assists you in customizing your presentation message according to audience type, size, and available time.

3. *Meeting Minder:* Allows you to prepare additional notes or minutes during a presentation that you can later save with the file or export to Word.

4. *Pack and Go Wizard:* Prepares your PowerPoint files on disk so that you can take them with you as you travel to different locations to make presentations.

5. *Presentation Conferencing:* Used simultaneously with remote workgroups to review presentations over the network. Provides controls to check notes, timing, and slides.

MICROSOFT POWERPOINT 7.0
FOR WINDOWS 95

1

PRESENTATION BASICS

OBJECTIVES

After completing this chapter, you will be able to

1 Explain the general capabilities of a presentation graphics program.
2 Describe the procedures to launch and exit Power-Point.
3 Explain the various components of the PowerPoint window.
4 Create a presentation by selecting a template and slide layout.
5 Enter text into the slide layout and save it as a file.
6 Compare and contrast the appearance and use of PowerPoint views.
7 Open and print a presentation.

OVERVIEW

This chapter introduces the PowerPoint presentation graphics package. After reviewing the Windows startup procedures, techniques for launching and exiting Power-Point are presented, and components of the PowerPoint window are explored, including the menu bar, status bar, and toolbars. Next, you will learn to create and save a simple presentation by using templates and slides. Additional slides are added, and then the presentation is organized and printed.

PG

PRESENTATION GRAPHICS

A **presentation graphics** program allows you to combine text, graphics, and visual special effects into a professional-looking presentation that can be specifically designed for individuals, small conferences, or large audiences. With PowerPoint and the appropriate materials, you can create color or black-and-white overhead transparencies, 35mm slides, printed handouts, speaker's notes, or fully automated on-screen presentations. You can choose from more than 100 templates that control the overall style, color, and layout of your presentation, and then you can modify them to suit your needs. You can choose from more than 1,000 prepared clip art images or draw your own graphics to emphasize or augment your text. You can also employ many of the graphic special effects used by professionals, such as dissolves and fades.

The instructions in this section pertain to PowerPoint 7.0 for Windows 95 (called "Windows" in this manual). PowerPoint, like other Windows programs, is based on a *graphical user interface,* or *GUI* (pronounced "gooey"), which communicates with the computer through symbols (icons), buttons, and menus. PowerPoint operates in a *what-you-see-is-what-you-get,* or *WYSIWYG* (pronounced "wizzy-wig"), environment, in which the screen image closely resembles the final product.

Although you can invoke PowerPoint's capabilities by mouse or keyboard, this manual presents the much-preferred mouse approach. Where appropriate, mouse shortcuts (toolbar buttons) will be shown in the left margin, and shortcut keystrokes will be shown at the right.

GETTING STARTED

Before you begin, be certain you have all the necessary tools: a hard disk or network that contains Windows 95, PowerPoint 7.0 for Windows 95, and a formatted disk on which you will save the presentations you create.

STARTING WINDOWS

Before launching any Windows application, you must first boot your computer and start Windows. Directions are given for hard-disk systems and networks. Follow the one appropriate for your system. If you are already familiar with your computer's boot procedure, start Windows95 now and skip this section.

USING A HARD-DISK DRIVE.   This text assumes that the Windows and PowerPoint programs are on your hard disk, which is identified as Drive C. To start Windows:

STEPS

1 Turn on your computer to boot the operating system. A "Starting Windows 95" message appears and Windows should start automatically. If it does, continue with Step 2. Your system may also do one of the following:

a. If a menu appears, select or type the appropriate commands in your menu to start Windows. You may want to write them here for future reference:

_____

2

b. If a C:\> prompt appears, type   **WIN**   and press   ↵

If a *Welcome to Windows 95* dialog box appears, press   **Esc**   for now to remove it

You should now be at the Windows desktop, recognizable by its taskbar and *Start* button at the bottom of the screen.

3   Insert your disk into Drive A (or Drive B as appropriate)

4   Continue with the "Mouse and Keyboard Operations" section

USING A NETWORK.   Windows and PowerPoint may be available to you through a local area network (LAN). In this case, the programs are kept on the hard-disk drive or another computer that is shared by many users. To launch PowerPoint, you must access the program from your own microcomputer. So many network configurations are available that it is difficult to know exactly which one you will use. Check with your instructor or lab technician for exact directions. In general, however, to start Windows:

STEPS

1   Boot the network operating system (perhaps with your own disk)

2   Type the command(s) and password(s) needed to access your network menu

In many networks, this is done by typing   **LAN**   and pressing   ↵

3   Select or type the appropriate command shown on your screen to start Windows.

4   If a *Welcome to Windows 95* dialog box appears, press   **Esc**   for now to remove it.

You should now be at the Windows desktop, recognizable by its taskbar and *Start* button at the bottom of the screen.

MOUSE AND KEYBOARD OPERATIONS

> Note: Skip this section if you are already familiar with using a mouse or keyboard to invoke commands and move around the window. The commands in PowerPoint can be invoked by mouse (the preferred approach) or keyboard.

USING A MOUSE.   A *mouse* is an input device that allows you to control a *mouse pointer* (graphical image) on your screen and select program features. Currently, it appears as a small arrow, but will change to other icons when you perform other tasks. As you move your mouse on a flat surface or mouse pad (a small rubber pad), the mouse pointer moves on your screen in a similar fashion.

PG

You can perform a number of mouse actions:

■ *Point:* Move the mouse, and thus the pointer, to another location on the screen.
■ *Click:* Press and release the left mouse button to select the item at which the mouse pointer is positioned.
■ *Right-click:* Press and release the right mouse button to invoke a *Shortcut* menu.
■ *Double-click:* Quickly click the mouse twice to initiate a command.
■ *Drag and drop:* Press and hold the left mouse button, move the mouse to a new location, and then release the mouse button. This action normally moves or resizes the selected object.

Try this brief exercise to practice all these actions before continuing:

STEPS

1 *Point* to the *Start* button on the taskbar by moving the mouse on a flat surface or pad. If you run out of space on your desk or pad, simply lift the mouse, replace it in a more convenient spot, and continue to move it. The screen's mouse pointer will not move until you replace the mouse on the surface.

2 *Click* the *Start* button to see the Windows menu, then click anywhere on the desktop to close the menu

3 *Right-click* the *My Computer* icon on the desktop to access its *Shortcut* menu. (Remember: point to the icon and click the right mouse button.) Now, click anywhere on the desktop to close the *Shortcut* menu.

4 *Double-click* the *My Computer* icon (point to it and double-click). The icon opens to a window on the desktop.

> **Tip:** If double-clicking does not open the icon to a window, try holding the mouse steady with one hand and then double-clicking with the other until you master the technique.

5 Point to the *My Computer* title bar. *Drag* the window about an inch lower on the desktop. (Remember: press and hold the left mouse button, then move the mouse.) Now, *drop* it (release the mouse) in its new location.

6 Click its *Close* button (as shown in the left margin) to return the window to its icon

USING A KEYBOARD. At times, Windows features may also be accessed by keyboard. Keystrokes required to operate PowerPoint's menu system are discussed under the heading "Menu Bar" later in this chapter. You can also access many of PowerPoint's commands directly through special keystrokes called **shortcut keys** that bypass the normal menu structure. Shortcut keys involve pressing an alphabetic or function key, in combination with Ctrl, Alt, or Shift keys. For example, to close a window using its shortcut key, you would press Ctrl + F4; that is, hold the Ctrl key, press the F4 key, then release both keys. This manual presents its tutorials using the mouse approach. Where appropriate, keyboard shortcuts will be shown in brackets at the right of the step. Mouse shortcut buttons will be shown in the left margin. You can then choose the approach you prefer.

LAUNCHING POWERPOINT

The procedure to launch (start) PowerPoint is the same as that used to launch any Windows application.

STEPS

1 Click the *Start* button to access the Windows menu   [**Ctrl** + **Esc**]

Remember that the keyboard shortcut is shown to the right of the numbered step.

2 Point to the *Programs* item in the menu list that appears

Note that the letter "P" is underlined in the menu and in this manual. The underlined letter indicates that you can press "P" on the keyboard to select this item as an alternative to pointing to it by mouse.

This tutorial assumes that PowerPoint is located within the Microsoft Office submenu item. If yours is in a different submenu, point to *it* instead of Microsoft Office in this step. If PowerPoint is contained in the *Programs* menu list, skip to Step 4.

3 Point to the *Microsoft Office* item in the menu list that appears to the right   [→ , ↵]

> **Note:**   You can also select menu items by keyboard by pressing an arrow key to move to them and then pressing the Enter key.

4 Click the PowerPoint program menu item.

A title screen will briefly appear, followed by a blank PowerPoint window.

5 If a *Tip of the Day* dialog box appears, click the *OK* button   [↵]

A PowerPoint dialog box now appears. For now, you can close it as follows:

6 Click the *Cancel* button to exit this dialog box for now   [**Tab** , **Tab** , ↵]

☑ **CHECKPOINT**

✓ Describe the procedure to start Windows in your computer system.
✓ Explain the difference among a click, right-click, and double-click procedure.
✓ What is the purpose of the *Start* button on the taskbar?
✓ What is a shortcut key?
✓ Describe the procedure to launch PowerPoint.

UNDERSTANDING POWERPOINT

The PowerPoint window should now appear as shown in Figure PG1-1. This is the main program window that appears when you first launch the program.

THE POWERPOINT WINDOW

The PowerPoint window has several standard Windows features as well as features unique to PowerPoint. The following is a brief summary of these features and their operation. Examine your screen as you read about each feature.

TITLE BAR.   The **title bar,** located at the top of the window, identifies the program (Microsoft PowerPoint). It also includes a presentation's name, if one is active and maximized on the screen. Double-clicking the title bar switches between a restored and maximized window (see the "Resizing Buttons" section for more information).

 PROGRAM ICON.   PowerPoint's program icon appears at the left of the title bar. Clicking the **program icon** activates a control menu, which can resize, move, or close

FIGURE PG1–1 ■ THE POWERPOINT WINDOW

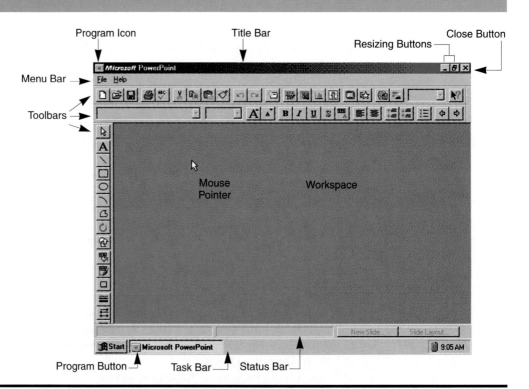

the program window. You can press the Esc key or click outside the menu to cancel it. Double-clicking the program icon is a mouse shortcut to exit from the program.

RESIZING BUTTONS.   Two resizing buttons are located to the right of the title bar. Clicking a **resizing button** will quickly resize the window. Three types of resizing buttons are avaiable:

- The *Minimize button* reduces the window to a taskbar button.

- The *Restore button* reduces the size of a maximized (full screen) window. The restore button appears only when a window is at maximum size.

- The *Maximize button* resizes the window to full screen. The *Maximize* button appears only when the window is not at its full size.

Try this:

 ▮1 **Click PowerPoint's *Restore* button to reduce the window's size**

 ▮2 **Now, click PowerPoint's *Maximize* button to return the window to a full screen**

▮✕ **CLOSE BUTTON.**   PowerPoint's ***Close*** **button** is located at the extreme right of the title bar. When clicked, it will close the PowerPoint program.

POINTER.   A *mouse pointer,* currently shaped like an arrow, will appear somewhere on the screen.

MENU BAR.   The row beneath the title bar contains PowerPoint's **menu bar,** which lets you invoke most PowerPoint commands by pointing with a mouse or pressing the appropriate keys. As you invoke commands, additional menus or dialog boxes appear as appropriate. Try this brief exercise:

▮1 **Click *File* to open its pull-down menu**   [**Alt** + **F**]

The *File* pull-down menu opens as in Figure PG1-2a. To open a menu bar item by keyboard, you must press and hold the Alt key, press the underlined (mnemonic) letter of the item, and then release both. Figure PG1-2b explains the entries you will see on a typical pull-down menu. Once a pull-down menu is opened, you can click the desired item, or you can use the arrow keys to highlight it and press the Enter key to invoke the command. For now,

▮2 **Click anywhere outside the pull-down menu to close it**   [**Alt** , **Esc** , **Esc**]

FIGURE PG1–2 ■ **USING THE MENU BAR**

(a) The *File* pull-down menu.
(b) A description of the items
in a typical pull-down menu.

(a)

(b)

Menu Items with	Description
Ellipsis (…)	Opens to a dialog box or another window
▶ at far right	Opens to a submenu
No notation	Invokes a command or other feature
Keys at far right	Shortcut key(s) to invoke the menu item by keyboard
✓ to left of item	A toggle feature that has been turned on
Dimmed (or not visible)	A menu item not currently available

STATUS BAR.   At the bottom of the window, just above the Windows taskbar, is the **status bar,** which displays messages and provides mouse shortcut buttons to add new slides or adjust the layout (as you will soon see).

TOOLBARS.   A number of **toolbars** appear on the screen. Toolbars include shortcut buttons that can be clicked by mouse to invoke various commands. By default, two toolbars appear directly below the menu bar. The Standard toolbar (on top) contains buttons that perform common file commands. The buttons on the Formatting toolbar (the lower toolbar) control text appearance. A Drawing toolbar, which contains graphics tools, is positioned vertically at the left of the window. Other toolbars and toolboxes will appear as you perform tasks in PowerPoint.

> **Tip:** To identify a toolbar button, simply point to it and wait a moment. Its title will appear below it in a small rectangle, and an explanation of its function will appear in the status bar.

WORKSPACE.   The blank area filling the remainder of the window is PowerPoint's **workspace.** Presentations and other views of your work appear here.

TASK BAR.   The Windows taskbar appears at the bottom of the screen. The *Start* button or other program buttons can be used to access other applications.

GETTING ON-LINE HELP

PowerPoint's on-line help feature includes a Contents section for general help, as well as Index and Find components to locate specific answers to questions you may have. Although you can access the Help feature through the menu bar, most dialog boxes also have a Help button, identified with a question mark, that can invoke help specific to the current task. In this exercise, you will briefly examine the Search feature in the Index component of Help to gather information about clip art.

GETTING HELP.   To initiate the Help feature, do the following:

STEPS

1   Click *Help* on the menu bar   [**F1**]

2   Click *Microsoft PowerPoint Help Topics*

A *Help* dialog box appears as in Figure PG1-3. By default, the *Help* dialog box opens to its Contents component, which offers general topics of interest. In general, you would click a topic and then click the *Open* button to access the information. For this exercise, however, try the following:

3   Click the *Index* tab if needed to open its screen   [**Ctrl** + **Tab**]

FIGURE PG1-3   ■   THE *HELP* DIALOG BOX

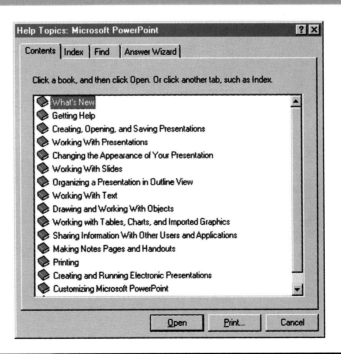

PG

4 Type **CLIP ART** (need not be in uppercase letters)

As you type, note that the list moves to topics that match your search characters. You can now select a specific topic. For example,

5 Click the *clip art* entry and then click the *Display* button

6 Click the *Insert clip art* entry in the *Topics Found* dialog box [↓ , ↵]

7 Click the *Display* button

8 Read the information box that appears. When you are done, [Esc]
click its *Close* button to exit the Help feature

Feel free to use the Help feature whenever you want to learn more about PowerPoint.

EXITING POWERPOINT

When you are finished using PowerPoint, you should exit it properly to ensure that none of your work is lost. If you want to continue, read the following steps to learn the procedure, but do not execute them. If you want to stop for now, perform the steps to exit PowerPoint:

STEPS

☒ **1** Click *File*, and then click *Exit* from the pull-down menu [Alt + F4]

2 Shut down Windows (click *Start, Shut down, Yes*) [Ctrl + Esc , U , Y]

☑ CHECKPOINT

✓ Launch PowerPoint.
✓ How many items appear in the menu bar?
✓ Use the Help feature to learn about Autolayouts.
✓ Which toolbars currently appear in the PowerPoint window?
✓ Exit PowerPoint.

CREATING AND SAVING A PRESENTATION

PowerPoint allows you to create presentations in a series of *slides,* or pages, that can (if used properly) effectively communicate your ideas to your audience. In this exercise, you will create the first slide of a presentation about PowerPoint itself. To prepare for this exercise, use the techniques you learned in the first section of this chapter. Namely,

1 **Boot your computer's operating system and start Windows**

2 **Launch PowerPoint**

3 **Maximize the PowerPoint window if it is not already at full size (click its *Maximize* button)**

CREATING A BASIC PRESENTATION

To create a new presentation, you simply invoke the File, New command and then select a number of variables that will define the look and feel of your presentation. Note that any selection you make can be changed at any time with ease.

1 **Click *File* and then click *New* from the pull-down menu**

The *New Presentation* dialog box appears as shown in Figure PG1-4a. You can now specify the presentation you want, using the tabs at the top of the dialog box. During this procedure, you will have the opportunity to specify three different **templates** (patterns) that determine the look of the overall presentation, its design, and each individual slide. The *Presentations* tab, the rightmost one, provides access to 28 *presentation templates* that provide preformatted presentations for business and marketing plans, reports, and other communications. However, for this exercise, you will create your own presentation from scratch by selecting the blank presentation template. Feel free to explore other presentation templates after you've learned the fundamentals.

> **Tip: Using shortcuts of clicking the *New* toolbar button or pressing Ctrl + N skips directly to Step 3 in the next section. You may want to explore this on your own in the future.**

2 **Click the *General* tab if it is not already selected**   [Ctrl + Tab]

3 **Click the *Blank Presentation* icon if it is not already selected**

SELECTING A TEMPLATE.   Now that you have selected the basic layout, you can apply a *design template* that controls the color scheme, font styles and sizes, background graphics, and general layout of the overall design. Selecting no design will leave the screen in plain black-and-white mode for now. Again, it does not matter which design template you choose—it can be easily changed at any time (as you will see). To select a design template, do the following:

PG

FIGURE PG1–4 ■ THE *NEW PRESENTATION* DIALOG BOX

(a) Selecting the blank presentation template.
(b) Selecting the *Multiple Bars* icon.

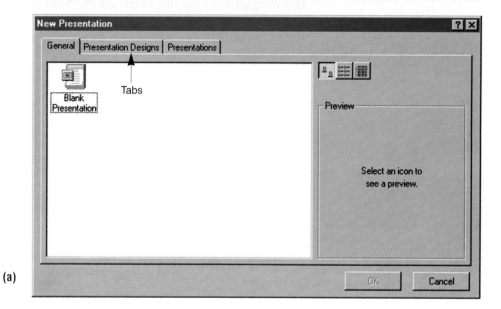

(a)

(b)

Selected Icon   Preview

---

1   Click the *Presentation Designs* tab   [**Ctrl** + **Tab**]

The first 12 of 23 design template icons appear (your screen may display fewer icons). A preview of the current selection appears to the right of the list. You can scroll through the list and click icons to preview their effect on your presentation. For example,

2 Scroll to and click the *Multiple Bars* template icon (usually fourth row,   [↓ , →]
rightmost icon)

As shown in Figure PG1-4b, a color preview of the design template appears to the right. For now, accept this design template as follows:

3 Click *OK* to accept the template

A *New Slide* dialog box appears, offering the first 12 of 24 *slide templates,* or **autolay-outs,** as in Figure PG1-5. This dialog box allows you to select the specific layout for the current slide in the presentation. Each autolayout contains placeholders for various objects (titles, bulleted lists, or graphics) that can be added to the slide.

SELECTING A SLIDE.   The first slide of any presentation should be a *title slide* that introduces the topic of the presentation to the audience. Note that the current autolay-out is identified at the right of the dialog box. In this example, you will create the title slide shown in Figure PG1-6, with your name in the lower portion of the screen.

STEPS

1 Click the title slide at the upper left, if it is not already selected

FIGURE PG1–5 ■ THE *NEW SLIDE* DIALOG BOX

The first 12 of 24 autolayouts are displayed.

Autolayouts →

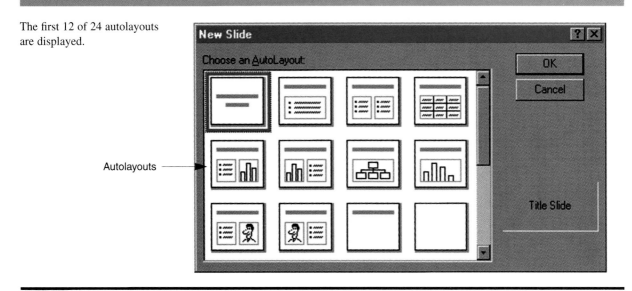

PG

FIGURE PG1–6 ■ **THE TITLE SLIDE**

Use this image as a guide in
creating your title slide.

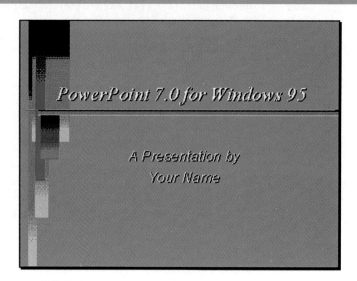

> **2** Click the *OK* button to select this autolayout

A presentation window appears, as shown in Figure PG1-7. Examine some of the new
window components as they are introduced in the following sections, before proceeding.

Placeholders.   A **placeholder** is an empty object area that can hold a title, text, graphic, or other data, depending on the autolayout you have selected. As shown in Figure
PG1-7, the title slide autolayout contains two placeholders, each contained within its
own dotted-line rectangle. The top placeholder will hold the title; the bottom one will
hold a subtitle. As you will see, you click a placeholder (or press Tab) to open it, enter
the appropriate text or graphic, and then click (or press Esc) to close it again.

> **Tip:** You need not fill every placeholder. An empty placeholder will not appear in the
> slide during a presentation.

Formatting Toolbar.   Appearing above the presentation window is a **formatting toolbar,** which allows you to change various text attributes, such as font, size, enhancements (bold, italic, underline), and alignment (aligned left, centered). As shown in
Figure PG1-8a, current settings are shown in the entry boxes for font and size and by
the depressed toolbar buttons.

View Buttons.   Five view buttons appear at the lower left corner of the presentation window. As you will see shortly, clicking a **view button** will change PowerPoint's view to
one of its five options as shown in Figure PG1-8b: slide view, outline view, slide sorter
view, notes pages view, and slide show. Currently, the *Slide* view button is depressed, indicating that the slide view is active.

FIGURE PG1–7 ■ THE TITLE SLIDE PRESENTATION WINDOW

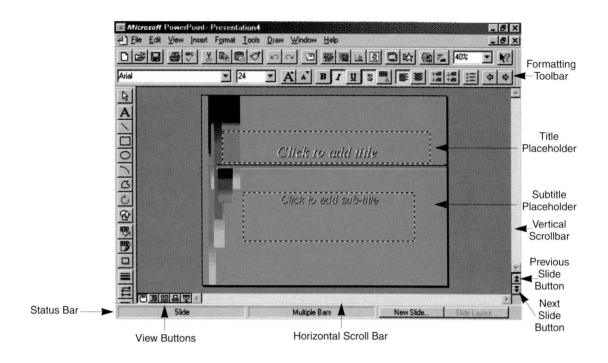

- Formatting Toolbar
- Title Placeholder
- Subtitle Placeholder
- Vertical Scrollbar
- Previous Slide Button
- Next Slide Button
- Status Bar
- View Buttons
- Horizontal Scroll Bar

FIGURE PG1–8 ■ PRESENTATION WINDOW COMPONENTS

(a) The Formatting Toolbar.
(b) The *View* Buttons.
(c) The Status Bar.

(a)
- Font
- Increase/Decrease Font Size
- Underline
- Text Color
- Bullet On/Off
- Indent Less (promote)
- Font Size
- Bold
- Italic
- Text Shadow
- Left Align
- Center
- Indent More (demote)

(b)
- Slide Sorter View
- Slide View
- Slide Show
- Outline View
- Notes Pages View

(c)
- View — Slide
- Design — Multiple Bars
- Command Buttons — New Slide... / Slide Layout...

Scroll Bars.   A horizontal scroll bar appears to the right of the view buttons. A vertical scroll bar appears down the right side of the presentation window. When objects in the window are too large to be seen all at once, you can click the arrow buttons on either end of the scroll bar (or drag the scroll bar elevator) to see other portions of the window.

Next/Previous Slide Buttons.   Additional movement buttons are located at the lower-right corner of the presentation window. When your presentation includes more than one slide, clicking the *Next Slide* button (shown by two downward-pointing triangles) advances you one slide further into your presentation. Clicking the *Previous Slide* button moves back one slide.

Status Bar Settings.   PowerPoint's status bar now displays information about the current presentation, as shown in Figure PG1-8c. Note that the status bar shows that you are currently viewing Slide 1 in a presentation that has only one slide (1 of 1), and that you are using the Multiple Bars template.

ENTERING TEXT

You are now ready to enter text into the placeholders of your title slide. When you first display a new slide, any text you type will immediately be placed into the title placeholder without having to click it to open it. Try this:

STEPS

1   Type   **PowerPoint 7.0 for Windows 95**

Your screen should resemble Figure PG1-9a. Note that a rectangular outline with diagonal lines in its border appeared around the placeholder immediately after you typed the first "P" in PowerPoint. This outline, called the **selection box,** indicates that the placeholder is active. Note, too, that an insertion point shows the current location of text entry. As shown in the formatting toolbar, the text appears in a Times New Roman font at 44-pt. size, with italic and shadow attributes.

> **Tip: If you make a mistake while entering text, simply press Backspace to erase it, or use the arrow keys and Delete as needed. Then retype the entry correctly.**

2   Click the *Subtitle* placeholder to open it

Note that the selection box moves from the top placeholder to the bottom one, showing that the subtitle placeholder is now active.

3   Type   **A Presentation by**

Your screen should now resemble Figure PG1-9b. Assume you want to type your own name on the next line. You can end the line as follows:

(a) The completed title.
(b) The subtitle awaits your
name to be complete.

(a)

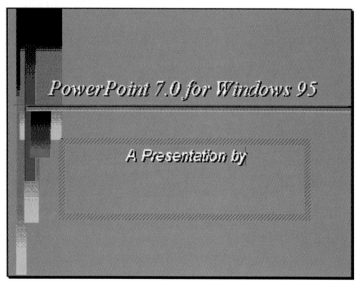

(b)

4 Press ↵ to end the line

The insertion point moves to the next line.

5 Type your name on this line

6 Click outside the placeholder box to deselect it

Although you could continue to add additional slides to your presentation, for now, one slide is sufficient for practicing the next important skill—saving your work.

SAVING THE PRESENTATION

As you work on your presentation, PowerPoint stores it in the computer's main memory. If you were to exit PowerPoint now, or if your computer were to lose power, all your work would be lost. It is important, therefore, to save your work frequently, so that you can return to it and continue whenever you want. **Save** copies the current presentation in main memory onto a file on disk. To save your work for the first time, do the following:

STEPS

1   Click *File* and then *Save* (or click the *Save* toolbar button)   [**Ctrl** **+** **S**]

Because this is the first time you are saving this presentation, a *File Save* dialog box appears, as shown in Figure PG1-10a. This dialog box lets you specify the destination and filename. Like all dialog boxes, the *File Save* dialog box has a variety of standard Windows options. To select an option by mouse, simply click it. By keyboard, press the Alt key with the underlined letter of the option.

> **Tip: You can also select dialog box options by pressing the Tab key to move the highlight to a desired option and then pressing the Enter key.**

To save your work, you need only set the proper folder and provide a filename for the presentation as follows:

2   Examine the *Save in* entry box. If the folder (or drive) displayed is correct, continue with Step 5. If it is not, follow Steps 3 and 4 to change it.

To change the *Save in* folder shown in the entry box,

3   Click the *Save in* drop-down arrow

4   Click the *3½ Floppy (A:)* or *(B:)* as appropriate

The folder or drive for saving documents is now set. You will not need to set it again as long as you stay in PowerPoint. When you save another document now, it will be placed in the folder you specified in the *Save in* entry box.

> **Tip: You can also save a presentation without changing the *Save in* drive, by including the disk identifier (and folder, if needed) in front of the presentation's name (as in A:POWER1) when you save it.**

You can now name the file:

5   Click the *File name* entry line

6   Type   POWER1   as in Figure PG1-10b

FIGURE PG1–10 ■ THE *FILE SAVE* DIALOG BOX

(a) The default settings.
(b) The POWER1
presentation will be saved in
Drive A.

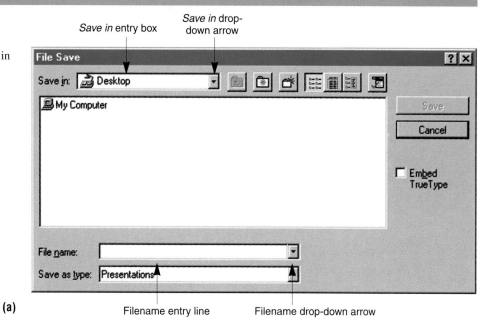

Save in entry box

Save in drop-
down arrow

(a)

Filename entry line   Filename drop-down arrow

(b)

Tip: A filename, including its drive letter and path can contain up to 255 characters.
You cannot use the following symbols in a filename: / \ > < * ? " : or ;

7 Click the *Save* button   [↵]

The light on the disk drive flashes briefly as the presentation is being saved. When the
process is finished, the presentation name should appear in the title bar. Although you

may not see it, PowerPoint automatically adds the filename extension ".ppt" to presentations that you save. This extension identifies the file as a PowerPoint presentation. You can now continue working on your document.

SAVE VERSUS SAVE AS.   Once you have saved a file, you can easily save it again as you work by invoking the Save command, as you did in Step 1. Because you have already named the file, the presentation is immediately saved to its original folder or disk with the same name, automatically replacing the old file that was there. For example,

---

STEPS

 1 Click *File* and then *Save* (or click the *Save* toolbar button)   [**Ctrl** + **S**]

The disk drive light flashes as the presentation is being saved again. Any changes you may have made in the presentation have been safely copied to your disk, replacing the previous file's contents.

At times, however, you may want to save a presentation with a different name than its current one so that you don't erase the previous file. To accomplish this, you must use the Save As command when you save the file instead of the Save command. Try this:

2 Click *File* and then *Save As*

The *File Save* dialog box appears as before. Note that the current *Save in* folder and filename automatically appear. If you wanted to change the filename, you could type a new one in its place. You could also identify a new *Save in* folder or disk if needed before clicking the *Save* button to accept the changes.

In this example, however, simply cancel the command as follows:

3 Click the *Cancel* button   [**Esc**]

CLOSING THE PRESENTATION WINDOW

At times you will want to close the current presentation before beginning work on another one. Try this:

STEPS

 1 Click *File* and then *Close* (or click the *Close* button)   [**Ctrl** + **F4**]

If you have already saved your presentation, the window will simply disappear. If you did not, a dialog box will appear asking if you want to save changes. If this happens, for now,

2 Click the *Yes* button

Note that you could choose to not save the presentation by clicking the *No* button.

If you do not close a presentation window, each new window would be placed on top of the preceding window in the workspace. Get into the habit of always closing one presentation before opening or creating another one.

You could now create a new presentation, open an existing one, or exit PowerPoint entirely.

3 If you want to stop for now, exit PowerPoint (by clicking *File, Exit*) and shut down Windows (by clicking *Start, Shut down, Yes*). Otherwise, continue on to the next section.

☑ CHECKPOINT

✓ Open a new presentation with a design template of your choice.
✓ Create a title slide with "About Me!" as the title.
✓ Type your name as the subtitle.
✓ Save the presentation with the name ALL ABOUT ME.
✓ Close the presentation window.

ORGANIZING A PRESENTATION

One slide alone does not make an effective presentation. The typical presentation may contain dozens of slides, which then have to be organized into an effective sequence and adjusted for best effect. Not only must you master the techniques of adding new slides to your initial title slide, but you must learn how to view them and adjust their sequence as needed.

OPENING A PRESENTATION

Once a presentation has been saved to disk, it can be opened again for additional work. The **open** command fetches a file from its folder or disk and then copies it into a presentation window on the screen. Note that the original file is still kept on the disk. Any changes you make to the screen copy must then be saved if you want to retain them.

STEPS

1 If PowerPoint is not already on your screen, start Windows and launch PowerPoint, following the procedures you learned earlier

2 Maximize the PowerPoint window if it is not at full size

You can now open the POWER1 presentation as follows:

 3 Click *File* and then *Open*   [**Ctrl** + **O**]

A *File Open* dialog box appears, similar to the one shown in Figure PG1-11.

PG

FIGURE PG1-11 ■ THE *FILE OPEN* DIALOG BOX

Look in entry box   Look in drop-down arrow   Preview button

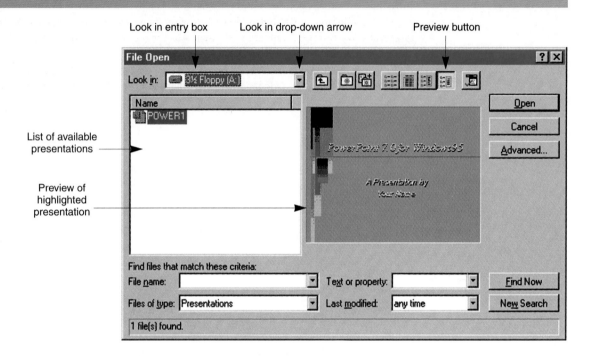

List of available
presentations

Preview of
highlighted
presentation

4 **Change the Look in entry to match your disk if needed by clicking its drop-down arrow and then clicking the *3½ Floppy (A:) (or B:)* drive**

As shown in Figure PG1-11, note that a list of available presentations appears at the left. Currently, only one presentation, POWER1, is on the disk. If the *Preview* button is depressed (the default), an image of the highlighted presentation's title slide appears on the right side of the dialog box. When you have more than one presentation saved, you can click each file (or move to it with the arrow keys) to see its first slide in the preview box. This technique helps you to identify the proper file before opening it into PowerPoint.

5 **Click the POWER1 presentation filename in the list to select it if it is not already highlighted**

6 **Click the *Open* button to open the selected presentation**   [↵]

Tip: There are three other ways to open a file. (1) Use the arrow keys to move to the filename in the list and press the Enter key. (2) Type the filename directly into the *File name* entry box and press the Enter key. (3) Double-click the desired file to open it immediately.

The POWER1 presentation window appears on the screen. Depending on how you last left the program, the window may not be at its maximum size. The larger a window is, the easier it will be to work with its objects. Check PowerPoint's title bar. If the title displays "POWER1" as in Figure PG1-12a, then the window is maximized. If, however, the "POWER1" title appears in its own window beneath the toolbars, as in Figure PG1-12b, you need to maximize it as follows:

[7] **If the POWER1 window is not at maximum, maximize it now by clicking its *Maximize* button**

ADDING NEW SLIDES

Slides can be added to your presentation at any time. You will now add a second slide to the presentation, as shown in Figure PG1-13. This slide will use a bulleted list to present some of the features of the PowerPoint Program.

CREATING A BULLETED LIST.   Using Figure PG1-13 as a guide, perform the following steps to insert a new slide after the current slide in the window:

FIGURE PG1-12 ■ MAXIMIZING THE PRESENTATION WINDOW

(a) When the presentation window is maximized, PowerPoint's title bar also displays the presentation's name.
(b) A non-maximized window displays a separate title bar.

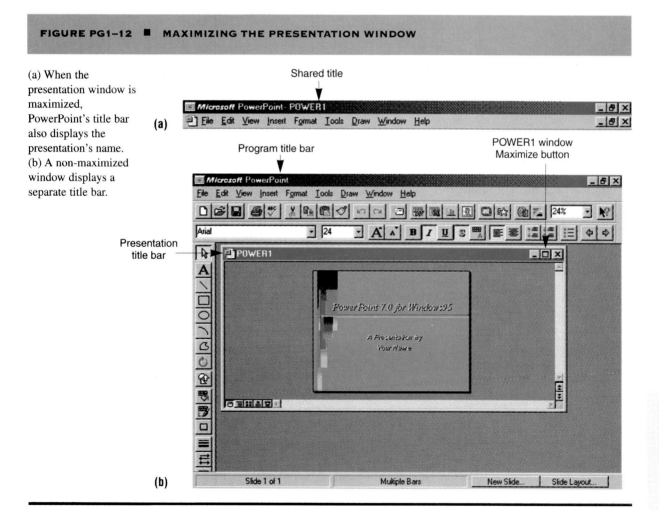

FIGURE PG1–13 ■ **THE SECOND SLIDE**

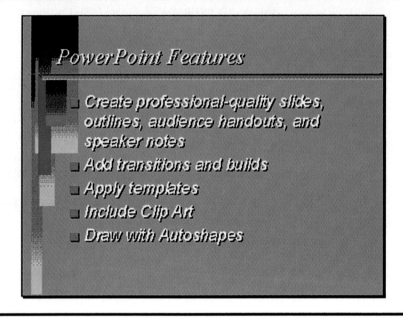

STEPS

1 Click the *New Slide* button on the status bar or click *Insert* and then *New Slide* in the menu

The *New Slide* dialog box appears again, as shown in Figure PG1-14. Now that the title slide has already been used, the second choice, a bulleted list, is highlighted. Although you could choose any slide autolayout by clicking it or moving to it with the arrow keys, you will use the bulleted list as follows for the second slide:

2 Click the *Bulleted List* autolayout template if it is not already highlighted   [→]

> Tip: The highlighted template's title will appear at the lower right of the dialog box for easy, and positive, identification.

3 Click the *OK* button to accept the highlighted template

An empty second slide template appears on the screen, as shown in Figure PG1-15. Note that the message "Slide 2 of 2" appears in the status bar.

4 Click the top title placeholder to select it

FIGURE PG1–14 ■ SELECTING A BULLETED LIST AUTOLAYOUT TEMPLATE

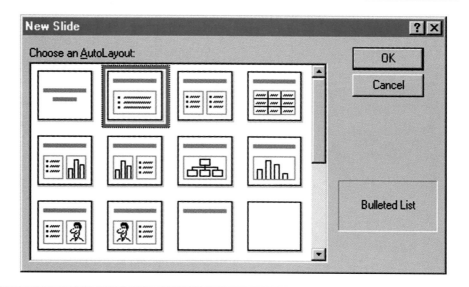

5 Type **PowerPoint Features**

6 Click the bottom text placeholder to select it

FIGURE PG1–15 ■ THE BULLETED LIST LAYOUT

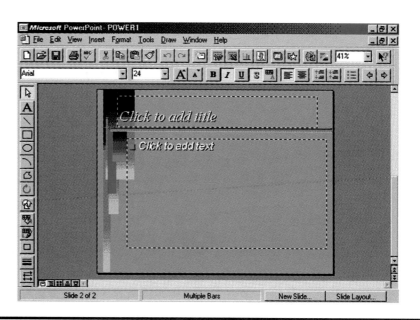

The insertion point moves to the first bulleted row. You need only type each bulleted item and press the Enter key at the end of each entry, except for the last one. Do not press the Enter key when you reach the end of the line, but allow PowerPoint's wordwrap to automatically move text as needed to fit within the margins of the slide. Only press the Enter key to end the entire bulleted entry as follows:

7 Type **Create professional-quality slides, outlines, audience handouts, and speaker notes**

8 Press ↵ to move to the next entry

The next bullet and row appear on the screen awaiting your entry.

9 Type **Add transitions and builds** and then press ↵

10 Type **Use Slide Masters** and then press ↵

11 Type **Apply Templates** and then press ↵

12 Type **Include Clip Art** and then press ↵

13 Type **Draw with Autoshapes,** but do not press the Enter key

If you pressed the Enter key in the last entry, an unwanted extra bullet will appear. Simply press the Backspace key to remove it.

> Tip: You can use the arrow keys to position the insertion point in any bulleted entry, and then insert or delete text as needed to correct typing errors.

14 Click outside the placeholder to deselect it

 15 Save the presentation again with the same name (click *File, Save*)

16 If you want to stop for now, exit PowerPoint and shut down Windows. When you return, you will have to launch PowerPoint and open the POWER1 presentation before continuing.

CREATING A SLIDE FOR CLIP ART.   Following a similar procedure, you can now add a third slide, which resembles Figure PG1-16. This slide uses a template that will allow you to add a clip art image later on. Create the slide as follows:

STEPS

1 Click the *New Slide* button on the status bar, or click *Insert* and then *New Slide* in the menu

2 Click the *Text and Clip Art* autolayout template in the   [↓ , ↓ , ←] lower-left corner, or move to it

FIGURE PG1–16 ■ **THE THIRD SLIDE**

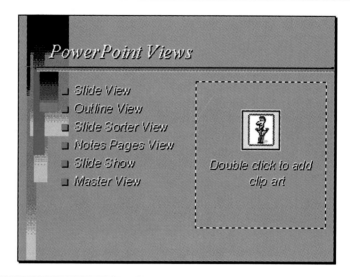

Be sure the title at the lower right of the dialog box displays "Text and Clip Art" before continuing.

3 Click the *OK* button to accept the highlighted template

An empty third slide template appears on the screen. This one has placeholders for a title, text, and clip art.

4 Click the top title placeholder to select it

5 Type   PowerPoint Views

6 Click the left-bottom text placeholder to select it

7 Type   Slide View   and press ↵

8 Type   Outline View   and press ↵

9 Type   Slide Sorter View   and press ↵

10 Type   Notes Pages View   and press ↵

11 Type   Slide Show   and press ↵

12 Type   Master View,   but do not press the Enter key

13 Click outside the placeholder to deselect it

> **Note: Clip art will be added in Chapter Two.**

14 **Save the presentation again with the same name (click** *File, Save***)**

15 **If you want to stop for now, exit PowerPoint and shut down Windows**

REVIEWING YOUR WORK

A typical presentation, as any creative work, requires careful review and adjustment before it is ready for an audience. You should examine the text content, slide order, design template, and individual slide layouts to see if they are effective. You might want to change them or add other color or text enhancements to better express your ideas. To help you, PowerPoint offers five views that provide different tools and screens in which you can review, and if need be alter, your work. As you saw in Figure PG1-8b, you can switch to a different view by clicking the appropriate view button in the bottom left corner of the presentation window. You can also click the view item on the menu bar to select a new view. It is important for you to examine each of them, so that you understand their uses and differences.

SLIDE VIEW.   PowerPoint's **slide view,** the default setting, presents one slide on the screen at a time. It is the main work window for creating new presentations, adding slides, and editing text.

STEPS

1 **If needed, launch PowerPoint and open the POWER1 presentation**

The *Slide* view button should appear depressed in the lower-left corner of the window, indicating that the slide view is active.

2 **If slide view is not active, click** *View* **and then** *Slides* **on the menu bar to change it, or click the** *Slide* **view button directly**

The status bar should display "Slide 1 of 3," indicating that you are looking at the first, or title, slide of your presentation.

3 **If the title slide is not displayed, press** Pg Up **or** Pg Dn **(or click the** *Next* **or** *Previous Slide* **button) as needed to move to it**

Your screen should now resemble Figure PG1-17, displaying the title slide in slide view. While in slide view, you can edit text, add new slides, change the design or slide layout, add prepared graphic pictures (clip art), or draw your own graphics, as you will see in Chapter 2. Try this:

4 **Press** Pg Dn **(or click the** *Next Slide* **button) to move to Slide 2**

Note how the status bar now shows "Slide 2 of 3."

FIGURE PG1–17 ■ SLIDE VIEW

One slide is presented at a time.

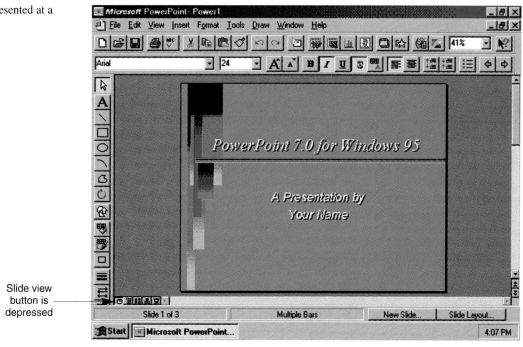

Slide view button is depressed

⬆ | **5** | Press **Pg Up** (or click the *Previous Slide* button) to return to the title slide

SLIDE SORTER VIEW.   The **slide sorter view** displays miniature images of your slides in sequence, as if you had dealt them out onto a table. To switch to slide sorter view, do the following:

STEPS

▦ | **1** | Click the *Slide Sorter* view button, or click *View* and then *Slide Sorter* on the menu bar

As shown in Figure PG1-18, the *Slide Sorter* view button is now depressed, and the message "Slide Sorter" appears in the status bar. All the slides in your presentation appear on the screen in rows. Each slide is numbered beneath its lower-right corner in the order it will appear in your presentation. The current slide is indicated by a rectangular box surrounding it. (If necessary, you can use the scroll bars to view large sets of slides.)

Unlike slide view, the slide sorter is not concerned with the contents of individual slides, but rather how they work together in your presentation. You can use the slide sorter to change the order of the slides. Try this:

2 | Click *Slide 3* to select it

PG

FIGURE PG1–18 ■ **SLIDE SORTER VIEW**

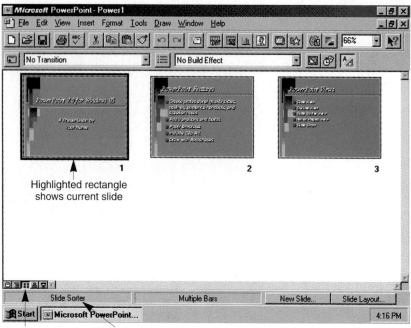

Highlighted rectangle
shows current slide

Slide Sorter view   Slide Sorter appears
button is depressed   in status bar

Note that the rectangular indicator has now moved to the slide, as in Figure PG1-19a, showing that it is selected.

3 **Click the slide and drag the mouse pointer so that it lies between Slides 1 and 2, as shown in Figure PG1-19b. A vertical line will help you position the new location of the slide**

4 **Release the mouse button**

The contents of Slide 3 have been moved in front of Slide 2, and both slides have been renumbered to show their new order. Of course, you could have also dragged Slide 2 past Slide 3 to obtain the same result.

> **Tip:** To move a slide by keyboard, press the appropriate arrow keys to move the rectangular indicator to the slide. Then, press Ctrl + X to cut the slide, move to its new location, and press Ctrl + V to paste it back in.

5 **Repeat Steps 2–4 to return the slides to their previous order for now**

The slide sorter can also be used to create transitions, or graphic changes, between slides, as you will see in Chapter 2.

FIGURE PG1–19 ■ **CHANGING SLIDE ORDER**

(a) Slide 3 is selected.
(b) Mouse pointer is dragged to desired location and then released.

(a)   1   2   3

(b)   1   2   3

NOTES PAGES VIEW. PowerPoint's **notes pages view** allows you to add notes to each slide. These notes can be printed for your own use when presenting your work or distributed to your audience as a handout. To switch to this view,

STEPS

   1   **Click the *Notes Pages* view button, or click *View* and then *Notes Pages* on the menu bar**

As shown in Figure PG1-20, a single slide appears on the screen, as in slide view, but with a large placeholder for text beneath it. As expected, the *Notes Pages* view button is depressed, and a "Notes" counter appears in the status bar. As with other placeholders, you could click the text area to select it for entry, type your notes, and then click outside the placeholder to deselect it. For example,

2   **Click within the notes placeholder**

Note that it is now available for text entry. For now, however,

3   **Click outside the notes placeholder to close it**

SLIDE SHOW. The **slide show** allows you to run your entire presentation in full-screen form, both for review and for when you actually want to present to an audience. Try this:

PG

FIGURE PG1–20   ■   THE NOTES PAGES VIEW

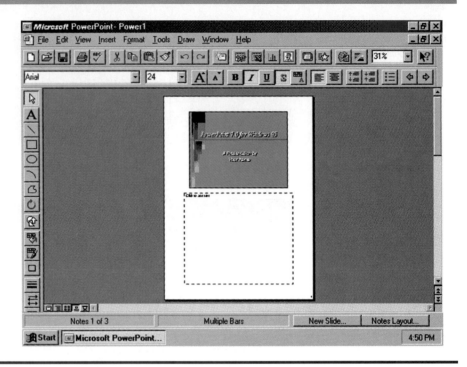

STEPS

1   Move to Slide 1 if you are not already there

 2   Click the *Slide Show* view button, or click *View, Slide Show,* and then *Show* on the menu bar

> **Tip:** If you click the *Slide Show* button, the show begins at the current slide. Using the menu starts the show at the *first* slide by default.

As shown in Figure PG1-21, the title slide completely fills the screen. For now, the slide show is set to manual operation; that is, to move to the next slide:

3   Click the mouse   [↵]

The first bulleted list fills the screen.

4   Click the mouse to see the third slide   [↵]

FIGURE PG1–21 ■ THE SLIDE SHOW

5 Click the mouse once more to end the show (if needed, press ↵ or click the
mouse again to return to the workspace)   [↵]

> **Tip: Clicking the mouse or pressing the Enter or Pg Dn key will move you to the next
> slide in the presentation. To move backward, press Pg Up. You can also end the slide
> show at any time by pressing the Esc key. Right-clicking a slide activates a *Shortcut*
> menu with various movement and show options. To cancel the *Shortcut* menu, click
> outside the menu.**

In the next chapter, you will learn how to automate the slide show so that it runs without the need for you to press any key at all.

OUTLINE VIEW.   The **Outline view** presents all the text contained in your presentation in outline form for review or editing purposes. To switch to outline view,

STEPS

   1 Click the *Outline* view button, or click *View*, *Outline* on the menu bar

As shown in Figure PG1-22, the text in your presentation appears in outline form, and
the message "Outline" appears in the status bar. Each slide is numbered with its title
appearing as a major heading in the outline. Bulleted lists or subtitles appear as subheadings in the outline. The current text is highlighted.

FIGURE PG1–22 ■ OUTLINE VIEW

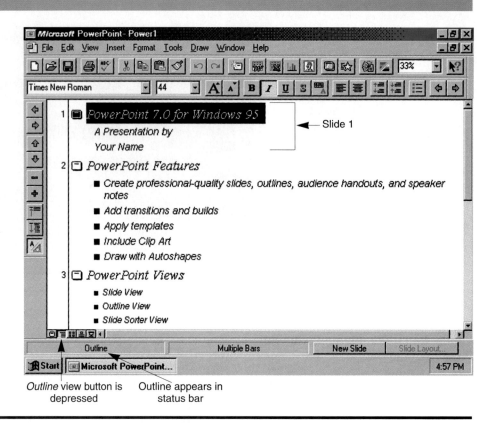

PowerPoint's outline is very similar to the outline found in Microsoft Word. You can add or delete text at any outline level, or you can use the toolbar buttons at the left of the outline to change the level of subheadings of any text line. All other text will adjust accordingly. For example, to add text in the second slide, try this:

2 **Click to the immediate left of the "A" in "Add transitions and builds"**

3 **Type** **Edit text** **and press** ↵

Note that a new bullet has been added to the list. Other bullets have moved down. To delete text, try this:

4 **Click to the immediate left of the "E" in "Edit text"**

5 **Press** **Delete** **until all characters are removed in the row**

Tip: If you click on the bullet itself, you can delete the entire item with one press of the Delete key.

Note how the remaining bullets move back up to fill the space.

Using the outline view allows you to review the flow of ideas in your presentation without being influenced by layout, color, or graphics. For now,

6   Click the *Slide* view button or click *View* and then *Slide View* on the menu bar to return to the slide view

7   You can exit PowerPoint for now or continue to the next section

Note: Text can be added or deleted in either *Slide* or *Outline* view.

USING FOOTERS

A **footer** is an item of information that you can add at the bottom of any or all slides. PowerPoint provides three placeholders for footers: date and time, footer text, and a slide number. You can add any or all of these items to your slides as follows:

STEPS

1   Launch PowerPoint and open POWER1 if needed

2   Switch to *Slide* view if it is not already active

3   Click *View* and then *Header and Footer*

A *Header and Footer* dialog box appears as in Figure PG1-23a. You can now select each item you desire by clicking its check box. In this example, you will select all three items.

4   Click the *Date and Time* check box to place a check mark in it

Note that a black rectangle appears in the preview in the lower-right corner, displaying where the date and/or time will appear in the slide. By default, the date will automatically be updated to display the computer's system date each time you view the presentation. You can now specify which format should be used to display the date. For example,

5   Click the drop-down arrow in the *Update Automatically* box

A drop-down list appears, as shown in Figure PG1-23b. For now,

6   Click the fourth format on the list that shows the month's name, followed by the day, a comma, and the year, as in April 25, 1996

Tip: You could also specify a fixed date by clicking its check box, typing a date, and choosing a format.

FIGURE PG1–23 ■ THE *HEADER AND FOOTER* DIALOG BOX

(a) The Slide tab allows you to specify date and time, the slide number, and a text footer.
(b) The Date and Time format drop-down list.

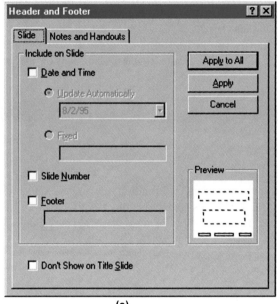

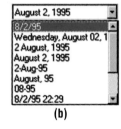

(b)

(a)

---

 7 Click the *Slide Number* check box to number the slide

 8 Click the *Footer* check box to allow you to specify text that will appear at the bottom center of the slide

 9 Type your name in the *Footer* entry box

 10 Click the *Don't Show on Title Slide* check box to eliminate these items from the title slide

 11 Click the *Apply to All* button to place these footer items on all slides, except the title slide.

The slide view returns. Note that there is no footer on the title slide, as expected.

 12 Press Pg Dn to move to Slide 2

As shown in Figure PG1-24, the footer information has been placed appropriately.

 13 Press Pg Dn to see the same footer information on Slide 3

 14 Save the POWER1 presentation again

 15 Exit PowerPoint or continue to the next section

FIGURE PG1–24 ■ EXAMINING FOOTER INFORMATION

The three footer items appear in all slides but the title slide.

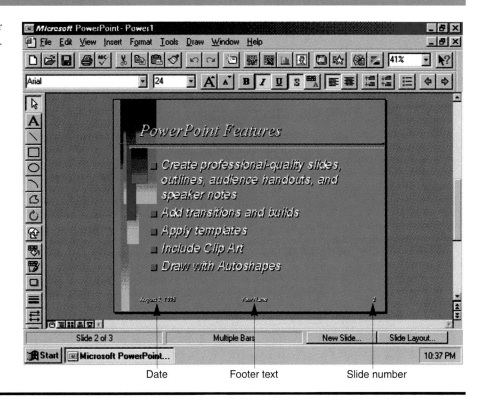

Date   Footer text   Slide number

To remove footer information, click *View* and then *Header and Footer* as before to access the *Header and Footer* dialog box. Then click each undesired item to remove its check mark. When you're done, click the *Apply All* button.

☑ **CHECKPOINT**

- ✓ Open the All About Me presentation in *Slide* view.
- ✓ Add a second slide entitled "Facts" with space for clip art, which lists four facts about you; then add a third slide entitled "My Class" that lists your class, semester, and instructor.
- ✓ Switch the order of the second and third slides using the slide sorter.
- ✓ Add a footer with your name and slide number. Run the slide show to see the results.
- ✓ Save the presentation again with the same name. Exit PowerPoint, if desired.

PRINTING A PRESENTATION

You can display your presentation in full color animation through the slide show view, prepare color slides by photographing each screen, or send your file to a profesional slide preparation service. You can also use PowerPoint's Print command to print your notes, outlines, or slides on paper or overhead transparencies. Presentations can be printed in full color or monochrome, depending on your printer. To prepare for these exercises,

STEPS

1 **Launch PowerPoint and open the POWER1 presentation if needed**

2 **Move to the title slide if you are not already there**

3 **Click *File* and then *Print***

> **Tip:** Do not use the *Print* toolbar button in this exercise. It will only print the complete slide view.

SPECIFYING PRINTING PARAMETERS

A *Print* dialog box appears as in Figure PG1-25. The *Printer* box at the top controls the printer that will be used. The *Print range* box lets you select the type and range of the materials that will be printed as follows:

FIGURE PG1–25 ■ THE *PRINT* DIALOG BOX

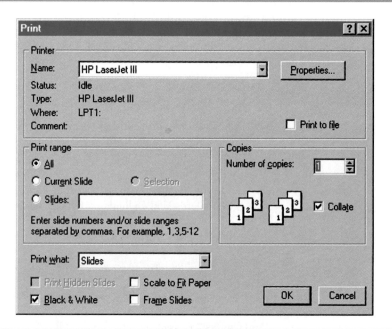

- *All* will print all slides in the presentation.
- *Current Slide* will print only the current slide page.
- *Slides* will print any range of slides. You can then type the desired range in the entry box to its right. For example, 1 will print only the first slide; 2–3 will print Slides 2 through 3; 1,3 prints Slide 1 and 3; –2 prints slides up to and including Slide 2; 2– prints from Slide 2 forward.

The *Copies* box lets you specify the number of copies that will print. The *Print what* entry box and drop-down arrow lets you select the type of image that will be printed— you can select from among slides, handouts (with two, three, or six slides to a page), notes pages, or outlines.

Assume you want to print the title and second slide in your presentation. Try the following:

1 Click the *Slides* option button in the *Print range* box

2 Type **–2** and delete any extra characters

> Note: The –2 indicates the first two slides in the series. You could have also typed 1,2 or 1–2 with the same result.

3 Make sure your printer is on and connected to your computer

> Tip: If you have a noncolor printer, you may get better results by also clicking the *Black & White* check box in the lower-left corner of the dialog box.

4 Click the *OK* button to print the selected slides

A *Print Status* dialog box appears as your slides print. When the final slide has been sent to the printer, the presentation window returns to the screen. Let's say you now wanted to print your entire presentation as a handout, with three images to a page. Try this:

5 Click *File* and then *Print*

6 Click the *All* option button in the *Print range* box to select all slides

7 Click the *Print what* drop-down arrow

8 Click the *Handouts (3 slides per page)* menu item in the drop-down list

9 Click the *OK* button

A one-page handout with all three slides should now print.

10 You may now exit PowerPoint

OTHER CONSIDERATIONS

In most cases, the default settings for printed slides will be acceptable. However, if the size or orientation of the printed slides do not meet your needs, you can use the *Slide Setup* dialog box to adjust some of these parameters. Click *File* and then *Slide Setup* to access this dialog box. You can then change the height, width, numbering scheme, and orientation of the slides that will be printed.

☑ CHECKPOINT

✓ Open the All About Me presentation.
✓ Print all slides in the presentation.
✓ Print only Slides 2 and 3 on a 3-slides-per-page handout.
✓ Print the outline of your presentation.
✓ Close the presentation window.

SUMMARY

- A presentation graphics program lets you combine text, graphics, and special effects into a professional-looking series of slides.
- A mouse is an input device that lets you control a screen pointer and select program commands or features. You can point, click, right-click, double-click, or drag and drop. Keyboard shortcut keys are available to bypass the normal menu structure.
- To launch PowerPoint, click *Start,* point to *Programs,* point to *MS Office* (or the appropriate submenu in your system), and click *Microsoft PowerPoint.* If a *Tip of the Day* dialog box appears, click *OK* and then click *Cancel.* To exit PowerPoint, click *File, Exit.*
- The PowerPoint window contains a program icon, a title bar, resizing buttons, a *Close* button, a mouse pointer, a menu bar, a status bar, three toolbars, and a workspace.
- PowerPoint's on-line help can be accessed through the menu or a *Help* button (?) that will invoke help specific to the current task.
- The first slide of any presentation should be a title slide that introduces the topic of the presentation to the audience.
- Predesigned templates, or patterns, determine the look of the overall presentation (presentation template), its design (design template), and each individual slide (autolayout). Templates control the color scheme, font styles and sizes, background graphics, and layout of the presentation.
- Autolayouts contain placeholders for objects that can be added to the slide. A placeholder is an empty object area that can hold a title, text, graphic or other data, depending on the autolayout you have selected. A selection box indicates when a placeholder is active.
- Clicking a view button will change PowerPoint's view to one of five options: slide view, outline view, slide sorter view, notes pages view, and slide show.
- To save a presentation, click *File, Save* (or click the *Save* toolbar button).

- A footer is information that can be added at the bottom of any or all slides. Power-Point provides three placeholders for footers: date and time, footer text, and a slide number.
- PowerPoint can print one or more slides, outlines, notes, or specially prepared hand-outs in various formats.

KEY TERMS

Shown in parentheses are the page numbers on which key terms are boldfaced.

Autolayout (PG13)
Close button (PG7)
Footer (PG35)
Formatting toolbar (PG14)
Menu bar (PG7)
Notes pages view (PG31)
Open (PG21)
Outline view (PG33)
Placeholder (PG14)

Presentation graphics
 (PG2)
Program icon (PG6)
Resizing button (PG7)
Save (PG18)
Selection box (PG16)
Shortcut keys (PG4)
Slide show (PG31)
Slide sorter view (PG29)

Slide view (PG28)
Status bar (PG8)
Template (PG11)
Title bar (PG6)
Toolbar (PG8)
View button (PG14)
Workspace (PG8)

QUIZ

TRUE/FALSE

____ 1. A presentation graphics program can combine visual special effects with text and graphics.

____ 2. No toolbars will appear in PowerPoint until you open a presentation window.

____ 3. PowerPoint creates a presentation as a series of slides.

____ 4. The autolayout template controls the overall color and design of a presentation.

____ 5. A slide must have all its placeholders filled before it can be saved.

____ 6. New slides are inserted before the current slide in the presentation window.

____ 7. Slide view is the default window setting in PowerPoint.

____ 8. Slide sorter view runs your presentation in sequence from beginning to end.

____ 9. PowerPoint offers three types of footers: date and time, text, and slide number.

____ 10. Entering a slide range of "4–" in the *Print* dialog box will print all slides that follow after Slide 4.

MULTIPLE CHOICE

____ 11. Which screen component does not normally appear when you launch PowerPoint?
   a. Title bar
   b. Presentation window
   c. Toolbars
   d. Status bar

____ 12. What feature in PowerPoint allows you to communicate by clicking icons or buttons instead of typing commands?
   a. WYSIWYG (what-you-see-is-what-you-get)
   b. Taskbar
   c. *Print* dialog box
   d. GUI (graphical user interface)

___ 13. Which button can you click to exit the PowerPoint program?
   a. *Close*
   b. *New*
   c. *Exit*
   d. *Minimize*

___ 14. Which of these templates controls the overall look of the entire presentation?
   a. Presentation template
   b. Design template
   c. Slide template
   d. Autolayout template

___ 15. Which of the following is an empty object area that can hold a title, text, or graphic?
   a. Autolayout
   b. Window
   c. Placeholder
   d. Template

___ 16. Which one of these is not offered as a view button in PowerPoint?
   a. Master view
   b. Slide view
   c. Slide show
   d. Outline view

___ 17. When entering text in a placeholder, if you type past the right margin without pressing the Enter key, how will the new text be affected?
   a. It will not be accepted.
   b. It will appear as dimmed characters.
   c. It will be moved to the next placeholder.
   d. It will wordwrap to the next line.

___ 18. How is the Save As command different from the Save command?
   a. Save As lets you change the filename or destination folder.
   b. Save As takes less time to save the file onto disk.
   c. Save As can only be accessed by mouse.
   d. There is no difference.

___ 19. Which autolayout arranges text in rows preceded by a small dot?
   a. Title
   b. Bulleted list
   c. Clip art
   d. Blank presentation

___ 20. Which screen view displays miniature images of your slides?
   a. Slide view
   b. Notes pages view
   c. Outline view
   d. Slide sorter view

MATCHING

Select the lettered item from the following figure that best matches each phrase.

___ 21. This PowerPoint feature provides quick mouse access to several frequently used file, text, or layout commands.

___ 22. Clicking this standard Windows feature will close the PowerPoint window.

FIGURE PG1–A ■ MATCHING FIGURE

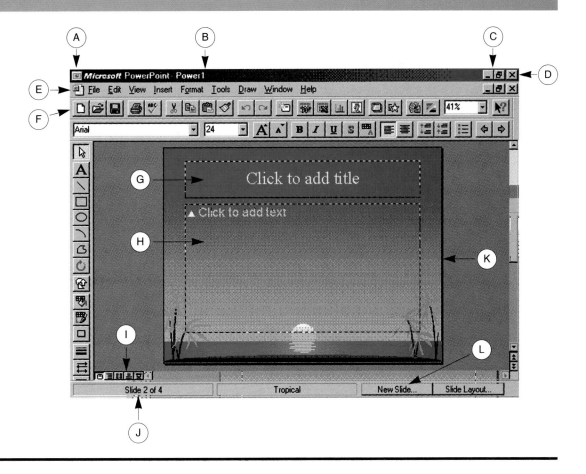

_____ 23. This PowerPoint feature allows you to place text in a bulleted list.
_____ 24. This standard Windows feature can be used to resize the program window by mouse only.
_____ 25. This feature displays information about the current slide.
_____ 26. This feature allows you to switch among screen views by clicking one button.
_____ 27. This item is also known as an autolayout.
_____ 28. This standard Windows feature provides access to PowerPoint's features through pull-down menus.
_____ 29. This item will activate a control menu.
_____ 30. This standard Windows feature identifies the current program window.

ANSWERS

True/False: 1. T; 2. F; 3. T; 4. F; 5. F; 6. F; 7. T; 8. F; 9. T; 10. F
Multiple Choice: 11. b; 12. d; 13. a; 14. b; 15. c; 16. a; 17. d; 18. a; 19. b; 20. d.
Matching: 21. f; 22. d; 23. h; 24. c; 25. j; 26. i; 27. k; 28. e; 29. a; 30. b.

EXERCISES

I. OPERATIONS

Provide the PowerPoint or Windows 95 actions required to do each of the following operations. For each operation, assume a hard-disk system with a disk in Drive A. You may want to verify each command by trying it on your computer system, where appropriate.

1. Start Windows and launch PowerPoint.

2. Enlarge the PowerPoint program window to full-screen size.

3. Obtain help information about creating a new presentation.

4. Create a new presentation title slide, using the blank presentation template and Azure design. (If you do not have this design template, you may substitute another one.)

5. Enter the title "Mastering Today's Software" and the subtitle "Practice #1."

6. Insert a new slide to hold a bulleted list.

7. Entitle the bulleted slide "Operations" and enter items 1–3 above as bulleted text.

8. Change the order of the slides in the presentation, and then change them back.

9. Run a slide show of your presentation.

10. In outline view, add item #4 above to the end of Slide 2's list.

11. Add your name and a slide number to the bottom of Slide 2 only.

12. Save your presentation as "PRACTICE1."

13. Print Slide 1 only in your presentation.

14. Print both slides in a handout.

15. Exit PowerPoint and shut down Windows.

II. COMMANDS

Describe what command is initiated or what is accomplished in PowerPoint by the actions described below. Assume that each exercise part is independent of any previous parts.

1. Clicking the *Maximize* button on the PowerPoint window.

2. Clicking the *Close* button on the PowerPoint window.

3. Clicking *File, New.*

4. Clicking a title placeholder in an autolayout.

5. Pressing the Enter key in a placeholder.

6. Clicking a view button.

7. Clicking the *Save in* drop-down arrow in the *File Save* dialog box.

8. Clicking *File, Save* after previously saving a file.

9. Right-clicking a slide in the Slide Show feature.

10. Clicking the *Slide Number* check box in the *Header and Footer* dialog box.

III. APPLICATIONS

Perform the following operations using your computer system. You will need a hard drive or network with Windows 95 and PowerPoint on it. You will also need one additional disk to store the results of this exercise. In a few words, describe how you accomplished each operation. *Note:* Of the six application exercises, each pair relates to school, home, and business, respectively.

APPLICATION 1: A COURSE HISTORY

1. Boot your computer; start Windows and launch PowerPoint.

2. Create the following slides, using a design template of your choice. Replace the words in brackets in the title slide with the appropriate data. Use bulleted list templates for all other slides. *Note*: If the course designations in Slides 2 and 3 are not appropriate for your school, you may change them.

Title Slide:	<Your School's Name> A Course History by <Your Name> <Date>

Slide 2:	Fall 1994 • English 101—A • Math 101—A- • Psy 105—B+ • Eco 200—Inc

Slide 3:	Spring 1995 • English 102—A • Math 105—B+ • Music 215—A • Eco 200—A-

3. Save the presentation as COURSES1, changing the *Save in* drive as needed.

4. Print a three-to-a-page handout of your presentation.

5. Add a fourth slide for Fall 1995, adding your own courses.

6. Add your name, the date, and slide numbers in a footer to all but the title slide.

7. Save the modified presentation with the same name.

8. Run the slide show to review your work.

9. Print an outline of your entire presentation.

10. Close the presentation and exit PowerPoint.

APPLICATION 2: A SCHOOL SAMPLER

1. Boot your computer; start Windows and launch PowerPoint.

2. Using an appropriate template, create a title slide to introduce a video presentation about your school. Replace the words in brackets in the title slide with the appropriate data.

> <Your School's Name>
> <Your School's Town and State>
> A Presentation by <Your Name>
> <Date>

3. Create a second slide, using the bulleted list template, entitled "Brief History." List five facts about your school, including its founding date.

4. Add a third slide, using a bulleted list and clip art placeholder. Title this slide "Courses of Study." List some of the areas of concentration in which students can major.

5. Save the presentation as SCHOOL1, changing the *Save in* drive as needed.

6. Change the order of Slides 2 and 3, and then print a three-to-a-page handout of your presentation.

7. Add a footer that displays your name centered in all but the title slide.

8. Save the modified presentation with the same name.

9. Run the slide show to review your work.

10. Print an outline of your entire presentation. Then close the presentation and exit PowerPoint.

APPLICATION 3: AN ONSCREEN RÉSUMÉ

1. Boot your computer; start Windows and launch PowerPoint.

2. Create the following title slide, using a design template of your choice. Replace the words in brackets in the title slide with the appropriate data.

> <Your Name>
> On-Screen Resume
> <Date>

3. Add two bulleted list slides with the following titles: Employment History, Education. Within each, add at least three facts about you that are appropriate to the specific slide.

4. Save the presentation as RESUME1, changing the *Save in* drive as needed.

5. Print the Employment History slide only.

6. Add a fourth slide, entitled "Personal Data" that presents bulleted items for date of birth, hobbies/interests, and other skills. Print an outline of the presentation.

7. Add your name and the date in a footer in all slides but the title slide.

8. Save the modified presentation with the same name.

9. Run the slide show to review your work.

10. Close the presentation and exit PowerPoint.

APPLICATION 4: A *STAR TREK* PRIMER

1. Boot your computer; start Windows and launch PowerPoint.

2. Create the following title slide, using a futuristic-looking design template of your choice. Replace the words in brackets in the title slide with the appropriate data.

> Introduction to *Star Trek*
> Produced by
> <Your Name>

3. Add the following three bulleted list slides:

Slide 2:   *Star Trek*
             • Ship: Enterprise
             • Captain: James T. Kirk
             • Actor: William Shatner
             • Notable Character: Mr. Spock

Slide 3:   *Star Trek: Next Generation*
             • Ship: Enterprise
             • Captain: Jean-Luc Picard
             • Actor: Patrick Stewart
             • Notable Character: Lt. Cmdr. Data

Slide 4:   *Star Trek: Deep Space Nine*
             • Ship: Defiant
             • Captain: Benjamin Sisko
             • Actor: Avery Brooks
             • Notable Character: Quark

4. Save the presentation as TREK1, changing the *Save in* drive as needed.

5. Print the presentation, using the six-slides-to-a-page handout format.

6. Add a fifth slide, entitled *Star Trek: Voyager* that presents these bulleted items: Ship: Voyager, Captain: Kathryn Janeway, Actor: Kate Mulgrew, Notable Character: Kes. Print an outline of the presentation.

7. Add the date and slide number in a footer on all slides.

8. Save the modified presentation with the same name.

9. Run the slide show to review your work.

10. Close the presentation and exit PowerPoint.

APPLICATION 5: VIDEO MARKETING

1. Boot your computer; start Windows and launch PowerPoint.

2. Using an appropriate environmentally-oriented or related template, create a title slide to introduce a video presentation about an imaginary product called Shrub-Garb Garbage Bags. Replace the words in brackets in the title slide with your name.

> Shrub-Garb Products
> Proudly Presents...
> Shrub-Garb Garbage Bags
> A Presentation by <Your Name>

3. Create a second slide as follows, using the bulleted list template:

> Shrub-Garb Garbage Bags
> • Fully disposable garbage product
> • Fully biodegradable
> • Environmentally pleasing
> • Durable and popular
> • Resemble native bushes and shrubs

4. Add a third slide, using a bulleted list and clip art placeholder, as follows:

> Available Shrub-Garb Sizes
> • Azalea—for single households
> • Rhododendron—for couples
> • Pine—for small families
> • Sequoia—for large families with pets

5. Save the presentation as SHRUB1, changing the *Save in* drive as needed.

6. Change the order of Slides 2 and 3, and then print the entire presentation.

7. Add a footer that displays the slide number in all slides including the title.

8. Save the modified presentation with the same name.

9. Run the slide show to review your work.

10. Print an outline of your entire presentation. Then close the presentation and exit PowerPoint.

APPLICATION 6: EXECUTIVE TRAINING

1. Boot your computer; start Windows and launch PowerPoint.

2. Using an appropriate template, create a title slide to introduce a presentation to be used in an executive training session to learn about Microsoft Office for Windows 95. Replace the words in brackets in the title slide with the appropriate data.

> Mar-Park Consulting Services
> Executive Summary
> Microsoft Office for Windows 95
> Prepared by <Your Name>
> <Date>

3. Add a second slide, using a bulleted list with a left clip art placeholder, as follows:

> Word
> • Enter, edit and print letters
> • Use writing tools
> • Prepare letters with mail merge
> • Combine graphics with text
> • Use linking and embedding

4. Add a third slide as follows, using the bulleted list template:

> Office 95 Professional Edition
> • Word Processing—Word
> • Spreadsheets—Excel
> • Database Management—Access
> • Presentation Graphics—PowerPoint
> • Communication—Mail

5. Save the presentation as OFFICE1, changing the *Save in* drive as needed.

6. Change the order of Slides 2 and 3, and then print the entire presentation.

7. Add a footer that displays the date, company name (Mar-Park Consulting) and slide number in all slides including the title.

8. Save the modified presentation with the same name.

9. Run the slide show to review your work.

10. Print an outline of your entire presentation. Then close the presentation and exit PowerPoint.

MASTERY CASES

The following mastery cases allow you to demonstrate how much you have learned about this software. Each case describes a fictitious problem or need that can be solved using the skills you have learned in this chapter. Although minimum acceptable outcomes are specified, you are expected and encouraged to design your presentation (files, data, lists) in ways that display your personal mastery of the software. Feel free to show off your skills. Use real data from your own experience in your solution, although you may also fabricate data if needed.

These mastery cases allow you to display your ability to

- Launch the program.
- Create a new presentation and select templates.
- Enter titles and bulleted lists.
- Add appropriate footers to slides.
- Save the presentation on disk.
- Run the presentation and print it in various forms.

CASE 1: COURSE OUTLINE

Your instructor has asked you to prepare a presentation about the course in which you are currently learning this software. Using your course syllabus or outline, prepare a set of slides that present the material included in this course in proper sequence. Save the presentation and then print its outline.

CASE 2: MUSIC COLLECTION

You are planning to sell your music collection and would like to prepare a presentation to show to potential buyers. Create a set of slides that each display an album title and artist, with bullets for the major songs included. Save the presentation and print one slide.

CASE 3: SOFTWARE PRESENTATION

Your boss would like you to demonstrate how PowerPoint can benefit your coworkers. Prepare a short presentation that introduces the basics of PowerPoint to your company. Save the presentation and print a three-slides-to-a-page handout.

2

ENHANCING THE PRESENTATION

OBJECTIVES

After completing this chapter, you will be able to

1 Add text, delete text, and check spelling in existing slides.

2 Emphasize text appearance with font enhancements.

3 Apply graphics (clip art and AutoShapes) to your slides.

4 Explain and create transitions and builds.

5 Automate the slide show and rehearse presentations.

6 Describe techniques for linking and embedding objects.

OVERVIEW

This chapter extends the skills introduced in Chapter 1 by exploring ways to enhance your presentations. Techniques for editing and checking text spelling are presented, followed by procedures for adjusting text appearance. Next, graphic images are added to slides through clip art and Autoshapes. Enhancing the show's progression are explored, including the use of transitions and builds. Next, you will learn to time and automate a presentation and to link or embed objects from other programs.

PG

EDITING A SLIDE

As with other application programs, PowerPoint's real value lies in its ability to let you alter your work anytime the need arises. You can edit your text—change text, add new text, or delete old text—to fine-tune the presentation, update it with new information, or correct errors. You can also change the look of the entire presentation by selecting another design template, as you will soon see. To prepare for these exercises,

STEPS

1 Start Windows and launch PowerPoint (Escape from the *Tip of the Day* and *PowerPoint* dialog boxes if needed)

 2 Open the POWER1 presentation

> **Tip:** PowerPoint offers another way to open a recently used presentation: click *File*. By default, the four most recent presentations should be listed just above the *Exit* option in the pull-down menu. You can now click the presentation's name to open it. (If this option is not active, you can set it for future use after you have opened a presentation: click *Tools*, *Options*, the *General* tab, the *Recently Used File List* check box, select the number of entries to display, and click *OK*.)

 3 By default, the slide view should be displayed when you open a presentation. Switch to the slide view if it is not

ADDING AND DELETING TEXT

PowerPoint offers many ways to add text to a slide. You can use the slide view or outline view. You can copy and paste text from another slide or type directly from the keyboard. If you type, the text is inserted into the existing screen text. Here are a few examples:

INSERTING TEXT.   The most direct way to add new text is to insert it. Try the following steps to add the word "graphics" into the bulleted list in Slide 2:

STEPS

1 Move to Slide 2   [Pg Dn]

2 Click to the right of the last "t" in "Include Clip Art" as shown in Figure PG2-1a

FIGURE PG2–1 ■ **INSERTING TEXT**

(a) Click at the desired position.
(b) The new text has been added.

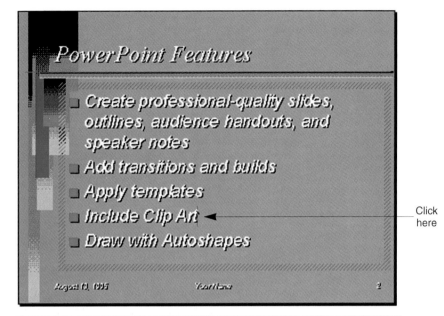

(a)

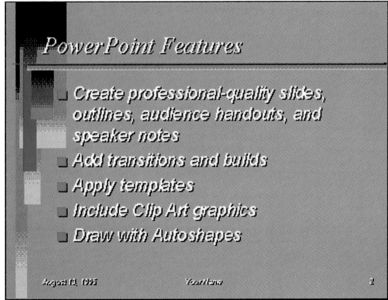

(b)

By clicking, you not only position the insertion point, but also open the placeholder for use. As expected, a frame appears around the list.

3 **Press** **Spacebar** **to insert a space after the word "Art"**

4 **Type** **graphics** **but do not press** ↵ **(pressing** ↵ **adds another bulleted item)**

> **Tip:** If you pressed ⏎ by mistake, press the Backspace key to correct it.

As shown in Figure PG2-1b, the new text has been inserted into the slide.

5 Click outside the placeholder to close it

6 Save this presentation with the new name, POWER2 (click *File, Save As*)

COPYING AND PASTING TEXT. Another way to insert text is to select a text block from another location in the presentation, copy it, and then paste it where you want it. For example, this exercise will copy text from Slide 2 and paste it into Slide 3:

STEPS

1 Move to Slide 2

You can now select the text to be copied.

2 Click to the left of "transitions and builds" in the second bullet as shown in Figure PG2-2a

3 Click and drag the pointer past the "s" in "builds" so that the entire phrase is highlighted, as shown in Figure PG2-2b   [**SHIFT** + →]

4 Click *Edit* and then *Copy,* or click the *Copy* toolbar button   [**Ctrl** + **C**]

The selected text block has been copied to the Windows holding buffer, called the Clipboard, and is now available for pasting.

5 Move to Slide 3

6 Click to the right of the last "w" in "Master View"

7 Click *Edit* and then *Paste* or click the *Paste* toolbar button   [**Ctrl** + **V**]

The text block has been pasted back into the presentation. Don't worry if the font size or style differs; you'll be deleting the text in the next section. You'll also learn how to change fonts shortly.

8 Click outside the placeholder to close it

> **Tip:** To *move* text, select *Cut* (Ctrl+X) in Step 4, instead of *Copy*. It will be removed from its previous location and placed in the Clipboard. It can then be pasted into the new location.

FIGURE PG2–2 ■ COPYING AND PASTING TEXT

(a)Click at the start of the text block to be copied.
(b) Drag the pointer to the end of the block.

Click here

(a)

(b)

DELETING TEXT.   Removing unwanted text from a presentation is a simple procedure, similar to inserting. Move to the slide, click to the left or right of the text to be deleted, and then press either the Delete or Backspace key, depending on the location of the insertion point. For example, to delete the word "Audience" in Slide 2, do the following:

1 Move to Slide 2   **[Pg Up]**

2 Click to the left of the "a" in "audience" on the second line of text

3 Press **Delete** nine times to remove the word and space after it

4 Click outside the placeholder to close it

Note that any remaining text moves left to fill in the gap. Try one more deletion, this time using the Backspace key as follows:

5 Move to Slide 3   **[Pg Dn]**

6 Click to the right of the last "s" in "builds" at the bottom of the list

7 Press **Backspace** ten times to remove the last two words

8 Press **Backspace** twelve more times to remove the word "transitions"

Note how the insertion point moves backward through the text to the previous bulleted item.

9 Press **Backspace** until you remove the entire "Master View" item and its bullet

10 Click outside the placeholder to close it, then save the POWER2 presentation

> **Tip:** You can also delete text by selecting a text block (as you did in copying and pasting) and then select *Edit* and then *Cut* from the menu or press the Delete key.

REPLACING TEXT. You can replace old text with new by using a combination of inserting and deleting. Simply insert the new text and then delete the portion that is no longer desired.

> **Tip:** If you no longer want an entire slide in your presentation, you can delete it in the slide view or note view by clicking *Edit* in the menu bar and then *Delete Slide*.

KEY FORMAT ENHANCEMENTS

The Design template that you select determines the overall appearance of each slide you create. It does this through a slide *master* that contains the basic format—color, layout, spacing, font (typestyle), and font size. Although these default settings will be fine for most purposes, there will be times when you want to adjust them to better suit your presentation's needs. PowerPoint offers two ways to do this: you can change the slide master itself, which will affect every slide in your presentation, or you can move to specific slides and make adjustments to some aspects of its format. You'll take a quick look at both in the following exercise. To prepare,

1   **Start Windows and launch PowerPoint if needed**

    2   **Open the POWER2 presentation**

VIEWING THE SLIDE MASTER.   Each autolayout in PowerPoint has its own master that controls the format and appearance of the slide. For example, there is a **title master** for the title slide and a **slide master** for each additional slide autolayout in your presentation. Master formats for handouts and notes are available as well. Although you will not make any changes in these masters for now, this exercise demonstrates the technique for your use in the future. Let's say you wanted to change the master layout for all the bulleted lists in your presentation.

1   **Move to Slide 2, the first bulleted list**

2   **Point to the *Slide View* button just above the status bar**

3   **Press and hold   Shift**

Note how the "Slide View" identifying label changes to "Slide Master." This indicates that you can access the master for this slide by holding the Shift key when clicking the view button as follows:

4   **Hold   Shift   and click the *Slide View* (now *Slide Master*) button, then release**

The slide master appears in the window, as shown in Figure PG2-3. Note that the status bar also displays the message "Slide Master." It's now a simple matter of clicking the desired placeholder to select it for change.

5   **Click the top placeholder for the title (which displays the message "Click to edit Master title style")**

6   **Now, click *Format* in the menu bar**

As shown in Figure PG2-4, the *Format* submenu allows you to alter various facets of the title. You could change the font, alignment, line spacing, color scheme, or background objects. If you select the font menu item, you could further adjust the typestyle, size, color, or text enhancement of the title. For now, however, leave this master as is by performing the following steps:

7   **Click outside the pull-down menu to cancel it**

PG

FIGURE PG2–3 ■ VIEWING A SLIDE MASTER

Holding the Shift key while
clicking a view button will
access a slide master.

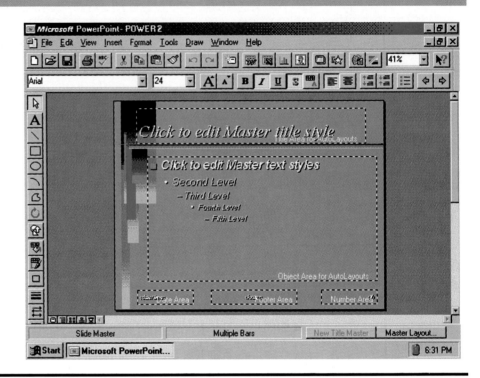

FIGURE PG2–4 ■ THE FORMAT SUBMENU

8 **Click outside the master slide to deselect the placeholder**

9 **Click the *Slide* view button to return to the normal view screen**

When you alter a slide master, every slide in the presentation will reflect the change. (The title slide is not affected unless the title master is changed.) For example, increasing the font size of a bullet item in the slide master will immediately affect every bulleted item throughout the presentation.

Changes made to the Title or Slide masters affect only the current presentation—not others that may use the same design template.

This opens the possibility of canceling master changes by simply changing the design template of the presentation to another design, and then back again.

> **Tip: You can access the slide masters by clicking *View, Master* and then selecting the desired master.**

CHANGING TEXT ATTRIBUTES.   You can also apply changes directly to one slide, or the text within it, without affecting the rest of your presentation. In this case, your adjustments will supersede, or take precedence over, the default settings of the master for the text you select. Let's say you want to change the look of the bulleted text in Slide 2. Perform the following steps to see this effect:

STEPS

1 **Move to Slide 2 and switch to the slide view if needed**

2 **In the first bulleted item, click to the immediate left of the "C" in "Create"**

3 **Now, click and drag the mouse pointer to the last "s" in "Autoshapes"   [Shift   + →] at the bottom of the list**

The selected text block should be highlighted as shown in Figure PG2-5.

4 **If the text is not highlighted correctly, click outside the slide and repeat Steps 2 and 3**

PowerPoint provides two ways to change the text attributes. You can use the *Format* menu option to access the *Font* dialog box, or you can change the enhancements directly on the Formatting toolbar. You'll try both for practice.

Using the Font Dialog Box.   The *Font* dialog box offers a bit more detail and control when adjusting text enhancements. It also provides the only way to change text enhancements by keyboard.

5 **Click *Format*, and then click *Font***

The *Font* dialog box appears, as shown in Figure PG2-6. Examine the types of changes you can make within this dialog box:

PG

FIGURE PG2–5 ■ **CHANGING TEXT ATTRIBUTES**

The selected text block is highlighted.

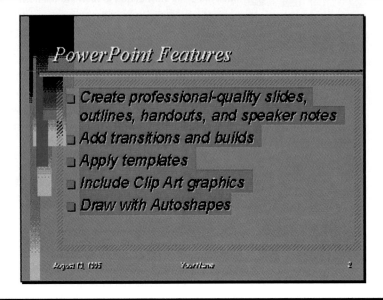

FIGURE PG2–6 ■ **THE *FONT* DIALOG BOX**

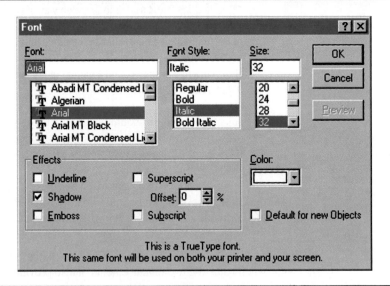

■ *Font:* The overall typestyle that will be applied to text. Depending on your system, more than 60 different fonts, or typestyles, will be offered in the scroll list beneath the current font entry.

- *Font Style:* An enhancement that changes the font from its regular style to either bold, italic, or a combination of both. You may only choose one of the choices offered.
- *Size:* The size of the font, measured in points. A point is approximately 1/72″ so that an uppercase character in the typical 12-pt. size measures just about ⅙″ in height.
- *Effects:* Additional text enhancements that provide emphasis. Check marks indicate which effects are currently active. You can apply up to three effects: (1) Underline, (2) Shadow or Emboss, (3) Superscript or Subscript, or none at all.
- *Color:* The current text color appears in the *Color* box. By clicking the drop-down arrow, you can choose from among eight coordinated colors. If you do not want any of these colors, you can click the *Other Color...* option to access hundreds of shades and hues.

You'll now change a few settings for the selected text:

6 Click *Regular* in the *Font Style* box   [**Alt** + **O** , then ↓ or ↑]

7 Click 28 in the Size box   [**Alt** + **S** , then ↓ or ↑]

8 Click the *Shadow* check box to cancel it   [**Alt** + **A**]

9 Click the *Color* drop-down arrow to access its colors   [**Alt** + **C** , then ↓]

10 Click the red color box (third on top) for now   [↑ , → , ↵]

11 Click the OK button to accept   [↵]

12 Click outside the placeholder to deselect the text block   [**Esc** , **Esc**]

The bulleted items should now reflect your changes. If not, repeat the above steps to correct the text attributes and enhancements as needed.

Using the Formatting Toolbar.   You can also change many text attributes or enhancements directly by mouse through the Formatting toolbar. Try the following changes:

13 Click the bottom placeholder to select it

Note that the current font settings are displayed in the Formatting toolbar, as shown in Figure PG2-7. Reading from left to right, you can see that an Arial font of 28 pt. size is in use. The central enhancement buttons are not depressed, indicating that the text is regular without any enhancement. In addition, the depressed *Left Alignment* button and Bullet *On/Off* buttons show that these features are active in this placeholder.

14 Select all the bulleted items as you did in Steps 2 and 3 earlier

You could change font size by clicking the drop-down arrow in the *Font Size* entry box and clicking a desired size, but you can also do it as follows:

 15 Click the *Increase Font Size* button

FIGURE PG2–7 ■ USING THE FORMATTING TOOLBAR

The current placeholder settings are shown in the toolbar.

Formatting toolbar ➤

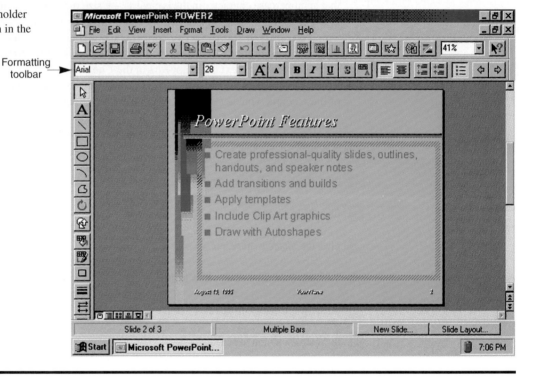

The font increases to the next available point size. Try these enhancements:

16 **Click the** *Shadow* **button to add a shadow enhancement to the text**

17 **Click the** *Text Color* **button**

18 **Click the white box in the lower-left corner**

One more change. Let's say you wanted to increase the spacing between bulleted items. Try this:

19 **Click the** *Increase Paragraph Spacing* **button twice**

Note how the spacing increases between lines.

20 **Click the** *Decrease Paragraph Spacing* **button once**

Your screen and Formatting toolbar should resemble Figure PG2-8. Repeat the necessary steps if it does not.

21 **Click outside the placeholder to deselect it**

FIGURE PG2–8 ■ THE ADJUSTED TEXT

The Formatting toolbar
displays the new settings.

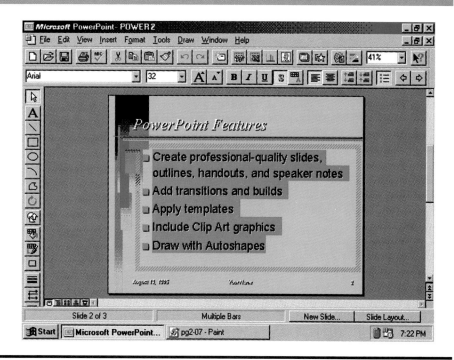

22 Save the POWER2 presentation

23 You can exit PowerPoint for now or continue

> **Tip:** To change text settings in a footer placeholder, first change to the slide master
> view and click the desired footer object. The change you make will affect all slides.

SPELL CHECKING

Like a word processor, PowerPoint includes a spell checker that you can use to check
for potential typographical errors and misspelled words in all parts (slides, notes, handouts, or outlines) of your presentation. To prepare, do the following:

STEPS

1 Start Windows and launch PowerPoint if needed

2 Open POWER1

> Tip: Windows 95 lets you access a file directly without having to first launch a pro-
> gram. Try this approach sometime instead of Steps 1 and 2: Start Windows, click
> *Start* and point to the *Documents* menu item. Click the POWER1 document if it appears
> in the list. PowerPoint will launch and open POWER1 without further commands.

You will now purposely misspell a word to see how the spell check operates.

3 Move to Slide 2

4 Click between the "t" and "e" in "Create" in the first bullet item

5 Press **Delete** to remove the final "e" in Create

Your screen should resemble Figure PG2-9. Fix it if it does not.

6 Click outside the placeholder to deselect it

7 Move to Slide 1

You are now ready to try the spell check feature.

 8 Click *Tools* and then click *Spelling* in the menu, or click the *Spelling*   [**F7**]
button on the toolbar

A *Spelling* dialog box appears, as shown in Figure PG2-10. PowerPoint checks each word
in your presentation against its dictionary of acceptable words. The first word that does
not appear in its dictionary will be highlighted on the slide and appears in the "Not in Dictionary" line of the dialog box. The dialog box may suggest alternative spellings in the

FIGURE PG2–9 ■ PREPARING FOR THE SPELL CHECK

The word "create" has been
purposely misspelled as
"creat".

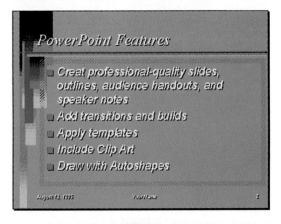

FIGURE PG2–10 ■ THE *SPELLING* DIALOG BOX

The first "misspelled" word
has been located.

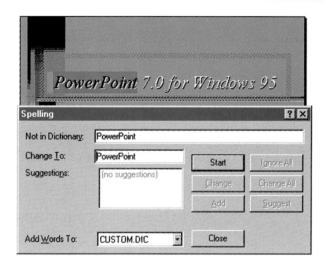

Change To or *Suggestions* box. The spelling command buttons located at the right of the
dialog box perform the functions displayed in Table PG2-1. (Remember, to select a button by mouse, click it. With the keyboard, press the Alt key and the underlined letter of the
button's command.)

Examine your screen and Figure PG2-10. Note that the word "PowerPoint" may be
highlighted at the top of the slide and that the spell check has no suggestions for a proper spelling. If your spell check does not stop at "PowerPoint," continue with step 10.

TABLE PG2–1 ■ *SPELLING* DIALOG BOX OPTIONS

Command Button	Function
Ignore	Skips the highlighted word once without correcting it. The program will high-light this word again if it appears later in the presentation.
Ignore All	Skips the highlighted word now and for the remainder of the presentation.
Change	Replaces the highlighted word at this point in the presentation with the word highlighted in the *Change To* box. To change the word in the *Change To* box to a different word in the *Suggestions* box, click the desired word, or press the down arrow to move the highlight to it.
Change All	Changes all occurrences of the highlighted word to the new word.
Add	Adds a word to the custom dictionary listed in the *Add Words To* box. This is useful for technical words, proper names or other words that are used often. You should not attempt to add words to the dictionary if you are not using your own computer system.
Suggest	List word suggestions in the *Suggestions* list box.

PG

9 If "PowerPoint" is highlighted, click the *Ignore All* button to continue

⊠ **Tip: You can exit the spell check at any time by clicking the *Close* button.**

Remember, selecting the *Ignore All* button tells the spell check to ignore "PowerPoint" while checking the remainder of the presentation.

10 If the spell check stops at your first name, click the *Ignore* button to continue

11 If the spell check stops at your last name, click the *Ignore* button to continue

The spell check has now found "Creat" and suggests that you change it to "Create."

12 Click the *Change* button to make this change

The spell check now locates "Autoshapes."

13 Click the *Ignore* button to continue past "Autoshapes"

When the spell check is completed, a *Microsoft PowerPoint* dialog box appears, advising you that the entire presentation has been checked.

14 Click the *OK* button to end the spell check procedure

15 If a placeholder is open, click outside it now to close it

As in word processing, the spell check is a useful tool, but it is not infallible. It will find most of your mistakes, but it will not look for capitalization, nor will it find words that are spelled correctly *but used wrong,* as in "Ewe wear write" instead of "You were right." Also, unlike more powerful word processing spellers, it will not find duplicate words, such as "the the"—a common typing error. Whether you use a spell check program or not, it is still *your* responsibility to check your own work for proper spelling, usage, and grammar.

⊠ **16** Close the POWER1 window, *without* saving it

Although you will not practice it here, PowerPoint also provides a means for you to check the style of your presentation through its *style checker.* By clicking *Tools* and then *Style Checker* in the menu, you will access a dialog box that allows you to check the spelling as well as the visual clarity (text size, number of diffferent fonts and bullets), case, and end punctuation of your presentation. You simply click the *Start* button in the dialog box and follow the instructions, much like the spell check procedure. When you're finished, click the *OK* button to end.

CHANGING THE DESIGN TEMPLATE

As your presentation develops, you may want to examine other designs to find the most effective one for your audience. You can easily change the design as follows:

1 Open the POWER2 presentation

2 Click the *Apply Design Template* in the Standard toolbar, or click *Format* and then *Apply Design Template* in the menu

An *Apply Design Template* dialog box appears, as shown in Figure PG2-11. The left *Name* box lists more than 20 available design templates. The right side displays a preview of the highlighted design. For example,

3 Scroll down the list to find the *Sparkle* design   [**Shift** + **Tab** , ↓]

> Note: If your computer does not have the Sparkle design, select another design of your choice.

4 Click the *Sparkle* design to highlight it

The Sparkle design appears in the preview box. To apply this design to your presentation:

5 Click the *Apply* button

FIGURE PG2–11 ■ THE *APPLY DESIGN TEMPLATE* DIALOG BOX

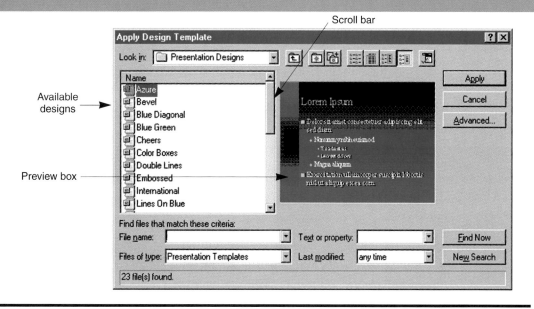

(In general, if you did not want to change the design, you could click the *Cancel* button.) The Sparkle design template has been applied to your entire presentation.

6 **Run the slide show or page through each slide in the slide view to see the effect of the new design**

7 **Save the presentation with the new name POWER3**

8 **Feel free to explore other design templates, but do not save the presentation again**

9 **Exit PowerPoint or continue to the next section**

Tip: At times, changing to another design may require you to adjust spacing or text attributes for best effect. It is important to review the presentation completely.

☑ CHECKPOINT

✓ Open the ALL ABOUT ME presentation. Increase the text size of the bullets in the My Class slide.
✓ In the Facts slide, delete the last fact in the list.
✓ Spell check the entire presentation and correct or ignore as needed.
✓ Increase the line spacing between the facts in Slide 3.
✓ Select and apply a new design template. Save the presentation.

ADDING CLIP ART

Even though your presentation may have enhanced text or a pleasing layout, it can often be improved by adding graphic images to some or all of its slides. PowerPoint allows you to add graphics to your presentations by selecting them from a library of **clip art**—professionally prepared graphic images—or by drawing your own using various drawing tools. You will first examine the clip art technique. To prepare for these exercises,

---

STEPS

---

1 **Start Windows and launch PowerPoint if needed**

2 **Open the POWER3 presentation**

You can add clip art into an existing slide placeholder, or you can place it yourself on a slide. The placeholder option automatically positions and sizes the image for you, and it will always adjust the image correctly if you change the design. Placing the clip art yourself involves resizing and positioning the image, which may then have to be resized or moved if you change designs. You will practice both techniques in the following exercises. Use whichever is appropriate for your needs. You may use either one or a combination of both in any presentation.

INSERTING A CLIP ART GRAPHIC IMAGE

Inserting a clip art image into a slide is a fairly simple process. You move to the desired slide, access the library of clip art images, and select the one you want.

USING A PLACEHOLDER.   The following exercise places a clip art image into the placeholder that already exists in Slide 3. This is the most direct way to add clip art to your presentation:

STEPS

1 **Move to Slide 3**

2 **Double-click the clip art placeholder on the right side of Slide 3 as shown in Figure PG2-12**

After a short wait, a *Microsoft ClipArt Gallery* dialog box appears, as shown in Figure PG2-13a. The *Pictures* box in the center currently displays the first few images in the collection. Hundreds more can be accessed by scrolling or selecting a given category. A rectangular highlight shows the current clip art selection. A brief description appears directly beneath the *Pictures* box. Although you can select any image at all, clip art should relate to the topic being presented. Because this slide displays various views, you'll use the image entitled "Future Forecast" found in the Cartoons category. To locate this image, do the following:

FIGURE PG2–12 ■ INSERTING CLIP ART INTO A PLACEHOLDER

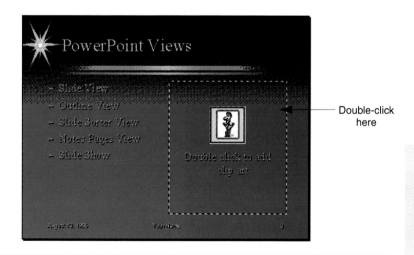

Double-click here

FIGURE PG2–13 ■ THE *MICROSOFT CLIPART GALLERY* DIALOG BOX

(a) The initial screen displays all categories.
(b) Moving to the "Future Forecast" image.

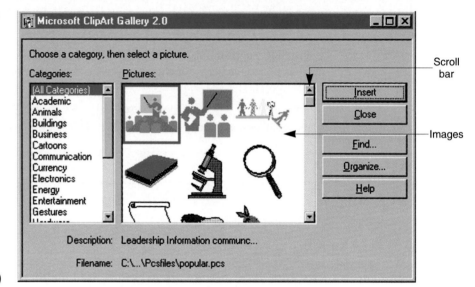

(a)

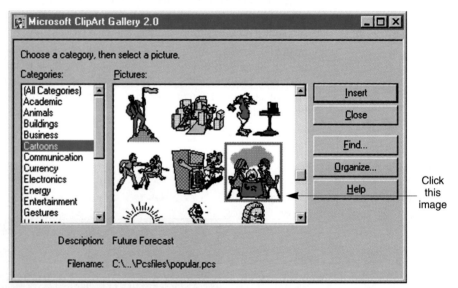

(b)

3 **Click the *Cartoons* Category**   [**Alt** + **G** , then ↓]

Tip: Although all images are contained in the "(All Categories)" selection, it is easier to view each set of related images by selecting a specific category.

The *Pictures* box now displays the cartoon subset of the clip art gallery.

4 In the *Pictures* box, scroll down to the ninth row   [**Alt** + **P** , then ↓]

The image in your *Picture* box may be located in a slightly different position than the one shown in the figure. If your computer does not have this image available, choose another cartoon.

5 Click the "Future Forecast" image as shown in Figure PG2-13b   [→ , →]

A highlighting rectangle appears around the chosen clip art and its description, "Future Forecast,"is displayed beneath the *Pictures* box. Make sure you find the correct clip art image before continuing.

6 Click the *Insert* button to accept it   [↵]

7 Click outside the clip art placeholder to deselect it for now

Your screen should resemble Figure PG2-14. The clip art image has been added to the slide, properly sized and positioned within the placeholder.

8 Save the POWER3 presentation

PLACING CLIP ART ON YOUR OWN.   You will now place another piece of clip art in your presentation. This time, you will add an image in the upper-right corner of Slide 2, without the advantage of an autolayout placeholder.

STEPS

1 Move to Slide 2

FIGURE PG2–14 ■ THE CLIP ART IS INSERTED IN THE PLACEHOLDER

2 Click the *Insert Clip Art* toolbar button, or click *Insert* and then *Clip Art* from the menu

The *Microsoft ClipArt Gallery* dialog box reappears as expected.

3 Click the "(All Categories)" option in the *Categories* box if it is not already highlighted

4 Click the clip art image in the upper left corner entitled "Professor Leadership Informat..."

Remember to check the description beneath the *Pictures* box to make certain you have the correct one. If you do not have this image, choose any other image for this exercise.

5 Click the *Insert* button

A tiny frame appears in the center of the slide containing the clip art image as in Figure PG2-15. (Your image may be larger.) Although the image has been successfully inserted into the slide, it is not useful in its current size and location. For now,

6 Click outside the clip art frame to deselect it

RESIZING AND POSITIONING AN OBJECT

When you insert clip art into a slide that does not have a clip art placeholder, Power-Point creates a small clip art object frame that is centered in the slide. You can now adjust its size and position it as desired. You can use these same techniques to change the image's size and position in the slide at any time.

FIGURE PG2–15 ■ THE INSERTED CLIP ART IMAGE

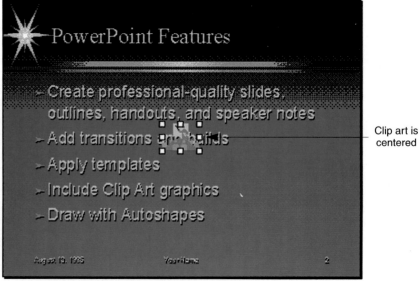

Clip art is centered

1 **Click the clip art object frame to select it**

As shown in Figure PG2-16a, the corners and sides of the object frame now display small squares, called *handles*. **Handles** can be dragged by mouse to alter the size of the object frame.

To resize the clip art image, perform the following steps:

2 **Point to the lower-right corner frame handle**

When your pointer is correctly positioned, it will appear as a diagonal line with arrows at both ends, as shown in Figure PG2-16b.

3 **Click and drag the pointer diagonally down and right until the image size (indicated by a dotted rectangle) expands to about twice its current size, as shown in Figure PG2-16c. Then release the mouse**

The exact size is not important for now, for you can always adjust it later after it has been moved. Simply click and drag a handle as needed and then release the mouse.

> **Tip:** Dragging a corner handle maintains the image's proportions, whereas dragging an edge handle will change only the height or width. To enlarge an image, drag a corner away from the center of the frame. To reduce the image, drag toward the center.

You can now reposition the clip art image in the upper-right corner, as shown in Figure PG2-17. Perform these steps:

4 **Point anywhere within the image frame**

5 **Using Figure PG2-17 as a guide, click and drag the image (which appears as a dotted rectangle) to the upper-right corner and then release the mouse**

FIGURE PG2–16 ■ RESIZING AN OBJECT

(a) Handles appear around a selected object.
(b) Pointing to the lower-right corner handle.
(c) Drag the pointer to resize the object.

Handles

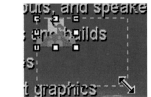

(a)   (b)   (c)

FIGURE PG2-17 ■ **THE REPOSITIONED CLIP ART**

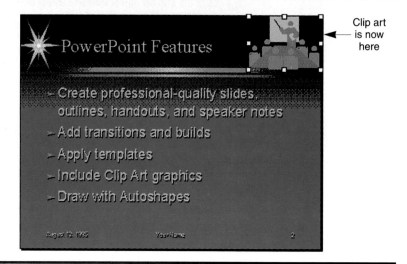

Clip art
is now
here

Tip: You can also press the arrow keys to move the graphic to the desired position.

6 Click outside the frame, away from the text placeholders, to deselect the frame

7 Save the presentation as POWER3A

DELETING AN OBJECT

When it is no longer needed, you can remove an object easily. Try this:

STEPS

1 Click the clip art image in Slide 2 to select it

As expected, a frame with handles appears around the image, as in Figure PG2-17.

2 Press **Delete**

It's gone. As in most Windows programs, PowerPoint also provides a way to undo your previous commands in case you make a mistake. For example,

 3 Click *Edit* and then *Undo Clear* or click the *Undo* button   [**Ctrl** + **Z** on the toolbar]

The deletion has been cancelled. The clip art image is back.

4 Now, close the presentation *without* saving it again

CHECKPOINT

- ✓ In the Fact slide of the ALL ABOUT ME presentation, add appropriate clip art in the placeholder provided by the autolayout.
- ✓ In the My Class slide, add, resize and position a clip art graphic in the lower-right corner.
- ✓ Move the clip art you just inserted to the upper-right corner of the My Class slide.
- ✓ Reduce the size of the inserted clip art in the My Class slide. Print the slide.
- ✓ Delete the clip art in the My Class slide. Save the presentation.

DRAWING ART WITH AUTOSHAPES

You can also draw images with PowerPoint's Drawing toolbar. For example, to add a shape in the upper-right corner of Slide 2, try the following:

STEPS

1 **Open the POWER3 presentation**

The Drawing toolbar that appears on the left side of the presentation window contains the tools you will need to create or alter your own graphic. Figure PG2-18 lists the function

FIGURE PG2–18 ■ THE DRAWING TOOLBAR

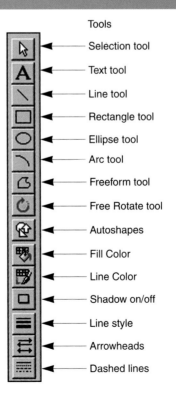

of each of its buttons. Although it is not required, you may want to place a ruler on the screen to help position a graphic on a slide. To do this,

2 **Click _View_ and then _Ruler_**

Vertical and horizontal rulers appear on the screen, as shown in Figure PG2-19, measuring distances in inches from the center of the slide (which is located at 0,0).

SELECTING A SHAPE

Here is one way to place an oval shape in the upper-right corner of Slide 2:

STEPS

1 **Press** **Pg Dn** **to move to Slide 2**

You can now select the shape you want to use, as follows:

 2 **Click the _Autoshapes_ toolbar button**

FIGURE PG2–19 ■ **SETTING THE RULER BARS**

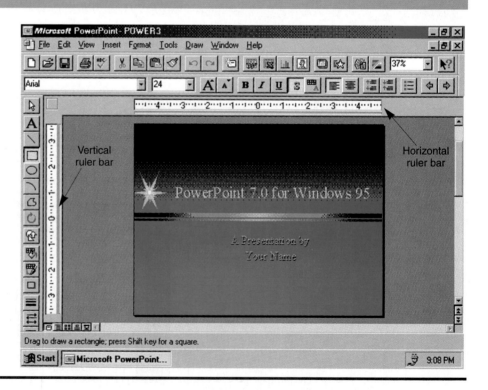

An Autoshapes toolbox now appears on the screen, as shown in Figure PG2-20a.

3 **Click the *Ellipse Tool* in the first column, third row**

The desired shape has been selected, and appears depressed in the AutoShapes toolbox. When you move the pointer arrow into the slide, it changes to a cross hair to allow more exact placement of the shape.

POSITIONING AND SIZING

Once you choose the shape, you need to position and size the image. You do this is in two steps: first, you position the pointer where you want the upper-left corner of the image to appear; then, you drag the pointer to the lower-right corner, thus sizing and positioning the image at the same time. Figure PG2-20b shows the desired position of the graphic.

STEPS

1 **Using Figure PG2-20b as a guide, identify the desired upper-left corner of the image by pointing to the top edge of the slide, 2" to the right of center**

Note that the ruler bars display the current vertical and horizontal position of the pointer with a line that moves along the ruler as you move the pointer.

FIGURE PG2–20 ■ POSITIONING AND SIZING A SHAPE

(a) The Autoshapes toolbox.
(b) The graphic has been placed.

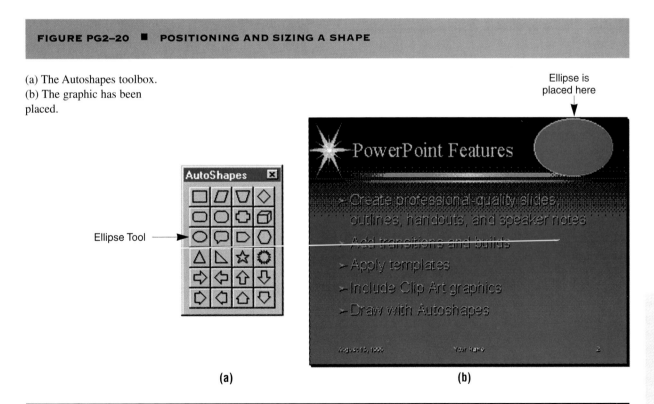

(a)   (b)

2 Now, click and drag the pointer right and down, so that it is approximately 4-½″ right and 2″ above the center of the slide. Then release the mouse

> **Tip:** If needed, you can click and drag a corner handle to fine-tune the size.

3 Click anywhere outside the ellipse frame to deselect it

4 Close the *Autoshapes* toolbox by clicking its *Close* button or by clicking its button on the Drawing toolbar

5 Save the presentation again as POWER3

6 You can exit PowerPoint or continue

EDITING THE ART

PowerPoint allows you to make many adjustments to a drawn image. You can adjust its size or position. You can change its **fill color** (its internal color) or **line color** (its border color). You can also select shades, patterns, or textures to add interest. This exercise will present each of these techniques briefly. To prepare,

STEPS

1 If needed, launch PowerPoint and open POWER3

2 Move to Slide 2

3 Click the ellipse to open its frame

ADJUSTING SIZE.   You can adjust the size of a drawn object with the same technique you used for clip art. Try this:

STEPS

1 Click the left edge handle of the image as shown in Figure PG2-21a

As expected, the pointer changes to a double-arrow. Because you are using an edge handle this time instead of a corner handle, the pointer is horizontal and will only affect the *width* of the image.

2 Drag the pointer approximately ½″ to the right, as shown in Figure PG2-21b, and then release the mouse

FIGURE PG2–21 ■ ADJUSTING GRAPHIC SIZE

(a) Click the left edge handle of the graphic.
(b) Drag the pointer to the right and release.

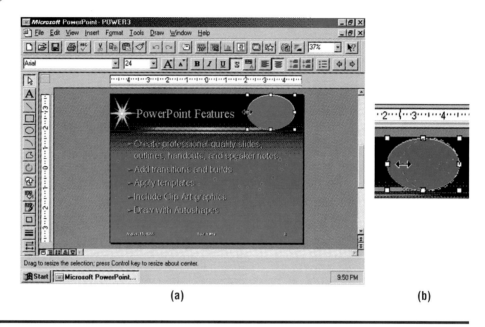

(a)   (b)

The image has become more circular in appearance. Note: You can use any handle to enlarge or reduce the frame size as desired.

ADJUSTING POSITION. You can also click the center of the image and then drag it, without changing its size, to a new location. Try this:

STEPS

1   Point anywhere within the center of the image

2   Click and drag the pointer approximately ¼″ to the right and then release the mouse (the distance need not be exact, simply move it slightly closer to the right edge of the slide)

3   For now, click outside the image, away from the text, to deselect it

CHANGING THE FILL COLOR. The internal color of the image can also be adjusted if it suits your needs. Try this:

STEPS

1   Click the ellipse image to select it for use

2 **Click the** *Fill Color* **button on the Drawing toolbar**

A color palette appears as shown in Figure PG2-22. If you click the *No Fill* option, the image will be filled with the same color as the background and appear transparent on the slide. Using the *Automatic* option allows PowerPoint to select an appropriate color. For now,

3 **Click the light blue-green color on the second row in the second column. The color of the image has been changed**

> Tip: The colors presented in the eight boxes of the palette are meant to complement the colors of the design. If none appeal to you, you can click the *Other Color* option to access a dialog box offering a full array of colors, tints, and hues. You can then click any color and accept it, or click the *Cancel* button to exit that dialog box.

ADDING A PATTERN TO THE FILL. You may prefer a texture or pattern in the fill color, rather than a plain background. This is easily done.

STEPS

1 **Click the** *Fill Color* **button on the Drawing toolbar**

The color palette reappears. Note the three options that appear in the center of the list: shaded, patterned, and textured. Each of these options accesses a distinct dialog box that provides literally thousands of combinations in color, design, and textures (including wood grains, marble, sand, and weaves). The three dialog boxes are displayed in Figure PG2-23 for your review. Feel free to explore each of them on your own. For now, to learn the technique, you will add a shaded option to your ellipse as follows:

FIGURE PG2–22 ■ **THE** *FILL COLOR* **PALETTE**

FIGURE PG2–23 ■ *FILL OPTION* DIALOG BOXES

(a) Shaded Fill.
(b) Patterned Fill.
(c) Textured Fill.

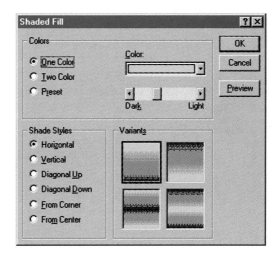

(a)

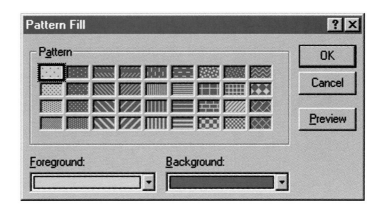

(b)

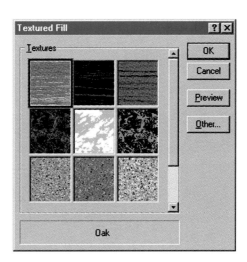

(c)

2 Click the *Shaded* option in the palette

The *Shaded Fill* dialog box appears, as shown in Figure PG2-23a. You can change colors, intensity (darkness), and shade styles as desired. In this example,

3 Make sure the options match those shown in the figure and change them if they do not: one color, horizontal shade, upper-left variant

4 Click the *OK* button to accept the shading

5 Click outside the image, away from any text frames, to deselect it

6 Save the POWER3 presentation again

> **Tip:** To cancel a shading, pattern, or texture, return to the *Fill Color* palette and simply click a solid color.

CHANGING THE LINE COLOR.   You can also adjust the color of the line (border) that surrounds the image. Try this:

STEPS

1 Click the ellipse image to select it for use

 2 Click the *Line Color* button on the Drawing toolbar

Another color palette appears. If you click the *No Line* option, the line will become transparent on the slide. You could also click any desired color. For now,

3 Click the *No Line* option

The line has "disappeared."

4 Click outside the image to deselect it

5 Save the POWER3 presentation

ADDING TEXT

You might want to add text to your image. The following exercise will allow you to place your initials in the shaded ellipse:

STEPS

1 Open POWER3 if needed and move to Slide 2

2 Click the *Text Tool* button in the Drawing toolbar

3 Now, point within the ellipse (approximately 3″ right and 2 ½″ high on the ruler bars) where the text will be placed

4 Click the mouse to open the text box at this point

A small shaded rectangle appears within the ellipse, as shown in Figure PG2-24a.

5 Type your initials, as has been done in Figure PG2-24b

6 Click outside the ellipse to deselect the text box

RESIZING TEXT.   The default font size is not always the best one to use. Try the following to learn how to adjust text size:

STEPS

1 Click your initials to open the text box

2 Click the *Increase Font Size* button on the Formatting toolbar five or six times

Note how your initials grew larger.

3 Click outside the text box to deselect it

REPOSITIONING TEXT.   You can also reposition the text as needed. For example,

STEPS

1 Click your initials to open the text box

FIGURE PG2-24 ■ ADDING TEXT TO A SLIDE

(a) The Text tool has opened a text box.
(b) Initials have been typed (yours will differ).
(c) Text has been resized.

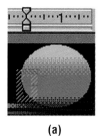
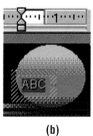

(a)   (b)   (c)

2 Press Esc to access a text frame with handles

3 Press ↑ and → as needed, or point within the image and then click and drag the box slightly up and right to center it in the ellipse

4 Press Esc again (or click outside the text) to deselect the frame

Your screen should resemble Figure PG2-24c. If not, you can repeat Steps 1–4 to fix it.

5 If you want to turn off the ruler bar, click *View, Ruler*

6 Save the POWER3 presentation

OTHER OBJECT TECHNIQUES

Many other object manipulations are available in PowerPoint, but they are outside the scope of this introduction. You can copy objects; change their shape; superimpose one above another; group them; add shading, lines, arrows; and rotate them in place. Feel free to experiment with shapes in the future. In addition, remember that you can easily delete an object by clicking it and then pressing the Delete key.

☑ CHECKPOINT

✓ In the ALL ABOUT ME presentation, add a shape of your choice in the upper-right corner of the My Class slide.
✓ Change the fill color of the added shape to a pattern.
✓ Add the current year as text inside the added shape.
✓ Enlarge the text and center it in the shape.
✓ Save the presentation, print the My Class slide, and close the window.

ADDING SPECIAL EFFECTS

By default, PowerPoint's slide show presents each slide in your presentation in sequence by simply replacing one slide with the next. Although this is satisfactory for some presentations, you can add various visual special effects, such as transitions and builds, that enhance the effect of your presentation. To prepare for these exercises,

STEPS

1 Launch PowerPoint and open the POWER3 presentation

2 Switch to the slide sorter view   [Alt + V , D]

USING TRANSITIONS

A **transition** is a visual effect that allows one slide to blend into the next. PowerPoint offers more than 40 transitions, including blinds, checkerboards, cuts, fades, dissolves, splits, and wipes. To select a transition with which to start Slide 1, do the following:

STEPS

1   Click, or move to, Slide 1 if the highlight is not already there

Note the Transition toolbar above the slide sorter, as shown in Figure PG2-25. The *Slide Transition Effects* box indicates that there is no transition for this slide.

 2   Click the *Slide Transition* toolbar button, or click *Tools* and then *Slide Transition*

A *Slide Transition* dialog box appears, as shown in Figure PG2-26. This dialog box lets you set a transition effect, adjust its speed from slow to fast, and choose a manual or automatic advance. You can also add sound effects during the transition if your computer has that capability. The small dog image on the right side lets you preview the effect.

FIGURE PG2–25 ■ ADDING A SLIDE TRANSITION

Transitions are added in the slide sorter window.

Slide Transition Effects box

Transition toolbar

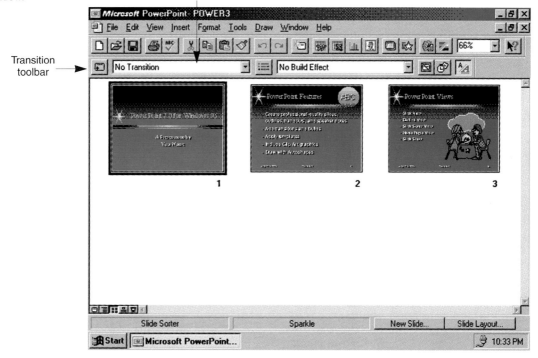

FIGURE PG2-26 ■ THE *SLIDE TRANSITION* DIALOG BOX

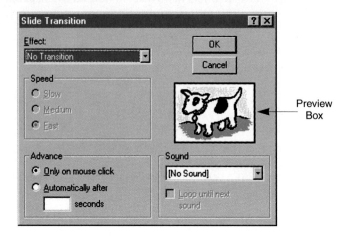

Preview
Box

3 **Click the drop-down arrow in the *Effect* box**

The drop-down list displays the first seven transition options. Table PG2-2 displays the complete transition list. For example,

4 **Watch the preview box and press ↓ to move to the *Blinds Horizontal* transition**

Note how the effect was displayed in the preview, which has now changed to a key image. You could continue to press the down arrow to preview all the effects, but for now,

5 **Click the *Box In* transition effect to select it**

> **Tip:** You can use the scroll bar to move through the list to a desired effect without having to display it in the preview box and then click the effect to select it.

TABLE PG2-2 ■ TRANSITION EFFECTS

No Transitions	Cover Left
Blinds Horizontal	Cover Up
Blinds Vertical	Cover Right
Box Out	Cover Down
Box In	Cut
Checkerboard Across	Cut Through Black
Checkerboard Down	Dissolve

The effect may occur too quickly for your needs. When this occurs, you can slow it down as follows:

6 Click the *Medium* option check box to set a medium speed

Note the transition speed shown in the *Preview* box. You can select any one of three transition speeds (slow, medium, or fast) by clicking the appropriate box. In typical use, you should spend less time on transitions and more time on your slides. For now, you will not change the advance setting, leaving it activated by your mouse click when the slide show is running.

7 If your computer is capable of producing sound, click the *Sound* drop-down arrow (or press **Alt** + **U**) and then click the *Camera* sound option

8 Click the *OK* button to accept the transition selections

 Note that a transition icon, as shown in the left margin, now appears at the lower left of Slide 1, indicating that a transition has been set for this slide. Now, using the same technique as in Steps 1–8,

9 For Slide 2, select a medium-speed *Uncover Left* transition effect with no sound

10 For Slide 3, select a fast *Dissolve* effect with no sound

11 Save the presentation as POWER4

12 Run the slide show to see the transition effects between slides

13 Close the POWER4 presentation window

14 If you want to stop for now, exit PowerPoint

USING BUILDS

A **build** is a graphic special effect that focuses attention on items in a bulleted list. Rather than displaying the entire list at once, a build *progressively discloses* the list. That is, it presents one item at a time, displaying the next item in sequence only when you command it to do so. The following exercise creates a build effect in Slide 2 of your presentation.

STEPS

1 Open the POWER4 presentation, switch to Slide view if needed, and move to Slide 2

2 Click the bulleted text on the slide to select the text frame

 3 Click the *Animation Effects* toolbar button to access its toolbox

4   Click the *Animation Settings* button in the resultant toolbox

An *Animation Settings* dialog box appears, as in Figure PG2-27, which lets you specify various build options. First, you will create the build:

5   Click the drop-down arrow in the *Build Options* box to access its drop-down list

6   Click *By 1st Level Paragraphs* to have the build reveal each item in sequence

SPECIFYING A BUILD EFFECT   As shown in Table PG2-3, PowerPoint offers numerous build effects that control how items are presented. A build effect can focus audience attention on a particular point and enhance interest in your presentation. In this exercise, you will specify the *Fly From Left* effect as follows:

STEPS

1   Click the drop-down arrow in the first *Effects* box (which currently displays No Build Effect) to access its drop-down list

2   Click the *Fly from Left* effect

CHANGING ITEM COLORS.   By default, each bulleted item remains on the screen after it has been revealed. You can focus additional attention on each new item by changing the color of previous bullets on the screen or by having them "hide"(that is disappear entirely, matching the background color). This exercise will dim existing bulleted items as follows:

FIGURE PG2–27 ■ THE *ANIMATION SETTINGS* DIALOG BOX

Build effects are controlled
by manipulating these
options.

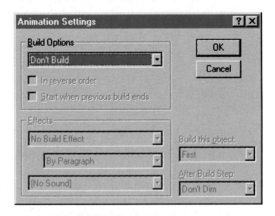

TABLE PG2–3 ■ BUILD EFFECTS

Fly from Left/Top/Right/Bottom	Dissolve
Blinds Vertical/Horizontal	Flash Once
Box Out/In	Random Bars Horizontal/Vertical
Checkerboard Across/Down	Split Horizontal Out/In

STEPS

▾   1   **Click the drop-down arrow in the _After Build Step_ box (which currently displays "Don't Dim")**

2   **Click the purple color in the upper-right corner**

3   **Click the _OK_ button to accept the build as specified**

4   **Click outside the text block to deselect it**

☒   5   **Close the _Animation Effects_ box if needed (click its _Close_ button)**

6   **Save the POWER4 presentation**

VIEWING THE BUILD EFFECT.   You can now examine the build effect by running the Slide Show starting with Slide 2 as follows:

STEPS

🖵   1   **Click the _Slide Show_ button**

As expected, only the title appears. The bulleted items have not yet been revealed.

> Tip: If you use the _View, Slide Show_ menu, you must set the _From_ entry to 2.

2   **Click the mouse**   [↵ or Pg Dn]

The first bulleted item, shown in Figure PG2-28a, "flies in" from the left as specified in the build effect. Note how your attention is drawn to it.

3   **Click the mouse to continue**   [↵ or Pg Dn]

The first item is now dimmed as the second item flies onto the screen. When presenting, you can pause as long as you want to discuss each item, clicking the mouse only when you are ready to reveal the next item.

PG

FIGURE PG2–28 ■ **VIEWING THE BUILD**

(a) The first bullet "flies" in
from the left.
(b) The completed build.

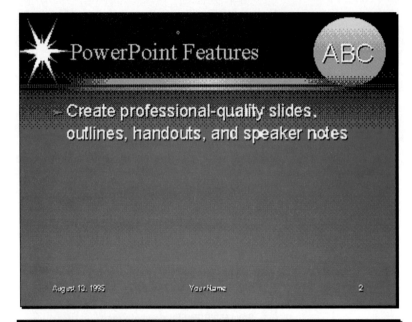

(a)

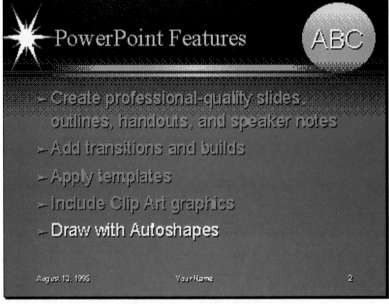

(b)

---

4 Click the mouse three more times to reveal the remaining items as in Figure PG2- 28b

5 Press Esc to close the slide show

Using a similar technique, you'll now set a build without dim for the list in Slide 3,
as follows:

1   Move to Slide 3

2   Repeat Steps 2–6 in the *Using Builds* section to turn on the build effect

3   Click the drop-down arrow in the *Effects* box

4   Scroll to, and then click, *Dissolve*

5   Click the *OK* button

6   Click outside the bullet list frame to deselect it

7   Save the POWER4 presentation again

8   Run the slide show until the end to see the differences between both builds

9   Close the *Animation Effects* toolbox when you are done

Feel free to explore other build colors, sounds, and transition effects.

> **Tip:** The *Animation Effects* toolbox contains a number of text effects that can be applied to the title text as well. Try these in the future to see their effect on your presentation.

☑ CHECKPOINT

✓ Open the ALL ABOUT ME presentation and add transitions between the slides.
✓ Create a build in Slide 2 without using the dim effect.
✓ Create a build in Slide 3 employing hidden bullets.
✓ Run the slide show to see the results.
✓ Save the ALL ABOUT ME presentation and close the window.

AUTOMATING A SLIDE SHOW

You may have noticed that when your slide show ends, a black screen or the view from which you invoked slide show returns to the window. Although this is fine for developing and reviewing a presentation, it does not provide a professional-looking ending to your presentation when you show it to an audience.

ENDING A PRESENTATION

To more effectively end your presentation, a PowerPoint tip suggests that you include a blank autolayout as the last slide in your presentation, providing a finished look to your project. You might even create a transition that would blend it into the presentation. To add a blank slide, follow these steps:

1 Open the POWER4 presentation if needed

2 Move to Slide 3

3 Click the *New Slide* button on the status bar

A *New Slide* dialog box appears, as you've seen in the first chapter.

4 Click the *Blank* autolayout in the lower right corner

Remember to check its title to make sure it is correct before continuing to the next step.

5 Click the *OK* button to accept it

Now remove the footer information from this last slide for a "cleaner" ending as follows:

6 Move to the final blank slide if you're not already there

7 Click *View* and then click *Header and Footer...*

8 Click the *Slide* tab if needed

9 Click the check boxes for Date, Slide Number, and Footer to remove   [D , N , F]
their check marks

10 Click the *Apply* button to remove those footer settings from the current slide only (do *not* click
the *Apply to All* button

11 Save the POWER4 presentation

12 If you want to add a transition to this slide, switch to *Slide Sorter* view, select a transition (try
Random Transition), and then save the POWER4 presentation again

13 Run the slide show to see the finished ending

14 Exit PowerPoint or continue

REHEARSING TIMINGS

Until now, you have been using the slide show in manual mode. That is, you have been controlling the progression of slides and builds by clicking the mouse or pressing the Enter or Pg Dn key. Although this is a reasonable way to display a presentation, you cannot be certain that your slides—and the speech you give to accompany them—will adequately fill the time you have been allotted. Your presentation may be much too long or too short for the intended audience. Even if overall time were not a concern, you may need to add or remove material or adjust your rate of speech to maximize the effectiveness of the presentation.

PowerPoint offers a built-in timer that lets you practice the pacing of your presentation, while it keeps track of time for each individual build, slide, and the overall presentation. You can rehearse as often as necessary and then record the timing for future use (as you will see). Here's how to do it:

STEPS

1   **If needed, launch PowerPoint and open the POWER4 presentation**

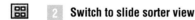   2   **Switch to slide sorter view**

In actual use, you would now have your prepared notes or speech ready to recite as you glance at the screen. For this exercise, you will simply wait a few seconds between each slide.

3   **Click the *Rehearse Timings* button**

The slide show starts and a *Rehearsal* dialog box, as shown in Figure PG2-29a, appears at the lower right of the screen. Two timers are running in the dialog box: the left timer records total presentation time, whereas the right timer records the time for the current slide only. At this point, you would make whatever introductory remarks desired.

4   **When you have finished, press   Pg Dn   or click the *Advance* button in the dialog box to move to the next slide**

Note that the left timer continues, while the right timer has reset to zero and begins again for the new slide.

5   **Keep pressing   Pg Dn   or clicking the *Advance* button to move through all of your builds and slides**

FIGURE PG2-29 ■ REHEARSING A SLIDE SHOW

(a)The *Rehearsal* dialog box.
(b) When the rehearsal is over, PowerPoint displays the total slide show time.

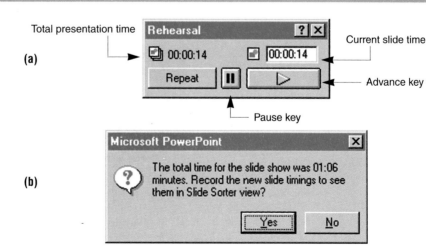

You may wait a few seconds between each or continue immediately as you wish. The timers will record all of your actions. When you reach the end of your presentation, the total time for your presentation will appear in a dialog box, as shown in Figure PG2-29b, with a messsage asking if you want to record the times in the slide sorter view.

6 **Click *Yes* to save the times you rehearsed**

The times for each slide now appear beneath each slide in slide sorter view. You could repeat the rehearsal process to improve or adjust your timing, saving the new times (and replacing the old times) when you complete the show.

7 **Save the POWER4 presentation**

> **Tip: You could also highlight a slide in the slide sorter view, click the *Transition* button, and then manually type a new time for that slide at the bottom of the dialog box.**

USING SLIDE TIMINGS

Once you have set times for each slide and build in your presentation, you can have the slide show run automatically, advancing each slide and build according to the last rehearsal you recorded. Here's how to set the slide show to run in automatic mode:

STEPS

1 **Click *View* and then *Slide Show* in the menu**

A *Slide Show* dialog box appears, as shown in Figure PG2-30. Within this box, you can specify a range of slides to be shown using the *From...To* entry boxes, or let *All* of them

FIGURE PG2–30 ■ THE *SLIDE SHOW* DIALOG BOX

appear in the show (the default). You can also instruct the show to loop continuously (repeat over and over again) until you press the Escape key to stop it. In this exercise,

2   Click *Use Slide Timings*

to instruct PowerPoint to run the show automatically, using your rehearsed (or entered) times.

3   Click *Show* to begin the slide show

The show will run to completion. Note how the final blank slide finishes the show in a professional manner.

4   Save the POWER4 presentation

> **Tip:** Once the automatic feature has been set in the *Slide Show* dialog box, the timed presentation will run whenever you click the *Slide Show* view button on the status bar. If you want to return to manual operation, you must first click *View* and then *Slide Show* in the menu, and then click the *Manual Advance* option.

5   You can exit PowerPoint or continue

ANNOTATING A SLIDE SHOW

Most presentations can be enhanced through the use of a pointer to draw attention to some item on the screen or a marker to underline or circle topics of discussion. An electronic presentation is no exception. PowerPoint provides both for your use. Here's how:

STEPS

1   If needed, launch PowerPoint and open the POWER4 presentation

It is better to run the presentation in manual mode to allow you time to use these new tools, so for now, make sure the automatic timer is off, by following these steps:

2   Click *View* and then *Slide Show* to open its dialog box

3   Click the *Manual Advance* option

4   Click the *Show* button to begin

As expected, the title slide appears on the full screen.

Tip: You can press F1 to see a list of slide show shortcut commands. Press *OK* to close the list.

5 Click the mouse or press **Pg Dn** to advance

6 Click the mouse or press **Pg Dn** to see the first bullet item

Now, let's say you wanted to point to this item on the screen for emphasis.

7 Move the mouse or press **A** to activate the arrow pointer

The arrow pointer appears on the screen, as in Figure PG2-31a. An options box also appears in the lower-left corner of the screen, as in Figure PG2-31b. (You can click this box to access a pop-up menu with additional features. To exit the menu, click outside of it.)

8 Practice moving the pointer around the screen

9 Press **A** when you are done to shut off the arrow pointer

Now assume you would like to draw on the screen to underline or circle something of interest.

10 Press **Ctrl** + **P** to activate the drawing pen

A pen pointer now appears on the screen, as in Figure PG2-31c. You can move this pen just as you would the arrow. However, when you want to draw with it, simply drag the mouse, that is, press and hold the left mouse button as you move. When you remove your finger from the left mouse button, the "pen" will stop writing. Try this:

11 Move beneath the letter "p" in the word "professional" in the first bullet

12 Press and hold the left mouse button and drag the pointer to the right to underline the entire word, now release the mouse

13 Draw an oval around the word "handouts"

FIGURE PG2–31 ■ ANNOTATING A SLIDE

(a) The mouse arrow pointer.
(b) The options box.
(c) The mouse pen pointer.

(a) (b) (c)

> **Tip:** Pen marks are only temporary. They will disappear when you move to the next slide. To erase pen marks immediately, press the letter "E."

14 Press **E** to erase the pen marks on the slide

15 To turn off the pen feature, press **Ctrl** + **H**

At times, you may want to discuss something without having your audience stare at a slide. You can easily blank the screen as follows:

16 Press **B** to black out the screen (or press **W** to white it out)

17 When you're ready to continue, press **B** again (or **W**) to restore it

18 Press **Esc** to end the slide show

19 Save the POWER4 presentation so that it will remain in manual mode

20 You can exit PowerPoint if desired

☑ CHECKPOINT

- ✓ Add a blank ending slide to the ALL ABOUT ME presentation.
- ✓ Rehearse the ALL ABOUT ME presentation and save the recorded times.
- ✓ Run the automated slide show.
- ✓ Manually change the timing on Slide 1 to 5 seconds.
- ✓ Change the ALL ABOUT ME presentation back to manual mode and save it.

SHARING DATA WITH OTHER APPLICATIONS

Microsoft Office is a **suite** program—a set of separate applications that work together as one large program. PowerPoint can easily incorporate data from other Microsoft Office applications, such as Word, Excel, or Access, into slides as text or objects. For example, opening a Word outline will directly convert it into the text of a PowerPoint presentation. Conversely, clicking the *Report It!* toolbar button in PowerPoint will move a PowerPoint outline into the Word program for detailed editing and adjustment.

PREPARING FOR THIS SECTION

In order for you to perform the linking and embedding exercise, your disk must contain an Excel file named EMPLOY. Check with your instructor or lab technician for the proper copying technique for your system. For example, if the file is stored on your Local Area Network (LAN), you may be able to copy it directly to your disk (in this case, follow your lab's instructions). If you have two floppy disk drives or a hard-disk drive, perform the following steps to quickly copy the needed file:

1 Start Windows (or remain in PowerPoint)

2 Click the *Start* button

Although you could use the My Computer window or Explorer to copy the file, try this approach, which may be faster:

3 Point to the *Programs* menu option

4 Click the *MS-DOS* prompt

A "C:\WINDOWS>" message should appear on your screen. Now follow Steps 5–10 in the column appropriate for your system:

USING ONE FLOPPY DISK AND A HARD-DISK DRIVE	USING TWO FLOPPY-DISK DRIVES
5 Remove your disk from Drive A and place the Dryden File disk in the drive	**5** Make sure your disk is in Drive A
6 Leaving a space before the A: and the C: in the following command, type `COPY A:\WORD\EMPLOY.XLS C:\` and press ↵	**6** Place the Dryden File disk in Drive B
	7 Leaving a space before the A: and the B: in the following command, type `COPY B:\WORD\EMPLOY.XLS A:`
7 When the copy is complete, remove the Dryden File disk from Drive A and place your disk back in the drive	**8** Press ↵
8 Leaving a space before the C: and the A: in the following command, type `COPY C:\EMPLOY.XLS A:` and press ↵	**9** If "Overwrite a:EMPLOY.XLS (Yes/No/All)?" appears, press **Y** and ↵
9 If "Overwrite a:EMPLOY.XLS (Yes/No/All)?" appears, press **Y** and ↵	**10** When the copying is done, remove the Dryden File disk from Drive B
10 Leaving a space before the C: in the following command, type `DEL C:\EMPLOY.XLS` and press ↵	

11 Type **EXIT** and press ⏎ to return to Windows (or PowerPoint)

You can now continue with the rest of this section.

LINKING AND EMBEDDING

You can also bring data from another program into PowerPoint using two additional techniques, namely, *linking* and *embedding.* These techniques are standard throughout Microsoft Office and Windows.

An **object** contains information. **Embedding** copies an object from one application to another. In effect, it takes a "snapshot" of the original object and places it elsewhere. You can embed an object in a PowerPoint slide. Embedding is appropriate when you plan to show your presentations on other computers that are not part of your network, because the objects no longer depend on the original source.

Linking, on the other hand, establishes an ongoing connection between the application that provides the object (known as the *source document*) and its destination (known as the *container document*). Change the object in the source and the container object is automatically updated. This is useful when a number of different users within the network want to access the same data in a source file and have it reflect future conditions. For example, the following exercise will link the EMPLOY Excel worksheet with PowerPoint. You can use a similar technique to link any Microsoft Office file with PowerPoint.

LINKING AN OBJECT. The following paragraphs describe how to link a block of data from an Excel worksheet into a PowerPoint slide. You do not need to know Excel to perform this brief task; just follow the instructions carefully.

STEPS

1 Open the POWER4 presentation in PowerPoint and move to Slide 3

2 In the slide view, click the *New Slide* button on the status bar

3 From the dialog box, click the *Title Only* autolayout (third row, third column) and then click the *OK* button

4 Click the title placeholder to open it, type **Example of Excel Link** and then click outside the placeholder

Your slide should resemble Figure PG2-32a. You are now ready launch Excel to link the EMPLOY worksheet with this slide.

5 While in PowerPoint, click the *Start* button on the Windows taskbar

6 Point to the *Programs* menu option

FIGURE PG2-32 ■ **PREPARING TO LINK AN OBJECT**

(a) The slide title has been prepared.
(b) The object has been identified in Excel.

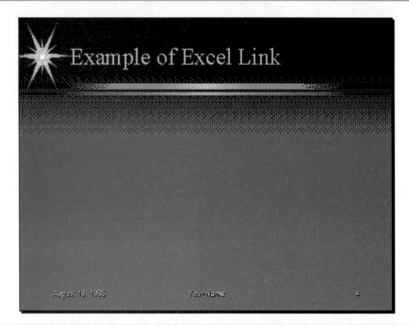

(a)

Start here
(A1)

	A	B	C	D
1	Employee List			
2		Home	Annual	Date
3	Sales Staff	Phone	Salary	Hired
4	Burstein, J.	408-555-1010	$23,450	06-Jul-78
5	Laudon, J.	914-555-9876	33,600	07-Oct-81
6	Martin, E.	718-555-1234	31,750	01-Nov-79
7	Parker, C.	505-555-5678	37,500	25-Apr-82
8	Williams, D.	312-555-0202	38,000	17-Feb-75
9	Total		$164,300	
10				
11				

(b)

Drag to
here (D10)

7 If the *Microsoft Excel* icon is not in this menu, point to the folder that contains it (typically, *MS Office*)

8 Click the *Microsoft Excel* icon to launch the program

9 Click *File* and then *Open* in the Excel menu bar   [**Ctrl** + **O**]

10 In the *File name* box, type **A:EMPLOY** and press ⏎

The EMPLOY worksheet appears. You now simply mark the text block as follows:

11 **Press Ctrl + Home to move to the upper-left cell in the worksheet (or just click the cell itself)**

12 **Click and drag the mouse to cell D10, or press Shift + → three times to move to Column D and then Shift + ↓ nine times to move to Row 10**

Your screen should resemble Figure PG2-32b. Repeat Steps 11–12 if it does not.

13 **Click *Edit* and then *Copy* from the menu**   [**Ctrl** + **C**]

The block of cells (object) has been copied to the Windows Clipboard and is now available for pasting.

14 **Click the *Microsoft PowerPoint* button on the taskbar to open PowerPoint**

15 **Click *Edit* and then *Paste Special* from the menu**

A *Paste Special* dialog box appears.

16 **Click the *Paste Link* option at the left to invoke it, then click the *OK* button**

As expected, a small frame appears in the slide.

17 **In the Drawing toolbar, click the *Fill Color* button and click *Automatic***

18 **Using Figure PG2-33 as a guide, first click and drag the frame's lower-right handle outward, as you have learned with clip art, to enlarge the size of the object appropriately**

FIGURE PG2–33 ■ THE LINK "GOAL"

The linked object is sized and positioned in the slide.

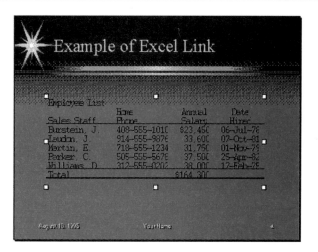

19 Now, drag the upper-left handle outward (Note: You may have to click the center of the image and drag it slightly down to match the figure.)

20 Click outside the frame to deselect it

21 Save the presentation as POWER5

The data from Excel now appears in PowerPoint container, dynamically linked to the source worksheet, still in Excel. For example, we will change Williams' salary:

22 Click the *Microsoft Excel* button on the taskbar to switch to Excel

23 Click Cell C8, then type `40000` , and press ↵

24 Click the *Microsoft PowerPoint* button on the taskbar to switch back

25 Click *Edit* and then *Links*

26 Click the link displayed in the *Links* dialog box to select it

27 Click the *Update Now* button

Note that the $40,000 has been updated in the PowerPoint slide. If you make any changes to the source document in the future, and PowerPoint were not currently active, a dialog box would ask you to update the link the next time you opened the presentation for use. You could click *OK* to update, or *Cancel* to leave the data unchanged.

28 Click the *Microsoft Excel* button on the taskbar

29 Click *File* and then *Exit* to exit Excel *without* saving changes

30 You may want to run the slide show to see the new slide

31 If you want to stop for now, close the presentation and exit from PowerPoint

EMBEDDING AN OBJECT.   Embedding an object simply copies it into the container program without creating a link between the two applications. To embed an object, you could identify the object as you did in linking by following Steps 1–14 above. Then, in Step 15, click *Edit* and then *Paste*. The object is now copied, but will now remain static regardless of changes made to the source document in the future.

WORKSHEETS, GRAPHS, AND TABLES

You can also create worksheets, graphs, and tables directly in PowerPoint by clicking one of the toolbar buttons shown in Figure PG2-34, or by double-clicking an appropriate autolayout placeholder, to open a frame and activate another Microsoft Office program while remaining in PowerPoint. Although you create these objects using another Microsoft Office application to edit them, they become part of the PowerPoint presentation. Familiarity with the editing program is essential in developing these objects. It is

FIGURE PG2–34 ■ CREATING NEW OBJECTS WITH THE TOOLBAR

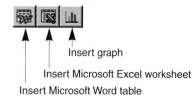

Insert graph
Insert Microsoft Excel worksheet
Insert Microsoft Word table

beyond the scope of this brief introduction to explore all the commands and nuances of each approach, but you are welcome to examine them on your own. Instead, the following exercise presents a small illustration of how you might create a graph using Microsoft Graph, an additional application supplied with PowerPoint.

STEPS

1   Open the POWER5 presentation

A dialog box may appear advising you to update the link in Power5. For now,

2   Click *Cancel* to leave the linked object unchanged for this exercise

3   Move to Slide 4

4   In the slide view, click the *New Slide* button on the status bar

5   From the dialog box, click the "Graph" autolayout (second row, fourth column)

6   Verify that the title is correct, and then click the *OK* button

7   Click the title placeholder to open it, type   Example of Graph   and then click outside the placeholder

You are now ready to insert a graph into this slide.

8   Double-click the bottom graph placeholder and wait

A sample datasheet appears, as shown in Figure PG2-35a, within a Microsoft Graph window. This datasheet's layout and commands closely match those of Excel. As shown in the figure, each column contains a set of data points that will appear on the graph. The top (unnumbered) row of each column contains a column heading that will identify the data when graphed. The left-most (unlabeled) column, contains a similar heading for rows. You can now modify this sample datasheet to create the data for your new graph. For example, to create the datasheet shown in Figure PG2-35b, do the following:

9   Click the gray "C" label in the frame to select the entire C column

PG

FIGURE PG2–35 ■ **CREATING A GRAPH**

(a) A sample datasheet appears.
(b) Deleting columns C and D and retyping data creates the desired graph datasheet.

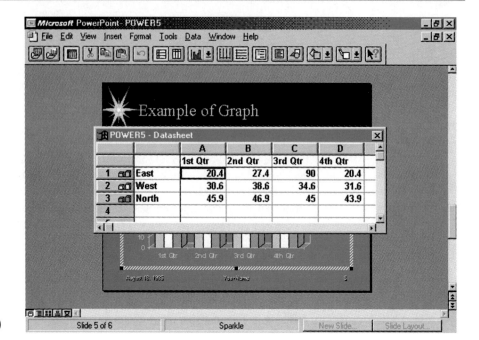

(a)

(b)

10 Press **Delete** to remove this data set

11 Repeat Steps 9–10 in Column D to delete it as well

12 In the remaining cells, click to move to each cell and then type the data shown in Figure PG2-35b

Of course, you could use the toolbar buttons to present the graph by row or column, change the chart type, add gridlines, change colors, adjust text, or make other enhancements to your graph. For now,

☒ 13 Click the *Close* button in the datasheet's upper-right corner

14 Click outside the frame twice to deselect it

The completed graph appears as in Figure PG2-36.

15   Save the POWER5 presentation once again

16   You can now create transitions to your two new slides if you want and then resave the presentation as POWER5

Feel free to click the graph slide frame again to open it and experiment with any of the graph enhancements available on the toolbar. When you are done, exit PowerPoint without saving the presentation.

☑ CHECKPOINT

✓   Add a new "Title only" after Slide 1 in the ALL ABOUT ME presentation, and title it "A Linking Example."

✓   Link and appropriately resize cells A1–C10 of the EMPLOY worksheet into this new slide (you may use another Excel worksheet if you have one).

✓   Add a new "Graph" slide after Slide 2 entitled "My G.P.A."

✓   Create a line graph showing your GPA for the years 1994, 1995, and 1996 (you may fabricate the data if needed).

✓   Save the presentation as ALL ABOUT ME #2

SUMMARY

■   Power Point lets you edit text, add new text, or delete unwanted text or slides.

■   A slide master contains a presentation's basic format and appearance—color, layout, spacing, font (typestyle), and font size. Each autolayout has its own master.

■   The *Font* dialog box or formatting toolbar buttons can change the font (overall typestyle), its style (bold or italic), size, or color. You can also underline, shadow, emboss, superscript, or subscript.

■   PowerPoint's spelling checker finds typographical errors and misspelled words in all parts (slides, notes, handouts, outlines) of the presentation.

FIGURE PG2–36   ■   THE FINISHED GRAPH SLIDE

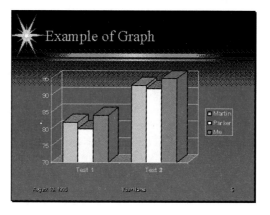

- You can change the look of a presentation by selecting another design template.
- You can add graphics to slides by selecting them from a library of *clip art*—professionally prepared graphic images—or by drawing your own.
- Graphic objects are placed in frames, which have handles that can be dragged to alter size. To delete unwanted frames, click the frame and press the Delete key.
- Images can be drawn with PowerPoint's Drawing toolbar. You can change a shape's *fill color* (internal) or *line color* (border). You can also select shades, patterns, or textures.
- A transition is a visual effect that allows one slide to blend into the next. A build is an effect that focuses attention on items in a bulleted list by progressively disclosing (revealing) each item in sequence.
- PowerPoint's built-in rehearsal timer lets you practice the pacing of your presentation and record it for future playback. Once times are set, you can run the slide show automatically.
- PowerPoint's arrow or pen marker can draw attention to items during the slide show.
- PowerPoint can easily incorporate data from other applications into slides, as text or objects. An object contains information. Embedding copies an object from one application to another. Linking establishes an ongoing connection between the application that provides the object (known as the *source document*) and its destination (known as the *container document*).
- You can also create worksheets, graphs, and tables directly in PowerPoint.

KEY TERMS

Shown in parentheses are the page numbers on which key terms are boldfaced.

Build (PG87)	Handle (PG73)	Slide master (PG57)
Clip art (PG68)	Line color (PG78)	Suite (PG97)
Embedding (PG99)	Linking (PG99)	Title master (PG57)
Fill color (PG78)	Object (PG99)	Transition (PG85)

QUIZ

TRUE/FALSE

_____ 1. Text can be edited in slide view or outline view.

_____ 2. Each presentation has one slide master that controls the format of all slides.

_____ 3. A point is approximately 1" in height.

_____ 4. PowerPoint's spell check also finds duplicate words.

_____ 5. Applying a new design will change all slides in the presentation.

_____ 6. Clip art must be placed in existing slide placeholders.

_____ 7. Frame handles are used to change the size of an object frame.

_____ 8. PowerPoint's rulers measure distances from the center of a slide.

_____ 9. The *AutoDraw* toolbox provides a variety of shapes for your selection.

_____ 10. A transition is used to reveal bulleted items one by one.

MULTIPLE CHOICE

___ 11. Where is text temporarily stored before it is pasted back into a slide?
   a. An object frame
   b. The presentation window
   c. The master slide
   d. The Windows clipboard

___ 12. What is the effect of pressing the Enter key at the end of a bulleted item?
   a. A blank bulleted item is added.
   b. A space is added.
   c. An error dialog box appears.
   d. The bullet list placeholder is closed.

___ 13. Which of these text attributes cannot be changed using the Formatting toolbar?
   a. Font
   b. Size
   c. Shadow effect
   d. Emboss effect

___ 14. Which button could you click to have the spell check skip over the current spelling of a word through the presentation?
   a. Ignore
   b. Ignore all
   c. No change
   d. Cancel

___ 15. Where should you insert clip art in a slide to be sure that it will adjust correctly when you apply a new design?
   a. Upper-left corner
   b. Title placeholder
   c. Clip art placeholder
   d. Center footer placeholder

___ 16. When resizing clip art, which one of these object components should be dragged to maintain the image's height and width proportions?
   a. Corner handle
   b. Edge handle
   c. Center
   d. Ruler bar

___ 17. The fill color refers to which portion of a drawn object?
   a. Border
   b. Internal
   c. Background
   d. Font

___ 18. The visual effect that moves from one slide to another is called a(n) ___.
   a. Build
   b. Transition
   c. Animation
   d. Clip art change

___ 19. An application document that receives a linked object is called a ___.
   a. Container
   b. Source
   c. Placeholder
   d. Linker

___ 20. Which of these procedures copies an object without creating a ongoing connection between the source and the container?

a. Linking

b. Embedding

c. Outlining

d. Using a placeholder

MATCHING

Select the lettered item from the following figure that best matches each phrase below:

___ 21. This item increases a selected text block's font size when clicked.

___ 22. This item displays distances left or right from the center of the slide.

___ 23. This item allows you to change the color of a graphic's interior.

___ 24. This item clicked with the Shift key, accesses the Slide Master view.

___ 25. This item increases line spacing when clicked.

___ 26. This item invokes the spell check program.

___ 27. This item allows you to insert clip art into the slide.

___ 28. This item opens the Animation toolbar.

___ 29. This item accesses a toolbox of available shapes.

___ 30. This item opens a box for text entry.

FIGURE PG2–A ■ MATCHING FIGURE

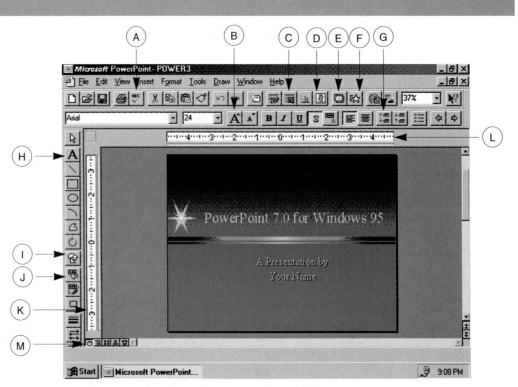

ANSWERS:

True/False: 1. T; 2. F; 3. F; 4. F; 5. T; 6. F; 7. T; 8. T; 9. F; 10. F
Multiple Choice: 11. d; 12. a; 13. d; 14. b; 15. c; 16. a; 17. b; 18. b; 19. a; 20. b
Matching: 21. b; 22. l; 23. j; 24. m; 25. g; 26. a; 27. d; 28. f; 29. i; 30. h

EXERCISES

I. OPERATIONS

Provide the PowerPoint actions required to do each of the following operations. For each operation, assume a hard-disk system with a disk in Drive A. You may want to verify each command by trying it on your computer system, where appropriate.

1. Insert a word into the subtitle of a presentation.
2. Spell check the presentation and outline.
3. Decrease the font size of the title to the next available size.
4. Add clip art to a graphic placeholder.
5. Reduce the size of a clip art image.
6. Draw a rectangle at the lower-right of a slide.
7. Add a wood texture to the interior of the rectangle created in Exercise 6.
8. Create a *Box Out* transition for the title slide.
9. Progressively disclose a bulleted list that will dissolve onto the screen without dimming.
10. Point to a bulleted item during a slide show.
11. Rehearse a complete presentation.
12. Have a presentation run automatically.
13. Link a paragraph of text from Word into a slide.
14. Delete the second slide of a presentation.
15. Insert a bar graph that compares the number of men and women voters.

II. COMMANDS

Describe what command is initiated or what is accomplished in PowerPoint by the actions described below. Assume that each exercise part is independent of any previous parts.

1. Holding the Shift key while clicking the *Slide View* button.
2. Clicking the *Text Color* button in the Formatting toolbar.
3. Clicking the *Ignore* button in the *Spell Check* dialog box.
4. Double-clicking a clip art placeholder in an autolayout.
5. Dragging a frame's corner handle away from the center of the frame.

6. Clicking outside a frame or placeholder that has already been selected.

7. Clicking *View* and then *Ruler* in the menu.

8. Clicking the *Slide Transition* toolbar button when in slide sorter view.

9. Clicking a color in the *After Build Step* box in the *Animation Settings* dialog box.

10. Clicking the *Rehearse Timings* toolbar button in slide sorter view.

11. Clicking the *Use Slide Timings* option in the *Slide Show* dialog box.

12. Pressing an "A" during a slide show.

III. APPLICATIONS

Perform the following operations using your computer system. You will need a hard drive or network with Windows 95 and PowerPoint on it. You will also need the disk used in Chapter 1 to store the results of this exercise. In a few words, describe how you accomplished each operation. *Note:* Of the six application exercises, each pair relates to school, home, and business respectively.

APPLICATION 1: ENHANCING THE COURSE HISTORY

1. Launch PowerPoint and open the COURSES1 presentation you created in Chapter 1.

2. Modify the text in the appropriate slides as listed below:

Title Slide:	Change "A Course History" to read "A Recent Course History"
Slide 2:	Delete the bullet for Psy 105
Slide 3:	Change the grade for Eco 200 to B+

3. Spell check the entire document, changing the text as needed. Save the presentation as COURSES2.

4. Apply a new design template that significantly differs in layout and color from the original choice.

5. Change Slide 3's layout to a bullet list with clip art placeholder. (Hint: move to the slide and click the *Slide Layout* button on the status bar.)

6. Add an appropriate cartoon clip art image into the new placeholder.

7. Draw and resize a rectangle in an appropriate corner of Slide 2 so it does not interfere with text. Save the COURSES2 presentation.

8. Add text showing the current year into the rectangle you drew in the previous exercise.

9. Create transitions between all your slides.

10. Close the presentation and exit PowerPoint.

APPLICATION 2: AMENDING THE SCHOOL SAMPLER

1. Launch PowerPoint and open the SCHOOL1 presentation you created in Chapter1.

2. Increase the font size by two sizes in the subtitle of the Title slide.

3. Change the bulleted text in the second slide so that it appears embossed.

4. Save the presentation as SCHOOL2 and then print the second slide.

5. Add a clip art image to the clip art placeholder in Slide 2.

6. Create builds in the two bulleted lists: one that dims previous bullets, and one that does not.

7. Add a blank final slide to your presentation that will use a random transition.

8. Rehearse your presentation and save the times.

9. Run the slide show in automatic mode.

10. Save the presentation with the same name and then exit PowerPoint.

APPLICATION 3: IMPROVING THE ON-SCREEN RÉSUMÉ

1. Launch PowerPoint and open the RESUME1 presentation you created in Chapter 1.

2. Apply a new design template to the entire presentation that differs significantly in layout and color scheme from the current design.

3. Increase the font size of the title to as large as will comfortably fit in the place-holder.

4. In the Education slide, add an appropriate clip art image.

5. Save the presentation as RESUME2, changing the *Save in* drive as needed.

6. Draw a "seal" shape in the Employment History slide and fill it with an appropriate shading.

7. Add a final blank slide with no footer that will finish the presentation. Select one transition and apply it to all slides. (Tip: Use Shift + Click to select all slides before selecting a transition.)

8. Create builds in the bulleted lists that use a checkboard effect, but will not dim pre-vious bullets.

9. Rehearse the slide show so that each bullet stays on the screen for no more that five seconds. Save the times.

10. Save the presentation again as RESUME2 and exit PowerPoint.

APPLICATION 4: "WARPING" THE STAR TREK PRIMER

1. Launch PowerPoint and open the TREK1 presentation you created in Chapter 1.

2. Change the title of the presentation to read "Introduction to the World of Star Trek." Change the text to the italic, shadow effect if it is not already set with these en-hancements.

3. Change the layout of Slide 2 to include a clip art placeholder. (Hint: move to the slide and click the *Slide Layout* button on the status bar.)

4. Insert a clip art image of your choice into the placeholder in Slide 2.

5. Save the presentation as TREK2.

6. Select and apply one transition to all slides.

7. Add a sixth slide that has a placeholder for a graph. Title the slide "Episodes." Then create and insert a bar graph that will display each show's title (Abbreviate: ST, ST-NG, ST-DS9, ST-VOY) and the number of episodes aired in each series (fabricate numbers between 20 and 200).

8. Using lines and arcs (not covered in the tutorial) try drawing a picture of a spaceship in Slide 3. If this proves too difficult, insert an appropriate clip art image in this slide. Save the presentation again as TREK2.

9. Run the slide show and, using the pen pointer, draw circles around the actors' names in each slide.

10. Close the presentation and exit PowerPoint.

APPLICATION 5: IMPROVING VIDEO MARKETING

1. Launch PowerPoint and open the SHRUB1 presentation you created in Chapter 1.

2. Add a clip art image to the title slide. Position and resize it appropriately.

3. Add a typewriter animation effect to the title of the second slide.

4. Add an appropriate clip art image to the empty placeholder in Slide 3.

5. Add a fourth slide with a placeholder for a graph. Using the names in Slide 2 (you may abbreviate), create a horizontal bar graph that displays a size for each name (fabricate a larger number for each size in the list).

6. Save the presentation as SHRUB2.

7. If you know how to use Excel, create a worksheet that exactly matches the datasheet in Exercise 5. Then add a "Title only" slide after Slide 3 and embed the Excel worksheet into the slide. (If you cannot use Excel, simply embed the EMPLOY worksheet you used in the chapter.)

8. Rehearse the presentation so that the title slide is displayed for no more than ten seconds, and each bullet item remains on the screen for as close to six seconds as possible. Graph and worksheet slides should remain for fifteen seconds each. Save the modified presentation with the same name.

9. Run the slide show to review your work.

10. Print the graph and worksheet slides, two on one page. Close the presentation and exit PowerPoint.

APPLICATION 6: EXECUTIVE TRAINING

1. Launch PowerPoint and open the OFFICE1 presentation you created in Chapter 1.

2. Change the template to a new layout and color scheme.

3. Decrease the size of the text in the subtitle of the presentation. Change the words "Executive Summary" to "Brief Executive Summary" and add italics to the font.

4. Change the date in the title slide to today's date.

5. Add an appropriate clip art image to the third slide, then reduce the font size of the bulleted items.

6. Increase the line spacing in the bullets in the second slide.

7. Create interesting transitions between each slide. Add builds to the bulleted items in Slide 2 only that dim each previous item.

8. Set the presentation to run in automatic mode with continuous looping.

9. Save the presentation as OFFICE2.

10. Print Slides 2 and 3 in a two-slides-to-a-page format and then exit PowerPoint.

MASTERY CASES

The following mastery cases allow you to demonstrate how much you have learned about this software. Each case describes a fictitious problem or need that can be solved using the skills you have learned in this chapter. Although minimum acceptable outcomes are specified, you are expected and encouraged to design your presentation (files, data, lists) in ways that display your personal mastery of the software. Feel free to show off your skills. Use real data from your own experience in your solution, although you may also fabricate data if needed.

These mastery cases allow you to display your ability to

- Edit text and change the presentation's appearance.
- Add clip art graphics.
- Draw shapes and text.
- Add transitions and builds to slides.
- Rehearse and automate a slide show.

CASE 1: ENHANCING THE COURSE OUTLINE

After reviewing your course outline from Chapter 1, your instructor has asked you to change the design and add appropriate clip art to enhance your presentation. Add transitions and builds where appropriate and then save the presentation.

CASE 2: MUSIC COLLECTION

Your music presentation was not as effective as you had planned. Select a new design and change each slide to include a clip art placeholder. Insert appropriate clip art that pertains to each artist and then automate the entire show. Save the presentation and print one slide.

CASE 3: SOFTWARE PRESENTATION

Your boss liked your PowerPoint presentation but wants it to show more. Add clip art and Autoshapes, provide interesting and different transition and build effects for each slide, and then automate the presentation so that it will run continuously but take no longer than 90 seconds for the entire show. Save the presentation and print it in a three-slides-to-a-page handout.

POWERPOINT 7.0 REFERENCE APPENDIX

This brief appendix extends your abilities by listing commands and features *not* included in the PowerPoint tutorials. Use the index to locate and review topics presented in the tutorial chapters. Use this appendix to explore additional topics of interest. Keyboard and mouse shortcuts are displayed first, followed by a toolbar reference, and finally selected features and commands arranged in alphabetical order.

KEYBOARD AND MOUSE SHORTCUTS

KEYBOARD SHORTCUTS

The following categories list selected shortcuts that you can access by pressing the appropriate keys.

COPY OR DELETE COMMANDS

To perform this	Press
Delete character left	Backspace
Delete word left	Ctrl + Backspace
Delete character right	Delete
Delete word right	Ctrl + Delete
Cut	Ctrl + X
Copy	Ctrl + C
Paste	Ctrl + V
Undo	Ctrl + Z

INSERTION POINT MOVEMENTS IN TEXT

To move the insertion point	Press
One character left	←
One character right	→
One line up	↑
One line down	↓
One word left	Ctrl + ←
One word right	Ctrl + →
To end of line	End
To beginning of line	Home
Up one paragraph	Ctrl + ↑
Down one paragraph	Ctrl + ↓
To end of page	Ctrl + End
To start of page	Ctrl + Home
To previous object	Shift + Tab
To next object	Tab
Repeat Find or Go To Commands	Shift + F4

MENU COMMANDS

Edit Menu

To	Press
Undo	Ctrl + Z
Repeat/Redo	Ctrl + Y
Clear	Delete
Cut	Ctrl + X
Copy	Ctrl + C
Paste	Ctrl + V
Select all	Ctrl + A
Find	Ctrl + F
Replace	Ctrl + H
Duplicate	Ctrl + D
Update links	Ctrl + Shift + F7

File Menu

To	Press
Open new presentation	Ctrl + N
Open existing presentation	Ctrl + O
Close	Ctrl + W or Ctrl + F4
Save	Ctrl + S
Save As	F12
Print	Ctrl + P
Exit PowerPoint	Ctrl + Q or Alt + F4

Format Menu

To	Press
Format character	Ctrl + T
Center paragraph	Ctrl + E
Justify paragraph	Ctrl + J
Left-align paragraph	Ctrl + L
Right-align paragraph	Ctrl + R

Help Menu

To	Press
Display Help Contents screen	F1
Display context-sensitive Help	Shift + F1

Insert Menu

To	Press
Create new slide	Ctrl + M
Add date	Alt + Shift + D
Add page number	Alt + Shift + P
Add time	Alt + Shift + T

SELECTING TEXT OR OBJECTS

To select this	Press
A character to the right	Shift + $\rightarrow$
A character to the left	Shift + $\leftarrow$

To end of word	Ctrl + Shift + →
To beginning of word	Ctrl + Shift + ←
A word	Double-click
A paragraph	Triple-click
Drag and drop copy	Ctrl + select and drag
A line up	Shift + ↑
A line down	Shift + ↓
All objects (slide view)	Ctrl + A
All slides (slide sorter)	Ctrl + A
All text (outline view)	Ctrl + Z

WINDOW CONTROLS

To	Press
Go to previous presentation window	Ctrl + Shift + F6
Go to next presentation window	Ctrl + F6
Maximize PowerPoint window	Alt + F10
Maximize presentation window	Ctrl + F10
Restore presentation window	Ctrl + F5

MOUSE SHORTCUT MENUS

TO INVOKE A SHORTCUT MENU

1 Select the object for which you want to use a shortcut menu.

2 Right-click the mouse to access its shortcut menu.

3 Click the desired command.

THE TOOLBARS

Toolbars provide quick access by mouse to frequently used PowerPoint features. Figure PGA-1 displays the various toolbars that appear in PowerPoint. The reference number beneath each button in the figure refers to its name and function in the chart that follows. (Note: See the "Toolbars Adjustments" reference in the "PowerPoint Features and Commands" section for toolbar customizing techniques.)

Toolbar	#	Button Name	Function
Standard	1	New	Creates a new presentation
	2	Open	Opens an existing presentation
	3	Save	Saves the active presentation
	4	Print	Prints the active presentation
	5	Spelling	Checks spelling in active presentation
	6	Cut	Cuts the selection and places it in the Clipboard
	7	Copy	Copies the selection and places it in the Clipboard
	8	Paste	Inserts the Clipboard contents at the insertion point
	9	Format Painter	Copies the selection's format to another object
	10	Undo	Reverses the last action

FIGURE PGA–1 ■ POWERPOINT TOOLBARS

Standard

1 2 3 4 5 6 7 8 9 10 11 12 13 14 15 16 17 18 19 20 21 22

Formatting

Times New Roman   44
23   24   25 26 27 28 29 30 31 32 33 34 35 36 37 38

Slide Sorter

39   40   41   42   43 44 45

Animation Effects   Outline
46 47 48 49 50 51 52 53 54 55 56 41   37 38 57 58 59 60 61 62 45

Drawing   Drawing +
63 64 65 66 67 68 69 70 71 72 73 74 75 76 77   78 79 80 81 82 83 84 85

AutoShapes
86 87 88 89 90 91 92 93 94 95 96 97 98 99 100 101 └─102─┘ └─103─┘

Microsoft
104 105 106 107 108 109 110 111

11	Redo	Redoes the last action that was undone
12	Insert New Slide	Inserts a new slide after the current slide
13	Insert Microsoft Word Table	Adds a table onto the current slide
14	Insert Microsoft Excel Worksheet	Adds a Excel Worksheet onto the current slide
15	Insert Graph	Adds a Microsoft Graph onto the current slide
16	Insert Clip Art	Adds clip art from the library onto the current slide
17	Apply Design Template	Applies a design to the current presentation
18	Animations Effects	Animation Toolbar toggle (on/off)
19	Report It	Transfers the contents to Microsoft Word
20	B&W View	Black-&-white view toggle (on/off)
21	Zoom Control	Adjusts the scale of the editing view
22	Help	Accesses the Help feature

Formatting

23	Font	Changes the font of the selected text
24	Font Size	Changes the font size of the selected text
25	Increase Font Size	Increases the font size of the selected text

	26	Decrease font size	Decreases the font size of the selected text
	27	Bold	Bold toggle (on/off)
	28	Italic	Italic toggle (on/off)
	29	Underline	Underline toggle (on/off)
	30	Text Shadow	Text shadow toggle (on/off)
	31	Text Color	Changes color of selected text
	32	Left Alignment	Aligns the text at the left
	33	Center Alignment	Centers the text
	34	Increase Paragraph Spacing	Increases spacing between bullets or items
	35	Decrease Paragraph Spacing	Decreases spacing between bullets or items
	36	Bullet On/Off	Bullet toggle (on/off)
	37	Promote (indent less)	Reduces level of indent
	38	Demote (indent more)	Increases level of indent
Slide Sorter	39	Slide Transition	Changes effects between slide changes
	40	Slide Transition Effects	Selects transition effect
	41	Text Build Effects	Selects build effects
	42	Hide Slide	Skip slide during show toggle (on/off)
	43	Rehearse Timings	Runs and rehearses a slide show
	44	Show Formatting	Character formatting display toggle (on/off)
Animation Effects	45	Animate Title	Title fly from top toggle (on/off)
	46	Build Slide Text	Build toggle (on/off)
	47	Drive-in Effect	Fly from right, with car sound
	48	Flying Effect	Fly from left, with whoosh sound
	49	Camera Effect	Box out, with camera sound
	50	Flash Once	Flash once, when previous build ends
	51	Laser Text Effect	Fly from top-right, with laser sound
	52	Typewriter Text Effect	Build by letter, with typewrite sound
	53	Reverse Text Build	Wipe right, in reverse order
	54	Drop-in Text Effect	Fly from top by word
	55	Animation Order	Sets the order in which selected text is animated
	56	Animation Settings	Animation Settings toolbar toggle (on/off)
Outline	**57**	Move Up	Moves a selected paragraph above the previous one
	58	Move Down	Moves the selected paragraph below the next one
	59	Collapse Selection	Displays only the titles in the selection
	60	Expand Selection	Displays all levels of text in the selection
	61	Show Titles	Displays only the titles for all slides
	62	Show All	Displays the titles and all levels of text for all slides
Drawing	63	Selection	Selects and edits an object
	64	Text	Create a text object
	65	Line	Creates a line
	66	Rectangle	Creates a rectangle
	67	Ellipse	Creates an ellipse
	68	Arc	Creates an arc
	69	Freeform	Creates a freeform object
	70	Free Rotate	Rotates a selected object
	71	Autoshapes	Autoshapes Toolbar toggle (on/off)
	72	Fill Color	Changes the fill color
	73	Line Color	Changes the line color
	74	Shadow On/Off	Shadow toggle (on/off)
	75	Line Style	Changes the line style
	76	Arrowheads	Creates arrowheads
	77	Dashed Lines	Creates dashed lines
Drawing +	78	Bring Forward	Brings selected object to the front
	79	Send Backward	Sends selected object to the back

	80	Group Objects	Groups the selected objects
	81	Ungroup Objects	Ungroups the selected group of objects
	82	Rotate Left	Rotates selection 90 degrees to the left
	83	Rotate Right	Rotates selection 90 degrees to the right
	84	Flip Horizontal	Flips selection left to right
	85	Flip Vertical	Flips selection top to bottom
Autoshapes	86	Rectangle	Rectangle tool
	87	Parallelogram	Parallelogram tool
	88	Trapezoid	Trapezoid tool
	89	Diamond	Diamond tool
	90	Rounded Rectangle	Rounded Rectangle tool
	91	Octagon	Octagon tool
	92	Cross	Cross tool
	93	Cube	Cube tool
	94	Ellipse	Ellipse tool
	95	Balloon	Balloon tool
	96	Pentagon	Pentagon tool
	97	Hexagon	Hexagon tool
	98	Isoceles Triangle	Isoceles Triangle tool
	99	Right Triangle	Right Triangle tool
	100	Star	Star tool
	101	Seal	Seal tool
	102	Thin Arrows	Thin Arrow; Right, Left, Up, Down tools
	103	Thick Arrows	Thick Arrow; Right, Left, Up, Down tools
Microsoft	104	Microsoft Mail	Starts or switches to Mail
	105	Microsoft Excel	Starts or switches to Excel
	106	Microsoft Word	Starts or switches to Word
	107	Microsoft Access	Starts or switches to Access
	108	Microsoft Schedule+	Starts or switches to Schedule+
	109	Microsoft FoxPro	Starts or switches to FoxPro
	110	Microsoft Publisher	Starts or switches to Publisher
	111	Microsoft Project	Starts or switches to Project

POWERPOINT FEATURES AND COMMANDS

Selected PowerPoint features and commands in the following list are presented in alphabetical order.

AUTOMATIC START-UP SETTINGS

You can control various settings (start-up switches) that will be invoked automatically
each time PowerPoint is launched.

1 In the Windows desktop, right-click the *Shortcut* icon for Microsoft PowerPoint, click *Properties* and then click the *Shortcut* tab. If you do not have a shortcut icon, you can create
one as follows:

    a. Click *Start* and then point to *Programs*
    b. Click *Windows Explorer*
    c. Click *Tools* and then point to *Find*

d. Click *Files or Folders*

e. Type   **POWERPNT.EXE**

f. Click *Find Now*

g. When the list appears, click *File* and then click *Create Shortcut*

h. Close the dialog box

i. Click and drag the *Shortcut to PowerPnt.exe* icon in the contents list onto the desktop and then release the mouse

j. Close the Explorer window

2 In the *Target* box or the *Command Line* box, add a start-up switch to the end of the path as follows:

a. To start a presentation in slide show view, type the path to the presentation, type the filename in quotes, and then type **/s,** as in "a:file.ppt" /s.

b. To print a presentation upon launching, add **/p.**

c. To create a new presentation using the named presentation as the template, add **/n.**

3 When done, click *OK*.

4 To have a presentation run in slide show view each time PowerPoint is launched, add the following steps:

a. Right-click a blank section of the Windows 95 taskbar.

b. Click *Properties* and then the *Start Menu Programs* tab.

c. Click *Add*.

d. Click *Browse* and move to the shortcut you want to use. Double-click the shortcut.

e. Click *Next*.

f. Click the *Start* menu.

g. Click *Next* and then *Finish*.

BRANCHING

Branching allows you to have your presentation jump, on command, to other slides or presentations that provide additional details. To create a branch, you draw a button on a given slide and then link the button to the desired branch destination. During the slide show, you can then point to the button until the mouse appears as a hand with a pointing finger and then click if you want to branch.

When you branch to another *presentation,* you will automatically return to the slide where you started when the branched presentation ends. However, when you branch to another *slide* within the current presentation, you must use the *Slide Navigator* to return or create a button in the slide to return you to the original slide.

TO SET UP A BRANCH WITHIN A PRESENTATION

1 Switch to the slide view.

2 Move to the slide in which you want to create a branch.

3   Draw a shape using the PowerPoint drawing tools or insert a clip art image to be used as a button.

4   Select the button, and then click *Tools, Interactive Settings.*

5   Click *Go To,* then click the slide option to which you want to branch. (The "Slide…" option lets you designate a particular slide.)

6   Click *OK* and then deselect the image.

TO SET UP A BRANCH TO ANOTHER PRESENTATION

1   In slide view, move to the slide where the branch will occur.

2   Click *Insert* and then *Object.*

3   Click the *Create from File* checkbox.

4   Type the desired path and filename or browse to it and then double-click to select it.

5   Click the *OK* button.

6   Adjust the image's size and position as desired.

7   Click the image.

8   Click *Tools, Interactive Settings, Object Action, Show, OK.*

9   Deselect the image, which now serves as the branch button.

TO USE A BRANCH IN A SLIDE SHOW

1   Click the branch button or image in the appropriate slide to branch.

2   If you do *not* click the button, the presentation will proceed in its original sequence.

CLIP ART TECHNIQUES

TO REPLACE A CLIP ART IMAGE IN A PRESENTATION

1   Switch to the slide view.

2   Double-click the clip art image to access the ClipArt Gallery. If the ClipArt Gallery does not appear, delete the image and then click the clip art icon and select a new one.

3   Double-click a new image.

TO ADD ART TO THE CLIP ART GALLERY

1 Click the *Insert Clip Art* button on the standard toolbar.

2 Click *Organize.*

3 Click *Add Pictures,* and then click *Other Pictures.*

4 In the *Look in* box, select the folder that contains the desired picture.

5 Click the picture and then *Open.*

6 Click the *OK* button.

7 Enter a category under *Current Picture Information* and include a brief description.

8 Click *Add.*

TO ACTIVATE OR DEACTIVATE AUTOCLIPART

AutoClipArt is a PowerPoint program that searches the text in your presentation and suggests possible clip art images that complement your work.

1 To activate AutoClipArt, click *Tools, AutoClipArt,* and, if desired, click the *Run In Background* check box.

2 To deactivate AutoClipArt, repeat Step 1 but clear the *Run In Background* check box.

MODIFYING ART. Any inserted picture can be resized, recolored, bordered, or shadowed. You can also use the Draw, Ungroup command to convert clip art into PowerPoint objects that can be modified as if you had drawn them yourself.

MEETING MINDER. The Meeting Minder feature can be used to take minutes or prepare action items during a presentation. When you take minutes, they are added to the notes pages, whereas the action items you record appear on the last slide in your presentation.

TO EXPORT MEETING MINUTES TO A WORD DOCUMENT

1 Switch to the slide view.

2 Click *Tools* and then *Meeting Minder.* (During a slide show, click the right mouse button, and then click *Meeting Minder.*)

3 Click the *Meeting Minutes* tab and then *Export.*

4 Click the *Export Meeting Minutes And Action Items To Word* check box.

5 Click *Export Now.*

MOVIES

When a movie is linked to a slide, it can be displayed either as a poster or an icon. In a poster, the first frame of the movie appears on the slide. An icon can also be used instead of the movie's first frame. The choice of display does not affect how the movie plays.

If you have access to animated movie images, you can add them to slides within your presentation. Once placed, movies are invoked by clicking either an icon or poster on the appropriate slide.

TO DISPLAY A MOVIE AS AN ICON

1 Switch to the slide view.

2 Move to the slide in which you want to insert a movie.

3 Click *Insert* and then *Object.*

4 Click *Create From File.*

5 Click *Browse,* and move to the desired movie.

6 Click the movie, and then click the *OK* button.

7 Click *Display As Icon,* and then click the *OK* button. To change the icon, click *Change Icon* and then select another one.

8 Drag the icon to the desired location.

TO DISPLAY A MOVIE AS A POSTER

1 Switch to the slide view.

2 Move to the slide in which you want to insert a movie.

3 Click *Insert* and then *Movie.*

4 Select the movie you want to insert.

5 Click the *OK* button.

6 Drag the movie to the location you want on the slide.

TO EDIT A MOVIE

1 Switch to the slide view.

2 Move to the slide that contains the movie.

3 Click the movie's icon or poster.

4 Click *Edit*, point to *Edit Media Clip Object*, and click *Edit*.

5 Use the Media Player tools and menus to edit the movie. The following list displays some of the controls you can use.

To	Perform this action
Change the poster	Display the desired frame in the movie to be used as the poster. On the *Media Player* menu, click *File, Update Presentation*, then *Exit And Return To Presentation.*
Set the volume	On the *Media Player* menu, click *Insert Clip, Volume Control.*
Set automatic rewind	On the *Media Player* menu, click *Edit, Options,* and click *Auto Rewind* check box.
Set continuous play	On the *Media Player* menu, click *Edit, Options,* and click *Auto Repeat* check box.
Add a border	On the *Media Player* menu, click *Edit, Options,* then click the *Border Around Object* check box.
Display the Control Bar	On the *Media Player* menu, click *Edit, Options,* then click the *Control Bar On Playback* check box.
Cut/copy one frame	Display the frame. Then on the *Media Player* menu, click *Edit, Cut* (or *Copy*).
Cut/copy a frame set	Display the first frame. Press Shift and drag the Media Player slider to the last frame in the sequence. Click *Edit, Cut* (or *Copy*).

6 When you finish editing, click outside the movie.

TO RESIZE A MOVIE

1 Switch to the slide view.

2 Move to the slide that contains the movie.

3 Click the movie's icon or poster.

4 Click *Draw* and then *Scale.*

5 Click the *Best Scale For Slide Show* check box.

TO TIME A MOVIE

1 Switch to the slide view.

2 Move to the slide that contains the movie.

3   Click the movie's icon or poster.

4   Click *Tools* and then *Animation Settings*.

5   In the *Play Options* box, click *Play* and then *More*.

6   Specify any desired options.

VIEWING MOVIES DURING A SLIDE SHOW. The following list displays some of the controls you can use to view a movie during a slide show.

To	Perform this action
Play	Click the movie icon or poster.
Pause	Click the movie or pause button.
Restart	Click the movie.
Advance/rewind frames	Drag the Control Bar slider forward or backward as needed.
Stop (exit)	Click outside the movie.

MUSIC AND SOUND

PowerPoint offers a sampling of sounds that can be added to a slide show. A few sounds can be accessed through toolbar buttons on the Animation Effects toolbar. Playing sounds or music requires that your computer have the appropriate hardware (for example, speakers and a sound card) installed.

TO PLAY A SOUND WHEN AN OBJECT OR TEXT APPEARS IN A SLIDE SHOW

1   Select the object or text.

2   Click the appropriate button on the Animation Effects toolbar.

TO ADD OTHER SOUNDS TO A SLIDE SHOW

1   Insert the music or sound object on the slide where you want to play.

2   Click *Tools*.

3   Use the Animation Settings command to set the music or sound.

NOTES PAGES

TO SET UP NOTES PAGES. The notes master works in a fashion similar to the slide master.

1 Click *View,* point to *Master,* and then click *Notes Master.*

2 Change or resize the slide image or the notes box as desired.

3 Add additional material as desired—clip art, text, headers or footers, date, time, or page number.

OBJECTS IN SLIDE MASTER

To Add the Same Object on Every Slide in the Presentation

1 Click *View,* point to Master, and then click *Slide Master.*

2 Add the object to the slide master.

3 Click *View* and then *Slides.*

4 If the object does not appear on your slides, click *Format* and then *Custom Background* and then clear the check mark in the *Omit Background Objects From Master* check box.

ORGANIZATION CHARTS

Organization charts use graphics to illustrate the reporting or communication relationships within the ranks and files of an organization.

TO EDIT AN ORGANIZATIONAL CHART

1 Double-click the organizational chart to open it.

2 Edit the chart using Microsoft Organization Chart tools and menus.

3 Click the *Organization Chart File* and then *Exit And Return To Presentation.*

TO INSERT AN ORGANIZATIONAL CHART

1 Switch to the slide view.

2 Move to the slide that will hold the organizational chart.

3 Click *Insert* and then *Object.*

4 Click *MS Organization Chart.*

5 Design the chart with Microsoft Organization Chart tools.

6 When you are finished, click the *Organization Chart File* and then *Exit And Return To Presentation.*

OUTLINES

In outline view, a presentation appears as an outline composed of the titles and main text from each slide. You can type an outline, use an outline from the AutoContent wizard, or import an outline from another application such as Microsoft Word. Each slide title appears to the right of a slide number and icon. The slide icon shows whether graphics are included in the slide. Body text appears indented beneath the title. You can rearrange bullet items within a slide, move slides, or edit titles and body text.

TO CHANGE THE INDENT LEVEL OF A BULLET ITEM

1 Use the *Demote* or *Promote* buttons in the Outline toolbar.

TO CREATE A PRESENTATION IN OUTLINE FORM

1 Open a new presentation.

2 Switch to the outline view.

3 Type a title for the first slide, and then press ↵ .

4 Click the *Demote* button on the Outline toolbar to create the first bullet level.

5 Type each bullet item, pressing ↵ at the end of each item.

6 Click the *Promote* or *Demote* buttons to create various indent levels.

7 When you're finished with the slide, click the *New Slide* button or press Ctrl + ↵ to create the next slide.

8 Continue as needed.

TO INSERT AN OUTLINE INTO AN EXISTING PRESENTATION

1 Switch to slide, outline, or slide sorter view.

2 Select the slide after which you want to add the outline.

3 Click *Insert* and then *Slides From Outline.*

4 Go to the folder in which you've stored the outline.

5 Double-click the desired outline file.

TO MOVE A BULLET ITEM OR SLIDE UP OR DOWN IN THE OUTLINE

1 Select a paragraph to be moved

  2 Use the *Move Up* or *Move Down* buttons in the Outline toolbar.

3 You can also use the remaining *Outline* buttons to show or hide slide formatting or to expand or collapse text.

4 To move a slide, drag its icon to a new location.

TO REARRANGE SLIDES OR BULLET ITEMS

1 Select the block to be moved.

2 Drag it to a new location.

TO SPLIT A SLIDE'S BODY TEXT INTO TWO SEPARATE SLIDES

1 Switch to the outline view.

2 Place the insertion point within the text you want to use for the new slide title.

 3 Click the *Promote* button in the Outline toolbar until a new slide icon and number appear next to the new slide title.

 4 To insert a new slide title, press ↵ at the end of the item prior to the new title, then click the *Promote* button until a slide icon appears to the left of the insertion point. Then type the new title.

SHARING DATA

Importing reads data from another application and converts it into a PowerPoint document.

IMPORTING OR CONVERTING FILES FROM ANOTHER OFFICE AP-PLICATION. To convert most files created in another Office application, just open the file in PowerPoint. If PowerPoint recognizes the file's format, it converts the document automatically. For example, when you open a Word document in PowerPoint, it is automatically converted into a PowerPoint presentation.

When importing Microsoft Word or Excel files, it is best to convert the documents to a text or rich text format (.RTF) and then edit them in the outline view. Additional import and export information is available in "converting file formats" in the Help index.

USING TEXT FROM OTHER APPLICATIONS. You can use text created in other applications to make a new presentation or to add slides to an existing presentation by importing text in the form of an outline. PowerPoint will import presentations from other applications using the outline structure from the imported document's styles: a first-level heading becomes a slide title, a second-level heading becomes the first level of text, and so on. If the document has no styles, PowerPoint creates the outline based on its paragraph indentations or tabs.

You can import outlines from word processing applications in rich-text or plain-text format. Using the slide master of the current presentation for format, PowerPoint creates separate slides for all first-level headings and adds body text as indent levels.

TO DRAG AND DROP INFORMATION BETWEEN APPLICATIONS. You can move or copy information between documents in applications that support OLE (object linking and embedding) by using drag and drop editing methods. Follow these general steps:

1 Arrange the two application windows so that the information in the source document and its location within the destination document can be seen.

2 Select the block of information you want to move or copy.

3 To move the block, point to the block, then press and hold the mouse button. After the pointer appears, drag it to the destination location and release the mouse button.

4 To copy the block, hold down the Ctrl key while performing the actions in Step 3. Then release both the mouse button and the Ctrl key at the end.

SLIDE SHOW TECHNIQUES

TO AUTOMATICALLY INSERT A BLACK SLIDE AT THE END OF A SLIDE SHOW

1 Click *Tools* and then *Options.*

2 Click the *View* tab, then click the *End With Black Slide* check box.

TO HIDE A SLIDE (HIDDEN DURING THE SLIDE SHOW)

1 Switch to the slide view.

2 Click *Tools, Hide Slide.*

TO OPEN AN APPLICATION (DURING THE SLIDE SHOW)

1 Switch to the slide view.

2 Move to the slide in which you want to open an application.

3 Draw an image using PowerPoint's drawing tools or insert a clip art image to be used as a button.

4 Select the image.

5 Click *Tools, Interactive Settings.*

6 Click *Run Program,* and then type the path to tell PowerPoint how to locate the application you want to open.

TABLES

Tables present data in columns. You can create tables within PowerPoint using Word techniques or import Word tables directly into your presentation.

TO EDIT A TABLE

1 Double-click the table to open it.

2 Edit the table using Word tools and menus.

3 Click outside the table to accept it.

TO INSERT A TABLE

1 Switch to the slide view.

2 Move to the slide in which you will add a table.

3 Click the *Insert Microsoft Word Table* button on the standard toolbar, then drag the pointer right and down to specify the desired number of rows and columns.

4 Enter data into the table's cells.

5 Format the table using Word tools and commands.

6 Click outside the table to accept it.

TOOLBAR ADJUSTMENTS

TO CHANGE THE SPACING BETWEEN TOOLBAR BUTTONS

1 To increase space between two toolbar buttons, press and hold Alt and then drag the rightmost (or lower) button farther away from the other (to the right or down as needed).

2 To decrease space between two buttons, repeat Step 1 but drag one button closer to the other one.

TO CREATE A CUSTOM TOOLBAR

1 Click *View, Toolbars,* and then *New.*

2 In the *Toolbar Name* box, enter a name for the toolbar.

3 In the *Make Toolbar Available To* box, click the template where you want the toolbar stored for future use.

4 Click the *OK* button.

5 In the *Categories* box, click the category that contains the command or item you want to add to the toolbar.

6 In *Buttons*, drag the button or item to the toolbar.

TO ADD OR DELETE A TOOLBAR BUTTON

1 Display the toolbar you want to change.

2 Click *Tools* and then *Customize*.

3 To add a button, click a category in the *Categories* box, and then drag the button from the Buttons area to a toolbar.

4 To delete a button, drag it off the toolbar.

> Note: The PowerPoint Help screen states that when you delete a standard (built-in) toolbar button, the button remains available in the *Customize* dialog box. However, when you delete a custom toolbar button that you have created yourself, it is permanently deleted. To solve this problem, you can create a toolbar to store your unwanted buttons, move the button to the storage toolbar, and then simply not display the storage toolbar.

TO MOVE A TOOLBAR

1 Point between two toolbar buttons, or point to a floating toolbar's title bar.

2 Drag the toolbar to its new location.

TO RESTORE A DEFAULT BUILT-IN TOOLBAR

1 Click *View* and then *Toolbars*.

2 In the Toolbars box, click the check box of the toolbar you want to restore.

3 Click *Reset*.

VIEWER

The PowerPoint Viewer is an auxiliary program that allows a presentation to be viewed on a computer that does not have PowerPoint installed. PowerPoint Viewer can be freely distributed without any additional license. Note that the viewer does not support all of PowerPoint's features, such as builds and branching.

TO CREATE A DISK THAT CONTAINS A PRESENTATION AND THE POWERPOINT VIEWER

1. In an open presentation, click *File* and then the *Pack And Go* Wizard.

2. Follow the directions to copy the PowerPoint Viewer and a presentation to a disk.

TO PRESENT A SLIDE SHOW WITH THE POWERPOINT VIEWER

1. Start Windows and move to the desktop.

2. In Windows Explorer, select *PowerPoint Viewer.*

3. Select the presentation you want to show.

4. Click *Show.*

STYLE CHECKER

TO CHECK A PRESENTATION FOR VISUAL CLARITY, CONSISTENCY, AND STYLE

1. Open the presentation.

2. Click *Tools* and then *Style Checker.*

3. Click the items you want to check in your presentation.

4. Click *Options* to see more choices.

5. Run the style check.

GLOSSARY

Autolayout A predesigned layout that contains placeholders for various objects (titles, bulleted lists, or graphics) that can be added to the slide. (PG13)

Build A graphic special effect that focuses attention on items in a bulleted list by progressively disclosing each item in sequence. (PG87)

Clip art Professionally prepared graphic images that can be electronically copied from a library collection and pasted into a slide. (PG68)

Close **button** A window component that exits and closes the window when clicked. (PG7)

Embedding A procedure used to copy an object from one application to another. (PG99)

Fill color The color of the internal part of a graphic object. (PG78)

Footer An item of information added at the bottom of any or all slides. (PG35)

Formatting toolbar A PowerPoint toolbar that allows you to change various text attributes, such as font, size, enhancements, and alignment. (PG14)

Handle A small square box, situated at a corner or side of an object frame, which can be dragged by mouse to alter the size of the object. (PG73)

Line color The color of the border of a graphic object. (PG78)

Linking A procedure that copies an object from the application that provides it (the *source*) to the one that receives it (the *container*) so that any changes in the source are automatically updated in the container. (PG99)

Menu bar A window component that lets you access most commands by point-ing with a mouse or pressing the appropriate keys. (PG7)

Notes pages view A PowerPoint screen mode that allows you to add notes to each slide. (PG31)

Object A collection of information. (PG99)

Open A command that fetches a file from its folder or disk and then copies it into a window on the screen. (PG21)

Outline view A PowerPoint screen mode that presents the text contained in your presentation in outline form. (PG33)

Placeholder An empty object area in a layout that can hold a title, text, graphic, or other data. (PG14)

Presentation graphics A program that allows you to combine text, graphics, and visual special effects into a professional-looking presentation. (PG2)

Program icon A window component, appearing at the upper-left corner, that activates a control menu when clicked. (PG6)

Resizing button A window component that resizes the window when clicked to one of three sizes: *minimized, restored,* or *maximized.* (PG7)

Save A command that copies the current presentation in main memory into a file on disk. (PG18)

Selection box A rectangular frame that indicates when a placeholder is active. (PG16)

Shortcut keys Keystrokes in combination with the Ctrl, Alt, and/or Shift keys that bypass the normal menu structure to invoke commands quickly. (PG4)

Slide master A design format that controls the layout and appearance of a specific autolayout slide template in a presentation. (PG57)

Slide view The default PowerPoint screen mode, which presents one slide on the screen at a time; the main work window for creating new presentations, adding slides, and editing text. (PG28)

Slide show A PowerPoint screen mode that runs your entire presentation in full-screen form. (PG31)

Slide sorter view A PowerPoint screen mode that displays miniature images of your slides in sequence. (PG29)

Status bar A window component located at the bottom of the window that displays messages and provides additional mouse shortcut buttons. (PG8)

Suite A collection of separate programs that function as if they were one large program. (PG97)

Template A predesigned pattern that determines some graphic aspect of a presentation: the look of the overall presentation, its design, color, or general layout. (PG11)

Title bar A window component, located at the top of the window, that identifies a program or document. (PG6)

Title master A design format that controls the layout and appearance of the title slide in a presentation. (PG57)

Toolbar A collection of shortcut buttons that can be clicked by mouse to invoke various commands. (PG8)

Transition A visual effect that allows slides to blend from one into the next when running the screen show. (PG85)

View button A feature that allows you to switch among PowerPoint's five screen views when clicked. (PG14)

Workspace A large blank area of a document window that contains your work. (PG8)

INDEX